THE MORE ECONOMIC APPROACH TO EU ANTITRUST LAW

In the late 1990s, the European Commission embarked on a long process of introducing a 'more economic approach' to EU antitrust law. One by one, it reviewed its approach to all three pillars of EU antitrust law, starting with Article 101 TFEU, moving on to EU merger control and concluding the process with Article 102 TFEU. Its aim was to make EU antitrust law more compatible with contemporary economic thinking.

On the basis of an extensive empirical analysis of the Commission's main enforcement tools, this book establishes the actual changes that the more economic approach has made to the Commission's enforcement practice over the past 15 years. It demonstrates that the new approach not only introduced modern economic assessment tools to the Commission's analyses, but fundamentally changed the Commission's interpretation of the law. Emulating one of the key credos of the US Antitrust Revolution 30 years earlier, the Commission reinterpreted the EU antitrust rules as aiming at the enhancement of economic consumer welfare only, and amended its understanding of key legal concepts accordingly.

This book argues that the Commission's new understanding of the law has many benefits. Its key principles are logical, translate into workable legal concepts and promise a great degree of accuracy. However, it also has a number of serious drawbacks as it stands. In particular, the Commission's review of Article 102 has yielded unsatisfactory results. Moreover, its revised interpretation of the law is largely incompatible with the case law of the Court of Justice of the European Union, which has not been swayed by the exclusive consumer welfare aim. This situation is undesirable from the point of view of legal certainty and the rule of law.

Volume 14 in the series Hart Studies in Competition Law

Hart Studies in Competition Law

Intellectual Property, Antitrust and Cumulative Innovation in the EU and the US
Thorsten Käseberg

State Aid and the European Economic Constitution
Francesco de Cecco

The Private Enforcement of Competition Law in Ireland
David McFadden

Cross-Border EU Competition Law Actions
Edited by Mihail Danov, Florian Becker and Paul Beaumont

Competition Laws, Globalization and Legal Pluralism: China's Experience
Qianlan Wu

Joint Ventures and EU Competition Law
Luis Silva Morais

Sanctions in EU Competition Law: Principles and Practice
Michael Frese

Fairness in Antitrust: Protecting the Strong from the Weak
Adi Ayal

European Merger Remedies: Law and Policy
Dorte Hoeg

Media Ownership and Control: Law, Economics and Policy in an Indian and International Context
Suzanne Rab and Alison Sprague

The Interface between Competition and the Internal Market: Market Separation under Article 102 TFEU
Vasiliki Brisimi

Anti-Cartel Enforcement in a Contemporary Age: Leniency Religion
Edited by Caron Beaton-Wells and Christopher Tran

Public Procurement and the EU Competition Rules
Albert Sánchez Graells

The Concept of Abuse in EU Competition Law: Law and Economic Approaches
Pınar Akman

The Competitive Effects of Minority Shareholdings: Legal and Economic Issues
Panagiotis Fotis and Nikolaos Zevgolis

The More Economic Approach to EU Antitrust Law

Anne C Witt

•HART•
OXFORD • LONDON • NEW YORK • NEW DELHI • SYDNEY

HART PUBLISHING
Bloomsbury Publishing Plc
Kemp House, Chawley Park, Cumnor Hill, Oxford, OX2 9PH, UK

HART PUBLISHING, the Hart/Stag logo, BLOOMSBURY and the Diana logo are trademarks of Bloomsbury Publishing Plc
First published in Great Britain 2016

First published in hardback, 2016
Paperback edition, 2019

A catalogue record for this book is available from the British Library.

Library of Congress Cataloging-in-Publication Data

Names: Witt, Anne C., author.

Title: The more economic approach to EU antitrust law / Anne C Witt.

Other titles: More economic approach to European Union antitrust law

Description: Oxford [UK] ; Portland, Oregon : Hart Publishing, 2016. | Series: Hart studies in competition law ; volume 14 | Includes bibliographical references and index.

Identifiers: LCCN 2016029109 (print) | LCCN 2016029331 (ebook) | ISBN 9781849466967 (hardback) | ISBN 9781509909223 (Epub)

Subjects: LCSH: Antitrust law—Economic aspects—European Union Countries. | Competition, Unfair—Economic aspects—European Union Countries.

Classification: LCC KJE6456 .W58 2016 (print) | LCC KJE6456 (ebook) | DDC 343.2407/21—dc23

LC record available at https://lccn.loc.gov/2016029109

Series: Hart Studies in Competition Law, volume 14

ISBN: HB: 978-1-84946-696-7
PB: 978-1-50992-795-1
ePDF: 978-1-50990-923-0
ePub: 978-1-50990-922-3

Typeset by Compuscript Ltd, Shannon

ACKNOWLEDGEMENTS

I would like to thank Claus-Dieter Ehlermann and Heike Schweitzer for encouraging me to write this book. I would like to thank Giorgio Monti, Harm Schepel and the EUI competition law group for their valuable feedback and input. My thanks further go to the European University Institute for granting me a visiting fellowship to carry out part of my research there, to the British Academy for funding this stay and to the University of Leicester for granting me study leave to complete the project. Finally, I would like to thank my family and friends for their unfailing patience and support.

TABLE OF CONTENTS

Acknowledgements v
Table of Cases xv
Table of Legislation xxix

Introduction 1

Part I

1. Triggers and Catalysts 7
    I. Introduction 7
    II. The Completion of the Internal Market 7
    III. Academic Criticism 10
    IV. Transatlantic Conflict 11
        A. The Boeing/McDonnell Douglas Crisis (1997) 11
        B. GE and Honeywell Run Afoul of Nineteenth-Century Thinking (2001) 14
            i. The US Investigation 15
            ii. The EU Investigation 15
            iii. The Controversy 16
        C. Microsoft (2004) 18
            i. The US Investigation 19
            ii. The EU Investigation 21
            iii. The Controversy 24
        D. Conclusion 25
    V. DG Competition's *annus horribilis* 27
        A. The Scope of Judicial Review 27
        B. Airtours 28
        C. Schneider Electric 29
        D. Tetra Laval 30
        E. Consequences 32
    VI. The Great Reformer 34
    VII. Increased International Cooperation 36
    VIII. Conclusion 39

2. The Process 40
I. Introduction 40
II. One Pillar at a Time 40
A. Article 101 40
B. EU Merger Law 41
C. Article 102 42
III. A 'Soft' Reform 43
A. Article 101 43
B. EU Merger Law 45
C. Article 102 46
IV. Changes in the Professional Composition of DG Competition 47
V. Public Consultations 49
VI. Conclusion 52

3. The Agenda 54
I. Introduction 54
II. Speeches, Interviews and Publications by the Commissioner for Competition Policy 54
III. Official Commission Acts 57
IV. The Broader Context 60
A. The Comparison with US Antitrust Law 60
i. The Key Substantive Provisions of US Antitrust Law 61
ii. The Objectives of US Antitrust Law 62
iii. The Concept of Harm 65
iv. *Per se* Rules v Rules of Reason 65
v. Conclusion 68
B. The Academic Debate 69
V. Conclusions and Consequences for the Structure of Part II 73

Part II

4. A More Economic Objective 77
I. Introduction 77
II. The Importance of Identifying a Provision's Legal Objective 77
III. A Few of the Usual Suspects 79
A. Economic Welfare 80
B. Fundamental Constitutional Values: Individual Freedom, Equality of Opportunity, Fairness and Democracy 83
C. Other Aims 86
D. One Aim or Several Aims? 88

IV. The Commission's Understanding of the EU Antitrust Rules' Legal Objective Prior to the More Economic Approach 88
A. The Legal Provisions 89
B. The Commission's Understanding 91
i. Legally Binding Commission Acts 91
ii. Commission Notices 92
iii. The Annual Reports on Competition Policy 93
a. The Internal Market 94
b. Preventing the Concentration of Economic Power 95
c. Economic Growth 96
d. Industrial Adaptability 96
e. Fighting Inflation 97
f. 'Competitiveness' of the European Economy 97
g. Consumer Interests 97
h. The Interests of Society as a Whole 98
i. Fairness 98
j. Individual Commercial Freedom and other Democratic Values 99
k. Employment 99
l. Innovation 100
m. Efficiency 100
n. Fundamental Union Objectives 101
o. Conclusion 102
iv. Conclusions on the Commission's Early Position 102
V. The Legal Objectives according to the More Economic Approach 103
A. The Legal Provisions 103
B. The Commission's Revised Understanding of the Objectives of EU Antitrust Law 104
C. Other Commission Publications 107
VI. Conclusion 108

5. A More Economic Concept of Competitive Harm 110
I. Introduction 110
II. Article 101 111
A. The Commission's Concept of Harm Prior to the Introduction of the More Economic Approach 111
i. Interpretative Notices and other Soft Law 111
ii. The Commission's Decision Practice 114
iii. Conclusion 118

B. The Commission's Concept of Harm after the Introduction of the More Economic Approach 118
i. Commission Notices and other Soft Law..........118
ii. The Commission's Decision Practice..........121
iii. Conclusion..........125
C. Conclusion..........125
III. Merger Control..........126
A. The Commission's Concept of Harm Prior to the Introduction of the More Economic Approach..........127
i. The Legal Basis: Council Regulation 4064/89..........127
ii. Commission Notices and other Soft Law..........127
iii. The Commission's Decision Practice..........128
iv. Conclusion..........132
B. The Commission's Concept of Harm after the Introduction of the More Economic Approach..........132
i. The New Legal Basis: Council Regulation 139/2004..........133
ii. Commission Notices and other Soft Law..........135
iii. The Commission's Decision Practice..........137
C. Conclusion..........140
IV. Article 102..........141
A. The Commission's Concept of Harm Prior to the Introduction of the More Economic Approach..........142
i. Commission Soft Law..........142
ii. The Commission's Decision Practice..........142
iii. Conclusion..........146
B. The Commission's Concept of Harm after the Introduction of the More Economic Approach..........146
i. Commission Notices and other Soft Law..........146
ii. The Commission's Decision Practice..........149
iii. Conclusion..........155
V. Conclusion..........156

6. A More Economic Concept of Countervailing Effects..........159
I. Introduction..........159
II. Article 101..........159
A. The Legal Basis: Article 101(3)..........159
B. The Commission's Understanding Prior to the Introduction of the More Economic Approach..........160
i. The Commission's Block Exemption Regulations..........160
ii. The Commission's Decision Practice..........162
iii. Conclusion..........165
C. The Commission's Understanding after the Introduction of the More Economic Approach..........165
i. Soft Law..........165
ii. The Commission's Block Exemption Regulations..........166

iii. The Commission's Decision Practice 167
iv. Conclusion 173
D. Conclusion 173
III. EU Merger Law 174
A. The Commission's Understanding Prior to the Introduction of the More Economic Approach 174
i. The Legal Basis 174
ii. The Decision Practice 175
iii. Conclusion 176
B. The Commission's Understanding after the Introduction of the More Economic Approach 177
i. The Legal Basis 177
ii. The Soft Law 177
iii. The Decision Practice 178
iv. Conclusion 179
C. Conclusion 179
IV. Article 102 181
A. The Legal Basis 181
B. The Commission's Understanding Prior to the Introduction of the More Economic Approach 181
C. The Commission's Understanding after the Introduction of the More Economic Approach 183
i. Soft Law 184
ii. The Decision Practice 186
iii. Conclusion 188
D. Conclusion 188
V. Conclusion 190

7. A More Economic Test 193
I. Introduction 193
II. A Few Preliminary Considerations 194
III. Article 101 196
A. The Legal Basis 196
B. The Commission's Approach Prior to the Introduction of the More Economic Approach 198
i. The Decision Practice 199
ii. Block Exemption Regulations 202
iii. Conclusion 203
C. The Commission's Approach after the Introduction of the More Economic Approach 204
i. Soft Law 204
ii. The Decision Practice 207
iii. Block Exemption Regulations 209
iv. Conclusion 211
D. Conclusion on the Changes under Article 101 211

IV. EU Merger Law 213
V. Article 102 214
A. The Commission's Approach Prior to the Introduction of the More Economic Approach 215
B. The Commission's Approach after the Introduction of the More Economic Approach 219
i. Soft Law 219
ii. The Decision Practice 221
iii. Conclusion 226
C. Conclusion on the Changes under Article 102 227
VI. Conclusion 228

8. A More Economic Methodology 231
I. Introduction 231
II. The Use of Economic Theory 231
A. The Commission's Approach Prior to the Introduction of the More Economic Approach 232
i. Articles 101 and 102 232
ii. Merger Control 234
B. The Commission's Approach after the Introduction of the More Economic Approach 236
III. The Use of Quantitative Analysis 239
A. The Use of Quantitative Analysis in the Commission's Decision Practice 240
B. The Significance of Quantitative Analysis in the Commission's Decision Practice 242
IV. More Empirical Evidence 244
V. The Length of Decisions 245
VI. Conclusion 245
Conclusions on Part II 246

Part III

9. Advantages 253
I. Introduction 253
II. Logic and Internal Consistency 253
III. Accuracy 254
IV. More Empirical Evidence 256
V. Reduction in the Number of Cases Caught by the Antitrust Provisions 256
VI. Approximation with US Antitrust Law 258
VII. Conclusion 260

10. Compatibility with the Case Law 261
I. Introduction 261
II. The Aims of EU Antitrust Law in the Case Law 262

III. The Concept of Harm in the Case Law....266
A. The Court's Concept of Harm under Article 101....266
B. The Court's Concept of Harm under EU Merger Law....271
C. The Court's Concept of Harm under Article 102....274
D. Conclusions on the Court's Concept of Harm....281
IV. The Relevance of Non-economic Policy Goals in the Case Law....281
V. Form- v Effects-based Tests in the Case Law....286
VI. Compatibility of the Commission's More Economic Approach with the Case Law and Consequences....289
A. The Points of Divergence....289
B. Consequences....290
VII. Conclusion....294

11. Other Concerns....296
I. Introduction....296
II. Consistency....296
III. Clarity....297
IV. Difficulty of Application....298
A. Manageability for Courts....298
B. Manageability for Undertakings....300
C. Cost....301
D. Conclusion....301
V. Consumer Welfare as the Only Relevant Value....302
VI. Conclusion....304

Conclusion....305

Annex: Tables on Decision Length....310

Bibliography....318
Index....333

TABLE OF CASES

Judgements of the European Court of Justice of the European Union

AKZO Chemie BV v Commission of the European Communities (Case C-62/86) ECLI:EU:C:1991:286 .... 138, 213, 215, 218, 276, 287

Albany International BV v Stichting Bedrijfspensioenfonds Textielindustrie (Case C-67/96) ECLI:EU:C:1999:430 .... 172, 284

Allianz Hungária and Others v Gazdasági Versenyhivatal (Case C-32/11) ECLI:EU:C:2013:160 197

Andrea Francovich and Danila Bonifaci and others v Italian Republic (Joined Cases C-6/90 and C-9/90) ECLI:EU:C:1991:428 78

Ascendi Beiras Litoral e Alta, Auto Estradas das Beiras Litoral e Alta SA v Autoridade Tributária e Aduaneira (Case C-377/13) ECLI:EU:C:2014:1754 77

AstraZeneca AB and AstraZeneca plc v European Commission (Case C-457/10 P) ECLI:EU:C:2012:770 .... 129, 223, 277

Brentjens' Handelsonderneming BV v Stichting Bedrijfspensioenfonds voor de Handel in Bouwmaterialen (Joined Cases C-115/97 to C-117/97) ECLI:EU:C:1999:434 .... 172, 284

British Airways plc v Commission of the European Communities (Case C-95/04 P) ECLI:EU:C:2007:166 .... 149, 226, 277

Commission of the European Communities v Anic Partecipazioni SpA (Case C-49/92 P) ECLI:EU:C:1999:356 119

Commission of the European Communities v French Republic (Case 167/73) ECLI:EU:C:1974:35 263

Commission of the European Communities v Tetra Laval BV (Case C-12/03 P) ECLI:EU:C:2005:87 .... 18, 32

Compagnie maritime belge transports SA (Case C-395/96 P), *Compagnie maritime belge SA* (Case C-395/96 P) *and Dafra-Lines A/S* (Case C-396/96 P) v *Commission of the European Communities* ECLI:EU:C:2000:132 276

Compagnie Royale Asturienne des Mines SA and Rheinzink GmbH v Commission of the European Communities (Joined Cases 29/83 and 30/83) ECLI:EU:C:1984:130 .... 196, 268

Competition Authority v Beef Industry Development Society Ltd and Barry Brothers (Carrigmore) Meats Ltd (Case C-209/07) ECLI:EU:C:2008:643 .... 169, 196, 286

Coop de France bétail et viande and others v Commission of the European Communities (Joined Cases C-101/07 P and C-110/07 P C-101/07 P) ECLI:EU:C:2008:741 168

Coöperatieve Vereniging 'Suiker Unie' UA and others v Commission of the European Communities (Joined Cases 40 to 48, 50, 54 to 56, 111, 113 and 114/73) ECLI:EU:C:1975:174 ... 267, 286

Dansk Rørindustri A/S (Case C-189/02 P), *Isoplus Fernwärmetechnik Vertriebsgesellschaft mbH and Others* (Case C-202/02 P), *KE KELIT Kunststoffwerk GmbH* (Case C-205/02 P), *LR af 1998 A/S* (Case C-206/02 P), *Brugg Rohrsysteme GmbH* (Case C-207/02 P), *LR af 1998 (Deutschland) GmbH* (Case C-208/02 P) and *ABB Asea Brown Boveri Ltd* (Case C-213/02 P) *v Commission of the European Communities* ECLI:EU:C:2005:408 ... 44

David Meca-Medina and Igor Majcen v Commission of the European Communities (Case C-519/04 P) ECLI:EU:C:2006:492 ... 172, 284, 285

Deutsche Telekom AG v European Commission (Case C-280/08 P) ECLI:EU:C:2010:603 ... 275, 277–78

Dow Benelux NV v Commission of the European Communities (Case 85/87) ECLI:EU:C:1989:379 ... 264

Établissements Consten S.à.R.L. and Grundig-Verkaufs-GmbH v Commission of the European Communities (Joined Cases 56 and 58/64) ECLI:EU:C:1966:41 ... 119, 196, 267

European Commission v Dimosia Epicheirisi Ilektrismou AE (DEI) (Case C-553/12 P) ECLI:EU:C:2014:2083 ... 149

Europemballage and Continental Can v Commission of the European Communities (Case 6/72) ECLI:EU:C:1973:22, ... 149, 262, 277, 283

Expedia Inc v Autorité de la Concurrence and Others (Case C-226/11) ECLI:EU:C:2012:795 ... 44

FNV Kunsten Informatie en Media v Staat der Nederlanden (Case C-413/13) ECLI:EU:C:2014:2411 ... 285

Ford-Werke AG and Ford of Europe Inc. v Commission of the European Communities (Joined Cases 25 and 26/84) ECLI:EU:C:1985:340 ... 268

France Télécom SA v Commission of the European Communities (Case C-202/07 P) ECLI:EU:C:2009:214 ... 149, 275

Franz Völk v S.P.R.L. Ets J. Vervaecke (Case 5/69) ECLI:EU:C:1969:35 ... 92, 112, 117, 257

French Republic and Société commerciale des potasses et de l'azote (SCPA) and Entreprise minière et chimique (EMC) v Commission of the European Communities (Joined Cases C-68/94 and C-30/95) ('Kali & Salz') ECLI:EU:C:1998:148 ... 27

General Motors BV v Commission of the European Communities (Case C-551/03 P) ECLI:EU:C:2006:229 ... 196

GlaxoSmithKline Services Unlimited v Commission of the European Communities (Case C-501/06 P) *and Commission of the European Communities v GlaxoSmithKline Services Unlimited* (Case C-513/06 P) *and European Association of Euro Pharmaceutical Companies (EAEPC) v Commission of the European Communities* (Case C-515/06 P) *and Asociación de exportadores españoles de productos farmacéuticos (Aseprofar) v Commission of the European Communities* (Case C-519/06 P) ECLI:EU:C:2009:610 ... 196-97, 265

Groupement des cartes bancaires v European Commission (Case C-67/13 P) ECLI:EU:C:2014:2204 196-97
Groupement des fabricants de papiers peints de Belgique and others v Commission of the European Communities (Case 73/74) ECLI:EU:C:1975:160 267
Hasselblad (GB) Limited v Commission of the European Communities (Case 86/82) ECLI:EU:C:1984:65 268
Hoechst AG v Commission of the European Communities (Joined Cases 46/87 and 227/88) ECLI:EU:C:1989:337 .... 262, 264
Hoffmann-La Roche & Co. AG v Commission of the European Communities (Case 85/76) ECLI:EU:C:1979:36 .... 23, 153, 215, 264
Huawei Technologies v ZTE (Case C-170/13) ECLI:EU:C:2015:477 277
Hugin Kassaregister AB and Hugin Cash Registers Ltd v Commission of the European Communities (Case 22/78) ECLI:EU:C:1979:138 277
Intel Corporation v Commission (Case C-413/14 P), Appeal brought on 28 August 2014 by Intel Corporation against the judgment in Case T-286/09: *Intel Corporation v European Commission* (pending) 277
Istituto Chemioterapico Italiano and Commercial Solvents v Commission of the European Communities (Joined Cases 6/73 and 7/73) ECLI:EU:C:1974:18 264
Italian Republic v Council of the European Economic Community and Commission of the European Economic Community (Case 32/65) ECLI:EU:C:1966:42 262
JCB Service v Commission of the European Communities (Case C-167/04 P) [2006] ECLI:EU:C:2006:594 44
Kanal 5 Ltd and TV 4 AB v Föreningen Svenska Tonsättares Internationella Musikbyrå (Case C-52/07) ECLI:EU:C:2008:703 282
Konkurrensverket v TeliaSonera Sverige (Case C-52/09) ECLI:EU:C:2011:83 .... 149, 264
Langnese-Iglo GmbH v Commission of the European Communities (Case C-279/95 P) ECLI:EU:C:1998:447 284
Maatschappij Drijvende Bokken BV v Stichting Pensioenfonds voor de Vervoer- en Havenbedrijven (Case C-219/97) ECLI:EU:C:1999:437 .... 172, 284
MasterCard Inc. and Others v European Commission (Case C-382/12 P) ECLI:EU:C:2014:2201 .... 123, 197, 209
Metro SB-Großmärkte GmbH & Co. KG v Commission of the European Communities (Case 26/76) ECLI:EU:C:1977:167 .... 162, 198, 283
Metro SB-Großmärkte GmbH & Co. KG v Commission of the European Communities (Case 75/84) ECLI:EU:C:1986:399 .... 198, 277, 283
Métropole télévision (M6), Suez-Lyonnaise des eaux, France Télécom and Télévision française 1 SA (TF1) v Commission of the European Communities (Case T-112/99) ECLI:EU:T:2001:215 165
Miller International Schallplatten GmbH v Commission of the European Communities (Case 19/77) ECLI:EU:C:1978:19 267
National Panasonic (UK) Limited v Commission of the European Communities (Case 136/79) ECLI:EU:C:1980:169 264
NV IAZ International Belgium and Others v Commission of the European Communities (Joined Cases 96-102, 104, 105, 108 and 110/82) ECLI:EU:C:1983:310 268
NV Nederlandsche Banden Industrie Michelin v Commission of the European Communities (Case 322/81) ECLI:EU:C:1983:313 .... 145, 234, 264

O. v Minister voor Immigratie, Integratie en Asiel (Case C-456/12) ECLI:EU:C:2014:135 77
Orkem v Commission of the European Communities (Case 374/87) ECLI:EU:C:1989:387 264
Pavel Pavlov and Others v Stichting Pensioenfonds Medische Specialisten (Joined Cases C-180/98 to C-184/98) ECLI:EU:C:2000:428. 285
Pfleiderer AG v Bundeskartellamt (Case C-360/09) ECLI:EU:C:2011:389 44
Pierre Fabre Dermo-Cosmétique SAS v Président de l'Autorité de la concurrence and Ministre de l'Économie, de l'Industrie et de l'Emploi (Case C-439/09) ECLI:EU:C:2011:649 198
Post Danmark A/S v Konkurrencerådet (Case C-209/10) ECLI:EU:C:2012:172 .... 277–280, 288–89, 291
Post Danmark A/S v Konkurrencerådet (Case C-23/14) ECLI:EU:C:2015:651 .... 279, 280–81, 289
Pronuptia de Paris GmbH v Pronuptia de Paris Irmgard Schillgallis (Case 161/84) ECLI:EU:C:1986:41 .... 162, 197, 286
Remia BV and others v Commission of the European Communities (Case 42/84) ECLI:EU:C:1985:327 .... 27, 162, 283
Roquette Frères SA v Directeur général de la concurrence, de la consommation et de la répression des fraudes, and Commission of the European Communities (Case C-94/00) ECLI:EU:C:2002:603 264
SA Binon & Cie v SA Agence et messageries de la presse (Case 243/83) ECLI:EU:C:1985:284 .... 197, 286
Société de Vente de Ciments et Bétons de l'Est SA v Kerpen (Case 319/82) ECLI:EU:C:1983:374 123
Sot. Lélos kai Sia EE and Others v GlaxoSmithKline (Joined cases C-468/06 to C-478/06) ECLI:EU:C:2008:504 266
Stergios Delimitis v Henninger Bräu AG (Case C-234/89) ECLI:EU:C:1991:91 268
T-Mobile Netherlands BV, KPN Mobile NV, Orange Nederland NV and Vodafone Libertel NV v Raad van bestuur van de Nederlandse Mededingingsautoriteit (Case C-8/08) ECLI:EU:C:2009:343 .... 197, 266
Telefónica and Telefónica de España v European Commission (Case C-295/12 P) ECLI:EU:C:2014:2062 223
Tepea BV v Commission of the European Communities (Case 28/77) ECLI:EU:C:1978:133 268
Tomra Systems ASA and Others v European Commission (Case C-549/10 P) EU:C:2012:221 .... 222, 275
United Brands Company and United Brands Continentaal BV v Commission of the European Communities (Case 27/76) ECLI:EU:C:1978:22 .... 17, 129, 215, 264, 275
Vereeniging van Cementhandelaren v Commission of the European Communities (Case 8/72) ECLI:EU:C:1972:84 267–68
Vereniging ter Bevordering van het Vlaamse Boekwezen, VBVB, and Vereniging ter Bevordering van de Belangen des Boekhandels, VBBB v Commission of the European Communities (Joined Cases 43/82 and 63/82) ECLI:EU:C:1984:9 267
Walt Wilhelm and others v Bundeskartellamt (Case 14/68) ECLI:EU:C:1969:4 263

Wouters v Algemene Raad van de Nederlandse Orde van Advocaten (Case C-309/99) ECLI:EU:C:2002:98 .... 172, 284

Opinions of Advocates General

Konkurrensverket v TeliaSonera AB (Case C-52/09), Opinion of Advocate General Mazák ECLI:EU:C:2010:483, ... 149, 264, 266, 275, 278, 288, 293
Post Danmark A/S (Case C-23/14), Opinion of Advocate General Kokott ECLI:EU:C:2015:343 277
Solvay v Commission (Case C-109/10 P), Opinion of Advocate General Kokott ECLI:EU:C:2011:256 292
Tomra Systems ASA and Others v European Commission (Case C-549/10 P), Opinion of Advocate General Mazák ECLI:EU:C:2012:55 .... 222, 275

Judgments of the General Court

Airtours plc v Commission of the European Communities (Case T-342/99) ECLI:EU:T:2002:146 .... 27, 244, 261
Akzo Nobel NV and Others v European Commission (Case T-47/10) ECLI:EU:T:2015:506 .... 197, 286
AstraZeneca AB and AstraZeneca plc v European Commission (Case T-321/05) ECLI:EU:T:2010:266 .... 223, 277
Automec Srl v Commission of the European Communities (Case T-24/90) ECLI:EU:T:1992:97 291
Cisco Systems and Messagenet v European Commission (Case T-79/12) ECLI:EU:T:2013:635. 273–74
Compagnie maritime belge transports and Others v Commission of the European Communities (Case T-24/93) ECLI:EU:T:1996:139 276
Der Grüne Punkt—Duales System Deutschland v Commission of the European Communities (Case T-289/01) ECLI:EU:T:2007:155 283
Deutsche Börse AG v European Commission (Case T-175/12) ECLI:EU:T:2015:148 .... 140, 180, 261
Éditions Odile Jacob SAS v European Commission (Case T-237/05) ECLI:EU:T:2010:224 273
Federal Republic of Germany v Commission of the European Communities (Case T-374/04) ECLI:EU:T:2007:332 78
Fédération nationale de la coopération bétail et viande (FNCBV) and Others v Commission of the European Communities (Joined Cases T-217/03 and T-245/03) ECLI:EU:T:2006:391 .... 168, 284
France Télécom SA v Commission of the European Communities (Case T-340/03) ECLI:EU:T:2007:22 276
Gencor Ltd v Commission of the European Communities (Case T-102/96) ECLI:EU:T:1999:65 .... 13, 28, 78, 261
General Electric Company v Commission of the European Communities (Case T-210/01) ECLI:EU:T:2005:456 .... 18, 271
GlaxoSmithKline Services Unlimited v Commission of the European Communities (Case T-168/01) ECLI:EU:T:2006:265 265

Gosselin Group NV (T-208/08) and *Stichting Administratiekantoor Portielje* (T-209/08) v *European Commission* ECLI:EU:T:2011:287 ....197, 286
Hilti AG v Commission of the European Communities (Case T-30/89) ECLI:EU:T:1991:70 282
Intel Corp v European Commission (Case T-286/09) ECLI:EU:T:2014:547....149, 277
Irish Sugar plc v Commission of the European Communities (Case T-228/97) ECLI:EU:T:1999:246 276
Italian Republic v European Commission (Joined Cases T-99/09 and T-308/09) ECLI:EU:T:2013:200....78
Kingdom of Spain v European Commission (Case T-398/07) ECLI:EU:T:2012:173....277
Koninklijke Wegenbouw Stevin v European Commission (Case T-357/06) ECLI:EU:T:2012:488....266
Langnese Iglo GmbH v Commission of the European Communities (Case T-7/93) ECLI:EU:T:1995:98 268
Lundbeck v European Commission (Case T-472/13) [2013] OJ C325/47 (pending). 124
Manufacture française des pneumatiques Michelin v Commission of the European Communities (Case T-203/01) ECLI:EU:T:2003:250 ....222, 276, 289
MasterCard, Inc. and Others v European Commission (Case T-111/08) ECLI:EU:T:2012:260 ....123, 209
Matra Hachette SA v Commission of the European Communities (Case T-17/93) ECLI:EU:T:1994:89 284
Metropole télévision SA and Reti Televisive Italiane SpA and Gestevisión Telecinco SA and Antena 3 de Televisión v Commission of the European Communities (Joined Cases T-528/93, T-542/93, T-543/93, T-546/93) ECLI:EU:T:1996:99....283
Microsoft Corp. v Commission of the European Communities (Case T-201/04) ECLI:EU:T:2007:289....23, 277
Nederlandse Vakbond Varkenshouders (NVV), Marius Schep and Nederlandse Bond van Handelaren in Vee (NBHV) v Commission of the European Communities (Case T-151/05) ECLI:EU:T:2009:144 273
Novácke chemické závody a.s. v European Commission (Case T-352/09) ECLI:EU:T:2012:673....283
Ryanair Holdings v European Commission (Case T-342/07) ECLI:EU:T:2010:280....139, 180, 272–73, 281
Schneider Electric SA v Commission of the European Communities (Case T-310/01) ECLI:EU:T:2002:254....27, 244
Società Italiana Vetro SpA, Fabbrica Pisana SpA and PPG Vernante Pennitalia SpA v Commission of the European Communities (Joined Cases T-68/89, T-77/89 and T-78/89) ECLI:EU:T:1992:38....268
Strintzis Lines Shipping SA v Commission of the European Communities (Case T-65/99) ECLI:EU:T:2003:336....264
Sun Chemical Group BV, Siegwerk Druckfarben AG and Flint Group Germany GmbH v Commission of the European Communities (Case T-282/06) ECLI:EU:T:2007:203 273
Telefónica, SA and Telefónica de España, SA v European Commission (Case T-336/07) ECLI:EU:T:2012:172,....223

Tetra Laval BV v Commission of the European Communities (Case T-5/02) ECLI:EU:T:2002:264 .... 18, 27, 244
Tetra Pak International SA v Commission of the European Communities (Case T-83/91) ECLI:EU:T:1994:246 276
Tomra Systems ASA and Others v European Commission (Case T-155/06) ECLI:EU:T:2010:370 .... 222, 277
United Parcel Service v European Commission (Case T-194/13) [2013] OJ C147/30 (pending) 180, 272
Van den Bergh Foods Ltd v Commission of the European Communities (Case T-65/98) ECLI:EU:T:2003:281 268
Visa Europe Ltd and Visa International Service v European Commission (Case T-461/07) ECLI:EU:T:2011:181 266

European Commission Decisions

ABG oil companies operating in the Netherlands (Case IV/28.841) [1977] OJ L117/1 .... 143, 216, 238
Acec-Berliet (Case IV/26045) [1968] OJ L201/7 162
AEG-Telefunken (Case IV/28.748) [1982] OJ L117/15 .... 116, 200, 232
Aerospatiale-Alenia/de Havilland (Case IV/M.053) [1991] OJ L334/42 .... 128, 175, 213, 235
Airtours/First Choice (Case IV/M.1524) [2000] OJ L93/1 .... 28, 131, 235
AOIP/Beyrard (Case IV/26.949) [1976] OJ L6/8 118
ARA (Case COMP/D3/35.470) and *ARGEV, ARO* (COMP/D3/35.473) [2004] OJ L75/59. 171
Arthur Bell and Sons Ltd (Case IV/29.440) [1978] OJ L235/15 .... 117, 199
Asahi/Saint-Gobain (Case IV/33.863) [1994] OJ L354/87 199
ASBL pour la promotion du tube d'acier soudé électriquement (Case IV/412) [1970] JO L 153/14 .... 116, 232
Assurpol (Case IV/33.100) [1992] OJ L37/16 165
AstraZeneca (Case COMP/A.37.507/F3) 152, 222, 239, 255
Atlas (Case No IV/35.337) [1996] OJ L239/23 162
Automotive Wire Harnesses (Case AT.39748) 208
Bandengroothandel Frieschebrug BV/NV Nederlandsche Banden-Industrie Michelin (Case IV/29.491) [1981] OJ L353/33 .... 144, 215, 233
Bayer Dental (Case IV/32.877) [1990] OJ L351/46 .... 117, 199
Bayer/Gist-Brocades (Case IV/27.073) [1976] OJ L30/13 162
Bayerische Motoren Werke AG (Case IV/14.650) [1975] OJ L29/1 .... 162, 202
Bearings (Case AT.39922) 208
Bertelsmann/Kirch/Premiere (Case IV/M.993) [1999] OJ L53/1 130
Bertelsmann/Springer (Case COMP/M.3178) 138
BIC/Gillette and Others (Case IV/33.486) [1993] OJ L116/21 .... 127, 215
Blackstone/Acetex (Case COMP/M.3625) Commission Decision 138
Blokker/Toys 'R' Us (Case IV/M.890) [1998] OJ L316/1 .... 130, 176, 213, 235
BMW Belgium NV and Belgian BMW dealers (Case IV/29/146) [1978] OJ L 46/33 199
Boeing/McDonnell Douglas (Case IV/M.877) OJ [1997] L336/16 11
BPB Industries plc (Case IV/31.900) [1989] OJ L10/50, ... 143, 182, 215

BPCL/ICI (Case IV/30.863) [1984] OJ L212/1 163
Breeders' rights—maize seed (Case IV/28.824) [1978] OJ L286/23 200
British Airways/American Airlines/Iberia (Case COMP/39.596) 167
British Dental Trade Association—BDTA (IV/31.593)
[1988] OJ L233/15 .... 116, 200, 232, 244
British Leyland (Case IV/30.615) [1984] OJ L207/11 .... 146, 215
British Telecommunications (Case IV/29.877) [1982] OJ L360/36 215
Cafeteros de Colombia (Case IV/30.077) [1982] OJ L360/31 116
Cauliflowers (Case IV/28.948) [1978] OJ L21/23 116
CECED (Case IV.F.1/36.718) [2000] OJ L 187/47 170
CEZ (Case AT/39727) 150, 226
Charles Jourdan (Case IV/31.697) [1989] OJ L35/31 162
Chiquita (Case IV/26699) [1976] OJ L95/1 .... 143, 219
CISAC (Case COMP/C2/38.698) 124, 171, 208, 243
Coapi (IV/33.686) [1995] OJ L122/37 199
Computerland (Case IV/32.034) [1987] OJ L222/12 162
Continental Can Company (Case IV/26.811) [1972] OJ L7/25
(no English version available) 127
Continental/Michelin (Case No IV/32.173) [1988] OJ L305/33 .... 116, 244
Continental/United/Lufthansa/Air Canada (Case COMP/AT.39595) 122, 167, 209
Convention chaufourniers (Case IV/242-295) [1969] OJ L122/8
(no English version available) 117
Copper Plumbing Tubes (Case COMP/E-1/38.069) 243
D.R.U.—Blondel (Case IV/3036) [1965] OJ 65/2194
(no English version available) 162
Danish Crown/Vestjyske Slagterier (Case IV/M.1313) [2000] OJ L20/1 175
De Beers (Case COMP/B-2/38.381) 239
Decca Navigator System (Cases IV/30.979 and 31.394) [1989] OJ L43/27 .... 144, 182, 215
Deutsche Bahn I (Case COMP/AT.39678) and *Deutsche Bahn II*
(COMP/AT.39731) 150, 186, 226
Deutsche Börse/NYSE Euronext (Case No COMP/M.6166) 137, 178, 239,
255, 272
Deutsche Telekom/BetaResearch (Case IV/M.1027) [1999] OJ L53/31 130
Distribution system of Ford Werke AG (Case IV/30.696)
[1983] OJ L327/31 .... 116, 200, 268
DSD (Case COMP/34.493) [2001] OJ L319/1 170
Du Pont/ICI (Case IV/M.214) [1993] OJ L7/13 .... 129, 235
Duro-Dyne—Europair (Case IV/560) [1975] OJ L 29/11 202
E-Books (Case COMP/39.847) 122
E.ON Gas (Case COMP/39.317) 150, 226
EBU/Eurovision System (Case IV/32.150) [1993] OJ L179/23 200
Eco System/Peugeot (Case IV/33.157) [1992] OJ L66/1 200
ECS/AKZO (Case IV/30.698) [1985] OJ L374/1 .... 91, 144, 218, 233
ENI (Case COMP/39.315) 150, 226
ENI/Montedison (Case IV/31.055) [1987] OJ L5/13 163
Enichem/ICI (Case IV/31.846) [1988] OJ L50/18 163
España v Telefónica (Case COMP/38.784) 239
Eurocheque—Helsinki Agreement (Case IV/30.717-A) [1992] OJ L95/50 201

Eurofix-Bauco v Hilti (Cases IV/30.787 and 31.488) [1988] OJ L65/19 ... 144, 182, 215
European Sugar Industry (Case IV/26 918) [1973] OJ L140/17 ... 144, 219
Exxon/Shell (Case IV/33.640) [1994] OJ L144/20 ... 165
Far Eastern Freight Conference (Case IV/33.218) [1994] OJ L378/17 ... 199
Fentanyl (Case COMP/AT.39685) ... 123, 167, 208, 243
Fiat Geotech/Ford New Holland (Case IV/M.009) ... 138
Fisher-Price/Quaker Oats Ltd—Toyco (Case IV/31.017) [1988] OJ L49/19 ... 200
Fittings (Case COMP/F-1/38.121) ... 168
Floras Bookshops v OUP/Burlington/Pearson (Case No COMP/39771) ... 154
Ford/Volkswagen (Case IV/33.814) [1993] OJ L20/14 ... 164, 200
French beef (Case COMP/C. 38.279/F3) OJ [2003] L209/12 ... 168
Gas Insulated Switchgear (Case COMP/F/38.899) ... 168, 208
Gaz de France (Case COMP/39.316) ... 150
GDF/ENEL (Case COMP/38662) ... 123–24
GEMA I (Case IV/26.760) [1971] OJ L134/15 (no English version available) ... 142
GEMA statutes (Case IV/29.971) [1982] OJ L94/12 ... 218
Gencor/Lonrho (Case IV/M.619) [1997] OJ L11/30 ... 130, 175, 235
General Electric/Honeywell (Case COMP/M.2220) [2004] OJ L48/1 ... 14–15, 130, 213, 236, 272
General Motors Continental (Case IV/28.851) [1975] OJ L 29/14 ... 218, 234
GERO-fabriek (Case IV/24.510) [1977] OJ L16/8 ... 116, 200
Glatfelter/Crompton Assets (Case No COMP/M.4215) ... 138
Glaxo Wellcome (Case IV/36.957/F3), *Aseprofar and Fedifar* (Case IV/36.997/F3), *Spain Pharma* (Case IV/37.121/F3), *BAI* (Case IV/37.138/F3), *EAEPC* (Case IV/37.380/F3) [2001] OJ L302/1 ... 124, 243, 269, 296
Goodyear Italiana-Euram (Case IV/23.013) [1975] OJ L38/10 ... 162, 202
Google (Cases COMP/C-3/39.740, COMP/C-3/39.775 & COMP/C-3/39.768) ... 259
Google/DoubleClick (Case No COMP/M.4731) ... 138
Groupement des cartes bancaires (Case COMP/D1/38606) ... 123, 192, 209, 239, 255
Guinness/Grand Metropolitan (Case No IV/M.938) [1998] OJ L 288/24 ... 130, 176, 213, 235
GVL (Case IV/29.839) [1981] OJ L370/49 ... 145, 182, 216, 232
Hasselblad (Case IV/25.757) [1982] OJ L161/18 ... 116, 232, 268
Hennessy-Henkell (Case IV/26.912) [1980] OJ L383/11 ... 115, 232
HOV SVZ/MCN (Case IV/33.941) [1994] OJ L104/34 ... 144, 215, 234
Hugin/Liptons (Case IV/29.132) [1978] OJ L22/23 ... 144, 182, 217, 234
Hutchison 3G Austria/Orange Austria (Case No M.6497) ... 179
IAG/BMI (Case No COMP/M.6447) ... 241
IATA Cargo Agency Programme (Case IV/32.792) [1991] OJ L258/29 ... 200
IBM Maintenance Services (Case COMP/39.692) ... 150, 186
Intel (Case COMP/C-3 /37.990) ... 149, 187, 221, 239, 294

International Private Satellite Partners (Case IV/34.768) [1994] OJ L354/75 162
Internationales Chininkartell (Case IV/26.623) [1969] OJ L192/5
(no English version available) 200
Irish Sugar plc (Case IV/34.621, 35.059/F-3) [1997] OJ L258/1 144
Italian flat glass (Case IV.29.988) [1981] OJ L326/32....................116, 200, 268
John Deere (Case IV/30.809) [1985] OJ L35/58....................199
Johnson & Johnson (Case IV/29.702) [1980] OJ L 377/16....................117, 199,
Kawasaki (Case IV/29.430) [1979] OJ L16/9....................117
KLM/Martinair (Case COMP/M.5141) 138, 178
Konica (Case IV/31.503) [1988] OJ L78/34 200
Langenscheidt/Hachette (Case IV/29.972) [1982] OJ L39/25 200
London European—Sabena (Case IV/32.318) [1988] OJ L317/47....................218
Long term electricity contracts in France (Case COMP/39.386) 150
Lufthansa/Austrian Airlines (Case COMP/M.5440) 179
Lufthansa/SN Airholding (Case COMP/M.5335) 138
Lundbeck (Case AT.39226) 124, 167,
208, 243
Magill TV Guide/ITP, BBC and RTE (Case IV/31.851) [1989] OJ L78/43 217
Magyar Suzuki Corporation (Case AT.40072) 154
MasterCard (Case COMP/34.579), *EuroCommerce* (Case COMP/36.518),
and *Commercial Cards* (Case COMP/38.580) ('Mastercard I') 123, 209, 241
MCI WorldCom/Sprint (Case COMP/M.1741) [2003] OJ L300/1 130
MELDOC (Case IV/31.204) [1986] OJ L348/50 200
Metso/Aker Kvaerner (Case No COMP/M.4187) 179
Microsoft (Case COMP/C-3/37.392) [2007] OJ L32/23....................21
Microsoft (tying) (Case COMP/C-3/39.530)....................150, 226, 239, 259
Microsoft/Skype (Case No COMP/M.6281) 273
Milchförderungsfonds (Case IV/28.930) [1985] OJ L35/35 200
Miller International Schallplatten GmbH (Case IV/29.018)
[1976] OJ L357/40 ....117, 200, 244
Moët et Chandon (Case IV/30.188) [1982] OJ L94/7 117
Morgan Stanley/Visa International and Visa Europe
(Case COMP/D1/37860) 123, 239, 243
Motorola—Enforcement of GPRS Standard Essential Patents
(Case AT.39985) 149, 186, 221,
239, 259, 297
MSG Media Service (Case IV/M.469) [1994] OJ L364/1 ....130, 176
Mushrooms (Case AT.39965) 208
Napier Brown—British Sugar (Case IV/30.178) OJ L284/41 ....144, 182, 219, 232
Nathan-Bricolux (Case COMP/F.1/36.516) [2001] OJ L54/1 206
National Panasonic (Case IV/30.070) [1982] OJ L 354/28....................117, 200, 233
National Sulphuric Acid Association (Case IV/27.958)
[1980] OJ L 260/24 ....116, 199
NAVEWA-ANSEAU (Case IV/29.995) [1982] OJ L167/39 ....116, 232, 268
Nederlandse Cement-Handelmaatschappij NV (Case IV/595)
[1972] OJ L 22/16 ....116, 200, 232, 244
Nestlé/Perrier (Case IV/M.190) [1992] OJ L356/1 ....129, 235
Nokia/Navteq (Case COMP/M.4942) 138, 178

Nutricia/de Rooij (Case IV/30.389) and *Nutricia/Zuid-Hollandse Conservenfabriek* (IV/30.408) [1983] OJ L376/22 200
Olympic/Aegean Airlines (Case No COMP/M.5830) 137, 178, 239, 255, 272
Omnis/Microsoft (Case COMP/39.784) 154
ONP (Case 39510) (no English version available) 208, 243
Outokumpu/INOXUM (Case COMP/M.6471) 179
Parfums Givenchy system of selective distribution (Case No IV/33.542) [1992] OJ L236/11 163
Peugeot (Case IV/31.143) [1986] OJ L295/19 ....116, 200
Philips/Osram (Case IV/34.252) [1994] OJ L378/37. 164
PO/Elevators and Escalators (Case COMP/E-1/38.823) 168, 208
Prokent-Tomra (Case COMP/E-1/38.113) 187, 222, 241, 255
Rabattbeschluss der Interessengemeinschaft der deutschen keramischen Wand- und Bodenfliesenwerke (Case IV/25107) [1971] OJ L10/15 (no English version available) 114, 232
Rank/Sopelem (Case IV/26.603) [1975] OJ L29/20 162
Repsol CPP (Case COMP/B-1/38.348) 122, 209
Reuters Instrument Codes (Case AT.39654) 150, 187, 226, 239
Rio Tinto Alcan (Case AT.39230) 122, 209
Rolled zinc products and zinc alloys (Case IV/29.629) [1982] OJ L362/40 ....116, 268
Romanian Power Exchange/OPCOM (Case AT.39984) 149, 152, 187, 223, 243
RTL/Veronica/Endemol (Case IV/M.553) [1996] OJ L134/32 130
Ryanair/Aer Lingus I (Case No COMP/M.4439) 137, 178, 239, 272
Ryanair/Aer Lingus III (Case COMP/M.6663) Summary Decision [2013] OJ C216/22 ....137, 178, 239, 255, 272
Ryanair/Aer Lingus III (Case No COMP/M.6663) 137, 178, 239, 255, 272
Ryanair/DAA-Aer Lingus (Case COMP/39.886) 154
SABA's EEC distribution system (Case IV/29.598) [1983] OJ L376/41 ....116, 163, 232, 244
Saint-Gobain/Wacker-Chemie/NOM (Case No IV/M.774) [1997] OJ L 247/1 ....130, 175, 236
Samsung—Enforcement of UMTS Standard Essential Patents (Case AT.39939) 150, 186
Sandoz (Case IV/31.741) [1987] OJ L222/28 ....117, 233
Schneider/Legrand (Case COMP/M.2283) OJ [2004] L101/1 29
Schöller Lebensmittel (Cases IV/31.533 and IV/34.072) [1993] OJ L183/1 200
Sea-Invest/EMO-EKOM (Case COMP/M.3848) 241
SEP et autres/Peugeot SA (Cases F-2/36.623/36.820/37.275) 124, 209, 243
Ship Classification (Case COMP/39.416) 122
Siemens/Fanuc (Case IV/30.739) [1985] OJ L376/29 200
Société Air France/Alitalia Linee Aeree Italiane (Case COMP/38.284/D2) 209

Soda-ash-ICI (Case IV/33.133-D) [1991] OJ L152/40 .... 143, 215, 234
Soda-ash-Solvay, ICI (Case IV/33.133-A) [1991] OJ L152/1 .... 200, 233
Souris—Topps (Case COMP/C-3/37.980) 124, 243
Stichting Baksteen (Case IV/34.456) [1994] OJ L131/15 163
Sugar beet (Case IV/32.414) [1990] OJ L31/32 199
Synthetic fibres (Case IV/30.810) [1984] OJ L207/17. 163
T-Mobile Austria/Tele.ring (Case No COMP/M.3916) 138, 179
Telefónica UK/ Vodafone UK/Everything Everywhere/JV (Case COMP/M.6314) 138
Telefónica/Portugal Telecom (Case COMP/39.839) 122
Telekomunikacja Polska (Case COMP/39.525) 149, 186, 221, 239
Tetra Laval/Sidel (Case COMP/M.2416) [2004] OJ L43/13 .... 31, 132, 176, 235
Tetra Pak I (BTG licence) (Case IV/31.043) [1988] OJ L272/27 216
Tetra Pak II (Case IV/31.043) [1992] OJ L72/1 182
The Distillers Company Limited (Case IV/28.282) [1978] OJ L50/16 .... 116, 199
Theal Watts (Case IV/28.812) [1977] OJ L 39/19 .... 116, 233, 268
Tipp-Ex (Case IV- 31.192) [1987] OJ L222/1 117
TNT/Canada Post, DBP Postdienst, La Poste, PTT Post & Sweden Post (Case IV/M.102) 138
Tom Tom/Tele Atlas (Case COMP/M.4854) 138, 178, 241
Trans-Atlantic Conference Agreement (Case IV/35.134) [1999] OJ L95/1 216
Transocean Marine Paint Association (Case IV/223) [1980] L39/73 162
UEFA Financial Fair Play Rules (Case AT.40105) 154
Uniform Eurocheques (Case IV/30.717) [1985] OJ L35/43 200
UPS/TNT Express (Case No COMP/M.6570 .... 137, 140, 178, 242, 272
Varta/Bosch (Case IV/M.012) [1991] OJ L 320/26 128
VBBB/VBVB (Case IV/428) [1982] OJ L54/36 200
Velcro/Aplix (Case IV/4.204) [1985] OJ L233/22 200
Vereeniging van Cementhandelaren (Case IV/324) [1972] OJ L 13/34 .... 116, 232, 268
Viho/Toshiba (Case No IV/32.879) [1991] OJ L287/39 199
Villeroy & Boch (Case IV/30.665) [1985] OJ L376/15 163
Visa MIF (Case COMP/39.398) 167
Vitamins (Case IV/29.020) [1976] OJ L223/27 .... 144, 219, 232
Volvo/Scania (Case COMP/M.1672) [2001] OJ L143/74 .... 130, 241
VW (Case COMP/35733) [1998] OJ L124/60 123
Wanadoo España v Telefónica (Case COMP/38.784) 152, 187, 222–23, 239, 255
Warner-Lambert/Gillette (Case IV/33.440) and *BIC/Gillette and Others* (Case IV/33.486) [1993] OJ L116/21 .... 127, 215
Welded steel mesh (Case IV/31.553) [1989] OJ L260/1 200
White lead (Case IV/29.535) [1979] OJ L21/16 200
Yves Rocher (Cases IV/31.428 to 31.432) [1987] OJ L8/49 162
Yves Saint Laurent Parfums (Case IV/33.242) [1992] OJ L12/24 163
Zera/Montedison (Case IV/31.550) and *Hinkens/Stähler* (Case IV/31.898) C [1993] OJ L272/28 199

Amicus curiae observations by the European Commission

Observations of the Commission under Article 15, paragraph 3 of Regulation 1/2003 in 2003 No 7764P *The Competition Authority v Beef Industry Development Society Ltd (BIDS) and Barry Brothers (Carrigmore) Meats Ltd*, http://ec.europa.eu/competition/court/amicus_curiae_2010_bids_en.pdf.................169

US cases

US Supreme Court

Addyston Pipe and Steel Co v United States, 175 U.S. 211 (1899).......................................194
Brooke Group Ltd v Brown & Williamson Tobacco Corp 509 U.S. 209 (1993) 64, 82, 258
Brown Shoe Co v. United States, 370 U.S. 294 (1962)...63
California Dental Association v FTC, 526 U.S. 756 (1999). 68
Continental T. V., Inc v GTE Sylvania Inc, 433 U.S. 36 (1977) 65, 67, 69, 194
FTC v Indiana Federation of Dentists, 476 U.S. 447 (1986)...67, 194
Hartford Fire Ins Co v California, 509 U.S. 764 (1993) 13
Leegin Creative Leather Products, Inc v PSKS, Inc, 127 S.Ct. 2705 (2007)....................67, 194
National Society of Professional Engineers v United States, 435 U.S. 679 (1978)...65
NCAA v Board of Regents of the University of Oklahoma, 468 U.S. 85 (1984) 64, 82, 258
Northern Pacific R. Co v United States, 356 U.S, 1 (1958)..66, 196
Northwest Wholesale Stationers, Inc v Pacific Stationery & Printing Co, 472 U.S. 284 (1985)...67, 194
Palmer v BRG of Georgia, Inc., 498 U.S. 46 (1990)...194
Reiter v Sonotone Corp, 442 U.S. 330 (1979)...64, 258
Standard Oil Co of New Jersey v United States, 221 U.S. 1 (1911) 65
State Oil Co v Khan et al, 522 U.S. 3 (1997)...67, 194
United States v Topco Associates, Inc 405 U.S. 596 (1972)...63
United States v Trenton Potteries Co, 273 U.S. 392 (1927) 194
United States v Arnold, Schwinn & Co, 388 U.S. 365 (1967)...67, 194
United States v Socony-Vacuum Oil Co, 310 U. S. 150 (1940) 194
United States v Trans-Missouri Freight Assn, 166 U.S. 290 (1897)...62

Circuit Courts

Addyston Pipe and Steel Company v United States, 85 F. 271 (1898)....................................65
Broadcom Corp v Qualcomm Inc, 501 F.3d 297 (2007)...64, 82, 258
Commonwealth of Massachusetts v Microsoft Corp, 373 F.3d 1199 (2004) 21
Rebel Oil Company, Inc, Auto Flite Oil Company, Inc v. Atlantic Richfield Company 51 F.3d 1421 (1995)...64, 82, 258
United States v Microsoft Corp, 147 F.3d 935 (1998)..19
United States v Microsoft Corp, 253 F.3d 34 (2001)..20
United States v Microsoft Corp, 56 F.3d 1448 (1995)..19
United States v Aluminium Co of America, 148 F.2d 416 (1945) 13

District Courts

United States v Microsoft Corp, 84 F. Supp.2d 9 (1999) (Findings of Fact) 19
United States v Microsoft Corp, 87 F. Supp.2d 30 (2000) (Conclusions of Law) 20
United States v Microsoft Corp, 97 F. Supp.2d 59 (2000) (Final Judgment) 20

Cases filed by the FTC

United States of America v Mahle GmbH, Mahle, Inc., Mabeg eV, Metal Leve, S.A., and Metal Leve, Inc., FTC matter/file number: 9610085a, CIVIL ACTION NUMBER: 961-0085 13

Decisions by national competition authorities

Germany (Bundeskartellamt)

Deutsche Post AG (Case B9-128/12) decision of 2 July 2015..............292
Deutsche Telekom (B7-11/09) decision of 6 August 2009..............293

France (Autorité de la Concurrence)

E-kanopi, Decision 13-D-07 of 28 February 2013..............293

Belgium (Autorité Belge de la Concurrence)

Lampiris v Electrabel (Affaire CONC-P/K-09/0002) decision ABC-2015-P/K-09-AUD of 26 March 2015 293

United Kingdom (Office of Fair Trading/Competition and Markets Authority)

Flybe Limited (Case MPINF-PSWA001) decision of 5 November 2010..............293
CH Jones Limited (Case reference: CE/9278/10) decision of 1 October 2013..............293

TABLE OF LEGISLATION

European Union legislation

Treaties

Treaty establishing the European Coal and Steel Community, as signed in Paris on 18 April 1951 8
Treaty Establishing the European Economic Community, as signed in Rome on 25 March 1957 .... 9, 85, 127
Single European Act, signed in Luxembourg on 17 February 1986 [1987] OJ L169/1 10
Treaty on European Union, as signed in Maastricht on 7 February 1992 [1992] OJ C191/1 90
Treaty Establishing the European Community, as signed in Nice on 26 February 2001 [2002] OJ C325/33 (consolidated version) 263
Treaty on European Union, as signed at Lisbon on 13 December 2007 [2012] OJ C326/13 (consolidated version) 3
Treaty on the Functioning of the European Union, as signed at Lisbon on 13 December 2007 [2012] OJ C326/47 (consolidated version) 3

Travaux Preparatoires

Intergovernmental Committee of the Messina Conference, Report by the Heads of Delegations to the Foreign Ministers (Spaak Report) of 21 April 1956, available at http://www.cvce.eu/en 85, 127
Entwurf eines Protokolls über die Sitzungen der Arbeitsgruppe vom 3.–5. September 1956 in Brüssel, 10. September 1956, document (57) in R Schulze and T Hoeren (eds), *Dokumente zum Europarecht, Band 3, Kartellrecht* (Berlin, Springer, 2000) 172 127

Council Regulations

Council Regulation (EEC) No 17: First Regulation implementing Articles 85 and 86 of the Treaty [1962] OJ L13/204 .... 57, 160
Council Regulation (EEC) No 19/65 on application of Article 85(3) of the Treaty to certain categories of agreements and concerted practices [1965] OJ L36/533 92
Council Regulation (EEC) No 2821/71 on application of Article 85(3) of the Treaty to categories of agreements, decisions and concerted practices [1971] OJ L285/46 92
Council Regulation (EEC) No 4064/89 of 21 December 1989 on the control of concentrations between undertakings OJ [1989] L 395/1 .... 15, 17, 41, 89, 213

Council Regulation (EC) 1310/97 of 30 June 1997 amending Regulation (EEC) No 4064/89 on the control of concentrations between undertakings [1997] OJ L180/1 138
Council Regulation (EC) No 1215/1999 of 10 June 1999 amending Regulation No 19/65/EEC on the application of Article 81(3) of the Treaty to certain categories of agreements and concerted practices [1999] OJ L148/1 45
Council Regulation (EC) No 1/2003 of 16 December 2002 on the implementation of the rules on competition laid down in Articles 81 and 82 of the Treaty [2003] OJ L1/1 ....1, 57, 91, 160
Council Regulation (EC) No 139/2004 of 20 January 2004 on the control of concentrations between undertakings [2004] OJ L 24/1 ....17, 41, 46, 89, 134, 177, 214

Commission Regulations

Commission Regulation 67/67/EEC on the application of Article 85(3) of the Treaty to certain categories of exclusive dealing agreements [1967] OJ 57/849....................161, 202
Commission Regulation (EEC) No 2779/72 on the application of Article 85(3) of the Treaty to categories of specialization agreements [1972] OJ L292/23 ....92, 161, 202
Commission Regulation (EEC) No 1983/83 of 22 June 1983 on the application of Article 85(3) of the Treaty to categories of exclusive distribution agreements [1983] OJ L173/1....................45, 92, 161
Commission Regulation (EEC) No 1984/83 of 22 June 1983 on the application of Article 85(3) of the Treaty to categories of exclusive purchasing agreements [1983] OJ L281/25....................45
Commission Regulation (EEC) No 1984/83 on the application of Article 85(3) of the Treaty to categories of exclusive purchasing agreements [1983] OJ L173/5 ....92, 161, 202
Commission Regulations (EEC) No 2349/84 on the application of Article 85(3) of the Treaty to certain categories of patent licensing agreements [1984] OJ L219/15 161
Commission Regulation (EEC) No 123/85 on the application of Article 85(3) of the Treaty to certain categories of motor vehicle distribution and servicing agreements [1985] OJ L15/16 ....161, 202
Commission Regulation (EEC) No 417/85 on the application of Article 85(3) of the Treaty to categories of specialization agreements [1985] OJ L53/1....................161
Commission Regulation (EEC) No 418/85 on the application of Article 85(3) of the Treaty to categories of research and development agreements [1985] OJ L53/5 161
Commission Regulation (EEC) No 4087/88 of 30 November 1988 on the application of Article 85 (3) of the Treaty to categories of franchise agreements [1988] OJ L359/46 ....45, 92, 161, 202
Commission Regulations (EEC) No 2672/88 on the application of Article 85(3) of the Treaty to certain categories of agreements between undertakings relating to computer reservation systems for air transport services [1988] OJ L239/13....................161, 203

Commission Regulations (EEC) No 556/89 on the application of Article 85(3) of the Treaty to certain categories of know-how licensing agreements [1989] OJ L61/1 161
Commission Regulation (EEC) No 82/91 on the application of Article 85(3) of the Treaty to certain categories of Agreements, Decisions and concerted practices concerning ground handling services [1991] OJ L10/7 161
Commission Regulation (EEC) No 1617/93 on the application of Article 85(3) of the Treaty to certain categories of agreements and concerted practices concerning joint planning and coordination of schedules, joint operations, consultations on passenger and cargo tariffs on scheduled air services and slot allocation at airports [1993] OJ L155/18....161, 203
Commission Regulation (EC) No 1617/93 on the application of Article 85(3) of the Treaty to certain categories of agreements and concerted practices concerning joint planning and coordination of schedules, joint operations, consultations on passenger and cargo tariffs on scheduled air services and slot allocation at airports [1993] OJ L155/18 ....161, 203
Commission Regulation (EC) No 870/95 on the application of Article 85(3) of the Treaty to certain categories of agreements, decisions and concerted practices between liner shipping companies [1995] OJ L89/7....161, 203
Commission Regulation (EC) No 2790/1999 of 22 December 1999 on the application of Article 81(3) of the Treaty to categories of vertical agreements and concerted practices [1999] OJ L336/21 ....45, 211
Commission Regulation (EU) No 461/2010 on the application of Article 101(3) of the Treaty on the Functioning of the European Union to categories of vertical agreements and concerted practices in the motor vehicle sector [2010] OJ L129/52 167
Commission Regulation (EU) No 1217/2010 on the application of Article 101(3) of the Treaty on the Functioning of the European Union to certain categories of research and development agreements [2010] OJ L 335/36....210
Commission Regulation (EU) No 1218/2010 on the application of Article 101(3) of the Treaty on the Functioning of the European Union to certain categories of specialisation agreements [2010] OJ L335/46 210
Commission Regulation (EU) No 330/2010 of 20 April 2010 on the application of Article 101(3) of the Treaty on the Functioning of the European Union to categories of vertical agreements and concerted practices [2010] OJ L102/1 ....45, 167, 210
Commission Regulation (EU) 316/2014 on the application of Article 101(3) of the Treaty on the Functioning of the European Union to categories of technology transfer agreements [2014] OJ L93/17....167

Directives

European Parliament and Council Directive 94/62/EC of 20 December 1994 on packaging and packaging waste [1994] OJ L365/10 171

Commission Notices and Communications

European Commission, Bekanntmachung über Alleinvertriebsverträge mit Handelsvertretern [1962] OJ 139/2921 (no English version) 112, 160, 198

European Commission, Bekanntmachung über Patentlizenzverträge [1962] OJ C113/2922 (no English version) 92
European Commission, Bekanntmachung über Vereinbarungen, Beschlüsse und aufeinander abgestimmte Verhaltensweisen, die eine zwischenbetriebliche Zusammenarbeit betreffen [1968] OJ C75/3 (no English version) 92, 112, 160, 198
European Commission, Bekanntmachung der Kommission vom 27. Mai 1970 über Vereinbarungen, Beschlüsse und aufeinander abgestimmte Verhaltensweisen von geringer Bedeutung [1970] OJ C64/1 (no English version) 92, 113, 160, 198, 257
European Commission, Commission Notice concerning agreements of minor importance of 19 December 1977 [1977] OJ C 313/3 ....92, 121, 113, 160, 257
European Commission, Notice of 18 December 1978 concerning its assessment of certain subcontracting agreements in relation to Article 85(1) of the EEC Treaty [1979] OJ C1/2 93
European Commission, Notice concerning Commission Regulations (EEC) No 1983/83 and (EEC) No 1984/83 of 22 June 1983 on the application of Article 85(3) of the Treaty to categories of exclusive distribution and exclusive purchasing agreements [1984] OJ C101/2 93
European Commission, Commission Notice concerning agreements of minor importance of 3 September 1986 [1986] OJ C 231/2 ....92, 113, 160, 257
European Commission, Notice regarding restrictions ancillary to concentrations [1990] OJ C203/5 ....93, 128
European Commission, Notice regarding the concentrative and cooperative operations under Council Regulation (EEC) No 4064/89 of 21 December 1989 on the control of concentrations between undertakings [1990] OJ C203/10 ....93, 128
European Commission, Guidelines on the application of EEC competition rules in the telecommunications sector [1991] OJ C 233/2 93
European Commission, Notice concerning the assessment of the cooperative joint ventures pursuant to Article 85 of the EEC Treaty [1993] OJ C43/2 ....113, 199
European Commission, Notice on the definition of the relevant market for the purposes of Community competition law [1997] OJ C372/5 ....93, 238
European Commission, Commission Notice concerning agreements of minor importance of 19 December 1997 [1997] OJ C 372/13 ....92, 113, 121, 160, 257
European Commission, Guidelines on Vertical Restraints of 13 October 2000 [2000] OJ C291/1 ....35, 41, 43, 58, 104, 119, 204
European Commission, Guidelines on the Applicability of Article 81 of the EC Treaty to Horizontal Cooperation Agreements of 6 January 2001 [2001] OJ C3/2 ....35, 41, 43, 50, 58, 119, 204
European Commission, Commission Notice concerning agreements of minor importance of 22 December 2001 [2001] OJ C368/13) 92, 258

European Commission, Guidelines on the assessment of horizontal mergers under the Council Regulation on the control of concentrations between undertakings [2004] OJ C31/5 .... 35, 42, 46, 58, 105, 135, 177, 238
European Commission, Guidelines on the Application of Article 81 of the Treaty to Technology Transfer Agreements [2004] OJ C101/2 .... 35, 41, 43, 50, 58, 104, 119, 204
European Commission, Guidelines on the Application of Article 81(3) of the Treaty [2004] OJ C101/97 .... 35, 41, 43, 50, 119, 165, 204, 238, 255, 296–97
European Commission, Notice on the handling of complaints [2004] OJ C101/65 154
European Commission, Notice on Immunity from fines and reduction of fines in cartel cases [2006] OJ C298/17 2
European Commission, Guidelines on the assessment of non-horizontal mergers under the Council Regulation on the control of concentrations between undertakings [2008] OJ C265/6 .... 42, 46, 58, 105, 135, 143, 177, 274
European Commission, Guidelines on the applicability of Article 101 of the Functioning of the European Union to horizontal co-operation agreements of 14 January 2011 [2011] OJ C11/1 .... 41, 119, 204
European Commission, Notice on agreements of minor importance which do not appreciably restrict competition under Article 101(1) of the Treaty on the Functioning of the European Union (De Minimis Notice) [2014] OJ C291/1 .... 92, 113, 121, 258

European Commission Reports

European Commission, *First Report on Competition Policy 1971* 87, 93, 95, 97, 99
European Commission, *Second Report on Competition Policy 1972* 95, 97, 142
European Commission, *Third Report on Competition Policy 1973* 97
European Commission, *Fifth Report on Competition Policy 1975* 95–97
European Commission, *Sixth Report on Competition Policy 1976* 95
European Commission, *Seventh Report on Competition Policy 1977* 95–96
European Commission, *Eighth Report on Competition Policy 1978* 95, 98–99
European Commission, *Ninth Report on Competition Policy 1979* 94, 96, 98
European Commission, *Tenth Report on Competition Policy 1980* 164
European Commission, *Eleventh Report on Competition Policy 1981* 94, 97, 99–100
European Commission, *Twelfth Report on Competition 1982* 96–97, 99–100, 164
European Commission, *Thirteenth Report on Competition Policy 1983* 97, 100, 102
European Commission, *Fourteenth Report on Competition 1984* 100
European Commission, *Fifteenth Report on Competition Policy 1985* 97–100
European Commission, *Seventeenth Report on Competition Policy 1987* 291
European Commission, *Twentieth Report on Competition Policy 1990* 98, 100
European Commission, *Twenty-first Report on Competition Policy 1991* 101
European Commission, *Twenty-second Report on Competition Policy 1992* 95, 98, 101–02

European Commission, *Twenty-third Report on Competition Policy 1993*....................93, 96, 100–02
European Commission, *Twenty-fourth Report on Competition Policy 1994*.................98, 100
European Commission, *Twenty-fifth Report on Competition Policy 1995*.....................95–96, 98, 100
European Commission, *Twenty-sixth Report on Competition Policy 1996*............96, 101–02
European Commission, *Thirtieth Report on Competition Policy 2000*................................55
European Commission, *Thirty-second Report on Competition Policy 2002*.......................107
European Commission, *Thirty-third Report on Competition Policy 2003*.........................107
European Commission, *Report on Competition Policy 2004*, Volume 1 257
European Commission, *Report on Competition Policy 2005*...108
European Commission, *Report on Competition Policy 2006*..................................87, 107–08
European Commission, *Report on Competition Policy 2007*...107
European Commission, *Report on Competition Policy 2008*...107
European Commission, *Report on Competition Policy 2010*...107
European Commission, *Report on Competition Policy 2011*...108
European Commission, *Report on Competition Policy 2013*...108

Commission Staff Working Papers, Reports, White Papers, Green Papers and other preparatory Commission instruments

European Commission, Green Paper On Vertical Restraints in EC Competition Policy COM(96) 721 of 22 January 1997............................. 11, 41, 236, 302
European Commission, Communication from the Commission on the application of the Community competition rules to vertical restraints—Follow-up to the Green Paper on vertical restraints [1998] OJ C365/3 ....50, 104
European Commission, White Paper on modernisation of the rules implementing Articles 85 and 86 of the EC Treaty [1999] OJ C132/1...57, 257
European Commission, Green Paper on the Review of Council Regulation (EEC) No 4064/89 COM(2001) 745..................................35, 50, 133
European Commission, 'Summary of the replies received' to the public consultation on the Green Paper on the Review of Council Regulation (EEC) No 4064/89 (COM/2001/0745 final), http://ec.europa.eu/competition/consultations/2002_council_regulation 177
European Commission, Draft Commission notice on the appraisal of horizontal mergers under the Council Regulation on the control of concentrations between undertakings [2002] OJ C331/18...51, 70
European Commission, Proposal for a Council Regulation on the control of concentrations between undertakings [2003] OJ C20/4 ....35, 41, 133
European Advisory Group on Competition Policy (EAGCP), 'An Economic Approach to Article 82', July 2005, ec.europa.eu/dgs/competition/economist/eagcp_july_21_05.pdf...59, 106, 146, 184, 195, 237
European Commission, DG Competition, Discussion Paper on the Application of Article 82 of the Treaty to Exclusionary Abuses, November 2005, http://ec.europa.eu/competition/antitrust/art82/discpaper2005.pdf................42, 51, 59, 69, 106, 147, 184

European Commission, Draft Commission Notice, Guidelines on the assessment of non-horizontal mergers under the Council Regulation on the control of concentrations between undertakings of 13 February 2008, http://ec.europa.eu/competition/mergers/legislation/draft_nonhorizontal_mergers.pdf 51, 70
European Commission, Communication 'Guidance on the Commission's enforcement priorities in applying Article 82 of the EC Treaty to abusive exclusionary conduct by dominant undertakings' [2009] OJ C45/7 ....43, 59, 106, 147, 184, 220, 238, 282
European Commission, Communication 'EUROPE 2020—A strategy for smart, sustainable and inclusive growth' COM(2010) 2020 final....108
European Commission, 'DG Competition Staff working paper on Best Practices for the submission of economic evidence and data collection in cases concerning the application of Articles 101 and 102 TFEU and merger cases', http://ec.europa.eu/competition/antitrust/legislation/best_practices_submission_en.pdf 241
European Commission, Staff Working Document 'Impact Assessment Report on the future of EU-US trade relations, accompanying the document Recommendation for a Council Decision authorising the opening of negotiations on a comprehensive trade and investment agreement, called the Transatlantic Trade and Investment Partnership, between the European Union and the United States of America' SWD(2013) 68 final....259
European Commission, 'Commission opens proceedings against Microsoft's alleged discriminatory licensing and refusal to supply software information', Press Release IP/00/906 of 3 August 2000....21
European Commission, 'Mergers: Commission prohibits Ryanair's proposed takeover of Aer Lingus', Press Release IP/07/893 of 27 June 2007 139
European Commission, 'Antitrust: Commission fines Microsoft for non-compliance with browser choice commitments', Press Release IP/13/196 of 6 March 2013....24

Other Commission publications

European Commission, 'Publication of A 2 post of Chief Competition Economist' [2003] OJ C39 A/5....48
European Commission, 'Merger Review Package in a Nutshell' (2004) *Competition Policy Newsletter Special Edition* 2....134
European Commission, 'European Union, Trade in goods with USA', http://trade.ec.europa.eu/doclib/docs/2006/september/tradoc_113465.pdf. 259
European Commission, 'Antitrust: Guidance on Commission enforcement priorities in applying Article 82 to exclusionary conduct by dominant firms—frequently asked questions', Memorandum MEMO/08/761 of 3 December 2008....293
European Commission, 'Antitrust: Commission confirms sending a Statement of Objections to Microsoft on the tying of Internet Explorer to Windows', Memorandum MEMO/09/15 of 17 January 2009 23
European Commission, 'The Chief Competition Economist', http://ec.europa.eu/dgs/competition/economist/role_en.html 237
European Commission, 'The Economic Advisory Group on Competition Policy (EAGCP)', http://ec.europa.eu/dgs/competition/economist/eagcp.html 48, 237

European Commission, '20 Years of the European Single Market' (Publications Office of the European Union, 2012), http://ec.europa.eu/internal_market/publications/docs/20years/achievements-web_en.pdf 10
European Commission, 'Publication of the post of Chief Competition Economist' [2013] OJ C33 A/1....48
European Commission, 'Cartel statistics', 6 April 2016, http://ec.europa.eu/competition/cartels/statistics/statistics.pdf 207

Other acts by the Union institutions

Committee of the Regions, Opinion on the 'Green Paper on vertical restraints in EC competition policy' [1997] OJ C244/38....49
Economic and Social Committee, Opinion on the 'Green Paper on vertical restraints in EC competition policy' [1997] OJ C296/19....49
European Parliament, Resolution on the Commission's Green Paper on vertical restraints in EC competition policy [1997] OJ C286/347 49

Non-European Union legislation

United States

Legal acts

Section 1 of the Sherman Act (15 U.S.C. Chapter 1, section 1).... 65, 67, 78, 194, 197, 258, 306
Section 2 of the Sherman Act (15 U.S.C. Chapter 1, section 2).... 19, 61, 81, 233, 258
Section 7 of the Clayton Act (15 U.S.C. Chapter 1, section 18).... 13, 61, 65, 78, 258
Hart-Scott-Rodino Act (15 U.S.C. Chapter 1, section 18a) 13

US FTC and DoJ guidelines

US Department of Justice and US Federal Trade Commission, Antitrust enforcement guidelines for international operations (April 1995)....13
US Federal Trade Commission and US Department of Justice, Antitrust Guidelines for Collaborations Among Competitors (April 2000) 64–65, 258
US Federal Trade Commission and US Department of Justice, Horizontal Merger Guidelines (19 August 2010) 65, 258

Press Releases and other publications by the US Antitrust Authorities

US Federal Trade Commission, 'FTC Allows Merger of the Boeing Company and McDonnell Douglas Corporation', Press Release of 1 July 1997 12
US Federal Trade Commission, 'Statement of Chairman Robert Pitofsky and Commissioners Janet D. Steiger, Roscoe B. Starek III and Christine A. Varney Concerning The Boeing Co./McDonnell Douglas Corp.', FTC File No 971-0051 (1 July 1997)....12
US Federal Trade Commission, 'Statement of Commissioner Mary L. Azcuenaga Concerning The Boeing Co.', FTC File No 971-0051 (1 July 1997)....12

US Department of Justice's International Competition Policy Advisory Committee, 'Final Report to the Attorney General and the Assistant Attorney General for Antitrust Enforcement', February 2000 37
US Department of Justice, 'Justice Department requires divestitures in merger between General Electric and Honeywell' Press Release of 2 May 2001 14
US Department of Justice, 'Justice Department Informs Microsoft of Plans for Further Proceedings in the District Court', Press Release of 6 September 2001 20
US Federal Trade Commission, 'Statement of the Federal Trade Commission Regarding Google's Search Practices', *In the Matter of Google Inc*, FTC File Number 111-0163 (Washington, DC, 3 January 2013) 25

Germany

Gesetz gegen Wettbewerbsbeschränkungen (GWB) of 27 July 1957, BGBl I 1081 85

United Kingdom

Enterprise Act 2002 134

International law

International Treaties

United Nations Conference on Trade and Employment, Havana Charter for an International Trade Organization, Chapter V, 24 March 1948, Final Act and Related Documents, www.wto.org/english/docs_e/legal_e/havana_e.pdf 36
OECD, Supplementary Protocol No. 1 to the Convention for European Economic Co-operation on the Legal Capacity, Privileges and Immunities of the Organisation, 16 April 1948 37

WTO Ministerial Declarations

Singapore WTO Ministerial Declaration (WT/MIN(96)/DEC) of 18 December 1996 36
Doha WTO Ministerial Declaration (WT/MIN(01)/DEC/1 20) of 14 November 2001 36

OECD documents

OECD, Recommendations and Best Practices on Competition Law and Policy, www.oecd.org/competition/recommendations.htm .... ??
OECD, Best Practice Roundtables on Competition Policy, www.oecd.org/competition/roundtables.htm .... ??

UNCTAD documents

UNCTAD, Competition and Consumer Policies Programme—mandate and key functions, http://unctad.org/en/Pages/DITC/CompetitionLaw/ccpb-Mandate.aspx 37

Introduction

In the late 1990s, the European Commission embarked on an extensive process of rethinking and redesigning its antitrust policy. One element of this review was the reform of the enforcement system, which culminated in the Council decentralising the enforcement of Articles 101 and 102 of the Treaty on the Functioning of the European Union (TFEU) in Regulation 1/2003.[1] Alongside the procedural reform, the Commission also began a review of the substantive law. Its aim was to give the EU antitrust rules a radical overhaul by introducing a 'more economic approach' that would increase the emphasis on sound economics and result in a competition policy fully compatible with economic learning.[2]

The substantive review process was significantly longer and its outcome less clear-cut than that of the procedural reform. The more economic approach was not introduced by means of formal legislative amendment of the antitrust rules. Rather, the Commission made the relevant changes in several stages by means of soft law instruments. Between 2000 and 2009, it published a number of legally non-binding Notices and Communications that spelled out a more economic approach to assessing business conduct under all three pillars of EU antitrust law: Article 101 TFEU, EU merger control and Article 102 TFEU. However, while the majority of these soft law instruments explained in their introductory statements that they were based on an economic or more economic approach, they neither defined the core principles of the approach, nor did they make clear what changes they were introducing. Even the most superficial comparison of the Commission's individual decisions prior to and after the introduction of the more economic approach allows the conclusion that some form of overhaul has indeed taken place. The decision practice has changed beyond recognition. Assessments are resplendent with economic terminology, contain complex quantitative studies and are on average 10 times longer than prior to the reform. Yet, these are only the most visible manifestations of the revised approach. In reality, it has made far more fundamental changes.

The aim of this book is to define the essence of the more economic approach to EU antitrust law in its entirety and to cast a critical look upon it, now that the

[1] Council Regulation (EC) No 1/2003 of 16 December 2002 on the implementation of the rules on competition laid down in Articles 81 and 82 of the Treaty [2003] OJ L1/1.

[2] M Monti, 'A Competition Policy for Today and Tomorrow' (2000) 23 *World Competition* 1.

Commission has had the opportunity to apply the principles set out in its most recent soft law instruments and that the Court of Justice has had the chance to pronounce itself on the revised approach. Part I of the book sets the scene for this analysis by retracing the origins of the approach and the process by which it was introduced. Part II contains the core analysis. It establishes on the basis of empirical evidence what changes the more economic approach has made to the Commission's understanding and application of the EU antitrust rules. It does so by comparing the Commission's manner of assessing the competitive nature of business conduct under Article 101 TFEU, Article 102 TFEU and the EU Merger Regulation both before and after the introduction of the new approach. This comparison takes into account every publicly available infringement, clearance and exemption decision since 1962, the Commission's Block Exemption Regulations, its interpretative guidelines, other substantive Notices and Annual Reports on Competition Policy since 1972.

The analysis focuses on the substantive changes that the Commission has made in its interpretation and application of the EU antitrust rules under the catchphrase of the more economic approach. In five separate chapters it explores the changes that the Commission introduced to its understanding of the antitrust rules' legal objective, its concept of competitive harm, its view on the nature and role of countervailing effects, the types of legal tests used to establish these effects, and general methodological issues. For each of these areas, the analysis initially establishes these changes separately for Articles 101, 102 and the EU Merger Regulation, and then draws out the parallels and discrepancies of the Commission's approach to these three prohibition provisions. This makes it possible eventually to establish a complete picture of the more economic approach to EU antitrust law.

The analysis in Part II does not aim to explore in depth the changes in the use of procedural instruments that occurred in the Commission's enforcement practice in recent years, such as the advent of the leniency programme, the cartel settlement procedure and the use of commitments decisions. These may to a certain extent also be seen as an expression of the increased relevance of economic thought and theory in EU antitrust law. The use of commitments decisions and the cartel settlement procedure, in particular, sacrifice in-depth legal assessments in the interest of procedural economy. Likewise, the leniency programme for cartel offences,[3] which is based on a game theoretical concept and sets incentives for cartel members to default and thereby not only increases detection but undermines the stability of cartels generally, forgoes the punishment of the guilty party in the interest of cost efficient enforcement.[4] It would go beyond the possibilities of a single

[3] European Commission, Notice on Immunity from fines and reduction of fines in cartel cases [2006] OJ C298/17.

[4] See eg M Motta and M Polo, 'Leniency Programs and Cartel Prosecution' (2003) 21 *International Journal of Industrial Organization* 347; G Spagnolo, 'Leniency and Whistleblowers in Antitrust' in P Buccirossi, *Handbook of Antitrust Economics* (Cambridge, MA, MIT Press, 2008) 259, 290.

monograph to cover both the substantive and procedural changes. Nonetheless, it is useful to bear in mind that they are connected to a degree. The significantly more complex and costly assessments required by the more economic approach make the use of commitments decisions a very attractive and even necessary tool for enforcement agencies that operate on a limited budget. Moreover, the increased use of commitments decisions over the past 10 years is significant for this monograph as it creates a considerable practical problem for its key analysis. The proliferation of commitments decisions has resulted in a significant reduction in the number of decisions that carry out formal legal assessments of the investigated conduct. Commitments decisions merely outline a summary of the Commission's concerns based on a preliminary assessment and explain why the parties' commitments seem suitable to address these concerns. As a result, there is relatively little hard evidence of how the Commission interprets and applies the antitrust rules in practice these days, and one needs to rely heavily on the theory outlined in its interpretative guidelines and other soft law instruments to gain an understanding of its current approach.

Part III concludes the book with a critical analysis of the changes introduced by the more economic approach. It identifies a number of strong points of the Commission's new approach, but also serious concerns, in particular its lack of compatibility with the case law of the European Court of Justice. The conclusion contains suggestions on how these issues could be addressed.

A few words on terminology. The book refers to EU 'antitrust law' instead of the probably more common EU 'competition law' in its title and throughout. The reason for this choice of wording was to make clear from the outset that the scope of the book is limited to the EU competition provisions addressed to businesses, and that it does not encompass the competition rules addressed to the Member States, in particular not the State Aid rules.

Further, it is necessary to address the awkward terminological problems created by the piece-by-piece development of the European Union and its successive Treaty amendments. Today's European Union evolved from the European Economic Community (EEC), which came into being in 1958, and was renamed European Community (EC) in 1992. In 2009, the European Union (EU) took the place of the European Community. For the sake of clarity, this book normally refers to the European Union or EU throughout even when discussing legal instruments that predate 2009. For the same reason, this book also refers to the current Treaty name and Article numbers, where possible, regardless of the historical period under discussion. The two substantive antitrust rules in the Treaty currently in force are Articles 101 and 102 TFEU. They started out life as Articles 85 and 86 EEC. In 1992, when the Treaty of Maastricht changed the name of the European Economic Community to European Community, Articles 85 and 86 EEC became Articles 85 and 86 EC. In 1999, the Treaty of Amsterdam renumbered the provisions of the EC Treaty, turning Articles 85 and 86 EC into Articles 81 and 82 EC respectively. In 2009, finally, the Treaty of Lisbon[5], which put an end to the Community system, integrated most of the provisions of the former EC Treaty, including Articles 81 and 82 EC, into the new TFEU. The two provisions in question are now known as Articles 101 and 102 of the TFEU. Except for a few minor tweaks of terminology,[6] their wording is the same as that of Articles 85 and 86 EEC in 1958. For the sake of simplicity and clarity, the following will use the current appellation, Articles 101 and 102, throughout even when discussing events that predate the Treaty of Lisbon.

Finally, Treaty Articles discussed in this book refer to the TFEU unless otherwise specified.

[5] Treaty on European Union, as signed at Lisbon on 13 December 2007 [2012] OJ C326/13 (consolidated version), Treaty on the Functioning of the European Union, as signed at Lisbon on 13 December 2007 [2012] OJ C326/47 (consolidated version).

[6] The Treaty of Lisbon replaced 'Community' with 'Union', and 'common market' with 'internal market'.

Part I

1

Triggers and Catalysts

I. Introduction

The more economic approach to EU antitrust law did not appear out of the blue. A number of factors contributed to its advent. In the mid-1990s, the European Union had realised its key aim of creating a single market to a great extent, which allowed the institutions to turn their attention to new tasks and objectives. Around the same times, the European Commission's antitrust policy came under increasing criticism from academics and practitioners for its lack of economic analysis. The 1990s and early 2000s saw the Commission clash repeatedly with the US antitrust authorities over cases with international dimensions, in which it was accused of being guided by the wrong values and applying outdated economic theories. In particular, the emotionally charged dispute over the Commission's decision to prohibit the merger between the two US companies General Electric and Honeywell triggered an extensive debate about the role of economics in antitrust analyses both at the academic level and within the European Commission's Directorate General for Competition Policy (DG Competition). The Court of Justice of the European Union is likely to have fuelled the Commission's review process further when, in an unprecedented move, it annulled three merger decisions in 2001 because of manifest errors of assessment. Another important factor was the appointment of an economist to the position of Commissioner for Competition in 1999. His professional background and personal convictions no doubt played a major part in driving forward the reform and shaping the Commission's more economic approach to EU antitrust law. Finally, the Commission's review process is likely to have been influenced by the exchange of ideas between antitrust authorities in the International Competition Network and other international forums of cooperation.

II. The Completion of the Internal Market

The creation of a common market between the six original Member States had been the cornerstone of the European project that dominated much of the Union's early activities. In order to understand the importance accorded to this aim, one must bear in mind that market integration not only served the purpose of creating economic welfare. In the 1950s, it was considered a key tool for preventing further military conflict in Europe. The European Communities were created in response to World Wars I and II, which ravaged the European continent in quick succession. Attempts at international peace-building following World War I had not been successful. 20 years after the Treaty of Versailles officially ended the state of war between Germany and the allied powers, World War II began, only to surpass the previous conflict in human loss, destruction and suffering. In 1946, the League of Nations, which had proved ineffective in preventing World War II, was therefore dissolved. The United Nations took its place as the key international body to promote international cooperation and peace. Given how powerless the League of Nations had been against the rise of war, however, there were serious doubts as to whether this successor organisation would be any more successful.

Against this background, the French Foreign Minister Robert Schuman proposed a novel and highly experimental method of securing a sustainable peace in Europe. Instead of focusing on the promotion and respect of certain ideological values in the image of the United Nations and the Council of Europe, the Schuman Declaration of May 1950[1] outlined a much more pragmatic plan. It was based on the key premise that in order to achieve a lasting peace in Europe it was necessary to eliminate the age-old opposition between France and Germany. This was not to be achieved through unilateral supervision of Germany, but through practical cooperation. The hope was that such cooperation, which was to start in small, well-defined areas, would result in mutual trust and could then be expanded to other spheres.

Today's European Union is the outcome of this plan. In 1951, France, Germany, Italy and the three Benelux countries agreed to create a common market for coal and steel. With this aim, they created a European Coal and Steel Community (ECSC) with independent institutions that would not only ensure the application of the Treaty's provisions but also had the power to make rules and take decisions with regard to this common market that were binding on the signatory States.[2] This system allowed the Member States and the independent Community institutions to monitor the trade of coal and steel within the Community's territory. The reasons for starting cooperation and trust-building in this specific area were obvious. Coal and steel were indispensable to the production of arms and military machinery, so that placing the trade in coal and steel under common supervision would have allowed the participating States to detect if one of them were rearming.

In 1957, the same six States agreed to create two further areas of cooperation. The Treaty establishing the European Atomic Energy Community (Euratom)

[1] Declaration of 9 May 1950 by Robert Schuman, available at: www.robert-schuman.eu/en/doc/questions-d-europe/qe-204-en.pdf.

[2] Treaty establishing the European Coal and Steel Community (1951).

related to the other area relevant to modern warfare, ie nuclear energy. The Treaty establishing the European Economic Community, the legal predecessor of today's Union, was not concerned with detecting and preventing rearmament, but pursued another method of conflict prevention: economic integration. In the ultimate aim of establishing an 'ever-closer union amongst the peoples of Europe' and the 'elimination of barriers which divide Europe',[3] the same six States decided to begin this process by abolishing the economic barriers that divided Europe. The key purpose of the European Economic Community was to create a common market between its members, within which goods, services, capital and the people engaged in economic activities could move around freely irrespective of national borders. The hypothesis was that national economies would become so intertwined that engaging in military conflict with one another would have disastrous economic consequences for the individual Member States. This was deemed a powerful deterrent not only for the Member States' governments but also for their citizens, who were dependent on good relations with neighbouring States either because they were engaged in trade with them or because they benefited from this trade as consumers. In addition to this effect, the signatory States also assumed that free trade would create economic prosperity and improve the 'living and working conditions of their peoples'.[4]

The key legal tools for creating the common market were the free movement rules that were aimed at abolishing state-imposed barriers to the free movement of goods, workers, the self-employed, services and capital.[5] As a complement to these rules, the signatory States also included 'rules on competition' that were addressed to undertakings. The main reason for including these competition rules was that they were deemed necessary to ensure that private parties did not replace the state-imposed barriers with private barriers to trade.

The creation of the three Communities was a remarkable victory of reason over emotion. France, Germany, Belgium and The Netherlands had geographically been at the centre of both world wars and many other previous European military conflicts. France and Germany in particular had repeatedly clashed over border territories and in the 1950s, there was a deeply embedded distrust between the citizens of these States stemming from centuries of conflict and suffering.

While the aim of peace-building may no longer be what most people nowadays associate with the internal market goal, it must have been prominent in the minds of the first generations of Community officials, who had experienced the traumas of World Wars I and II first-hand. This experience, and the desire to prevent another conflict between the original Member States, undoubtedly explains the importance, urgency and almost mythical status accorded to the common market goal in the early days of the Communities. Not surprisingly, therefore, the

[3] Treaty Establishing the European Economic Community (1957) Preamble, points 1 and 2.
[4] ibid, Preamble, point 3.
[5] Now TFEU, Arts 28–37, 45–48, 49–55, 56–62 and 63–66.

creation of the common market was the focus of the institutions' policy during the first 35 years of the Union's existence,[6] including its antitrust policy. While the process faltered in the 1970s and early 1980s when the oil crises, recession and empty chair crisis almost paralysed the Union's political institutions, it was revived in the mid-1980s, when the Commission published a White Paper outlining a plan for completing the common market by 1992 under the guidance of its new president Jacques Delors. The functional rather than institutional approach of Delors' plan appealed to most Member States, prompting them to convene an intergovernmental conference, which resulted in the adoption of the Single European Act in 1986.[7] This Treaty amended the Treaty of Rome in apparently modest ways.[8] At its heart lay the proposal and goal to complete the common market, redubbed 'single market', by 31 December 1992. Between 1986 and 1992, the European Union adopted nearly 280 pieces of legislation to achieve this aim.[9] The single market was formally considered in place on 1 January 1993.

While the aim of protecting the single market, renamed 'internal market' by the Treaty of Lisbon, remains a valid and important objective of the Union, it lost some of its immediate urgency after 1 January 1993. This is also reflected in the growing number of objectives not related to the internal market in the Union Treaties after 1993. Consequently, the institutions, including the Commission, were able to turn their attention to other projects and causes, more in line with that of a modern nation state than an experimental supranational organisation focused on eliminating barriers to trade.

III. Academic Criticism

In the late 1980s and early 1990s, EU antitrust law came under attack from a number of academics. Barry Hawk famously published a particularly critical analysis of the treatment of vertical restraints under EU antitrust law, which he deemed too legalistic and lacking in economic analysis.[10] The European Commission explicitly engaged with his views in a Green Paper on Vertical Restraints from 1997, which opened a public consultation on ways of modernising the

[6] JHH Weiler, 'The Transformation of Europe' (1991) 100 *Yale Law Journal* 2403; DJ Gerber, *Law and Competition in Twentieth Century Europe* (Oxford, Clarendon Press, 2001) 346 ff; R Wesseling, *The Modernisation of EC Antitrust Law* (Oxford, Hart Publishing, 2002) 22 ff.

[7] Single European Act [1987] OJ L169/1.

[8] GA Bermann, 'The Single European Act: A New Constitution for the Community' (1989) 27 *Columbia Journal of Transnational Law* 529, 536; JW de Zwaan, 'The Single European Act: Conclusion of a Unique Document' (1986) 23 *Common Market Law Review* 747.

[9] European Commission, 20 Years of the European Single Market (Luxembourg, Publications Office of the European Union, 2012).

[10] BE Hawk, 'System Failure: Vertical Restraints and EC Competition Law' (1995) 32 *Common Market Law Review* 973. See also BE Hawk, 'The American (Anti-trust) Revolution: Lessons for the EEC?' (1988) 9 *European Competition Law Review* 53.

Commission's approach to assessing vertical restraints.[11] Hawk was by no means the only person to criticise the lack of economic analysis in the Commission's antitrust policy. A number of other eminent academics, practitioners and even Commission officials expressed similar views.[12] Most of these critiques drew on a comparison of EU antitrust law with US antitrust law, which had been guided by the objectives and tools of economic theory since the late 1970s, and the Commission's approach usually came off very much worse in these comparisons.

IV. Transatlantic Conflict

What a number of academics had detected in the 1980s already became more or less public knowledge in the late 1990s: EU and US antitrust law did not follow the same substantive principles. This became painfully obvious when the US and EU antitrust authorities investigated a number of cases with international dimensions and reached opposite findings. All of a sudden, these discrepancies were no longer merely of academic interest. They had very real implications.

A. The Boeing/McDonnell Douglas Crisis (1997)

In 1997, both the US Federal Trade Commission (FTC) and the European Commission investigated the proposed merger between Boeing and McDonnell Douglas. Both of these businesses were US companies operating in the aerospace industry. At the time of the proposed transaction, Boeing had a market share of 64 per cent in the market for new large commercial aircraft and McDonnell Douglas had a market share of 6 per cent. The only other significant competitor, the European Airbus consortium, had a market share of around 30 per cent.[13] After the transaction, McDonnell Douglas was to become a wholly owned

[11] European Commission, 'Green Paper on Vertical Restraints in EC Competition Policy' COM(96) 721 of 22 January 1997, fn 4.

[12] eg N Kyriazis and L Gyselen, 'Article 86 EEC: the Monopoly Power Measurement Issue Revisited' (1986) 11 *European Law Review* 134; AS Pathak, 'Articles 85 and 86 and Anti-competitive Exclusion in EEC Competition Law: Part 1' (1989) 10 *European Competition Law Review* 74 and 'Articles 85 and 86 and Anti-competitive Exclusion in EEC Competition Law: Part 2' (1989) 10 *European Competition Law Review* 256; V Korah, 'The Judgment in Delimitis: A Milestone towards a Realistic Assessment of the Effects of an Agreement—or a Damp Squib?' (1992) 14 *European Intellectual Property Review* 167 and 'The Paucity of Economic Analysis in the EEC Decisions on Competition: Tetra Pak II' (1993) 46 *Current Legal Problems* 148; D Ridyard, 'Economic Analysis of Single Firm and Oligopolistic Dominance under the European Merger Regulation' (1994) 15 *European Competition Law Review* 255; R van den Bergh, 'Modern Industrial Organisation versus Old-Fashioned European Competition Law' (1996) 17 *European Competition Law Review* 75.

[13] *Boeing/McDonnell Douglas* (Case IV/M.877) [1997] OJ L336/16, recital 9.

subsidiary of Boeing. It was undisputed that the merger would have repercussions on European markets.

The FTC cleared the transaction unconditionally by majority vote, despite the fact that the merger would reduce the number of players in the market from three to two. Its reasoning was that McDonnell Douglas, whose market shares had been steadily decreasing over the previous 10 years, no longer constituted a meaningful competitive force in the commercial aircraft market.[14] The European Commission, on the other hand, made clear that it intended to block the merger under the EU Merger Regulation unless the parties submitted commitments that would alleviate its concerns.[15] It took the view that Boeing already had a dominant position in the market for large commercial aircraft, which would be further strengthened if Boeing were to acquire McDonnell Douglas.[16] The merger would reduce the number of competitors from three to two in the market for large commercial aircraft, and increase Boeing's market share from 65 to 70 per cent. Further, Boeing would acquire McDonnell Douglas' existing customer base, fleet in service, skilled work force, as well as considerable financial and other resources. It would be the only manufacturer able to offer a full family of aircraft and to commit itself to new aircraft models, which would strengthen its ability to induce airlines into long-term exclusivity agreements, thus denying its competitors access to customers.[17] The Commission was also concerned about the effects of Boeing acquiring McDonnell Douglas' space and defence business, which would increase Boeing's intellectual property portfolio. Further, McDonnell Douglas' R&D activities in this area received significant financial contributions from the US government. The Commission considered it likely that Boeing could use some of these monies to cross-subsidise its activities in the commercial aircraft sector, allowing it to offer aircraft at lower prices than its one remaining competitor, Airbus.[18]

The case was highly politicised, both in the United States and in Europe. The US government reportedly exerted considerable pressure on the European Commission and warned it of a damaging political conflict should the Commission

[14] FTC Press Release, 1 July 1997, 'FTC Allows Merger of the Boeing Company and McDonnell Douglas Corporation'; 'Statement of Chairman Robert Pitofsky and Commissioners Janet D. Steiger, Roscoe B. Starek III and Christine A. Varney Concerning The Boeing Co./McDonnell Douglas Corp.', FTC File No 971-0051 (1 July 1997). 1 Commissioner dissented and wrote a separate statement in which she disagreed with her colleagues' assessment of McDonnell Douglas's competitive significance, arguing that the evidence showed that McDonnell Douglas had added an element of competition and had continued to win some business: 'Statement of Commissioner Mary L. Azcuenaga Concerning The Boeing Co.', FTC File No 971-0051 (1 July 1997). Both statements are available at: www.sec.gov/Archives/edgar/data/63917/0000063917-97-000017.txt.

[15] P Chalmers, 'EU Threatens Being/McDonnell Douglas Deal' *Reuters News* (4 July 1997); 'Brussels v Boeing' *The Economist* (17 July 1997).

[16] *Boeing/McDonnell Douglas* (n 13) recitals 21–71.

[17] The Commission estimated that such exclusivity deals would foreclose around 40% of the world market; ibid, recital 71.

[18] *Boeing/McDonnell Douglas* (n 13) recitals 72–112.

oppose the merger.[19] The Commission, on its part, was digging in its heels. In late-night talks, just days before the final decision, neither side seemed prepared to cede grounds, and the parties walked away without finding a solution to what threatened to turn into a major conflict between the two jurisdictions.[20]

Public opinion in the United States was fiercely critical of the Commission's decision. There was a fair deal of resentment that the European Commission should assume the right to assess and block a merger between two US companies.[21] From the point of view of US antitrust lawyers, however, the extra-territorial scope of the EU Merger Regulation[22] was not the true bone of contention. US courts have long interpreted the US antitrust provisions as also applying to business conduct taking place in another jurisdiction, at least if they were 'intended to affect imports and did affect them'.[23] The US Department of Justice and the FTC have issued enforcement guidelines for international operations that explain in more detail under what conditions they intend to apply the US antitrust rules to foreign businesses,[24] and the FTC has repeatedly assessed mergers between non-US companies under section 7 of the Clayton Act.[25]

While the Commission's scrutiny of the proposed acquisition of McDonnell Douglas by Boeing could therefore not really come as a shock to US antitrust experts, the Commission's reasons for opposing this particular merger were met with great scepticism. Primarily, the Commission was accused of being guided

[19] B Coleman, 'Clinton Hints U.S. May Retaliate if EU Tries to Block Boeing-McDonnell Deal' *Wall Street Journal* (New York, 18 July 1997) A2.

[20] A Torres, 'EU Issues Tough Warning over Boeing-McDonnell Merger' *Reuters News* (15 July 1997); B Coleman, 'EU Still Threatening To Vote Down Boeing-McDonnell Douglas Deal' *Dow Jones Business News* (21 July 1997); J Wolf, 'Boeing-McDonnell Merger Plan Is Closer to Rejection in Europe' *Wall Street Journal* (New York, 16 July 1997) B4.

[21] eg EL Andrews, 'Boeing, Threatened, Sees Trade War' *New York Times* (21 May 1997).

[22] The General Court established in *Gencor* that the application of the Merger Regulation is justified under public international law when it is foreseeable that a proposed concentration between undertakings established outside the Union will have an immediate and substantial effect within the Union (Case T-102/96 *Gencor Ltd v Commission* ECLI:EU:T:1999:65, para 90).

[23] The extra-territorial scope of s 2 of the Sherman Act was first recognised in *US v Aluminium Co. of America*, 148 F.2d 416, 444 (2d Cir 1945). For s 1 of the Sherman Act, see *Hartford Fire Ins. Co v California*, 509 U.S. 764 (1993). (This is a much-simplified summary of a very complex legal question. For an in-depth account, see F Wagner-von Papp, 'Competition Law and Extraterritoriality' in A Ezrachi, *Research Handbook on International Competition Law* (Cheltenham, Edward Elgar, 2012) 21–59).

[24] US Department of Justice and US Federal Trade Commission, 'Antitrust enforcement guidelines for international operations' (April 1995), available at: www.justice.gov/atr/public/guidelines/internat.htm.

[25] Only a few weeks before approving the Boeing/McDonnell Douglas merger, eg, the FTC filed a complaint against a German company, Mahle GmbH, and its Brazilian competitor, Metal Leve SA, for failing to notify the US antitrust authorities of their intention to merge under the Hart-Scott-Rodino Act. Mahle and Metal Leve agreed to pay a (then record) $5.6 million civil penalty to resolve the charges (*United States of America (filed at the request of the FTC) v Mahle GmbH, Mahle, Inc, Mabeg eV, Metal Leve, SA, and Metal Leve, Inc*). Mahle also undertook to divest certain parts of its US business, which was made binding by a FTC consent order of 6 June 1997 (FTC File No 961-0085, Docket Number: C-3746).

by protectionist motives rather than concerns for competition.[26] Unlike in the subsequent *GE/Honeywell* case, only few analysts engaged with the substance and theoretical underpinnings of the Commission's analysis in *Boeing/McDonnell Douglas* in detail. Those who did, however, reached the conclusion that *Boeing/ McDonnell Douglas*, far from being a case of national protectionism, was dealt with in good faith on both sides of the Atlantic and that the different positions were expressions of different philosophies as to the purpose of merger control and different economic assumptions about markets.[27]

The 'dirty trade war' predicted by journalists[28] was eventually averted after Boeing offered a number of last-minute structural and behavioural commitments that the Commission deemed capable of addressing its concerns.[29] Despite some sabre-rattling on both sides, the conflict thus eventually blew over. However, people were quick to recall the incident when the European Commission and the FTC clashed over the ill-fated *GE/Honeywell* merger in 2001. That crisis ended less happily.

B. GE and Honeywell Run Afoul of Nineteenth-Century Thinking (2001)

In 2001, both the US and the EU antitrust authorities investigated another proposed merger between two US companies in the aerospace industry, General Electric Company (GE) and Honeywell International Inc (Honeywell). Both GE and Honeywell were diversified manufacturing and services companies. Amongst others, GE was active in the markets for aircraft engines, household appliances, lighting, power generation, industrial controls, medical imaging equipment, engineering plastics, broadcasting, financial services and transportation systems. Honeywell's activities included aerospace products and services, automotive products, electronic materials, speciality chemicals, performance polymers, transportation and power systems as well as home, building and industrial controls.[30] GE and Honeywell's turnovers were such that the proposed acquisition had a 'Community dimension' within the meaning of Regulation 4064/89 (the original Merger

[26] HW Jenkins, 'Business World: What's a Little Antitrust between Friends?' *Wall Street Journal* (New York, 28 January 1997); Editorial, 'Distrustful', *The Economist* (London, 26 July 1997) 60. For a particularly scathing review of the European position, see Editorial, 'A "'Dangerous" Merger?' *Wall Street Journal* (New York, 21 July 1997).

[27] EM Fox, 'Antitrust Regulation Across National Borders: The United States of Boeing Versus the European Union of Airbus' 1998 16 *Brookings Review* 30; EJ Stock, 'Explaining the Differing U.S. and EU Positions on the Boeing/McDonnell-Douglas Merger: Avoiding Another Near-Miss' 1999 (20) *University of Pennsylvania Journal of International Economic Law* 825.

[28] Editorial, 'Brussels v Boeing' *The Economist* (17 July 1997).

[29] *Boeing/McDonnell Douglas* (n 13) recitals 114–19.

[30] US Department of Justice, Press Release (2 May 2001), and Commission Decision of 3 July 2001 in *General Electric/Honeywell* (Case COMP/M.2220) OJ [2004] L48/1, recitals 3 and 4.

Regulation),[31] which meant that, although both companies were established in the United States, the transaction also fell within the scope of EU merger law.

Like in the case of *Boeing/McDonnell Douglas*, the US antitrust authorities reached the conclusion that the proposed acquisition, as modified by the parties, did not raise significant competitive concerns,[32] and again, the European Commission took the opposite view. This time, however, the European Commission prohibited the acquisition, only a few weeks after it had been cleared by its US counterparts.[33] The two agencies had cooperated closely during the fact-finding stages of the investigation. They had conducted several joint witness interviews[34] and the factual basis for the US Department of Justice's and European Commission's competitive analyses was therefore not appreciably different. The two antitrust authorities reached different conclusions because they carried out different analyses.

i. The US Investigation

The US Department of Justice had originally had competition concerns for certain markets on which both GE and Honeywell were active, as well as for certain related after-sales service markets. GE and Honeywell were the two premier manufacturers of US military helicopter engines. The US Department of Justice had feared that GE's acquisition of its competitor would substantially lessen competition in this market and result in higher prices, lower quality and reduced innovation in the production of the next generation of advanced military helicopter engines for the US military. It also predicted that the acquisition was likely to result in a substantial lessening of competition in the market for the maintenance, repair and overhaul of Honeywell aircraft engines and auxiliary power units, resulting in higher prices and lower quality for commercial business aircraft users. To resolve these concerns, GE agreed to divest Honeywell's helicopter business after the acquisition and to license a new competitor to service certain Honeywell engines. The Department considered these undertakings sufficient to mitigate its concerns in substance.

ii. The EU Investigation

In line with Article 2(3) of Regulation 4064/89, the Commission assessed whether the acquisition would result in the creation or strengthening of a dominant position and found that this was likely to be the case. It held that the transaction would

[31] Regulation (EEC) No 4064/89 of 21 December 1989 on the control of concentrations between undertakings OJ [1989] L 395/1, Art 1(2).

[32] US Department of Justice, Press Release (n 30).

[33] *General Electric/Honeywell* (Case COMP/M.2220) OJ [2004] L48/1.

[34] Remarks of Deborah Platt Majoras, then Deputy Assistant Attorney General, Antitrust Division, US Department of Justice, before the Antitrust Law Section State Bar of Georgia, 29 November 2001.

strengthen an already dominant position in markets in which both entities were competitors because it would reduce the number of competitors in these markets and eliminate the undertaking that had exercised the only significant competitive constraint on GE's business practices. This part of the Commission's analysis was, in theory at least, not radically different from that carried out by its US counterpart, even though they drew different conclusions from the facts. The Commission's analysis looked at most of the factors relevant in a market power analysis under section 7 of the US Clayton Act, such as market shares, potential competition, barriers to entry and countervailing buyer power.

Had the Commission limited its assessment to this part of its analysis, the reaction of US antitrust experts may not have been quite so vehement. However, it also based its prohibition on a further argument. In the second part of its competitive assessment, it established that the merger would moreover result in anticompetitive effects on vertically related and adjacent markets. It held that the acquisition would create or strengthen dominant positions on these markets because the combination of GE and Honeywell's activities would allow the merged entity to exclude other businesses from these markets. According to the Commission, there were two mechanisms by which the merged entity could be expected to 'leverage' its existing dominance to create new dominant positions in other markets. First, it took the view that GE's considerable financial power would allow it to cross-subsidise Honeywell's former activities in vertically related markets. This would give it such an advantage in these markets that it would be able to exclude its competitors therein and thus create a new dominant position. Second, the Commission predicted that the combined portfolio of the two companies' diversified activities would allow the merged entity to offer its customers bundles of products and services that were so attractive that competitors would be forced out of the market because they would be unable to match these.[35]

iii. The Controversy

There seems to have been the unspoken expectation that the Commission would eventually follow the example of the US Department of Justice and clear the acquisition. When the Commission eventually prohibited the acquisition, the reaction of US government officials, antitrust experts but also journalists and the wider business community alternated between indignation and disbelief. There were, on the one hand, accusations of obstructionism and protectionism.[36] The European Commission was said to have an official policy of favouring national champions[37]

[35] *General Electric/Honeywell* (n 33) recitals 342–444.

[36] See eg Editorial, 'Europe to GE: Go Home' *Wall Street Journal* (15 June 2001) A14: 'In the Honeywell case, novel antitrust theories have been dreamed up simply because it would be unthinkable to let a large U.S. company go about its business unmolested'.

[37] HR Varian, 'Economic Scene: In Europe, GE and Honeywell Ran Afoul of 19th Century Thinking' *New York Times* (28 June 2001) C2.

or at least of having caved in to powerful interests in this instance.[38] More fundamentally, however, the Commission was accused of adhering to 19th century thinking[39] and dangerously outdated economic theories.[40] The Commission's leveraging or portfolio arguments in particular incited more or less open derision.[41]

It can of course not be excluded that industrial policy considerations tacitly played a role—on either side of the Atlantic—even though they did not find expression in the authorities' final decisions and official statements. Notwithstanding this possibility, it is unlikely to have been the only reason why the two jurisdictions reached different conclusions. A comparison of the two authorities' assessments shows that they assessed very different types of effects. In line with the substantive test of Regulation 4064/89,[42] the Commission examined whether the merger would have had the effect of creating or strengthening a 'dominant position', ie a

> position of economic strength enjoyed by an undertaking which enables it to prevent effective competition being maintained on the relevant market by affording it the power to behave to an appreciable extent independently of its competitors, customers and ultimately of its consumers.[43]

By contrast, the US antitrust authorities had assessed whether the merger would result in the creation of market power, which would result in higher prices, lower quality and reduced innovation for consumers.

If one discards the accusations of protectionism and bias against US companies, the key criticism of US antitrust experts was that the Commission had not made its findings dependent on the merger's effects on consumers, but had instead based its conclusions on the concern that competitors could be forced to leave the market as a consequence of the merged entity's combined abilities. Their overarching conclusion was that EU competition law protected competitors while US antitrust law protected competition.[44] Indeed, the merger's effects on end prices

[38] G Becker, 'Economic View Point: What US Courts Could Teach Europe's Trust Busters' *Business Week* (6 August 2001) 20.

[39] Varian, 'Economic Scene' (n 37) C2.

[40] GL Priest and F Romani, 'Antique Antitrust: The GE/Honeywell Precedent' *The Wall Street Journal* (21 June 2001) 6.

[41] See Varian (n 37) C2; Priest, 'The GE/Honeywell Precedent and Franco Romani' (n 40) A18.

[42] Art 2(3) of Council Regulation (EEC) No 4064/89 of 21 December 1989 on the control of concentrations between undertakings OJ [1989] L 395/1 reads as follows: 'A concentration which creates or strengthens a dominant position as a result of which effective competition would be significantly impeded in the common market or in a substantial part of it shall be declared incompatible with the common market'. Regulation 4064/89 was superseded by the current EU Merger Regulation (Council Regulation (EC) No 139/2004 of 20 January 2004 on the control of concentrations between undertakings [2004] OJ L 24/1) with effect from 1 May 2004.

[43] Case 27/76 *United Brands v Commission* ECLI:EU:C:1978:22, para 65.

[44] W Kolasky, 'Conglomerate Mergers and Range Effects: It's a Long Way from Chicago to Brussels' (2002) 10 *George Mason Law Review* 533; CA James, 'Statement on the EU's Decision Regarding the GE/Honeywell Acquisition' (3 July 2001) available at: www.justice.gov/archive/atr/public/

were not part of the European Commission's analysis. The head of the European Commission's former Merger Task Force, responsible for assessing the transaction and drafting the decision, defended the Commission's approach against the onslaught of criticism by arguing that it was simplistic to believe that competitors should never be the focus of antitrust law as there could be no competition without competitors, and described the US position as 'Darwinian'.[45]

GE subsequently lost its action for annulment before the General Court.[46] It was a bittersweet victory for the Commission, as the Court severely criticised the decision's standard of proof. It found in particular that the Commission had failed to establish to the required legal standard that the merged entity was actually likely to engage in bundling or cross-subsidisation.[47] Importantly, however, it did not disapprove of the controversial theory underlying these assessments.[48] The Court ultimately dismissed the action in its entirety because it saw no manifest errors of assessment in the first part of Commission's analysis, relating to the markets on which both parties were competitors, which it deemed sufficient to justify a prohibition of the transaction.[49]

C. Microsoft (2004)

In 2004, only three years after *GE/Honeywell*, the next crisis loomed on the horizon when both the US and the EU authorities investigated the US software giant Microsoft for a number of business practices considered questionable in both jurisdictions. Despite shared concerns, the investigations again resulted in different outcomes. The first business practice considered problematic by both the US and EU antitrust authorities was Microsoft's strategy of integrating diverse types of software into its 'Windows' operating system. This led to accusations of anticompetitive tying in both the United States and Europe. The second practice concerned Microsoft's refusal to reveal interoperability information to other

press_releases/2001/8510.htm; Becker, 'What US Courts Could Teach Europe's Trust Busters' (n 38) 20; DS Evans, 'The New Trustbusters, Brussels and Washington May Part Ways' (2002) 81 *Foreign Affairs* 14.

45 G Drauz, 'Unbundling GE/Honeywell: The Assessment of Conglomerate Mergers under EC Competition Law' in B Hawk (ed), *International Antitrust Law and Policy 2001, Annual Proceedings of the Fordham Corporate Law Institute* (New York, Juris Publishing, 2002).

46 Case T-210/01 *General Electric Company v Commission* ECLI:EU:T:2005:456.

47 ibid, paras 311 and 340.

48 This was in line with the ruling in *Tetra Laval* 2 years earlier. Although in that case, too, the Court found that the evidence adduced by the Commission had not met the high standard of proof required for predicting uncertain future effects, which ultimately led to the annulment of the Commission decision, it did not object to the Commission's leveraging theory: Case T-5/02 *Tetra Laval BV v Commission* ECLI:EU:T:2002:264, upheld on appeal in C-12/03P *Commission v Tetra Laval BV* ECLI:EU:C:2005:87.

49 *GE v Commission* (n 46) paras 474–620.

software developers, which the latter required to produce software capable of operating efficiently in Windows.

i. The US Investigation

In the United States, the process was long, complex and involved several actors. The following is a much-simplified account.[50] The FTC began its antitrust investigation into Microsoft's business practices in the early 1990s, but decided to close the case in 1993 after several internal deadlocks. The US Department of Justice subsequently initiated its own investigation, and brought its first lawsuit against Microsoft under section 2 of the Sherman Act in 1994 for unlawfully maintaining a monopoly in the operating system market by means of anticompetitive terms in its licensing and software developer agreements. Microsoft chose to enter into a consent decree, in which it agreed to eliminate certain contractual restrictions on PC manufacturers and thus avoided a trial on the merits.[51]

In 1998, the Department of Justice brought a second lawsuit under sections 1 and 2 of the Sherman Act against Microsoft for various types of exclusionary conduct, ie exclusive dealing arrangements, unlawfully tying its web-browser 'Internet explorer' to its operating system 'Windows', maintaining a monopoly through predatory practices and attempts to monopolise the web-browser market.[52] A number of States also brought claims accusing Microsoft of violating various State antitrust laws. These cases were joined with the Department of Justice's action. After several months of fruitless settlement negotiations, the DC District Court issued its conclusions of law. It agreed with the Department of Justice in all but one count. It found that Microsoft had violated section 1 by tying its web browser to its operating system. It further found that Microsoft had a monopoly within the meaning of section 2 of the Sherman Act in the market for Intel-compatible PC operating systems, based on its market share of 95 per cent and the high barriers to entry characterising the market. It further held that Microsoft had unlawfully maintained this monopoly by anticompetitive exclusionary practices that significantly restricted the ability of other firms to compete on the merits of what they offered customers, in particular by integrating the web browser into the operating system, by contractually requiring key players in the market to give preference to Microsoft products and through its efforts to

[50] Amongst the many detailed accounts of the US Microsoft litigation under s 2 of the Sherman Act, see eg RJR Peritz, 'The Microsoft Chronicles' in L Rubini (ed), *Microsoft on Trial* (Cheltenham, Edward Elgar, 2010) 205–57, or AD Melamed and DL Rubinfed, '*U.S. v. Microsoft*: Lessons Learned and Issues Raised' in EM Fox and DA Crane (eds), *Antitrust Stories* (New York, Foundation Press, 2007) 287–310; AI Gavil and H First, *The Microsoft Antitrust Cases* (Cambridge, MA, MIT Press, 2014).

[51] *United States v Microsoft Corp*, 56 F.3d 1448 (DC Cir 1995). The Department of Justice subsequently filed a civil contempt action against Microsoft, alleging that Microsoft had violated one of the consent decree's clauses. The DC Circuit Court dismissed the action as unfounded (*United States v Microsoft Corp*, 147 F.3d 935 (DC Cir 1998)).

[52] *United States v Microsoft Corp*, 84 F. Supp. 2d 9 (D.D.C. 1999) (Findings of Fact).

contain and subvert competing technology.[53] The District Court also held that Microsoft's anticompetitive efforts to maintain its monopoly power in the market for Intel-compatible PC operating systems amounted to an unlawful attempt to monopolise a second market, ie the market for Internet browsers.[54] The final judgment ordered Microsoft to submit a plan of divestiture that would split the company into an operating systems business and an applications business, and also ordered a number of behavioural remedies.[55]

On appeal, the DC Circuit Court affirmed in part, reversed in part, and remanded in part the District Court's judgment.[56] It agreed with the District Court that Microsoft had monopoly power in the market for PC operating systems and that Microsoft had unlawfully maintained this power by engaging in various forms of exclusionary conduct, harming the competitive process and thereby consumers.[57] However, it reversed the District Court's finding of section 2 liability for attempted monopolisation of the second market on the grounds that the Department of Justice had failed to 'flesh out' the claim.[58] Regarding the allegation of tying, it found that the District Court had applied the wrong test by assessing the practice under a *per se* rule instead of a rule of reason and remanded the case for assessment under the latter.[59] Most significantly for Microsoft, perhaps, the Circuit Court also vacated the remedial order in its entirety as it rested on findings that it did not uphold. It vacated in full the final judgment embodying the remedial order and remanded the case to the District Court for reassignment to a different trial judge for further proceedings consistent with the Circuit Court's opinion.[60]

Shortly thereafter, the Department of Justice, recently re-staffed with appointments by the new Bush administration,[61] announced that it would not pursue its original aim of breaking up Microsoft and also decided to abandon the claim that Microsoft had engaged in illegal tying.[62] With regard to the other allegations it reached a settlement with Microsoft.[63] The District Court approved the parties' agreement in substance, but amended a number of provisions that would have prevented it from enforcing the decree. According to the settlement, Microsoft was required to share certain interoperability information with third party manufacturers of middleware software, and was prohibited from retaliating against users of competing software. Microsoft was not prohibited from integrating any

[53] *United States v Microsoft Corp*, 87 F. Supp. 2d 30 (D.D.C. 2000) (Conclusions of Law) 34–44.
[54] ibid, 45–46.
[55] *United States v Microsoft Corp*, 97 F. Supp. 2d 59, 64–65 (DDC 2000) (Final Judgment).
[56] *United States v Microsoft Corp*, 253 F.3d 34 (DC Cir 2001).
[57] ibid 58, 59–79.
[58] ibid 84.
[59] ibid 84–96.
[60] ibid 119.
[61] Peritz, 'The Microsoft Chronicles' (n 50) 219.
[62] US Department of Justice, Press Release, 'Justice Department Informs Microsoft of Plans for Further Proceedings in the District Court' (6 September 2001).
[63] *US v Microsoft Corp*, Civil Action No 98-1232, 12 November 2002.

of its software programs into Windows.[64] Most of the plaintiff States joined the settlement. Others chose to litigate to judgment. The judgment entered by the District Court closely paralleled the consent decree negotiated by the Department of Justice and Microsoft.[65] In addition to the enforcement attempts by the federal and State antitrust authorities, there were a number of private law suits brought primarily by other software developers, all of which were eventually settled.[66]

ii. The EU Investigation

The European Commission began investigating Microsoft under the EU antitrust rules in February 2000 while the US Department of Justice was litigating its second case against Microsoft in the DC District Court. Four months after the District Court issued its conclusions in law finding Microsoft guilty of infringing both sections 1 and 2 of the Sherman Act, the European Commission formally opened proceedings against Microsoft by sending it its first Statement of Objections.[67]

While the European Commission's investigation also centred on Microsoft's near monopoly power on the market for Intel-compatible PC operating systems and its attempts to maintain and extend this power into neighbouring markets, the Commission focused on different business practices from those investigated by the US antitrust authorities. The US Department of Justice had accused Microsoft of tying its browser to its operating system. The European Commission, by contrast, investigated Microsoft for tying its media player to its operating system. The European Commission further objected to Microsoft's refusal to supply designers of 'work group server operating systems'[68] with interoperability information for its operating systems software so as to allow them to develop interoperable software. The US Department of Justice had been concerned about Microsoft's refusal to share such information with producers of middleware software.

In May 2004, almost four years after sending out its initial Statement of Objections, the Commission issued an infringement decision according to which Microsoft had infringed Article 102 on both counts.[69] According to the Commission's assessment, Microsoft's practice of exclusively selling its PC operating system 'Windows' with a pre-installed 'Windows Media Player' amounted to an

[64] At the plaintiffs' request, the District Court agreed to extend parts of the Final Judgments for 2 years. The remaining provisions of the Final Judgments expired as originally ordered on 12 November 2007 (*United States v Microsoft Corp*, Civil Action No 98-1232 (CKK) (DDC 7 September 2006)).

[65] Affirmed on appeal in *Commonwealth of Massachusetts v Microsoft Corp*, 373 F.3d 1199 (DC Cir 2004).

[66] For a more detailed account, see Peritz (n 50) 221–22.

[67] European Commission, Press Release IP/00/906, 3 August 2000, 'Commission Opens Proceedings against Microsoft's Alleged Discriminatory Licensing and Refusal to Supply Software Information'.

[68] Work group server services are the basic services that are used by office workers in their day-to-day work, namely sharing files stored on servers, sharing printers and having their rights as network users administered centrally by their organisation's information technology department. Work group server operating systems, in turn, are operating systems designed and marketed to deliver these services collectively to relatively small numbers of PCs linked together in small to medium-sized networks.

[69] *Microsoft* (Case COMP/C-3/37.392) OJ [2007] L32/23.

abuse of a dominant position by means of tying. In line with the findings of the US courts, it found that Microsoft was dominant in the market for PC operating system because of its market share of over 95 per cent and the market's high barriers to entry. According to the Commission, Microsoft's conduct formally amounted to tying as Microsoft was selling two separate products as a bundle and did not give consumers a choice to purchase the tied product separately, which was sufficient to make this practice anticompetitive according to the case law. In view of Microsoft's highly specific defences, however, the Commission additionally chose to assess the practice as to its actual effects as it considered it possible that this specific instance of tying did not in fact have any negative effects on competition, or that any potential anticompetitive effects could be outweighed by efficiencies. The Commission found that the practice did have anticompetitive effects: Microsoft's ubiquity on the market for PC operating systems and the network effects characterising this market gave Microsoft a competitive advantage unrelated to the merits of the products as it offered software developers the ability to reach almost all PC users worldwide by relying on the Windows monopoly. Software developers were hence induced to rely primarily on Windows technology to reach consumers. Consequently, consumers would also prefer to use Microsoft's media player over competing media players, since a wider array of complementary software would be available for this product. The Commission therefore concluded that Microsoft's practice of tying its media player to Windows risked (1) excluding competitors from the media player market by placing them at a competitive disadvantage; (2) stifling innovation in the media player market; and (3) causing a spill-over effect on competition in complementary software markets with further detrimental effects on innovation. It did not find any of the efficiency defences offered by Microsoft sufficient to outweigh these anticompetitive effects.[70]

With regard to Microsoft's refusal to supply interoperability information to designers of 'work group server operating systems', the Commission established that in view of its market shares and the high market entry barriers Microsoft was dominant in both the market for PC operating systems and in the market for work group server operating systems. It then assessed whether Microsoft had 'abused' these positions by refusing to supply competing manufacturers of work group server operating systems with the interoperability information they needed to make their products compatible with Windows. It held that while undertakings were generally free to choose their contractual partners, a refusal to supply on the part of a dominant undertaking could be considered abusive, because dominant undertakings had a special responsibility not to distort competition. Under exceptional circumstances this could even apply to refusals to license intellectual property rights. On the basis of a lengthy analysis of the facts, the Commission reached the conclusion that there were several factors that justified qualifying

[70] ibid, recitals 793–993.

Microsoft's refusal to supply interoperability information as 'exceptional' and therefore abusive within the meaning of Article 102: (1) Microsoft had held a quasi-monopoly position in the PC operating systems market for many years; (2) it had progressively diminished the level of disclosures; (3) interoperability with Windows was necessary for a work group server operating system vendor in order to stay in the market; (4) Microsoft's market share had increased swiftly in the market for work group server operating systems to a position of extraordinary strength as a result of the interoperability advantage; (5) data showed that there was a risk that competition would be completely eliminated in the market for work group server operating systems and (6) Microsoft's refusal to supply stifled innovation in the market for work group server operating systems and diminished consumer choice by locking them into a homogeneous Microsoft solution. It did not find that Microsoft's practice was objectively justified.[71]

Microsoft argued, amongst others, that the Commission had not established to the required standard that consumers were harmed as a consequence of its conduct. The Commission took the view that it had demonstrated consumer harm, and that, in any event, actual consumer harm was irrelevant under Article 102. According to longstanding case law Article 102 prohibited not only conduct that could prejudice consumers directly but also conduct that harmed them indirectly by impairing an effective competitive structure.[72]

The Commission fined Microsoft a (then) record €497,196,304 for the two infringements. It further imposed a number of behavioural remedies, ordering Microsoft to make available a version of Windows without Windows Media Player within 90 days,[73] and to make available interoperability information to any undertaking having an interest in developing work group server operating system products on reasonable and non-discriminatory terms.[74] Microsoft brought an action for annulment against the Commission decision. In 2007, the General Court upheld the decision in its entirety.[75] The Commission subsequently fined Microsoft a further €899 million for failure to comply with the remedies imposed in the infringement decision.[76]

Incidentally, Microsoft's troubles with EU antitrust law did not end there. In 2008, the Commission turned its attention to Microsoft's practice of tying its web browser to its operating system the very strategy that the US Department of Justice had tried to put an end to in 1998.[77] Microsoft offered commitments to

[71] ibid, recitals 546–791.

[72] ibid, recitals 702–08, citing Case 85/76 *Hoffmann-La Roche v Commission* ECLI:EU:C:1979:36, para 125.

[73] ibid, Art 6.

[74] ibid, Art 5.

[75] Case T-201/04 *Microsoft Corp v Commission* ECLI:EU:T:2007:289.

[76] *Microsoft* (n 69).

[77] European Commission, Memorandum MEMO/09/15 of 17 January 2009, 'Antitrust: Commission confirms sending a Statement of Objections to Microsoft on the tying of Internet Explorer to Windows'.

address the Commission's concerns, which the Commission considered satisfactory and made legally binding by means of a decision.[78] However, Microsoft failed to fulfil these commitments to the satisfaction of the Commission,[79] which fined Microsoft another €561 million for non-compliance in March 2013.[80]

iii. The Controversy

Like in the case of the failed *GE/Honeywell* merger five years earlier, the Commission's decision in *Microsoft* met with great disapproval in the United States. US Senators are reported to have been 'particularly incensed' at the Commission's demand that Microsoft give its rivals access to the computer code underlying Windows, which they considered an infringement of a US company's intellectual property.[81] Again, there was talk of a transatlantic trade war.[82] All in all, however, the political reaction to the European Commission's decision in *Microsoft* was more muted than in the case of *GE/Honeywell*. The Assistant Attorney General for the Antitrust Division of the US Department of Justice resigned himself to expressing the view that EU competition law favoured 'gentlemanly' over 'Darwinian' competition.[83] This relatively mild reaction may be explained by the fact that there had been serious doubt about Microsoft's conduct in the United States as well. Not only had the Department of Justice brought proceedings against Microsoft, joined by no fewer than 20 States, but the DC District Court had found Microsoft guilty of breaching both sections 1 and 2 of the Sherman Act and had taken the radical step of attempting to break Microsoft into two separate companies. The Court of Appeals, while partially reversing this judgment, had upheld the finding of a section 2 infringement for maintaining a monopoly by anticompetitive means, including tying, and had remanded the case for a separate assessment of Microsoft's tying under the correct section 1 test, making clear that it did not find Microsoft's technological integration welfare-enhancing or that it should be absolved of tying liability.[84] In the end, the new federal administration preferred to settle with Microsoft. The settlement, which was partially extended for another two years,

[78] This possibility had not existed during the first Microsoft investigation. Commitments decisions are a relatively new tool in EU antitrust law, which were introduced by Council Regulation (EC) 1/2003 (the so-called Modernisation Regulation) with effect from 1 May 2004.

[79] European Commission, Press Release IP/13/196, 6 March 2013, 'Antitrust: Commission Fines Microsoft for Non-compliance with Browser Choice Commitments.

[80] *Microsoft (Tying)* (Case AT.39530).

[81] R Wray, 'Microsoft Ruling is 'First Shot in Trade War'' *Guardian* (London, 26 May 2004) 17.

[82] ibid; J Burgess, 'Europeans Come down Hard on Microsoft' *Washington Post* (Washington, DC, 25 March 2004).

[83] Address by R Hewett Pate, 'Antitrust in a Transatlantic Context—From the Cicada's Perspective' (Brussels, 7 June 2004) available at: www.usdoj.gov/atr/public/speeches/203973.htm. Commissioner Monti, appearing to take offence at this characterisation, replied that he did not oppose the Darwinian concept of competition as long as it was 'Darwinian competition on the merits' (M Monti, 'Comments to the Speech of Hew Pate at the Conference "Antitrust in a Transatlantic Context"' (Brussels, 7 June 2004) www.ec.europa.eu/comm/competition/speeches).

[84] *United States v Microsoft Corp* (n 56).

imposed restrictions on Microsoft that addressed at least a few of the Department of Justice's initial concerns. Moreover, several States refused to join the federal government's settlement and litigated the case to the end in the attempt to obtain more stringent remedies. Even in the United States, there were voices that argued that Microsoft had got away with anticompetitive conduct.[85]

At the academic level, by contrast, the European Commission's decision met with clearer criticism. US commentators, as well as many EU academics, found that the Commission's analysis in Microsoft suffered from similar shortcomings as its assessments in *Boeing/McDonnell-Douglas* and *GE/Honeywell*. The Commission's assessment was generally found to lack solid economic foundations.[86] Also, the Commission was once more criticised for assessing the effects on competitors rather than on consumer welfare.[87]

D. Conclusion

Parallel investigations of the same conduct by the US and EU antitrust regimes continue to happen. In so far, the above cases are not unique. In 2013, for example, both the US Federal Trade Commission and the European Commission independently investigated claims under their respective antitrust rules that the US technology company Google had been giving preference to its own services in its research results (this time, Microsoft was the complainant). Google eventually settled the case with both authorities.[88]

At first sight, US and EU antitrust law contain very similar rules: a prohibition of anticompetitive agreements, a prohibition of anticompetitive conduct on the part of economically powerful undertakings and a prohibition of anticompetitive mergers. In both antitrust systems, these prohibitions are worded broadly and in somewhat antiquated language, that requires substantial interpretation by the antitrust authorities and courts. However, *GE/Honeywell*, at the very latest, made obvious that the US and EU antitrust authorities and courts in fact did not interpret their antitrust rules identically. They assessed different types of effects

[85] See eg S Houck, 'The EC Decision Against Microsoft: Windows on the World, Glass Houses, or Through the Looking Glass?' *The Antitrust Source* (September 2004) 1, 10.

[86] See eg R Pardolesi and A Renda, 'The European Commission's Case Against Microsoft: Kill Bill?' (2004) 27 *World Competition* 513; D Ridyard, 'Compulsory Access under EC Competition Law—a New Doctrine of "Convenient Facilities" and the Case for Price Regulation' (2004) 25 *European Competition Law Review* 669; DS Evans and AJ Padilla, 'Tying under Article 82 EC and the Microsoft Decision: a Comment on Dolmans and Graf' (2004) 27 *World Competition* 503; J-Y Art and G McCurdy, 'The European Commission's Media Player Remedy in its Microsoft Decision: Compulsory Code Removal despite the Absence of Tying or Foreclosure' (2004) 25 *European Competition Law Review* 694.

[87] eg D Ridyard, 'Tying and Bundling—Cause for Complaint?' (2005) 26 *European Competition Law Review* 316.

[88] US FTC, 'Statement of the Federal Trade Commission Regarding Google's Search Practices', *In the Matter of Google Inc*, FTC File Number 111-0163 (Washington, DC, 3 January 2013).

and relied on different theories of harm. US antitrust experts found the European Commission's analyses to be strangely out of sync with contemporary economic theory. Yet more fundamentally, antitrust experts began to wonder whether the two antitrust regimes might not even pursue the same aim. From the point of view of US antitrust lawyers, it seemed that EU antitrust law aimed to protect businesses from the anticompetitive conduct of their competitors, whereas the objective of US antitrust law was to protect consumers from anticompetitive conduct.

This recognition contributed to a major transatlantic debate about the appropriate objective of antitrust law, key concepts of antitrust law as well as the role of economics in antitrust assessments. The debate took place both at the academic and political level, and involved a fair deal of exchange between the two.[89]

[89] Amongst many, see eg M Monti, 'Antitrust in the US and Europe: A History of Convergence' (General Counsel Roundtable American Bar Association, Washington, DC, 14 November 2001); G Drauz, 'Unbundling GE/Honeywell' (n 45); A Schaub, 'Continued Focus on Reform: Recent Developments in EC Competition Policy' in Hawk (ed), *International Antitrust Law and Policy 2001, Annual Proceedings of the Fordham Corporate Law Institute* (n 45) 31; D Ridyard, 'Exclusionary Pricing and Price Discrimination Abuses under Article 82—An Economic Analysis' (2002) 23 *European Competition Law Review* 286; W Kolasky, 'Conglomerate Mergers and Range Effects' (n 44); D Ridyard and S Bishop, 'EC Vertical Restraints Guidelines: Effects-Based or Per Se Policy?' (2002) 23 *European Competition Law Review* 35; O Odudu, 'A New Economic Approach to Article 81(1)?' (2002) 27 *European Law Review* 100; E Fox, 'US and European Merger Policy—Fault Lines and Bridges—Mergers that Create Incentives for Exclusionary Practices' (2002) 10 *George Mason Law Review* 471; J Temple Lang and R O'Donoghue, 'Defining Legitimate Competition: How to Clarify Pricing Abuses under Article 82 EC' (2002) 26 *Fordham International Law Journal* 83; J Vickers, 'How to Reform the EC Merger Test?' in G Drauz and M Reynolds (eds), *EC Merger Control—A Major Reform in Progress* (Oxford, Oxford University Press, 2003); AJ Riley, 'EC Antitrust Modernisation: The Commission Does Very Nicely—Thank You! Part 1' (2003) 11 *European Competition Law Review* 604 and 'Part 2' (2003) 11 *European Competition Law Review* 657; SB Völker, 'Mind the Gap: Unilateral Effects Analysis Arrives in EC Merger Control' (2004) 25 *European Competition Law Review* 395; V Verouden, C Bengtsson and S Albaek, 'The Draft EU Notice on Horizontal Mergers: A Further Step toward Convergence?' (2004) 49 *Antitrust Bulletin* 243; C Veljanovski, 'EC Merger Policy After GE/Honeywell and Airtours' (2004) 49 *Antitrust Bulletin* 153; B Sher, 'The Last of the Steam-Powered Trains: Modernising Article 82' (2004) 25 *European Competition Law Review* 243; P Lowe, 'DG Competition's Review of the Policy on the Abuse of Dominance' in Hawk (n 45) 163; DS Evans and AJ Padilla, 'Tying under Article 2 EC and the Microsoft Decision' (2004) 27 *World Competition* 503; L-H Röller, 'Der ökonomische Ansatz in der europäischen Wettbewerbspolitik' in Monopolkommission, *Zukunftsperspektiven der Wettbewerbspolitik* (Baden-Baden, Nomos, 2005); R Hewett Pate, "Antitrust in a Transatlantic Context" (n 83); M Monti, 'Comments to the Speech of Hew Pate at the Conference' (n 83); K-U Kühn, "Antitrust in a Transatlantic Context" R Stillman and C Caffarra, 'Economic Theories of Bundling and their Policy Implications in Abuse Cases: an Assessment in Light of the Microsoft Case' (2005) 1 *European Competition Journal* 85; JS Venit, 'Article 82: The Last Frontier—Fighting Fire With Fire?' (2005) 28 *Fordham International Law Journal* 1157; D Waelbroeck, 'Michelin II: A *Per Se* Rule Against Rebates by Dominant Companies?' (2005) 1 *Journal of Competition Law and Economics* 149; G Niels and H Jenkins, 'Reform of Article 82: Where the Link Between Dominance and Effects Breaks Down' (2005) 26 *European Competition Law* Review 605; L-H Röller, 'Antitrust Economics—Catalyst for Convergence?' George Mason Law Review Symposium (Washington, DC, 20 September 2005); A Christiansen and W Kerber, 'Competition Policy with Optimally Differentiated Rules Instead of "*Per Se* Rules v Rule of Reason"' (2006) 2 *Journal of Competition Law & Economics* 215; Bundeskartellamt/Competition Law Forum, 'Debate on Reform of Article 82: A Dialectic on Competing Approaches' (2006) 2 *European Competition Journal* 211; R Nazzini, 'The Wood Began to Move: An Essay on Consumer Welfare, Evidence and Burden of Proof in Article 82 EC Cases' (2006)

It contributed greatly to the substantive modernisation process that transformed EU antitrust law in the first decade of the twenty-first century.

V. DG Competition's *annus horribilis*

A further chain of events that influenced and drove forward the Commission's substantive reform took place in 2002. Within a period of only three months, the General Court struck down three separate Commission decisions in the field of EU merger control because of serious errors of assessment.[90] This unprecedented situation led to important organisational changes within DG Competition but also to some soul-searching on the quality of its competitive assessments.

A. The Scope of Judicial Review

It is unusual for the Court of Justice to second-guess the Commission's assessments in the area of antitrust law. According to longstanding practice, the Court exercises judicial self-restraint when it comes to reviewing assessments of an economic nature and limits itself to verifying whether the relevant procedural rules have been complied with, whether the decision's statement of reasons is adequate, whether the facts have been accurately stated and whether there has been a manifest error of appraisal or misuse of powers.[91] This is particularly so in the field of merger control where the Commission is required to make a prospective assessment of likely future effects. The Court takes the view that Article 2 of the Merger Regulation confers upon the Commission a discretionary margin, which the Union judicature must take into account when reviewing assessments of an economic nature.[92] Notwithstanding this principle, the General Court found that

31 *European Law Review* 518; A Schmidt, 'Wie ökonomisch ist der "more economic approach"? Einige Anmerkungen aus ordnungsökonomischer Sicht' (2006) *Freiburger Diskussionspapiere* 06/10; J Vickers, 'Market Power in Competition Cases' (2006) 2 *European Competition Journal* 3; S Voigt and A Schmidt, 'Der "more economic approach" in der Mißbrauchsaufsicht' (2006) 56 *Wirtschaft und Wettbewerb* 1097; G Monti, 'The Concept of Dominance in Article 82' (2006) 3 *European Competition Journal* 31; P Lowe, 'Consumer Welfare and Efficiency—New Guiding Principles of Competition Policy?' 13th International Conference on Competition (Munich, 27 March 2007); M Dreher and M Adam, 'Abuse of Dominance under Reform—Sound Economics and Established Case Law' (2007) 28 *European Competition Law Review* 278; ILO Schmidt, 'The Suitability of the More Economic Approach for Competition Policy: Dynamic vs. Static Efficiency' (2007) 28 *European Competition Law Review* 408.

[90] Case T-342/99 *Airtours plc v Commission* ECLI:EU:T:2002:146; Case T-310/01 *Schneider Electric SA v Commission* ECLI:EU:T:2002:254; Case T-5/02 *Tetra Laval BV v Commission* ECLI:EU:T:2002:264.

[91] See eg Case 42/84 *Remia BV and others v Commission* ECLI:EU:C:1985:327, para 34.

[92] Joined Cases C-68/94 and C-30/95 *France and Others v Commission* ('Kali & Salz') ECLI:EU:C:1998:148, paras 223 and 224.

the Commission had committed assessment errors of such gravity in the cases of *Airtours, Schneider Electric* and *Tetra Laval* that they exceeded the permissible margin of discretion.

B. Airtours

In the case of *Airtours*, the Commission had prohibited a merger between two UK tour operators, Airtours and First Choice, on the grounds that it would create a collective dominant position in the UK market for short-haul foreign package holidays as a result of which competition would be significantly impeded on this market.[93] A position of collective dominance is one held by the parties to the concentration together with one or more undertakings not party thereto. According to the Court, it refers to a situation in which effective competition would be significantly impeded by the members of the collective dominant position, in particular because of factors giving rise to a connection between them as a result of which they would be able to adopt a common policy on the market and act to a considerable extent independently of their competitors, their customers and ultimately consumers.[94] In the case of *Airtours*, the General Court further clarified that a collective dominant position could only exist under three conditions: (1) the market had to be sufficiently transparent for each member to know how the other members were behaving in order to monitor whether they were adopting the common policy; (2) the situation of tacit coordination had be sustainable over time, ie there had to be an incentive not to depart from the common policy, which was only the case if there was a sufficient deterrent not to depart from the common course of conduct; and (3) the Commission had to establish that the foreseeable reaction of current and future competitors, as well as of consumers, would not jeopardise the results expected from the common policy.[95]

The General Court found that the Commission had failed to prove any of these conditions to the required legal standard in this case and that its decision was 'vitiated by a series of errors of assessment as to factors fundamental to any assessment of whether a collective dominant position might be created'.[96] It found, for instance, that the Commission had been wrong to infer that there was already a tendency to collective dominance prior to the merger from factors such as the market participants' cautious capacity planning or from the fact that the same institutional investors were found to some extent in the three major market players.[97] It also criticised the Commission for not having taken into account that the main

[93] *Airtours/First Choice* (Case IV/M.1524) OJ [2000] L93/1.
[94] Case T-102/96 *Gencor v Commission* ECLI:EU:T:1999:65, paras 125 and 163.
[95] *Airtours plc v Commission* (n 90) para 61.
[96] ibid, para 294.
[97] Ibid, paras 91, 92.

tour operators' market shares had been volatile in the past and that such volatility was counter-indicative of coordination.[98] It further held that the Commission had failed to prove key factors on which it based its assumption that the market was conducive to oligopolistic coordination, that the Commission had frequently misinterpreted the available data,[99] and that it had ignored economic theory by not considering demand volatility a factor likely to destabilise any attempt at collusion by the remaining market players post-merger.[100] It also found that the Commission had underestimated the likely reaction of smaller competitors, potential competitors and consumers as factors capable of destabilising the alleged dominant oligopoly.[101] In particular, it had failed to take into account the lack of barriers to entry.[102] Finally, the Court rebuked the Commission for having ignored 'economic logic' by not taking into consideration that every business was motivated by profit maximisation in its attempts to predict the likely impact of the merger on the remaining market participants' conduct.[103] The Court found the Commission's assessment so flawed that it annulled the decision in its entirety. This was a damning criticism of the Commission's evidentiary standards and economic know-how.

C. Schneider Electric

In *Schneider Electric*, the General Court was asked to review a Commission decision prohibiting a merger in the electrical distribution sector.[104] Schneider Electric, a company incorporated under French law, was the parent of a group engaged in the manufacture and sale of products in the electrical distribution sector. It proposed to acquire all publicly held shares in Legrand, another French company, specialising in the manufacture and sale of electrical equipment for low-voltage installations. The Commission prohibited the acquisition on the basis that it would create new dominant positions in nine markets and would strengthen pre-existing dominant positions in another five markets.[105]

On review, the Court found that, like the in the case of *Airtours*, the Commission had committed serious errors in its assessment of the merger's likely impact that by far exceeded the permissible margin of discretion. Amongst others, it held

[98] ibid, paras 112, 120. The Commission had excluded growth by acquisition when it assessed the evolution of the key actors' market share, and thus reached the conclusion that the market participants' market shares had been stable. The Court did not find this convincing.

[99] ibid, paras 133, 172–80.

[100] ibid, para 147.

[101] ibid, paras 208–61.

[102] ibid, para 269.

[103] ibid, paras 290–93.

[104] *Schneider Electric v Commission* (n 90), reviewing Commission Decision of 10 October 2001 in *Schneider/Legrand* (Case COMP/M.2283) OJ [2004] L101/1.

[105] *Schneider/Legrand* (n 104) recitals 782 and 783.

that the Commission had overestimated the merged entity's power by presuming the existence of 'transnational effects' capable of increasing the concentration's impact on the relevant national markets, but had failed to prove the likelihood of such effects on the basis of cogent evidence.[106] It also found that, having defined the separate product markets as being national in dimension, the Commission had failed to carry out a detailed country-by-country analysis and had instead repeatedly relied on general European-wide considerations[107] or on characteristics of other national markets.[108] It further found that the Commission had failed to prove its contention that the merged entity would become an unavoidable trading partner for wholesalers and that these had no countervailing buyer power. It took the view that the data contained in the decision was at odds with the Commission's findings and criticised the Commission for imputing specific future market conduct on the part of the merged entity without providing any evidence in support of this critical assumption.[109] Also, when calculating the competing companies' market shares for the purpose of assessing their strength, the Commission had been wrong not to take into consideration the proportion of sales that these competitors made to vertically integrated groups.[110]

In unusually stern language, the Court concluded that it considered these 'errors, omissions and inconsistencies' in the Commission's analysis to be 'of undoubted gravity', and that they were such as to 'deprive of probative value the economic assessment of the impact of the concentration.'[111] To add insult to injury, the Court also found that the Commission had infringed Schneider's rights of defence by basing a key objection to the merger on a concern that was not formulated in the Statement of Objections with sufficient precision to allow Schneider to identify it as such, submit practical comments and propose appropriate remedies.[112] Again, the General Court annulled the decision in its entirety.

D. Tetra Laval

The final blow came only three days after the judgment in *Schneider Electric* when the General Court struck down a third prohibition decision because of similar assessment errors.[113] The case concerned a proposed merger in the liquid food packaging industry. Tetra Laval SA, a French company wholly owned by the Dutch company Tetra Laval BV (Tetra), intended to acquire Sidel, a company incorporated under French law. Tetra comprised amongst others the Tetra Pak

[106] *Schneider Electric SA v Commission* (n 90) paras 152–91.
[107] ibid, para 193–97.
[108] ibid, paras 237, 238.
[109] ibid, paras 203–30.
[110] ibid, paras 292–296.
[111] ibid, paras 404, 411.
[112] ibid, paras 421–62.
[113] *Tetra Laval BV v Commission* (n 90).

company, which was active in the area of liquid food carton packaging and was the worldwide market leader for the production of carton packaging equipment and cartons. Tetra also had more limited activities in the plastic packaging sector, mainly as a converter[114] of high-density polyethylene (HDPE) bottles. Sidel designed and produced packaging equipment and systems, in particular stretch blow moulding (SBM) machines, which were used in the production of polyethylene terephthalate (PET) plastic bottles. It was the worldwide leader for the production and supply of such machines. It was also active in barrier technology, used to make PET compatible with products that are sensitive to gas and light, and the manufacture of filling machines for PET and HDPE bottles.[115]

The Commission prohibited the merger.[116] It held that pre-merger, Tetra already had a dominant position in the market for aseptic cartons and that it had a leading position in the market for non-aseptic cartons. Sidel had a leading, although not yet dominant, position in the market for PET packaging equipment. According to the Commission, the merger would turn the latter into a dominant position.[117] It would also further strengthen Tetra's already dominant position in the market for carton packaging systems, because it would create the only vertically integrated entity that was involved in the production of three separate packaging systems (carton, PET and HDPE). According to the Commission, the merged entity's dual position as supplier and competitor of converters would create a 'channel conflict' and be likely to incite it to raise competing converters' costs.[118] It further predicted that the merged entity would use its presence in several packaging markets to 'leverage' its dominant position in the carton sector, and turn its already leading position in PET packaging equipment into a dominant position. Tetra could achieve this by tying carton packaging equipment with PET packaging equipment, and using its knowledge of clients' needs from its carton side of the business to offer them timely and bespoke PET solutions, enabling them to switch from carton to PET with a single supplier.[119] The Commission found Tetra's commitments insufficient to address these concerns.

On review, the General Court found multiple issues with this analysis, which it deemed too serious to withstand review. Its comments on the Commission's analysis of the merger's horizontal and vertical effects were as brief as they were critical. It held that, if the commitments were taken into account, the potential negative horizontal and vertical effects identified by the Commission were merely minimal if not non-existent.[120] The Court went through the Commission's

[114] Converters manufacture and supply empty packaging to producers who then fill the packaging themselves.

[115] ibid, paras 9–13.

[116] *Tetra Laval/Sidel* (Case COMP/M.2416) OJ [2004] L43/13.

[117] ibid, recitals 263–90.

[118] ibid, recitals 291–324.

[119] ibid, 325–408.

[120] *Tetra Laval BV v Commission* (n 90) paras 132, 136–39.

assessment of the merger's likely conglomerate effects in more detail. It found that the Commission had committed 'manifest errors of assessment' in predicting that the merged entity could and would use its dominant position in the carton packaging market successfully as a 'lever' to achieve dominance in the neighbouring PET packaging equipment market by means of bundling or other exclusionary practices. First, the Commission had failed to take into account that such practices would be illegal pursuant to Article 102, which had to be considered a disincentive for the parties to engage in such behaviour. Also, Tetra had submitted behavioural commitments that left little room for such conduct.[121] While the Court did not exclude that it would in theory be possible for the merged entity to engage in leveraging practices, for example, by enticing existing carton customers to switch to PET or by offering attractive bundles of PET-related products, it held that the Commission had failed to adduce sufficiently convincing evidence to prove that this would allow the merged entity to achieve a dominant position in any of the PET-related markets.[122] It also dismissed the Commission's finding that the merger would reinforce Tetra's dominant position on the markets for aseptic carton packaging by eliminating the competitive constraint represented by Sidel as a potential competitor coming from the neighbouring PET markets on the grounds that the Commission had not adduced any evidence for the key assumption on which this prediction was based, namely that there would be considerable growth in PET use for sensitive products.[123] The Court concluded that the contested decision did not establish any of the alleged anticompetitive effects to the requisite legal standard and annulled it in its entirety.

This time the Commission appealed against the General Court's judgment to the Court of Justice, claiming that the former had exceeded its role by substituting its view for that of the Commission. The Court of Justice dismissed the appeal as unfounded. It confirmed that the Commission had a margin of discretion with regard to economic matters. This, however, did not mean that the Union Courts had to refrain from reviewing the Commission's interpretation of information of an economic nature. On the contrary: not only did the General Court have the duty to establish that the evidence relied on was factually accurate, reliable and consistent, but it also had to ascertain whether the evidence contained all the information necessary for assessing a complex situation and whether it was capable of substantiating the conclusions drawn from it.[124]

E. Consequences

The General Court's criticism of the Commission's assessments in these three merger decisions was unprecedented in its detail and outspokenness. It occurred

[121] ibid, paras 158–61.
[122] ibid, paras 226–307.
[123] ibid, paras 312–33.
[124] C-12/03P *Commission v Tetra Laval* ECLI:EU:C:2005:87.

only one year after the *GE/Honeywell* crisis incited equally vehement criticism of the Commission's competitive assessments from US antitrust experts and academics. One could easily jump to the conclusion that the General Court and the US antitrust community were making the same point when they criticised the quality of the Commission's assessments. However, that is not quite the case.

US antitrust experts primarily criticised that the Commission's analyses were not guided by the appropriate legal objective and did not focus on the correct type of harmful effect. In their view, a modern antitrust regime had to be guided by the objective of economic theory, ie the maximisation of economic welfare, be it in the form of general welfare or consumer welfare. Any antitrust test should therefore ask whether the conduct in question reduced economic welfare. This was not the approach taken by the Commission in *GE/Honeywell* or *Microsoft*. The Commission had instead assessed whether the merger would lead to the creation of a dominant position, and in particular whether this position would allow the merged entity to exclude competitors. Essentially, US antitrust experts thus took issue with the concept of competitive harm of EU antitrust law. In addition, they criticised the economic theories used by the European Commission to support their assumptions as being seriously outdated.

By contrast, the concept of competitive harm and the relevance of consumer harm were not the point of contention in the three judgments from 2001. The General Court did not criticise the Commission for looking at the wrong type of effect and asking the wrong questions. The General Court's main issue in 2002 was one of slapdash fact-finding and poor evidentiary standards. In its view, the Commission had 'merely' failed to support its key assumptions with sufficiently convincing evidence and had ignored fundamental economic reasoning in its conjecture.

Despite these differences, there is little doubt that both the *GE/Honeywell* crisis and the events of 2002 played an important role in encouraging the Commission to rethink key concepts and develop the more economic approach to EU antitrust law. Two weeks after the General Court handed down its judgment in *Tetra Laval*, the then Commissioner for Competition Policy, Mario Monti, stated that it had in fact long been his intention to submit a reform package on merger control to the Council. In so far, the General Court's judgments, however painful, had come at an opportune moment. Monti acknowledged that there were lessons to be drawn from the Court's criticism, and rather than allowing these setbacks to distort its view of the EU merger control policy, the Commission should turn them into an opportunity for even deeper reform than originally envisaged.[125] In fact, the Commission's reforms over the following years went far beyond addressing the Court's concerns in *Airtours, Schneider Electric* and *Tetra Laval*, which has led to a new and still ongoing conflict between the Court and the Commission.[126]

[125] M Monti, 'Merger Control in the European Union: A Radical Reform', Speech at the European Commission/IBA Conference on EU Merger Control (Brussels, 7 November 2002).

[126] This issue is discussed in Ch 10.

VI. The Great Reformer

There is little doubt that the professional background and beliefs of Mario Monti played a major role in introducing and shaping the Commission's more economic approach to EU antitrust law as we know it today. Since the earliest days of the European Economic Community, Commissioners for Competition Policy had traditionally been politicians with a background in law or political science. Hans von der Groeben (1958–67), the first Commissioner for Competition, was a lawyer and senior civil servant in the German post-war government. His successor Maan Sassen (1967–71), a Dutch politician, also held a law degree. Albert Borschette (1971–76) was a Luxembourgian diplomat and writer who had studied literature and politics. Raymond Vouel (1976–81) was a Luxembourgian politician and journalist, with a background in political economics. Frans Andriessen (1981–85) was a Dutch politician who had studied law. Peter Sutherland (1985–1989) and Leon Brittan (1989–93) were both barristers by profession. Karel van Miert (1993–99), a Dutch politician, had a degree in diplomatic sciences.

This tradition came to end when Mario Monti took over as Commissioner for Competition Policy in 1999. Monti was the first economist to be appointed Commissioner for Competition Policy. He held a degree in economics and business from Bocconi University in Italy and had pursued graduate studies at Yale University in the United States.[127] Prior to joining the European Commission he was a professor of economics. His research outputs include the Klein-Monti model, an econometric model aimed at describing the behaviour of banks operating under monopoly circumstances.[128] Monti was appointed European Commissioner for Internal Market, Financial Services and Financial Integration, Customs and Taxation in 1995, and became Commissioner responsible for Competition Policy in 1999.

Monti made clear from the beginning that he would make it a priority of his office to give EU competition law a radical overhaul and increase the emphasis on sound economics.[129] Throughout his term as Commissioner for Competition Policy, he continued to promote his aim of elevating EU antitrust law from its 'legalistic approach' to one 'based on sound economic principles' in line with current economic thinking.[130]

[127] www.ec.europa.eu/civil_service/docs/special_advisers/2015/monti_cv_en.pdf.

[128] M Monti, 'Deposit, Credit and Interest Rate Determination under Alternative Bank Objective Functions' in GP Szegö and K Shell (eds), Mathematical Methods in Investment and Finance (Amsterdam, North-Holland Publishing, 1972).

[129] M Monti, 'A Competition Policy for Today and Tomorrow' (2000) 23 *World Competition* 1.

[130] See eg M Monti, 'Antitrust in the US and Europe: A History of Convergence' (n 89); 'EU Competition Policy', Fordham Annual Conference on International Antitrust Law and Policy (New York, 31 October 2002); 'The New EU Policy on Technology Transfer Agreements', Speech at École des Mines (Paris, 16 January 2004); 'EU Competition Policy after May 2004', Speech at the Fordham Annual Conference on International Antitrust Law and Policy (New York, 24 October 2003), 'A Reformed Competition Policy: Achievements and Challenges for the Future', Speech at the Center for European

This is not to say that discussions about a substantive reform had not already started under the previous Commissioner or that the reform process came to an abrupt end when Monti left the Commission in 2004. The first public signs that the Commission was exploring the possibility of giving greater weight to economic theory in its antitrust policy in fact predate Monti's term. In 1996, the Commission published the aforementioned Green Paper on Vertical Restraints,[131] in which it outlined several ideas for modernising its approach to assessing vertical agreements under Article 101. This preparatory document proposed several policy options for a new approach to vertical restraints and signalled that it considered it useful to take into account the emerging consensus amongst economists on the effects of vertical agreements in this review.[132] Nonetheless, the Green Paper was still markedly cautious on the possible role and significance of economic theory in antitrust policy. Its opening paragraphs stressed that economic theory could not be the only factor in the design of its policy, as it was only one of many relevant policy sources. It also stressed that a full evaluation of every individual case according to economic principles would be too costly in terms of resource and would lead to legal uncertainty.[133]

This caution disappeared during Monti's office, and it is during his time as Commissioner that the Commission published the key documents introducing the more economic approach: the interpretative guidelines on Article 101,[134] the policy documents initiating the reform of EU merger law[135] and the interpretative horizontal merger guidelines accompanying the new Merger Regulation.[136] He also set in motion the ultimately very lengthy process of reforming the Commission's approach to Article 102 before the end of his term,[137] earning himself the epithet of 'Great Reformer'.[138]

Reform (Brussels, 28 October 2004). These speeches are available at: www.ec.europa.eu/competition/speeches. See also M Monti, 'The New Shape of European Competition Policy', Speech at the Inaugural Symposium of the Competition Policy Research Center (Tokyo, 20 November 2003).

[131] European Commission, 'Green Paper on Vertical Restraints in EC Competition Policy' (n 11).

[132] ibid, para 10.

[133] ibid, paras 13, 86.

[134] Guidelines on Vertical Restraints of 13 October 2000, [2000] OJ C291/1; Guidelines on the Applicability of Article 81 of the EC Treaty to Horizontal Cooperation Agreements of 6 January 2001, [2001] OJ C3/2; Guidelines on the Application of Article 81 of the Treaty to Technology Transfer Agreements [2004] OJ C101/2; and Guidelines on the Application of Article 81(3) of the Treaty [2004] OJ C101/97.

[135] European Commission, 'Green Paper on the Review of Council Regulation (EEC) No 4064/89', COM(2001) 745/6 of 11 December 2001; European Commission, Proposal for a Council Regulation on the control of concentrations between undertakings [2003] OJ C20/4.

[136] Guidelines on the assessment of horizontal mergers under the Council Regulation on the control of concentrations between undertakings [2004] OJ C31/5.

[137] Monti, 'EU Competition Policy after May 2004' (n 130).

[138] M Bloom, 'The Great Reformer: Mario Monti's Legacy in Article 81 EC and Cartel Policy' (2005) 1 *Competition Policy International* 55.

VII. Increased International Cooperation

One final factor that is likely to have contributed to shaping and facilitating the substantive reform of EU antitrust law is the increase in cooperation and exchange in best practices between antitrust authorities at the international level. Many attempts had been made in the twentieth century to establish binding international antitrust rules under the auspices of an international organisation.[139] None of these was successful, not least because of the US Congress and government's repeated opposition to a world antitrust system with centralised enforcement powers.[140]

In 2001, the *GE/Honeywell* dispute between the United States and European Union reignited the discussion on how to address the issue of diverging antitrust standards at the international level.[141] Although the concept of an enforceable international competition agreement under the auspices of the WTO remained, and continues to remain, popular at the academic level,[142] governments appeared to abandon such ambitions as unrealistic for the time being and decided to focus on a less invasive and more pragmatic form of international

[139] eg the ill-fated Havana Charter from 1948, proposed by John Maynard Keynes, had contained a chapter on restrictive practices, requiring its members to act against anticompetitive business conduct (Havana Charter for an International Trade Organization, Chapter V, United Nations Conference on Trade and Employment, held at Havana, Cuba from 21 November 1947 to 24 March 1948, Final Act and Related Documents (available at: www.wto.org/english/docs_e/legal_e/havana_e.pdf)) or the Draft International Antitrust Code from 1993 (reprinted in 'Draft International Antitrust Code as a GATT-MTO-Plurilateral Trade Agreement 10 July 1993' (1993) 5 *World Trade and Arbitration Materials* 126), and the subsequent unsuccessful attempts by the WTO (eg Singapore WTO Ministerial Declaration (WT/MIN(96)/DEC) of 18 December 1996, para 20; Doha WTO Ministerial Declaration (WT/MIN(01)/DEC/1 20) of 14 November 2001, paras 23–25). For a detailed account, see P Marsden, *A Competition Policy for the WTO* (London, Cameron May, 2003).

[140] The Havana Charter was signed by 53 States, but ultimately abandoned owing to opposition in the US Congress (see eg K Kennedy, *Competition Law and the WTO: Limits of Multilateralism* (London, Sweet & Maxwell, 2001). For the US position on establishing a World Competition Order under the auspices of the WTO, see the speech of former US Assistant Attorney General Joel Klein, 'Anticipating the Millennium: International Antitrust Enforcement at the End of the Twentieth Century' Fordham Corporate Law Institute, 24th Annual Conference on International Law and Policy (New York, 9 November 2000).

[141] See eg 'International Antitrust in the 21st Century: Cooperation and Convergence', Address by Charles A James, Assistant Attorney General, Antitrust Division, US Department of Justice, Speech before the OECD Global Forum on Competition (Paris, 17 October 2001); W Kerber, 'An International Multi-Level System of Competition Law: Federalism in Antitrust' in J Drexl (ed), *The Future of Transnational Antitrust—From Comparative to Common Competition Law* (Berne/The Hague, Staempfli Publishers/Kluwer Law International 2003) 269; A Geiger and W von Meibom, 'A World Competition Law as an Ultima Ratio' (2002) 23 *European Competition Law Review* 445.

[142] See eg DJ Gerber, 'Competition Law and the WTO: Rethinking the Relationship' (2007) 10 *Journal of International Economic Law* 707; M Taylor, *International Competition Law: A New Dimension for the WTO?* (Cambridge, Cambridge University Press 2006); J Drexl, 'International Competition Policy after Cancún: Placing a Singapore Issue on the WTO Development Agenda' (2004) 27 *World Competition* 419.

cooperation: harmonisation through informal dialogue and persuasion, rather than binding agreement.[143]

The Organisation for Economic Cooperation and Development (OECD) is one such forum for discussion. The OECD Competition Committee promotes regular exchanges of views and analysis of competition policy issues in roundtable discussion. The proceedings from these discussions, which include submissions from representatives of antitrust enforcement authorities and invited experts, are made publicly available.[144] The European Commission participates in these discussions alongside the national competition authorities of the European Union.[145] The OECD Competition Committee issues non-binding guidelines and best practices recommendations.[146] It is assisted by the Competition Division, which provides analytical support, promotes the Competition Committee's recommendations internationally and offers hands-on support to governments seeking to strengthen their competition frameworks. The OECD Global Forum on Competition further regularly brings together high-level competition officials from around the world to facilitate a policy dialogue between OECD countries and non-OECD economies.

The United Nations Conference on Trade and Development (UNCTAD) also has a Competition and Consumer Policies Programme, which provides a forum for intergovernmental deliberations, undertakes research to inform these deliberations and provides technical assistance to developing countries.[147] The European Commission is also involved in this programme.

The most recent, most specialised and probably most important addition to these forums is the International Competition Network (ICN). Launched in 2001 after the *GE/Honeywell* crisis on the initiative of the United States, the ICN was explicitly intended as an alternative to the WTO route. It was designed to provide competition authorities with a specialised, yet informal venue for maintaining regular contacts, addressing practical competition concerns and elaborating best practice on the procedural and substantive level.[148] Where members reach

[143] N Kroes, 'European Competition Policy in the Age of Internationalisation—Towards a Global Competition Order?', Speech at the FIW (Innsbruck, 7 February 2008); M Monti, 'Competition Policy in a Global Economy' (2004) 7 *International Finance* 495; O Budzinski, 'Towards an International Governance of Transborder Mergers?—Competition Networks and Institutions between Centralism and Decentralism' (2004) 36 *New York University Journal of International Law and Politics*; A Burnside and Y Botteman, 'Networking Amongst Competition Agencies' (2004) 10 *International Trade Law & Regulation* 1; A Burnside and H Crossley, 'Cooperation in Competition: a New Era?' (2005) 30 *European Law Review* 234.

[144] www.oecd.org/daf/competition/roundtables.htm.

[145] Supplementary Protocol No 1 to the Convention on the OECD.

[146] www.oecd.org/daf/competition/recommendations.htm.

[147] www.unctad.org/en/Pages/DITC/CompetitionLaw/ccpb-Mandate.aspx.

[148] See US Department of Justice's International Competition Policy Advisory Committee in *Final Report to the Attorney General and the Assistant Attorney General for Antitrust Enforcement* (February 2000) www.justice.gov/atr/international-competition-policy-advisory-committee-delivers-final-report-attorney-general-reno.

consensus on recommendations or best practices, the individual competition authorities decide whether and how to implement the recommendations. 104 competition agencies from 92 jurisdictions are members of the ICN, including those of the United States, the European Union and its Member States. It is also open to international organisations such as the OECD and the WTO, industry and consumer associations, antitrust practitioners and members of the academic community.

The ICN is based on the idea that regular contact and exchange will lead to converging views, which will de facto eventually result in common standards, without any need for overarching Treaty rules. The Network does not have the mandate to discuss the creation of binding international competition rules. It does not have a permanent seat either, but is of a virtual nature. It has no organs capable of deciding on behalf of its members and can therefore not be qualified as an international organisation within the meaning of public international law. It is in many ways a poster child of new governance: rules are replaced by best practices and recommendations, peer review replaces enforcement and instead of purely governmental actors, the ICN involves a multitude of stakeholders, including non-governmental organisations, private sector entities, civic society actors and individuals.

The ICN has been described as a success story that by far surpassed its creators' expectations.[149] Although there is little data on the degree of convergence that has resulted globally from the exchanges and discussions that have taken place within the ICN, it stands to reason that the discussions and search for best practices with other competition authorities will have influenced the Commission's substantive review at least to some degree. The ICN working groups have explored a number of issues highly relevant to the Commission's substantive reform process, including the aims of antitrust law,[150] the assessment of dominance,[151] substantive merger analysis[152] and the role of economists and economic evidence in competitive analyses.[153] In 2007, the then EU Commissioner for Competition, Neelie Kroes, in fact explicitly stated that the Commission had taken into account the ICN recommendations when reviewing its procedural merger rules, and that it considered the discussions of the ICN's unilateral conduct working group a key opportunity to gather useful input into its then still ongoing reform of Article 102.[154]

[149] E Fox, J Fingleton and S Mitchell, 'The Past and Future of International Antitrust: Gaps, Overlaps and the Institutional Challenge' in D Lewis (ed), *Building New Competition Law Regimes* (Cheltenham, Edward Elgar 2013) 163, 172.

[150] ICN Unilateral Conduct Working Group, Unilateral Conduct Workbook, Ch 1: The Objectives and Principles of Unilateral Conduct Laws.

[151] ibid, Ch 3: Assessment of Dominance.

[152] ICN Merger Working Group, Recommended Practices for Merger Analysis.

[153] ICN, Merger Working Group, 'The Role of Economists and Economic Evidence in Merger Analysis' Presented at the 12th Conference of the ICN (Warsaw, 24–26 April 2013) www.internationalcompetitionnetwork.org/uploads/library/doc903.pdf.

[154] N Kroes, 'The International Competition Network—Achievements and Goals', Speech at the International Competition Network (ICN) Annual Conference (Moscow, 30 May 2007).

VIII. Conclusion

In sum, a multitude of factors contributed to the advent of the European Commission's more economic approach to EU antitrust law. The Commission's antitrust policy had been subject to criticism from a number of different angles. Commentators and US antitrust experts were comparing it unfavourably with the 'more economic' US antitrust law. The Court had criticised the quality of the Commission's competitive assessments in *Airtours, Schneider Legrand* and *Tetra Laval* in scathing words. Crucially, the timing was also right for a review of the Commission's substantive antitrust policy. In the early 1990s, the internal market had been completed and the market integration aim had lost somewhat of its urgency. Before this background, and under the guidance of an economist with a vision, DG Competition embarked on the long process of introducing a more economic approach to EU antitrust law.

2

The Process

I. Introduction

This chapter explores the process and means by which the European Commission introduced the more economic approach to EU antitrust law. Bringing the legal provisions into line with contemporary economic thinking did not happen overnight, nor did it happen in one step. It was a lengthy, multistage process that was characterised by a number of peculiarities. It can be roughly situated between 1999 and 2009. While there are signs that the Commission began thinking about the necessity of reviewing its traditional approach as early as the mid-1990s, the key policy changes occurred as of 1999.

II. One Pillar at a Time

The Commission did not introduce the more economic approach to all three pillars of EU antitrust all at once, but reviewed its approach one prohibition provision at a time. The following briefly sketches out the timeline.

A. Article 101

Article 101 was first in line. The Commission's treatment of vertical agreements under Article 101 had been the subject of severe criticism by a number of academics even before any *GE/Honeywell* or other political crisis.[1] Commentators took the

[1] Most famously maybe: B Hawk, 'System Failure: Vertical Restraints and EC Competition Law' (1995) 32 *Common Market Law Review* 973, but see also L Gyselen, 'Vertical Restraints on the Distribution Process: Strength and Weakness of the Free Rider Rationale Under EEC Competition Law' (1984) 21 *Common Market Law Review* 647; V Korah, 'EEC Competition Policy—Legal Form or Economic Efficiency' [1986] 39 *Current Legal Problems* 85; AS Pathak, 'Articles 85 and 86 and Anti-competitive Exclusion in EEC Competition Law: Part 1' (1989) 10 *European Competition Law Review* 74 and 'Articles 85 and 86 and Anti-competitive Exclusion in EEC Competition Law: Part 2' (1989) 10 *European Competition Law Review* 256.

view that the Commission's assessment of vertical agreements was out of touch with economic theory, in particular in that the Commission did not sufficiently take into account their potential for generating economic efficiency effects. Not surprisingly therefore, the Commission began its review of Article 101 by reconsidering its approach to assessing vertical agreements. The first tentative steps in this process can be traced back to its Green Paper on Vertical Restraints from 1997, which outlined a few options for reforming its approach to vertical agreements.[2] Following a public consultation, this reform eventually resulted in the adoption of the first general Block Exemption Regulation for vertical agreements in 1999 and a set of guidelines on vertical restraints in 2000,[3] both of which were explicitly based on an 'economic approach' to assessing vertical agreements under Article 101.[4] These two instruments were soon followed by three further sets of guidelines on Article 101, spelling out 'more economic' approaches to horizontal cooperation agreements,[5] technology transfer agreements[6] and the exemption provision contained in Article 101(3).[7]

B. EU Merger Law

In 2002, the Commission turned its attention to the area of EU merger law. It submitted a legislative proposal for a revised Merger Regulation to the Council.[8] Based on this proposal, the Council recast the original Merger Regulation in 2004.[9] The main novelty of the new Regulation was that it introduced a revised substantive test for assessing mergers with a Union dimension. The Commission subsequently published two sets of merger guidelines that explained its understanding of the new test and the manner in which it intended to assess future mergers under this test. The 'horizontal merger guidelines' date from 2004, while

[2] European Commission, 'Green Paper on Vertical Restraints in EC Competition Policy' COM(96) 721 of 22 January 1997.

[3] Commission Notice, Guidelines on Vertical Restraints of 13 October 2000 [2000] OJ C291/1. These guidelines were reviewed in 2010, and have since been replaced by a new Commission Notice, Guidelines on Vertical Restraints of 19 May 2010 [2010] OJ C130/1.

[4] ibid, para 7.

[5] Commission Notice, Guidelines on the Applicability of Article 81 of the EC Treaty to Horizontal Cooperation Agreements of 6 January 2001 [2001] OJ C3/2 (replaced in 2011 by Guidelines on the applicability of Article 101 of the Functioning of the European Union to horizontal co-operation agreements [2011] OJ C11/1).

[6] Commission Notice, Guidelines on the Application of Article 81 of the Treaty to Technology Transfer Agreements [2004] OJ C101/2 (replaced in 2014 by the Guidelines on the application of Article 101 to technology transfer agreements [2014] 0J C101/97).

[7] Commission Notice, Guidelines on the Application of Article 81(3) of the Treaty [2004] OJ C101/97, para 5.

[8] European Commission, Proposal for a Council Regulation on the control of concentrations between undertakings (The EC Merger Regulation) [2003] OJ C20/4.

[9] Council Regulation (EC) No 139/2004 of 20 January 2004 on the control of concentrations between undertakings (the EC Merger Regulation) [2004] OJ L24/1, replacing Council Regulation (EEC) 4064/89 on the control of concentrations between undertakings [1989] OJ L395/1.

the 'non-horizontal merger guidelines' took longer to complete and were not published until 2008.[10] In contrast to the Commission's guidelines on Article 101, the merger guidelines did not explicitly state that they were based on an 'economic' or 'more economic' approach. Nonetheless, as will be shown in Part II of this book, the changes they made to the Commission's merger practice mirror those introduced by the more economic approach to Article 101.

C. Article 102

After Article 101 and EU merger law, only Article 102 remained. The process of modernising the Commission's approach to this provision proved lengthier and more difficult than the reform of the previous two pillars. Bringing Article 102's concepts of dominance and abuse into line with mainstream economics raised fundamental questions as to the objectives and key concepts of EU competition law. These issues, which were somewhat swept under the carpet in the Commission's' review of its approach to Article 101 and horizontal mergers, could no longer be ignored in the context of so-called exclusionary abuses under Article 102. Similar problems, incidentally, arose in the context of introducing the economic approach to the assessment of non-horizontal mergers, which may explain why the non-horizontal merger guidelines took four years longer to finalise than their horizontal counterparts. A further key difficulty in the context of Article 102 was that bringing the Commission's approach to this provision into line with the Commission's more economic approaches to Article 101 and the EU Merger Regulation would have been plainly incompatible with the Court of Justice's interpretation of Article 102.[11]

The Commission officially got the reform of Article 102 underway in 2003 by commissioning an opinion from the European Advisory Group for Competition Policy (EAGCP) on how the Commission's assessments of abusive conduct could be improved from the point of view of economic theory. The EAGCP outlined its recommendations in a report entitled 'An Economic Approach to Article 82' in 2005.[12] A few months later, DG Competition published a 'Staff Discussion Paper' outlining its own vision of a more economic approach to Article 102.[13]

[10] European Commission, Guidelines on the assessment of horizontal mergers under the Council Regulation on the control of concentrations between undertakings [2004] OJ C31/5, and European Commission, Guidelines on the assessment of non-horizontal mergers under the Council Regulation on the control of concentrations between undertakings [2008] OJ C265/6.

[11] See Ch 10.

[12] Report by the EAGCP, *An Economic Approach to Article 82* (July 2005), www.ec.europa.eu/dgs/competition/economist/eagcp_july_21_05.pdf.

[13] DG Competition, Discussion Paper on the Application of Article 82 of the Treaty to Exclusionary Abuses (November 2005) www.ec.europa.eu/competition/antitrust/art82/discpaper2005.pdf.

The Commission made both of these documents available on its website and invited comments from interested third parties. The public consultation process was officially closed in June 2006. It took another two and a half years until the Commission formally concluded the review of Article 102 with the publication of a Communication setting out new enforcement priorities for applying Article 102 to exclusionary conduct in February 2009.[14]

III. A 'Soft' Reform

A further feature of the review process, which may already have become apparent from the preceding paragraphs, is that the review was carried out primarily by means of soft law instruments and individual decisions rather than formal amendment of the antitrust provisions.

A. Article 101

The European Commission introduced the key principles of its more economic approach to Article 101 by means of interpretative guidelines. Article 101 was not formally amended. Its wording has remained essentially the same since the signature of the Treaty of Rome in 1957. Instead, the Commission published four sets of guidelines, in which it spelled out a 'more economic' or 'economic' approach to Article 101. Three of these guidelines have in the meantime been reviewed and replaced by somewhat updated versions.[15] Their key principles, however, remain the same.

The guidelines' express purpose is to help companies self-assess the compatibility of their conduct with Article 101 and to provide guidance to the courts and competition authorities of the Member States in their application of Article 101.[16] In this aim, they spell out the Commission's interpretation of the conditions of Article 101 and indicate what types of evidence the Commission considers suitable and sufficient for proving that these conditions are fulfilled. For those conditions

[14] Communication from the Commission, 'Guidance on the Commission's enforcement priorities in applying Article 82 of the EC Treaty to abusive exclusionary conduct by dominant undertakings' [2009] OJ C45/7.

[15] Commission Notice, Guidelines on Vertical Restraints of 13 October 2000 [2000] OJ C291/1, para 7; Commission Notice, Guidelines on the Applicability of Article 81 of the EC Treaty to Horizontal Cooperation Agreements of 6 January 2001 [2001] OJ C3/2; Guidelines on the Application of Article 81 of the Treaty to Technology Transfer Agreements [2004] OJ C101/2; Commission Notice, Guidelines on the Application of Article 81(3) of the Treaty [2004] OJ C101/97, para 5.

[16] eg Guidelines on Article 81(3) (n 15) para 4, and 2000 Vertical Restraints Guidelines (n 15) para 3.

that require assessments of an economic nature, they also establish a number of assumptions and rules of thumb that the Commission intends to apply. As Part II of this book shows, the Article 101 guidelines introduced a number of fundamental changes to the Commission's legal interpretation of Article 101. Remarkably, however, they do not mention this. Neither do they define the essence and implications of the more economic approach on which they are based.

As mere Communications, the Commission's guidelines do not have formal legal effect. They explicitly acknowledge that the interpretation of Article 101 which they spell out is 'without prejudice to the interpretation by the Court of Justice'.[17] The Court has confirmed repeatedly that the guidelines are not legally binding on individuals, on the national enforcement authorities or on the Court itself.[18] Although the guidelines thus have no direct legal effect, they are tremendously influential in practice. First, the Commission itself may not deviate from the approach spelled out in its guidelines in individual cases. The principle of equal treatment and the protection of legitimate expectations, general principles of EU law, require that the Commission not deviate from an established enforcement practice in individual cases without legitimate reason. This also applies to rules of conduct that the Commission has published with the express intention of henceforth applying to relevant cases.[19] The guidelines are thus indirectly binding on the Commission up until the time that it publicly revokes them for all future cases.

Second, despite not being formally binding on businesses, in practice, these types of guidelines exert considerable influence on undertakings' behaviour. The Commission investigates and prosecutes infringements of the EU antitrust rules. It also decides whether the conduct in question is compatible with the EU antitrust rules. Guidelines that spell out the Commission's understanding of the law and assessment methods are therefore bound to constitute one of the first sources of reference for businesses and their legal representatives when establishing a rational business strategy. Acting in a way that the Commission considers illegal is likely to result in enforcement proceedings, and business that are keen to avoid costly proceedings will therefore follow the Commission's guidelines, notwithstanding the fact that they are not formal legal acts.

Third, although the Commission guidelines are not formally binding on national competition authorities and courts, they are likely to have a strong persuasive effect in practice. It will be tempting for national Courts and enforcement agencies to fall back on the detailed, ready-made guidance spelled out in the Commission's Notices when applying Article 101. Overall, despite lacking formal

[17] eg 2000 Vertical Restraints Guidelines (n 15) para 4.

[18] Case C-226/11 *Expedia Inc v Autorité de la Concurrence and Others* ECLI:EU:C:2012:795, para 29, and Case C-360/09 *Pfleiderer* ECLI:EU:2011:389, para 21.

[19] eg Case C 167/04 P *JCB Service v Commission* ECLI:EU:C:2006:594, paras 207 and 208; Case C-189/02 P *Dansk Rørindustri and Others v Commission* ECLI:EU:C:2005:408, paras 209–11.

legal status, the persuasive effect of these interpretative Commission guidelines is bound to be very high indeed.

For the sake of completeness, it should be added that one of the first steps in the Commission's reform of its substantive approach to Article 101 actually took the form of a legal act. In 1999, the Commission enacted its first general Block Exemption Regulation for vertical agreements.[20] This Block Exemption Regulation replaced a number of awkwardly complex and rigid Block Exemption Regulations for different types of distribution and supply agreements[21] and was the Commission's first step in introducing a more economic approach to the assessment of vertical agreements.[22] However, this Block Exemption Regulation was limited in its scope and purpose to exempting certain vertical agreements from the prohibition of Article 101(1). The general principles of the more economic approach were introduced by means of legally non-binding guidelines.

B. EU Merger Law

At first sight, the reform of EU merger law might appear a little less soft law-heavy and less led by the Commission than the review of Article 101. After all, it was the Council that recast the original Merger Regulation and introduced the new substantive test on which the Commission subsequently based its more economic approach.

However, this impression is misleading. The Commission and its soft law played a crucial role in introducing the more economic approach to EU merger review. It was the Commission that submitted the proposal for amending the original Merger Regulation to the Council. The Commission also played a key role during the difficult negotiation process in the Council of Ministers, during which it mediated between the conflicting positions and came up with the compromise that is the new test of EU merger law. Finally, it is the Commission's interpretative guidelines that gave the new legal test the meaning it nowadays has in the

[20] Commission Regulation (EC) No 2790/1999 of 22 December 1999 on the application of Article 81(3) of the Treaty to categories of vertical agreements and concerted practices [1999] OJ L336/21, based on Council Regulation (EC) No 1215/1999 of 10 June 1999 amending Regulation No 19/65/EEC on the application of Article 81(3) of the Treaty to certain categories of agreements and concerted practices [1999] OJ L148/1. Regulation 2790/1999 has since been replaced by Commission Regulation (EU) No 330/2010 of 20 April 2010 on the application of Article 101(3) of the Treaty on the Functioning of the European Union to categories of vertical agreements and concerted practices [2010] OJ L102/1.

[21] Commission Regulation (EEC) No 1983/83 of 22 June 1983 on the application of Article 85(3) of the Treaty to categories of exclusive distribution agreements [1983] OJ L173/1; Commission Regulation (EEC) No 1984/83 of 22 June 1983 on the application of Article 85(3) of the Treaty to categories of exclusive purchasing agreements [1983] OJ L281/25; Commission Regulation (EEC) No 4087/88 of 30 November 1988 on the application of Article 85(3) of the Treaty to categories of franchise agreements [1988] OJ L359/46.

[22] For a detailed analysis of the changes introduced by the new Block Exemption Regulation, see Ch 5.

Commission's decision practice. The new Merger Regulation essentially replaced one vaguely worded test with another vague test. Regulation 4064/89 had prohibited mergers that would result in the creation or strengthening of a dominant position, as a result of which effective competition would be significantly impeded.[23] Regulation 139/2004 now prohibits mergers that would significantly impede effective competition, in particular as a result of the creation or strengthening of a dominant position.[24] Neither of these tests is self-explanatory, and in fact the recitals of Regulation 139/2004 suggest that the Council did not intend to change the former standard of competitive harm, but merely intended to clarify that the creation of certain oligopolistic market structures also fell within the scope of the Merger Regulation.[25]

The Commission's merger guidelines from 2004 and 2008[26] give substance to the new test. They explain the Commission's understanding of the provision and other key concepts of EU merger control. They also explain in detail how the Commission intends to assess cases under these principles. Like in the case of Article 101, the Commission's merger guidelines introduced important conceptual changes to the Commission's understanding of EU merger law. These went well beyond what would have strictly been necessary based on the wording and legislative history of the new test.

Finally, like the guidelines on the interpretation of Article 101, the Commission's merger guidelines do not formally have the status of EU law. They are not legally binding on individuals or on the national competition authorities. They 'merely' spell out the Commission's understanding of the law. Nonetheless, for the same reasons as those applying to the guidelines on Article 101, they are more or less on a par with legal acts as far as their persuasive effect is concerned.

C. Article 102

Soft law finally also dominated the reform of Article 102. The Commission completed the long review of its approach to Article 102 with the publication of yet another legally non-binding Communication that spells out a more economic approach to Article 102. However, there is one significant difference from its soft law instruments on Article 101 and EU merger control. Instead of publishing interpretative guidelines that spell out a revised interpretation of Article 102, the Commission merely chose to revise its enforcement priorities for Article 102 in a

[23] Council Regulation (EEC) No 4064/89 [1990] OJ L257/13, Art 2(3).

[24] Council Regulation (EC) No 139/2004 [2004] OJ L24/1, Art 2(3).

[25] ibid, recitals 25, 26.

[26] European Commission, Guidelines on the assessment of horizontal mergers under the Council Regulation on the control of concentrations between undertakings [2004] OJ C31/5, and European Commission, Guidelines on the assessment of non-horizontal mergers under the Council Regulation on the control of concentrations between undertakings [2008] OJ C265/6.

Communication entitled 'Guidance on the Commission's enforcement priorities in applying Article 102 to abusive exclusionary conduct by dominant undertakings'.[27] In essence, the Commission did not formally change its interpretation of Article 102, but simply chose no longer to enforce Article 102 in cases that do not raise competitive concerns according to the principles of the more economic approach. The Communication spells out in great detail how the Commission intends to carry out such an economic assessment. It also provides guidance to national antitrust authorities and courts on how to carry out an assessment under Article 102 in line with the more economic approach.

This unusual and indirect method of reform is most likely explained by the fact that an interpretation of Article 102 in line with the Commission's more economic approach to Article 101 and EU merger law would have been incompatible with the Court of Justice's interpretation of Article 102.[28] While the Commission's solution may have avoided a direct clash with the case law, it has a number of other drawbacks that are discussed in Part III of this book. These concerns and the atypical approach of the Notice notwithstanding, there is little doubt that the Guidance is as influential in practice as the guidelines on Articles 101 and the EU Merger Regulation.

IV. Changes in the Professional Composition of DG Competition

The interpretative guidelines and the Communication on enforcement priorities were important instruments for implementing the more economic approach to EU antitrust law. Another crucial tool was the integration of more economists into the daily work of DG Competition. During his term as Commissioner for Competition Policy, Mario Monti significantly increased the ratio of economists in DG Competition, which had traditionally been dominated by lawyers.

Monti, as mentioned previously, was the first economist to hold the position of Commissioner for Competition Policy, while his predecessors had predominantly been lawyers and political scientists. Three years into his term, he broke with another tradition. Up until then, all Directors General of DG Competition had been (German) lawyers.[29] In 2002, Monti appointed a (UK) economist as

[27] Communication from the Commission, 'Guidance on the Commission's enforcement priorities in applying Article 82 of the EC Treaty to abusive exclusionary conduct by dominant undertakings' (n 14).

[28] See Ch 10.

[29] Ernst Albrecht, Willy Christoph Schlieder, Manfred Caspari, Claus-Dieter Ehlermann and Alexander Schaub.

his Director General.[30] He also established a number of new key positions for economists within or closely associated with DG Competition. At his recommendation, the Commission created the position of 'Chief Competition Economist', also commonly referred to simply as 'Chief Economist'.[31] According to the original job description, the Commission sought an economist, specialised in industrial organisation and with practical experience in the analysis of individual competition cases. His key functions were to provide guidance on methodological issues of economics and econometrics in the application of the EU competition rules in individual cases and to contribute to the development of general policy instruments with the aid of a dedicated staff of 10 specialised economists.[32] Since 2003, four eminent PhD economists have held the position of Chief Competition Economist[33] and the size of the Chief Economist's Team has grown. When the job was re-advertised in 2013,[34] the number of specialised economists on the Chief Competition Economist's team had increased from the original 10 to 24.[35]

The Chief Economist and his team get involved in the day-to-day work of the case-teams from an early stage, offering economic guidance and methodological assistance. They also participate in creating general policy instruments, such as the aforementioned guidelines and Block Exception Regulations. The Chief Economist further provides the Commissioner with an independent opinion on the economic aspects before the latter proposes a final decision to the College of Commissioners. Another function of the Chief Economist is to increase the economic expertise within DG Competition by contributing to its training plan. His team organises and facilitates courses, seminars and conferences for the staff of DG Competition, and maintains contacts with the academic world.[36] To this end, the Commission's first Chief Economist initiated the creation of the European Advisory Group for Competition Policy (EAGCP), which is a group of around 15 leading academics in the field of industrial organisation theory. Its role is to provide advice and input on important issues of antitrust policy for the internal debate of DG Competition. At the request of the Commissioner, the Chief Economist or the Director General, the EAGCP prepares opinions on such policy issues, which are often made publicly available on DG Competition's website.[37]

[30] Lowe was succeeded by another economist, Alexander Italianer, in February 2010. Since 2015, there seems to have been a return to the status quo, when Johannes Laitenberger, a German lawyer, became the new Director General.

[31] M Monti, 'EU Competition Policy', Speech at Fordham Annual Conference on International Antitrust Law and Policy (New York, 31 October 2002).

[32] European Commission, 'Publication of A 2 post of Chief Competition Economist' [2003] OJ C39 A/5.

[33] Lars-Hendrik Röller (2003–06), Damien Neven (2006–11), Kai-Uwe Kühn (2011–13) and currently Massimo Motta (since 2013).

[34] The position is assigned for 3 years, and nowadays renewable for another 2.

[35] European Commission, 'Publication of the post of Chief Competition Economist' [2013] OJ C33 A/1.

[36] L-H Röller and P Buigues, 'The Office of the Chief Competition Economist at the European Commission' (2005) 8 *Global Competition Review* 3.

[37] www.ec.europa.eu/dgs/competition/economist/eagcp.html.

Increasing the economic expertise within DG Competition was not limited to appointing economists to leadership positions. Over the past 15 years, a more general demographic shift can be observed within DG Competition. Up until the mid-1990s, the ratio of economists to lawyers within DG Competition had reportedly been about 1 to 7.[38] In 2007, it had increased to 1 to 2.[39] At the time of the writing of this book, it is now 1 to 1.7.[40]

Boosting the number of economists working within DG Competition no doubt fulfilled its primary aim of enhancing the economic expertise in the case teams and policy groups. Economic know-how seems like an indispensable condition for an enforcement policy based on sound economic reasoning. In addition to this practical consideration, appointing more economists is also likely to have increased the personal motivation and willingness within DG Competition to advance the use of economics in the Commission's antitrust practice. It stands to reason that economists are more likely to be enthusiastic about bringing the key beliefs and tools of economic theory to the discipline of antitrust policy than officials with a background in law. This psychological effect may well be another contributing factor to the success and extent of the Commission's more economic approach.

V. Public Consultations

One last factor that characterises the reform process is the heavy involvement of stakeholders and other interested third parties. When the Commission first began exploring options for reforming its approach to vertical agreements under Article 101, it set the ball rolling by publishing a Green Paper on Vertical Restraints. This document, which outlined several policy options, was intended to provide the basis for a 'wide reaching public consultation involving Parliament, Member States, the Economic and Social Committee and Committee of Regions as well as all interested parties'.[41] The European Parliament, the Economic and Social Committee and the Committee of the Regions all duly submitted comments,[42]

[38] S Wilks and L McGowan, 'Competition Policy in the European Union: Creating a Federal Agency' in GB Doern and S Wilks (eds), *Comparative Competition Policy: National Institutions in a Global Market* (Oxford, Clarendon Press, 1996) 225 ff

[39] D Neven, 'Competition Economics in Europe' (2007) *The Handbook of Competition Economics* 4.

[40] According to a survey in the Global Competition Review in 2015, 50% of DG Competition's staff were lawyers, while 30% were economists (www.globalcompetitionreview.com/surveys/article/38830/european-commissions-directorate-general-competition).

[41] European Commission, 'Green Paper on Vertical Restraints in EC Competition Policy' (n 2) para 5.

[42] European Parliament, Resolution on the Commission's Green Paper on vertical restraints in EC competition policy [1997] OJ C286/347; Opinion of the Economic and Social Committee on the 'Green Paper on vertical restraints in EC competition policy' [1997] OJ C296/19; Opinion of the Committee of the Regions on the 'Green Paper on vertical restraints in EC competition policy' [1997] OJ C244/38.

and so did the business community, national competition authorities, practitioners and academics. In total, the Commission received 227 written submissions. It engaged with the views expressed in these submissions in a Follow-up Communication to the Green Paper.[43] The Commission's guidelines on vertical restraints from 2000, which outline the more economic approach to assessing vertical agreements under Article 101, are the outcome of this process. However, no such consultation was carried out for the other three sets of Article 101 guidelines introducing the more economic approach to Article 101.[44]

By contrast, the review of EU merger law involved a great degree of input from third parties throughout. The Commission again initiated the review process by means of a Green Paper, in which it examined the existing merger system as to possible weaknesses and suggested potential solutions.[45] It invited all interested parties to submit their views on the issues raised in the paper, as well as on any other matters of relevance to the implementation of merger control in Europe.[46] The public consultation in fact proved decisive for the direction and outcome of the reform process. The emphasis of the Commission's Green Paper had lain on addressing problems of a jurisdictional and procedural nature. It had also briefly looked at the workability of the substantive test of Regulation 4064/89, which all in all it had found satisfactory. Rather in passing and more for the purpose of completeness, one gets the impression, this section of the Green Paper had also mentioned 'one of the more specific hypothetical questions that has occasionally been raised about the reach of the dominance test in the Merger Regulation', namely the question whether the existing test would allow the Commission to prohibit mergers that created an oligopolistic situation likely to result in price increases, even though the oligopolists were unlikely to engage in collusion. The Green Paper had concluded that, while interesting as a hypothetical discussion, there was little cause for concern as the Commission had never encountered a situation of the kind.[47]

[43] European Commission, Communication from the Commission on the application of the Community competition rules to vertical restraints—Follow-up to the Green Paper on vertical restraints [1998] OJ C365/3.

[44] Guidelines on the Applicability of Article 81 of the EC Treaty to Horizontal Cooperation Agreements of 6 January 2001 [2001] OJ C3/2; Guidelines on the Application of Article 81 of the Treaty to Technology Transfer Agreements [2004] OJ C101/2; Guidelines on the Application of Article 81(3) of the Treaty [2004] OJ C101/97. The Commission carried out public consultations when reviewing the horizontal cooperation and technology transfer guidelines in 2010 and 2013 respectively (www.ec.europa.eu/competition/consultations/2010_horizontals/index.html and www.ec.europa.eu/competition/consultations/2013_technology_transfer/index_en.html).

[45] European Commission, 'Green Paper on the Review of Council Regulation (EEC) No 4064/89' COM(2001) 745.

[46] ibid, para 254.

[47] ibid, para 166.

The comments submitted during the consultation process, an Economic Study commissioned by DG Competition[48] and the accompanying academic debate[49] persuaded the Commission that non-collusive oligopolies might in fact constitute a serious competitive concern after all. The Commission consequently submitted an initially cautious legislative proposal to the Council that suggested that the Council retain the dominance test of the original Merger Regulation but clarify that the concept of dominance also included the creation of oligopolies non-inclined to cooperation.[50] The Council ultimately went beyond this proposal and ended up enacting a significantly amended substantive test. The public consultation was hence a key contributor to the formal legislative change. The Commission subsequently also carried out public consultations on its draft horizontal and non-horizontal guidelines before enacting the final version.[51]

Likewise, the Commission's review of its approach to Article 102 involved an intense and fertile consultation of a wide variety of private parties. The Commission made both the EAGCP's study on how to reform the Commission's approach to Article 102[52] and DG Competition's own 'Staff Discussion Paper' on the review of Article 102[53] publicly available on its website, and invited comments from interested third parties. It received over 100 written comments from antitrust scholars, law firms, individual businesses and business associations within and outside the European Union, which it published on its website.[54] It concluded the consultation process by holding a public hearing in June 2006 at which leading antitrust experts were invited to present their views.[55] Both the EAGCP report and the

[48] M Ivaldi, B Jullien, P Rey, P Seabright, J Tirole, *The Economics of Tacit Collusion* (March 2013) available at: www.ec.europa.eu/competition/mergers/studies_reports/the_economics_of_tacit_collusion_en.pdf.

[49] See eg J Vickers, 'How to Reform the EC Merger Test?' in G Drauz and M Reynolds (eds), *EC Merger Control—A Major Reform in Progress* (Oxford, Oxford University Press, 2003); N Levy, 'Dominance versus SLC: A Subtle Distinction?' in G Drauz and M Reynolds (eds), *EC Merger Control—A Major Reform in Progress* (Oxford, Oxford University Press, 2003); D Parker and Z Biro, 'A New EC Merger Test? Dominance v Substantial Lessening of Competition' (2002) 1 *Competition Law Journal* 157–66; E Müller and U Böge, 'From the Market Dominance Test to the SLC Test: Are there Any Reasons for Change?' (2002) 23 *European Competition Law Review* 495.

[50] European Commission, Proposal for a Council Regulation on the control of concentrations between undertakings (The EC Merger Regulation) [2003] OJ C 20/4, Art 2(2).

[51] European Commission, Draft Commission Notice on the Appraisal of Horizontal Mergers under the Council Regulation on the Control of Concentrations Between Undertakings [2002] OJ C331/18, para 99; and Draft Commission Notice, Guidelines on the Assessment of Non-horizontal Mergers under the Council Regulation on the Control of Concentrations Between Undertakings of 13 February 2008,: http://ec.europa.eu/competition/mergers/legislation/draft_nonhorizontal_mergers.pdf.

[52] EAGCP, *An Economic Approach to Article 82* (n 12).

[53] DG Competition, Discussion Paper on the Application of Article 82 of the Treaty to Exclusionary Abuses (n 13).

[54] www.ec.europa.eu/competition/antitrust/art82/contributions.html.

[55] These contributions remain available at: www.ec.europa.eu/comm/competition/antitrust/art82/contributions.html.

Discussion Paper triggered a considerable academic debate outside the Commission's consultation, which continued long after the latter was formally closed.[56] In addition to this highly visible public consultation of private actors, DG Competition also involved the Member States and their competition authorities in the review of Article 102. In the summer of 2008, it sent a draft of the Communication to the national competition authorities and the responsible national ministries in order to discuss the document within the European Competition Network before submitting it to the College of Commissioners for formal adoption.[57]

VI. Conclusion

In sum, the introduction of the more economic approach did not happen by way of a formal legislative revision. It happened by means of a process that one would not be able to find in the EU Treaties. Instead of being introduced by the Member States or the Union's legislative bodies, the Commission carried out this radical legislative overhaul by means of soft law instruments, spelling out a revised interpretation of the key legal rules, revised assessment methods and revised enforcement priorities. The recasting of the Merger Regulation by the Council in 2004 was the one exception to this rule. However, as Chapter 5 explains in more detail, it is the Commission's merger guidelines spelling out its interpretation of the recast merger test that gave the latter its 'more economic' meaning in practice.

[56] See eg G Niels and H Jenkins, 'Reform of Article 82: Where The Link Between Dominance and Effects Breaks Down' (2005) 26 *European Competition Law Review* 605; T Eilmansberger, 'How to Distinguish Good From Bad Competition under Article 82 EC: In Search of Clearer and More Coherent Standards for Anticompetitive Abuses' (2005) 42 *Common Market Law Review* 129; B Sher, 'The Last of the Steam-Powered Trains: Modernising Article 82' (2005) 25 *European Competition Law Review* 243; Competition Law Forum Article 82 Review Group, 'The Reform of Article 82: Recommendations on Key Policy Objectives' (2005) 1 *European Competition Journal* 179; A Bavasso, 'The Role of Intent under Article 82 EC: from "Flushing the Turkeys" to "Spotting Lionesses in Regent's Park"' (2005) 26 *European Competition Law Review* 616; E Rousseva, 'Modernizing by Eradicating: How the Commission's New Approach to Article 81 EC Dispenses with the Need to Apply Article 82 EC to Vertical Restraints' (2005) 42 *Common Market Law Review* 587; P Akman, 'Article 82 Reformed? The EC Discussion Paper on Exclusionary Abuses' (2006) *Journal of Business Law* 816; J Drexl, S Enchelmaier, M Leistner, M-O Mackenrodt and B Conde Gallego, 'Comments of the Max Planck Institute for Intellectual Property, Competition and Tax Law on the Directorate-General Competition Discussion Paper of December 2005 on the Application of Art.82 of the EC Treaty to Exclusionary Abuses' (2006) 37 *International Review of Intellectual Property and Competition Law* 558; R Nazzini, 'The Wood Began to Move: an Essay on Consumer Welfare, Evidence and Burden of Proof in Article 82 Cases' (2006) 31 *European Law Review* 518; the many excellent contributions in the (2006) 2 *European Competition Journal* (Special Supplement, July 2006); R O'Donoghue and AJ Padilla, *The Law and Economics of Article 82 EC* (Oxford, Hart Publishing, 2006), now in its 2nd edition: *The Law and Economics of Article 102* (Oxford, Hart Publishing, 2013); M Dreher and M Adam, 'Abuse of Dominance Under Reform—Sound Economics and Established Case Law' (2007) 28 *European Competition Law Review* 278, amongst many others.

[57] N Kroes, 'Exclusionary Abuses of Dominance—the European Commission's Enforcement Priorities', Speech at the Fordham University Symposium (New York, 25 September 2008).

Increasingly, the Commission involved private parties in the reform, submitting draft documents and internal discussion papers for public consultation and inviting comments from the business community, practitioners and academics. This feature was less consistent in the early days of the reform, ie the reform of the Commission's approach to Article 101, but became more and more significant as the Commission started to address the areas of merger control and Article 102. It engendered a well-publicised debate that resulted in a great degree of cross-fertilisation and contributed to making the relevant issues more transparent than they had been during the early days of the review process.

3

The Agenda

I. Introduction

Having identified the triggers for the more economic approach as well as the process by which it was introduced, a key question remains to be answered: what is the more economic approach? If the answer to this question were self-evident, there would be little point in writing this book. Part II is entirely dedicated to establishing the changes that the more economic approach made to the Commission's assessment practice. The current Chapter explores the Commission's agenda at the outset of its review process. This provides a first glimpse of the relevant issues and sets the scene for the ensuing analysis of the actual changes.

A number of sources are capable of shedding light on the Commission's intentions and aspirations in its review process. First and foremost, there are the Commission acts introducing the more economic approach and the public statements of the key Commission officials under whose watch these instruments were created. As the following shows, none of these sources is particularly clear as to the actual implications of the approach. However, if one reads them in their broader context and takes into consideration the academic debate accompanying the reform process, it is possible to gain an adequate idea of the issues that the Commission intended to address.

II. Speeches, Interviews and Publications by the Commissioner for Competition Policy

Between 1999 and 2004, Commissioner Monti spoke and wrote extensively about his mission to introduce a more economic approach to EU antitrust law and policy. In a guest editorial for *World Competition* in 2000, he announced that he intended to give the European Union's cumbersome and complicated competition provisions a radical overhaul in order to bring them into holding with modern economic thinking.[1] This statement conveys not only how important he considered

[1] M Monti, 'A Competition Policy for Today and Tomorrow' (2000) 23 *World Competition* 1.

this mission, but also gives an idea of the magnitude of the changes he aimed to achieve. A 'radical overhaul' of the law suggests more than a mere tweaking of established principles. What is less clear, however, is the actual nature of these changes.

The editorial further promised that the reform would result in an antitrust law that was 'in line with modern economic thinking'.[2] The great majority of his publications and speeches of the time contained variations on the same theme. In the introduction to the Commission's 2000 Report on Competition Policy, he explained that the more economic approach aimed at a 'better integration of economic reasoning into the legal framework'.[3] At other occasions, he described the approach as a shift from 'a legalistic based approach to an interpretation of the rules based on sound economic principles',[4] an antitrust policy 'fully compatible with economic learning',[5] and one that recognised the 'importance that economic arguments and considerations should have in a competition assessment, in line with the general competition policy approach of our main trading partners'.[6]

None of these characterisations allows a definitive conclusion as to what the new approach was to look like in practice. They suggest an interdisciplinary approach that integrates economic theory into the design or the application of the competition rules. This, however, could mean a multitude of things. One possible understanding is that the approach advocates the use of economic theory to help enforcement agencies understand how markets work when assessing business conduct under the antitrust rules, for example to gain a better understanding of the factors that influence businesses' decision-making or to be able to understand the effects of certain types of business conduct. Then again, it could also mean the use of certain tools commonly used by economists, such as econometrics and game theoretical models, in order to understand or even measure certain market phenomena. That the more economic approach had this aim is suggested by a number of speeches in which Monti highlighted the need for 'rigorous economic and/or econometric analysis' in the Commission's assessments and his determination to strengthen DG Competition's economic expertise.[7] To this end, he created the position of Chief Competition Economist within DG Competition, who was to ensure that the Commission's competition enforcement and policy actions

[2] ibid.

[3] European Commission, *Thirtieth Report on Competition Policy 2000*, 9.

[4] M Monti, 'EU Competition Policy after May 2004', Speech at the Fordham Annual Conference on International Antitrust Law and Policy (New York, 24 October 2003). This and the following speeches are available at: www.ec.europa.eu/competition/speeches/.

[5] M Monti, 'A Reformed Competition Policy: Achievements and Challenges for the Future', Speech at the Center for European Reform (Brussels, 28 October 2004).

[6] M Monti, 'The New EU Policy on Technology Transfer Agreement', Speech at École des Mines (Paris, 16 January 2004).

[7] M Monti, 'EU Competition Policy', Speech at the Fordham Annual Conference on International Antitrust Law and Policy (New York, 31 October 2002).

were economically sound.[8] Many speeches and publications of the Commission's first Chief Economist supported the impression that more economic approach was primarily about making use of industrial organisation theory and micro-economic analytical tools when assessing the likely competitive impact of a particular transaction.[9] In other words, the more economic approach could have merely been a new methodology in which the Commission was to make use of contemporary economic theory and tools in its assessments.

A speech towards the end of Monti's term as Commissioner for Competition Policy, however, suggests that the more economic approach amounted to more than a policy that favoured the use economic tools in competitive assessments under the otherwise unchanged antitrust rules. At a conference in 2004, Monti stated:

> Th[e] focus on ensuring that competition enforcement in Europe is grounded in sound economics is one that I cannot over-emphasise. It is fair to say that the far-reaching policy shift which occurred in US antitrust enforcement during the 1980s—namely, the shift towards a focus on the economic welfare of consumers—has been mirrored in the policy priorities of the European Commission during the 1990's.[10]

This statement suggests that the Commission's economic approach went beyond introducing mere methodological changes. It alludes to substantive change. The policy shift in US antitrust law referred to in this speech, commonly known as the 'US Antitrust Revolution', had in fact led to major changes in the legal interpretation of the US antitrust statutes in the late 1970s and 1980s. Even presupposing a solid background knowledge on the history of US antitrust law, Monti's statement does not allow an exact conclusion as to how exactly the far-reaching policy shift in question had changed the Commission's antitrust policy.

In sum, Commissioner Monti, the driving force behind the introduction of the more economic approach to EU antitrust law, did not articulate the exact implications of the more economic approach in his public statements. While stressing that the reform was a priority of his office, and making clear that the changes were radical, important and aimed at increasing the relevance of economics in antitrust assessments, he did not elaborate on the nature of these changes. As the following shows, the official Commission documents referring to and introducing the approach were not much more concise.

[8] ibid.

[9] See eg L-H Röller, 'Antitrust Economics—Catalyst for Convergence?', Speech at the George Mason Law Review Symposium (Washington, DC, 20 September 2005) and 'Der ökonomische Ansatz in der europäischen Wettbewerbspolitik' (2004) available at: www.ec.europa.eu/competition/speeches.

[10] M Monti, 'Convergence in EU-US Antitrust Policy Regarding Mergers and Acquisitions: an EU Perspective', Speech at the UCLA Law First Annual Institute on US and EU Antitrust Aspects of Mergers and Acquisitions (Los Angeles, 28 February 2004).

III. Official Commission Acts

There are a fair number of Commission acts referring to the 'economic' or 'more economic' approach to EU antitrust law. The Green Paper on Vertical Restraints from 1997 is the earliest Commission document that engages with the need to bring the Commission's assessments under Article 101 more into line with economic theory, at least with regard to vertical restraints.[11] This document was published at a stage where the Commission was only just beginning its reflection process and had not yet decided what its new approach should look like in practice. However, the document makes clear that the Commission aimed to integrate the findings of economists on the effects of vertical restraints into its assessments under Article 101. In particular, it intended to find a way of taking into account that vertical restraints were overall less likely to result in anticompetitive effects than their horizontal counterparts, and that they had a greater potential for creating beneficial efficiency effects.

The first Commission document that actually refers to a 'more economic approach', albeit in passing, is the White Paper on Modernisation of the Rules Implementing Articles 101 and 102 from 1999.[12] This document explored ways of reforming the highly centralised enforcement system set up in 1962,[13] which had become unmanageable for the Commission in a Union of 15 Member States, especially in view of the expected further eastward expansion in 2004. The White Paper explored several options for reform and essentially recommended decentralising the enforcement by abolishing the authorisation system and making Article 101(3) directly applicable. The Council eventually followed this recommendation and made the relevant changes in Council Regulation 1/2003.[14] The White Paper contains one highly significant statement for the purposes of this monograph. Hidden away in the section outlining the need to end the prior notification and authorisation systems, the document parenthetically mentioned that the Commission intended to adopt a 'more economic approach' to the application of Article 101(1) under the new enforcement system, which would 'limit the scope of its application to undertakings with a certain degree of market

[11] European Commission, 'Green Paper on Vertical Restraints in EC Competition Policy' COM (96) 721 final, 22 January 1997.

[12] European Commission, 'White Paper on Modernisation of the Rules Implementing Articles 85 and 86 of the EC Treaty' [1999] OJ C132/1.

[13] Council Regulation (EEC) No 17: First Regulation implementing Articles 85 and 86 of the Treaty [1962] OJ L13/204.

[14] Council Regulation (EC) No 1/2003 of 16 December 2002 on the implementation of the rules on competition laid down in Articles 81 and 82 of the Treaty [2003] OJ L1/1.

power'.[15] This is suggestive of a change in the interpretation of Article 101 rather than a mere change in methodology.

The Commission's guidelines on vertical restraints from 2000 are the first Commission act to be explicitly based on the more economic approach.[16] These guidelines, which set out the Commission's principles for assessing vertical agreements under Article 101, stated in their introductory remarks that the Commission intended to adopt an economic approach in applying the EU competition rules that was 'based on the effects on the market'.[17] While the document hence made an attempt at defining the economic approach, the definition is far from clear. It is not evident what an approach 'based on the effects of the market' actually entails. This is the only explicit reference to the new approach in the vertical restraints guidelines.

The next Commission act that explicitly referred to and incorporated the approach was the Commission's guidelines on the application of Article 101(3).[18] These guidelines set out the Commission's interpretation of Article 101(3), under which agreements that are restrictive of competition are nonetheless legal if they generate certain benefits for consumers. In their opening statements, the guidelines stated that they developed a methodology for applying Article 101(3) that was 'based on the economic approach already introduced and developed in the guidelines on vertical restraints, horizontal co-operation agreements and technology transfer agreements'.[19] It did not contain any further explanation of the term. As shown above, the vertical restraints guidelines had not defined the economic approach beyond indicating that it was based on the effects on the market. The other two guidelines in question, ie the guidelines on horizontal cooperation agreements[20] and the guidelines on technology transfer agreements[21] had, for their part, not even mentioned that they were based on an economic or more economic approach.

The Commission's merger guidelines[22] outlining its approach to assessing horizontal and non-horizontal mergers under the recast EU Merger Regulation

[15] European Commission, 'White Paper on Modernisation of the Rules Implementing Articles 85 and 86 of the EC Treaty' (n 12) 30.

[16] European Commission, Guidelines on Vertical Restraints [2000] OJ C 291/1.

[17] ibid, para 7.

[18] European Commission, Guidelines on the Application of Article 81(3) of the Treaty [2004] OJ C 101/97.

[19] ibid, para 5.

[20] European Commission, Guidelines on the Applicability of Article 81 of the EC Treaty to Horizontal Cooperation Agreements of 6 January 2001, [2001] OJ C3/2.

[21] European Commission, Guidelines on the Application of Article 81 of the Treaty to Technology Transfer Agreements [2004] OJ C101/2.

[22] European Commission, Guidelines on the assessment of horizontal mergers under the Council Regulation on the control of concentrations between undertakings [2004] OJ C31/5; and European Commission, Guidelines on the assessment of non-horizontal mergers under the Council Regulation on the control of concentrations between undertakings [2008] OJ C265/6.

did not explicitly mention the concept of a more economic approach either, nor did they indicate that they actually introduced a revised approach. Nonetheless, it is clear from the speeches of Commissioner Monti towards the end of his term that EU merger law had undergone a major shift since 2004, and that the new substantive test of the recast EU Merger Regulation as interpreted in the Commission's horizontal merger guidelines had ensured that EU merger law was now 'firmly grounded in sound micro-economics' and had made a significant step towards convergence with US merger law.[23]

The Commission documents accompanying and concluding the reform of the Commission's approach to Article 102 were rhetorically equally reticent. While the 2005 Report commissioned from the EAGCP in preparation of the public consultation was very clear about the fact that it outlined an 'economics-based approach to Article 102 in a way similar to the reform of Article 101 and merger control',[24] DG Competition's own Staff Discussion Paper from 2005[25] did not explicitly refer to any 'economic approach' or the aim of bringing the Commission's approach more into line with economic theory. The only general principle that the Discussion Paper identified as guiding its proposals was that it was 'based on the likely effects on the market'.[26] This is an open-ended concept, similar to that used in the vertical restraints guidelines on Article 101 from 2000.[27] The Communication that eventually concluded the Commission's reform of its Article 102 policy in 2009 did not mention that it introduced an analysis based on the 'effects on the market', an economic approach or increased reliance on economic theory in any form. Instead, the only statement that can be interpreted as laying down a key value guiding the analytical framework of the Communication is the information that, in applying Article 102, the Commission would focus on those types of abuse that are the most harmful to consumers.[28]

In sum, the official Commission documents introducing the more economic approach do not explain its agenda clearly and consistently. They articulate a number of key principles: the incorporation of economic theory on the effects of certain types of conduct, a restriction of the scope of Article 101 to conduct by undertakings with market power, an analysis based on the effects on the market and a restriction of the enforcement under Article 102 to conduct that is most

[23] M Monti, 'International Antitrust—A Personal Perspective', Speech at the Fordham Corporate Law Institute (New York, 7 October 2004), and 'A Reformed Competition Policy: Achievements and Challenges for the Future', Speech at the Center for European Reform (Brussels, 28 October 2004).

[24] European Advisory Group on Competition Policy (EAGCP), 'An Economic Approach to Article 82' (July 2005), www.ec.europa.eu/dgs/competition/economist/eagcp_july_21_05.pdf.

[25] DG Competition, Discussion Paper on the Application of Article 82 of the Treaty to Exclusionary Abuses (November 2005) www.ec.europa.eu/competition/antitrust/art82/discpaper2005.pdf.

[26] ibid, para 4.

[27] European Commission, Guidelines on Vertical Restraints (2000) (n 16) para 7.

[28] Communication from the Commission, 'Guidance on the Commission's enforcement priorities in applying Article 82 of the EC Treaty to abusive exclusionary conduct by dominant undertakings' [2009] OJ C45/7, para 5.

harmful to consumers. These definitions do not allow a clear conclusion as to the key features and implication of the more economic approach.

An in-depth analysis of the assessment guidelines contained in these documents is in fact very informative, and a careful comparison of these findings with the Commission's approach prior to the reform allows a solid conclusion as to the key features of the more economic approach. Part II of this book is entirely dedicated to this extensive exercise. However, it remains that an objective onlooker would struggle to grasp the exact intentions and implications of the more economic approach from an unprejudiced first reading of these key legal documents.

IV. The Broader Context

Seen in isolation, both the statements of Commissioner Monti and the official Commission documents introducing the approach are thus vague and inconclusive. Nonetheless, they highlight a number of different issues that the Commission seems to have considered in need of reforming and as such give a good first indication of the relevant issues. These become much clearer when examined in the broader context surrounding the introduction and progression of the more economic approach. Two sets of factors are particularly helpful for this purpose: the juxtaposition of the Commission's approach with that of its US counterparts in the *GE/Honeywell* crisis, and the intense academic debate surrounding the Commission's reform process.

A. The Comparison with US Antitrust Law

As outlined in the previous chapter, the Commission's decision not to follow the lead of its US counterparts in the *GE/Honeywell* and *Microsoft* cases triggered vehement criticism in the United States. First, there were a number of stinging jibes about the datedness of the economic theories used by the Commission.[29] In light of this criticism, Monti's promise to bring EU antitrust law into holding with 'modern economic thinking'[30] suggests that one focus of the more economic

[29] See eg HR Varian, 'In Europe, GE and Honeywell Ran Afoul of 19th Century Thinking' *New York Times* (28 June 2001) C2: 'The European Commission's merger task force naturally considered Cournot's 1838 analysis of "merger of complementors" in preparing its report'. Likewise: GL Priest, 'The GE/Honeywell Precedent and Franco Romani' *Wall Street Journal* (20 June 2001) A18: 'The Commission's Merger Task Force is relying on economic theories that, though dressed in modern garb, were discarded in the U.S. 30 years ago'.

[30] Monti, 'A Competition Policy for Today and Tomorrow' (n 1).

approach was to increase DG Competition's expertise in contemporary economic theory and to steer clear of Cournot in future.

The second key criticism, however, was more fundamental and concerned a key substantive principle of EU antitrust law: the Commission was admonished for pursuing the wrong aim in its antitrust policy. US antitrust experts took the view that instead of protecting consumers, as they held should be the aim of any modern antitrust law, the Commission interpreted its antitrust rules as protecting corporate rivals and additionally took into account a wide variety of other policy aims in its assessments, including objectives of social and industrial policy.[31] For a better understanding of the meaning and implications of these arguments, it is useful to take a closer look at the key substantive principles of US antitrust law.

i. The Key Substantive Provisions of US Antitrust Law

The Sherman Antitrust Act dates back to the late-nineteenth century, and its wording has remained substantially unchanged since it was enacted in 1890. Both sections 1 and 2 of the Act are worded broadly. Essentially, section 1 prohibits 'contracts in restraints of trade'.[32] It is the US equivalent of Article 101. Section 2 prohibits the 'monopolisation of trade'.[33] It is broadly comparable to Article 102. Section 7 of the Clayton Act contains the merger prohibition. It outlaws mergers that would have the effect of substantially lessening competition.[34]

Neither the Sherman Act nor the Clayton Act defines the legal objective of these provisions, nor is it obvious from their wording what amounts to a 'restraint of trade', 'monopolisation' or 'substantial lessening of competition'. Another problem that these provisions have in common with their EU equivalents is that they do not specify how the likelihood of a restraint of trade or monopolisation is to

[31] G Becker, 'What US Courts Could Teach Europe's Trust Busters' *Economic View Point, Business Week* (6 August 2001) 20; W Kolasky, 'Conglomerate Mergers and Range Effects: It's a Long Way from Chicago to Brussels' (2002) 10 *George Mason Law Review* 533; DS Evans, 'The New Trustbusters, Brussels and Washington May Part Ways' (2002) 81 *Foreign Affairs* 14; DE Patterson and C Shapiro, 'Transatlantic Divergence in GE/Honeywell: Causes and Lessons' (2001–02) 16 *Antitrust* 18.

[32] Section 1(1) of the Sherman Act reads: 'Every contract, combination in the form of trust or otherwise, or conspiracy, in restraint of trade or commerce among the several States, or with foreign nations, is hereby declared to be illegal' (15 U.S.C. § 1).

[33] Section 2 of the Sherman Act reads: 'Every person who shall monopolize, or attempt to monopolize, or combine or conspire with any other person or persons, to monopolize any part of the trade or commerce among the several States, or with foreign nations, shall be deemed guilty of a felony' (15 U.S.C. § 2).

[34] Section 7 of the Clayton Act is the equivalent of Art 2(2) of the EU Merger Regulation. It states the following: 'No person engaged in commerce or in any activity affecting commerce shall acquire, directly or indirectly, the whole or any part of the stock or other share capital and no person subject to the jurisdiction of the Federal Trade Commission shall acquire the whole or any part of the assets of another person engaged also in commerce or in any activity affecting commerce, where in any line of commerce or in any activity affecting commerce in any section of the country, the effect of such acquisition may be substantially to lessen competition, or to tend to create a monopoly' (15 U.S.C. § 18).

be assessed. Is it necessary, for example, to assess the conduct's actual effects in every single case or is it possible to infer its legality or illegality from its form? The answers to these questions have changed over the 125-year period since the Sherman Antitrust Act was enacted. The following briefly retraces the key stages of this evolution.

ii. The Objectives of US Antitrust Law

While the protection of consumer welfare may have been the undisputed objective of US antitrust law at the time of the *GE/Honeywell* merger, this has actually not always been the case. It is well established that US courts used to take a very different view of the aims of the Sherman Act and that the key values guiding US antitrust law have undergone many adjustments since the Sherman Act was enacted.[35] In *Trans-Missouri Freight Assn* (1897), for instance, the US Supreme Court held that the plain intention of the law was to protect the liberty of contract and the freedom of trade.[36] It explained that 'trusts induced by motives of individual or corporate aggrandizement' were incompatible with the public interest because they restrained trade or commerce

> by driving out of business the small dealers and worthy men whose lives have been spent therein, and who might be unable to readjust themselves to their altered surroundings. Mere reduction in the price of the commodity dealt in might be dearly paid for by the ruin of such a class.[37]

During the 1940s and 1960s, US courts often defined the primary aim of the antitrust rules as preventing the concentration of economic power to the detriment of the economy and wider political values. In *Alcoa* (1945), for example, the Second Circuit Court of Appeals held that monopolies were not only undesirable for economic reasons, but that great industrial consolidations were inherently detrimental. It held that it was possible, because of its indirect social or moral effect, to prefer a system of small producers, each dependent for his success upon his own skill and character, to one in which the great mass of those engaged must accept the direction of a few.[38] It further took the view that one of the purposes of

[35] EM Fox and LA Sullivan, 'Antitrust—Retrospective and Prospective: Where Are We Coming from—Where Are We Going?' (1987) 62 *New York University Law Review* 936; EM Fox, 'The Modernization of Antitrust: A New Equilibrium' (1981) 66 *Cornell Law Review* 1140; WE Kovacic and C Shapiro, 'Antitrust Policy: A Century of Economic and Legal Thinking' (2000) 14 *Journal of Economic Perspectives* 43; JD Wright and DH Ginsburg, 'The Goals Of Antitrust: Welfare Trumps Choice' (2013) 81 *Fordham Law Review* 2405; DH Ginsburg, 'Originalism and Economic Analysis: Two Case Studies of Consistency and Coherence in Supreme Court Decision Making' (2010) 33 *Harvard Journal of Public Policy* 217.

[36] *United States v Trans-Missouri Freight Assn.*, 166 US 290, 355 (1897).

[37] ibid, 323.

[38] *United States v Aluminum Co of America et al*, 148 F. 2d 416, 427 (1945).

Congress in enacting the Sherman Act had been to put an end to great aggregations of capital 'because of the helplessness of the individual before them', and that the antitrust statutes aimed to perpetuate and preserve, for its own sake and in spite of possible cost, an organisation of industry in small units which could effectively compete with each other.[39] Likewise, in *Brown Shoe* (1962), the US Supreme Court argued that the primary vice of vertical mergers or tying arrangements was that they foreclosed competitors and deprived them of a fair opportunity to compete.[40] It considered that Congress had appreciated the occasional higher costs and prices that might result from the maintenance of fragmented industries and markets, but that it had resolved these competing considerations in favour of decentralisation,[41] and considered itself bound to protect the 'economic way of life' that Congress had sought to preserve by means of the antitrust statutes, namely 'viable, small, locally owned businesses'.[42] Finally, as late as 1972, the US Supreme Court described the US Antitrust laws as the 'Magna Carta of free enterprise' that guaranteed each and every business, no matter how small, the freedom to compete.[43] In sum, the courts interpreted the antitrust rules as protecting the freedom of small companies to compete, both in the interest of the individual, the economy and society in general.

This understanding underwent a major shift in the late 1970s when a group of gifted young scholars, many of them associated with the University of Chicago, called for a fundamental reinterpretation of the law. They argued that antitrust law should be interpreted and applied in holding with economic theory. This, in their view, first and foremost required aligning the aims of antitrust law with that of economic theory, ie the maximisation of economic welfare.[44] On that basis, they argued that only such business conduct should be deemed anticompetitive under the US antitrust rules that would result in a reduction of economic welfare. Their arguments set in motion a major process of thinking and reinterpreting the US antitrust statutes, which became known as the 'US Antitrust Revolution' or the 'Chicago Revolution'.[45] Crucially, the movement won over the US Supreme Court, which was persuaded that the antitrust rules should be guided by the exclusive aim of enhancing economic welfare.

[39] ibid, 428, 429.

[40] *Brown Shoe Co v United States*, 370 U.S. 294, 323 (1962).

[41] ibid, 344.

[42] ibid, 332.

[43] *United States v Topco Associates, Inc* 405 U.S. 596, 610 (1972).

[44] See esp R Bork, 'The Goals of Antitrust Policy' (1967) 57 *American Economic Review* 242; Bork, *The Antitrust Paradox: A Policy at War With Itself* (New York, The Free Press, 1978) 81 and R Posner, *Antitrust Law*, 2nd edn (Chicago, Chicago University Press, 2001) 29.

[45] Many of the key figures in this movement were not actually associated with the University of Chicago. Robert Bork, frequently cited by the Supreme Court in support of these revised views, wrote his *Antitrust Paradox* at Yale Law School, and Phillip Areeda was a professor at Harvard Law School.

However, to this day, a dispute remains over the correct welfare standard. Whereas most true Chicago scholars and economists advocate a 'total welfare' standard, ie aggregate economic efficiency consisting of the sum of both consumer and producer surplus,[46] the US Supreme Court adopted a more limited 'consumer welfare' standard in the late 1970s, that does not take into account the welfare gains of producers but only considers consumer welfare relevant. *Reiter v Sonotone Corp* from 1979 is the first case in which it expressed this new understanding of the aims of US antitrust law. It held that Congress had designed the Sherman Act as a 'consumer welfare prescription'[47] and quoted the writings of Robert Bork in support of this view.[48] It is now widely accepted that the Supreme Court misunderstood Bork's somewhat loose use of the term consumer welfare, which the latter had actually equated with efficiency.[49] Be that as it may, the US Supreme Court and the majority of lower courts continue to adhere to the consumer welfare aim[50] despite criticism and suggestions for a more appropriate welfare standard in the literature.[51]

The Chicago Revolution was by no means limited to the US judiciary. The Chicago school's position that very little state intervention is needed to achieve the aim of enhancing welfare because most anticompetitive practices are untenable in competitive markets,[52] sat well with the Reagan and Bush administrations' political agendas of cutting back business regulation. It strongly influenced the enforcement practice of the DoJ and FTC, which also adopted the consumer welfare aim as the exclusive objective of the US antitrust statutes.[53]

[46] Bork, *The Antitrust Paradox: A Policy at War With Itself* (n 44) 81; Posner, *Antitrust Law* (n 44) 29. According to Posner, efficiency should be the aim of all law because in a world of scarce resources waste should be considered immoral: R Posner, *Economic Analysis of Law*, 9th edn (The Hague, Wolters Kluwer, 2014) s 2.4.

[47] *Reiter v Sonotone Corp.*, 442 U.S. 330, 343 (1979).

[48] ibid, quoting Bork (n 44) 66.

[49] B Orbach, How Antitrust Lost Its Goal (2013) 81 *Fordham Law Review* 2253, 2274; RD Blair and DD Sokol, 'The Rule of Reason and the Goals of Antitrust: An Economic Approach' (2012) 78 *Antitrust Law Journal* 471, 473.

[50] eg *Brooke Group Ltd v Brown & Williamson Tobacco Corp* 509 U.S. 209, 221 (1993); *NCAA v Board of Regents of the University of Oklahoma*, 468 U. S. 85, 107 (1984) for the US Supreme Court. Likewise, *Broadcom Corp v Qualcomm Inc*, 501 F.3d 297, 308 (2007); *Rebel Oil Company, Inc, Auto Flite Oil Company, Inc v Atlantic Richfield Company* 51 F.3d 1421, 1433 (1995).

[51] See eg SC Salop, 'Question: What Is the Real and Proper Antitrust Welfare Standard? Answer: The True Consumer Welfare Standard' (2010) 22 *Loyola Consumer Law Review* 336; B Orbach, 'The Antitrust Consumer Welfare Paradox' (2011) 7 *Journal of Competition Law and Economics* 133. See also the many excellent contributions in the April issue of the *Fordham Law Review* (2013) 81 following from the Antitrust Law Association Symposium 'The Goals of Antitrust' (Washington DC, 26 October 2012).

[52] Easterbrook, eg, advocates an antitrust policy that consists of pursuing 'plain vanilla cartels and mergers to monopoly' (FH Easterbrook, 'Workable Antitrust Policy' (1986) 84 *Michigan Law Review* 1701).

[53] The FTC and DoJ enforcement guidelines spelling out the authorities' approach to assessing anticompetitive conduct do not explicitly define the aims of the antitrust statutes, but make clear that the authorities will only assess the effects for consumers, in particular in terms of price, output, quality, service or innovation (US Federal Trade Commission and US Department of Justice, Antitrust

iii. The Concept of Harm

Having decided that the true aim of the US antitrust statutes was to protect consumer welfare, the US Supreme Court drew the necessary consequences and also adopted a new understanding of competitive harm. It construed the broad wording of sections 1 and 2 of the Sherman Act and section 7 of the Clayton Act to mean that a 'restraint of trade', 'monopolisation' and a 'significant lessening of competition' all implied a reduction in consumer welfare. In other words, business conduct is these days only deemed anticompetitive under the US antitrust rules if it results in higher prices, reduced output, less innovation or harms consumers in other ways as a result of diminished competitive constraints or incentives.[54]

iv. Per se *Rules v Rules of Reason*

The Chicago school had another axe to grind with the courts. In their view, the judiciary relied too heavily on the use of *per se* rules instead of assessing suspect business conduct under the rule of reason.

The rule of reason is a doctrine developed by the US Supreme Court in the interpretation of section 1 of the Sherman Act. As previously explained, section 1 prohibits arrangements 'in restraint of trade'. The courts soon recognised that this prohibition would catch too many situations if restraint of trade were interpreted as meaning 'any restraint of trade'. The US Supreme Court solved this problem in *Standard Oil Co of New Jersey v United States* by interpreting the provision as containing a 'rule of reason', according to which only unreasonable restraints were prohibited by Section 1.[55] Under the rule of reason, an agreement's reasonableness must be established by considering and weighing all of the circumstances, including the facts peculiar to the business, the history of the restraint and the reason why it was imposed.[56] However, the understanding of what makes a restraint of trade unreasonable has undergone significant changes over the past 100 years. Since the Antitrust Revolution, the only relevant factors are the agreement's effects on consumer welfare. In practice, a rule of reason therefore nowadays amounts to balancing the agreement's anticompetitive (ie consumer welfare-reducing) effects against its pro-competitive (ie consumer welfare-increasing) effects. If the

Guidelines for Collaborations Among Competitors (issued: April 2000) s 2.2; and Horizontal Merger Guidelines (issued: 19 August 2010) s 1).

[54] US Department of Justice and the Federal Trade Commission, Horizontal Merger Guidelines (19 August 2010) s 1, and Federal Trade Commission and US Department of Justice, Antitrust Guidelines for Collaborations Among Competitors (April 2000) s 2.2.

[55] *Standard Oil Co of New Jersey v United States*, 221 U.S. 1 (1911), following the reasoning of the Court of Appeals for the 6th Circuit under Chief Judge William Howard Taft in *Addyston Pipe and Steel Company v United States*, 85 F. 271 (6th cir. 1898).

[56] eg *Continental T. V., Inc v GTE Sylvania Inc*, 433 U.S. 36 (1977); *National Society of Professional Engineers v United States*, 435 U.S. 679 (1978).

anticompetitive effects outweigh the pro-competitive effects, the agreement is considered overall anticompetitive and thus unreasonable.

Given that assessing agreements under the rule of reason is a complex and costly process, the Supreme Court excluded certain types of restraint from the application of the rule of reason. If an agreement's nature and inevitable effects are so plainly anticompetitive that an elaborate study of the industry is not necessary to establish their anticompetitive effects, their anticompetitive nature may be presumed.[57] These types of agreements are deemed 'per se illegal'.

In the period between the First World War and the mid-1930s, US courts relied heavily on the rule of reason to determine the legality of agreements and applied *per se* rules only sparingly. Generally, the US antitrust authorities also took a permissive attitude towards suspect business conduct during this period.[58] The trend was reversed in the late 1930s when antitrust enforcement was rediscovered as an instrument to create economic wealth under the Roosevelt administration. To facilitate the enforcement and lighten the antitrust authorities' burden of proof, courts started relying increasingly on *per se* rules.[59] Their use reached its height during the 1940s to 1960s.

Robert Bork was one of the most forceful and prolific critics of the *per se* rule, arguing, amongst others, that a *per se* rule of illegality could not fully appreciate the economic phenomena underlying the suspect conduct[60] and that it was unfair to punish individuals whose conduct could not conceivably have had 'anti-consumer consequences'.[61] He was not alone in this view. Critics generally agreed that *per se* rules were too rigid and inflexible to measure the actual effects (both anticompetitive and pro-competitive) of the agreement, and that they were too easily circumventable if everything turned on the bare form of the transaction.[62]

57 In *Northern Pacific R Co v United States*, the US Supreme Court held: '[T]here are certain agreements or practices which because of their pernicious effect on competition and lack of any redeeming virtue are conclusively presumed to be unreasonable and therefore illegal without elaborate inquiry as to the precise harm they have caused or the business excuse for their use. This principle of *per se* unreasonableness not only makes the type of restraints which are proscribed by the Sherman Act more certain to the benefit of everyone concerned, but it also avoids the necessity for an incredibly complicated and prolonged economic investigation into the entire history of the industry involved, as well as related industries, in an effort to determine at large whether a particular restraint has been unreasonable—an inquiry so often wholly fruitless when undertaken'. (*Northern Pacific R Co v United States*, 356 US 1, 5 (1958)).

58 Kovacic and Shapiro, 'Antitrust Policy' (n 35) 43, 46.

59 ibid, 49, 50.

60 R Bork, 'The Rule of Reason and the *Per Se* Concept: Price Fixing and Market Division [I]' (1965) 74 *Yale Law Journal* 775, 777.

61 R Bork, 'The Rule of Reason and the *Per Se* Concept: Price Fixing and Market Division [II]' (1966) 75 *Yale Law Journal* 373, 384, 385.

62 eg R Posner, 'Antitrust Policy and the Supreme Court: An Analysis of the Restricted Distribution, Horizontal Merger and Potential Competition Decisions' (1975) 75 *Columbia Law Review* 282, 287; DI Baker, 'Vertical Restraints in Times of Change: From White to Schwinn to Where?' (1975) 44 *Antitrust Law Journal* 537, 538.

Chicago scholars therefore argued in favour of assessing a suspect agreement's anti- and pro-competitive effects in every individual case, instead of inferring its nature from its form.[63]

The *Sylvania* case from 1977[64] marks the first major victory of the Chicago school on this issue. In *Sylvania*, the US Supreme Court faced the question whether a contractual clause, in which a manufacturer prohibited its distributors from selling out of locations other than those specified in the distribution agreement, was an unreasonable restraint of trade under section 1 of the Sherman Act. Only 10 years earlier, the Court had ruled in *Schwinn* that non-price restrictions in distribution agreements had to be presumed *per se* illegal.[65] In *Sylvania*, the Court overruled this precedent. It noted that scholarly opinion had been highly critical of the ruling in *Schwinn*, and therefore took the *Sylvania* case as the opportunity to reconsider its position. The Court referred to the writings of Posner and Bork, in particular, and was convinced by their arguments that the type of restraint in question, while restricting intra-brand competition, also had 'great economic utility'.[66] It concluded that the inherent potential of non-price restrictions in distribution agreements for yielding economic efficiencies meant that they could not be presumed to be unreasonable within the meaning of section 1 of the Sherman Act, and that they should be assessed as to their actual effects under a traditional rule of reason instead.

Sylvania was only the first in a series of judgments, in which the US Supreme Court, step by step, curtailed the use of *per se* rules. In *State Oil Co v Khan*, it overruled the precedent that maximum resale price maintenance should be considered *per se* illegal.[67] Most recently, in *Leegin Creative Leather Products*,[68] it reversed the precedent according to which minimum resale price maintenance was considered *per se* illegal. It has also narrowed down the circumstances under which a concerted refusal to deal is deemed *per se* illegal.[69]

[63] Easterbrook summarised the situation in the following terms: 'As time goes by, fewer and fewer things seem appropriate for *per se* condemnation. We see competitive benefits in practices that once were thought uniformly pernicious. (…) We cannot condemn so quickly anymore. What we do not condemn, we must study. The approved method of study is the Rule of Reason (FH Easterbrook, The Limits of Antitrust (1984) 63 *Texas Law Review* 1, 10).

[64] *Continental T. V., Inc v GTE Sylvania Inc* (n 56).

[65] *United States v Arnold, Schwinn & Co*, 388 U.S. 365 (1967).

[66] *Continental T. V., Inc v GTE Sylvania Inc* (n 56) 51–58, citing Bork, 'The Rule of Reason and the *Per Se* Concept: Price Fixing and Market Division [I]' (n 60) and 'The Rule of Reason and the *Per Se* Concept: Price Fixing and Market Division [II]' (n 61); Posner, 'Antitrust Policy and the Supreme Court' (n 62) amongst many others.

[67] *State Oil Co v Khan*, 522 U.S. 3, 19 (1997).

[68] *Leegin Creative Leather Products, Inc v PSKS, Inc*, 127 S.Ct. 2705 (2007).

[69] *Northwest Wholesale Stationers, Inc v Pacific Stationery & Printing Co*, 472 U.S. 284, 298 (1985), in which the Court of Appeals of the 9th Circuit had applied a *per se* rule, and *FTC v Indiana Federation of Dentists*, 476 U.S. 447 (1986), in which the Court declined to 'resolve this case by forcing the Federation's policy into the "boycott" pigeonhole and invoking the *per se* rule' (458).

Per se illegality is now generally the exception rather than the rule under US antitrust law again, and except for a handful of hard-core restraints, such as horizontal price fixing and market sharing, most agreements are now assessed as to their actual effects (on consumer welfare). However, as full market analyses are expensive, make for lengthy processes and generate vast evidentiary records, the past 10 years have also seen the proliferation of many different types of intermediary 'quick look rules' or 'bright-line tests' for the more obviously suspect cases.[70] This is said to have led to some degree of confusion at the district court level, triggering academic attempts to develop a uniform model of intermediary rule.[71]

In sum, the Chicago school's mission to bring US antitrust law into line with economics was not primarily about introducing the use of microeconomic theory and its many practical applications in individual assessments. First and foremost, the Chicago school fought for a more fundamental change: it proposed to reinterpret the old federal antitrust statutes as aiming at the maximisation of efficiency and economic welfare exclusively. By winning over the federal judiciary, it gave US antitrust law a new legal objective and a new concept of competitive harm, even though it would presumably have preferred to see the US Supreme Court embrace the total welfare rather than the consumer welfare standard. It also convinced the US Supreme Court to move away from presumptions of illegality and to assess most business conduct as to its actual effects under a rule of reason.

v. Conclusion

That the EU institutions had not followed the US Supreme Court's change of heart in the 1970s only really became evident to the wider public when the US and EU antitrust authorities reached different conclusions in *Boeing/McDonnell Douglas*, *GE/Honeywell* and *Microsoft*. Before this background, the reaction of US antitrust experts to the Commission's approach in *GE/Honeywell* and *Microsoft* also becomes much more understandable. The Commission was criticised for pursuing the 'wrong' aim because it had not been exclusively guided by the consumer welfare aim of current US law and had consequently not assessed the investigated conduct's impact on consumer welfare either.

[70] Under one 'quick look' rule of reason, a defendant must offer a legitimate justification for inherently suspect behaviour before the court will proceed to a more comprehensive competitive analysis. According to the US Supreme Court, conduct is inherently suspect if 'an observer with even a rudimentary understanding of economics could conclude that the arrangements in question would have had an effect on customers and markets' and the 'great likelihood of anticompetitive effects can easily be ascertained' (*California Dental Association v FTC*, 526 U.S. 756 (1999).

[71] See eg TC Arthur, 'A Workable Rule of Reason: A Less Ambitious Antitrust Role for the Federal Courts' (2002) 68(2) *Antitrust Law Journal* 337; TJ Muris, 'The Rule of Reason after California Dental' (2002) 68(2) *Antitrust Law Journal* 527; WK Tom and C Pak, 'Toward a Flexible Rule of Reason' (2000) 68(2) *Antitrust Law Journal* 391.

The background of the US Antitrust Revolution is also helpful for interpreting the somewhat cryptic definitions of the more economic approach in the Commission's various Communications. The vertical restraints guidelines and DG Competition's Discussion Paper on Article 102 had defined the Commission's more economic approach as one that was 'based on the effects on the market'.[72] Given that a key feature of the Chicago school's prescription for US antitrust law was to assess the suspect conduct's actual effects and to abandon *per se* rules, it is conceivable that a more economic approach to EU antitrust law 'based on the effects on the market' also implied curtailing the use of rules that inferred the competitive nature of conduct from its form, in favour of rules that required establishing its actual effects in a case-specific analysis. Possibly, an approach based on the effects on the market even meant an approach that assessed the effects on consumer welfare. The Guidance Paper's focus on consumer welfare seems to point that way.

Incidentally, Richard Posner, commenting on the US Supreme Court's decision in the *Sylvania* case in 1977, referred to the ruling as containing an 'economic approach' to section 1 Sherman Act.[73] This term is conspicuously similar to the Commission's 'more economic approach' to EU antitrust law. Part II of this book demonstrates that the similarities do not stop at the name, but that the Commission's more economic approach in fact emulates many of the changes, although not all, that the Chicago Revolution introduced to US antitrust law.

B. The Academic Debate

A second source that is helpful for gaining a better understanding of the Commission's reform agenda is the extensive academic debate accompanying the process. The political clashes between the EU and US antitrust authorities over the *GE/Honeywell* and *Microsoft* cases fostered an animated interdisciplinary and inter-jurisdictional scholarly discussion of the validity of the European Commission's approach in these two cases.[74] Soon, the contributions shifted their focus from

[72] European Commission, Guidelines on Vertical Restraints (2000) (n 16) para 7; DG Competition, Discussion Paper on the Application of Article 82 of the Treaty to Exclusionary Abuses (n 25) para 4.

[73] R Posner, 'The Rule of Reason and the *Economic Approach*: Reflections on the Sylvania Decision' (1977) 45 *University of Chicago Law Review* 1, commenting on *Continental T. V., Inc v GTE Sylvania Inc* (n 56).

[74] On the *GE/Honeywell* case, see eg F Romano, 'General Electric/Honeywell—Victory of the Commission … or Failure?' (2007) 3 *International Business Law Journal* 368; S Baxter, F Dethmers and N Dodoo, 'The GE/Honeywell Judgment and the Assessment of Conglomerate Effects: What's New in EC Practice?' (2006) 2 *European Competition Journal* 141; DJ Gerber, 'The European Commission's GE/Honeywell Decision: US Responses and their Implications' (2003) 1 *Zeitschrift für Wettbewerbsrecht* 87; M Pflanz and C Caffarra, 'The Economics of G.E./Honeywell' (2002) 23 *European Competition Law Review* 115; Patterson and Shapiro (n 31); EM Fox, 'Mergers in Global Markets: GE/Honeywell and the Future of Merger Control' (2002) 23 *University of Pennsylvania Journal of International Economic Law* 457; W Kolasky, 'GE/Honeywell: Continuing the Transatlantic Dialog' (2002)

the Commission's analyses in these specific decisions to a more general discussion of the economic foundations of the Commission's antitrust assessments.[75] The academic community subsequently followed the Commission's modernisation process with interest and carefully scrutinised the first Commission guidelines on Article 101 TFEU.[76]

Whereas the scholarly contributions on the Commission's reform of Article 101 primarily happened in the academic press,[77] antitrust scholars from all over the world were given a great deal of opportunity to contribute to the review of the Commission's approach to EU merger control and Article 102 more directly. In the area of merger control, the Commission carried out public consultations on both its draft horizontal and non-horizontal merger guidelines,[78] and it involved interested third parties at an even earlier stage in its review of Article 102.[79] The

23 *University of Pennsylvania Journal of International Economic Law* 513; DS Evans and M Salinger, 'Competition Thinking at the European Commission: Lessons from the Aborted GE/Honeywell Merger' (2001–02) 10 *George Mason Law Review* 489; G Drauz, 'Unbundling GE/Honeywell: The Assessment of Conglomerate Mergers under EC Competition Law' (2001–02) 25 *Fordham International Law Journal* 885 on the *GE/Honeywell* case. On the European Commission's *Microsoft* decision, see eg S Vezzoso, 'The Incentives Balance Test in the EU Microsoft Case: a Pro-innovation "Economics-based" Approach?' (2006) 27 *European Competition Law Review* 382; M Furse, 'Article 82, Microsoft and Bundling, or "The Half Monti"' (2004) 3 *Competition Law Journal* 169; DS Evans and AJ Padilla, 'Tying under Article 82 EC and the Microsoft Decision' (2004) 27 *World Competition* 503; K-U Kühn, R Stillman and C Caffarra, 'Economic Theories of Bundling and their Policy Implications in Abuse Cases: an Assessment in Light of the Microsoft Case' (2005) 1 *European Competition Journal* 85; M Dolmans and T Graf, 'Analysis of Tying under Article 82 EC: the European Commission's Microsoft Decision in Perspective' (2004) 27 *World Competition* 225; R Pardolesi and A Renda, 'The European Commission's Case against Microsoft: Kill Bill?' (2004) 27 *World Competition* 513.

[75] See eg J Vickers, 'Merger Policy in Europe: Retrospect and Prospect' (2004) 25 *European Competition Law Review* 445; P Muysert, 'Price Discrimination—an Unreliable Indicator of Market Power' (2004) 25 *European Competition Law Review* 350; J Kallaugher and B Sher, 'Rebates Revisited: Anti-competitive Effects and Exclusionary Abuse under Article 82' (2004) 25 *European Competition Law Review* 263; J Vickers, 'Competition Economics and Policy' (2003) 24 *European Competition Law Review* 95; DS Evans and AJ Padilla, 'Demand-side Efficiencies in Merger Control' (2003) 26 *World Competition* 167; D Ridyard, 'Exclusionary Pricing and Price Discrimination Abuses Under Art.82—An Economic Analysis' (2002) 23 *European Competition Law Review* 286.

[76] eg P Lugard and L Hancher, 'Honey, I Shrunk the Article! A Critical Assessment of the Commission's Notice on Article 81(3) of the EC Treaty' (2004) 25 *European Competition Law Review* 410; the (2004) 49(1&2) issue of *Antitrust Bulletin* on 'Antitrust in the U.S. and the EU—Converging or Diverging Paths?'; S Bishop and D Ridyard, 'E.C. Vertical Restraints Guidelines: Effects Based or *per se* Policy?' (2002) 23 *European Competition Law Review* 35; L Peeperkorn, 'E.C. Vertical Restraints Guidelines: Effects Based or *per se* Policy?—a Reply' (2002) 23 *European Competition Law Review* 38.

[77] The Commission did carry out a public consultation on its Green Paper on Vertical Restraints (European Commission, 'Green Paper on Vertical Restraints in EC Competition Policy' (n 11)).

[78] European Commission, Draft Commission Notice on the appraisal of horizontal mergers under the Council Regulation on the control of concentrations between undertakings [2002] OJ C331/18, para 99; and Draft Commission Notice, Guidelines on the assessment of non-horizontal mergers under the Council Regulation on the control of concentrations between undertakings of 13 February 2008, available at: www.ec.europa.eu/competition/mergers/legislation/draft_nonhorizontal_mergers.pdf.

[79] See Ch 2.

inclusive and transparent manner in which the Commission conducted the reform of this last pillar, and the public exchange of views amongst a wide variety of interested third parties, resulted in the key issues being defined much more clearly than during the review of Article 101.

The EAGCP study proposing an 'economic approach' to Article 102[80] clearly spelled out the key characteristics of such an approach in its introductory statements. According to the report, assessments in line with economic theory were (1) 'effects-based' rather than 'form-based'; (2) focused on anticompetitive effects that harmed consumers; and (3) based on sound economics and grounded in facts.[81] Instead of inferring the competitive nature and legality of the investigated conduct from its form, competition authorities were expected to assess the conduct's actual effects on competition in every individual case, identify the actual harm inflicted on consumers and assess the extent to which such a negative effect was potentially outweighed by efficiency gains generated by the conduct. According to the EAGCP, an economic approach also required that competition authorities prove these effects on the basis of consistent theories of business behaviour grounded in sound economics and supported by empirical evidence.[82]

A few months later, DG Competition published its internal Staff Discussion Paper, that outlined an approach 'based on the effects on the market'[83] and opened a public consultation on the document. This exercise engendered numerous responses from academics, practitioners, national competition authorities and the wider business community. Over 100 contributions were published on the Commission's website[84] and the scholarly debate carried on beyond the consultation in many other forums.[85] A survey of this vast body of literature reveals that

[80] EAGCP, 'An Economic Approach to Article 82' (n 24).

[81] ibid, 2.

[82] ibid, 3.

[83] See s III of this chapter.

[84] These contributions remain available at: www.ec.europa.eu/comm/competition/antitrust/art82/contributions.html.

[85] See eg the 2006 special issue of the *European Competition Journal* ((2006) 2(1) Supp); CD Ehlermann and I Atanasiu (eds), *European Competition Law Annual 2003—What is an Abuse of a Dominant Position?* (Oxford, Hart Publishing, 2006); D Ridyard, 'Exclusive Contracts and Article 82 Enforcement: an Effects-based Perspective' (2008) 4 *European Competition Journal* 579; M Dreher and M Adam, 'Abuse of Dominance under Reform—Sound Economics and Established Case Law' (2007) 28 *European Competition Law Review* 278; Bundeskartellamt/Competition Law Forum, 'Debate on Reform of Article 82: A Dialectic on Competing Approaches' (2006) 2 *European Competition Journal* 211; R O'Donoghue and AJ Padilla, *The Law and Economics of Article 82 EC* (Oxford, Hart Publishing, 2006), now in its second edition (Oxford, Hart Publishing, 2013); D Geradin and N Petit, 'Price Discrimination under EC Competition Law: Another Antitrust Doctrine in Search of Limiting Principles?' (2006) 2 *Journal of Competition Law and Economics* 479; T Eilmannsberger, 'How to Distinguish Good from Bad Competition under Article 82: In Search of Clearer and More Coherent Standards for Anti-Competitive Abuse' (2005) 42 *Common Market Law Review* 129; G Federico, 'When are Rebates Exclusionary?' (2005) 26 *European Competition Law Review* 477; G Niels and H Jenkins, 'Reform of Article 82: Where the Link between Dominance and Effects Breaks Down' (2005) 26 *European Competition Law Review* 605; B Sher, 'The Last of the Steam-powered Trains: Modernising Article 82' (2004) 25 *European Competition Law Review* 243; Kallaugher and Sher, 'Rebates Revisited' (n 75).

commentators had different ideas on what should be done to bring EU antitrust law and policy more into line with mainstream economics. Nonetheless, it is possible to identify a number of recurring themes.

In the aftermath of *GE/Honeywell* and the three annulment judgments of 2002, supporters of a more economic approach pressed the Commission to make better use of contemporary economic theory, in particular industrial organisation theory, to establish or predict the investigated conduct's consequences for the market.[86] Others advised the Commission to verify and support the conclusions it reached by means of 'quantitative' analysis, ie by employing the mathematical tools developed by economists especially for the purpose of proving, measuring and predicting the effects of certain types of business conduct in the market.[87]

The relevance of consumer welfare in antitrust assessments was another major bone of contention. Many commentators criticised the EU institution's antitrust practice for not considering a negative effect on consumer welfare a key requirement of anticompetitiveness, or at least for carrying out such assessments very badly. The Commission was advised to focus on the conduct's consequences for consumers exclusively, and that if the conduct did not affect their welfare adversely, it was not to be considered anticompetitive.[88]

Other commentators focused on the issue of form- and effects-based tests. They argued that in order to guarantee accurate outcomes, EU antitrust law should employ effects- rather than form-based tests, ie require the enforcement bodies to assess and prove the conduct's actual effects in every single case rather than infer the likelihood of anticompetitive effects from the conduct's form. Form-based tests were too blunt to be able to capture all of the conduct's effects reliably and therefore often resulted in pro-competitive conduct being prohibited, while truly anticompetitive conduct was not caught.[89]

Finally, there was wide agreement that EU antitrust law did not adequately take into account economic efficiency effects generated by the investigated conduct.

[86] EAGCP (n 24) 15 ff; R Van den Bergh, 'Modern Industrial Organisation versus Old-fashioned European Competition Law' (1996) 17 *European Competition Law Review* 75; F Maier-Rigaud, 'Article 82 Rebates: Four Common Fallacies' (2006) 2 Supp (Special issue) *European Competition Journal* 85; L-H Röller, 'Economic Analysis and Competition Policy Enforcement in Europe' in PAG Kloosterhuis and E Bergeijk (eds), *Modelling European Mergers* (Cheltenham, Edward Elgar, 2005) 11; Niels and Jenkins, 'Reform of Article 82' (n 85); A Lofaro and D Ridyard, 'Beyond Bork: New Economic Theories in Merger Cases' (2002) 23 *European Competition Law Review* 151.

[87] EAGCP (n 24) 13; Röller, 'Economic Analysis and Competition Policy Enforcement in Europe' (n 86) 11; D Hildebrand, *The Role of Economic Analysis in the EC Competition Rules* (Alphen aan den Rijn, Wolters Kluwer, 2002), now in its 3rd edn (2009).

[88] EAGCP (n 24) 2; Sher, 'The Last of the Steam-powered Trains' (n 85); O'Donoghue and Padilla, *The Law and Economics of Article 82 EC* (n 85) 174 ff; Competition Law Forum, Article 82 Review Group, 'The Reform of Article 82: Recommendations on Key Policy Objectives' (2005) 1 *European Competition Journal* 179.

[89] eg EAGCP (n 24) 5 ff; John Vickers, 'Abuse of Market Power' (2005) 115 *The Economic Journal* 244; D Waelbroeck, 'Michelin II: A *Per Se* Rule Against Rebates by Dominant Companies?' (2005) 1 *Journal of Competition Law and Economics* 149; Kallaugher and Sher, (n 75); Ridyard, 'Exclusionary Pricing and Price Discrimination Abuses under Article 82' (n 75); S Bishop, 'Pro-competitive Exclusive Supply Agreements: How Refreshing!' (2003) 24 *European Competition Law Review* 229; Bishop and Ridyard, 'E.C. Vertical Restraints Guidelines' (n 76).

As efficiency increased economic welfare, efficiency effects engendered by the investigated conduct should be considered countervailing factors capable of cancelling out the conduct's anticompetitive effects.[90]

In sum, the academic view of what an economic approach to EU antitrust law should entail went far beyond the use of more up to date economic theory in order to understand the purpose and wider consequences of business behaviour in the market. Its proponents' wish list closely emulated the changes that were made in the interpretation of the US antitrust statutes in the 1970s and 1980s.

To avoid creating the impression that the Commission's mission to introduce a more economic approach to EU antitrust law reform was universally accepted in academic circles, it should be pointed out that this was not the case. A fair number of commentators, especially those coming from a German legal background, were dubious of or even vehemently opposed to the suggested changes. A key concern was that effects-based tests, combined with the use of complex economic theories and econometric models, would result in legal uncertainty as their outcomes were difficult to predict for individuals.[91] Also, many opposed the belief that economic surplus should be the exclusive aim and guiding value of EU antitrust law.[92]

V. Conclusions and Consequences for the Structure of Part II

While the Commission documents introducing the more economic approach themselves were not particularly clear as to the actual changes the new policy

[90] EAGCP (n 24) 35; European Commission, Summary of The Replies Received During The Consultation Process on The Green Paper on the Review of Council Regulation (EEC) NO 4064/89, paras 112–27, available at: www.ec.europa.eu/competition/consultations/2002_council_regulation; PD Camesasca, *European Merger Control: Getting the Efficiencies Right* (Antwerp, Intersentia, 2000); D Neven, P Papandropoulos and P Seabright, *Trawling for Minnows. European Competition Policy and Agreements between Firms* (Center for Economic Policy Research, 1998); D Gerard, 'Merger Control Policy: How to Give Meaningful Consideration to Efficiency Claims?' (2003) 40 *Common Market Law Review* 1367; M Motta, 'E.C. Merger Policy and the Airtours Case' (2000) 21 *European Competition Law Review* 199; Niels and Jenkins (n 85).

[91] This was the position, eg, of the then President of the German Federal Cartel Office: U Böge, 'Reform der Europäischen Fusionskontrolle' (2004) 54 *Wirtschaft und Wettbewerb* 138, and U Böge, 'Der "more economic approach" und die deutsche Wettbewerbspolitik' (2004) *Wirtschaft und Wettbewerb* 726. For similar doubts, see A Christiansen, 'Die "Ökonomisierung" der EU-Fusionskontrolle: Mehr Kosten als Nutzen?' (2005) 55 *Wirtschaft und Wettbewerb* 285; A Schmidt and S Voigt, 'Der "more economic approach" in der Mißbrauchsaufsicht' (2006) 56 *Wirtschaft und Wettbewerb* 1097.

[92] J Drexl, S Enchelmaier, M Leistner, M-O Mackenrodt and B Conde Gallego, 'Comments of the Max Planck Institute for Intellectual Property, Competition and Tax Law on the Directorate-General Competition Discussion Paper of December 2005 on the Application of Art.82 of the EC Treaty to Exclusionary Abuses' (2006) 37 *International Review of Intellectual Property and Competition Law* 558; ILO Schmidt, 'The Suitability of the More Economic Approach for Competition Policy: Dynamic vs. Static Efficiency' (2007) 28 *European Competition Law Review* 408; J Basedow, 'Konsumentenwohlfahrt und Effizienz—Neue Leitbilder der Wettbewerbspolitk?' (2007) 57 *Wirtschaft und Wettbewerb* 712; see also: Bundeskartellamt/Competition Law Forum 'Debate on Reform of Article 82' (n 85).

intended to make, the historical context of the US Antitrust Revolution and the academic debate accompanying the Commission's review process make it possible to gain a clearer understanding of the Commission's reform agenda.

For one, it is likely to have aimed to incorporate the conclusions of contemporary economic theory on the effects of business conduct on the market into its individual assessments and into the design of general policy instruments. This is probably the most obvious understanding of a competition law and policy 'fully compatible with economic learning'. However, there are clear indications that the Commission's more economic approach aimed to go beyond mere methodological changes and also targeted the substance of the law. Before the background of the changes introduced by the US Antitrust Revolution, an approach 'based on the effects on the market' could be interpreted as an approach that seeks to establish the effects on economic welfare. The US Antitrust Revolution essentially aligned the aims of US antitrust law with the ultimate aim of contemporary economic theory: the maximisation of economic welfare. In particular, the debate surrounding the reform of Article 102 suggests that the Commission intended to focus its enforcement activities on pursuing conduct that would harm consumer welfare. Finally, the relevant Commission acts, as interpreted in the context of the US Antitrust Revolution and the broader academic debate, suggest that the Commission's more economic approach also aimed to review the type of legal test employed for assessing the competitive nature of conduct: instead of inferring the likelihood of competitive harm from the conduct's form, it seems that a more economic approach would have favoured establishing the conduct's actual effects in individual assessments.

To avoid any misunderstandings, the fact that the Commission documents introducing the more economic approach, and speeches by key Commission officials prior to 2004 in particular, did not define the substance of the approach more clearly and precisely is not interpreted as a sign of underhandedness or an intentional lack of transparency. Rather, it seems likely that there was no ready masterplan in the late 1990s for how to bring EU antitrust law more into line with economic theory, but that the agenda and substance of the approach crystallised and evolved little by little over a period of 10 years and more.

The following five chapters establish what changes have actually occurred in the Commission's assessment practice since the introduction of the more economic approach, and show that these are both significant and fundamental in nature. The more economic approach went well beyond a mere tweak in methodology. Rather, the ambition to introduce an antitrust policy fully compatible with economic learning led the Commission to revise its understanding of the law's objective, adopt a new concept of competitive harm, change its position on countervailing effects and reject a number of old-established presumptions of illegality.

Part II

4

A More Economic Objective

I. Introduction

This chapter explores one of the most fundamental premises of the more economic approach, the purpose of EU antitrust law, and demonstrates that the Commission's understanding of the antitrust rules' objective underwent a major change in the late 1990s. From an initially broad and holistic position, it narrowed down the legal objective to two distinct aims: the enhancement of consumer welfare and the protection of the internal market.

II. The Importance of Identifying a Provision's Legal Objective

Before delving into the intricate process of identifying the European Commission's understanding of the goals of EU antitrust law, it is worth reflecting on why the issue matters at all. At first sight, attempting to capture the objective of EU antitrust law may appear like little more than a philosophical exercise without much practical relevance. That, however, is not the case. A clear understanding of the purpose a rule is supposed to achieve is, for one, key during the drafting process. When dealing with existing rules, a clear grasp of their objectives is essential for interpreting unclear terms in a coherent way and setting consistent enforcement priorities. Teleology is a key method of interpretation of EU law. According to the teleological approach, ambiguous legal terms need to be read in light of the purpose that the law pursues.[1] In other words, unclear terms need to be given the meaning that ensures that the purpose pursued by the provision

[1] See eg Case C-377/13 *Ascendi Beiras Litoral e Alta, Auto Estradas das Beiras Litoral e Alta SA v Autoridade Tributária e Aduaneira* ECLI:EU:C:2014:1754, para 48; Case C-456/12 *O. v Minister voor Immigratie, Integratie en Asiel*, ECLI:EU:C:2014:135, para 37.

is realised. Teleology is by no means the only method of interpretation under EU law. The Union institutions also look at the plain meaning of the text, the history and the wider context of the ambiguous rule.[2] They are further guided by the principle of effectiveness of EU law.[3] However, teleology is a very important, if not the most important, instrument in the Union institutions' interpretative tool kit.[4]

There is no lack of ambiguous terms in EU antitrust law. Article 101(1) prohibits 'restrictions of competition'. Article 102 prohibits the 'abuse of a dominant position'. The current Merger Regulation prohibits mergers that would result in a 'significant impediment to effective competition'. These are key concepts, yet what do they mean? There is no obvious answer to these questions. One gets the general idea that these provisions outlaw conduct that harms competition. Yet, even this key term requires interpretation. What is competition within the meaning of these provisions, and when is it harmed? Although competition is a term commonly used in everyday situations, it is not all that easy to define. The *Concise Oxford English Dictionary* suggests the following: 'the activity or condition of competing against others'.[5] In the first instance, it thus replaces an ambiguous noun with an ambiguous verb. Under 'to compete' one finds 'to gain or win something by defeating or establishing superiority over others'.[6]

This is a definition that broadly makes sense in the market environment too. But immediately, further questions arise. Article 101 prohibits agreements and similar arrangements that restrict competition. When is competition restricted? Is this the case when businesses no longer strive 'to gain or win something by defeating or establishing superiority over others' and, if so, how does one prove this? Or does a restriction of competition within the meaning of Article 101 require something else entirely? Likewise, the EU Merger Regulation prohibits mergers that would lead to a significant impediment of effective competition. Is an impediment to competition the same as a restriction of competition? When is this impediment significant? And when is competition effective? Article 102 is particularly ambiguous: it prohibits the abuse of a dominant position and actually does not mention any harmful effects on competition at all. How to make sense of this concept of harm?

Ambiguous wording is by no means a problem that is peculiar to EU antitrust law. As explained in the previous chapter, the key US antitrust statutes are hardly any clearer. Competitive harm within the meaning of section 1 of the Sherman Act is a 'restraint of trade or commerce'. Section 2 seeks to prevent the 'monopolisation of trade or commerce'. Section 7 of the Clayton Act outlaws mergers that could

[2] See eg Case T-374/04 *Germany v* Commission ECLI:EU:T:2007:332, para 92, or Joined Cases T-99/09 and T-308/09 *Italian Republic v European Commission* ECLI:EU:T:2013:200, para 42.

[3] eg Joined Cases C-6/90 and C-9/90 *Francovich and Bonifaci v Italian Republic* ECLI:EU:C:1991:428, para 33.

[4] See eg Case T-102/96 *Gencor v Commission* ECLI:EU:T:1999:65, para 4.

[5] *The Concise Oxford English Dictionary*, 11th edn (Oxford, Oxford University Press, 2008).

[6] ibid.

'substantially lessen competition' or 'tend to create a monopoly'. These concepts of harm are just as ambiguous as their EU counterparts, and it is only the enforcement authorities' and courts' interpretation that gives them their true meaning.

This is where a clear idea of the rules' purpose comes in useful. If one assumes that the objective of a prohibition rule is to protect X, it makes sense to interpret this rule as only being breached if X has been harmed or at least endangered. As Bork famously stated in 1970s: 'Antitrust policy cannot be made rational until we are able to give a firm answer to one question: What is the point of the law—what are its goals? Everything else follows from the answer we give'.[7]

Having a clear idea of the law's objective is, of course, not the be all and end all when trying to interpret a prohibition provision in a coherent manner. There remains the question, for example, of how harm to X, once it has been defined, is to be established when applying the rule. May it be inferred on the basis of a legal rule of thumb? Or should it be established in a detailed assessment of the particular circumstances of every single case? And, if so, what is the appropriate standard of proof? Notwithstanding these issue, knowing that the law's aim is to protect X is the indispensable starting point for a coherent interpretation.

So what is X in the case of antitrust law? The answer to this question is not set in stone. It differs from jurisdiction to jurisdiction, and even within individual jurisdictions, it has been known to change over time. In a number of jurisdictions, there even appears to be no clear concept of the law's objective at all. The following gives a short overview of the objectives most commonly associated with antitrust law, before moving on to exploring the European Commission's understanding of the goals of EU antitrust law.

III. A Few of the Usual Suspects

In 2007, the ICN working group on unilateral conduct carried out a study of the legal objectives guiding its members' unilateral conduct rules.[8] The study established that the participants[9] cited a multitude of reasons for protecting competition against the unilateral behaviour of powerful businesses. Likewise, in academia, there is no shortage of views on what the proper objective should be.[10] The following does not aim to replicate this in-depth debate. It merely

[7] RH Bork, *The Antitrust Paradox* (New York, Basic Books Inc, 1978) 50.

[8] ICN, Unilateral Conduct Working Group, *Report on the Objectives of Unilateral Conduct Laws, Assessment of Dominance/Substantial Market Power, and State-created Monopolies* (2007) available at: www.internationalcompetitionnetwork.org/uploads/library/doc353.pdf.

[9] The study was based on the responses of 33 ICN Member States and 14 non-governmental advisors.

[10] See eg the many thoughtful contributions in D Zimmer (ed), *The Goals of Competition Law* (Cheltenham, Edward Elgar, 2012), and C-D Ehlermann and I Laudati (eds), *Objectives of Competition Law* (Oxford, Hart Publishing, 1997).

intends to summarise the goals most commonly advocated in order to provide the intellectual background for the key purpose of this chapter, which is to determine and understand the European Commission's concept of the objectives of EU antitrust law both before and after the introduction of the more economic approach.

A. Economic Welfare

The majority of antitrust experts these days would probably subscribe to the idea that the primary objective of antitrust law is to enhance economic welfare. However, there is some disagreement as to whose welfare. The supporters of an economic welfare aim can be broadly split into two camps: those who consider that the goal of antitrust law is to enhance total welfare, and those who hold that the objective is to protect and enhance the welfare of consumers only.

In simplified terms, proponents of the 'total' or 'general' welfare aim assert that the objective of antitrust law is to enhance aggregate economic welfare, ie the welfare of all groups of citizens in an economy. While more complete measures of aggregate welfare might also take into account economic factors such as taxes, government subsidies and externalities, the most commonly used standard of aggregate welfare only considers consumer welfare and producer welfare. In economic terms, this objective is defined as 'total surplus', which amounts to the sum of consumer surplus and producer surplus.[11] When total surplus is maximised, the allocation of resources is deemed efficient.

Total welfare, or efficiency, is the aim advocated by two of the most influential schools of thought in the domain of antitrust law and policy: the Harvard school and the Chicago school. The Harvard school originated in the 1930s. Harvard economists Edward Mason and Joe Bain are credited with developing the original thesis that certain types of market structure would almost inevitably result in specific types of anticompetitive conduct, and that antitrust law should therefore focus on avoiding or correcting these types of undesirable structure.[12] Other key individuals who contributed to developing the school and later moved away from a strictly

[11] In mainstream economics, an individual consumer's surplus is defined as the difference between his valuation of relevant good and the price he effectively has to pay for it, whereas an individual producer's surplus is defined as the profit made by that producer from the sale of his product. 'Consumer surplus' is the aggregate measure of all consumers' surplus, whereas 'producer surplus' is the aggregate measure of all producers' surplus. 'Total surplus' is the sum of consumer and producer surplus (see eg M Motta, *Competition Policy* (Cambridge, Cambridge University Press, 2004) 18–22).

[12] JS Bain, *Barriers to New Competition: Their Character and Consequences in Manufacturing Industries* (Cambridge Mass, Harvard University Press, 1956); ES Mason, *Economic Concentration and the Monopoly Problem* (New York, Atheneum, 1964).

structuralist approach are Carl Kaysen, Phillip Areeda, Donald Turner and Stephen Breyer.[13]

The competing Chicago school of thought rose to fame in the 1970s. It was highly critical of the then prevalent Harvard school's structural approach and the high level of interventionism of the US antitrust authorities and courts since World War II. Key figures associated with the Chicago school are Richard Posner, Robert Bork and Frank Easterbrook. It is probably the Chicago school rather than the more moderate Harvard school which is most immediately associated with promoting the total welfare aim, at least in the mind of many European lawyers. Its key members wrote eloquently and memorably about the relevance of defining the objective of antitrust law in line with neo-classical economics as total surplus (or allocative efficiency),[14] and, as explained in the previous chapter, their views influenced the position of the US Supreme Court enduringly on this point.[15] However, Harvard scholars, while generally less focused on the issue of objectives in their work, started assessing the effects of business conduct on total surplus as early as the 1930s.[16] Since the late 1970s, the total welfare objective has found wide acceptance amongst academics generally[17] and appears to be the preferred welfare standard amongst of economists.[18]

By contrast, the supporters of the more restricted consumer welfare aim take the view that the objective of antitrust law should be to enhance consumer welfare, or 'consumer surplus', and disregard the effects on producer welfare. The US judiciary overwhelmingly considers consumer welfare the true objective of US

[13] On the origins and evolution of the Harvard School, and its influence on current antitrust law, see E Elhauge, 'Harvard, Not Chicago: Which Antitrust School Drives Recent U.S. Supreme Court Decisions?' (2007) 3 *Competition Policy International* 59; WE Kovacic, 'The Intellectual DNA of Modern U.S. Competition Law for Dominant Firm Conduct: The Chicago/Harvard Double Helix' (2007) *Columbia Business Law Review* 1; H Hovenkamp, *The Antitrust Enterprise: Principle and Execution* (Cambridge, Mass, Harvard University Press, 2008) 35–38.

[14] Bork, *The Antitrust Paradox* (n 7) 50; RA Posner, *Antitrust Law*, 2nd edn (Chicago, University of Chicago Press, 2001) ix; F Easterbrook, 'Is There a Ratchet in Antitrust Law?' (1981–82) 60 *Texas Law Review* 705.

[15] See Ch 3.

[16] eg ES Mason, 'Monopoly Law in Law and Economics' (1937–38) 47 *Yale Law Journal* 34 and 'The Current State of the Monopoly Problem in the United States' (1949) 62 *Harvard Law Review* 1265.

[17] RD Blair and DD Sokol, 'Welfare Standards in US and EU Antitrust Enforcement' (2013) 81 *Fordham Law Review* 2497; AJ Meese, 'Debunking the Purchaser Welfare Account of Section 2 of the Sherman Act: How Harvard Brought Us a Total Welfare Standard and Why We Should Keep It' (2010) 85 *New York Law Review* 659; DW Carlton, 'Does Antitrust Need to be Modernized?' (2007) 21 *Journal of Economic Perspectives* 155; P Akman, 'Searching for the Long-Lost Soul of Article 82 EC' (2009) 29 *Oxford Journal of Legal Studies* 267.

[18] See eg Motta, *Competition Policy* (n 11) 22; KG Elzinga, 'The Goals of Antitrust: Other than Competition and Efficiency, What Else Counts?' (1977) 125 *University of Pennsylvania Law Review* 1191. For more conciliatory views, see J Farrell and ML Katz, 'The Economics of Welfare Standards in Antitrust' (2006) *UC Berkeley Competition Policy Center*, available at: www.escholarship.org/uc/item/1tw2d426; and DJ Neven and L-H Röller, 'Consumer Surplus vs. Welfare Standard in a Political Economy Model of Merger Control' (2005) 23 *International Journal of Industrial Organization* 829.

antitrust law these days.[19] Likewise, many members of the Post-Chicago school of thought are proponents of the consumer welfare aim. Post-Chicagoans are critical of many of the Chicago school's key assumptions about market conditions, which they consider overly simplified and unrealistic. In their view, the objective of antitrust law should also not be to enhance general economic welfare, but to protect consumer welfare against the detrimental effects of certain business behaviour. As mentioned previously,[20] it is Robert Bork, the staunch Chicagoan, who is often credited, or discredited, depending on the stance, with having convinced the US Supreme Court to adopt the consumer welfare standard.[21] In his hugely influential work *The Antitrust Paradox*, Bork somewhat misleadingly used the term 'consumer welfare prescription' to describe the legal objective of the Sherman Act,[22] while a closer analysis of his arguments reveals that he actually equated this concept with economic efficiency, ie total surplus.[23]

There are different rationales for the consumer welfare aim and different concepts of consumer welfare. Commonly, proponents of the consumer welfare aim argue that the purpose of antitrust law is to prevent an unfair transfer of wealth, often equated with 'theft', from consumers to the businesses engaging in anticompetitive conduct.[24] Others prefer the consumer surplus standard to the total surplus standard for the very pragmatic reason that it is easier to apply.[25] Like the total welfare standard, the consumer welfare standard has a healthy following in academia. Most of its supporters seem to subscribe to the consumer surplus model,[26] although a number of alternatives have been proposed, including a 'qualified consumer welfare standard'[27] and a 'consumer choice model'.[28]

[19] eg *Brooke Group Ltd v Brown & Williamson Tobacco Corp* 509 U.S. 209, 221 (1993); *NCAA v Board of Regents of the University of Oklahoma*, 468 U.S. 85, 107 (1984) for the US Supreme Court. Likewise, *Broadcom Corp v Qualcomm Inc*, 501 F.3d 297, 308 (2007); *Rebel Oil Company, Inc, Auto Flite Oil Company, Inc v Atlantic Richfield Company* 51 F.3d 1421, 1433 (1995).

[20] See Ch 3, s IV.A.ii.

[21] eg H Hovenkamp, 'Implementing Antitrust's Welfare Goals' (2013) 81 *Fordham Law Review* 2471, 2472; B Orbach, 'The Antitrust Consumer Welfare Paradox' (2010) 7 *Journal of Competition Law & Economics* 133, 134.

[22] Bork (n 7) 66.

[23] See also the epilogue of the reprinted version of 1993: Bork, *The Antitrust Paradox* (New York, Free Press, 1993) 427.

[24] See eg R Lande, 'A Traditional and Textualist Analysis of the Goals of Antitrust: Efficiency, Preventing the Theft from Consumers, and Consumer Choice' (2013) 81 *Fordham Law Review* 2349, in which he disagrees strongly with Bork's analysis in 'Legislative Intent and the Policy of the Sherman Act' (1966) 9 *Journal of Law and Economics* 7.

[25] Hovenkamp, 'Implementing Antitrust's Welfare Goals' (n 21).

[26] JB Kirkwood, 'The Essence of Antitrust: Protecting Consumers and Small Suppliers From Anticompetitive Conduct' (2013) 81 *Fordham Law Review* 2425; SC Salop, 'Question: What Is the Real and Proper Antitrust Welfare Standard—Answer: The True Consumer Welfare Standard' (2009–10) 22 *Loyola Consumer Law Review* 336.

[27] JB Baker, 'Economic and Politics: Perspectives on the Goals and Future of Antitrust' (2013) 81 *Fordham Law Review* 2175.

[28] Most prominently: NW Averitt and RH Lande, 'Using the Consumer Choice Approach to Antitrust Law' (2007) 74 *Antitrust Law Journal* 175.

These days, many commentators take the view that despite the fundamental philosophical differences between the total and the consumer welfare aims the distinction is not all that relevant in practice, and that few if any cases have ever actually turned on the difference.[29] According to the above-mentioned ICN study, a 'vast majority' of the respondent States identified both efficiency and consumer welfare as one of the key objectives or at least intended benefits of their competition laws.[30]

B. Fundamental Constitutional Values: Individual Freedom, Equality of Opportunity, Fairness and Democracy

While economic aims have predominated in the academic debate since the 1980s, this has not always been the case, and even today, not everybody subscribes to the idea that economic welfare, however, defined, should be considered the only objective of antitrust law. An alternative view is that antitrust law (also) aims to protect fundamental constitutional rights and values against the misuse of private economic power. More specifically, proponents of this approach argue that one of its key aims is to protect individual freedom of action, in particular individuals' freedom to participate in the market, and their commercial autonomy against unfair business strategies of economically powerful businesses that use their power to drive out their less powerful opponents, or make it impossible for them to enter the market in the first place. The proponents of this view also often cite the protection of 'fairness' and 'equality of opportunity' as key aims of antitrust law. Finally, there are those who hold that in addition to protecting these key civil freedoms, antitrust law also has a role to play in safeguarding the political system. In their view, the concentration of private economic power in the hands of a few corporate giants is a danger to democratic institutions, especially in times of political stress.

The ordoliberal school of thought is a key proponent of this position. Ordoliberalism was developed by a group of legal and economic scholars at the University of Freiburg in Germany in the early 1930s, around the same time as the Harvard school made its debut in the United States. It is therefore also known as the Freiburg school. Walter Eucken, Leonhard Miksch and Franz Böhm are key names associated with this movement.[31] Their fundamental premise was that individual freedom was an indispensable prerequisite for a democratic, moral, socially just and prosperous society. According to ordoliberals, the protection of the

[29] Hovenkamp (n 21); Blair and Sokol, 'Welfare Standards in US and EU Antitrust Enforcement' (n 17); Motta (n 11) 20.

[30] ICN, Unilateral Conduct Working Group, *Report on the Objectives of Unilateral Conduct Laws* (n 8) 5.

[31] See eg W Eucken, *Die Grundlagen der Nationalökonomie* (Jena, Gustav Fischer, 1940); L Miksch, *Wettbewerb als Aufgabe* (Stuttgart, Kohlhammer, 1937); and F Böhm, *Wettbewerb und Monopolkampf* (Cologne, Carl Heymann, 1933).

individual's freedom of action was therefore the central means of organising society. They believed that the greatest threat to individual freedom emanated from the concentration of power, both in the public and the private sphere. One of the most dangerous forms of private power, in their view, was the concentration of economic power in the hands of cartels or monopolists, which could be used to infiltrate and corrupt the political system.[32] In contrast to many other neo-liberals, ordoliberals therefore argued the necessity of a legal order (hence 'ordo') restraining the exercise of both public and private economic power so as to protect individual freedom. They envisaged a legal framework that would lay down clear and general rules within which businesses could operate. This statutory law was to be embedded in a constitutional framework that clearly established the limits of state intervention in the market.[33] Unlike the Harvard and Chicago schools, which considered economic prosperity the main purpose of competition, ordoliberalism was therefore in many respects a political theory. It defined competition as a state in which the individual was free to exercise his commercial autonomy, and the restraint of 'undue economic power' was a particular focus of the system.[34]

Ordoliberalism was very much a child of its time and place. The scholars at the University of Freiburg were greatly influenced by two key events: the global economic crisis of the 1920s and the demise of the Weimar Republic, both of which they had experienced first-hand. In their view, cartelisation and the resulting concentration of economic power had significantly contributed to both of these events, confirming their belief that it was a key responsibility of the State to protect society against the misuse of such power.[35]

Although not currently the most fashionable school of thought, ordoliberalism deserves mentioning alongside the more prevalent Harvard, Chicago and Post-Chicago schools as many of its concepts can be spotted in the Commission's early antitrust policy. While ordoliberal ideas were not compatible with the

[32] W Eucken, 'Staatliche Strukturwandlungen und die Krisis des Kapitalismus' (1932) 84 *Weltwirtschaftliches Archiv* 297.

[33] W Eucken, '*Die Wettbewerbsordnung und ihre Verwirklichung*' (1949) 2 *ORDO* 1. To this day, the economic constitution remains an important notion of German public law. See eg W Frotscher, *Wirtschaftsverfassungs- und Wirtschaftsverwaltungsrecht* (Munich, Beck, 2008); P Badura, *Wirtschaftsverfassung und Wirtschaftsverwaltung* (Tübingen, Mohr Siebeck, 2008).

[34] F Böhm, 'Das Problem der privaten Macht—Ein Beitrag zur Monopolfrage' (1928) 3 *Die Justiz*, reprinted in H-J Mestmäcker, *Franz Böhm—Reden und Schriften* (Karlsruhe, CF Müller, 1960) 25; see also M Streit and M Wohlgemuth, 'Walter Eucken und Friedrich A. von Hayek: Initiatorien der Ordnungsökonomik' *Max-Planck-Institut zur Erforschung von Wirtschaftssystemen Discussion Paper* No 9911 (1999); C Ahlborn and C Grave, 'Walter Eucken and Ordoliberalism: An Introduction from a Consumer Welfare Perspective' (2006) 2(2) *Competition Policy International*; W Möschel, 'Competition Policy from an Ordo Point of View' in A Peacock and H Willgerodt (eds), *German Neo-Liberals and the Social Market Economy* (London, Palgrave MacMillan, 1989) 146.

[35] W Eucken, *Grundlagen der Nationalökonomik*, 9th edn (Berlin, Springer, 1989) 196 ff. Eucken went further than most ordoliberals and argued, after the war, that the State not only had the obligation to fight the misuse of economic power but to combat its very existence by breaking up powerful corporations (Eucken, *Konzernentflechtung und Kartellauflösung* (Freiburg, 1947)).

political and economic ideologies of the Nazi regime,[36] many of its key members continued their discussions and work on a liberal political and economic model for a post-war/post-Nazi Germany underground.[37] In the post-war period, they rejoined the international neo-liberal academic circle. Many were also appointed to key positions in the new German government and their ideas became very influential in German post-war law and politics.[38] They formed the intellectual basis for post-war Germany's concept of 'social market economy' adopted and implemented by the first post-war Minister of Economics, Ludwig Erhard, even though Erhard later distanced himself from some of their views.[39] Erhard did, however, see eye to eye with the Freiburg Circle on matters of competition and the necessity of protecting the economy against cartelisation. Ordoliberal thought therefore played a decisive role in shaping the first German post-war antitrust statute from 1957.[40]

By the same token, ordoliberalism also influenced the early EU antitrust law and policy. Germany played an instrumental role in creating the Union's competition rules, and also took a leading role in developing their interpretation and enforcement during the early years of the Union. Many members of the German delegation negotiating the Community Treaties were closely associated with or at least strongly influenced by the ordoliberal school. Alfred Müller Armack, a high-ranking civil servant in Erhard's Ministry of Economic Affairs, was head of the German delegation negotiating the EEC Treaty. Although not an ordoliberal in the strict sense of the term, he was influenced by many of its fundamental ideas.[41] His deputy, Hans von der Groeben, also from the German Ministry of Economic Affairs and one of the authors of the Spaak Report,[42] chaired the working group

[36] See eg N Goldschmidt, 'Die Entstehung der Freiburger Kreise' (1997) 4 *Historisch-Politische Mitteilungen* 1.

[37] C Blumenberg-Lampe, *Das wirtschaftspolitische Programm der 'Freiburger Kreise'* (Berlin, Duncker & Humblot 1973); H Peukert, 'Die wirtschafts- und sozialpolitischen Zielsetzungen der Freiburger Kreises' in N Goldschmidt (ed), *Wirtschaft, Politik und Freiheit* (Tübingen, Mohr Siebeck, 2005) 267–87.

[38] See eg B Löffler, 'Soziale Marktwirtschaft und administrative Praxis: das Bundeswirtschaftsministerium unter Ludwig Erhard' (2003) 162 *Vierteljahrschrift für Sozial- und Wirtschaftsgeschichte* 72 ff.

[39] See eg VR Berghahn, 'Ludwig Erhard, die Freiburger Schule und das "Amerikanische Jahrhundert"' (2010) *Freiburger Diskussionspapiere zur Ordnungsökonomik* 10/1; R Klump, 'Der Beitrag der Freiburger Kreise zum Konzept der Sozialen Marktwirtschaft' in Goldschmidt (ed), *Wirtschaft, Politik und Freiheit* (n 37) 383–401.

[40] Gesetz gegen Wettbewerbsbeschränkungen (GWB) of 27 July 1957, BGBl I 1081. The US occupational forces had made the enactment of such an anti-cartel legislation a precondition for Germany regaining its sovereignty. For a history of the beginnings of postwar German competition law in English language, see DJ Gerber, *Law and Competition in Twentieth Century Europe* (Oxford, Clarendon Press, 1998) 266 ff; H Buch-Hansen and A Wigger, *The Politics of European Competition Regulation* (Abingdon, Routledge, 2011) 31 ff.

[41] Löffler, 'Soziale Marktwirtschaft und administrative Praxis' (n 38) 75.

[42] Intergovernmental Committee of the Messina Conference, Report by the Heads of Delegations to the Foreign Ministers (Spaak Report) of 21 April 1956. This document constituted the basis for negotiating the Treaty establishing the European Economic Community.

charged with drafting the EEC Treaty's competition rules. Walter Hallstein, a German law professor and close friend of Franz Böhm, was later appointed the first president of the European Commission, and under his presidency, von der Groeben became the EEC's first Commissioner for Competition Policy. Moreover, all Directors General of DG Competition up until 2010 had been German lawyers.[43]

This is not to say that the objectives of individual freedom, democracy and fairness are exclusive to ordoliberalism. Commentators outside of this school of thought, on both sides of the Atlantic, have argued and continue to argue that at least one of the objectives of antitrust law is to protect the political system and/or individual economic freedom.[44] The above-mentioned ICN study on the goals of antitrust law from 2007 reveals that 13 out of 35 respondent competition enforcement agencies identified the protection of economic freedom as an objective of their competition laws.[45] Seven agencies recognised the aim of ensuring a level playing field for small and medium size enterprises,[46] and six agencies cited 'fairness and equality' as an objective of their antitrust regime.[47] Only one State mentioned the connection between competition and the democratic system.[48]

C. Other Aims

The enhancement of economic welfare and the protection of individual freedom and democracy are the key rationales advanced for why competition should be protected. Most other legal objectives proposed in the literature tend to be variations upon this theme. Instead of economic welfare in the sense of total or consumer surplus it has, for example, been suggested that a country's economic

[43] See Ch 2, s IV.

[44] D Millon, The Sherman Act and the Balance of Power (1987–88) 61 *Southern California Law Review* 1219; R Pitofsky, 'The Political Content of Antitrust' (1979) 127 *University of Pennsylvania Law Review* 1051; L Schwartz, '"Justice" and Other Non-Economic Goals of Antitrust' (1979) 127 *University of Pennsylvania Law Review* 1076; more recently: L Lovdahl Gormsen, *A Principled Approach to Abuse of Dominance in European Competition Law* (Cambridge, Cambridge University Press, 2013) 84–112; ME Stucke, 'Reconsidering Antitrust's Goals' (2012) 53 *Boston College Law Review* 551; VJ Vanberg, 'Consumer Welfare, Total Welfare and Economic Freedom—on the Normative Foundations of Competition Policy' in J Drexl, W Kerber, R Podszun (eds), *Competition Policy and the Economic Approach—Foundations and Limitations* (Cheltenham, Edward Elgar, 2011) 44; E-J Mestmäcker, 'Die Interdependenz von Recht und Ökonomie in der Wettbewerbspolitik' in Monopolkommission (ed), *Zukunftsperspektiven der Wettbewerbspolitik* (Baden-Baden, Nomos, 2005) 19–35.

[45] ICN, Unilateral Conduct Working Group (n 8) 14.

[46] ibid, 17.

[47] ibid, 18.

[48] The Israeli Antitrust Authority's response included the statement that 'free competition is a basic pillar of any democratic regime, being a prominent characteristic of the individual's freedom to implement his autonomy'; ibid, 15.

growth (or 'productivity growth') would be a better objective.[49] Many States also consider the promotion of 'international competitiveness' (ie the strengthening of national enterprises vis-à-vis foreign competitors) an objective of their national competition laws,[50] although this is not an objective that is commonly advocated in academia.

A wide variety of other policy objectives are also often thrown into the pot when discussing the objectives of antitrust law. This is, for one, because competition is deemed capable of indirectly contributing to the realisation of many other benefits. For example, effective competition has been linked to social justice and even environmental protection.[51] Effective competition is also said to result in a 'better use of labour', which in turn is deemed to lead to an adequate payment of skilled workers.[52] This does not mean that achieving these benefits is considered the legal purpose of antitrust law. They are generally deemed welcome side effects, or bonuses, but not the primary reason for protecting competition.

The second reason why 'other' objectives often enter the goals debate is that there are situations in which the goals of antitrust law, be they defined in terms of economic welfare or individual freedom, clash with other legitimate policy aims. For example, a specific instance of business conduct may restrict competition, but at the same time result in environmental benefits or create jobs. Economic welfare and the protection of individual freedom are not the only objectives pursued by governmental bodies. The question therefore arises whether the restriction of competition should be allowed in the interest of realising the other benefit. However, taking environmental or social concern into account when deciding whether to make an exception from the prohibition of anticompetitive conduct does not necessarily mean that one considers environmental or social protection an objective of antitrust law, let alone its primary objective. It is usually considered under the aspect of balancing conflicting policy goals, for example by means of an objective justification or other form of derogation.

In sum, it remains that the two categories of legal antitrust objectives most commonly advocated in the literature and recognised by jurisdictions are the enhancement of economic welfare on the one side and the protection of individual freedom on the other.

[49] ME Porter, 'Competition and Antitrust: A Productivity-Based Approach to Evaluating Mergers and Joint Ventures' (2001) 46 *Antitrust Bulletin* 919.

[50] ICN, Unilateral Conduct Working Group (n 8) 20.

[51] In 2007, the then Commissioner for Competition, Neelie Kroes, stated: 'Free competition is not an end in itself—it is a means to an end. When we strive to get markets working better, it is because competitive markets provide citizens with better goods and better services, at better prices. Competitive markets provide the right conditions for companies to innovate and prosper, and so to increase overall European wealth. More wealth means more money for governments to use to sustain the fabric of our societies and to guarantee social justice and a high-quality environment for generations to come'; European Commission, *Report on Competition Policy 2006*, 3.

[52] European Commission, *First Report on Competition Policy 1971*, 11.

D. One Aim or Several Aims?

One last theoretical issue remains to be addressed. Should the legal objective of antitrust law be limited to one aim or can it accommodate several aims? Opinions are divided on this matter. Most proponents of a total welfare aim are adamant that economic welfare should be the exclusive aim of antitrust law.[53] On the other hand, those who consider that political and societal aims should be taken into account rarely dispute that economic aims are also relevant. They tend to take the view that the objectives of antitrust law should not be narrowed down to one single aim, but that the law could and should pursue a multitude of legitimate policy aims.[54] Whereas the first position makes for a clear and relatively straightforward interpretation of key legal concepts, the latter position requires further reflection. Should all of the relevant aims be of equal standing or should there be a hierarchy amongst them? The answer to this question is relevant when it comes to defining what constitutes competitive harm, as it is imaginable that one and the same conduct could have positive consequences for one aim but detrimental effects on another.

Before this theoretical background, the following examines the European Commission's understanding of the legal objectives of EU antitrust law. It begins with the period predating the more economic approach. The subsequent section looks at the period after the introduction of the more economic approach from 1999 onwards.

IV. The Commission's Understanding of the EU Antitrust Rules' Legal Objective Prior to the More Economic Approach

In preparation of this analysis, it makes sense to take a quick look at the prohibition provisions of EU antitrust law themselves and to examine whether they define or at least give any guidance as to their legal objective.

[53] Amongst many others: RH Bork, *The Antitrust Paradox* (New York, Basic Books, 1978) 50; Posner, *Antitrust Law* (n 14) ix; O Odudu, 'The Wider Concerns of Competition Law' (2010) 30 *Oxford Journal of Legal Studies* 599. For a somewhat more accommodating position, see KG Elzinga, 'The Goals of Antitrust: Other Than Competition and Efficiency, What Else Counts?' (1977) 125 *University of Pennsylvania Law Review* 1191.

[54] Pitofsky, 'The Political Content of Antitrust' (n 44); TE Kauper, 'The "Warren Court" and the Antitrust Laws: Of Economics, Populism, and Cynicism' (1968–69) 67 *Michigan Law Review* 325; Stucke, 'Reconsidering Antitrust's Goals' (n 44); B van Rompuy, 'Economic Efficiency: The Sole Concern of Modern Antitrust Policy? Non-Efficiency Considerations under Article 101 TFEU' (Alphen aan den Rijn, Kluwer, 2012); C Townley, *Article 81 EC and Public Policy* (Oxford, Hart Publishing, 2009); Lovdahl Gormsen, *A Principled Approach to Abuse of Dominance in European Competition Law* (n 44).

A. The Legal Provisions

The relevant prohibition provisions for the time predating the advent of the more economic approach are the two Treaty provisions now known as Articles 101 and 102 and Regulation (EEC) No 4064/89 on the control of concentrations, commonly known as the first Merger Regulation.[55] One brief look at Articles 101 and 102 dashes any hope one may have had of finding a precise definition of their purpose. Both provisions outlaw specific types of conduct in general terms, ie agreements that restrict competition and abuses of a dominant position, and give examples of behaviour that are deemed to amount to such conduct. However, neither provision explains the ultimate rationale for prohibiting these types of business behaviour, other than implying that they are bad for competition.

In comparison, Regulation 4064/89 was a little more expansive on the issue. The Council enacted the Regulation in 1989 to complete the Treaties' anti-trust system, which does not provide a system for *ex ante* merger control. The Regulation entered into force in 1990, and was replaced by Regulation (EC) No 139/2004, the current EU Merger Regulation, in 2004.[56] As a piece of secondary EU legislation, Regulation 4064/89 was longer and more detailed than the two Treaty provisions. While its legally binding provisions did not define the objectives of merger control, its recitals at least touched on the issue.[57]

According to the recitals of the first Merger Regulation, the Council pursued the aim of 'instituting a system ensuring that competition in the common market is not distorted' when enacting this piece of legislation. This is a verbatim replica of one of the original Community policies enshrined in ex Article 3 EEC/EC.[58] The Regulation's recitals explained that this objective was essential for the achievement of the common market, and stated that the Council considered it necessary to ensure that concentrations did not result in 'lasting damage to competition'. As the Treaty provisions themselves were insufficient to cover all operations that jeopardised the system of undistorted competition, it was necessary to create this new legal instrument to permit effective monitoring of all concentrations from the point of view of their 'effect on the structure of competition.' The recitals finally also stated that the Commission was to assess whether concentrations were compatible with the common market from the point of view of the need to preserve and develop effective competition, and that it was to place this appraisal within

[55] Council Regulation (EEC) No 4064/89 on the control of concentrations between undertakings [1989] OJ L395/1.

[56] Council Regulation (EC) No 139/2004 of 20 January 2004 on the control of concentrations between undertakings (the EC Merger Regulation) [2004] OJ L24/1.

[57] The purpose of a Regulation's recitals is to set out its legal basis the reasons for which it was enacted. This obligation follows from TFEU, Art 296(2). While recitals are not legally binding, they are important interpretative tools.

[58] Ex Art 3(f)EEC/3(g)EC. The Treaty of Lisbon removed this objective from the main body of the Treaty, and relegated it to Protocol 27 of the Treaty of Lisbon [2010] OJ C83/309.

the general framework of fundamental objectives listed in Article 2 of the Treaty as well as the aim of strengthening the Community's economic and social cohesion laid down in Article 130a EEC.[59]

While these explanations are neither particularly concise nor clear, they allow a number of conclusions. The immediate goal of Regulation 4064/89 was defined as the protection of competition and in particular its structure. While the recitals did not exhaustively define the underlying rationale for protecting competition, they explained that the protection of competition was at least crucial for achieving the Treaty's aim of creating and safeguarding the common market. In fact, the very way in which the merger prohibition of Regulation 4064/89 was worded suggests that the aim of market integration was a key objective of merger control: Article 2(3) prohibited anticompetitive concentrations on the grounds that they were incompatible with the common market.[60] However, the objective of market integration was not the only aim that the Commission was to take into account when assessing the legality of mergers. According to the recitals, the Commission was to consider all of the fundamental Treaty objectives when assessing the compatibility of a concentration with the common market. When the Council enacted the original Merger Regulation in 1989, the fundamental objectives listed in Article 2 EEC were: the establishment of a common market; the approximation of the economic policies of Member States; the promotion of a harmonious development of economic activities; a continuous and balanced expansion; an increase in stability; an accelerated raising of the standard of living; and closer relations between the States belonging to it. Article 130a EEC added the objective of strengthening the Union's economic and social cohesion, in particular by reducing the disparities between the various regions and the backwardness of the least-favoured regions. In 1992, the Treaty of Maastricht added several more objectives to Article 2, including a number of non-economic policy aims, such as the respect of the environment; a high level of employment and of social protection; the raising of the standard of living and the quality of life; and solidarity between Member States.[61]

In sum, while Articles 101 and 102 were silent on their objectives beyond the general message that their aim was to protect competition, the first Merger Regulation provided a few more clues as to the Council's understanding of the purpose of merger control. It especially emphasised the aim of market integration, but considered all of the other fundamental Treaty objectives relevant as well. Interestingly, the recitals did not even mention consumer welfare or any other type of economic welfare. The question therefore arises what the Commission, as the main enforcement body, made of these open-ended prohibition provisions

[59] This aim is now included in the general provision of TEU, Art 3.

[60] Regulation 4064/89, Art 2(3) read: 'A concentration which creates or strengthens a dominant position as a result of which effective competition would be significantly impeded in the common market or in a substantial part of it shall be declared incompatible with the common market'.

[61] TEU, Art 3, as signed in Maastricht on 7 February 1992.

and Regulation 4064/89's vague guidance on the objectives of EU antitrust law in practice.

B. The Commission's Understanding

The Commission enacted a great number of legal and non-legal enforcement instruments during the first 40 years of EU antitrust law, including individual decisions, Regulations and diverse soft law instruments. An analysis of these acts reveals an incoherent and not particularly well-thought-out understanding of the aims of EU antitrust law.

i. Legally Binding Commission Acts

The Commission's legally binding enforcement instruments of the first 40 years rarely made any mention of the aims they sought to achieve. Its individual decisions, for example, usually did not elaborate on the goals of the prohibition provision on which they were based. The Commission's decision *ECS/AKZO*[62] is a rare exception to this rule. In this case from 1985, the Commission was confronted with the question of when below-cost pricing should be considered abusive within the meaning of Article 102. As part of its assessment, it briefly considered whether the so-called 'Areeda and Turner' test, which informed the predatory pricing test of US antitrust law, would also be suitable for EU antitrust law.[63] It concluded that this was not the case, because the Areeda and Turner test was based on the premise that efficiency was the exclusive aim of antitrust law. According to the Commission, the objectives of EU antitrust law were broader than mere efficiency and also included the aim of protecting the 'structure of competition'.[64]

The other legal instruments enacted by the Commission in its enforcement practice during this period are mostly inconclusive as to their underlying objectives. Prior to the introduction of the more economic approach, the Commission enacted a great number of sector- and contract-specific Block Exemption Regulations to facilitate the enforcement of Article 101. Block Exemption Regulations transfer the benefits of Article 101(3) *en bloc* on entire categories of agreements. This tool was particularly useful at a time when the exemption in Article 101(3) did not apply automatically but had to be expressly granted by the Commission.[65] Like any Regulation, Block Exemption Regulations need to explain their legal basis and the reasons for which they are enacted. The early Block Exemption Regulations' recitals indeed duly explained the rationale for

[62] *ECS/AKZO* (Case IV/30.698) [1985] L374/1.
[63] ibid, recital 75.
[64] ibid, recital 77.
[65] This authorisation system, set up in 1962 by Regulation No 17 [1962] OJ 13/204, was abolished on 1 May 2004 by Council Regulation (EC) No 1/2003 [2003] OJ L1/1.

conferring the effect of Article 101(3) on specific types of contract insofar as they elaborated on why the Commission considered the relevant categories of contract particularly likely to meet the requirements of Article 101(3).[66] However, while indicating that the purpose of Article 101 was to protect competition against distortion, they did not touch on the ultimate rationale for protecting competition. Incidentally, the enabling Council Regulations, from which the Commission derived the power to enact the individual Block Exemption Regulations, were equally silent on the objectives of Article 101.[67]

ii. Commission Notices

The Commission Notices of the first 40 years were no clearer. Guidelines and other forms of soft law instruments really started to proliferate in the late 1990s and have since become key instruments in the Commission's enforcement practice. However, even during the early years of EU antitrust law, the Commission occasionally made use of legally non-binding Communications to explain how it intended to apply certain legal concepts in practice. In 1962, for example, it published two highly specific Notices that explained under what circumstances the Commission considered exclusive dealing contracts with commercial agents and patent licence agreements to contravene Article 101(1).[68] In 1968, it published the first general Notice on the application of 101(1).[69] This Notice was replaced two years later by the first *de minimis* Notice,[70] which integrated the Court's ruling in *Völk v Vervaecke*[71] on agreements of minor importance into the previous Notice.

[66] eg Commission Regulation (EEC) No 1983/83 on the application of Article 85(3) of the Treaty to categories of exclusive distribution agreements [1983] OJ L 173/1, recitals 1–15; Commission Regulation (EEC) No 1984/83 on the application of Article 85(3) of the Treaty to categories of exclusive purchasing agreements [1983] OJ L173/5, recitals 1–23; Commission Regulation (EEC) No 4087/88 on the application of Article 85(3) of the Treaty to categories of franchise agreements [1988] OJ L359/46, recitals 1–17; or Regulation (EEC) No 2779/72 on the application of Article 85(3) of the Treaty to categories of specialization agreements [1972] OJ L292/23.

[67] See eg Council Regulation (EEC) No 19/65 on application of Article 85(3) of the Treaty to certain categories of agreements and concerted practices [1965] OJ L36/533 and Council Regulation (EEC) No 2821/71 on application of Article 85(3) of the Treaty to categories of agreements, decisions and concerted practices [1971] OJ L285/46.

[68] European Commission, Bekanntmachung über Alleinvertriebsverträge mit Handelsvertretern [1962] OJ C113/2921; Bekanntmachung über Patentlizenzverträge [1962] OJ C113/2922 (no English versions available).

[69] European Commission, Bekanntmachung über Vereinbarungen, Beschlüsse und aufeinander abgestimmte Verhaltensweisen, die eine zwischenbetriebliche Zusammenarbeit betreffen [1968] OJ C75/3 (no English version available).

[70] The first *de minimis* Notice dates from 17 May 1970 (Bekanntmachung der Kommission vom 27. Mai 1970 über Vereinbarungen, Beschlüsse und aufeinander abgestimmte Verhaltensweisen von geringer Bedeutung [1970] OJ C64/1—English version not available), which was subsequently revised repeatedly (Commission Notices concerning agreements of minor importance of 19 December 1977 [1977] OJ C 313/3, of 3 September [1986] OJ C 231/2, of 19 December 1997 [1997] OJ C 372/13, of 22 December 2001 [2001] OJ C368/13). The current version dates from 30 August 2014 (Notice on agreements of minor importance which do not appreciably restrict competition under Article 101(1) of the Treaty on the Functioning of the European Union (De Minimis Notice) [2014] OJ C291/1).

[71] Case 5/69 *Völk v Vervaecke* ECLI:EU:C:1969:35.

It would have made sense to start this type of Notice by defining the purpose of Article 101(1) and developing a general rationale for when an agreement should be considered contrary to Article 101(1) based on this legal objective. However, none of these early Notices touched on the provision's objective. Instead they focused entirely on spelling out specific rules of thumb and presumptions of legality for different types of contractual clauses. The situation is the same for the other substantive Commission Notices from this early era.[72] They contained highly specific lists of acceptable and inacceptable conduct, but rarely touched on the general purpose of the rule in question. The 1991 guidelines on the application of the antitrust rules in the telecommunications sector, dating back to a time in which this sector was first being opened to competition, were an exception to this rule, insofar as they stated that the competition rules were essential for completing the internal market, and that their purpose was to allow the Commission to stop States or private undertakings from building or maintaining 'artificial barriers incompatible with the single market'.[73]

iii. The Annual Reports on Competition Policy

The Commission's Annual Reports on Competition Policy, by contrast, were much more effusive on the issue of the antitrust rules' objective. The purpose of these Reports is for the Commission to explain the main developments and cases of competition policy to the other institutions, the Member States as well as industry at large and the general public.[74] While they are not legally binding instruments, they provide insight into the policy considerations guiding the Commission's enforcement practice. In particular the first separate Report on Competition Policy from 1971[75] and the Reports dating from times of economic crisis explained the Commission's rationale for applying the EU antitrust rules in some detail. The latter is explained by the fact that in times of recession, antitrust agencies tend to come under considerable political pressure from the business community to relax the enforcement of the antitrust rules, and hence feel compelled to explain the reasons for continuing to do so.

[72] eg European Commission, Bekanntmachung über Alleinvertriebsverträge mit Handelsvertretern (n 68); Bekanntmachung über Patentlizenzverträge (n 68); Commission Notice of 18 December 1978 concerning its assessment of certain subcontracting agreements in relation to Article 85(1) of the EEC Treaty [1979] OJ C1/2; Notice concerning Commission Regulations (EEC) No 1983/83 and (EEC) No 1984/83 of 22 June 1983 on the application of Article 85(3) of the Treaty to categories of exclusive distribution and exclusive purchasing agreements [1984] OJ C101/2; Notice on the definition of relevant market for the purposes of Community competition law [1997] OJ C372/5. Likewise, in the area of merger control: Notice regarding restrictions ancillary to concentrations [1990] OJ C 203/5, Notice regarding the concentrative and cooperative operations under Council Regulation (EEC) No 4064/89 [1990] OJ C203/10.

[73] European Commission, Guidelines on the application of EEC competition rules in the telecommunications sector [1991] OJ C 233/2, ss I.2., II.4 and 5.

[74] European Commission, *Twenty-third Report on Competition Policy 1993*, 13.

[75] European Commission, *First Report on Competition Policy 1971*, 11.

One could therefore assume that it would be relatively easy to gain a clear picture of the Commission's understanding of the objectives of EU antitrust law during this early period. Unfortunately, it is not all that straightforward. A number of problems arise. First, the Reports' explanations on the aims of the EU competition rules rarely distinguish clearly between the antitrust rules and the State aid rules. They therefore need to be read with a degree of caution, and the following will only take into account those statements that clearly relate to the aims of the EU competition rules addressed to undertakings. Second, it is not always possible to say with certainty whether a report is describing an objective of EU antitrust law or whether it is simply pointing out an additional benefit of competition that also makes the antitrust rules worth enforcing. Third, despite the great number of references to the aims and benefits of antitrust law, the Commission did not use a consistent formula. Different Reports name different objectives. More often than not, they list several objectives. And while their explanations are often long and elaborate, they are rarely models of clarity and concision.

For example, the Ninth Report on Competition Policy (1979) unequivocally identified three basic objectives of European antitrust policy: (1) to keep the common market open and unified; (2) to ensure that at all stages of the common market's development there exists the right amount of competition in order for the Treaty's requirements to be met and its aims attained; and (3) to ensure that the conditions under which competition takes place remain subject to the principle of fairness.[76] Two years later, the Eleventh Report on Competition (1981) stated, just as unequivocally, that the purpose of competition was to ensure that available resources were allocated to the most productive sectors, to stimulate firms to make use of their know-how and skills and to encourage them to invent, develop and exploit efficiently new techniques and new products.[77] These two definitions could hardly be any more different.

Before this background, the following identifies a number of recurring values that the Commission regularly referred to as objectives of EU antitrust law and policy in its Annual Reports between 1967 and 1998.

a. The Internal Market

The aim of market integration appears in the Commission's Reports on Competition Policy from their earliest days. The first Report on Competition Policy (1971) explained that the Commission's primary purpose in applying the antitrust rules was to prevent governmental restrictions and barriers to trade, which had been outlawed by the Treaty's free movement rules, from being replaced by similar

[76] European Commission, *Ninth Report on Competition Policy 1979*, 9 and 10.
[77] European Commission, *Eleventh Report on Competition Policy 1981*, 11.

measures of a private nature. Agreements on quotas and agreements that aimed to divide the common market by regions or other means were therefore in flagrant contradiction to the provisions of the Treaties.[78] While the internal market aim featured as a key purpose of EU antitrust law throughout the Commission's Annual Reports prior to the introduction of the more economic approach, it is possible to make out a shift of focus in the mid-1980s. Whereas the Reports of the 1970s typically referred to the antitrust rules' role in achieving the aim of market integration first and described it as the very basis of the Commission's antitrust policy,[79] the Reports of the 1980s and 1990s tended to place the emphasis on other objectives and referred to the objective of market integration last.[80] Nonetheless, the aim of market integration remained a valid objective of EU antitrust law throughout the first 40 years. It was in fact one of the few constants in the Commission's perception of the law's objectives.

b. Preventing the Concentration of Economic Power

The Reports of the 1970s and 1980s also frequently stated that one of the Commission's key objectives in enforcing the antitrust rules was to prevent the concentration of economic power.[81] To this end, the Commission regularly argued in favour of the creation of a separate legal basis that would allow it to exercise *ex ante* merger control, as it did not consider Articles 101 and 102 sufficient to enable it to stop undertakings from becoming too powerful.[82] In meantime, it proposed to assist small and medium-sized undertakings so that they could compete more effectively with bigger undertakings, in particular by exempting anticompetitive agreements between small and medium-sized enterprises, which would allow them to stand up to their bigger competitors.[83]

While there is therefore ample evidence that the Commission considered the concentration of economic power dangerous, it is not entirely clear what type of harm the Commission was expecting economically powerful undertakings to cause. The Fifth Report on Competition Policy (1975) explained that a decentralised structure of the market economy needed to be safeguarded so that competition could 'do its job of guiding and stimulating the economy'.[84] The Seventh

[78] European Commission, *First Report on Competition Policy 1971*, 11.

[79] See eg European Commission, *First Report on Competition Policy 1971*, 11; *Second Report on Competition Policy 1972*, 15; *Sixth Report on Competition Policy 1976*, 9; *Eighth Report on Competition Policy 1978*, p. 9; *Ninth Report on Competition Policy 1979*, 9.

[80] European Commission, *Twelfth Report on Competition 1982*, 12; *Thirteenth Report on Competition Policy 1983*, 11; *Twenty-second Report on Competition Policy 1992*, 19; *Twenty-fifth Report on Competition Policy 1995*, 15.

[81] European Commission, *Fifth Report on Competition Policy 1975*, 13; *Seventh Report on Competition Policy 1977*, 10.

[82] This proved to be a long battle, and it was not until 1989 that the Council finally enacted Regulation (EEC) No 4064/89.

[83] European Commission, *First Report on Competition Policy 1971*, 16; *Eleventh Report on Competition Policy 1981*, 14.

[84] European Commission, *Fifth Report on Competition Policy 1975*, 13.

Report (1977) argued that the existence of a healthy and strongly developed sector of small and medium-sized firms was a condition for the 'smooth functioning of a modern economy'.[85] The Ninth Report (1979) stated that an excessive concentration of economic, financial and commercial power could produce such far-reaching structural changes that free competition was no longer able to fulfil its role as an 'effective regulator of economic activity' and that competition policy had to ensure that there was the right amount of competition 'in order for the Treaty's requirements to be met and its aims attained'.[86] The Twelfth Report (1982) explained that the 'economic fabric woven by such smaller businesses' could make a significant contribution towards adapting the European economy to the constraints of the world market, and consequently to improving its competitiveness and safeguarding employment.[87] These statements offer a number of different reasons for fighting the concentration of economic power: the guidance and stimulation of the economy; the smooth functioning of a modern economy; the effective regulation of economic activity; the attainment of the Treaties' aims; the adaptability and competitiveness of the European economy, as well as employment. Many of the aforementioned concepts are really rather ambiguous. Interestingly, protecting consumer welfare is not cited as a rationale for fighting the concentration of economic power.

c. Economic Growth

Another aim that featured occasionally in the Commission's Annual Reports was the growth of the European economy. The Twenty-third Report on Competition Policy (1993), for example, explained that the stimulation of growth had always been 'one of the raisons d'être of competition policy'.[88]

d. Industrial Adaptability

During the recession of the 1970s and early 1980s, in particular, the Commission's Annual Reports regularly stressed that it was the function of antitrust policy to enhance the ability of industry to adapt to changing economic conditions. The Fifth Report on Competition Policy (1975), for example, stated that the function of antitrust policy was to preserve a situation in which the structural changes that were needed could take place.[89] Other Reports explained that the prohibition of entering into structural crisis cartels increased 'businessmen's capacities

[85] European Commission, *Seventh Report on Competition Policy 1977*, 10.

[86] European Commission, *Ninth Report on Competition Policy 1979*, 10.

[87] European Commission, *Twelfth Report on Competition 1982*, 13.

[88] European Commission, *Twenty-third Report on Competition Policy 1993*, 22. Likewise *Twenty-fifth Report on Competition Policy 1995*, 7.

[89] European Commission, *Fifth Report on Competition Policy 1975*, 7. Likewise *Seventh Report on Competition Policy 1977*, 9; *Twenty-fifth Report on Competition Policy 1995*, 15; *Twenty-sixth Report on Competition Policy 1996*, 7.

for adjustment'[90] and encouraged adaptation of industrial structures away from defunct to new, profitable sectors.[91] Competition policy measures consequently had to be analysed in terms of their effects both on economic sectors as a whole and on individual operators therein.[92]

e. Fighting Inflation

The Reports of the 1970s, somewhat surprisingly, also regularly emphasised the role of the antitrust rules as 'a means of fighting inflation' by prohibiting and punishing additional price increases that were the result of anticompetitive agreements.[93] The First Report on Competition Policy (1971) explained that inflation had to be fought because it was a 'structural obstacle to adaptation'.[94] Generally, the Reports suggest that the Commission was primarily concerned with fighting inflation because it was holding back economic recovery rather than because of its effects on consumers.

f. 'Competitiveness' of the European Economy

Safeguarding the 'competitiveness' of the European economy is a goal often found in the Reports of the 1980s. By 'competitiveness', these Reports meant the ability of European businesses to stand up to competition from outside the internal market.[95] It was an important function of the antitrust rules to ensure that European companies remained able to compete internationally.

g. Consumer Interests

Many Reports also cited 'consumer interests' as a rationale for protecting competition. The Commission's First Report on Competition Policy (1971), for example, explained that competition policy encouraged the best possible use of productive resources for the greatest possible benefit of the economy as a whole and for the benefit, in particular, of consumers.[96] Interestingly, however, the benefit of consumers generally did not take a prominent place in the narrative of these early Reports and was never portrayed as a key goal of EU antitrust policy. In the Fifteenth Report on Competition Policy (1985) the Commission in fact went to great lengths to explain why, in in its view, a vigorous competition policy, which played a key role in the Commission's overall strategy for dynamic economic development

[90] European Commission, *Twelfth Report on Competition Policy 1982*, 12.
[91] ibid, 9.
[92] European Commission, *Eleventh Report on Competition Policy 1981*, 11.
[93] European Commission, *First Report on Competition Policy 1971*, 11; *Second Report on Competition Policy 1972*, 9; *Third Report on Competition Policy 1973*, 26; *Fifth Report on Competition Policy 1975*, 13.
[94] European Commission, *First Report on Competition Policy 1971*, 11.
[95] European Commission, *Twelfth Report on Competition 1982*, 13; *Thirteenth Report on Competition Policy 1983*, 11.
[96] European Commission, *First Report on Competition Policy 1971*, 11; likewise, *Twelfth Report on Competition Policy 1982*, 12.

(ie prosperity and employment) was 'also ultimately' in the interest of the consumer. The Commission argued that in situations where there was little or no competition, consumers could be faced with inferior or outdated products, a limited choice, high prices or sub-standard service. Therefore, 'aside from the beneficial effects of competition as such' the enforcement of the competition rules 'also' brought direct, tangible benefits for the consumer in practice. The Report concluded that competition and competition policy were therefore clearly relevant to the man in the street.[97] One can gather from these extensive explanations that the Commission did not consider the connection between competition and the welfare of consumers self-evident in the 1980s. The other Reports from this time that mention consumer interests at all likewise portray competition's positive effects on consumers as a bonus rather than as the primary objective of antitrust policy.[98]

h. The Interests of Society as a Whole

Other Reports defined the aim of antitrust law as the protection of society in general. The Twenty-fourth Report on Competition Policy (1994), for instance, explained that the Commission pursued cartels because these did serious harm to 'public well-being by depriving society of the benefits of an open and competitive single market', and because the advantages stemming from an optimum use of the means of production were usurped by the cartel members rather than being 'redistributed to society as a whole' and benefiting 'general development'.[99]

i. Fairness

Another objective occasionally cited in the Commission's Annual Reports was the preservation of fairness in the marketplace. This objective did not take a prominent place in the Commission's Reports, and was rarely discussed in isolation from other principles. Nonetheless, it is a concept that regularly cropped up in the late 1970s and early 1980s. The Eighth Report on Competition Policy (1978) described the antitrust rules as a 'body of rules governing fair conduct'.[100] The Ninth Report (1979) went as far as characterising the principle of fairness as one of the key principles guiding the Commission's competition policy.[101] While it held that the main application of this principle related to the area of State aid control, one aim of which was to preserve equality of opportunity for all commercial operators, it stressed that the principle of fairness also guided the Commission's antitrust enforcement and therefore required it to adapt the antitrust rules so as

[97] European Commission, *Fifteenth Report on Competition Policy 1985*, 145.
[98] European Commission, *Twentieth Report on Competition Policy 1990*, 11; *Twenty-second Report on Competition Policy 1992*, 19; *Twenty-fifth Report on Competition Policy 1995*, 15.
[99] European Commission, *Twenty-fourth Report on Competition Policy 1994*, 19.
[100] European Commission, *Eighth Report on Competition Policy 1978*, 9.
[101] European Commission, *Ninth Report on Competition Policy 1979*, 10.

to pay special regard to small and medium firms that lacked market strength.[102] The Reports from 1981 and 1982 stated that the Union's economy was based on a system of fair, undistorted and workable competition.[103]

j. Individual Commercial Freedom and other Democratic Values

The Commission's early Competition Reports also frequently cited the protection of market participants' freedom and opportunity as a key aim of EU antitrust law. According to the Eighth Report on Competition Policy (1978), for example, the Commission intervened against attempts to ban exports or imports, to fix production or sales quotas, to partition markets, to abuse dominant positions by refusing to supply longstanding customers and to charge discriminatory or excessive prices in order to 'protect the equality of opportunity and the freedom of access to business'.[104] Likewise, the Fifteenth Report (1985) characterised the role of competition as follows:

> The Member States of the European Community share a common commitment to individual rights, to democratic values and to free institutions. It is those rights, values and institutions at the European and national levels that provide necessary checks and balances in our political systems. Effective competition provides a set of similar checks and balances in the market economy system. It preserves the freedom and right of initiative of the individual economic operator and it fosters the spirit of enterprise. (...) Competition policy should ensure that abusive use of market power by a few does not undermine the rights of the many.[105]

In other words, the Report likened competition to a system of checks and balances that curbed the power of private entities to protect the other market participants' freedom and other constitutional rights. This view of the aims of competition is reminiscent of the ordoliberal school of thought. It is a far cry from the position of US antitrust law in the 1980s.

k. Employment

Prior to the introduction of the more economic approach, the Commission's Annual Reports further regularly emphasised the relevance of antitrust law for employment policy. The First Report on Competition Policy (1971), for example, stressed that antitrust policy contributed considerably to the better use of labour, since ill-adjusted structures, encouraged by inflation, gave rise to under-utilisation of the Union's labour potential and to underpayment of skilled workers.[106] Subsequent Reports highlighted the relevance of antitrust policy for combating

[102] ibid.

[103] European Commission, *Eleventh Report on Competition Policy 1981*, 11; *Twelfth Report on Competition 1982*, 9.

[104] European Commission, *Eighth Report on Competition Policy 1978*, 9.

[105] European Commission, *Fifteenth Report on Competition Policy 1985*, 11.

[106] European Commission, *First Report on Competition Policy 1971*, 11.

structural unemployment[107] and increasing employment through improved economic performance and growth.[108] The Twenty-third Report on Competition Policy (1993) plainly stated that the stimulation of growth, competitiveness and employment had always been one of the key rationales of antitrust policy, as competition was the mechanism by which resources and jobs were redirected towards growing sectors and away from those with less promising futures.[109] This view was reiterated in many Reports throughout the 1990s.[110]

l. Innovation

In the 1980s, innovation started featuring as a key aim of EU antitrust policy in the Commission's Annual Reports. The Eleventh Report (1981) introduced the notion that the role of competition was to stimulate firms to make use of their know-how and skills and to encourage them to invent, develop and exploit efficiently new techniques and new products.[111] This aim became a fixture in subsequent Reports.[112]

m. Efficiency

In the mid-1980s, the term 'efficiency' also first appeared amongst the ranks of the Commission's objectives. The Fourteenth Report (1984) introduced the notion that competition could, amongst other beneficial effects, also be expected to perform a resource allocation function by encouraging better use of available factors of production, so that firms' technical efficiency was increased.[113] The Fifteenth Report (1985) picked up on the idea of efficiency and explained that competition created an environment within which European industry could grow and develop in the most efficient manner, while at the same time taking account of social goals.[114] These statements were vague at best, and did not explain how competition contributed to achieving these benefits, but they were forerunners of things to come.

Five years later, the Twentieth Report (1990) stated that competition policy was an important instrument used both to promote economic integration and to ensure an efficient allocation of resources.[115] Economists would probably

[107] European Commission, *Thirteenth Report on Competition Policy 1983*, 11.

[108] European Commission, *Fifteenth Report on Competition Policy 1985*, 11 and 145.

[109] European Commission, *Twenty-third Report on Competition Policy 1993*, 22.

[110] eg European Commission, *Twenty-fourth Report on Competition Policy 1994*, 18 and 19; *Twenty-fifth Report on Competition Policy 1995*, 7.

[111] European Commission, *Eleventh Report on Competition Policy 1981*, 11.

[112] eg European Commission, *Twelfth Report on Competition 1982*, 9; *Thirteenth Report on Competition Policy 1983*, 11; *Fifteenth Report on Competition Policy 1985*, 11; *Twentieth Report on Competition Policy 1990*, 11.

[113] European Commission, *Fourteenth Report on Competition 1984*, 11.

[114] European Commission, *Fifteenth Report on Competition Policy 1985*, 11.

[115] European Commission, *Twentieth Report on Competition Policy 1990*, 11.

recognise and subscribe to the second half of this definition. While the Twenty-first Report (1991) limited itself to stating that the link between competition and economic efficiency was now generally recognised by governments throughout the world,[116] the Twenty-second Report (1992) was more forceful. It unequivocally defined the damage caused by restrictive agreements as being one of two kinds: a 'loss of efficiency' because the restriction of competition discouraged undertakings from their 'constant search for ways of improving efficiency' and an impediment to market integration, which resulted in undermining the 'improvement in the economic efficiency of the production structure which integration ought to produce'.[117] In other words, not only did this report suggest that the key harm caused by anticompetitive behaviour was the loss of efficiency, it even defined the ultimate aim of market integration as efficiency, without however explaining the mechanism by which market integration would achieve efficiency. Subsequent Reports were less clear again. Many did not mention the concept at all. The Twenty-sixth Report (1996) defined the aim of antitrust policy as ensuring that markets acquired or maintained the flexibility they needed to allow scope for initiative and innovation, and to allow an 'effective and dynamic allocation of society's resources'.[118] An economist would presumably have expected to read 'efficient' rather than 'effective' allocation of resources here.

In sum, while the term 'efficiency' started to appear in the Commission's Annual Reports on Competition Policy as of the mid-1980s, the term was initially mostly used in a non-technical manner and did not appear to amount to much more than a catchphrase without practical implications at that point.

n. Fundamental Union Objectives

Finally, a number of Reports defined the aims of EU antitrust law in yet another manner. The Twenty-second (1992) and Twenty-third (1993) Reports explained that antitrust policy was one of the Treaties' two great strategies for achieving the Union's fundamental objectives, ie the promotion of a harmonious and balanced economic development, an improved standard of living, and closer relations between the Member States.[119] The Twenty-sixth Report (1996) took a similar stance. It stated that antitrust policy was both a Commission policy in its own right and an integral part of a large number of Union policies, all of which sought to achieve the objectives set out in ex Article 2 EC, including the promotion of harmonious and balanced development of economic activities; sustainable and non-inflationary growth which respected the environment; a high level of

[116] European Commission, *Twenty-first Report on Competition Policy 1991*, 11.
[117] European Commission, *Twenty-second Report on Competition Policy 1992*, 19.
[118] European Commission, *Twenty-sixth Report on Competition Policy 1996*, 17.
[119] European Commission, *Twenty-second Report on Competition Policy 1992*, 13; *Twenty-third Report on Competition Policy 1993*, 14.

employment and of social protection; the raising of the standard of living and quality of life; and economic and social cohesion.[120]

o. Conclusion

The number of aims and values cited in these Reports is almost overwhelming. Nonetheless, it is possible to draw a number of conclusions from the preceding account. The Commission did not operate on the basis of an exhaustively defined legal objective. Rather, it considered a wide variety of economic and non-economic objectives relevant. While one cannot necessarily infer from the Report's accounts that the Commission regarded all of the above-mentioned benefits as the law's primary objective, it seems clear that it took a broad view of its purpose. In a number of Reports, it even explicitly stated that the aims of EU antitrust policy could not be encapsulated by one sole objective, but that antitrust law was an instrument for achieving all of the Treaties' objectives.[121] Likewise, the Twenty-third Report on Competition Policy (1993) stressed that the link between the Union objectives and antitrust policy was a two-way process, and that it was inconceivable that antitrust policy could be applied without reference to the Union's priorities.[122] Competition law had always been an instrument of Union policy, which had helped the Union achieve fundamental goals such as the creation of the common market, a harmonious development of economic conditions and an accelerated raising of the standard of living as well as goals of industrial policy. The increasingly broad goals of the Treaties, for example deepened industrial, cultural and environmental objectives, did not affect the validity of this approach. On the contrary, an antitrust policy that did not have an impact on these policies or was not influenced by them would be marginalised and of less relevance.[123]

iv. Conclusions on the Commission's Early Position

In sum, while the Commission's legally binding acts tended not to engage with the objectives of EU antitrust law, its Annual Reports on Competition Policy, in which it gave yearly accounts of its antitrust enforcement activities to the European Parliament, revealed that the Commission was guided by a multitude of different aims, including all of the Union's fundamental objectives, in particular the creation of the internal market, a variety of macroeconomic aims, individual rights, freedom of opportunity, fairness, employment, the interests of society at large, consumer interests, efficiency and innovation.

There was no apparent hierarchy amongst these objectives.

[120] European Commission, *Twenty-sixth Report on Competition Policy 1996*, 17.
[121] eg European Commission, *Thirteenth Report on Competition Policy 1983*, 11; *Twenty-second Report on Competition Policy 1992*, 13.
[122] European Commission, *Twenty-third Report on Competition Policy 1993*, 13.
[123] ibid, 14. See also European Commission, *Twenty-sixth Report on Competition Policy 1996*, 17.

V. The Legal Objectives according to the More Economic Approach

The more economic approach changed this position fundamentally and led the European Commission to adopt a much narrower understanding of the aims of EU antitrust law.

A. The Legal Provisions

The legal bases for assessing potentially anticompetitive agreements and conduct by dominant undertakings remain the same. With effect of 1 January 2009, the Treaty of Lisbon renumbered the provisions and replaced 'common market' with 'internal market' to bring their terminology up to date. Other than that, it made no substantive changes to Articles 101 and 102. By contrast, the original Merger Regulation was replaced in 2004.[124] The new Merger Regulation, Regulation (EC) 139/2004, contains a revised substantive test. As Chapter 5 demonstrates, this formal legislative amendment triggered a major change of course in the Commission's assessment practice and its concept of competitive harm in EU merger control. However, the Regulation itself did not expressly stipulate any change in policy. On the contrary, its recitals made clear that it was merely the Council's intention to clarify in the interest of legal certainty that the Merger Regulation was meant to allow the Commission to prohibit mergers that were likely to result in an oligopolistic market situation inclined to non-collusive parallel conduct, while adhering to the previous standards of competitive harm applied by the Commission and the Court.[125] Most importantly for the purposes of this chapter, the new Merger Regulation did not depart from the original Merger Regulation's account of the objectives of merger control.

Like its predecessor, Regulation (EC) 139/2004's recitals open by citing the objective of setting up a system ensuring that competition is not distorted, and stress the relevance of this objective for the goal of developing the internal market.[126] They also repeat the principle that merger assessments have to be placed within the general framework of the Union's fundamental objectives listed in ex Article 2 EC and ex Article 2 TEU.[127] When the new Merger Regulation entered into force on 1 May 2004, Article 2 EC set out an even wider variety of economic and non-economic objectives than had been the case when the first

[124] Council Regulation (EC) No139/2004 of 20 January 2004 on the control of concentrations between undertakings (the EC Merger Regulation) (n 56).

[125] ibid, recitals 25–26.

[126] ibid, recital 2.

[127] ibid, recital 23.

Merger Regulation was enacted in 1989. In 2004, this list included the harmonious, balanced and sustainable development of economic activities, a high level of employment and of social protection, equality between men and women, sustainable and non-inflationary growth, a high degree of competitiveness and convergence of economic performance, environmental protection, the raising of the standard of living and quality of life, and economic and social cohesion and solidarity among Member States.

In sum, the prohibition provisions themselves did not change their tune. Nonetheless, as the following shows, the Commission's understanding of these rules' purpose and legal objective started to undergo a significant change around the turn of the millennium.

B. The Commission's Revised Understanding of the Objectives of EU Antitrust Law

While the Commission's individual decisions and Block Exemption decisions continue to avoid fundamental statements on the aims of the relevant legal provisions, the many preparatory consultation papers and interpretative guidelines resulting from the reform make a clear point of defining the aims of EU antitrust law. They do so in a manner that clearly breaks with the broad and holistic approach characterising the first 40 years.

The Commission began its review process with Article 101.[128] The guidelines on vertical restraints from 2000 were the first set of interpretative guidelines based on the more economic approach. Their introductory statements explained that the protection of competition was the primary objective of EU antitrust policy, because it enhanced consumer welfare and created an efficient allocation of resources. Market integration was an additional goal of EU antitrust policy according to these guidelines, as market integration enhanced competition in the Union.[129] The Commission's follow-up Communication on the public consultation on the Vertical Restraints Green Paper had already used an equivalent definition.[130]

The Commission's subsequent interpretative guidelines on Article 101 took a similar stance. The technology transfer guidelines from 2004, for example, explicitly defined the aim of Article 101 as the 'protection of competition on the market with a view to promoting consumer welfare and an efficient allocation of resources'.[131] They made no mention of market integration. The guidelines on

[128] See Ch 2.

[129] European Commission, Guidelines on Vertical Restraints [2000] OJ C291/1, para 7.

[130] Communication from the Commission on the application of the Community competition rules to vertical restraints—Follow-up to the Green Paper on vertical restraints [1998] OJ C365/3.

[131] European Commission, Guidelines on the application of Article 81 of the EC Treaty to technology transfer agreements [2004] OJ C101/2, para 5.

the Application of Article 101(3) explained that the objective of Article 101 was to 'protect competition on the market as a means of enhancing consumer welfare and of ensuring an efficient allocation of resources'. They added that competition and market integration served these ends since the creation and preservation of an open single market promoted an efficient allocation of resources throughout the Union for the benefit of consumers.[132] One can conclude that, according to these guidelines, the ultimate reason for protecting both competition and the internal market was to enhance consumer welfare and efficiency.

In 2010, the Commission updated its original vertical restraints guidelines. This revision did not change any of the key legal principles. In particular, they are based on the same understanding of Article 101's legal objective. If anything, the new guidelines are even clearer than the original. According to their opening statements, the objective of Article 101 is to ensure that undertakings do not use agreements to restrict competition on the market to the detriment of consumers.[133] They add that assessing vertical restraints is also important in the context of the wider objective of achieving an integrated internal market.[134] In other words, consumer welfare is defined as the specific objective of Article 101. Market integration is referred to as a 'wider objective'. Likewise, the revised technology transfer guidelines from 2014 do not deviate from the approach taken in the original guidelines from 2004, but reiterate that consumer welfare and an efficient allocation of resources are the objectives of Article 101.[135]

The Commission's reform of its approach to merger control reveals a similar development. After the Council recast the original Merger Regulation in 2003, the Commission reviewed the fundamental principles guiding its merger assessments. It issued two substantive sets of guidelines spelling out a revised approach to merger review. Both the horizontal merger guidelines[136] and the non-horizontal merger guidelines[137] clearly define the Commission's understanding of the objectives of merger control. They state that it is the Commission's aim to prevent mergers that would deprive consumers of the benefits of effective competition, such as low prices, high quality products, a wide selection of goods and services, and innovation.[138] In other words, the merger guidelines define the legal objective as the enhancement of consumer welfare. Neither set of guidelines even mentions the aim of market integration. Neither, incidentally, do they mention the

[132] Guidelines on the Application of Article 101(3) [2004] OJ C101/97, para 13.

[133] European Commission, Guidelines on Vertical Restraints [2010] C130/1, para 7.

[134] ibid.

[135] European Commission, Guidelines on the application of Article 101 of the Treaty on the Functioning of the European Union to technology transfer agreements [2014] OJ C89/3, para 5.

[136] European Commission, Guidelines on the assessment of horizontal mergers under the Council Regulation on the control of concentrations between undertakings [2004] OJ C31/5.

[137] European Commission, Guidelines on the assessment of non-horizontal mergers under the Council Regulation on the control of concentrations between undertakings [2008] OJ C265/6.

[138] Horizontal merger guidelines (n 136) para 8; Non-horizontal merger guidelines (n 137) para 10.

aim of ensuring an efficient allocation of resources, which features in a few of the Article 101 guidelines.

The reform of the Commission's approach to Article 102 was the last piece of the puzzle. The preparatory study commissioned from the European Advisory Group on Competition Policy (EAGCP)[139] had explicitly engaged with the matter of the appropriate legal objective and recommended an interpretation of the law that focused on the effects on consumers.[140] DG Competition's Discussion Paper,[141] which outlined DG Competition's initial vision for reforming its approach to Article 102, also contained a clear definition of the objectives of Article 102. In fact, it reiterated the definition of the Commission's guidelines on Article 101(3) word for word, and defined the objective of Article 102 as the protection of competition on the market as a means of enhancing consumer welfare and of ensuring an efficient allocation of resources.[142]

The Commission Notice that eventually concluded the review three years later, by contrast, is much more ambiguous.[143] While it clearly earmarks the Commission's new enforcement priorities as 'those types of conduct that are most harmful to consumers',[144] it does not explicitly define the legal objective of Article 102. Unlike the soft law instruments concluding the review of Article 101 and EU merger control, it limits itself to a number of vague and ambiguous references to the purpose and benefits of Article 102. Amongst others, it explains that Article 102 is important for the process of market integration and that its enforcement is beneficial to businesses and consumers.[145] It further states that the Commission's emphasis in enforcing Article 102 is on safeguarding the competitive process and ensuring that dominant undertakings do not exclude their competitors by other means than competition on the merits. It stresses that what really matters is protecting an effective competitive process and not simply protecting competitors, which means that competitors who deliver less to consumers in terms of price, choice, quality and innovation might leave the market.[146] This latter passage defines the protection of the competitive process, and not of consumer welfare, as the objective of Article 102. The only indication that consumer welfare might be relevant in assessments under Article 102 follows from the suggestion that competitors who do not deliver to consumers in terms

[139] EAGCP, 'An Economic Approach to Article 82', available at: www.ec.europa.eu/dgs/competition/economist/eagcp_july_21_05.pdf.

[140] ibid 7–8.

[141] DG Competition, Discussion paper on the application of Article 82 of the Treaty to exclusionary abuses, available at: www.ec.europa.eu/competition/antitrust/art82/discpaper2005.pdf.

[142] ibid, para 4; Article 81(3) Guidelines, para 13.

[143] European Commission, Guidance on the Commission's enforcement priorities in applying Article 82 of the EC Treaty to abusive exclusionary conduct by dominant undertakings [2009] OJ C45/7.

[144] ibid, paras 5 and 19.

[145] ibid, para 1.

[146] ibid, para 6.

of price, choice, quality and innovation may have to leave the market. All in all, however, these explanations are remarkably unfocused.

After the forceful and unequivocal definition of consumer welfare (and sometimes market integration) as the legal objective of Article 101 and the Merger Regulation, the absence of a similar statement in the Guidance on Article 102 is striking, and one cannot help but get the impression that the Guidance is beating about the bush. This is in line with the overall cautious approach of the guidance, which, unlike the guidelines on Article 101 and the Merger Regulation, does not spell out a revised interpretation of the law but officially merely revises the Commission's enforcement priorities. A reasonable explanation for this uncharacteristic reticence is that an interpretation of Article 102 in line with the revised approach to Article 101 and the EU Merger Regulation would not be compatible with the Court of Justice's case law, and that the Commission did not want to spell out an interpretation of the law that was in conflict with the Court's interpretation.[147]

Overall, however, it is clear from the guidelines on Article 101 and the merger guidelines that the Commission adopted consumer welfare, and at times an efficient allocation of resources, as the primary objective of EU antitrust law from 1999 onwards. Market integration remains a valid consideration in competitive assessments. It is sometimes categorised as a 'wider' objective of EU antitrust law, and sometimes as a mere instrument for achieving consumer welfare.

C. Other Commission Publications

The Commission's Reports on Competition Policy from 2000 onwards reflect this more restricted understanding of the aims of EU competition law to some extent. In particular during the Monti's term as Commissioner for Competition Policy, the Commission's Annual Reports clearly stated that the ultimate reason for protecting competition was to protect consumers[148] and to ensure efficient market outcomes.[149] Under Monti's successors, the Reports' portrayal of EU antitrust law's aims became a little less focused again. Consumer welfare, in the form of high quality products and low prices, is sometimes identified as an aim of antitrust law.[150] So is the aim of market integration.[151] Most Reports, however, are less concise. They go to great lengths to explain why and how competition policy advances most, if not all, of the European Union's objectives. Often these Reports

[147] See Ch 10.

[148] European Commission, *Thirty-second Report on Competition Policy 2002*, 3.

[149] European Commission, *Thirty-third Report on Competition Policy 2003*, 3.

[150] eg European Commission, *Report on Competition Policy 2006*, 3; *Report on Competition Policy 2007*, 3; *Report on Competition Policy 2008*, 3; *Report on Competition Policy 2010*, 5.

[151] European Commission, *Report on Competition Policy 2006*, 3; *Report on Competition Policy 2007*, 3; *Report on Competition Policy 2008*, 3; *Report on Competition Policy 2010*, 5.

focus on politically particularly pressing or topical aims. The 2011 Report,[152] for example, explains how the enforcement of competition law, including the antitrust law rules, contributes to achieving the political objectives laid down in the Commission's 'Europe 2020 strategy', which sets out a growth strategy for the European Union between 2010 and 2020 that aims to make the European Union a smart, sustainable and inclusive economy and includes concrete objectives on employment, innovation, education, social inclusion and climate/energy.[153] The 2013 Report, by contrast, is dedicated to explaining the role of competition policy as a tool for achieving European competitiveness following the global financial and economic crisis.[154] Job creation is another benefit ascribed to healthy competition.[155] The 2006 Report even stresses the link between 'overall European wealth' and 'more money for governments to use to sustain the fabric of our societies' and to guarantee 'social justice and a high-quality environment for generations to come'.[156] All in all, the Reports after Monti's time as Commissioner tend not to focus on legal objectives, but to laud the benefits of competition generally and aim to explain how, by protecting competition, the Commission contributes to furthering almost every goal of the European Union, be it economic, social, environmental or political.

VI. Conclusion

The more economic approach has significantly changed the Commission's understanding of the objectives of EU antitrust law. Despite the importance of a well-defined legal objective, the Commission's legally binding acts of the first 40 years rarely addressed the issue. Likewise, its interpretative guidelines did not contain any attempts at defining the legal objectives of the rule they were explaining. Its Annual Reports on Competition Policy, by contrast, suggest that the Commission pursued a multitude of aims by means of the antitrust rules. Market integration, economic growth, the protection of individual economic freedom, fairness, job creation, the competitiveness of the European industry, industrial policy, consumer interests and efficiency are but a few of the objectives and values cited in these Reports. While they were not legally binding acts, their purpose was to inform the other EU institutions, in particular the European Parliament, of the Commission's activities in the area of antitrust law and the principles guiding its

[152] European Commission, *Report on Competition Policy 2011*, 2, 15 ff.

[153] European Commission, Communication 'EUROPE 2020—A strategy for smart, sustainable and inclusive growth' COM(2010) 2020 final.

[154] European Commission, *Report on Competition Policy 2013*.

[155] European Commission, *Report on Competition Policy 2005*, 3; *Report on Competition Policy 2006*, 3.

[156] European Commission, *Report on Competition Policy 2006*, 3.

actions. They must therefore be considered a relatively accurate reflection of the beliefs of DG Competition's officials at the time.

The guidelines introducing the more economic approach to EU antitrust law appreciably altered this position. They are based on a much narrower concept. According to the more economic approach, EU antitrust law pursues only two aims: the enhancement of consumer welfare and market integration. The Commission's consumer welfare aim is more or less identical to that of the US antitrust authorities, who also take the view that the purpose of the US antitrust rules is to ensure that the conduct does not increase businesses' ability or incentive profitably to raise price above or reduce output, quality, service or innovation below what likely would prevail in the absence of the relevant conduct.[157] It is a 'more economic' objective than the Commission's previous understanding of the law's objective, because it, partially at least, embraces the aim of economic theory, which is to maximise economic welfare. However, it is not a 'fully economic' approach, because the Commission has chosen to focus on the welfare of consumers, rather than total welfare, and maintains the market integration goal. Consumer welfare and market integration are two distinct objectives. It is entirely possible to imagine constellations, in which a certain business practice discourages the flow of trade between two Member States, but does not negatively affect consumer welfare in terms of price, output, quality or innovation. The Commission guidelines do not explicitly establish a clear hierarchy between these two aims. The findings on the Commission's concept of harm in the following chapter, however, suggest that they have equal value, because the Commission considers business conduct illegal if it obstructs either of these two aims.

The Commission's change of attitude towards the values guiding its antitrust enforcement raises important philosophical questions—is competition really only worth protecting in the interest of low prices?[158] However, the more economic approach was much more than an abstract intellectual debate on values. The Commission's new understanding of the purpose of antitrust law had real life consequences, because it led the Commission to make significant changes to its interpretation and assessment of key legal concepts. These changes are the subject of the following four chapters.

[157] See eg US Federal Trade Commission and US Department of Justice, Antitrust Guidelines for Collaborations Among Competitors (March 2000) 4 and 6; and Horizontal Merger Guidelines (8 April 1997) 2, fn 6.

[158] See Ch 11.

5

A More Economic Concept of Competitive Harm

I. Introduction

This chapter explores how the more economic approach changed the Commission's concept of competitive harm within the meaning of EU antitrust law. What is it that makes conduct anticompetitive? Article 101 prohibits restrictions of competition, Article 102 outlaws abuses of a dominant position, and the Merger Regulation bans mergers that would result in a significant impediment to effective competition. All of these concepts are vague and in need of interpretation. One gets the general idea that the investigated conduct needs to harm competition, or at least be likely to do so. But what is harm to competition? The issue is distinct from the equally thorny matter of how to establish whether competitive harm, however defined, has occurred or is likely to occur, which will be addressed at a later point.[1] This chapter is about the concept of competitive harm.

The following examines the Commission's understanding of competitive harm separately for each of the three pillars of EU antitrust law, both before and after the reform. The order chosen for this analysis is the order in which the Commission introduced the more economic approach: Article 101, then the Merger Regulation and finally Article 102. The chapter concludes with a comparison between the Commission's current concepts of harm. It shows that, while the Commission has formally revised its understanding of competitive harm under Article 101 and the Merger Regulation in line with the new consumer welfare aim, its review of Article 102 has been less effective.

[1] See Chs 7 and 8.

II. Article 101

The wording of Article 101 does not contain a clear-cut concept of competitive harm. It prohibits agreements that result in a 'restriction of competition'. But what is a restriction of competition? Article 101 does not define the concept in general terms, but merely gives a number of examples of agreements that are deemed to amount to such a restriction: (a) fixing of prices or of other trading conditions; (b) limiting or controlling production, markets, technical development or investment; (c) sharing markets or sources of supply; (d) applying dissimilar conditions to equivalent transactions with other trading parties, thereby placing them at a competitive disadvantage; and (e) making the conclusion of contracts subject to acceptance by the other parties of supplementary obligations which have no connection with the subject of such contracts.

This list of contractual clauses does not allow a definite conclusion as to the underlying concept of harm. The rationale for deeming restrictions (a) to (c) anticompetitive could be that the parties to the contract coordinate their conduct instead of behaving independently, and hence reduce the degree of competition between them. Or their anticompetitive nature could arise from the negative effects that this lack of competition produces, for example, on non-participating undertakings, consumers or even the political system. Examples (d) and (e) might be interpreted as condemning unfair conduct. In sum, the concept of a restriction of competition is far from clear and therefore wide open to interpretation. The following demonstrates how the Commission interpreted 'restriction of competition' prior to the advent of the more economic approach and how this understanding underwent a fundamental change around the turn of the millennium. The analysis focuses on the Commission's interpretative guidelines and its individual decisions. The Commission's many Block Exemption Regulations both prior to and after the introduction of the more economic approach, while of great practical relevance, do not give any useful insights into the Commission's concept of competitive harm. Their recitals tend to explain the expected benefits of certain types of agreements, but do not explain what made the agreements anticompetitive in the first place.

A. The Commission's Concept of Harm Prior to the Introduction of the More Economic Approach

i. Interpretative Notices and other Soft Law

During the first 40-odd years of EU antitrust law, the Commission did not issue guidelines that spelled out a comprehensive interpretation of Article 101 in the manner of the guidelines introducing the more economic approach from

2000 onwards. However, it did publish a number of more specific interpretative Notices. A few of these allow at least some degree of insight into the Commission's concept of competitive harm during this period.

The earliest of these Notices, the Communication on exclusive dealing contracts with commercial agents from 1962,[2] is not particularly helpful. The main purpose of this short Notice was to clarify that the Commission considered agreements between a seller and his commercial agents to fall outside the scope of Article 101 even where they included an exclusivity clause, because sellers and agents had to be considered an economic unit. However, the Notice also indicated that exclusive distribution agreements with independent distributors were capable of being caught by Article 101, and explained that the restriction of competition in this constellation consisted in (a) the 'reduction of supply' where the seller undertook to sell exclusively to the buyer, and (b) the 'reduction of demand' where the buyer undertook to buy exclusively from the seller.[3] Again, this concept of harm is relatively vague. It is not clear why exactly the Commission considered a reduction of supply or demand harmful and who was expected to suffer as a consequence.

The second Notice on Article 101 dates from 1968.[4] Its purpose was to specify a few types of horizontal agreements that the Commission considered unproblematic from the point of view of Article 101. While it did not define in a general manner what constituted a restriction of competition, the Notice listed agreements that the Commission deemed innocuous to competition, such as agreements to exchange opinions and experience or to cooperate in market research or management. It explained that, despite the general presumption of innocuousness, these activities could amount to a restriction of competition where they restricted the 'freedom of action' of the undertakings involved or led to a 'coordination of market conduct'.[5] In sum, the Notice identified two indicators of competitive harm: the restriction of the participating undertaking's freedom of action and the coordination of their market conduct.

The Commission's *de minimis* Notices of the period under examination, implementing the Court's ruling in *Völk v Vervaeke*,[6] contained yet another formula. According to *Völk v Vervaeke*, merely insignificant restrictions of competition and trade are not caught by Article 101.[7] The primary purpose of the Commission's *de minimis* Notices is to quantify this concept of insignificance on the basis of

[2] European Commission, Bekanntmachung über Alleinvertriebsverträge mit Handelsvertretern [1962] OJ 139/2921 (no English version).

[3] 'Verkürzung des Angebots'/'Verkürzung der Nachfrage' in the German version, 'réduction de l'offre'/'réduction de la demande' in the French version (ibid, s II).

[4] European Commission, Bekanntmachung über Vereinbarungen, Beschlüsse und aufeinander abgestimmte Verhaltensweisen, die eine zwischenbetriebliche Zusammenarbeit betreffen [1968] OJ C75/3 (no English version).

[5] ibid, s II.1.

[6] Case 5/69 *Völk v Vervaecke* [1969] ECR 295.

[7] ibid, paras 5–6.

a minimum market share or turnover thresholds. However, the first *de minimis* Notice from 1970s, and the revised versions of 1977 and 1986, also explained the Commission's understanding of the rule's rationale. According to these early *de minimis* Notices, only such agreements were prohibited by Article 101 that had an appreciable 'impact on market conditions, in that they appreciably altered the market position, in other words the sales or supply possibilities, of third undertakings and of users'.[8] This passage does not contain an explicit definition of what constitutes a restriction of competition. However, read in conjunction with the Court ruling that it aimed to implement and quantify, it suggests that the Commission considered the effects both on other undertakings and on consumers relevant in a competitive assessment.

The Notice concerning the assessment of cooperative joint ventures from 1993[9] contains a similar approach. Its purpose was to help undertakings self-assess the legality of agreements establishing joint ventures under Article 101. The Notice set out a list of contractual clauses generally deemed compatible with Article 101. For all other cases, it proposed a two-step test. In order to be considered anticompetitive, the joint venture first had to be likely to restrict competition between the parties, and second, it had to be likely to affect appreciably the competitive position of third parties.[10] The second part of this analysis involved establishing whether the operation would affect the choice available to suppliers or customers, whether it would exclude the parties' traditional suppliers and customers from the market, and whether it would create barriers to market entry for potential competitors or impede the growth of the parties' competitors.[11] In other words, when assessing the anticompetitive effects of a joint venture, the Commission considered the effects on the parties' customers, suppliers and competitors, and in particular their ability to enter and stay in the market.

In conclusion, while the Commission's interpretative Notices from the 1960s to the early 1990s did not define the concept of a restriction of competition in a general manner, a number of them contained indications of what made conduct anticompetitive in the eyes of the Commission: a reduction of demand or supply, a restriction of the parties' freedom of action and opportunity, abandoning independent decision-making, coordination, a reduction in choice for undertakings and customers, the exclusion of other undertakings from the market, impeding their growth or creating barriers to entry for potential competitors. These are all

[8] European Commission, Bekanntmachung vom 27. Mai 1970 über Vereinbarungen, Beschlüsse und aufeinander abgestimmte Verhaltensweisen von geringer Bedeutung, die nicht unter Artikel 85 Absatz 1 des Vertrages zur Gründung der Europäischen Wirtschaftsgemeinschaft fallen [1970] OJ C64/1 (no English version available), s I. [1977] OJ C313/3, s I; [1986] OJ C231/2, para 2. The Notices from 1997 and 2014 ([1997] OJ C372/13; [2014] OJ C291/1) do not belong to period under consideration in this section, but will be discussed in the following section.

[9] European Commission, Notice concerning the assessment of cooperative joint ventures pursuant to Article 85 of the EEC Treaty [1993] OJ C43/2.

[10] ibid, para 17.

[11] ibid, paras 24–25.

different formulas. Nonetheless, it is possible to establish one common feature. The assessments described in these early Commission Notices did not focus on the agreements' effects on economic welfare, however defined, but on the freedom of the parties and the opportunities of their customers and competitors. These opportunities were not defined in monetary terms but in terms of independence, freedom and choice.

ii. The Commission's Decision Practice

The Commission's decision practice on Article 101 prior to the reform provides rich pickings. Between early 1964 and the end of 1998, the Commission decided 311 cases by means of substantive decision, ie either declaring agreements compatible with Article 101(1), exempting them under Article 101(3) or establishing an infringement. Although these decisions rarely explain the Commission's theories of harm in abstract terms, an analysis of the substantive assessments makes it possible to extract the underlying concept of competitive harm, which confirms and complements the initial conclusions drawn from the Commission's interpretative guidelines.

In a nutshell, the Commission equated restrictions of competition with restrictions of the commercial freedom or opportunity of any person affected by the investigated commercial transaction. This was the case for both horizontal and vertical agreements.[12] In fact, the Commission did not commonly differentiate between horizontal and vertical constellations during this period, but applied similar theoretical considerations to both types of agreement. It also considered discrimination and obstacles to market integration relevant factors in determining whether an agreement restricted competition. However, it often looked at these effects as restrictions of individual freedom as well, rather than considering them distinct concepts of harm. The following two decisions, chosen because they typify the Commission's approach of this time, illustrate these findings. The first case examines a horizontal constellation, the second concerns a vertical agreement.

In 1970, the Commission investigated the decision of an association of German ceramic tile manufacturers to adopt a common rebate policy.[13] Its members had agreed to grant their customers incremental quantity rebates, which the association would set for each of its members at the beginning of every calendar year. The Commission found that this decision had the object and effect of restricting competition for a number of reasons. One, it restricted the economic freedom of the association members to determine their own rebate policy. Two, it affected the 'competitive position' of customers who lost the opportunity to obtain

[12] Horizontal agreements being agreements between competitors, and vertical agreements being agreements between undertakings in the same market but at different stages of the production or distribution chain.

[13] *Rabattbeschluss der Interessengemeinschaft der deutschen keramischen Wand- und Bodenfliesenwerke* (Case IV/25107) [1971] OJ L10/15.

individualised rebates from the association members and to trigger a 'rebate competition' between manufacturers. Three, the incremental nature of the quantity rebates incited German customers to concentrate on German manufacturers, as purchases made from foreign manufacturers did not count towards the rebate. The Commission considered this problematic as it restricted the opportunities of foreign tile manufacturers to sell in the German market. It also considered that the policy discriminated between customers who bought tiles exclusively from German manufacturers and those who had bought some of their requirements from foreign manufacturers, as the latter were not entitled to the same rebate as the former.[14] On this basis, the Commission found that the common rebate policy restricted competition. As it did not consider the conditions for an exemption met, it found an infringement of Article 101 and prohibited the policy. In sum, the Commission looked at the effects of the practice on the opportunities of the investigated undertakings themselves, on the opportunities of their customers and on the opportunities of their competitors.

The Commission's approach to vertical agreements during this period was indistinguishable from its assessment of horizontal agreements. In fact, the terms horizontal and vertical, so commonplace today, do not appear in its decisions of the first 40 years. In 1980, for example, the Commission assessed a distribution agreement between Hennessy, a French manufacturer and distributor of Cognac, and Henkell, a German producer and distributor of alcoholic beverages.[15] Hennessy and Henkell concluded an agreement in which Hennessy made Henkell its exclusive distributor of Hennessy cognac for Germany and guaranteed it a price that would protect Henkell against parallel imports. In return, Henkell agreed not to distribute any competing brands of cognac in Germany and to resell Hennessy cognac at a set list price, from which it would not deviate without Hennessy's consent. The Commission identified several restrictive effects. It held that the agreement made it impossible for other manufacturers of cognac to use Henkell's distribution network to market their products in Germany. It also limited Henkell's freedom to distribute competing brands of cognac. The agreement further aimed to stop French distributors from selling Hennessy cognac into Germany. Finally, the resale price clause limited Henkell's freedom to set its own resale prices.[16] On this basis, the Commission held that the agreement restricted competition within the meaning of Article 101(1) and prohibited the agreement. Like in the case of the German ceramic tiles association, the Commission therefore saw the restriction of competition in the fact that the agreement restricted the parties' own freedom as well as the opportunities of their competitors. The effects on customers and end consumers are not even mentioned in this assessment.

[14] ibid, II.2.
[15] *Hennessy-Henkell* (Case IV/26.912) [1980] OJ L383/11.
[16] ibid, recitals 16–20.

These two cases are typical for the Commission's assessments of agreements under Article 101 prior to the introduction of the more economic approach. The Commission deemed that competition was restricted if the agreement restricted at least one of the parties' freedom to determine their own commercial strategies in areas such pricing,[17] advertising,[18] purchasing of inputs,[19] contracting with other parties,[20] granting licences[21] or determining its own production,[22] amongst many others.[23] The restriction of actual or potential competitors' freedom of action was equally considered a restriction of competition.[24] The interests of the parties' immediate customers were sometimes, although by no means always, considered relevant. Where the Commission did take these effects into account, it usually focused on whether the agreement would reduce the customers' opportunity to choose between manufacturers with independent business strategies[25] rather than the specific benefits this would have for them in terms of prices.[26] Discrimination on the part of the parties to the agreement, be it vis-à-vis competitors or customers, was also often considered a relevant factor for considering an agreement anticompetitive.[27]

Finally, export bans, ie contractual prohibitions imposed on distributors to sell into another EU Member State (usually to protect the commercial interests of an exclusive distributor assigned to that Member State or the manufacturer himself) were always considered restrictions of competition. The Commission's rationale for considering export prohibitions anticompetitive was not always the same, neither was it always clear on this point. A number of early decisions suggest that

[17] *Nederlandse Cement-Handelmaatschappij NV* (Case IV/595) [1972] OJ L 22/16, recital 7; *Vereeniging van Cementhandelaren* (Case IV/324) [1972] OJ L 13/34, recital 16(b).

[18] *ASBL pour la promotion du tube d'acier soudé électriquement* (Case IV/412) [1970] JO L 153/14, II; *SABA's EEC distribution system* (Case IV/29.598) [1983] OJ L376/41, II.C.3; *British Dental Trade Association—BDTA* (Case IV/31.593) [1988] OJ L233/15, recital 23.

[19] *National Sulphuric Acid Association* (Case IV/27.958) [1980] OJ L 260/24, recitals 32–33; *Italian flat glass* (Case IV.29.988) OJ L326/32, II.3.

[20] *Distribution system of Ford Werke AG* (Case IV/30.696) OJ L327/31, recital 30; *Peugeot* (Case IV/31.143) [1986] OJ L295/19, recital 34.

[21] *Continental/Michelin* (Case No IV/32.173) [1988] OJ L305/33, recital 15.

[22] *Rolled zinc products and zinc alloys* (Case IV/29.629) [1982] OJ L362/40, III.A.1.

[23] eg in *Cafeteros de Colombia*, the Commission held that prohibiting roasting plant owners from buying green coffee for resale in the green state amounted to a restriction of the plant owner's commercial freedom and therefore a restriction of competition: *Cafeteros de Colombia* (Case IV/30.077) [1982] OJ L360/31, recitals 35–39.

[24] *Theal Watts* (Case IV/28.812) [1977] OJ L 39/19, II.A; *Cauliflowers* (Case IV/28.948) [1978] OJ L21/23, s II.

[25] *Preserved Mushrooms* (Case IV/27.039) [1975] OJ L 29/26, II.2.a; *GERO-fabriek* (Case IV/24.510) [1977] OJ L16/8, II(a)3(b)

[26] Very occasionally, decisions did explicitly refer to higher end prices as a detriment for consumers, but only in addition to the restrictions of freedom, eg *The Distillers Company Ltd* (Case IV/28.282) [1978] OJ L50/16, 26.

[27] *NAVEWA-ANSEAU* (Case IV/29.995) [1982] OJ L167/39, recital 56; *Rabattbeschluss der Interessengemeinschaft der deutschen keramischen Wand- und Bodenfliesenwerke* (n 13) II.2.b; *ASBL pour la promotion du tube d'acier soudé électriquement* (n 18); *Hasselblad* (Case IV/25.757) [1982] OJ L161/18, recital 56; *AEG-Telefunken* (Case IV/28.748) [1982] OJ L117/15, recitals 53 ff.

export bans or measures intended to prevent parallel imports were not permissible under Article 101 because they led to the compartmentalisation of the market, which was incompatible with the Union's fundamental objective of establishing an internal market.[28] In other cases, the Commission relied on its usual freedom approach and argued that export prohibitions restricted competition because they restricted the addressee's freedom to sell and compete in another market.[29] In a handful of cases, the Commission also touched on the consequences for consumers, who were being prevented from buying from the most economical source.[30] In many other cases, the Commission did not offer any explanation at all, but merely stated that preventing exports to other EU countries clearly had the object and effect of restricting competition.[31]

Significantly, the parties' degree of economic power played no role in these assessments. In fact, the decisions from the 1960s to mid-1990s rarely contained any information on the parties' market shares or other indicators of economic power at all. Where they did, this type of information was mentioned in the facts, but did not enter into the actual assessment of whether the agreement restricted competition. The decisions did not define the relevant market either. The facts typically focused on summarising the terms of the investigated agreement, and the competitive assessments analysed the contractual terms as to whether they limited the parties' economic freedom or resulted in restricting other businesses' opportunities.

There was one exception to this rule: the *de minimis* case. In a handful of cases, the Commission applied the Court's ruling in *Völk v Verwaecke*, according to which an agreement escapes the application of Article 101 because it is not capable of having an appreciable effect on competition and trade because of the parties' weak position.[32] These were rare occurrences.[33] Normally, decisions did not mention the requirement of appreciability at all. Presumably, cases in which the combined market share of the parties was below 5 per cent rarely reached the decision stage because of the *de minimis* Notice's presumption of non-appreciability, which also removed the parties' obligation to notify the agreement. Where the Commission did explicitly refer to the requirement of appreciability, it usually limited itself to stating in one sentence that the parties' market shares or their turnover were sufficiently significant to make the restriction appreciable, without

[28] eg *Theal Watts* (n 24) 24; *National Panasonic* (Case IV/30.070) [1982] OJ L 354/28, recital 48; *Sandoz* (Case IV/31.741) [1987] OJ L222/28, recital 29.

[29] eg *Johnson & Johnson* (Case IV/29.702) [1980] OJ L 377/16, recital 29; *Moët et Chandon* (Case IV/30.188) [1982] OJ L94/7, recital 12; *Tipp-Ex* (Case IV/31.192) [1987] OJ L222/1, recitals 51 ff.; *Bayer Dental* (Case IV/32.877) [1990] OJ L351/46, recital 16.

[30] *Kawasaki* (Case IV/29.430) [1979] OJ L16/9, recital 44.

[31] *Miller International Schallplatten GmbH* (Case IV/29.018) [1976] OJ L357/40; *Arthur Bell and Sons Ltd* (Case IV/29.440) [1978] OJ L235/15; *The Distillers Company Limited* (n 26).

[32] *Völk v Vervaecke* (n 6) paras 5/7.

[33] eg *Convention chaufourniers* (Case IV/242–295) [1969] OJ L122/8, recitals 10–11.

attempting to approximate their actual degree of economic strength.[34] The *de minimis* rule is best understood as an emergency break, rather than a requirement to assess and factor in an undertaking's exact degree of economic power in every competitive assessment. Beyond the *de minimis* threshold, the parties' degree of economic power was deemed irrelevant.

iii. Conclusion

In sum, the Commission's Notices and decision practice show that during this first era, the Commission defined restrictions of competition as restrictions of the market participants' commercial freedom. Market participant within the meaning of this definition is to be understood in the widest sense of the term. It included not only competing undertakings and customers, but also the contracting parties themselves. Discrimination was also considered problematic. This finding sits well with a concept of harm that is based on the notion of individual rights and freedoms. Both freedom of action and the right to equal treatment are fundamental civil freedoms of constitutional rank. Finally, agreements that ran counter to the aim of market integration, because they contributed to (re-)compartmentalising the internal market along the lines of national borders, were also considered incompatible with Article 101. Sometimes this type of infringement was presented as a restriction of the market participants' freedom to trade in another Member State. In other decisions, it seemed to constitute a type of competitive harm *sui generis* that was based on the Treaty' aim of market integration.

B. The Commission's Concept of Harm after the Introduction of the More Economic Approach

The more economic approach significantly changed the Commission's concept of competitive harm under Article 101(1). The Commission abandoned its former freedom-based concept of a competitive restriction and adopted a new interpretation of Article 101(1), according to which a restriction of competition requires consumer harm.

i. Commission Notices and other Soft Law

Whereas the Commission's soft law of the first 40 years had not placed much emphasis on explaining the theoretical foundations of the Commission's approach, this changed with the advent of the more economic approach. The new generation of interpretative guidelines goes to great lengths to explain key concepts, the

[34] eg *VW* (Case IV/35.733) [1998] OJ L124/60, recitals 147–48; *AOIP/Beyrard* (Case IV/26.949) [1976] OJ L6/8, recital 4.a.

rationale behind them and how the Commission proposes to carry out its assessments in practice.

Between 2000 and 2004, the Commission enacted four key sets of guidelines on Article 101 that profess to be based on an 'economic' or 'more economic' approach: the vertical restraints guidelines, the horizontal cooperation guidelines, the guidelines on technology transfer agreements, and the guidelines on the application of Article 101(3).[35] All but the latter have in the meantime been revised[36] and updated in a number of points. However, the amendments have not changed any their predecessors' key concepts, in particular not the concept of competitive harm, which remains the same as in the original four guidelines. Incidentally, this second generation of substantive guidelines no longer mentions that they are based on an economic or more economic approach. As they are based on the same principles as the first sets of guidelines, this omission may be interpreted as the Commission no longer considering it necessary to emphasise the economic orientation of these guidelines, because it has in the meantime become the status quo.

Despite its name, it is the Notice on the application of Article 101(3) that explains the notion of competitive harm under Article 101(1) most systematically and exhaustively. The Article 101(3) guidelines distinguish clearly between restrictions by object, the anticompetitive nature of which is presumed, and restrictions by effect, in which case the anticompetitive nature of these effects needs to be established in an individual assessment.[37] Although the Commission in practice often did not distinguish between object and effect restrictions in its early decision practice, but usually generically stated that an agreement had both the object and effect of restricting competition, this theoretical distinction was not new. The Court established it in the 1960s.[38] The novelty lies in the type of effect that the Article 101(3) guidelines consider relevant in a competitive assessment. In their guidance on when an agreement can be considered to have the object of restricting competition, the guidelines explain that the presumption of illegality of object restrictions is based on the presumption that they are likely to produce negative effects 'on the market' and to jeopardise the objectives pursued by the EU antitrust rules. They add, by way of example, that price fixing and market sharing are object restrictions as they reduce output and raise prices. This leads to a misallocation of resources, because goods and services demanded by customers are not produced,

[35] European Commission, Guidelines on Vertical Restraints [2000] OJ C291/1, para 7; Guidelines on the applicability of Article 81 to horizontal cooperation agreements [2001] OJ C3/2; Guidelines on the Application of Article 81 of the Treaty to Technology Transfer Agreements [2004] OJ C101/2, para 5; Guidelines on the Application of Article 81(3) of the Treaty [2004] OJ C101/97, para 13.

[36] Guidelines on Vertical Restraints [2010] OJ C130/1; Guidelines on the applicability of Article 101 to horizontal co-operation agreements [2011] OJ C11/1; Guidelines on the application of Article 101 to technology transfer agreements [2014] OJ C89/3.

[37] Guidelines on the application of Article 81(3) (n 35) para 20.

[38] Joined Cases 56/64 and 58/64 *Consten and Grundig v Commission*, ECLI:EU:C:1966:41, 342; see also Case C-49/92 P *Anic Partecipazioni* ECLI:EU:C:1999:356, para 99.

as well as a reduction in consumer welfare, because consumers have to pay higher prices for the goods and services in question.[39] This is a very different rationale for prohibiting price fixing than that given in the decisions of the first 40 years. Instead of deeming price fixing anticompetitive because it restricts the cartel members' freedom to set prices independently, the guidelines focus on the practice's harmful effects on the market, and more particularly consumers, in the form of higher prices, which reduces their economic welfare.

The guidelines' explanations on how to assess the legality of an agreement that is not restrictive by object, but needs to be assessed as to its actual effects, confirm this conclusion. According to the Article 101(3) guidelines, the first step of such a competitive assessment consists in establishing whether an agreement has the effect of restricting inter-brand competition (competition between suppliers of competing brands) or intra-brand competition (competition between distributors of the same brand).[40] Such restrictions are deemed to occur when the parties themselves agree not to compete with each other, or if the agreement has the effect of foreclosing their competitors' access to the market.[41] Up to this point, the approach does not sound radically different from that used during the first 40 years of the Commission's enforcement practice. However, the guidelines then add the novel proposition that for an agreement to be restrictive by effect, it must affect actual or potential competition to such an extent that negative effects on prices, output, innovation or the variety or quality of goods and services on the relevant market can be expected with a reasonable degree of probability.[42] According to the guidelines, this rule 'reflects the economic approach which the Commission is applying'. They further add that such an assessment requires a 'proper market analysis'. The finding that the parties' market shares exceed the *de minimis* thresholds is insufficient.[43] According to the guidelines, such negative effects on consumers are likely to occur when the parties have some degree of market power and the agreement contributes to the creation, maintenance or strengthening of that power, or allows the parties to exploit such market power.[44] The guidelines define market power as the ability to maintain prices above competitive levels for a significant period of time or to maintain output in terms of product quantities, product quality and variety or innovation below competitive levels for a significant period of time.[45] According to the Article 101(3) guidelines, market power is a question of degree, and the degree of market power normally required for finding an infringement under Article 101(1) is less than the degree of market power required for a finding of dominance under Article 102. They also stipulate that

[39] Guidelines on the application of Article 81(3) (n 35) para 21.
[40] ibid, para 17.
[41] ibid, para 19.
[42] ibid, para 24.
[43] ibid.
[44] ibid, para 25.
[45] ibid.

analysing the restrictive effects of an agreement normally requires defining the relevant market.[46]

In other words, the guidelines suggest that restrictions of competition, which appear to be defined as the coordination of competitors' conduct or the foreclosure of competitors, are only prohibited by Article 101(1) if they also affect consumer welfare negatively. According to the more economic approach, consumer harm is thus an indispensable component of competitive harm. This is a more restrictive reading of Article 101(1) than the Commission's previous approach, and significantly narrows down the scope of the prohibition provision.

In line with this more permissive view of anticompetitiveness, the Commission also raised the *de minimis* threshold under which an agreement is deemed not to have an appreciable effect on competition. Whereas the *de minimis* Notices from 1970, 1977 and 1986 required that the combined market share of the parties to the agreement not exceed 5 per cent,[47] the *de minimis* Notice from 1997 amended this figure. It is based on the position of contemporary economic theory that vertical agreements are as a rule less dangerous to consumer welfare than agreements between competitors. It therefore raised the combined *de minimis* market share threshold for vertical agreements to 10 per cent.[48] The most recent *de minimis* Notice increased the safe harbour even further. Horizontal agreements are now deemed not have appreciable effects on competition if the parties' combined market share does not exceed 10 per cent. Vertical agreements are considered non-appreciable if the market share of each of the parties does not exceed 15 per cent.[49] However, while containing a much more generous *de minimis* threshold than the original *de minimis* Notices, the 2014 Notice now generally excludes restriction by object from its scope.[50]

ii. The Commission's Decision Practice

The following section looks at whether the Commission's decision practice has implemented the consumer welfare-based concept of harm spelled out in its Notices. It shows that, mostly, it does, although the decision practice is conceptually less rigorous and clear-cut than the guidelines.

Two trends in the enforcement practice of the past 10 years complicate the exercise of trying to understand the Commission's interpretation of Article 101 in practice. First, since Regulation 1/2003 decentralised EU antitrust enforcement by making Article 101(3) directly applicable, the Commission has concentrated its

[46] ibid, para 26.

[47] Bekanntmachung der Kommission vom 27. Mai 1970 über Vereinbarungen, Beschlüsse und aufeinander abgestimmte Verhaltensweisen von geringer Bedeutung (n 8) II; Commission Notice of 19 December 1977 concerning agreements of minor importance which do not fall under Article 85 (1) [1977] OJ C 313/3, II; Commission Notice of 3 September 1986 on agreements of minor importance which do not fall under Article 85 (1) [1986] OJ C231/1, para 7.

[48] European Commission, Notice on agreements of minor importance [1997] OJ C372/13, para 9.

[49] European Commission, Notice on agreements of minor importance [2014] C 291/1, para 8.

[50] ibid, para 13.

resources on pursuing hard-core cartels (ie price fixing, output reduction, market allocation and bid-rigging) and has primarily left the enforcement of other cases to the national competition authorities. Hard-core cartel activities are restrictive by object, which means that their anticompetitive effects are presumed. In practice, the focus of such Commission decision will lie on proving that the cartel members participated in the activity, and how much they should be fined. They tend not to engage with or even identify the harmful effects of the conduct. Cartel decisions are therefore as a rule far less informative on the Commission's understanding of competitive harm than decisions on less obviously anticompetitive conduct.[51]

The second trend that obscures the Commission's current understanding of key legal concepts is the heavy use of commitments decisions. Regulation 1/2003 not only decentralised the enforcement of Articles 101 and 102, but also introduced a new procedural tool, which allows the Commission to accept and make legally binding commitments offered by the investigated parties that address the competition concerns identified in the Commission's Statement of Objection.[52] If the Commission considers the commitments sufficient to address its concerns, it adopts a decision that makes the commitments legally binding on the parties and closes the case without reaching a final conclusion on the legality or illegality of the conduct. While this instrument has many procedural advantages for both sides, in particular cost and time savings, it also has a number of drawbacks. One of their disadvantages is that their lack of formal competitive assessments has resulted in a lack of information on the Commission's current approach to assessing anticompetitive effects. Commitment decisions do not carry out detailed competitive analyses that result in an unequivocal finding of competitive harm (or lack thereof), but merely express 'concerns' that are based on a preliminary assessment of the facts. These assessments are normally relatively superficial and informal. Not surprisingly, therefore, the Commission's commitments decisions of the past 10 years do not paint a clear picture of the Commission's current concept of harm. Whereas a handful clearly identify that the expected anticompetitive effect was a reduction of consumer welfare,[53] others seem concerned that the agreements would cause competitors disadvantages[54] or difficulties entering the market,[55] without touching on the effects on consumers. Many do not specify what anticompetitive effects they were concerned about at all.[56]

[51] See eg *Telefónica/Portugal Telecom* (Case COMP/39.839).

[52] Regulation 1/2003, Art 9.

[53] eg *E-Books* (Case COMP/39.847) recitals 90–93; *Rio Tinto Alcan* (Case COMP/AT.39230) recital 99.

[54] *Ship Classification* (Case COMP/39.416) recital 13.

[55] *Repsol CPP* (Case COMP/B-1/38.348) recitals 20–24.

[56] eg *Continental/United/Lufthansa/Air Canada* (Case COMP/AT.39595). In substance, the preliminary assessment in recitals 40–54 of the parties' closeness, the remaining competition, likelihood of entry and buyer power suggests a market power analysis.

It is the Commission's relatively few infringement decisions in non-cartel cases since the introduction of the more economic approach[57] that are most enlightening. The case of *MasterCard*[58] is one of them. In 2007, the Commission investigated the business model of MasterCard, a world-wide payment organisation, of collectively determining the multilateral interchange fees (MIFs) that its member banks were to charge merchants for being able to use the organisation's payment system.[59] The Commission defined the relevant product and geographic markets as those for acquiring payment cards, which it deemed national in scope. It did not commit itself as to whether this agreement restricted competition by object, but focused on establishing its anticompetitive effects instead. In the 40-page analysis, it argued that the agreement had the effect of restricting competition because it fixed a floor for the fee charged to merchants. Because MasterCard had market power, this resulted in higher merchant fees than would have prevailed absent the agreement. The higher merchant few would also result in higher end prices for consumers, because merchants were likely to pass on the charge at least partially.[60] In short, the assessment focused on demonstrating that the agreement would raise prices for merchants and/or end consumers. By contrast, the fact that the agreement limited the participating banks' freedom of action was not the rationale for finding the agreement anticompetitive. In fact, the word 'freedom' did not figure in the analysis at all. This concept of harm can be found in many of the Commission's Article 101 infringement decisions of the past 10 years.[61] While the quality of the assessment and evidence varies from case to case, their analysis allows the conclusion that the theoretical concept of harm was the reduction of consumer welfare in the form of higher prices.

However, there are also cases in which the Commission seemingly reverted to its prior approach. In *GDF/ENEL* from 2004, for example, in which the Commission assessed an agreement imposing a territorial restriction, it relied on a Court ruling from 1983 and a decision prior to the reform according to which contractual clauses that restricted the freedom of one of the parties to use the goods supplied in accordance with his own economic interests always amounted to a restriction of competition within the meaning of Article 101.[62] Similarly, in *Lundbeck*, a decision

[57] Between 2000 and July 2015, the Commission published 11 Art 101 infringement decisions in non-cartel cases, as opposed to 97 cartel infringements (see Ch7, III.C.i).

[58] *MasterCard and Others* (Cases COMP/34.579, COMP/36.518 and COMP/38.580), upheld on appeal in Case T-111/08 *MasterCard and Others v Commission* ECLI:EU:T:2012:260 and Case C-382/12 *MasterCard and Others v Commission* ECLI:EU:C:2014:2201.

[59] This is a very simplified account of a somewhat more complex system. The fee is in fact charged by the cardholder's bank (the 'issuing bank') to the merchant's bank (the 'acquiring bank') for each sales transaction made at a merchant outlet with a MasterCard payment card.

[60] *MasterCard* (n 58) recitals 408–523.

[61] See eg *Fentanyl* (Case COMP/AT.39685) recitals 212–15; *Groupement des cartes bancaires* (Case COMP/D1/38606) recitals 256, 257, 262, 263; *Morgan Stanley/Visa International and Visa Europe* (Case COMP/D1/37860) recitals 122–28, 201.

[62] *GDF/ENEL* (Case COMP/38662) recital 87, citing Case 319/82 *Société de Vente de Ciments et Bétons de l'Est SA v Kerpen* ECLI:EU:C:1983:374, para 6 and *VW* (Case COMP/35733) [1998] OJ L124/60, recital 143.

from 2013 that examined a 'pay-for-delay' agreement or 'reverse payment patent settlement' in the pharmaceutical sector, there was no mention of consumer welfare in the competitive assessment. Instead, the decision emphasised that the ultimate aim of Article 101 was to protect the competitive process and rivalry.[63]

In practice, the Commission also continues to consider agreements that create obstacles to market integration anticompetitive, even in the absence of consumer harm. Whereas prior to the reform, the decision practice was not entirely clear on the nature of the harm caused by agreements that imposed export prohibitions (sometimes the Commission focused on the restriction of the market participants' freedom, sometimes on the process of market integration), the decision practice since 2000 clearly focuses on the harm to the process of market integration. In the case of *SEP et autres/Peugeot SA*,[64] for example, the Commission found that Peugeot, a French car manufacturer, had taken steps to restrict parallel trade in new Peugeot cars in the internal market by adopting a remuneration policy that discouraged dealers from selling cars to consumers in other Member States. The Commission's assessment of the competitive nature of this practice was short and to the point. It held that Peugeot's agreements with its dealers contained restrictions of competition by object because they discouraged parallel trade by setting incentives for dealers not to exports to other Member States.[65] It additionally assessed the scheme's actual effects, and found that there had been a decline in exports and that there was a clear price differential for Peugeot cars between the Member States affected by the agreement.[66] It concluded that the scheme had both the object and effect of restricting competition.

This decision is typical of the Commission's approach to agreements that prohibit or discourage exports into other Member States, or limit the provision of services to specific national markets. The Commission's analyses in these cases do not assess whether the parties have market power, or whether the agreement will lead to a reduction of consumer welfare. It considers these types of agreements restrictive by object because they are clearly incompatible with the aim of establishing a single market.[67] Sometimes, the Commission nonetheless also assesses the effects of such agreements 'for the sake of completeness'. These effects analyses establish whether the agreement has affected exports, or whether there is a marked price differential for the relevant product between the national markets.[68] The Commission makes no attempts to present these findings as harm to consumer welfare, for example by arguing that market integration is good for consumers

[63] *Lundbeck* (Case COMP/AT.39226) recitals 656 ff (appeal pending: Case T-472/13 *Lundbeck v Commission* [2013] OJ C325/47).

[64] *SEP et autres/Peugeot SA* (Cases F-2/36.623/36.820/37.275).

[65] ibid, recitals 102–29.

[66] ibid, recitals 130–35.

[67] eg *CISAC* (Case COMP/C2/38.698) recitals 203–12.

[68] *Glaxo Wellcome and others* (Case IV/36.957/F3) recitals 126, 130; *Souris—Topps* (Case COMP/C-3/37.980) recital 48; *GDF/ENEL* (Case COMP/38662) recitals 86 ff.

because it will ultimately result in lower prices or the greatest possible choice. Harm to the functioning of the internal market is considered a separate form of harm caught by Article 101.

iii. Conclusion

In sum, the guidelines introducing a more economic approach to Article 101 spell out a very clear, new concept of competitive harm: restrictions of competition (by means of coordination of conduct or foreclosure of other undertakings) that lead to a reduction in consumer welfare. Although the Commission's focus on hardcore cartels and great use of commitments decisions has resulted in reducing the number of decisions that give a clear understanding of its current understanding of key theoretical concepts, the few suitable infringement decisions show that the Commission mostly adheres to the guidelines' concept of harm in practice. However, it also reveals that despite spelling out an entirely welfare-based concept of harm in the guidelines, the Commission continues to consider partitioning the single market along national borders a separate type of harm prohibited by Article 101, irrespective of consumer harm. The Commission guidelines do not mention this type of harm in their general principles on how to assess a restriction of competition, which focus entirely on the effects on consumer welfare.[69]

C. Conclusion

The comparison of the Commission's concept of harm prior to and after the introduction of the more economic approach shows a significant change in interpretation. Previously, restrictions of competition as such had been sufficient to make agreements anticompetitive, and the restriction of competition had been understood as a restriction of economic freedom, be it that of the parties, that of actual or potential competitors, or that of consumers. Now, post reform, the restriction of freedom or opportunity is considered the mere mechanism that can lead to the ultimate anticompetitive result, namely consumer harm. Whereas the early decision practice on price fixing, for example, reasoned that the practice was anticompetitive because it eliminated the parties' freedom to determine their own prices, the Commission now bases the anticompetitive nature of price fixing on the assumption that it will result in higher prices for consumers than would have existed in the absence of the agreement.

[69] There is eg no mention of market integration in the Art 101(3) or the Horizontal Cooperation Agreements guidelines' 'Basic principles for assessing agreements under Article 101(1)', which set out the Commission's key principles for assessing restrictions of competition (Guidelines on the application of Article 81(3) (n 35) paras 17–27, or Guidelines on the applicability of Article 101 to horizontal co-operation agreements (n 36) paras 26–31)).

This shift in values is not only of philosophical interest, although it raises challenging moral questions. After all, as a consequence of this reinterpretation of Article 101, 'anything goes' as long as it not likely to result in higher prices or affect other parameters of economic consumer welfare. Fairness and individual opportunities to participate in the market no longer count. These issues aside, the new reading of Article 101(1) has great practical implications. It has led to an entirely different test from that applied previously, that requires enforcement agencies and businesses to carry out a very different assessment. In order to prohibit conduct as incompatible with Article 101, the Commission now needs to prove the requirement that it has read into the wording of Article 101, ie a reduction in consumer welfare. In the case of object restrictions, this new condition may not make a great difference in practice. Their anticompetitive nature will continue to be presumed, although the new concept of harm raises the question whether the old object rules are still suitable, given that they were developed for a different type of harm, ie a restriction of economic freedom. In cases in which the Commission needs to assess the agreement's actual effects, however, this new condition makes a great deal of difference. Instead of merely assessing whether the agreement restricts somebody's economic freedom, it now needs to establish, on the basis of convincing evidence, whether the agreement has resulted in a tangible reduction of consumer welfare in terms of price, output, quality or levels of innovation, or whether it is at least likely to do so in future. Chapters 7 and 8 will look in more detail at what such an assessment of an agreement's effects on consumer welfare entails in practice.

One last point is worth signalling. Although the more economic approach thus made a fundamental change to the interpretation of Article 101, with significant practical consequences, the guidelines introducing this approach did not make this clear. It is only a careful analysis of the Commission's early decisions practice, and its comparison with the guidelines' principles that allowed this conclusion. In the interest of transparency, it would have been desirable if the guidelines could have made the fundamental change they were introducing more explicit.

III. Merger Control

This section retraces the evolution of the Commission's concept of harm in the area of EU merger control. It is not concerned with the quality of the Commission's assessments, or about the credibility of the evidence used to support its assumptions, which will be explored in Chapters 7 and 8. This part explores the Commission's understanding of what makes mergers anticompetitive. It does so by analysing the Commission's key enforcement instruments both before and after the introduction of the more economic approach, and comparing the findings. For both periods, it starts by taking a quick look at the guidance provided in the relevant prohibition provision.

A. The Commission's Concept of Harm Prior to the Introduction of the More Economic Approach

i. The Legal Basis: Council Regulation 4064/89

EU merger control is a relatively young area of EU antitrust law. The Treaty establishing a European Economic Community, the predecessor of today's Treaty on the Functioning of the European Union, did not provide a specific legal basis for merger control. While the Spaak Report had suggested including a system of merger control[70] and it is known that the German delegation negotiating the Treaty had strongly argued in favour of doing so,[71] the final version of the Treaty establishing a European Economic Community did not replicate the merger provisions of the Treaty of Paris.

During the first 30 years of EU antitrust law, the Commission sporadically assessed mergers and acquisitions under Article 102 (ex Article 86 EEC).[72] It was not until 1989 that the Council, after long and difficult negotiations, enacted the first merger-specific legal basis: Council Regulation 4064/89, also known as the first Merger Regulation.[73] Article 2(3) of this Regulation contained the substantive test. It prohibited concentrations that 'created or strengthened a dominant position as a result of which effective competition would be significantly impeded in the common market or in a substantial part of it'. This test was taken from German merger law, a fact that has been described as 'the last triumph in what had been 30 years of German influence on the development of European competition law'.[74] Like the 'restriction of competition' within the meaning of Article 101(1), 'dominance as a results of which effective competition would be significantly impeded' is a vague concept of harm. Regulation 4064/89 defined neither the concept of dominance nor that of a significant impediment to effective competition. Both were therefore wide open to interpretation by the Union institutions.

ii. Commission Notices and other Soft Law

Interpretative soft law on Regulation 4064/89 is sparse and not of much help for determining the Commission's concept of competitive harm under the first Merger

[70] Intergovernmental Committee of the Messina Conference, Report by the Heads of Delegations to the Foreign Ministers (Spaak Report) of 21 April 1956, Title II, Ch I, 60 (available at: www.cvce.eu/en).

[71] *Entwurf eines Protokolls über die Sitzungen der Arbeitsgruppe vom 3.—5. September 1956 in Brüssel, 10. September 1956,* document (57) in R Schulze and T Hoeren (eds), *Dokumente zum Europarecht, Band 3, Kartellrecht* (Berlin, Springer, 2000) 172 ff.

[72] *Continental Can Company* (Case IV/26.811) [1972] OJ L7/25; *Warner-Lambert/Gillette and Others* (Case IV/33.440); *BIC/Gillette and Others* (Case IV/33.486) [1993] OJ L116/21.

[73] Council Regulation (EEC) No 4064/89 of 21 December 1989 on the control of concentrations between undertakings [1990] OJ L257/ 13.

[74] A Weitbrecht, 'From Freiburg to Chicago—The First 50 Years of European Competition Law' (2008) 29 *European Competition Law Review* 81, 84.

Regulation. The Commission did publish two interpretative Notices, but they dealt with highly specific issues. The 'Notice concerning concentrative and cooperative operations'[75] explained the difference between concentrative and merely cooperative situations, but provided no guidance on the concept of harm. The 'Notice on restrictions ancillary to concentrations'[76] explained the concept of ancillary restrictions within the meaning of Article 8(3) of the Merger Regulation, which were to be assessed together with the concentration under the Merger Regulation, rather than under Articles 101 and 102, to avoid parallel assessments. In essence, this Notice listed a number of contractual restrictions and explained under what circumstances the Commission would consider them ancillary (because directly related and necessary) to the transaction. It contained little guidance on the theoretical principles underlying the Commission's assessment, and in particular no guidance on what constituted a 'dominant position as a result of which effective competition would be significantly impeded'. However, it did contain one interesting morsel: the Notice defined restriction within the meaning of ancillary restriction as an agreement between the parties that limited their own freedom of action in the market.[77] This freedom-based definition was perfectly in line with the Commission's early understanding of competitive restrictions under Article 101. Other than that, however, the Commission did not provide any general guidance on what it considered harmful under the original Merger Regulation. The following section therefore turns to its decision practice.

iii. The Commission's Decision Practice

An analysis of the Commission's decision practice on the basis of the first Merger Regulation reveals a very blurry concept of competitive harm. The Merger Regulation itself prescribed a two-prong test: (1) the creation of strengthening of a dominant position; (2) as a result of which effective competition would be significantly impeded. In fact, the Commission rarely followed this approach to the letter.[78] The vast majority of decisions did not explicitly assess either of these concepts, but carried out substantive analyses that more often than not failed to make clear what they were assessing until the conclusion wrapped them up with the finding that the concentration was (or was not) likely to result in the creation of a dominant position as a result of which effective competition was likely to be impeded.

The Commission's assessment in *Aerospatiale-Alenia/de Havilland*,[79] its very first prohibition decision under the original Merger Regulation, is a representative

[75] European Commission, Notice regarding the concentrative and cooperative operations under Council Regulation (EEC) No 4064/89 of 21 December 1989 on the control of concentrations between undertakings [1990] OJ C203/10.

[76] European Commission, Notice regarding restrictions ancillary to concentrations [1990] OJ C203/5.

[77] ibid, para 3.

[78] *Varta/Bosch*, a very early decision clearing a proposed concentration, is one of these exceptional cases, in which the Commission separately assessed dominance and its impact on competition (*Varta/Bosch* (Case IV/M.012) [1991] OJ L320/26, recitals 32 and 44–63).

[79] *Aerospatiale-Alenia/de Havilland* (Case IV/M.053) [1991] OJ L334/42.

example of this practice. The case concerned a proposed concentration in the air transport sector. Aerospatiale, a French company active in the aerospace industry, and Alenia, an Italian competitor, had collectively wished to acquire de Havilland, which manufactured regional turboprop aircraft. In its competitive assessment, the Commission first defined the markets likely to be affected by the transaction. It then assessed the 'impact of the concentration' by analysing (1) the effect on the 'position' of the leading producer of regional aircraft, ATR, which was controlled by the parties;[80] (2) the 'strength of the remaining competition';[81] (3) customers;[82] and (4) potential entry into the market.[83] It found that the acquisition would significantly strengthen ATR's position, so as to allow it to act 'independently of its competitors' who would not be able to compete effectively because of ATR's many competitive advantages such as its broad sales base and coverage of all the markets,[84] and 'independently of its customers' who would have little bargaining power and difficulties switching to another manufacturer.[85]

The Commission's concern about ATR's ability to act independently of its competitors and customers suggests that its assessment was at least loosely based on the concept of dominance as defined by the Court of Justice for Article 102. According to longstanding case law, the Court defines dominance within the meaning of Article 102 as a

> position of economic strength enjoyed by an undertaking which enables it to prevent effective competition being maintained on the relevant market by giving it the power to behave to an appreciable extent independently of its competitors, customers and ultimately of its consumers.[86]

The assumption that the Commission looked to the case law on Article 102 for inspiration in its interpretation of the Merger Regulation is supported by the fact that a number of early merger decisions actually explicitly defined dominance in line with the Court's formula for Article 102.[87]

A key problem with this definition of dominance is that it is broad and vague. Clearly, the concern is that the merged entity will become too powerful in economic terms. However, the Court's and Commission's concept of dominance of this period did not specify the type of power that the law sought to prevent, or the type of danger that was likely to result from this power. It suggested, generally, that the ability to behave independently from competitors, customers and consumers would be harmful. But what type of harm is actually caused by an undertaking's ability to behave independently? This remained unclear. Moreover, under Article 101, the Commission considered that *losing* the freedom to behave independently

[80] ibid, recitals 27–33.
[81] ibid, recitals 34–42.
[82] ibid, recitals 43–50.
[83] ibid, recitals 53–64.
[84] ibid, recital 34.
[85] ibid, recital 43.
[86] Case 27/76 *United Brands v Commission* ECLI:EU:C:1978:22, para 65, most recently reaffirmed in Case C-457/10 P *AstraZeneca v Commission* ECLI:EU:C:2012:770, para 175.
[87] eg *Nestlé/Perrier* (Case IV/M.190) [1992] OJ L356/1, recitals 110, 116, 132; *Du Pont/ICI* (Case IV/M.214) [1993] OJ L7/13, recital 47; *Aerospatiale-Alenia/de Havilland* (n 79) recitals 34 and 43.

from one's competitors amounted to competitive harm. In sum, this concept of dominance was vague at best. If understood literally, it was even inconsistent with the concept of harm under Article 101.

That being said, many merger decisions of this early period did not even attempt to define, explain or elaborate on the concept of dominance.[88] They were even less clear on how the Commission interpreted the condition of 'significant impediment to effective competition'. There is no definition or explanation to be found of this concept in the Commission's early decision practice. In fact, not every assessment mentioned the condition.

What one finds instead, in the manner of *Aerospatiale-Alenia/de Havilland*, are substantive assessments that leapt straight into the analysis of 'relevant factors' without explaining the ultimate purpose of the analysis or the type of harm the Commission was keen to prevent. Like the early approach to Article 101, the early merger practice did not distinguish between horizontal and non-horizontal constellations. Typically, the Commission's competitive assessments considered the following factors: (1) the effect on the parties' position (most commonly in terms of market share[89] but also in terms of competitive advantages over other undertakings);[90] (2) the effect on the position of existing competitors (usually in terms of market share and capacity);[91] (3) the possibility and likelihood of new competitors successfully entering the market;[92] and (4) customers' ability to switch suppliers and other forms of buying power.[93] In substance, many of these factors are relevant in modern-day market power analyses. However, while a market power analysis specifically seeks to determine whether the parties will have the power to raise prices or harm consumer welfare in other ways, the purpose of the Commission's competitive assessments was conceptually unclear.

A closer analysis of these decisions suggests that, in a number of cases, the Commission sought to establish whether the parties would face effective competition after the merger. In a few decisions, it found that this would not be

[88] eg *Varta/Bosch* (n 78); *MSG Media Service* (Case IV/M.469) [1994] OJ L364/1; *RTL/Veronica/Endemol* (Case IV/M.553) [1996] OJ L134/32; *Saint-Gobain/Wacker-Chemie/NOM* (Case No IV/M.774) [1997] OJ L 247/1, amongst many others.

[89] See eg *Aerospatiale-Alenia/de Havilland* (n 79) recitals 28–30; *Nestlé/Perrier* (n 87) recitals 38–48; *Volvo/Scania* (Case COMP/M.1672) [2001] OJ L143/74, recitals 297–98; *General Electric/Honeywell* (Case COMP/M.2220) [2004] OJ L48/1, recitals 45–73; *Deutsche Telekom/BetaResearch* (Case IV/M.1027) [1999] OJ L53/31, recitals 25–27.

[90] According to the Commission, owning a portfolio of brands as opposed to merely marketing a single brand constituted such a competitive advantage (eg *Guinness/Grand Metropolitan* (Case No IV/M.938) [1998] OJ L 288/24, recitals 38–46; *Nestlé/Perrier* (n 87) recitals 49–56, 83).

[91] See eg *Du Pont/ICI* (n 87) recitals 38–41; *Blokker/Toys 'R' Us* (Case IV/M.890) [1998] OJ L316/1, recitals 69–81.

[92] eg *Nestlé/Perrier* (n 87) recitals 90–107; *Gencor/Lonrho* (Case IV/M.619) [1997] OJ L11/30, recitals 86–90; *MCI WorldCom/Sprint* (Case COMP/M.1741) [2003] OJ L300/1, recitals 165–67; *Deutsche Telekom/BetaResearch* (n 89) recitals 29–41; *Bertelsmann/Kirch/Premiere* (Case IV/M.993) [1999] OJ L53/1, recitals 48–68.

[93] eg *Nestlé/Perrier* (n 87) recitals 77–89; *Volvo/Scania* (n 89) recitals 299–302; *MCI WorldCom/Sprint* (n 92) recitals 168–74; *General Electric/Honeywell* (n 89) recitals 224–28.

the case because the remaining competitors were so weak that they would not be able to compete against the parties.[94] In others, it found that effective competition was likely to be impeded because the merger would make the entry of new competitors more difficult.[95] What these decisions left open, however, was why exactly the Commission considered the inability of competitors to 'stand up' to the merged entity or to enter the market in the first place problematic and why it sought to prevent such a situation from arising. In particular, it remained unclear whether the concern was about competitors' opportunities to participate in the market (as had been the concern under Article 101 during the same period), whether it was about the existence of competition as such, or whether the Commission was concerned about possible detrimental results for consumers. In other cases, the Commission's key question was whether actual or potential competitors would be able to constrain the merged entity's 'freedom of action'.[96] If they were, the merger was not deemed anticompetitive. Again, it remains unclear from these decisions what type of danger the Commission sought to avert. They contained no indication as to what harm the parties were likely to inflict or what type of behaviour they might engage in, were their freedom of action not constrained by competitors.

It is possible to make out the first portents of change in the late 1990s. This was the period when the Commission started reviewing its approach to Article 101, leading it to adopt the consumer welfare aim and a reduced concept of harm under this provision. Around the same time, the term 'consumer welfare' also first appears in the Commission's merger practice under Regulation 4064/89. A number of prohibition decisions mentioned, albeit in passing and only in the conclusion, that one of the Commission's key concerns and reasons for prohibiting the transaction had been that the merged entity would be able to raise prices or reduce output to the detriment of consumers.[97] Two decisions even used the term market power,[98] without however explaining or engaging with the concept. This is not to say that the Commission adopted consumer harm as its concept of harm under Regulation 4068/89. Its general approach to assessing mergers did not change at this point in time and the theory underlying these decisions remained extremely hazy.

A second sign of change can be observed around the same period. In the early 2000s, when the Commission had just reviewed its approach to vertical agreements under Article 101, it also started to distinguish more systematically between horizontal and non-horizontal situations in the area of merger

[94] *Aerospatiale-Alenia/de Havilland* (n 79) recital 42; *RTL/Veronica/Endemol* (n 88) recitals 47–64; *Blokker/Toys 'R' Us* (n 91) recitals 103, 104.

[95] *MSG Media Service* (n 88) recitals 60–72.

[96] *Du Pont/ICI* (n 87) recital 47; *Varta/Bosch* (n 78) recital 57.

[97] *Gencor/Lonrho* (n 92) recitals 205, 206; *Saint-Gobain/Wacker-Chemie/NOM* (n 88) recital 236; *Airtours/First Choice* (Case IV/M.1524) OJ [2000] L93/1, recital 158.

[98] *Gencor* (n 92) recital 173, 214; *Airtours/First Choice* (n 97) 127.

control.[99] It recognised that mergers between competitors and mergers between undertakings in vertically related, or even adjacent, markets produced different types of harmful effects. It specifically started assessing the impacts of non-horizontal concentrations as to whether they would result in foreclosure effects, ie as to whether they would result in the exit of competitors from the market or whether they would make it more difficult for new competitors to enter the market.[100] Significantly, this did not entail an analysis of the effects on consumer welfare. The mere foreclosure of competitors was deemed sufficient to make the merger anticompetitive. The key novelty at this point was that Commission started to distinguish more clearly between the horizontal and non-horizontal aspects of mergers, and to tailor its assessments more specifically to these constellations.

iv. Conclusion

In sum, the Commission's concept of harm under the original Merger Regulation was broad and indeterminate. While its competitive assessments contained many elements of a modern market power analysis, and were insofar somewhat 'more economic' than the Commission's early approach to Article 101, its analyses were conceptually unclear. The majority revealed a generalised concern about too much economic power in too few hands, but did not explain what danger emanated from such a position or what harm it expected a powerful undertaking to inflict on society. The Commission specifically frowned upon mergers that would lead to the exclusion of competitors or would make the entry of new competitors more difficult. Again, it is not clear from the relevant decisions what the ultimate concern was. Did it consider the exclusion of competitors problematic because it restricted these businesses' opportunities or because the lack of competitors would ultimately lead the powerful undertaking to cause another type of harm? Whatever the underlying rationale may have been, the Commission did not consider it necessary to prove any harm other than the exclusion of competitors. Their foreclosure was sufficient to make a merger anticompetitive.

B. The Commission's Concept of Harm after the Introduction of the More Economic Approach

This situation changed radically in 2004 when the new Merger Regulation entered into force and the Commission issued its interpretative guidelines on the new legal basis.

[99] eg *Tetra Laval/Sidel* (Case COMP/M.2416) recitals 263 and 291; and *General Electric/Honeywell* (n 89).

[100] *Tetra Laval/Sidel* (n 99) recitals 291 ff; *General Electric/Honeywell* (n 89) recitals 342 and 437.

i. The New Legal Basis: Council Regulation 139/2004

In contrast to Articles 101 and 102, the legal basis of European merger control has been formally amended over time. In 2001, the Commission took its legal duty to review the Regulation's turnover thresholds and case referral rules as the opportunity to examine the operation of the Merger Regulation as a whole, in order to identify other areas in which improvements could be made. It published a Green Paper outlining its initial views[101] and launched a consultation of Member States, the business and legal communities and other interested parties.[102] The consultation persuaded the Commission that the original Merger Regulation might contain a significant 'gap'.[103] The concern was that the dominance test might not allow the Commission to prohibit mergers resulting in an oligopolistic situation likely to lead to price increases even though the oligopolists were unlikely to engage in collusion. While this was not a case the Commission had ever considered before,[104] there was broad agreement amongst practitioners and academics alike that EU merger law should be able to prevent such a situation. However, while some took the view that the concept of (collective) dominance was broad and flexible enough to catch such a situation,[105] others were more doubtful.[106] Eventually, the Commission sided with the latter, and agreed that relying on the concept of collective dominance in the eventuality of a future 'gap case' was too risky, as the Court might not agree with this approach. It therefore submitted an initially cautious legislative proposal to the Council that would have clarified that mergers leading to the creation of oligopolies non-inclined to cooperation fell within the scope of the Merger Regulation.[107] The negotiations at the ministerial level proved extraordinarily difficult. A number of Member States believed that the Community should seize the opportunity to adopt the 'substantial lessening of competition' (SLC)

[101] European Commission, 'Green Paper on the Review of Council Regulation (EEC) No 4064/89' COM(2001) 745/6 of 11 December 2001.

[102] The comments received by the Commission in the course of the consultation process are available at: ec.europa.eu/competition/consultations/2002_council_regulation/index.html.

[103] For more background information, see SB Völker, 'Mind the Gap: Unilateral Effects Analysis Arrives in EC Merger Control' (2004) 25 *European Competition Law Review* 395; VSV Selvam, 'The EC Merger Control Impasse: Is there a Solution to this Predicament?' (2004) 25 *European Competition Law Review* 52.

[104] 'Green Paper on the Review of Council Regulation (EEC) No 4064/89' (n 101) para 166.

[105] V Verouden, C Bengtsson and S Albaek, 'The Draft EU Notice on Horizontal Mergers: A Further Step toward Convergence?' (2004) 49 *Antitrust Bulletin* 243; E Müller and U Böge, 'From the Market Dominance Test to the SLC Test: Are there Any Reasons for Change?' (2002) 23 *European Competition Law Review* 495.

[106] J Vickers, 'How to Reform the EC Merger Test?' in G Drauz and M Reynolds (eds), *EC Merger Control—A Major Reform in Progress* (Oxford, Oxford University Press, 2003); R Whish, Competition Law, 5th edn (Oxford, Oxford University Press, 2003) 878; Z Biro and D Parker, 'A New EC Merger Test? Dominance v Substantial Lessening of Competition' (2002) 1 *Competition Law Journal* 157; N Levy, 'Dominance versus SLC: A Subtle Distinction?' in G Drauz and M Reynolds (eds), *EC Merger Control—A Major Reform in Progress* (Oxford, Oxford University Press, 2003).

[107] European Commission, Proposal for a Council Regulation on the control of concentrations between undertakings (Merger Regulation) [2003] OJ C20/4.

test of US merger law. The United Kingdom, which had recently adopted the SLC test in its own domestic merger law,[108] was the main proponent of this view. Others, Germany in particular, were vehement that the dominance criterion was a typically European concept that had served the Union well and should not be sacrificed 'at the altar of globalisation'.[109] Member States were deeply divided and repeatedly the negotiations came close to breaking down. Eventually, however, the Council agreed on what the Commission described as a 'truly European' solution combining 'the best of the substantive standards in our various jurisdictions and preserving existing precedent'.[110] Article 2(3) of the recast Merger Regulation, Regulation 139/2004, now prohibits mergers 'which would significantly impede effective competition in the common market or a substantial part of it, in particular as a result of the creation or the strengthening of a dominant position'.[111]

According to the wording of this test, the concept of dominance thus continues to exist. This was primarily due to the fact that Germany would not have agreed to a new test without its inclusion. Also Article 2(1), which lists the factors that the Commission is meant to take into account in its assessment under the new test, remained substantially unchanged. However, the wording of the recast Article 2(3) also suggests that dominance is no longer an essential condition for a merger's incompatibility with EU merger law. The new test primarily enquires whether the merger will lead to a 'significant impediment of effective competition'. The creation or strengthening of a dominant position is merely an example of a situation in which the merger is likely to lead to a significant impediment to competition.

Competitive harm within the meaning of the new Merger Regulation therefore is a significant impediment to effective competition. But what does this really mean and how does one measure it? It is yet another concept of harm that is vague and open to interpretation. The Regulation's recitals, which explain the Council's motivations and considerations for enacting the Regulation, do not define the concept. However, they do suggest that it had not been the Council's intention to introduce a new concept of harm. Recitals 23 and 24 state that the assessment of a concentration's compatibility with the internal market should happen in terms of the 'need to maintain and develop effective competition', the general framework of fundamental objectives listed in ex Articles 2 EC and 2 TEU and the principle of an open market economy with free competition. This is identical to the guidance given in the original Merger Regulation's recitals.[112] Recital 26 of Regulation

[108] Enterprise Act 2002, s 35(2).

[109] Reply by the Bundeskartellamt to the Green Paper on the review of Regulation (EEC) No 4064/89, available at: ec.europa.eu/competition/consultations/2002_council_regulation/bundeskartellamt.pdf.

[110] European Commission, 'Merger Review Package in a Nutshell' (2004) *Competition Policy Newsletter Special Edition* 2.

[111] Council Regulation (EC) No 139/2004 of 20 January 2004 on the control of concentrations between undertakings (the EC Merger Regulation) [2004] OJ L24/1.

[112] Regulation 4064/89 (n 73) recital 13.

139/2004 further stipulates that a significant impediment to effective competition can usually be expected to result from the creation or strengthening of a dominant position, and that the guidance from past judgments or Commission decisions on Regulation 4064/89 should be preserved and consistency with the former standards of competitive harm maintained.

In sum, Regulation 139/2004's recitals reveal that the Council did not intend to change the scope of Article 2(3), but merely to clarify that mergers leading to oligopolies non-inclined to cooperation but likely to align their market conduct were included within this scope. Neither the binding parts of the Merger Regulation nor the recitals introduced the notion that competitive harm within the meaning of this new Regulation equalled or presupposed consumer harm. Likewise, Commissioner Monti and his Director General emphasised at the time that the review of the merger test had not meant to change the existing merger practice, but that it had aimed to maintain precedent while clarifying that the Regulation also caught 'gap cases'.[113]

ii. Commission Notices and other Soft Law

While many signs at the time of the recasting process therefore pointed towards maintaining the status quo, the Commission's soft law paints a very different picture. In 2004, in time for the entry into force of the new Merger Regulation, the Commission published a set of guidelines on the assessment of horizontal mergers under the new legal instrument.[114] The guidelines on the assessment of non-horizontal mergers followed in 2008.[115] Both sets of guidelines spell out the Commission's legal interpretation of the new substantive test and its assessment methods in a systematic and comprehensive manner.

In contrast to the earlier merger Notices, the horizontal merger guidelines clearly define the Commission's concept of harm under Regulation 139/2003. Under the heading 'anticompetitive effects', they explain that horizontal mergers may significantly impede effective competition in two ways. One is by eliminating important competitive constraints on firms, which consequently would have increased market power without resorting to coordinated behaviour (non-coordinated effects).[116] Market power is defined as the ability of one or more firms profitably to increase prices, reduce output, choice or quality of goods and services,

[113] eg M Monti, 'Merger Control in the European Union: A Radical Reform' (Brussels, 7 November 2002) and 'Private Litigation as a Key Complement to Public Enforcement of Competition Rules and the First Conclusions on the Implementation of the New Merger Regulation' (Fiesole, 17 September 2004); P Lowe, 'Current Issues of E.U. Competition Law: the New Competition Enforcement Regime' (2004) 24 *Northwestern Journal of International Law & Business* 567, 578.

[114] Commission Notice, Guidelines on the assessment of horizontal mergers under the Council Regulation on the control of concentrations between undertakings [2004] OJ C31/5.

[115] Commission Notice, Guidelines on the assessment of non-horizontal mergers under the Council Regulation on the control of concentrations between undertakings [2008] OJ C265/6.

[116] ibid, para 22.

diminish innovation, or otherwise influence parameters of competition.[117] The second way in which a merger can result in anticompetitive effects, according to the horizontal merger guidelines, is by changing the nature of competition in such a way that firms that previously were not coordinating their behaviour are now significantly more likely to coordinate and raise prices or otherwise harm effective competition (coordinated effects).[118] In sum, both types of anticompetitive effect presuppose an increase in prices, a reduction in output, choice or quality of goods and services, a lessening of innovation, or other negative effects on parameters of consumer welfare. In other words, competitive harm within the meaning of the horizontal merger guidelines requires a reduction in consumer welfare.

The non-horizontal merger guidelines are based on the same concept of harm. They also take the view that non-horizontal mergers may significantly impede effective competition in two manners: by means of non-coordinated effects and coordinated effects.[119] In the context of non-horizontal mergers, non-coordinated effects are said to arise if the merger leads to foreclosure, because actual or potential rivals' access to supplies or markets is hampered or eliminated as a result of the merger, thereby reducing these companies' ability to compete. Where as a result of such foreclosure, the merging companies may be able to increase the price charged to consumers profitably, this amounts to a significant impediment to effective competition or 'anticompetitive foreclosure'.[120] According to the non-horizontal guidelines, coordinated effects arise where the merger changes the nature of competition in such a way that firms that previously were not coordinating their behaviour are now significantly more likely and able to coordinate to raise prices or otherwise harm effective competition.[121] In other words, what makes a non-horizontal merger anticompetitive according to these guidelines is its negative effect on consumer welfare. The exclusion of rivals is a mere mechanism through which competitive harm, ie consumer harm, may be caused. In itself, it is not deemed a significant impediment to effective competition.

This is an important departure from the Commission's former approach to assessing non-horizontal mergers. In the cases of *GE/Honeywell* and *Tetra Laval*, for example, the Commission had considered the likely exclusion of competitors sufficient to make the merger anticompetitive, and had not examined the likely effects on consumers.[122] This had been the key bone of contention between the EU and US antitrust authorities in the dispute over the ill-fated *GE/Honeywell* merger.

The Commission's new concept of harm under Regulation 130/2004 is perfectly consistent with the guidelines' understanding of the Regulation's objective. Both sets of merger guidelines define the purpose of merger control as preventing concentra-

[117] ibid, para 8.
[118] ibid, para 22.
[119] ibid, para 17.
[120] ibid, para 18.
[121] ibid, para 19.
[122] *Tetra Laval/Sidel* ((n 99) recitals 291 ff; *General Electric/Honeywell* (n 89) recitals 342 and 437.

tions that would be likely to deprive customers of the benefits of effective competition, namely low prices, high quality products, a wide selection of goods and services, and innovation, by significantly increasing the market power of firms.[123]

The horizontal merger guidelines from 2004 had predicted that the Commission would continue to base most cases of incompatibility on a finding of dominance and that it intended to preserve the guidance that could be drawn from past decisional practice and case law.[124] Interestingly, the non-horizontal guidelines, which were issued four years after the horizontal merger guidelines, contain no such caveat. This is a reflection of the fact that the concept of dominance, as is demonstrated in the following section, has in reality not retained much relevance in the Commission's decision practice after the horizontal guidelines introduced the 'more economic' concept of competitive harm. It does not play a meaningful role in the non-horizontal guidelines either.

Much like in the context of Article 101, the guidelines introducing the more economic approach to EU merger control did not make clear that they introduced a new, or at least a more clearly defined and restricted, concept of harm. It is only the comparison with the Commission's previous decision practice that allows the above conclusion that the merger guidelines departed from the Commission's previous practice.

iii. The Commission's Decision Practice

Under the new Merger Regulation, the Commission has so far cleared (with or without conditions) over 3,200 mergers by means of a formal decision.[125] There is therefore plenty of material to examine. However, one development is worth highlighting from the outset: to date, the Commission has only prohibited five mergers on the basis of the new Merger Regulation.[126] This is a marked drop in prohibitions compared to the 19 infringement decisions that the Commission had imposed under the first Merger Regulation between 1990 and 2004, in particular in view of the fact that the Union has grown by 13 Member States since 2004 and notifications have steadily increased in numbers.[127] In contrast to the

[123] Horizontal merger guidelines (n 114) para 8, Non-horizontal merger guidelines (n 115) para 10. See Ch 4.

[124] Horizontal merger guidelines (n 114) para 4.

[125] A search of the Commission's decisions available on its website (www.ec.europa.eu/competition/elojade/isef/index.cfm?clear=1&policy_area_id=2) reveals that it has to date cleared a total of 3,165 mergers in Phase I, and 73 in Phase II.

[126] *Ryanair/Aer Lingus* (Case No COMP/M.4439); *Olympic/Aegean Airlines* (Case No COMP/M.5830); *Deutsche Börse/NYSE Euronext* (Case No COMP/M.6166); *UPS/TNT Express* (Case No COMP/M.6570); and *Ryanair/Aer Lingus III* (Case No COMP/M.6663).

[127] Between 1990 and 2003, 2,342 proposed transitions were notified to the Commission. Between 2004 and June 2015, the Commission received 3,526 notifications (source: www.ec.europa.eu/competition/mergers/statistics.pdf). For an interesting comparison of figures of the Commission's merger enforcement activities between 1994–2003 and 2004–08, see F Maier-Rigaud and K Parplies, 'EU Merger Control Five Years after the Introduction of the SIEC Test: what Explains the Drop in Enforcement Activity?' (2009) 30 *European Competition Law Review* 565.

situation under Article 101, this development is not the result of a decentralisation of enforcement, as the assessment of mergers with a Union dimension remains firmly in the hands of the Commission. Also, unlike in the context of Articles 101 and 102, the Commission had in practice always taken into consideration commitments by the parties in the early stages of the investigation and cleared the notified transaction if it deemed that these commitments addressed its competitive concerns.[128]

An analysis of the Commission's decision practice shows that its clearance decisions generally follow the welfare-based approach outlined in the merger guidelines with regard to its theories and concept of harm. In the great majority of cases, they assess both horizontal and vertical mergers as to whether they will result in coordinated or non-coordinated effects. When assessing the likelihood of coordinated effects, the Commission's clearance decisions since 2004 generally examine whether the remaining competitors would be able to coordinate their behaviour after the merger so as to reduce capacity[129] or raise prices.[130] In the case of horizontal mergers that are unlikely to lead to coordination, the decisions assess whether the merger is likely to result in the creation of market power as the result of the elimination of an important competitive constraint.[131] In other words, they examine whether the remaining competitors would have the ability to raise prices or reduce output. Where the potential scenario is one of foreclosure, ie in non-horizontal constellations, the assessments are based on the premise that the exclusion of competitors is only anticompetitive if this is also likely to result in consumer harm.[132] The Commission tends not to rely on the concept of dominance, even in cases where the notifying parties' market share is so high that, according to the case law at least,[133] dominance should have been presumed. Instead, it assesses even these cases as to whether the merger is likely to result in market power as the result of coordinated or non-coordinated effects.[134] In sum, this is perfectly in line with the theory spelled out in the horizontal and non-horizontal merger

[128] See eg *Fiat Geotech/Ford New Holland* (Case No IV/M.009) recitals 30, 31, or *TNT/Canada Post, DBP Postdienst, La Poste, PTT Post & Sweden Post* (Case IV/M.102) recitals 6 and 47. This power was formalised by Art 1(5) of Council Regulation (EC) 1310/97 of 30 June 1997 amending Regulation (EEC) No 4064/89 on the control of concentrations between undertakings [1997] OJ L180/1, which allowed the Commission the power to make these commitments legally binding.

[129] eg *Blackstone/Acetex* (Case COMP/M.3625) recitals 96–103, 116–20, 127–34.

[130] eg *T-Mobile Austria/Tele.ring* (Case No COMP/M.3916) recital 127.

[131] See eg *Telefónica UK/Vodafone UK/Everything Everywhere/JV* (Case COMP/M.6314) recital 524; *KLM/Martinair* (Case COMP/M.5141) recitals 292–303, 332–34, also 221, 231 and 240; *Blackstone/Acetex* (n 129) recitals 88–95, 107–115 and 122–26; *Google/DoubleClick* (Case No COMP/M.4731) recitals 202 and 203; *T-Mobile Austria/Tele.ring* (n 130) recitals 40–126; *Lufthansa/SN Airholding* (Case COMP/M.5335) recitals 155–57, 334, amongst many others.

[132] See eg *Telefónica UK/Vodafone UK/Everything Everywhere/JV* (Case COMP/M.6314) recital 246; *Tom Tom/Tele Atlas* (Case COMP/M.4854) recitals 231–37; *Nokia/Navteq* (Case COMP/M.4942) recital 268.

[133] eg C-62/86 *AKZO Chemie v Commission* ECLI:EU:C:1991:286, para 60.

[134] See eg *Bertelsmann/Springer* (Case COMP/M.3178) recitals 99–153; *Glatfelter/Crompton Assets* (Case No COMP/M.4215) recitals 79, 95, 98, 104.

guidelines: the key criterion for establishing the competitive nature of a merger is whether it is likely to reduce consumer welfare.

While the Commission's clearance decisions, with rare exceptions, tend to follow the guidelines' theories of harm closely, several of its prohibition decisions are conceptually much more ambiguous. In three out of the five prohibition decisions based on the revised Merger Regulation, *Ryanair/Aer Lingus I*, *Olympic/Aegean Airlines* and *Ryanair/Aer Lingus III*,[135] there is no mention of coordinated or non-coordinated effects at all. Equally absent is the concept of market power. Instead, the term 'dominance' figures prominently in these assessments. These three decisions are moreover very evasive about the underlying concept of harm, despite the extraordinary detail of the assessment and the evidence collated to support its conclusions. Without spelling out any theory of harm, these decisions leap straight into the assessment of 'relevant' factors, much in the fashion of the Commission's merger decisions prior to the reform, without explaining what type of harmful effect they are seeking to establish.[136] Reading between the lines of these decisions, it is clear that the Commission feared in practice that the merged entities would be able to increase prices after the merger in all three cases.[137] The press releases and summary decisions in both *Ryanair/Aer Lingus* decisions are very emphatic on this point.[138]

At first sight, this seems like an irrational phenomenon. An extraordinary amount of work must have gone into proving the anticompetitive nature of these mergers and into writing the decision. Each *Ryanair/Aer Lingus* decision was over 500 pages long, and contained complex econometric analyses. The decision in *Olympic/Aegean Airlines* spanned 450 pages. Also, prohibition decisions usually attract far more attention and scrutiny than the much more common clearance decisions. Why not spell out the key purpose of the assessment and the commitment to the welfare-based concept of harm more clearly in such important decisions? One possible explanation for the conceptual caginess of these prohibition decisions is that the Commission wanted to ensure that these prohibition decisions were immune to possible actions for annulments and therefore avoided basing its assessments on an exclusively welfare-based concept of harm.[139] As Chapter 10

[135] *Ryanair/Aer Lingus* (n 126); *Olympic/Aegean Airlines* (n 126); *Ryanair/Aer Lingus III* (n 126).

[136] *Ryanair/Aer Lingus* (n 126) recitals 339 ff; *Olympic/Aegean Airlines* (n 126) recitals 490 ff; *Ryanair/Aer Lingus III* (n 126) recitals 423 ff.

[137] eg *Ryanair/Aer Lingus* (n 126) recitals 433, 491, 498, and 541–54; *Olympic/Aegean Airlines* (n 126) recitals 1482, 1483; *Ryanair/Aer Lingus III* (n 126) recitals 607, 629, 1068, 1630.

[138] *Ryanair/Aer Lingus* (n 126) Summary Decision [2008] OJ C47/9, recital 29; European Commission, 'Mergers: Commission Prohibits Ryanair's Proposed Takeover of Aer Lingus' Press Release IP/07/893 of 27 June 2007; *Ryanair/Aer Lingus III* (n 126) Summary Decision [2013] OJ C216/22, recitals 51 and 52; European Commission, 'Mergers: Commission Prohibits Ryanair's Proposed Takeover of Aer Lingus' Press Release of 27 February 2013.

[139] Ryanair indeed appealed against the Commission's first prohibition, arguing legal errors and manifest errors of assessment. The General Court rejected the action as unfounded (Case T-342/07 *Ryanair Holdings v European Commission* ECLI:EU:T:2010:280).

demonstrates, the Court of Justice does not share the Commission's 'more economic' interpretation of the EU antitrust rules in every point. In particular, it does not consider consumer harm an indispensable component of competitive harm. Be this as it may, the Commission's other two prohibition decisions, *Deutsche Börse/NYSE Euronext* and *UPS/TNT* are much more clearly based on the approach outlined in the horizontal merger guidelines,[140] although even *Deutsche Börse/NYSE Euronext* contains a number of passages that suggest that the anticompetitive effects consist in the loss of competition as such and that consumer harm is merely a further undesirable consequence of this loss.[141]

In sum, while not always as explicit or consistent as the merger guidelines, the Commission's decision practice under the new Merger Regulation is predominantly based on the same understanding of competitive harm. Only such restrictions of competition are deemed caught by the Merger Regulation that are likely to result in consumer harm.

C. Conclusion

In conclusion, although the changes may be less immediately obvious than those under Article 101, the more economic approach has also altered the Commission's concept of harm under EU merger law. While its concept of competitive harm used to be broad and vague, the Commission now operates on the basis of a very specific concept of harm. It interprets an impediment to effective competition within the meaning of Regulation 139/2004 as a lessening in competition that will lead to a reduction in consumer welfare, in particular in the form of higher prices, lower output, lower quality, less choice and lower levels of innovation. It has also established clear theories on how such consumer harm may occur, namely through coordination or through non-coordinated effects.

That being said, the new concept of harm has not significantly influenced the factors that the Commission assesses in the case of horizontal mergers or non-horizontal mergers that are likely to result in cooperation. Even prior to the reform, the Commission's competitive assessments of these constellations had included many elements of a modern market power analysis (for example, the analysis of market shares, presence of competitors, potential competition, barriers to entry and countervailing buyer power). The key difference is that these assessments are now conceptually much clearer as to what type of harmful effect is being established and how it is likely to be caused.

However, in the case of foreclosure effects resulting from non-horizontal mergers, the new understanding of competitive harm has significant practical

[140] *Deutsche Börse/NYSE Euronext* (n 126) recital 494, upheld on appeal in Case T-175/12 *Deutsche Börse AG v Commission* ECLI:EU:T:2015:148; and *UPS/TNT Express* (Case No COMP/M.6570) recitals 721–40.

[141] eg *Deutsche Börse/NYSE Euronext* (n 126) recitals 495, 1126.

implications. The Commission now only considers such instances of foreclosure anticompetitive that are liable to result in consumer harm. Previously, the mere likelihood of competitors being excluded was sufficient to make the merger anticompetitive. If the European Commission therefore were to reassess the *GE/Honeywell* merger today under its current approach, it would have to do what it did not consider necessary in 2001: assess the effects of the predicted foreclosure on end consumers. This theoretical dispute between the US and EU antitrust authorities therefore seems to have been laid to rest.

IV. Article 102

Like Article 101 and the EU Merger Regulation, Article 102 does not contain a clear concept of harm. The provision prohibits the 'abuse of a dominant position', but defines neither the concept of abuse nor that of dominance. Similarly to Article 101, it lists examples of conduct that may be considered anticompetitive, ie abusive, within the meaning of this prohibition: (1) imposing unfair purchase or selling prices or other trading conditions; (2) limiting production, markets or technical development to the prejudice of consumers; (3) applying dissimilar conditions to equivalent transactions with other trading parties, thereby placing them at a competitive disadvantage; and (4) making the conclusion of contracts subject to acceptance of supplementary obligations which have no connection with the subject of such contracts.

It is not possible to extract one single, incontrovertible concept of harm for Article 102 from these examples. For one, the provision's wording suggests that the four examples are not exhaustive.[142] Moreover, they do not appear to protect one single, clearly defined value or interest, although all of them could in fact be interpreted as containing a moral concept of harm, namely unfairness. This interpretation would sit nicely with the term 'abuse', which is in itself suggestive of unethical conduct. The term is certainly more value-laden than Article 101's and the Merger Regulation's more neutral concepts of 'restriction of competition' and 'significant impediment to effective competition'. The first example given in Article 102 explicitly uses the term 'unfair' to describe the type of conduct that may be considered abusive: unfair pricing or other unfair trading practices, apparently regardless of who is the addressee of the unfair treatment. The second example, by contrast, appears to condemn types of conduct that specifically cause prejudice to consumers. Again, the use of the term 'prejudice' rather than the more neutral 'disadvantage' suggests a moral objection to these actions. The third example condemns dominant undertakings discriminating amongst trading partners in a way that results in competitive disadvantages for these undertakings. The term

[142] 'Such abuse may, in particular, consist in'.

discrimination is evocative of unfairness again, and this example could be interpreted as protecting the rights of the businesses being discriminated against. Finally, the last example does not specify whether the conduct is addressed to consumers or trading partners, but appears to condemn the practice of making the conclusion of contracts subject to acceptance of supplementary, unrelated obligations, ie tying, for its own sake. As such, this example could also easily be interpreted as condemning unfair conduct. However, this is not the only possible reading of Article 102. Its wording is so vague that other interpretations are possible, and the following shows that the Union institutions have indeed interpreted these terms in many different ways.

A. The Commission's Concept of Harm Prior to the Introduction of the More Economic Approach

i. Commission Soft Law

There was very little general guidance on the Commission's interpretation of Article 102 prior to the reform of the mid-2000s. The Commission had not issued any interpretative Notices on Article 102 at all. Its annual Reports on Competition Policy allowed the occasional glimpse into the Commission's early understanding of harm under Article 102. For example, the Second Report on Competition Policy (1972) explained that the Commission had attacked 'improper practices' under Article 102 that had been designed to 'curtail the commercial freedom of dealers or to cut off supplies to a competitor'.[143] This suggests a concept of harm similar to the Commission's early understanding of competitive harm under Article 101, ie restrictions of commercial freedom. However, this type of information was sporadic and was not intended as interpretative guidance in any event, so that one should not read too much into it. The Commission's decision practice is really the only exhaustive and reliable source for gaining an understanding of the Commission's concept of competitive harm under Article 102 prior to the introduction of the more economic approach.

ii. The Commission's Decision Practice

The Commission was relatively slow to start enforcing Article 102 in comparison to Article 101. The first substantive decision on Article 102 dates from 1971,[144] whereas the Commission had been prohibiting and exempting agreements under Article 101 on a regular basis since 1964. The number of cases was also significantly

[143] European Commission, *Second Report on Competition Policy 1972*, 15.

[144] *Gema I* (Case IV/26.760) [1971] OJ L134/15, closely followed by the more famous decision in *Continental Can* (n 72).

lower. Between 1964 and 1998, the Commission decided 311 cases pursuant to Article 101. During the same period, it decided only 44 cases under Article 102. In contrast to its early approach under Article 101, however, the vast majority of the Article 102 decisions established infringements,[145] whereas many of the above-mentioned 311 Article 101 decisions cleared or exempted the investigated cases. In sum, there is a solid amount of material to examine for the purposes of identifying the Commission's early concept of harm.

The decision practice shows that the Commission's early assessments under Article 102 usually consisted in three steps: the definition of the relevant market, an assessment of whether the investigated undertaking was dominant in this market and, finally, whether the undertaking in question had abused this dominant position. For the purposes of determining the Commission's concept of harm, the last two steps in these assessments are most revealing and contain the key to determining its understanding of competitive harm.

The very early decision practice contains different definitions of dominance that are nonetheless mostly variations upon the same theme: the power to behave independently, without taking into account to any substantial extent competitors, purchasers and suppliers. The Commission considered that this was the case where the undertaking's market share, know-how, access to raw materials, capital or other advantages such as trade mark ownership, enabled it to determine prices or to control the production or distribution of a significant part of the relevant goods.[146] From the late 1970s on, the Commission's decisions usually faithfully reiterated the Court's landmark definition in *United Brands*, according to which dominance is a position of economic strength that enables the undertaking to 'prevent effective competition being maintained' on the relevant market by giving it the 'power to behave to an appreciable extent independently of its competitors, customers and ultimately of its consumers'.[147] This latter formula, as argued earlier, contains a broad and relatively unspecific concept of economic power.[148] In contrast to the concept of market power on which the more economic approach to Article 101 and the Merger Regulation is based, and which specifically refers to the ability to reduce consumer welfare,[149] the concept of dominance as defined in *United Brands* refers to the ability to behave independently of competitors, customers and consumers.

[145] Out of these 44 decisions, 39 were prohibitions and 5 were clearance decisions.

[146] eg *Continental Can Company* (n 72) B.3 (no English version), *Chiquita* (Case IV/26699) [1976] OJ L95/1, II.A.2; *ABG oil companies operating in the Netherlands* (Case IV/28.841 [1977] OJ L117/1, II.A.

[147] *United Brands v Commission* (n 86) para 65. See eg *BPB Industries plc* (Case IV/31.900) [1989] OJ L10/50, recital 114; *Soda-ash—ICI* (Case IV/33.133-D) [1991] OJ L152/40, recital 41.

[148] Ch5, s III.A.iii.

[149] eg European Commission, Guidelines on the application of Article 81(3), para 25, and Guidelines on the assessment of non-horizontal mergers under the Council Regulation on the control of concentrations between undertakings [2008] OJ C265/6, para 8.

While the Commission thus operated on the basis of an established if vague concept of dominance, an analysis of the decision practice reveals no single definition of 'abuse'. It is clear, however, that the concept comprised a multitude of sins. Decisions of the 1970s and 1980s often based the finding of abuse on the fact that the dominant undertaking's conduct had restricted its trading partners' commercial freedom. In *Chiquita*, for example, the Commission found the dominant undertaking's request that their distributors not sell and advertise competing brands abusive because it had undermined the buyers' freedom to determine their business interests, to choose which products to sell and to define their own sales policy.[150] Likewise, in *Vitamins* and *Michelin I*, the Commission found that a rebate system that was conditional on the customer buying exclusively from a dominant undertaking was abusive because it removed all freedom of choice from purchasers in their selection of sources of supply.[151] This understanding of abuse, which focuses on the effects on other businesses' freedom, is perfectly in line with its early understanding of a competitive restriction under Article 101.

The Commission further always considered conduct abusive that led to the exclusion of one or several competitors, although its rationale for this conclusion was not always the same. At times, it portrayed the harm caused by the exclusion as harm to the commercial freedom and opportunity of the excluded competitor.[152] In other instances, it condemned instances of exclusion because of the harm it caused to the 'structure of competition'.[153] In a number of cases, the Commission also argued that the exclusion of competitors was abusive because it reduced consumers' choice as to where to obtain the relevant good or service.[154] Many cases contain several of these very different rationales.

The Commission also considered discriminatory conduct on the part of a dominant abusive. Most of these cases concerned discrimination amongst the dominant undertaking's customers, usually in terms of prices[155] or rebate systems.[156] Applying unequal trading conditions to trading partners for similar transactions was (and remains) explicitly prohibited by Article 102(c). It is therefore not surprising

[150] *Chiquita* (n 146) II. A.3(d).

[151] *Vitamins* (Case IV/29.020) [1976] OJ L223/27, recital 24; *Bandengroothandel Frieschebrug BV/NV Nederlandsche Banden-Industrie Michelin* (Case IV/29.491) [1981] OJ L353/33, recital 47. In a similar vein: *Napier Brown-British Sugar* (Case IV/30.178) [1988] OJ L284/41, recital 59.

[152] eg *European Sugar Industry* (Case IV/26 918) [1973] OJ L140/17, E.3; *Chiquita* (n 146) II.A.3.a; *Hugin/Liptons* (Case IV/29.132) [1978] OJ L22/23, II.A; *Decca Navigator System* (Cases IV/30.979 and 31.394) [1989] OJ L43/27, recital 112; *Irish Sugar plc* (Cases IV/34.621 and 35.059/F-3) [1997] L258/1, recital 134.

[153] eg *ABG oil companies operating in the Netherlands* (n 146) II.B; *ECS/AKZO* (Case IV/30.698) [1985] L374/1, recitals 73 and 83; *BPB Industries plc* (n 147) recital 122.

[154] *Hugin/Liptons* (n 152) II.A.b; *Eurofix-Bauco v Hilti* (Cases IV/30.787 and 31.488) [1988] OJ L65/19, recital 75; *Decca Navigator System* (n 152), recital 112.

[155] *HOV SVZ/MCN* (Case IV/33.941) [1994] OJ L104/34, recitals 157 ff; *Irish Sugar* (n 152) recital 136.

[156] eg *European Sugar Industry* (n 152) E.3; *Vitamins* (n 151) recital 26; *Bandengroothandel Frieschebrug BV/NV Nederlandsche Banden-Industrie Michelin* (n 151) recital 41; *Eurofix-Bauco v Hilti* (n 154) recital 81.

to find that these decisions tend to contain little in way of rationale. Nonetheless, it is striking that the assessments of discriminatory conduct rarely even mention the effects on competition, let alone establish them. They tend to have a moralising undertone and condemn 'unfair' prices,[157] the 'arbitrariness' and 'subjectivity' of rebate schemes[158] and the 'exploitation' of trading partners.[159] One could conclude that the relevant harm here was not any negative effect on the 'structure of competition' or even knock-on effects on consumers, but the fairness of the competitive process or even the individual rights of businesses to be treated equally and fairly by the dominant undertaking. This interpretation is supported by the Commission's use of the concept of 'special responsibility' in a number of these decisions.[160] According to this concept, coined by the Court of Justice, a dominant undertaking has a 'special responsibility not to allow its conduct to impair genuine undistorted competition on the common market'.[161] The term 'responsibility', as opposed to a mere 'obligation' for example, again has moral connotations.[162] In fact, in the case of *ECS/AKZO*, the Commission explicitly stated that any unfair commercial practice on the part of a dominant undertaking intended to eliminate, discipline or deter smaller competitors fell within the scope of the prohibition of Article 102.[163]

One further case is worth mentioning in the context of discriminatory conduct. In *GVL*, the Commission held that discrimination on the basis of nationality had to be considered a separate form of abuse from Article 102(c), irrespective of its actual or potential effects on competition. It explained that the prohibition of abuses had to be viewed in the light of the general principles of EU law, including the prohibition of discrimination on grounds of nationality. As a rule, the Commission therefore concluded in *GVL*, discriminatory treatment by a dominant undertaking on grounds of nationality had to be regarded as an automatic infringement of Article 102.[164]

Finally, like in the case of Article 101, the Commission regularly considered conduct designed to or likely to discourage imports from another Member State abusive within the meaning of Article 102. However, the rationale for finding this type of conduct abusive was not always the same. In a few decisions, the Commission's assessment of the abusive nature of this conduct explicitly criticised its effect of partitioning the internal market.[165] In other cases, it condemned the

[157] *Chiquita* (n 146) II.A.3.c.

[158] *Bandengroothandel Frieschebrug BV/NV Nederlandsche Banden-Industrie Michelin* (n 151) recital 45.

[159] *Eurofix-Bauco v Hilti* (n 154) recital 81.

[160] eg *Irish Sugar* (n 152) recitals 115 and 123.

[161] Case 322/81 *Michelin v Commission* ECLI:EU:C:1983:313, para 57

[162] The same is true eg for the terms 'responsabilité' and 'Verantwortung' of the French and German versions of these judgments.

[163] *ECS/AKZO* (n 153) recitals 74 and 80.

[164] *GVL* (Case IV/29.839) [1981] OJ L370/49, recital 46.

[165] eg *Eurofix-Bauco v Hilti* (n 154) recital 76; *Irish Sugar* (n 152) recital 143.

fact that such conduct discriminated between foreign and domestic goods.[166] In yet others, it based the finding of abuse on the fact that this conduct limited the potential importers' or foreign suppliers' freedom of action and opportunity.[167] A few decisions criticised that this conduct 'limited markets to the prejudice of consumers'.[168] Then again, certain assessments contained no explicit rationale for condemning such conduct at all.[169]

iii. Conclusion

In sum, the decision practice reveals that the Commission considered several types of harm pertinent under Article 102: restrictions of the freedom of action or commercial opportunity of competitors and trading partners, discrimination of any kind and in particular on the basis of nationality, other unfair conduct, limitations of consumers' choices on where to source their supplies and obstacles to market integration. In other words, its concept of abusive conduct was by no means limited to conduct that caused consumer harm. Its broad understanding of dominance also supports the conclusion that the Commission's apprehension about economic power was not limited to the powerful undertaking's ability to reduce consumer welfare. It was more generalised.

B. The Commission's Concept of Harm after the Introduction of the More Economic Approach

By the mid-2000s, this broad reading of Article 102 was no longer in line with the Commission's 'more economic' concepts of harm under Article 101 and the EU Merger Regulation. Having read a consumer harm requirement into both Article 101 and Article 2 of the revised Merger Regulation, the Commission was faced with the dilemma of how to align the concept of abuse with its concept of harm under the other two pillars. The review of Article 102 proved more difficult than the reform of Article 101 and EU merger law, and the final outcome was less clear-cut.

i. Commission Notices and other Soft Law

Both the preparatory European Advisory Group on Competition Policy (EAGCP) Report and DG Competition's Staff Discussion Paper had proposed reinterpreting Article 102 in line with the Commission's more economic

166 *Gema I* (n 144) II.C.5 (no English version available).

167 eg *European Sugar Industry* (n 152) E.2; *BPB Industries* (n 147) recitals 148–52; *Irish Sugar* (n 152) recitals 134, 135.

168 *Irish Sugar* (n 152) recitals 129, 144.

169 *British Leyland* (Case IV/30.615) [1984] OJ L207/11, recital 26.

approach to Article 101 and the EU Merger Regulation. The EAGCP had recommended dropping the controversial concept of dominance altogether and essentially making the finding of abuse dependent on whether the conduct was likely to harm consumer welfare.[170] DG Competition's proposals were not quite as radical, but based on the same general idea. Instead of abandoning the criterion of dominance, it proposed to reinterpret it as meaning 'market power', ie the ability to influence market prices, output, innovation, the variety or quality of goods and services, or other parameters of consumer welfare to the detriment of consumers for a significant period of time.[171] This would have brought its concept of harm into line with its more economic approach to Article 101 and the Merger Regulation.

The Notice that finally concluded the reform process in February 2009, however, did not choose this solution. Instead of issuing interpretative guidelines outlining a more economic interpretation of Article 102, as it had done for Article 101 and EU merger law, the Commission published a Notice providing guidance on its 'enforcement priorities' in applying Article 102 to exclusionary abuses.[172] This Notice is very careful to stress that it is not intended to contain a statement of the law.[173] It does not claim to spell out the Commission's interpretation of Article 102. In particular, it does not claim that the Commission only deems such conduct abusive that results, or is likely to result, in consumer harm. In fact, the Notice faithfully reiterates many of the old legal doctrines from the 1970s, including the Court's concepts of dominance and special responsibility.[174] Neither of these is compatible with a concept of competitive harm that is limited to a measurable reduction in consumer welfare. As argued before, the concept of dominance is far broader than the concept of market power. Also, there is no place for 'special responsibilities' in an interpretation guided by the premise that only such conduct should be considered anticompetitive that is likely to result in a reduction of consumer welfare. This is either the case, or it is not. Special responsibilities and other moral duties do not enter into the equation. The Guidance is also uncharacteristically cagey about the legal objective of Article 102. Unlike the Notices on Articles 101 and the Merger Regulation, it does not explicitly state that consumer welfare is the exclusive aim of Article 102, but instead stresses the importance of safeguarding the 'competitive process'.[175]

[170] Report by the EAGCP, *An Economic Approach to Article 82* (July 2005) available at: www.ec.europa.eu/dgs/competition/economist/eagcp_july_21_05.pdf.

[171] DG Competition, Discussion Paper on the Application of Article 82 of the Treaty to Exclusionary Abuses, November 2005, www.ec.europa.eu/competition/antitrust/art82/discpaper2005.pdf, paras 23, 24.

[172] Communication from the Commission, 'Guidance on the Commission's enforcement priorities in applying Article 82 of the EC Treaty to abusive exclusionary conduct by dominant undertakings' [2009] OJ C45/7.

[173] ibid, para 3.

[174] ibid, paras 1 and 10.

[175] ibid, para 6.

However, this rhetorical reticence is somewhat misleading. Although the Notice does not define the legal objective of Article 102 as the protection of consumer welfare, or competitive harm as consumer harm, it redefines the Commission's enforcement priorities as being directed against 'those types of conduct that are most harmful to consumers'.[176] Consequently, the Commission will now only intervene under Article 102 where the allegedly abusive conduct is likely to lead to foreclosure resulting in consumer harm ('anticompetitive foreclosure'),[177] which is the case where the dominant undertaking has market power.[178] The main part of the Guidance then spells out in great detail how the Commission intends to go about assessing whether conduct is likely to result in such anticompetitive foreclosure.

In sum, instead of explicitly reinterpreting dominance as market power and reinterpreting the concept of abuse as requiring consumer harm, the Guidance evades the issue of legal interpretation. Instead, it redefines the Commission's enforcement priorities as those cases in which the abuse is likely to result in consumer harm. In practice, the outcome is the same as if the Commission had reinterpreted the provision on the basis of the consumer welfare aim: it will no longer enforce Article 102 against exclusionary conduct on the part of a powerful undertaking if this conduct is not going to reduce consumer welfare.

Considerations of fairness play no role in the Guidance's analytical framework for assessing abusive conduct under Article 102. Even if the dominant undertaking's conduct towards its competitors is 'unfair' or morally reprehensible, the Commission will only take action under Article 102 if it is likely to result in higher prices for consumers or other forms of consumer harm. Interestingly, the Guidance does not even mention the issue of discriminatory conduct against trading partners, which figured heavily in its enforcement practice of the first 40 years and is explicitly mentioned in Article 102(c). This may be because the scope of the Guidance is limited to explaining the Commission's (revised) approach to exclusionary abuses, ie conduct that harms consumers by excluding actual and potential competitors, insofar as this creates a situation in which the dominant undertaking can profitably raise prices or otherwise reduce consumer welfare. It explicitly does not cover exploitative abuses, ie conduct that is directly exploitative of consumers, although it indicates that the Commission theoretically considers exploitative abuse capable of infringing Article 102, and that it might decide to intervene in relation to such conduct, in particular where the protection of consumers and the proper functioning of the internal market could otherwise be adequately ensured.[179] However, discrimination against trading partners is not an exploitative abuse. It could in theory, however, be considered an exclusionary abuse if it resulted in the trading partners who are being discriminated against

[176] ibid, para 7.
[177] ibid, para19.
[178] ibid, paras 10, 11.
[179] ibid, para 7.

being driven from the market. Based on the principles spelled out in the Notice, it seems that the Commission would now only enforce Article 102 in such a case if the foreclosure of competitors would allow the dominant undertaking to raise prices. Discrimination as such, therefore, no longer seems to constitute a reason for triggering the application of Article 102 according to the Notice.

Why did the Commission choose to amend its enforcement priorities rather than spell out a revised concept of harm in the context of Article 102? It is a very roundabout way of implementing the premise that only such conduct should be prohibited under the antitrust rules that is likely to harm consumers. The Commission gave no official explanation for why it chose this method. The most likely explanation is that an interpretation of abuse as requiring consumer harm would have been incompatible with the case law. The Court of Justice has steadfastly refused all suggestions that only conduct that results in direct consumer harm should be considered abusive within the meaning of Article 102,[180] just as it continues to adhere to its broad and 'non-economic' definition of dominance[181] rather than aligning it with the concept of market power.[182]

The Commission's solution of not formally challenging the Court's interpretation of the law by spelling out a conflicting interpretation of Article 102, but simply announcing that it intends to focus its resources on those cases that cause harm to consumers while no longer pursuing Article 102 infringements that do not, is pragmatic and rather ingenious. However, it also raises a number of concerns. These are addressed in Chapter 10.

ii. The Commission's Decision Practice

The Commission's actual decision practice since the review paints a confusing picture of the Commission's concept of harm under Article 102. Since publishing the guidance in February 2009, the Commission has enacted four infringement decisions on the basis of Article 102.[183] Like in the context of EU merger control, the great majority of substantive decisions have been commitments decisions.[184]

The commitments decisions under Article 102 tend to be conceptually hazy. They do not contain in-depth legal assessments, but merely summarise the

[180] See eg Cases C-553/12 P *Commission v DEI* ECLI:EU:C:2014:2083, para 68; T-286/09 *Intel v Commission* ECLI:EU:T:2014:547, para 105; C-202/07 P *France Télécom v Commission* ECLI:EU:C:2009:214, para 105; C-95/04 P *British Airways* ECLI:EU:C:2007:166, para 106, all reaffirming the principle first established in Case 6/72 *Europemballage and Continental Can v Commission* ECLI:EU:C:1973:22, para 26.

[181] eg Case C-52/09 *Konkurrensverket v TeliaSonera Sverige* ECLI:EU:C:2011:83, para 23, or C-202/07 P *France Télécom v Commission* (n 180) para 103, amongst many others.

[182] See Ch 10 for a detailed analysis of the Court's concept of harm.

[183] *Intel* (Case COMP/C-3 /37.990); *Telekomunikacja Polska* (Case COMP/39.525); *Romanian Power Exchange/OPCOM* (Case AT.39984); *Motorola—Enforcement of GPRS standard essential patents* (Case AT.39985).

[184] Between 1 March 2009 and 1 August 2015, the Commission enacted 19 commitments decisions under Article 102.

Commission's competitive concerns. As a rule, they do not outline theories of harm, but focus on describing and classifying the investigated conduct on the basis of its form in a recognised category of abusive conduct, eg tying, fidelity rebates, refusal to deal, margin squeeze etc. When they touch on the potentially harmful effects of these types of conduct, they tend to refer to the exclusion or foreclosure of competitors,[185] the further strengthening of the dominant position[186] or the effects on the 'structure of the market'.[187] One decision additionally mentioned the negative effects on the 'liberalisation process' in a market.[188] By contrast, the effects on consumer welfare are generally not the focus of these decisions. In fact, the majority of commitments decisions do not mention the effects on consumers at all.[189] The others limit themselves to adding, usually in the final sentence, that the expected foreclosure effects would be to the detriment of consumers.[190] With few exceptions, they generally do not distinguish between the mere exclusion of a competitor and the Guidance Paper's key concept of 'anticompetitive foreclosure', ie foreclosure that is likely to result in consumer harm.[191] By contrast, they tend to use the term 'dominance' throughout,[192] sometimes combined with the Court's traditional definition coined in *United Brands* in 1976.[193] The term 'market power' tends not to figure in the Commission's commitment decisions. This conceptual vagueness is not particularly surprising, given that the same phenomenon can be observed in commitment decisions under Article 101.

One could have expected a clearer stance in the Commission's infringement decisions. However, the Commission's four infringement decisions since enactment of the 2009 guidance are remarkably ambiguous as to the underlying legal concept of harm. While it is clear from these decisions that the Commission was concerned about the effects on consumer welfare and also established these in its assessment, it formally based the abusive nature of the investigated conduct on its foreclosure effects. The decisions contain an odd mix of economic concepts and the established principles from the 1970s, which are not compatible

[185] eg *CEZ* (Case AT/39727) recitals 21–33; *Gaz de France* (Case COMP/39.316) recitals 22–25; *Long term electricity contracts in France* (Case COMP/39.386) recitals 30–35; *Microsoft (tying)* (Case COMP/C-3/39.530) recitals 39–54; *Samsung* (Case AT.39939) recital 62.

[186] *Microsoft (tying)* (n 185) recitals 57, 58.

[187] *Deutsche Bahn I* (Case COMP/AT.39678) and *Deutsche Bahn II* (Case COMP/AT.39731) recitals 44–47.

[188] *Long term electricity contracts in France* (n 185) recitals 36–38.

[189] eg *Deutsche Bahn I and II* (n 187) *CEZ* (n 185); *Gaz de France* (n 185); *Long term electricity contracts in France* (n 185); *Samsung* (n 185).

[190] eg *ENI* (Case COMP/39.315) recitals 15, 40; *IBM Maintenance Services* (Case COMP/39.692) recital 39.

[191] The decision in *E.ON Gas* alludes to the fact that the foreclosure would be likely to result in consumer harm, and cites the Guidance Paper's relevant passage on anticompetitive foreclosure in a footnote: *E.ON Gas* (Case COMP/39.317) recital 41.

[192] eg *CEZ* (n 185) recitals 14, 15; *Deutsche Bahn I and II* (n 187) recital 36; *Gaz de France* (n 185) recital 18–22; *Microsoft (tying)* (n 185) recitals 24–30; *IBM Maintenance Services* (n 190) recitals 26–30; *Reuters Instrument Codes (RICs)* (Case AT.39654) recitals 33–36.

[193] eg *Deutsche Bahn I and II* (n 187) recital 36.

with an interpretation of the law that is guided by the exclusive aim of protecting economic consumer welfare.

Intel was the first prohibition decision after the Commission concluded the reform of Article 102.[194] It is a borderline case insofar as the Commission started the investigation before the publication of the Guidance and therefore did not formally apply it to the case. However, the decision indicated that the Commission considered the assessment to be in line with the 'orientations' set out in the Guidance.[195]

The case concerned the practice of Intel, a major manufacturer of computer chips, of granting rebates and discounts to customers in exchange for exclusivity. Formally, the Commission's assessment was based on the old-established principles and the case law from the 1970s.[196] It thus reiterated the broad *United Brands* definition of dominance, although it added that this presupposed 'substantial market power'.[197] More importantly, it stated that the relevant test, as established in the case law, was whether the conduct was capable of 'eliminating a competitor' and thereby reinforcing the dominant undertaking's position by having recourse to means other than those within the scope of competition on the merits.[198] The relevant competitive harm according to this formula is the exclusion of competitors. Consumer harm is irrelevant. The Commission then dutifully applied this test and concluded without any difficulties in a very brief assessment that the rebates tended to 'remove or restrict the buyers' freedom to remove or to choose its sources of supply'.[199] In other words, the conditions of illegality according to the case law were fulfilled.

The Commission acknowledged this, but stated that, whilst these findings were in themselves sufficient to find an infringement under Article 102, the Commission would 'in addition' demonstrate that the conditional rebates were also capable of resulting in anticompetitive foreclosure, ie result in consumer harm.[200] This additional assessment, which the Commission stressed was legally not required, was far longer than the assessment under the 'legal' test. It included both qualitative and quantitative analyses, and spanned almost 200 pages.[201] In comparison, the assessment under the Court's test, which the Commission characterised as being 'the law', was only a few sentences long. In fact, a number of infringement decisions from the period of the Commission's review process contain a similar approach. Between 2004 and 2006, the Commission carried out 'additional assessments' of the investigated conduct's effects on consumer welfare in the cases of *Microsoft*, *AstraZeneca* and *Wanadoo España*, while stressing that

[194] *Intel* (n 183).
[195] ibid, recital 916.
[196] ibid, recitals 920–25.
[197] ibid, recitals 837–39.
[198] ibid, recital 915.
[199] ibid, recital 923.
[200] ibid, recital 925.
[201] ibid, recitals 1002–616.

the law did not require it to do so. The official rationale for prohibiting the conduct, like in *Intel*, had been that it was expected to foreclose competitors in all three of these cases.[202]

After *Intel* came *Telekomunikacja Polska.*[203] It is the only infringement decision under Article 102 to date to apply the relevant principles set out in the Guidance Paper explicitly. In *Telekomunikacja Polska*, the Commission examined a complaint that the Polish telecommunications operator and former monopolist, *Telekomunikacja Polska*, had consistently denied its competitors remunerated access to its network and wholesale broadband services, making it near impossible for them to offer their own telecommunications services in the Polish market. The assessment started with a summary of the case law on refusals to deal, including the Court's broad definition of dominance, the concept of special responsibility and the principle that direct consumer harm is not a requisite of abusive conduct because harm to an 'effective competition structure' is sufficient to make the conduct anticompetitive.[204] The decision then pointed out that, according to the Commission's Guidance Paper, refusals to deal were only an enforcement priority if they were likely to eliminate competition and cause consumer harm.[205] On that basis, the decision first applied the Court's test on refusals to supply a service, according to which such a refusal is abusive if it is likely to eliminate all competition in the market, it is not objectively justified and the service is indispensable to carrying out that person's business.[206] It easily established that these conditions were fulfilled, which made the conduct illegal. In a second step, the decisions then proved in great detail that the conduct was also likely to lead to 'anticompetitive foreclosure' within the meaning of the Guidance Paper, while stressing that this was not necessary in order to prove the existence of an abuse.[207] This assessment included a careful analysis of the conduct's effects on consumer welfare, and established, on the basis of qualitative and quantitative evidence, that the conduct would lead to consumer harm in the form of lower broadband penetration, higher broadband prices and lower average broadband connection speeds.[208] In other words, the decision first applied the law, which was explained as not requiring consumer harm, and then established, in a much longer assessment, that the conduct was an enforcement priority because it was likely to result in actual foreclosure and consumer harm.

The following prohibition, *Romanian Power Exchange/OPCOM*,[209] was surprisingly old school. In this case, the Commission objected to OPCOM, the operator

[202] *Microsoft* (Case COMP/C-3/37.792), recitals 693 ff; *AstraZeneca* (Case COMP/A.37.507/F3), recitals 758–72 and 848–59; *Wanadoo España v Telefónica* (Case COMP/38.784) recitals 543–618.
[203] *Telekomunikacja Polska* (n 183).
[204] ibid, recitals 695–702.
[205] ibid, recital 703.
[206] ibid, recitals 708–811.
[207] *Telekomunikacja Polska* (n 183) recital 813.
[208] ibid, recitals 829–63.
[209] *Romanian Power Exchange/OPCOM* (Case AT.39984).

of the only power exchange in Romania, requiring its trading partners to have a Romanian VAT registration and business premises in Romania. The decision did not refer to the Guidance Paper, its substantive principles or enforcement priorities at all. It used the traditional definition of dominance,[210] and did not mention the concept of market power. The competitive assessment was based on precedent set in decisions prior to the reform and case law according to which dominant undertakings may not engage in unfair and discriminatory conduct.[211] The Commission did not assess foreclosure effects, let alone 'anticompetitive foreclosure' effects. Instead, it based the abuse on the discriminatory nature of OPCOM's conduct. In its view, OPCOM's requirement that its trading partners have a Romanian VAT registration amounted to discrimination against businesses from other Member States who were already registered in their home State and for whom OPCOM's request resulted in a dual burden. It held that where market behaviour raised barriers to trade between Member States and consequently to the internal market by discriminating against trading partners on the grounds of nationality, this restricted competition within the internal market.[212] Consumer harm was not part of this analysis.

Finally, the case of *Motorola* investigated the decision of the US telecommunications company Motorola to obtain and enforce an injunction to prevent a competitor from using one of Motorola's smartphone patents, which the latter had committed to license on fair, reasonable and non-discriminatory (FRAND) terms. The Commission decided to treat this conduct as a novel type of abuse, rather than operate on the basis of established categories of abuse, such as a refusal to deal for example. Its competitive assessment was officially based on the general principles established in the case law. It reiterated the old definition of abuse coined by the Court in *Hoffmann-La Roche*[213] according to which abuse is an objective concept relating to the behaviour of an undertaking in a dominant position, which is such as to influence the structure of a market where, as a result of the very presence of the undertaking in question, the degree of competition is weakened and which, through recourse to methods different from those which condition normal competition, has the effect of hindering the maintenance of the degree of competition still existing in the market or the growth of that competition. It also cited the doctrine of the dominant undertaking's special responsibility, used the traditional definition of dominance[214] and stressed that direct consumer harm was not a legal requirement of competitive harm under Article 102.[215] Unlike in the case of *Telekomunikacja Polska*, the Commission did not

[210] ibid, recitals 114–21.
[211] ibid, recitals 125–35.
[212] ibid, recital 173.
[213] Case 85/76 *Hoffmann-La Roche v Commission* ECLI:EU:C:1979:36, para 91.
[214] *Motorola* (n 183) recitals 221, 239.
[215] ibid, recitals 271–73.

carry out a separate assessment whether the case was an enforcement priority in *Motorola*. The only mention of the Guidance can be found in a footnote, according to which the decision met the Commission's enforcement priorities as set out in the Guidance.[216]

Instead, the decision identified and proved three specific 'anticompetitive effects', apparently on the basis of the Court's general concept of abuse: a temporary ban on the sale of competing products; an initial settlement agreement that imposed disadvantageous terms on the competitor; and a negative impact on standard-setting in the telecommunications industry.[217] These analyses also mentioned, rather in passing, that the identified anticompetitive effects were detrimental to consumer welfare: the ban on selling competing products was disadvantageous to consumers because it reduced consumer choice;[218] the disadvantageous terms of the settlement could possibly be passed on to consumers in the form of higher prices;[219] and undermining confidence in the standard-setting process would deprive consumers of its benefits.[220] However, the effects on consumer welfare were neither presented as an essential element of the abuse, nor were they *de facto* the focus of the assessment. They were primarily based on conjecture rather than empirical evidence. Finally, the last instance of consumer harm referred to by the Commission, ie consumers being deprived of the benefits of the standard-setting process in the telecommunications industry, is based on a very broad concept of consumer welfare that risks undermining one of the key advantage of the economic welfare-based concept of harm: clarity and measurability.

All in all, the Guidance Paper's principles do not play a major role in the competitive assessments of the Commission's commitments and infringement decisions—at least not openly. Remarkably, they do not figure in its rejection decisions either. Many complaints against allegedly dominant undertakings under Article 102 are rejected for lack of priority. However, even after 2009, the Commission has usually justified a lack of priority on the traditional concept of 'Union interest' as set out in the Commission's Notice on the handling of complaints from 2004,[221] and not on the basis of the Guidance's priorities. The most common reasons in the Commission's decision practice for rejecting a case as a non-priority are that a national court would be well placed to handle the case,[222] the disproportionality of a Commission investigation in view of the limited impact of the conduct on the functioning of the internal market, the complexity of the case and the limited chances of proving the infringement.[223] No decision to date appears to

[216] ibid, fn 4.
[217] ibid, recitals 311–420.
[218] ibid, recital 312.
[219] ibid, recital 377.
[220] ibid, recital 415.
[221] European Commission, Notice on the handling of complaints [2004] OJ C101/65, paras 41–45.
[222] eg *UEFA Financial Fair Play Rules* (Case AT.40105) recitals 28–36.
[223] eg *Floras Bookshops v OUP/Burlington/Pearson* (Case No COMP/39771) recitals 13–20; *Omnis/Microsoft* (Case COMP/39.784) recitals 18–20; *Ryanair/DAA-Aer Lingus* (Case COMP/39.886) recitals 25–127; *Magyar Suzuki Corporation* (Case AT.40072) recitals 16–43, amongst many others.

have rejected a complaint on the basis of that it would not harm consumer welfare despite the conduct fulfilling the legal conditions of an abuse.

iii. Conclusion

During the first 40 years of EU antitrust law, the Commission's decision practice on Article 102 reveals a broad concept of competitive harm, in line with its early concept of harm under Article 101. Driving other businesses out of the market, harming the 'structure of competition', discriminating against competitors, trading partners or end users, or any other type of unfair conduct in the market were all considered abusive if committed by a dominant undertaking. Dominance was defined broadly, in line with the Court's definition in *United Brands*, as a position of economic strength that allowed the undertaking to prevent effective competition being maintained by giving it the power to behave independently of its competitors, customers and consumers. This concept was far wider and less clearly defined than the economic concept of market power, which refers specifically to the ability to reduce consumer welfare.

Formally, the Commission has not changed its legal interpretation of Article 102, despite much deliberation during the consultation process whether 'dominance' should be reinterpreted as meaning market power, and whether 'abuse' should be reinterpreted as referring to a restriction of competition that caused consumer harm. This would have brought the Commission's interpretation of Article 102 into line with its current concepts of harm under Article 101 and the EU Merger Regulation. Instead, the Commission published a Notice spelling out revised enforcement priorities, according to which it would simply no longer enforce Article 102 against conduct that was not likely to result in consumer harm. In particular, as the Guidance cites many of the Court's 'less economic' principles that the Commission used to follow prior to the review, this mere revision of the Commission's enforcement priorities suggests that the Commission formally continues to adhere to its original broad concept of harm under Article 102.

The Commission's decision practice since the publication of the Guidance is relatively unclear on the underlying concept of competitive harm. The commitments decisions are as a rule too vague to allow any reliable conclusion as to the concept of harm on which they are based. The four infringement decisions since 2009 do not employ a common approach. They all stress that they are based on the Court's interpretation of Article 102, according to which the mere exclusion of competitors is sufficient to prove an abuse, whereas consumer harm is not a legal requirement. One decision then nonetheless proves the presence of consumer harm for the sake of completeness, another does so to demonstrate that the case is a priority within the meaning of the Guidance, yet another does not mention consumer welfare at all, while the last decision claims that consumers are also affected, but does not prove this effect on the basis of any solid evidence. Finally, it appears, from the publicly available decisions at least, that the Commission has never formally rejected a complaint because it failed to meet the Guidance Paper's priorities. Instead it continues to justify the non-priority of cases on the basis that they lack 'Union interest' within the meaning of the general Notice on the Handling of Complaints.[224]

V. Conclusion

To conclude, the more economic approach has significantly changed the Commission's understanding of what constitutes competitive harm under Article 101 and the EU Merger Regulation. Under Article 101, the Commission used to consider agreements restrictive of competition if they restricted any market participant's commercial freedom or opportunity, including that of competitors, trading partners, unrelated businesses and end consumers. Now, post-reform, it reads Article 101 in line with its revised legal objective as prohibiting only such restrictions of competition that have a detrimental effect on consumer welfare, or create an impediment to market integration. The aim of market integration is therefore not a mere paper tiger. It remains a genuine legal objective in the eyes of the Commission that is capable of carrying a prohibition decision on its own without regard to the conduct's impact on consumer welfare. The Commission's concept of competitive harm under the original Merger Regulation was broad and ill defined. Now, the Commission unequivocally defines a significant impediment to effective competition as a lessening of competition through the elimination of important competitive constraints that will lead to a reduction in consumer welfare. In sum, the Commission has read a consumer harm requirement into both Article 101 and Article 2(3) of the EU Merger Regulation. Only if consumer welfare is (or is likely to be) diminished will an agreement or merger be deemed anticompetitive. Negative effects on competitors or other businesses as such are no longer considered injurious to competition.

This change in interpretation is not only of academic interest. It is highly relevant in practice. Having read a consumer harm element into both of these antitrust provisions, the Commission now needs to establish that consumer harm has occurred or is likely to occur before finding an infringement and prohibiting a businesses' conduct. It normally does so by means of a market power analysis. Under Article 101, the Commission had not taken the undertakings' economic strength into account at all prior to the more economic approach, beyond excluding entirely insignificant restrictions by means of the *de minimis* rule. In the context of merger control, the change in interpretation has had the greatest practical implications for the assessment of non-horizontal mergers. While the Commission used to consider the merging parties' ability to exclude competitors sufficient to make a merger anticompetitive, it now only considers such instances

[224] European Commission, Notice on the handling of complaints (n 221) paras 41–45.

of post-merger foreclosure illegal that are likely to result in consumer harm, and therefore has to prove the likelihood of consumer harm before prohibiting a merger.

The Commission's concepts of consumer harm and market power are broader than that advocated by many mainstream economists, who define market power more specifically and narrowly as the ability profitably to raise prices above a competitive level for a certain period of time.[225] The Commission's concept of consumer harm is not limited to price increases or output reductions leading to price increases, but also encompasses reductions in quality, choice and innovation and even more distant parameters of consumer welfare. Its understanding of market power is equally broad.

The Commission's attempts to make similar adjustments to its interpretation of Article 102 have been less successful. Despite plenty of ambition, a great deal of expert economic input and a long public consultation, the outcome of this last stage of the reform has not been as far-reaching and clear-cut as the reforms of the two previous pillars. Prior to the reform, the Commission had interpreted Article 102 as prohibiting a number of different types of harm: the exclusion of other businesses, discriminatory and unfair conduct on the part of a dominant undertaking, and the creation of obstacles to market integration. It had provided several rationales for deeming the exclusion of other undertakings abusive. Sometimes, prohibition decisions portrayed such exclusion as harm to the commercial freedom and opportunity of others. In other instances, it qualified the exclusion of competitors as harm to the 'structure of competition'. In a number of cases, the Commission argued that the exclusion of competitors was abusive because it reduced consumers' choice as to where to obtain the relevant good or service. Discrimination and other unfair conduct appeared to be prohibited primarily because of their amoral nature.

After the Commission's reinterpretation of Article 101 and the Merger Regulation as prohibiting only such conduct that caused tangible harm to consumers, one might have expected a similar reform of Article 102. The Commission's preparatory documents and the public consultation suggest that this was the aim. However, the Commission Notice that eventually emerged from the long reform process took another approach. Instead of reinterpreting the concept of abuse in Article 102 in a way that would have been in line with its new understanding of harm under Article 101 and the Merger Regulation, the Commission published a Notice that spelled out revised enforcement priorities. According to this Notice, the Commission no longer considers abuses that do not result in consumer harm a priority, and will therefore no longer enforce Article 102 against them. As a result, it is actually not entirely clear what the Commission's current legal understanding

[225] S Bishop and M Walker, *The Economics of EC Competition Law: Concepts, Application and Measurement*, 3rd edn (London, Sweet & Maxwell, 2010) para 3.001; M Motta, *Competition Policy* (Cambridge, Cambridge University Press, 2004) 40.

of harm is under Article 102. The Commission's commitments decisions are conceptually too vague to allow a clear conclusion. Its infringement decisions since the reform, by contrast, are officially based on the Court's legal tests, according to which exclusion as such is a type of competitive harm, as are discrimination and creating obstacles to market integration. Nonetheless, a few of these decisions still include an assessment of the conduct's effects on consumer welfare under one guise or another. This leaves us with one 'economic' concept of competitive harm for Article 101 and the Merger Regulation, and a different, much broader and somewhat ambiguous, concept for Article 102. Whether this is a desirable situation is discussed in Chapter 11.

6

A More Economic Concept of Countervailing Effects

I. Introduction

Business conduct is capable of producing many and often conflicting effects in the market. While it may on the one hand have the effect of harming competition, whatever one's understanding of competitive harm may be, it may by the same token also produce effects that are considered desirable by society. A key question that therefore arises in any antitrust system is: what type of benefit, if at all, should be considered capable of compensating for a business conduct's anticompetitive effects so that such conduct should be allowed despite its negative effects on competition?

The Commission's answer to this question changed with the advent of the more economic approach. Adopting consumer welfare as the key objective of EU antitrust law not only influenced its concept of competitive harm. It also affected its views on which type of value should be considered capable of offsetting or justifying such harm. The following retraces these changes under all three pillars of EU antitrust law in the chronological order of the Commission's reform.

II. Article 101

A. The Legal Basis: Article 101(3)

Article 101 explicitly acknowledges that anticompetitive conduct can also produce beneficial effects, and stipulates the conditions under which such benefits should be deemed to outweigh the conduct's anticompetitive effects. According to Article 101(3), agreements that are restrictive of competition are exempted from the prohibition of Article 101(1) if they fulfil four cumulative conditions: they must (1) contribute to improving the production or distribution of goods, or to promoting technical or economic progress; (2) allow consumers a fair share of the resulting benefit; (3) not impose restrictions that are not indispensable to the attainment of these objectives; and (4) not afford such undertakings the possibility of eliminating competition in respect of a substantial part of the products in question. The first condition thus defines the categories of benefit that are deemed capable of offsetting and justifying an agreement's anticompetitive effects: 'improving the production or distribution of goods', and 'promoting technical or economic progress'. Like most of Article 101's conditions, this prerequisite is broadly worded and wide open to interpretation.

The Commission's understanding of this first condition underwent a fundamental change with the advent of the more economic approach. While it used to interpret it broadly, the more economic approach significantly restricted the type of benefit deemed capable of offsetting a contractual restriction of competition.

B. The Commission's Understanding Prior to the Introduction of the More Economic Approach

The Commission's interpretative Notices on Article 101[1] prior to the introduction of the more economic approach did not provide any insight into the Commission's views on what types of beneficial effects should be deemed capable of offsetting competitive harm in an assessment under Article 101(3). By contrast, its Block Exemption Regulations and individual decision practice of that period are much more enlightening.

i. The Commission's Block Exemption Regulations

Block Exemption Regulations were an indispensable tool in the Commission's antitrust policy in the days when Article 101(3) was not yet automatically applicable, but the Commission had to authorise the exemption.[2] They continue to exist even after the Modernisation Regulation abolished the authorisation system in 2004 and made Article 101(3) directly applicable.[3] During the period under consideration in this section, the Commission enacted a great number of highly specific Block Exemption Regulations. As a rule, their recitals clearly identified

[1] eg European Commission, Bekanntmachung über Alleinvertriebsverträge mit Handelsvertretern [1962] OJ 139/2921, and Bekanntmachung über Vereinbarungen, Beschlüsse und aufeinander abgestimmte Verhaltensweisen, die eine zwischenbetriebliche Zusammenarbeit betreffen [1968] OJ C75/3 (no English versions available); as well as the Notices on agreements of minor importance (de minimis) [1970] OJ C64/1 (no English version), [1977] OJ C313/3; [1986] OJ C231/2; [1997] OJ C372/13.

[2] Art 9(1) of Council Regulation (EEC) No 17: First Regulation implementing Articles 85 and 86 of the Treaty [1962] OJ L13/204.

[3] Council Regulation (EC) No 1/2003 on the implementation of the rules on competition laid down in Articles 81 and 82 of the Treaty [2003] OJ L1/1, Art 1(2).

the benefits that the Commission expected the relevant agreements to yield and that, in its view, justified exempting the agreements from the prohibition of Article 101(1). They usually also specified which benefits the Commission considered to fall within the category of 'improving the production or distribution of goods' and which were deemed to 'promote technical or economic progress' within the meaning of Article 101(3).

The benefits most commonly identified as improving the production or distribution of goods in these early Block Exemption Regulations were: the rationalisation of the production or distribution process to achieve cost savings;[4] economies of scale;[5] ensuring the continuity of supply of goods of services;[6] intensifying marketing efforts;[7] increasing inter-brand competition;,[8] enabling an undertaking to enter a new market;[9] enabling small and medium size undertakings to compete in the market;[10] increasing the quantity and quality of goods produced;[11] and ensuring a high standard of services.[12] Benefits that were found to promote technical or economic progress were: encouraging the production of new goods,[13] as well as the dissemination of technical knowledge and avoiding the duplication of research and development work.[14] It is not always apparent from the recitals'

[4] eg Commission Regulations (EEC) No 2779/72 on the application of Article 85(3) of the Treaty to categories of specialization agreements [1972] OJ L292/23; 67/67/EEC on the application of Article 85(3) of the Treaty to certain categories of exclusive dealing agreements [1967] OJ 57/849; 1984/83 on the application of Article 85(3) of the Treaty to categories of exclusive purchasing agreements [1983] OJ L173/5, recital 5; 123/85 on the application of Article 85(3) of the Treaty to certain categories of motor vehicle distribution and servicing agreements [1985] OJ L15/16, recital 4; 417/85 on the application of Article 85(3) of the Treaty to categories of specialization agreements [1985] OJ L53/1, recital 4; 1617/93 on the application of Article 85(3) of the Treaty to certain categories of agreements and concerted practices concerning joint planning and coordination of schedules, joint operations, consultations on passenger and cargo tariffs on scheduled air services and slot allocation at airports [1993] OJ L155/18, recital 6.

[5] Commission Regulations (EEC) No 2672/88 on the application of Article 85(3) of the Treaty to certain categories of agreements between undertakings relating to computer reservation systems for air transport services [1988] OJ L239/13, recital 4; No 870/95 on the application of Article 85(3) of the Treaty to certain categories of agreements, decisions and concerted practices between liner shipping companies [1995] OJ L89/7, recital 4.

[6] Commission Regulations No 67/67/EEC (n 4); 1984/83 (n 4) recital 5; 82/91 on the application of Article 85(3) of the Treaty to certain categories of Agreements, Decisions and concerted practices concerning ground handling services [1991] OJ L10/7, recital 3; 1617/93 (n 4) recital 3.

[7] Commission Regulations No 67/67/EEC (n 4); 1984/83 (n 4) recital 6.

[8] Commission Regulations (EEC) No 1984/83 (n 4) recital 6; 4087/88 on the application of Article 85(3) of the Treaty to categories of franchise agreements [1988] OJ L359/46, recital 7.

[9] Commission Regulations (EEC) No 1984/83 (n 4) recital 6; 1983/83 on the application of Article 85(3) of the Treaty to categories of exclusive distribution agreements [1983] OJ L173/1, recital 6; 4087/88 (n 8) recital 7; 1617/93 (n 4) recital 4.

[10] Commission Regulations No 67/67/EEC (n 4); 4087/88 (n 8) recital 7; 1617/93 (n 4) recital 4.

[11] Commission Regulations (EEC) No 2349/84 on the application of Article 85(3) of the Treaty to certain categories of patent licensing agreements [1984] OJ L219/15, recital 12; 556/89 on the application of Article 85(3) of the Treaty to certain categories of know-how licensing agreements [1989] OJ L61/1, recital 7.

[12] Commission Regulation (EEC) No 82/91 (n 6) recital 3.

[13] Commission Regulation (EEC) No 2349/84 (n 11) recital 12.

[14] Commission Regulation (EEC) No 418/85 on the application of Article 85(3) of the Treaty to categories of research and development agreements [1985] OJ L53/5, recital 4.

explanations whom the Commission considered the relevant beneficiary of these effects. Many of these benefits were welfare enhancing effects. However, they also included the ability of competitors to enter and remain in the market.

ii. The Commission's Decision Practice

The Commission's decision practice reveals an even broader interpretation of the first condition of Article 101(3). The Commission regularly took into account all of the above-mentioned benefits in its individual assessments under Article 101(3). In fact, the majority of decisions exempting restrictive agreements under Article 101(3) directly did so because the agreement resulted in welfare-increasing effects or increased the number of competitors in the market.[15] In line with the case law of the period, the Commission sometimes also took into account similar beneficial effects under Article 101(1) already when assessing whether an agreement restricted competition. In *Remia,*[16] the Court had established the principle that clauses, which restricted the market participants' commercial freedom, but were directly related to and necessary for the implementation of a main operation that itself contributed to the promotion of competition because it lead to an increase in the number of undertakings in the market, did not to restrict competition within the meaning of Article 101(1).[17] The Commission applied this doctrine of 'ancillary restraints' in several cases.[18] Likewise, it regularly applied the Court's ruling in *Pronuptia*, according to which restrictive clauses that are strictly necessary for the functioning of a franchise system do not constitute restrictions of competition for the purposes of Article 101(1), because the existence of this type of distribution is considered to be both in the interest of competition and consumers.[19] Following the principle established in *Metro,*[20] the Commission further did not consider selective distribution agreements restrictive of competition as long as the nature of the good necessitated the use of such a system; the manufacturer chose the

[15] eg *Acec-Berliet* (Case IV/26045) [1968] OJ L201/7, III.1 (production of a new good); *Bayerische Motoren Werke* (Case IV/14650) [1975] OJ L29/1, recital 24 (improving standards of distribution and after-sales services); *D.R.U.—Blondel* (Case IV/3036) [1965] OJ 65/2194, III.1 (rationalisation of the distribution process); *Bayer/Gist-Brocades* (Case IV/27.073) [1976] OJ L30/13, III (rationalisation of the production process); *Rank/Sopelem* (Case IV/26.603) [1975] OJ L29/20, III (economies of scale); *Goodyear Italiana-Euram* (Case IV/23.013) [1975] OJ L38/10, recital 12 (ensuring regular supply); *Transocean Marine Paint Association* (Case IV/223) [1980] L39/73 (enabling smaller undertakings to compete with bigger undertakings).

[16] Case 42/84 *Remia v Commission* ECLI:EU:C:1985:327.

[17] ibid, paras 17–20.

[18] eg *International Private Satellite Partners* (Case IV/34.768) [1994] OJ L354/75, recitals 61–62; *Atlas* (Case No IV/35.337) [1996] OJ L239/23, recital 42.

[19] Case 161/84 *Pronuptia de Paris* ECLI:EU:C:1986:41. Applied eg in: *Yves Rocher* (Cases IV/31.428 to 31.432) [1987] OJ L8/49, recitals 39–48; *Computerland* (Case IV/32.034) [1987] OJ L222/12, recitals 21–23; *Charles Jourdan* (Case IV/31.697) [1989] OJ L35/31, recitals 26–31.

[20] Case 26/76 *Metro SB v Commission* ECLI:EU:C:1977:167, paras 20–22.

distributors in a non-discriminatory manner on the basis of objective and proportionate qualitative criteria; and the number of similar distribution systems did not preclude the possibility of other forms of distribution or resulted in a rigid price structure. The rationale for this rule was that selective distribution systems, despite restricting the dealers' commercial freedom and despite often resulting in higher prices for consumers, were also deemed to yield benefits. On this basis, the Commission regularly found selective distribution non-restrictive of competition because they created distribution channels with a high level of sales and after-sales service for consumers,[21] or because they preserved the 'aura of exclusivity' of certain luxury products in the interest of those consumers who valued such an image.[22] In sum, the Commission considered both increases in economic welfare and increases in the number of competitors in the market capable of offsetting an agreement's anticompetitive effects both under Article 101(3) and 101(1).

In addition to these effects, however, the decision practice sometimes also took into account very different types of effects because the Commission considered them desirable from the point of view of other Union policies.[23] In the 1980s, for example, the Commission exempted several crisis cartels in distressed industries, including the petrochemical sector,[24] the synthetic fibres industry[25] and the Dutch brick manufacturing industry,[26] in which competitors had agreed to reduce capacity in order to restore profitability. According to the Commission, these agreements, which contained clear restrictions by object, could be exempted under Article 101(3) because the reduction in excess capacity re-established market conditions in which producers could charge profit-making prices and therefore contributed to restoring the profitability and competitiveness of the sector.[27]

Restoring the profitability of an industry sector is not a benefit that directly increases the welfare of these products' users, nor does it increase the number of competitors. On the contrary—prices were likely to increase in the short term as a consequence of the capacity reduction and competitors were actually to exit the market under the terms of the agreements in question. The agreements were allowed because they were thought to save an industry. In its *Tenth Report on*

[21] *Villeroy & Boch* (Case IV/30.665) [1985] OJ L376/15, recitals 20–25; *SABA's EEC distribution system* (Case IV/29.598) [1983] OJ L376/41, II.A.

[22] *Yves Saint Laurent Parfums* (Case IV/33.242) [1992] OJ L12/24, II.A; *Parfums Givenchy system of selective distribution* (Case No IV/33.542) [1992] OJ L236/11, II.A.

[23] For a more detailed analysis, see AC Witt, 'Public Policy Goals Under EU Competition Law—Now is The Time to Set The House in Order' (2012) 8 *European Competition Journal* 443.

[24] *BPCL/ICI* (Case IV/30.863) [1984] OJ L212/1; *ENI/Montedison* (Case IV/31.055) [1987] OJ L5/13; *Enichem/ICI* (Case IV/31.846) [1988] OJ L50/18.

[25] *Synthetic fibres* (Case IV/30.810) [1984] OJ L207/17.

[26] *Stichting Baksteen* (Case IV/34.456) [1994] OJ L131/15.

[27] *BPCL/ICI* (n 24) recital 36; *ENI/Montedison* (n 24) recitals 26–32; *Enichem/ICI* (n 24) recitals 31–38; *Synthetic fibres* (n 25) recitals 28–36; *Stichting Baksteen* (n 26) recital 18.

Competition Policy (1980), the Commission explicitly stated that its competition policy not only aimed at sustaining effective competition but also at supporting its industrial policy, which encouraged restructuring measures for certain industries in order to adapt to the consequences of the oil crisis and the rapid rise in international trade.[28]

In several of the above decisions, the Commission also deemed the agreements' social benefits capable of offsetting their anticompetitive effects. In *Synthetic Fibres* and *Stichting Baksteen*, for example, it took into account that the coordination of plant closures by the competing manufacturers would make it easier to cushion the social effects of restructuring the market by making suitable arrangements for the retraining and redeployment of workers made redundant.[29] According to the above-mentioned *Tenth Report on Competition Policy*, 'pouring oil on waters troubled by intolerable social tensions' was also part of a healthy competition policy.[30] *Ford/Volkswagen*, a case from 1992, is the last decision in which the Commission explicitly took into account an agreement's social effects under Article 101(3).[31] Although the Commission considered that the notified joint venture had the effect of restricting competition, it exempted the agreement because of multiple beneficial effects. It held, for one, that the pooling of the parties' technical knowledge would promote technical progress.[32] However, it also took into account that the parties' investment would create 5,000 jobs in Portugal, and indirectly result in the creation of another 10,000 jobs, as well as attracting other investments in the supply industry. It would hence promote several primary Treaty aims: the harmonious development of the Union, the reduction of regional disparities and tying Portugal into the single market.[33]

Environmental protection is another category of benefit that the Commission took into account under Article 101(3) prior to the introduction of the more economic approach. In *Philips/Osram*,[34] it exempted an anticompetitive agreement on the grounds that it would eliminate obsolete energy plants, lower total energy usage and increase the prospect of realising energy reduction and waste emission programmes. The use of more efficient and cleaner facilities would result in less air pollution and hence in direct and indirect benefits for consumers from reduced negative externalities.[35] 'In addition', the Commission considered that the parties would be able to achieve economies of scale and pool their efforts to develop lead-

[28] Commission of the European Communities, *Tenth Report on Competition Policy 1980*, 9. Likewise in *Twelfth Report on Competition Policy 1982*, paras 38 and 39.

[29] *Synthetic Fibres* (n 25) recital 37; *Stichting Baksteen* (n 26) recital 27.

[30] Commission, *Tenth Report on Competition Policy 1980*.

[31] *Ford/Volkswagen* (Case IV/33.814) [1993] OJ L20/14.

[32] ibid, recital 25.

[33] ibid, recital 36.

[34] *Philips/Osram* (Case IV/34.252) [1994] OJ L378/37.

[35] ibid, recital 25.

free materials.[36] Likewise, in *Exxon/Shell*,[37] the Commission took into account that the as such anticompetitive agreement, in addition to achieving cost savings and improving product quality, would reduce the use of raw materials, the volume of plastic waste, and the health and environmental risks inherent in the transport of polyethylene.[38] It argued that this would benefit consumers because these effects were 'perceived as beneficial by many consumers at a time when the limitation of natural resources and threats to the environment are of increasing public concern'.[39]

iii. Conclusion

In sum, during the first 40 years of EU antitrust law, the Commission took into account beneficial effects created by agreements both under Article 101(1) and (3). The benefits it considered under Article 101(1) were usually effects that either strengthened competition by increasing the number of competitors in the market or benefited consumers directly by making different types of distribution channel available to them or safeguarding the key feature of a product. It took a broader view of the benefits capable of offsetting an agreement's anticompetitive effects under the exemption provision of Article 101(3). The majority of beneficial effects considered under Article 101(3) were also of the kind that increased economic welfare, albeit in a very broad sense of the term, or increased the number of competitors in the market. However, it also took into account effects that were deemed beneficial from the point of other Union policies and considered them capable of outweighing an agreement's anticompetitive effects. These benefits included effects as diverse as job creation, cushioning the social effects of unemployment, redeployment, restructuring an industry and environmental protection.

C. The Commission's Understanding after the Introduction of the More Economic Approach

i. Soft Law

The Commission's guidelines on the application of Article 101(3)[40] reiterate the principle established in the case law that ancillary restraints, ie restraints that are necessary for the implementing of a main non-restrictive transaction and proportionate to it, are compatible with Article 101(1).[41] However, they spell

36 ibid.
37 *Exxon/Shell* (Case IV/33.640) [1994] OJ L144/20.
38 ibid, recitals 67, 68.
39 ibid recital 71. See also *Assurpol* (Case IV/33.100) [1992] OJ L37/16, recitals 37–38.
40 European Commission Notice, Guidelines on the application of Article 81(3) of the Treaty [2004] OJ C101/97.
41 ibid, paras 28–31, citing Case T-112/99 *Métropole télévision (M6) and other v Commission* ECLI:EU:T:2001:215, para 104.

out a revised interpretation of Article 101(3). According to the guidelines on Article 101(3), 'improvement of the production or distribution of goods, and the promotion of technical or economic progress' within the meaning of Article 101(3) refers to efficiency gains only.[42] The guidelines explain in some detail the most important types of efficiencies the Commission intends to take into account in its assessments, namely cost efficiencies, and efficiencies of a qualitative nature that create value in the form of new or improved products, greater product variety etc.[43]

That economic efficiency gains fall within the scope of the first condition of Article 101(3) is not ground-breaking. Many exemption decisions of the first 40 years were based on exactly such efficiency effects, even though the terminology used in these decisions tended to be less technical. As shown in the previous section, the Commission had regularly exempted restrictive agreements because they led to cost savings, the creation of a new product, or better quality products and services. The novelty lies in the fact that the guidelines consider no other effect capable of offsetting competitive harm. More specifically, one has to conclude from the guidelines on Article 101(3) that social benefits, industrial policy considerations, environmental benefits, the reduction of regional disparities or furthering the harmonious development of the Union cannot as such outweigh an agreement's anticompetitive effects. Likewise, it would seem that the mere increase in the number of competitors in the market is no longer a reason to exempt an agreement under Article 101(3). This constitutes a clear departure from the Commission's position during the 1970s–90s.

The efficiency gains must further fulfil the other three conditions of Article 101(3) in order to justify an exemption: they must be at least partially passed on to consumers, the agreement must be indispensable to achieving them and the restriction of competition must not result in the elimination of competition. According to the guidelines, the second condition, ie the pass-on requirement, means that the efficiencies passed on to consumers must at least compensate them for any actual or likely negative impact caused to them by the restriction of competition.[44] In other words, the reduction in consumer welfare caused by the restriction of competition must be at least compensated by the increase in consumer welfare engendered by the efficiency effects. Overall, the effect on consumer welfare in terms of prices, quality, choice and innovation must be at least neutral.

ii. The Commission's Block Exemption Regulations

The new generation of Block Exemption Regulations since 2004, much more streamlined and limited in number, take a similar stance. Their recitals now only

[42] European Commission Notice, Guidelines on the application of Article 81(3) of the Treaty (n 40) paras 50–63.

[43] ibid, paras 64–82.

[44] ibid, para 85.

refer to economic efficiency gains as potentially countervailing effects within the meaning of Article 101(3).[45]

iii. The Commission's Decision Practice

The Commission has consistently implemented this new interpretation in its decision practice since 2004. Where decisions assess an agreement's alleged beneficial effects, they take into account economic efficiencies only.[46] At the same time, there has been a marked drop in successful Article 101(3) defences in the Commission's decision practice. Between 1965 and 1998, the Commission exempted 141 agreements by decision under Article 101(3) because of countervailing effects. Since 2004, the Commission has not once found in a decision in which it carried out a full assessment of a case that the efficiencies invoked by the parties were capable of offsetting the agreement's anticompetitive effects.[47]

This is a remarkable development. However, it does not necessarily mean that the Commission is not seriously committed to the theory that efficiencies are capable of offsetting an agreement's anticompetitive effects. There are a number of alternative explanations for this phenomenon. First, since Regulation 1/2003 made Article 101(3) directly applicable, there has been no more need for the Commission to grant formal exemption decisions. These days, the Commission will only declare Article 101 inapplicable by means of a decision if this is required by the public interest, for example in order to create precedent.[48] Second, many cases are already filtered out by the application of increasingly generous Block Exemption Regulations that confer the exemption of Article 101(3) on entire categories of agreements likely to generate efficiencies and unlikely to generate serious anticompetitive effects. Third, since Regulation 1/2003 decentralised the enforcement of Article 101, the Commission has been concentrating on pursuing the most serious cases, and leaving run of the mill cases to the national competition authorities. This means that, in practice, the Commission has been focusing on

[45] eg Commission Regulation 330/2010/EU on the application of Article 101(3) of the Treaty to categories of vertical agreements and concerted practices [2010] OJ L102/1, recitals 6 and 7; eg. Commission Regulation (EU) 461/2010 on the application of Article 101(3) of the Treaty on the Functioning of the European Union to categories of vertical agreements and concerted practices in the motor vehicle sector [2010] OJ L129/52, recitals 7, 8; Commission Regulation (EU) 1218/2010 on the application of Article 101(3) of the Treaty on the Functioning of the European Union to certain categories of specialisation agreements [2010] OJ L335/43, recital 6; Commission Regulation (EU) 316/2014 on the application of Article 101(3) of the Treaty on the Functioning of the European Union to categories of technology transfer agreements [2014] OJ L93/17, recitals 4, 5.

[46] eg *Fentanyl* (Case AT.39685) recitals 400–39; *Lundbeck* (Case AT.39226) recitals 1112–230; *MasterCard* (Case COMP/34.579) recitals 670–733; *Visa MIF* (Case COMP/39.398) recital 21; *Continental/United/Lufthansa/Air Canada* (Case COMP/AT.39595) recitals 55–65; *British Airways/American Airlines/Iberia* (Case COMP/39.596) recitals 91–94.

[47] See *Fentanyl* (n 46); *Lundbeck* (n 46); *MasterCard* (n 46); *Visa MIF* (n 46); *Continental/United/Lufthansa/Air Canada* (n 46); *British Airways/American Airlines/Iberia* (n 46).

[48] Regulation 1/2003 (n 3), Art 10.

hard-core cartels, in which parties usually do not even attempt to argue that they would produce efficiencies benefiting consumers.[49] Finally, many in-depth legal assessments are cut short by the fact that parties offer commitments that address the Commission's competitive concerns. These days, the only opportunity for an in-depth assessment of efficiencies under Article 101(3) in a Commission investigation is therefore the occasional less typical infringement of Union interest that raises serious competitive concerns and where the parties have not offered acceptable commitments. These defences tend not to succeed because the parties do not manage to demonstrate to the Commission's satisfaction that the efficiencies are likely to materialise, that they would be passed on to consumers, that they would be sufficient to outweigh the expected harm to consumers and that they would not eliminate competition.[50]

By contrast, since 2000, no individual decision has openly assessed or even considered social and industrial policy considerations either under Article 101(3) or 101(1). The Commission has only had one opportunity to assess an actual crisis cartel since the reform. The *French Beef* case[51] concerned an agreement between French cattle farmers, trade unions and associations of meat processors to fix minimum purchase prices and suspend beef imports into France to stabilise prices after an outbreak of BSE had caused a significant drop in beef consumption. The Commission found that the agreement amounted to a clear restriction of competition. It did not pronounce itself conclusively on whether the agreement could be exempted under Article 101(3) for industrial policy reasons on the formal grounds that the parties had not applied for an exemption.[52] It nonetheless indicated that even if the agreement had been notified it 'most likely' would not have qualified for exemption as it did 'not in any way contribute to improving the production or distribution of goods or to promoting technical or economic progress'.[53]

Since *French Beef*, the Commission has not discussed industrial or social policy benefits in an actual decision. There is nonetheless some guidance on the Commission's current stance on applying Article 101(3) to crisis cartels. In the wake of the financial crisis of 2008 and ensuing global recession, businesses started lobbying the Commission to relax its enforcement of the antitrust rules until the economy had recovered.[54] While no actual case presented itself at Union level, the

[49] eg *Fittings* (Case COMP/F-1/38.121) recital 622; *PO/Elevators and Escalators Commission* (Case COMP/E-1/38.823) recital 591; *Gas Insulated Switchgear* (Case COMP/F/38.899) recital 221.

[50] eg *Fentanyl* (n 46) recitals 400–39; *Lundbeck* (n 46) recitals 1212–31; *MasterCard* (n 46) recitals 666–753.

[51] *French beef* (Case COMP/C. 38.279/F3) [2003] OJ L209/12, upheld on appeal in Joined Cases T-217/03 and T-245/03 *FNCBV and Others v Commission* ECLI:EU:T:2006:391; and Joined cases C-101/07 P and C-110/07 P, C-101/07 P *Coop de France bétail et viande and others v Commission* ECLI:EU:C:2008:741.

[52] The decision just predated the entry into force of Regulation (EC) 1/2003, which made Art 101(3) directly applicable.

[53] *French beef* (n 51) recital 130.

[54] OECD Global Forum on Competition, 'Crisis Cartels—Contribution from the European Union' (27 January 2011) DAF/COMP/GF/WD(2011)20, para 2.

Commission took the opportunity to outline its views on the matter in *amicus curiae* observations in a case pending before the Irish High Court in 2010.[55] The case concerned another restructuring agreement, this time in the Irish beef industry, which was also suffering from significant overcapacity following yet another outbreak of BSE.[56] The Commission identified two types of benefit likely to result from restructuring agreements. First, it held that capacity-reducing agreements could lead to efficiency gains if the agreement removed inefficient capacity from the market. Second, agreements facilitating the exit of certain players from the market could lead to cost savings if the remaining players could be expected to increase output and utilise capacity more efficiently.[57] However, it also made clear that, in its view, cyclical overcapacity, ie overcapacity resulting from a general economic crisis, could never justify an exemption under Article 101(3) because market forces, which tended to eliminate the least efficient competitor, were generally the best means of correcting overcapacity.[58] In cases of overcapacity that was not the result of a temporary recession, but was of an industry-specific and lasting nature, an exemption could be justified in situations where market forces alone were exceptionally unable to ensure an efficient outcome, for example, where undertakings found themselves in a prisoner's dilemma likely to result in a war of attrition, which would ultimately harm the competitiveness of the industry and consumers.[59] In other words, the Commission considered that even if an agreement were capable of producing efficiencies, the third condition of Article 101(3), requiring that the agreement be indispensable, was rarely likely to be fulfilled. The second conclusion one can draw from this submission is that the only types of benefit the Commission now considers relevant in the assessment of restructuring agreements under Article 101(3) are indeed economic efficiency gains. Social and employment considerations, by contrast, no longer seem to enter into the equation.

[55] Observations of the Commission under Art 15, para 3 of Regulation 1/2003 in 2003 No 7764P *The Competition Authority v Beef Industry Development Society Ltd (BIDS) and Barry Brothers (Carrigmore) Meats Ltd*, available at: http://ec.europa.eu/competition/court/amicus_curiae_2010_bids_en.pdf. The Commission later reiterated these principles in a contribution to the session on crisis cartels organised by the OECD's Global Forum on Competition in February 2011 (n 54) paras 17–56.

[56] The Court of Justice had previously had the opportunity to give a preliminary ruling on the interpretation of Art 101(1) in the same case. It ruled that agreements aimed at reducing overcapacity in a market always had the object of restricting competition within the meaning of Art 101(1), regardless of potentially legitimate objectives, as the latter was a factor that had to be considered under Art 101(3). As the question referred by the Irish Supreme Court only concerned the interpretation of Art 101(1), the Court of Justice was not able pronounce itself on the application of Art 101(3) to crisis cartels; Case C-209/07 *Competition Authority v Beef Industry Development Society Ltd and Barry Brothers (Carrigmore) Meats Ltd* ECLI:EU:C:2008:643.

[57] Observations of the Commission (n 55) paras 19–28.

[58] ibid, para 34.

[59] According to the Commission, this is not the case where the drop in demand is the result of a recession, but can only arise where, irrespective of a general economic crisis, undertakings have been experiencing a significant reduction in their rates of capacity utilisation and drop in output, and no lasting improvements can be expected in the medium-term and the undertakings find themselves in a prisoner's dilemma-type situation; ibid, para 36.

The Commission's revised approach to dealing with restrictive agreements yielding environmental benefits has taken longer to crystallise. The process reflects the Commission's dilemma of being, on the one hand, clearly in favour of environmental protection, but, on the other hand, determined to adhere to the 'more economic' interpretation of Article 101(3). *CECED*[60] was the first case since the Commission started introducing the more economic approach to Article 101 in which it was confronted with an agreement that it expected to yield environmental benefits. The case concerned an agreement between producers of domestic appliances to stop producing and importing washing machines that did not meet a minimum standard of energy efficiency. While finding that this agreement clearly had the object of restricting competition,[61] the Commission exempted the agreement under Article 101(3) because it considered it likely to deliver both individual and collective benefits for users and consumers.[62] It first took into account the agreement's likely efficiency effects, arguing that washing machines that used less electricity resulted in lower electricity bills for consumers. Also, it held that the restriction of competition on one product dimension, ie energy consumption, was likely to increase competition on other product characteristics, for example price. In addition to these effects, however, it also held that the agreement's 'collective environmental benefits' translated into further economic benefits in the form of 'savings on the cost of pollution'. It then estimated the savings in marginal environmental damage from avoided emissions and found on the basis of 'reasonable assumptions' and *CECED's* own estimates that the benefits to society brought about by the agreement appeared to be more than seven times greater than the increased purchase cost of more energy-efficient washing machines.[63] These environmental advantages for society, it held, would allow consumers a fair share of the benefits, even if no benefits accrued to individual purchasers of washing machines.[64]

One year after *CECED*, the Commission examined another agreement that was deemed to yield beneficial effects for the environment.[65] DSD, a German company, had set up a system for collecting used sales packaging from end consumers that would allow participating producers and distributors of sales packaging to acquit themselves of their statutory obligation under German law to take back used wrappings from consumers and recycle them. DSD did not perform the actual collection itself but employed local collecting companies for this purpose. The Commission found that several clauses of the collection agreement, in particular a number of long-term exclusive contracts, restricted competition in an

[60] *CECED* (Case IV.F.1/36.718) [2000] OJ L187/47.
[61] ibid, recitals 30–37.
[62] ibid, recitals 47–57.
[63] It estimated the savings to amount to EUR 41 to 61 per tonne of carbon dioxide, from sulphur dioxide to EUR 4,000 to 7,000 per tonne, and from nitrous oxide to EUR 3,000 to 5,000 per tonne; ibid, recital 56.
[64] *CECED* (n 60).
[65] *DSD* (Case COMP/34.493) [2001] OJ L319/1.

appreciable manner. However, it exempted the agreement under 101(3) on the basis that the exclusivity clauses contributed to improving the production of goods and to promoting technical and economic progress. The first benefit the Commission took into account in this assessment was that the DSD system gave 'direct practical effect to national and Union environmental policy' and in so doing provided a 'high level of environmental protection'. It further considered that the agreement would enable the parties to plan and organise the provision of services on a long-term basis, and was thus likely to yield substantial efficiencies of scale and scope.[66] Consumers would benefit both from the improvement in environmental quality and the cost savings.[67] Unlike in *CECED*, the Commission did not attempt to determine the economic value of these environmental benefits, but nonetheless took them into account.

Rather than signalling a return to old times, however, the approach in *DSD* must be seen as a one-off slip-up in terms of the more economic approach. Since *DSD*, the Commission has not taken into account environmental benefits in their own right or attempted to translate them into economic benefits in assessments under Article 101(3). In 2003, for example, only two years after the decision in *DSD*, the Commission investigated a similar recycling system set up by an Austrian company, ARA.[68] In line with its approach in *DSD*, the Commission found that the exclusive long-term service contracts concluded by ARA with local collecting companies were incompatible with Article 101(1),[69] but that they could be exempted under Article 101(3). Unlike in *DSD*, however, the Commission did not take into account the likely environmental benefits in its assessment under Article 101(3) at all. While acknowledging parenthetically that the collection agreements were designed to fulfil the requirements of Council Directive 94/62/EC,[70] the aim of which was to mitigate the impact of packaging waste on the environment, the Commission exempted the agreement because it allowed the contracting parties to ensure the long-term planning and organisation of the relevant services, and also had the potential to achieve significant economies of scale and scope.[71] In other words, it took into consideration economic efficiency gains only.

In 2008, the Commission was confronted with the claim that an as such anti-competitive agreement should be exempted for reasons of cultural protection. The *CISAC* case[72] concerned an agreement between 24 European collecting societies who had agreed not to offer their services to authors and commercial users outside their domestic territories. The parties argued that this agreement was necessary to preserve cultural diversity. The Commission discussed this issue

66 ibid, recital 148.
67 ibid.
68 *ARA* (Case COMP/D3/35.470) and *ARGEV, ARO* (Case COMP/D3/35.473) [2004] OJ L75/59.
69 ibid, recitals 193–212.
70 The Austrian Packaging Ordinance from 1996, implementing Directive 94/62/EC on packaging and packaging waste [1994] OJ L365/10.
71 *ARA* (n 68) recitals 268–72.
72 *CISAC* (Case COMP/C2/38.698).

under the heading 'legal and policy context' in the assessment of the agreement's anticompetitive effects under Article 101(1) rather than Article 101(3). It acknowledged that Article 167(4) TFEU[73] required the Commission, like any other Union institution, to take cultural aspects into account in its action under other provisions of the Treaty, and to respect and to promote the diversity of its cultures.[74] However, it left open how this obligation could be accommodated in an assessment under Article 101, ie whether it was relevant under Article 101(1) or (3), because it took the view that cultural diversity in the music sector was simply not jeopardised by its decision to prohibit the agreement in question. It did not generally oppose a system of reciprocal representation and territorial delineation as such, but merely objected to a systematic territorial delineation by national territory, which led to market segmentation in a way that it deemed incompatible with the single market objective.[75] In other words, the Commission did not consider the agreement the least restrictive means for achieving the parties' objectives. Under Article 101(3), the Commission merely engaged with the parties' (unsuccessful) claim that the agreement would generate efficiencies.[76]

One last case in which the Commission was confronted with a non-economic defence was *ONP*.[77] The case concerned the decision by the Ordre National des Pharmaciens (ONP), the professional body of pharmacists in France, to impose minimum prices on the French market for clinical laboratory tests. According to the ONP, imposing a minimum price was necessary to protect public health and safety. The Commission did not assess this claim under Article 101(3) but under Article 101(1), where it considered whether the agreement should fall outside the scope of Article 101(1) according to the exception established by the Court in the *Wouters* line of case law. According to the Court's ruling in *Wouters*,[78] certain agreements, despite their restrictive effects on competition, fall outside the scope of Article 101(1) if they pursue a legitimate policy goal and if the restrictive effects on competition are inherent in and proportionate to the pursuit of that objective. In *Wouters*, the Court had held that a regulation adopted by the Bar Association of a Member State, that prohibited its members from entering into professional partnerships with members of other liberal professions, did not infringe Article 101(1) as it was necessary for the proper practice of the legal profession.[79] The Commission decided that the *Wouters* exception did not apply in the case of *ONP*.

[73] Ex Art 151(4) EC.

[74] *CISAC* (n 72) recital 92.

[75] *CISAC* (n 72) recital 93.

[76] *CISAC* (n 72) recital 233.

[77] *ONP* (Case 39.510) (no English version available).

[78] Case C-309/99 *Wouters* ECLI:EU:C:2002:98, paras 97–110. See also Cases C-67/96 *Albany International* ECLI:EU:C:1999:430, para 59; C-219/97 *Maatschappij Drijvende Bokken* ECLI:EU:C:1999:437, para 47; Joined Cases C-115/97 to C-117/97 *Brentjens' Handelsonderneming* ECLI:EU:C:1999:434, para 57; *Fédération nationale de la coopération bétail et viande (FNCBV) and Others v Commission* (n 51) para 98; C-519/04 P *David Meca-Medina* ECLI:EU:C:2006:492, para 45. See Ch 10, s IV for a more in-depth discussion of this case law.

[79] *Wouters* (n 78) paras 97–110.

Unlike the Dutch bar association in *Wouters*, the ONP had no regulatory powers for the conduct in question. Also, it considered that the existing legislation relating to laboratory tests was sufficient to safeguard public health and safety, and that the French State would have intervened if this had not been so.[80] In other words, the Commission did not consider the ONP's actions proportionate. Its assessment under Article 101(3) was limited to stating that ONP had not submitted any evidence that suggested that the conditions for exemption under Article 101(3), which required economic advantages benefiting consumers, could be fulfilled.[81]

iv. Conclusion

The Commission's interpretative guidelines, Block Exemption Regulations and decision practice on Article 101 after 2000 reveal a relatively coherent position on the issue of countervailing effects. Since the introduction of the more economic approach, the Commission only considers economic efficiency effects capable of justifying a restriction of competition under Article 101(3). After initial, and not particularly convincing,[82] attempts to translate non-economic benefits into economic benefits, the Commission now seems to have abandoned this approach and simply no longer takes non-economic benefits into account under Article 101(3) at all.

Regarding the Court's requirement that Article 101(1) be interpreted restrictively to exclude certain types of agreement that are concluded for legitimate reasons other than facilitating the implementation of a non-restrictive main transaction, the Commission's current position could be clearer. None of its many guidelines on the interpretation of Article 101 mentions this line of case law, and the Commission has only explicitly referred to it in one decision since the introduction of the more economic approach, in which it found that the principles established by the Court did not apply. In the case of *CISAC*, it vaguely discussed the relevance of cultural values in its assessment under Article 101(1), but did not place this discussion in the context of *Wouters* or any other theoretical mechanism, limiting itself instead to finding that the agreement was not necessary for achieving the parties' aim in any event.

D. Conclusion

While there is therefore some uncertainty on the Commission's current position on whether non-economic policy aims of the Union should be taken into account

[80] *ONP* (Case 39.510) recitals 686–91.
[81] ibid, recitals 703–06.
[82] For more detailed criticism of the Commission's approach in *CECED*, see Witt, 'Public Policy Goals Under EU Competition Law—Now is The Time to Set The House in Order' (n 23).

under Article 101(1), it is possible to say with certainty that the Commission no longer considers it appropriate to take such values into account under Article 101(3). While it used to take into account a broad range of socially and economically desirable effects under the first condition of Article 101(3), the more economic approach has reduced the type of eligible benefit to economic efficiency effects only.

This reading of Article 101(3) is perfectly in line with the new exclusive consumer welfare objective adopted by the Commission. The type of benefit that is deemed capable of cancelling out an agreement's anticompetitive effects under Article 101(3) is the counterpart to the Commission's new concept of competitive harm under Article 101(1). According to Article 101(1), only such effects are anticompetitive that result in a reduction of consumer welfare. According to Article 101(3), only efficiency gains that are passed on to consumers, ie consumer welfare-enhancing effects, are capable of offsetting anticompetitive effects. All other detrimental and beneficial effects are deemed irrelevant in an assessment under Article 101. In practice, however, even efficiency defences are rarely successful these days, at least where the agreement is considered likely to produce important anticompetitive effects.

III. EU Merger Law

A. The Commission's Understanding Prior to the Introduction of the More Economic Approach

i. The Legal Basis

Regulation 4064/89 did not contain an exemption provision similar to Article 101(3). This does not mean that it would have been theoretically impossible for the Commission to take into account the investigated concentrations' beneficial effects in its competitive assessments under the original Merger Regulation. Two possibilities come to mind: using the legal concept of an 'objective justification' or integrating the assessment of the concentration's beneficial effects into a more holistic assessment of the concentration's effects that would have balanced competing effects against each other to determine its overall competitive nature. Article 2(1) of Regulation 4064/89 in fact listed a number of factors that the Council expected the Commission to take into account in competitive assessments. This non-exhaustive list included factors such as the need to maintain and develop effective competition, the structure of the market, actual and potential competition, the undertakings' market position and economic and financial power, the alternatives available to suppliers and users, barriers to entry, and supply and demand trends, but also the development of technical and economic progress, provided that it was to consumers' advantage and did not form an obstacle to competition. This last factor, ie the 'development of technical and economic progress, provided that it is to consumers' advantage and does not form an obstacle to competition' is reminiscent of Article 101(3), and could reasonably have been used to consider countervailing effects in the overall competitive assessment. As the Commission did not issue any guidelines on its interpretation of the original Merger Regulation, it is only an analysis of its decision practice that is capable of casting light on whether, and if so how, the Commission took into account any countervailing effects in its competitive assessments under Regulation 4064/89.

ii. The Decision Practice

A study of the Commission's merger decisions under the original Merger Regulation reveals that potential beneficial effects played a negligible role in the Commission's assessments. The great majority of decisions did not examine the investigated merger's possible benefits for competition or other Union policies but focused on its anticompetitive effects exclusively. In particular, there were no decisions that openly took into account a merger's industrial, social or environmental benefits as potentially redeeming features. This is a marked difference from its approach under Article 101 during the same period.

Efficiency effects did not play a significant role in the Commission's assessments either, at least not under the aspect of countervailing effects. In *Aerospatiale-Alenia/de Havilland*, the first prohibition decision under Regulation 4064/89, for instance, the parties had argued that the concentration would lead to cost savings. The Commission briefly addressed this point under 'other general considerations'. It was doubtful whether cost savings could be considered relevant in a competitive assessment at all, but ultimately left the question open because it considered that the cost savings invoked by the parties in this specific case were negligible at any rate.[83] Only three other merger decisions under the first Merger Regulation touch on the issue of efficiencies as countervailing effects.[84] In all three cases, the parties had claimed that the merger would lead to 'synergies' and cost savings. The Commission briefly assessed these claims under the heading 'economic and technological progress'. While it did not question the theoretical possibility of taking into consideration cost savings in these decisions, it did not consider that the legal requirements for taking them into account were met. In *Gencor/Lonrho*, it was not convinced that the synergies invoked by the parties would actually materialise.[85] In *Saint-Gobain/Wacker-Chemie/NOM*, it did not question the potential for cost savings, but held that there was no mechanism whereby these could be passed on

[83] *Aerospatiale-Alenia/de Havilland* (Case IV/M.053) [1991] OJ L334/42, recital 65.

[84] *Gencor/Lonrho* (Case IV/M.619) [1997] OJ L11/30; *Saint-Gobain/Wacker-Chemie/NOM* (Case No IV/M.774) [1997] OJ L247/1; *Danish Crown/Vestjyske Slagterier* (Case IV/M.1313) [2000] OJ L20/1, recital 198.

[85] *Gencor/Lonrho* (n 84) VIII.

to consumers.[86] In *Danish Crown/Vestjyske Slagterier*, finally, it stated that it could only take into account the 'development of technical and economic progress' to the extent that it was to the consumers' advantage and did not form an obstacle to competition, which was excluded in cases, such as the one under investigation, in which the merger created a dominant position in the relevant markets.[87] As the creation or strengthening of a dominant position was a key condition of the substantive test under Regulation 4064/89, the Commission's position in *Danish Crown/Vestjyske Slagterier* suggests that there was not much scope for an efficiency defence at all.

On the contrary, in a number of cases, the Commission actually considered the prospect that the merger would make the parties more efficient a detrimental development and a further reason for prohibiting the transaction. In *Aerospatiale-Alenia/de Havilland, Blokker/Toys 'R' Us, Guinness/Grand Metropolitan* and *MSG Media Service*, for example, the Commission was concerned that the cost savings achieved by the merger would further strengthen the merged entity and give it an advantage over its competitors, who might not remain able to compete against this stronger undertaking and might be forced to leave the market.[88] Economies of scale and scope were thus not considered a potentially beneficial effect, but were seen as anticompetitive, at least in the hands of a dominant entity, because they could result in the exclusion of competitors. In a number of cases, one can even find parties explicitly arguing in their defence that the transaction would not lead to efficiencies.[89]

iii. Conclusion

It is difficult to make out the Commission's theoretical standpoint on the ability of efficiencies to act as countervailing factors in competitive assessments under the old Merger Regulation. Only a handful of cases alluded to the issue in response to efficiency defences raised by the parties, but avoided committing to a clear answer. In practice, however, it is clear that cost savings on the part of a dominant merged entity were often considered anticompetitive rather than pro-competitive, because they conferred a competitive advantage on the merged entity that might have resulted in the exclusion of competitors. This position is consistent with a concept of competitive harm that consists in the exclusion of competitors and harm to the structure of the market. It is less compatible with a concept of harm that only considers such restrictions of competition problematic that result in a reduction of consumer welfare. If the concern of antitrust law is to maximise

[86] *Saint-Gobain/Wacker-Chemie/NOM* (n 84) recital 246.

[87] *Danish Crown/Vestjyske Slagterier* (n 84) recital 198.

[88] *Aerospatiale-Alenia/de Havilland* (n 83) recital 32; *Blokker/Toys 'R' Us* (Case IV/M.890) [1998] OJ L316/1, recitals 63–66, 96; *Guinness/Grand Metropolitan* (Case No IV/M.938) [1998] OJ L288/24, recital 40; *MSG Media Service* (Case IV/M.469) [1994] OJ L364/1, recital 70.

[89] *Tetra Laval/Sidel* (Case No COMP/M. 2416) [2004] OJ L43/13, recital 325.

consumer welfare, and competitive harm is defined as a reduction in consumer welfare, then efficiency effects, which create welfare, must be deemed capable of offsetting competitive harm insofar as they are passed on to consumers.

B. The Commission's Understanding after the Introduction of the More Economic Approach

i. The Legal Basis

Before the background of the review of its Article 101 policy, and the Commission's ambition to introduce a similar welfare-based approach to EU merger control, it is therefore not surprising that the role of efficiencies as countervailing effects took a prominent place in the consultation process accompanying the recasting of the original Merger Regulation.[90] One might have expected the Council to clarify the issue when it recast the substantive test of EU merger law. However, this did not happen. The new substantive test of Regulation 139/2004 merely asks whether the merger is likely to result in a substantial impediment to effective competition. Like its predecessor, it does not contain an exemption provision similar to Article 101(3). It is only in one of the legally non-binding recitals that the Council explained that it was appropriate for the Commission to take into consideration any substantiated and likely efficiencies put forward by the undertakings concerned, and that efficiencies brought about by a concentration could under certain circumstances counteract its effects on competition and consumers. It further advised the Commission to publish guidance on the conditions under which it would take efficiencies into account in the assessment of a concentration.[91]

ii. The Soft Law

The Commission heeded this invitation. Both its horizontal and non-horizontal merger guidelines address the issue of efficiencies. They take the position that efficiencies brought about by a merger are in theory capable of counteracting a concentration's effects on competition and the potential harm to consumers,[92] and state that the Commission intends to consider both its possible anticompetitive effects and possible pro-competitive effects stemming from substantiated

[90] European Commission, 'Green Paper on the Review of Council Regulation (EEC) No 4064/89' (COM/2001/0745 final) paras 170–172; and responses received (European Commission, 'summary of the replies received' paras 112–27, available at: www.ec.europa.eu/competition/consultations/2002_council_regulation).

[91] Regulation 139/2004 [2004] OJ L24/1, recital 29.

[92] Commission Notice, Guidelines on the assessment of horizontal mergers under the Council Regulation on the control of concentrations between undertakings [2004] OJ C31/5, para 76; and Commission Notice, Guidelines on the assessment of non-horizontal mergers under the Council Regulation on the control of concentrations between undertakings [2008] OJ C265/6, para 21.

efficiencies benefiting consumers in an overall assessment.[93] They further stress that the fact that rivals may be harmed because a merger creates efficiencies cannot in itself give rise to competition concerns.[94] This is a clear change from the position found in the decision practice under Regulation 4064/89, which had been undecided as to the pro-competitive nature of efficiencies, but very clear on its anticompetitive exclusionary effects.

Having established the principle that efficiencies are relevant in competitive assessments, the horizontal merger guidelines then spell out three key conditions that need to be met for the Commission to take efficiency claims into account: the efficiencies need to benefit consumers, be merger-specific and verifiable.[95] In order to benefit consumers, efficiencies must be substantial, timely and sufficient to counteract its potential anticompetitive effects.[96] In order to qualify as merger-specific, they must not be achievable to a similar extent by less anticompetitive alternatives.[97] Finally, efficiencies are only deemed verifiable if they are precisely and convincingly proven on the basis of sound evidence. Where possible, the Commission expects the parties to quantify the expected efficiencies.[98] As the following shows, these requirements are not easy to meet in practice.

iii. The Decision Practice

The decision practice in theory fully embraces the principles spelled out in the guidelines. Efficiency defences are now a standard element in any competitive assessment under Regulation 139/2004. All five prohibition decisions enacted on the basis of the new Merger Regulation to date contain extensive analyses of the parties' efficiency claims,[99] and in all five cases, the parties put a great deal of effort into demonstrating the merger's potential efficiencies on the basis of detailed data and calculations, often supported by quantitative analyses commissioned from economic experts. In *Ryanair/Aer Lingus I*, the Commission even explicitly praised the merging parties' efforts to prove that the claimed efficiencies met the relevant criteria of verifiability, merger specificity and consumer benefit, as well as their attempts to provide indications of their magnitude.[100] Efficiency analyses are by no means limited to prohibition decisions. They nowadays also figure in clearance[101]

[93] Horizontal merger guidelines (n 92) para 76; and Non-horizontal merger guidelines (n 92) para 21.

[94] Non-horizontal merger guidelines (n 92) para 16.

[95] Horizontal merger guidelines (n 92) para 78.

[96] ibid, paras 79–84.

[97] ibid, para 85.

[98] ibid, paras 86–88.

[99] *Ryanair/Aer Lingus I* (Case No COMP/M.4439) s 7.10; *Olympic/Aegean Airlines* (Case No COMP/M.5830) s 7; *Deutsche Börse/NYSE Euronext* (Case No COMP/M.6166) s 12; *UPS/TNT Express* (Case No COMP/M.6570) s 7.10 and 7.11; and *Ryanair/Aer Lingus III* (Case No COMP/M.6663) s 9.

[100] *Ryanair/Aer Lingus I* (n 99) recital 1127.

[101] *TomTom/Tele Atlas* (Case COMP/M.4854) recitals 283–50; *Nokia/NAVTEQ* (Case COMP/M.4942) recitals 364–76; *KLM/Martinair* (Case No COMP/M.5141) recitals 408–11.

and commitments[102] decisions in which the parties formally plead efficiencies, although their assessment tends to be much more superficial than in prohibition decisions.

However, although efficiency analyses are now an integral part of competitive assessments under the new Merger Regulation, the reality is that efficiency defences are rarely successful in practice. The Commission routinely rejects efficiency claims on the basis that the efficiencies are not merger-specific,[103] not verifiable,[104] unlikely to be passed on to consumers,[105] not timely enough[106] or not of sufficient magnitude to make up for the merger's anticompetitive effects.[107] Often, efficiency claims fail to clear any of these hurdles. While there are a handful of decisions in which the Commission found that the efficiencies invoked by the parties were likely to meet its requirements, these were cases in which the Commission had not had any serious competitive concerns to begin with.[108] Not once has the Commission allowed a merger that in its view was likely to result in significant anticompetitive effects because of countervailing efficiencies.

iv. Conclusion

In sum, since the overhaul of its approach to EU merger control, the Commission now takes the view, in theory at least, that economic efficiency effects are capable of offsetting competitive harm. If the efficiency effects are merger-specific, verifiable and are passed on to consumers to such a degree that they neutralise the reduction in welfare expected from the merger's anticompetitive effects, the merger is not considered anticompetitive overall. It is for the parties to plead and prove such efficiencies. In practice, this is something that parties, even with expert economic advice, have rarely been able to do to the Commission's satisfaction.

C. Conclusion

The more economic approach has thus led the Commission to review and clarify its position on the role of efficiency effects in EU merger control.

[102] eg *Hutchison 3G Austria/Orange Austria* (Case No M.6497) s 7; *T-Mobile Austria/Tele.ring* (Case COMP/M.3916) recital 47; *Metso/Aker Kvaerner* (Case No COMP/M.4187) recitals 106, 107; *Outokumpu/INOXUM* (Case COMP/M.6471) recitals 836–53; *Lufthansa/Austrian Airlines* (Case COMP/M.5440) recital 326.

[103] *Ryanair/Aer Lingus I* (n 99) recital 1145; *Olympic/Aegean Airlines* (n 99) recital 1807; *Hutchison 3G Austria/Orange Austria* (n 102) recitals 414–20, 430.

[104] eg *Ryanair/Aer Lingus I* (n 99) recital 1142; *UPS/TNT Express* (n 99) recital 892; *Deutsche Börse/NYSE Euronext* (n 99) recitals 1166–76; *Olympic/Aegean Airlines* (n 99) recital 1783; *T-Mobile Austria/Tele.ring* (n 102) recital 47; *Hutchison 3G Austria/Orange Austria* (n 102) recital 412.

[105] eg *Ryanair/Aer Lingus I* (n 99) recital 1131; *Deutsche Börse/NYSE Euronext* (n 99) 1178–86; *Olympic/Aegean Airlines* (n 99) recital 1797.

[106] eg *UPS/TNT Express* (n 99) recitals 901 ff.

[107] eg *Ryanair/Aer Lingus* (n 99) 1150; *UPS/TNT Express* (n 99) recitals 922–1018.

[108] *TomTom/Tele Atlas* (n 101) recitals 283–50; *Nokia/NAVTEQ* (n 101) recitals 364–76.

While the Commission's theoretical position under the original Merger Regulation had been unclear, in practice, efficiency effects had often been considered anticompetitive. They were seen as giving the merging parties an advantage over their competitors that could undermine the latter's ability to exert competitive pressure on them or could even lead to them exiting the market. Unlike in the case of Article 101, public policy considerations had never openly played a role in assessments under the old Merger Regulation.

Since the introduction of the more economic approach, the Commission recognises in theory that efficiency effects are capable of offsetting the anti-competitive effects of a merger. This is in keeping with the fundamental canon of its more economic approach, according to which the primary purpose of EU antitrust law is to enhance consumer welfare. If the reduction in consumer welfare caused by the merger's anticompetitive effects is neutralised or even outweighed by an increase in consumer welfare resulting from its efficiency effects, then the overall effect must be neutral or even positive. It also brings the Commission's theoretical concept of countervailing effects in EU merger control into line with its revised approach to Article 101(3) under which it considers efficiency effects (only) capable of outweighing restrictions of competition.

However, despite this coherent theoretical approach, it cannot be ignored that in practice parties are rarely successful in convincing the Commission that the merger will generate efficiencies capable of offsetting the expected anticompetitive effects. In contrast to the situation under Article 101, this phenomenon cannot be explained away by speculating that the Commission has been focusing its enforcement activities on the most worrying cases, leaving the less precarious mergers to the national competition authorities, or that efficiencies are already being taken account at an earlier stage through Block Exemption Regulations. The Commission is the only institution that has the power to enforce the EU Merger Regulation and there are no Block Exemption Regulations in the context of merger law. This raises the question whether the standard of proof required by the Commission is unrealistic and even whether it is has fully embraced the theory underlying the efficiency defence. Incidentally, the Court has not found fault with the Commission's standards of proof to date. Both *Ryanair* and *Deutsche Börse* had challenged the Commission's assessments of their efficiency defences on appeal, but the General Court failed to find any manifest errors in either case.[109]

[109] Case T-175/12 *Deutsche Börse AG v Commission* ECLI:EU:T:2015:148, paras 200–08; Case T-342/07 *Ryanair v Commission* ECLI:EU:T:2010:280 paras 386–443. UPS's action for annulment against the prohibition of its acquisition of *TNT Express* is currently pending. It is also arguing, amongst others, that the Commission used an arbitrary standard for the verifiability of the transaction's efficiencies and assigned insufficient weight to the efficiencies it had accepted in principle (Case T-194/13 *United Parcel Service v Commission* [2013] OJ C147/30, point 2).

IV. Article 102

A. The Legal Basis

Unlike Article 101, Article 102 does not contain a specific exemption provision. There are several ways in which this could be interpreted. The absence of an explicit exemption provision in the vein of Article 101(3) could be understood as meaning that countervailing effects are not meant to be taken into account under Article 102. A second possibility would be to take such effects into account when deciding whether the conduct should be considered abusive, ie integrating their assessment into one overall analysis in the manner the Commission nowadays does under Regulation 139/2004. One could also consider whether it might be appropriate to apply Article 101(3) in analogy. A final option would be to use the general legal concept of an objective justification. The following establishes how the Commission has been dealing with beneficial effects created by potentially abusive conduct under Article 102 both before and after the introduction of the more economic approach.

B. The Commission's Understanding Prior to the Introduction of the More Economic Approach

The Commission did not issue any interpretative guidelines on Article 102 prior to the introduction of the more economic approach, and did not enact any implementing Regulations either. The only relevant source is therefore its decision practice. An analysis of the Commission's decisions on Article 102 shows that the Commission did in principle take into consideration countervailing effects in its assessments, and that it mostly chose to do so under the aspect of an objective justification.[110] It is equally clear that such defences were hardly ever successful. Even where the dominant undertaking managed to identify a legitimate benefit of its conduct, the Commission tended to consider the conduct disproportionate to this aim, ie not suitable, not indispensable or out of proportion to the harm inflicted on competition.

As for the type of benefit the Commission was prepared to take into account in theory, it is possible to identify two broad categories. The first category of beneficial effect was the protection of the dominant undertaking's own rights or legitimate commercial interests. For example, the Commission took the view that the protection of the dominant undertaking's intellectual property rights were, in

[110] Recognised as early as 1976 in *Chiquita* (Case IV/26.699) [1976] OJ L95/1, s II.A.3.b.

principle, a type of interest that could objectively justify abusive conduct, subject to the principle of proportionality.[111] Protecting oneself against liability[112] and protecting one's reputation[113] also seem to have been recognised as legitimate aims in principle, even though the Commission did not consider the abusive conduct necessary to achieve these aims in any of the relevant cases. In *GVL,* a German collecting society set up to manage authors' rights and claims pursuant to the German copyrights laws, attempted to justify its policy of not offering its service to non-German nationals residing outside of Germany with the argument that this would be too difficult because of the non-uniform and complex legal position on the recognition of performing rights within the Union. The Commission found this 'understandable' but nonetheless insufficient to justify discrimination between nationals and non-nationals established in other Member States.[114] In *Napier Brown-British Sugar*, in which the Commission investigated a refusal to supply, the dominant undertaking claimed that it had not supplied certain undertakings because of a shortage of supply. The Commission did not dispute that, in theory, a shortage of supply could be a legitimate reason for such conduct, but took the view that there had not actually been a shortage of supply.[115] Finally, in *BPB Industries*, the Commission accepted that abusive rebates could be justified for a certain period of time if they were part of a time-limited test exercise by the dominant undertaking designed to gain experience in a new delivery system.[116]

Another category of benefit sometimes invoked by dominant undertakings was the protection of consumers and the general public. In the cases of *Hilti*, *Hugin/Liptons* and *Tetra Pak II*, the investigated undertakings argued that their conduct was necessary to protect consumers against inferior competing products and services, or to ensure the proper functioning of the dominant undertaking's own product.[117] The Commission neither questioned nor acknowledged that consumer protection was a legitimate aim that should be taken into account under the aspect of an objective justification, but found in all three cases that the abusive conduct was not the least restrictive means possible for achieving this aim.[118] In *Hilti* and *Tetra Pak*, the dominant undertakings had further argued that their refusals to supply were motivated by the desire to protect public health against the dangers arising from faulty products. In both cases, the Commission held that the undertakings' conduct was disproportionate, because unnecessary,

[111] *Decca Navigator System* (Cases IV/30.979 and 31.394) [1989] OJ L43/27, recitals 105–07.

[112] *Eurofix-Bauco v Hilti* (Cases IV/30.787 and 31.488) [1988] OJ L65/19, recital 95.

[113] *Tetra Pak II* (Case IV/31.043) [1992] OJ L72/1, recital 121.

[114] *GVL* (Case IV/29.839) [1981] OJ L370/49, recitals 56–60.

[115] *Napier Brown-British Sugar* (Case IV/30.178) [1988] OJ L284/41, recital 23.

[116] *BPB Industries plc* (Case IV/31.900) [1989] OJ L10/50, recital 131.

[117] *Eurofix-Bauco v Hilti* (n 112); *Hugin/Liptons* (Case IV/29.132) [1978] OJ L22/23, I.E. and II.A(c); *Tetra Pak II* (n 113) recital 118.

[118] *Eurofix-Bauco v Hilti* (n 112) recital 88; *Hugin/Liptons* (n 117) II.A(a); *Tetra Pak II* (n 113) recital 119.

as there were adequate legal safety standards and product liability rules at the national level.[119]

There is only one case, in which a dominant undertaking invoked efficiencies as a justification prior to the review. In *Tetra Pak II*,[120] a case from 1992, the investigated undertaking claimed that the exclusive purchase obligation criticised by the Commission created economies of scales, other cost savings, as well as technical synergies.[121] The Commission did not dispute that efficiency effects were beneficial in principle. However, it refused to take them into account on the grounds that it did not consider Tetra Pak's practice of contractual tying necessary for achieving these benefits. It argued that if the claimed synergies really were to materialise and be passed on to consumers, then consumers would realise this and choose Tetra Pak's cheaper and better supply system over competing systems. In the Commission's view, it was 'up to the user', and not the producer, to compare such advantages with those offered by competing systems, and to make his choice freely.[122]

In sum, the Commission in principle recognised that abusive conduct on the part of a dominant undertaking could be objectively justified for legitimate reasons, as long as the conduct was proportionate to the aim. This meant that the conduct had to be suitable and indispensable for achieving the legitimate aim, and that the harm inflicted on competition was not out of proportion to the gain. While the Commission's decision practice did not define in a conclusive manner what type of aim it deemed capable of offsetting the harm caused by abusive conduct, it took into consideration a wide variety of beneficial effects in practice. This included both the dominant undertaking's own commercial interests and rights (for example, intellectual property rights or protecting itself against liability), as well as third parties' interests (for example, public health, consumer protection and, in one case, even efficiency effects that might have been passed on to consumers). However, in nearly every case, the dominant undertaking's defence failed because the abusive conduct was not deemed indispensable for achieving these as such legitimate aims.

C. The Commission's Understanding after the Introduction of the More Economic Approach

Article 102 was the last step in the Commission's substantive modernisation project. The review process was officially opened in 2005 when DG Competition

[119] *Eurofix-Bauco v Hilti* (n 112) recitals 89–91; *Tetra Pak II* (n 113) recital 119. In Hilti's case, the Commission also questioned the defence because it found Hilti's actions inconsistent with that of a business concerned about the safety of consumers (*Eurofix-Bauco v Hilti* (n 112) recitals 92, 93).

[120] *Tetra Pak II* (n 113).

[121] ibid, recital 118.

[122] ibid, recital 119.

submitted its Staff Discussion Paper for public consultation,[123] and formally concluded with the publication of the Commission's Guidance Notice in February 2009.[124] The following establishes the Commission's treatment of countervailing effects in assessments under Article 102 both in the Guidance and individual decision practice since the reform.

i. Soft Law

The role of efficiencies in competitive assessments was a key topic during the review of the Commission's approach to Article 102. Most commentators and practitioners argued that the Commission should align its approach to Article 102 with its more economic interpretation of Article 101 and the EU Merger Regulation in this point, so as to officially recognise efficiencies, and efficiencies only, as being capable of offsetting the anticompetitive effects of abusive conduct.[125] The EAGCP's Report from 2005, commissioned by the Commission's Chief Economist to inject expert economic input into the debate, also clearly took the view that efficiencies could outweigh the negative effects on consumers caused by abusive conduct, and that any assessment under Article 102 should balance these opposite effects against each other.[126] DG Competition's Discussion Paper from the same year suggested that abusive conduct should escape the prohibition of Article 102 either if the dominant undertaking could provide an objective justification for its behaviour,[127] or if it could demonstrate that its conduct generated efficiencies that outweighed its negative effects on competition.[128] It therefore seemed to view efficiencies as a permissible but *sui generis* type of defence that was distinct from the general concept of objective justification. The Discussion Paper roughly moulded this efficiency defence on the conditions of Article 101(3), and stipulated that efficiencies would be deemed capable of offsetting the abusive conduct's anticompetitive effects if (1) the conduct was indispensable for realising

[123] DG Competition, Discussion Paper on the Application of Article 82 of the Treaty to Exclusionary Abuses (November 2005) www.ec.europa.eu/competition/antitrust/art82/discpaper2005.pdf.

[124] Communication from the Commission, 'Guidance on the Commission's enforcement priorities in applying Article 82 of the EC Treaty to abusive exclusionary conduct by dominant undertakings' [2009] OJ C45/7.

[125] See eg the many contributions available under 'Comments on the public consultation on discussion paper on the application of Article 82 to exclusionary abuses' (March 2006) www.ec.europa.eu/competition/antitrust/art82/contributions.html.

[126] Report by the European Advisory Group on Competition Policy (EAGCP), *An Economic Approach to Article 82* (July 2005) www.ec.europa.eu/dgs/competition/economist/eagcp_july_21_05.pdf, 3.

[127] The Discussion Paper identified 2 categories of objective justification: an 'objective necessity defence' (the conduct is necessary due to external factors, eg because of reasons of safety or health related to the dangerous nature of the product in question) and the 'meeting competition defence' (the otherwise abusive conduct is a loss-minimising reaction to competition from others); ibid, paras 80 and 81–83.

[128] DG Competition, Discussion Paper on the Application of Article 82 of the Treaty to Exclusionary Abuses (n 123) para 77.

the efficiencies; (2) the efficiencies benefited consumers; and (3) competition was not eliminated in respect of a substantial part of the products concerned.[129]

The Commission's Guidance on its enforcement priorities in applying Article 102 to exclusionary abuses,[130] while not formulated as interpretative guidelines, takes a similar approach in substance. It is careful to stress that it is not intended as a statement of the law.[131] It does not even purport to spell out the Commission's own interpretation of Article 102. As explained in previous chapters, it merely aims to indicate what types of abusive conduct the Commission intends to focus its limited resources on, and how it will assess whether a case qualifies as a priority.

In assessing whether the conduct is a priority, the Commission intends to take into account whether the conduct is justified. According to the Guidance, this is the case if the conduct is either objectively necessary or if it produces substantial efficiencies that outweigh the anticompetitive effects on consumers, as long as the conduct is indispensable and proportionate to the aim pursued by the dominant undertaking.[132] The Guidance does not define in general terms what type of benefit the Commission deems capable of justifying abusive conduct under the 'objective necessity' defence. As an example, however, it explains that exclusionary conduct could be objectively necessary for health or safety reasons related to the nature of the product in question. It is also quick to point out, though, that in its assessment of the conduct's indispensability the Commission will normally consider it the task of public authorities and not that of dominant undertakings to set and enforce public health and safety standards.[133] This is in line with its former decision practice in *Hilti*, *Hugin/Liptons* and *Tetra Pak II*.[134] As the Guidance does not provide an exhaustive list of benefits deemed capable of justifying abusive conduct, one could assume that environmental and social benefits, or any other value protected by the EU Treaties, could in principle also be called upon to justify an abuse. However, the Guidance's observations on the role of private entities in protecting public health are likely to be equally valid for other public policy values. Based on these principles, it seems highly unlikely that a public policy defence, absent an emergency situation, would ever be able to take the hurdle of indispensability in practice.

In addition to 'objectively necessary' conduct, the Guidance states that the Commission will also consider abusive behaviour justified on the grounds of

[129] ibid, para 84.

[130] Communication from the Commission, 'Guidance on the Commission's enforcement priorities in applying Article 82 of the EC Treaty to abusive exclusionary conduct by dominant undertakings' (n 124).

[131] ibid, para 3.

[132] ibid, para 28.

[133] ibid, para 29.

[134] *Eurofix-Bauco v Hilti* (n 112); *Hugin/Liptons* (n 117) I.E and II.A(c); *Tetra Pak II* (n 113) recital 118 (see the discussion in section IV.B of this chapter).

efficiencies if these effects are sufficient to prevent net harm to consumers. The dominant undertaking is expected to demonstrate, with a sufficient degree of probability and on the basis of verifiable evidence, that four cumulative conditions are fulfilled: (1) the efficiencies have been, or will be, realised as a result of the conduct; (2) the conduct is indispensable (ie the least anticompetitive means) for realising the efficiencies; (3) the efficiencies outweigh any likely negative effects on competition and consumer welfare in the affected markets; and (4) the conduct does not eliminate effective competition by removing all or most existing sources of actual or potential competition.[135] In the assessment of the third condition, the Commission intends to weigh up any apparent anticompetitive effects against substantiated efficiencies in order to determine whether the conduct is likely to result in consumer harm.[136] These conditions are similar to those that the Commission applies in a modern-day assessment under Article 101(3) and EU merger law.[137] The only difference is that the Guidance Paper does not present them as being legally required by Article 102. It formally merely describes the assessment that the Commission intends to carry out for determining whether a case is an enforcement priority.

ii. The Decision Practice

The Commission's decision practice since 2009 is in line with the substantive approach on countervailing effects spelled out in the Guidance, although, in contrast to the guidelines on Article 101 and the EU Merger Regulation, the Guidance itself is hardly ever cited in individual decisions in support of this approach. Only one decision refers to the Guidance's principles on objective justifications,[138] whereas the vast majority, formally at least, rely on the Court's dicta.

The Commission's decision practice also recognises two permissible types of defences for justifying abusive conduct: 'objective necessity' or the generation of efficiencies that are passed on to consumers to such an extent that they offset the conduct's anticompetitive effects.[139] Examples of benefits that the Commission has recognised as being, in principle and subject to limitations, capable of justifying abusive conduct under the aspect of 'objective necessity' in practice are: the protection of the dominant undertaking's intellectual property rights;[140] its legitimate interest in not dealing with a trading partner who is unable or unwilling

[135] ibid, para 30.

[136] ibid, para 31.

[137] See ss II.C.i and III.B.iii above.

[138] *Telekomunikacja Polska* (COMP/39.525) recital 874).

[139] See eg ibid, recital 873; *Motorola—Enforcement of GPRS Standard Essential Patents* (Case AT.39985) recital 421; *Deutsche Bahn I* (Case COMP/AT.39678) and *Deutsche Bahn II* (COMP/AT.39731), recital 64.

[140] eg *Samsung—Enforcement of UMTS Standard Essential Patents* (Case AT.39939), recital 66; *IBM Maintenance Services* (Case COMP/39.692), recital 40.

to pay;[141] meeting competition;[142] not making itself criminally liable;[143] and the protection of its reputation.[144] There have not been any decisions in which public policy benefits, such as environmentally, socially or culturally desirable effects, were discussed or even argued by the parties.

In two out of the four infringement decisions since 2009, *Motorola* and *Intel*, the parties raised efficiency defences. In both decisions, the Commission explicitly recognised that efficiencies were in theory capable of offsetting an abuse's anti-competitive effects as long as (1) they counteracted any likely negative effects on competition and consumer welfare in the affected markets; (2) those gains were, or were likely to be, brought about as a result of that conduct; (3) the conduct was necessary for the achievement of those efficiency gains; and (4) the conduct did not eliminate effective competition by removing all or most existing sources of actual or potential competition.[145] These are, albeit in a different order, the same conditions as those listed in the Guidance on the Commission's enforcement priorities.

In fact, even decisions predating the official publication of the Guidance in February 2009 recognised the relevance of efficiency effects. Since 2004, when the role of efficiencies as countervailing factors had been formally recognised in the guidelines on Article 101 and the EU Merger Regulation, parties also regularly started raising efficiency defences under Article 102, and the Commission at least implicitly recognised the relevance of efficiencies by engaging with them in substance. This was the case, for example, in the first *Microsoft* case, *Prokent-Tomra* and *Wanadoo España v Telefónica*.[146]

What is striking, however, is that in practice neither efficiency nor objective necessity defences have ever been successful, at least not in cases closed by means of a formal decision. The Commission most commonly rejects efficiency defences as unfounded because the undertaking failed to prove to its satisfaction that the conduct would result in the creation of efficiencies quantified to the required legal standard;[147] the conduct was indispensable for achieving them;[148] the efficiency gains would be passed on to consumers;[149] or that the efficiencies

[141] eg *Samsung—Enforcement of UMTS Standard Essential Patents* (n 140) recital 67.

[142] *Intel* (Case COMP/C-3 /37.990) recitals 1626–31.

[143] *Romanian Power Exchange/OPCOM* (Case AT.39984) recitals 193–95.

[144] *Reuters Instrument Codes* (Case AT.39654) recital 44.

[145] *Motorola—Enforcement of GPRS Standard Essential Patents* (n 139) recitals 480–91; *Intel* (n 142) recitals 1632–39.

[146] *Microsoft* (Case COMP/C-3/37.792) recitals 955–70; *Prokent-Tomra* (Case COMP/E-1/38.113) recitals 349–57; *Wanadoo España v Telefónica* (Case COMP/38.784) recitals 641–59.

[147] eg *Intel* (n 142) recitals 1632–39; *Prokent-Tomra* (n 146) recital 349; *Microsoft* (n 146) recital 962.

[148] eg *Wanadoo España v Telefónica* (n 146), recital 647; *Prokent-Tomra* (Case n 146) recitals 350–57; *Microsoft* (n 146) recitals 963–67; *Motorola—Enforcement of GPRS Standard Essential Patents* (n 139) recital 485–87.

[149] *Wanadoo España v Telefónica* (n 146) recitals 655–68.

would have outweighed the competitive harm caused by the conduct.[150] Likewise, the defence that the investigated abusive conduct was objectively necessary in order to achieve legitimate aims, for example, the protection of intellectual property rights or the undertaking's commercial interests, tend to fail because the conduct is deemed unsuitable,[151] unnecessary[152] or disproportionate for achieving this aim.[153]

iii. Conclusion

In sum, since the review of its approach to Article 102, the Commission in theory recognises two categories of benefit as capable of justifying abusive conduct: efficiencies and 'other legitimate aims'. Efficiencies are in principle deemed capable of justifying an abuse under the same conditions as those spelled out in Article 101(3). The other legitimate aims need to be pursued in a manner that is proportionate to the harm caused to competition. Like under Article 101(3) and the EU Merger Regulation, neither defence tends to be successful in individual assessments.

D. Conclusion

If one compares the situation prior to the introduction of the more economic approach to that after the publication of the Guidance, one has to reach the conclusion that the Commission's position has changed to a lesser degree than under Article 101 and EU merger control. While there was no soft law prior to the reform that explained the Commission's position on this point in a clear and unequivocal manner, the decision practice allows the conclusion that the Commission had always considered that abusive conduct could be objectively justified if it pursued legitimate aims in a proportionate manner. There was no exhaustive list or definition of eligible legitimate aims, but in practice the Commission took into consideration the dominant undertaking's own rights and commercial interests, consumer protection and public health, as well as, in one case, economies of scale and other 'synergies' that were likely to benefit consumers.[154] The great majority of these defences failed in practice because the Commission did not deem the conduct indispensable for achieving these aims, or because it considered the harm caused by the conduct disproportionate to the benefit.

[150] ibid, recitals 655–58; *Deutsche Bahn I* (n 139) and *Deutsche Bahn II* (n 139) recital 66; *Motorola—Enforcement of GPRS Standard Essential Patents* (n 139) recital 482.

[151] *Intel* (n 142) recitals 1626–31.

[152] *Wanadoo España v Telefónica* (n 146) recitals 630, 637–39; *Motorola—Enforcement of GPRS Standard Essential Patents* (n 139) recital 423; *Romanian Power Exchange/OPCOM* (n 143) recitals 193–95 and 196–227; *Telekomunikacja Polska* (n 138) recitals 878–83.

[153] *Microsoft* (n 146) recitals 709–12.

[154] *Tetra Pak II* (n 113) recital 118.

Now, after the reform, the Commission recognises two formal categories of justification: efficiencies and 'objective necessity'. Neither the Guidance nor the decision practice contain a precise definition of when conduct is deemed objectively necessary, but they suggest that in principle any legitimate aim and benefit, be it of an economic or non-economic nature, is deemed capable of justifying abusive conduct as long as it is compatible with the principle of proportionality. This is not significantly different from the Commission's stance prior to the reform. Also, in practice, objective justifications still tend to fail at the hurdle of proportionality. Despite pursuing a legitimate aim, the Commission tends to find that there would have been a less restrictive means of achieving the aim in question, or that the harm inflicted on competition and consumers was disproportionate to the benefit. With regard to public policy aims, which have not played any role in practice but appear to be capable of justifying an abuse in theory, the Guidance suggests that the Commission would normally take the view that the abusive conduct was not necessary, because it is the task of public authorities, or not that of a dominant undertaking, to set and enforce such aims.

Efficiencies have now acquired the status of a distinct category of defence, but the Commission had in principle considered them legitimate benefits capable of justifying abusive conduct under the aspect of an objective justification even prior to the reform, as long as the conduct was proportionate. Now, it considers them capable of justifying abusive conduct if the latter is causal and necessary for achieving the efficiencies, the efficiencies outweigh the negative effects on competition and consumer welfare, and the conduct does not eliminate effective competition. In essence, these conditions are an adaptation of the general principle of proportionality, and closely follow the model of Article 101(3). The one condition that would not necessarily have been required by the principle of proportionality is the requirement that the efficiencies be passed on to consumers. However, it is the logical consequence of adopting the consumer welfare aim rather than a total welfare aim as the guiding objective of EU antitrust law. In fact, even in the one decision prior to the reform in which the Commission had considered the undertaking's efficiency defence under the aspect of a general objective justification, it had required that these efficiencies be passed on at least partially to consumers. In so far, the legal interpretation of Article 102 with regard to efficiencies, and any other countervailing factor, has not changed in a meaningful way.

One notable practical change is that the number of efficiency defences made by dominant undertakings has greatly increased since the introduction of the more economic approach to Article 102. This is likely to be a consequence of the increased academic and political debate about the role of efficiencies as countervailing factors under all three pillars of EU antitrust law, as well as the formal recognition of the defence in the Guidance. However, this does not mean that the success rate of such defences has increased. Since the introduction of the more economic approach, the Commission has not recognised a single efficiency defence under Article 102 as founded.

One last point worthy of note is that the Guidance's principles on efficiencies are far less detailed and emphatic than its counterparts in the Commission's guidelines on Article 101 and the EU Merger Regulation. They also play a lesser role in the Commission's decision practice than the guidelines on Article 101 and merger review. Instead, the Commission has so far relied almost entirely on case law in its assessments of efficiency defences under Article 102.

V. Conclusion

In conclusion, the more economic approach has markedly changed the Commission's theory on what type of beneficial effect should be deemed capable of offsetting a conduct's anticompetitive effects under Article 101 and the EU Merger Regulation. In line with the overarching consumer welfare aim and its new concept of competitive harm, it now takes the view that efficiency effects, and efficiency effects only, are capable of offsetting anticompetitive effects, in so far as they are passed on to consumers to such an extent that they are no worse off than without the conduct. Under Article 101, the Commission has accommodated this view by adopting a restrictive interpretation of Article 101(3). Whereas it had previously taken a broad view of 'improving the production or distribution of goods' or 'promoting technical or economic progress' so as to include any type of benefit that is desirable from the point of view of EU policy (for example, social, environmental, industrial benefits), the more economic approach has put an end to this. It now interprets the first condition of Article 101(3) as referring to economic efficiencies only.

Under EU merger law, the Commission had never, at least not openly, even considered any other benefit than efficiencies as potentially capable of justifying a merger's anticompetitive effects. In so far, the more economic approach did not lead to a restriction of the benefits capable of offsetting harm to competition as it did under Article 101. However, it did lead to the Commission officially recognising that efficiency effects are capable of offsetting a merger's anticompetitive effects and that their analysis should be part of the overall competitive assessment. Prior to the reform, the Commission's theoretical position on the relevance and role of efficiency effects was unclear at best. In the handful of cases in which the parties actually raised an efficiency defence, the Commission avoided giving a clear answer as to whether it deemed efficiencies capable of counterbalancing the merger's anticompetitive effects. By contrast, in a number of decisions it even considered cost savings to be anticompetitive rather than pro-competitive, because it feared that this advantage would allow the merged entity to drive its competitors out of the market.

The changes under Article 102 are less pronounced. Efficiency effects are now explicitly recognised as being capable of justifying an abuse and have been given their own status of justification, separate from 'other' legitimate aims. However, this is not a radical change in legal interpretation. The Commission had always considered that abusive conduct could be objectively justified if it pursued a legitimate aim in a proportionate manner. Efficiency effects that were passed on to consumers seem to have been deemed such a legitimate aim in principle in the one case prior to the reform in which the parties raised an efficiency defence. The Commission merely did not consider the conduct necessary for achieving them. Nonetheless, the reform has had the effect of clarifying the Commission's position on the role of efficiency effects under Article 102 and of raising the defence's profile. In so far, its position on countervailing effects is in line with its more economic approach to Article 101 and the EU Merger Regulation. Where it differs, however, is with regard to benefits other than the creation of economic welfare. In contrast to Article 101 and EU merger law, the Commission has not formally excluded public policy benefits as countervailing factors. It has made clear, however, that it will normally consider defences based on such aims as unfounded, because national legislators are likely to have taken appropriate measures to protect the public good, so that the abusive conduct is unnecessary. Nonetheless, *de lege*, public policy values remain capable of justifying abusive conduct. In so far, the Commission's reform of Article 102 has, formally at least, not gone as far as that of Article 101 and EU merger review. This tallies with the findings made with regard to the concept of harm, which were not as far-reaching and consequent under Article 102 as they were under Article 101 and EU merger law.

While there is hence a different legal position with regard to the type of benefit deemed capable of justifying anticompetitive conduct under the 'more economic' approach to Article 101 and merger law on the one hand, and the 'less economic' approach to Article 102 on the other, it has to be said that there is little difference in practice. Although public policy defences remains admissible under Article 102 in theory, none has been made since the reform. And while efficiency has been officially recognised as being capable of offsetting anticompetitive conduct under all three pillars of EU antitrust law, and efficiency defences are now regularly raised by investigated undertakings, such defences have simply not succeeded in practice to date. In no case in which the Commission had serious competitive concerns, be it under Article 101, the EU Merger Regulation or Article 102, has a party been able to demonstrate to the Commission's satisfaction that the conduct would create efficiencies that fulfilled the four conditions of the Commission's test.

After so much debate about the importance of efficiencies and so much effort to introduce the efficiency defence to all three pillars of EU antitrust law, this discrepancy between theory and practice is somewhat puzzling. In fact, the development even appears counterproductive. At the moment, the key effect of an efficiency defence is the generation of additional costs for all parties involved. The parties invoking the defence regularly require expert economic input to present the efficiencies in a way that complies with the Commission's guidelines. They often commission complex econometric analyses to prove and quantify the efficiencies expected from the merger. Consequently, disproving the validity of such detailed efficiency defences to a standard that will withstand an action for annulment before the General Court also requires a great deal of time and effort on the part of the Commission. The Commission regularly engages with these efficiency claims in depth, examining the validity of the data, the calculations and the very models used to predict the efficiencies.[155] Efficiency defences are thus a costly and time-consuming business. Without realistic chances of success, this additional cost makes little sense.

[155] See eg *UPS/TNT Express* (n 99) recitals 922–1018; *MasterCard* (n 46) recitals 666–753; *Groupement des cartes bancaires* (Case COMP/D1/38606) recitals 375–503.

7

A More Economic Test

I. Introduction

After settling on appropriate concepts of harm and countervailing effects, the next question facing any architect of antitrust law is how to design the legal test. Should one, for example, outlaw specific types of conduct outright, or should the relevant enforcement body carry out an individual assessment of the conduct's actual effects on competition, however defined, in order to establish its competitive nature? And if it is the latter, what should this assessment look like? This issue is distinct from the matter of defining the type of harm one wants to prevent or the type of benefit one wants to encourage by means of the antitrust rules. It is no less important, but logically, it is necessary to decide the key values first in order to decide what the most appropriate legal test would be.

The issue was highly polarised in the Commission's review process. Many practitioners and academics argued that the tests traditionally applied by the Commission and the Court to determine the competitive nature of the investigated conduct under the EU antitrust rules were too form-based, meaning that the institutions inferred the competitive nature from the form of the conduct rather than assessing its actual effects on competition. The resulting debate was often carried out under the motto of 'form- v effects-based tests'. While this is a handy catchphrase, it somewhat oversimplifies the issue. It refers to two types of test that are at opposite sides of the spectrum. A form-based test, in the strict sense of the term, establishes an irrefutable presumption that a specific form of conduct will result in harm to the protected value. An effects-based test requires the enforcement agency to demonstrate and prove the actual effect on the protected value. However, these are not the only two possibilities. There are many intermediary options in between these two extremes that do not simply infer the competitive nature of the conduct from its form but do not require a full-scale assessment of its effects either.

This chapter examines whether the more economic approach has changed the Commission's approach to carrying out competitive assessments, more particularly whether it has influenced the type of test the Commission uses under the EU antitrust rules. It begins with providing some background information on the context of the debate and a few general thoughts on the different types of legal tests.

II. A Few Preliminary Considerations

During the Commission's substantive modernisation process, the academic and political debate on the best type of test for antitrust assessments drew heavily on comparisons with US antitrust law. As explained in Chapter 3, US antitrust law operates on the basis of two main types of test under section 1 of the Sherman Act: rules of *per se* illegality and rules of reason. Certain types of conduct are deemed *per se* illegal, with the consequence that their anticompetitive effects are presumed, and others need to be assessed as to their actual effects under a rule of reason.[1] *Per se* rules reached their height of popularity in the 1940s to 1960s,[2] but in the 1970s, the Antitrust Revolution reversed the trend. One by one, the US Supreme Court started to abandon its former rules of *per se* illegality for specific types of contracts. In 1977, it overruled the precedent that non-price restrictions in distribution agreements had to be presumed *per se* illegal, and ordered that this type of restraint be assessed as to its actual effects under a traditional rule of reason.[3] In 1997, it overruled the precedent that maximum resale price maintenance must be deemed *per se* illegal,[4] and in 2007, the precedent according to which minimum resale price maintenance was deemed *per se* illegal met the same fate.[5] The US Supreme Court also narrowed down the circumstances under which a concerted refusal to deal has to be considered *per se* illegal.[6] While horizontal price fixing agreements,[7] bid-rigging[8] and market sharing[9] are still unreservedly deemed *per se* illegal, the great majority of agreements are now assessed under the rule of reason as to their actual effects on competition and consumer welfare, rather than being irrefutably presumed illegal under section 1 of the Sherman Act.

As the Commission's more economic approach was emulating many of the changes introduced during the US Antitrust Revolution, in particular the consumer welfare aim and the welfare-based concept of harm, it is only natural that the issue of legal presumption v individual assessment also appeared on the reform

[1] See Ch 3, s IV.A.iv.

[2] For a brief historical overview, see eg E Fox and L Sullivan, 'Antitrust—Retrospective and Prospective: Where Are We Coming From? Where Are We Going?' (1987) 62 *New York University Law Review* 336; WE Kovacic and C Shapiro, 'Antitrust Policy: A Century of Economic and Legal Thinking' (2000) 14 *Journal of Economic Perspectives* 43.

[3] *Continental T. V., Inc v GTE Sylvania Inc*, 433 U.S. 36 (1977), overruling *United States v Arnold, Schwinn & Co*, 388 U.S. 365 (1967).

[4] *State Oil v Khan*, 522 U.S. 3 (1997).

[5] *Leegin Creative Leather Products, Inc v PSKS, Inc*, 127 S.Ct. 2705 (2007).

[6] *Northwest Wholesale Stationers, Inc v Pacific Stationery & Printing Co*, 472 US 284, 298 (1985), and *FTC v Indiana Federation of Dentists*, 476 U.S. 447 (1986).

[7] eg *United States v Trenton Potteries Co*, 273 U.S. 392 (1927); *United States v Socony-Vacuum Oil Co.*, 310 U. S. 150, 223 (1940).

[8] eg *Addyston Pipe and Steel Co v United States*, 175 U.S. 211, 237 (1899).

[9] eg *Palmer v BRG of Georgia, Inc*, 498 U.S. 46 (1990).

agenda. Many academics, in particular economists, were of the view that the EU institutions relied too strongly on form-based presumptions, and recommended that the Commission adopt a more effects-based approach in the vein of current US antitrust law.[10]

There are advantages and drawbacks to either type of rule. The key advantage of carefully assessing a conduct's actual effects on competition before prohibiting it is of course that it promises a more accurate outcome. To use the language of economists, it is less likely to result in Type I and Type II errors.[11] If the assessment is carried out correctly, one should in theory only end up prohibiting conduct that actually was harmful to competition and not accidentally ban conduct that was neutral or even beneficial (Type I error). Also, conduct with truly anticompetitive effects should in principle always be detected, and not erroneously escape prohibition because it does not happen to take the exact form of conduct prohibited by a *per se* rule (Type II error). Both failing to deter truly anticompetitive conduct and deterring conduct that is actually pro-competitive is detrimental to competition, and therefore not in the interest of competition law.

The key disadvantage of assessing and establishing business conduct's actual effects in every single case before deciding on its competitive nature is equally obvious: such assessments are more difficult and therefore more resource-intense than applying a legal presumption, especially if one takes the view that the relevant effect is consumer harm. Proving conclusively that a certain business practice has caused a quantifiable reduction in consumer welfare in terms of price, quantity, quality, levels of innovation or other parameters of welfare is not usually a straightforward exercise. It requires accurate and detailed data, human resources, economic know-how and a fair amount of time. It can therefore be a lengthy and expensive process for all parties involved. Also, an accurate outcome is only guaranteed if the competent institutions operate on the basis of representative data, reliable theories of harm and apply the latter correctly to the facts. There is also room for error in this process. Moreover, there is the issue of predictability and justiciability of such tests. Will undertakings be able to self-assess the legality of their conduct under the law if the latter requires a complex economic assessment?

[10] eg European Advisory Group on Competition Policy (EAGCP), 'An Economic Approach to Article 82' (July 2005) 2, www.ec.europa.eu/dgs/competition/economist/eagcp_july_21_05.pdf, 5 ff; J Vickers, 'Abuse of Market Power' (2005) 115 *The Economic Journal* 244; D Waelbroeck, 'Michelin II: A *Per Se* Rule Against Rebates by Dominant Companies?' (2005) 1 *Journal of Competition Law and Economics* 149; J Kallaugher and B Sher, 'Rebates Revisited: Anti-competitive Effects and Exclusionary Abuse under Article 82' (2004) 25 *European Competition Law Review* 263; D Ridyard, 'Exclusionary Pricing and Price Discrimination Abuses under Article 82—An Economic Analysis' (2002) 23 *European Competition Law Review* 286; S Bishop, 'Pro-competitive Exclusive Supply Agreements: How Refreshing!' (2003) 24 *European Competition Law Review* 229; S Bishop and D Ridyard, 'E.C. Vertical Restraints Guidelines: Effects Based or *per se* Policy?' (2002) 23 *European Competition Law Review* 35.

[11] A Type I error (or a false positive) occurs when a test finds the presence of an effect that does not really exist, whereas a Type II error (or a false negative) occurs when the test fails to detect an effect that is really there.

And will judges be able to review these assessments in a meaningful way on appeal? Applying a legal presumption is certainly easier.

Establishing the actual effects in every case and relying on *per se* rules of legality or illegality are of course only two extremes on the scale of many possible tests. In theory, at least, there is plenty of scope for intermediary tests that strike a better balance between accuracy and ease of application.[12] The purpose of this chapter is not to develop such a rule, but to establish whether, and if so in what manner, the more economic approach has led the Commission to change the type of test it uses in its assessments under the EU antitrust rules.

III. Article 101

A. The Legal Basis

Article 101(1) distinguishes between agreements that have the object of restricting competition and restrictions that have the effect of restricting competition. Since 1962, the Court of Justice of the European Union has interpreted this as stipulating two different kinds of test. Agreements that have the object of restricting competition are presumed to be anticompetitive, so that there is no need to establish and prove the agreement's actual effects.[13] The Court's rationale for this rule is that certain types of agreement are so likely to have negative effects on competition that it would be redundant to prove their actual effects.[14] This reasoning is similar to that used by the US Supreme Court to justify the use of *per se* rules of illegality under US antitrust law.[15] Whether an agreement has the object of restricting competition within the meaning of Article 101(1) needs to be determined in each individual case on the basis of the agreement's content and the economic context in which it is to be applied.[16] There are many uncertainties as to how to do this in practice, and much academic effort continues to go into

[12] See eg TC Arthur, 'A Workable Rule of Reason: A Less Ambitious Antitrust Role for the Federal Courts' (2002) 68 *Antitrust Law Journal* 337; TJ Muris, 'The Rule of Reason after California Dental' (2002) 68 *Antitrust Law Journal* 527; WK Tom and C Pak, 'Toward a Flexible Rule of Reason' (2000) 68 *Antitrust Law Journal* 391; A Christiansen and W Kerber, 'Competition Policy with Optimally Differentiated Rules Instead of "Per Se Rules v Rule of Reason"' (2006) 2 *Journal of Competition Law & Economics* 215; DS Evans, 'How Economists Can Help Courts Design Competition Rules: A EU and US Perspective' (2005) 28 *World Competition* 93; F Fisher, 'Economic Analysis and 'Bright-Line' Tests' (2007) *Journal of Competition Law and Economics* 129.

[13] Joined cases 56 and 58-64 *Consten and Grundig v Commission* ECLI:EU:C:1966:41, 342.

[14] C-67/13 P *Groupement des cartes bancaires* ECLI:EU:C:2014:2204, para 51.

[15] See eg *Northern Pacific R Co v United States*, 356 US 1, 5 (1958).

[16] eg Cases C-209/07 *Competition Authority v Beef Industry Development Society and Barry Brothers* ECLI:EU:C:2008:643, para 15; C-501/06 P *GlaxoSmithKline v Commission* ECLI:EU:C:2009:610, para 55; C-551/03 P *General Motors v Commission* ECLI:EU:C:2006:229, para 66; 29/83 and 30/83 *Compagnie royale asturienne des mines and Rheinzink v Commission* ECLI:EU:C:1984:130, para 26.

extracting a clear and coherent rule from the case law.[17] The Court's standard formula is that restrictions by object are restrictions that are by their very nature injurious to the proper functioning of normal competition.[18] Examples of horizontal restrictions that the Court considers restrictive by object are price fixing,[19] output reduction,[20] customer allocation,[21] market allocation and bid-rigging.[22] Vertical restrictions that it considers restrictive by object are absolute territorial protection and agreements designed to restrict parallel trade[23] and resale price maintenance.[24]

According to the Court, agreements that do not have the object of restricting competition need to be assessed as to their actual effects. In this case, the Commission needs to establish and prove to the required legal standard that the agreement actually restricts competition in order to find it illegal.[25]

In sum, the wording of Article 101(1) itself, at least as interpreted by the Court of Justice, prescribes two distinct types of assessment: certain types of agreement are presumed to be restrictive of competition on the basis of their 'object', others require an individual assessment of their effects on competition. This distinction is to some extent comparable to the two types of test that the US Supreme Court has read into the wording of section 1 of the Sherman Act. However, they differ in that under Article 101 an object restriction can theoretically still be saved under Article 101(3), whereas a contract that is deemed *per se* illegal under section 1 of the Sherman Act is irrefutably presumed anticompetitive.

That being said, despite formally only operating on the basis of these two types of test (restriction by object and restriction by effect), the Court also uses tests that could qualify as types of intermediary or 'quick look' rules, because they neither infer the competitive nature from the agreement's object alone, nor do they require a detailed assessment of its effect on competition. Specifically for the assessment of selective distribution agreements, for example, the Court has developed a

[17] See eg J Goyder, 'Cet obscur objet: object restrictions in vertical agreements' (2011) 2 *Journal of European Competition Law and Practice* 327; C Graham, 'Methods for Determining whether an Agreement Restricts Competition: Comment on Allianz Hungaria' (2013) 38 *European Law Review* 542; D Bailey, 'Restrictions of Competition by Object under Article 101 TFEU' (2012) 49 *Common Market Law Review* 559; A Jones, 'Left Behind by Modernisation? Restrictions by Object under Article 101(1)' (2010) 6 *European Competition Journal* 649; S King, 'The Object Box: Law, Policy of Myth?' (2011) 7 *European Competition Journal* 269, amongst many others.

[18] eg Cases C-32/11 *Allianz Hungária and Others v Gazdasági Versenyhivatal* ECLI:EU:C:2013:160, para 41; C-382/12 P *MasterCard Inc and Others v Commission* ECLI:EU:C:2014:2201, para 185; *Groupement des cartes bancaires v Commission* (n 13) para 50.

[19] Case T-47/10 *Akzo Nobel v Commission* ECLI:EU:T:2015:506, para 230.

[20] *Beef Industry Development Society (BIDS)* (n 16) para 40.

[21] eg *Akzo Nobel v Commission* (n 19) para 230.

[22] Case T-208/08 *Gosselin Group NV v Commission* ECLI:EU:T:2011:287, para 67.

[23] eg *Consten and Grundig* (n 13) 340; Joined cases C-501/06 P, C-513/06 P, C-515/06 P and C-519/06 P *GlaxoSmithKline and Others v Commission* ECLI:EU:C:2009:610, para 61.

[24] Case 243/83 *Binon v Agence et messageries de la presse* ECLI:EU:C:1985:284, para 44; Case 161/84 *Pronuptia de Paris* ECLI:EU:C:1986:41, paras 23–25.

[25] eg Case *GlaxoSmithKline v Commission* (n 23) para 55; Case C-8/08 *T-Mobile Netherlands* ECLI:EU:C:2009:343, para 28.

test according to which this type of agreement is restrictive by object unless it fulfils a number of conditions: (1) the characteristics of the product in question necessitate such a network in order to preserve its quality and ensure its proper use; (2) the resellers are chosen on the basis of objective criteria of a qualitative nature, laid down uniformly for all potential resellers and not applied in a discriminatory fashion; (3) the criteria laid down do not go beyond what is necessary; and (4) the number of similar distribution systems in the market do not preclude the possibility of other forms of distribution or result in a rigid price structure.[26] This test goes beyond merely presuming selective distribution agreements to be anticompetitive on the basis of their form. It does not require a detailed assessment of the agreements' actual effects on competition either. However, it does require an assessment of relatively detailed conditions that are, presumably, supposed to allow an approximation of the agreement's likely anticompetitive and pro-competitive effects.

In comparison, the wording of Article 101(3), which states that anticompetitive agreements can be exempted from the prohibition of Article 101(1) if the agreement produces certain types of benefit, does not make a distinction similar to that in Article 101(1). It does not clarify at all whether countervailing effects may be presumed in all or certain cases, or whether they need to be proved by means of an individual assessment.

Before this background, the following analyses the Commission's approach to determining the anticompetitive nature of agreements and their redeeming effects in its enforcement practice both before and after the introduction of the more economic approach.

B. The Commission's Approach Prior to the Introduction of the More Economic Approach

There were no general interpretative guidelines prior to the introduction of the more economic approach that exhaustively explained the Commission's approach to assessing whether an agreement was likely to result in these types of harm or benefit, and the few highly specific soft law instruments on Article 101 that did exist[27] were silent on the issue. The Commission's early approach can therefore

[26] eg Case 26/76 *Metro SB-Großmärkte v Commission* ECLI:EU:C:1977:167, para 20; Case 75/84 *Metro SB-Großmärkte v Commission* ECLI:EU:C:1986:399, para 40; Case C-439/09 *Pierre Fabre Dermo-Cosmétique* ECLI:EU:C:2011:649, para 41.

[27] eg European Commission, Bekanntmachung über Alleinvertriebsverträge mit Handelsvertretern [1962] OJ 139/2921 (no English version); European Commission, Bekanntmachung über Vereinbarungen, Beschlüsse und aufeinander abgestimmte Verhaltensweisen, die eine zwischenbetriebliche Zusammenarbeit betreffen [1968] OJ C75/3 (no English version); European Commission, Bekanntmachung vom 27. Mai 1970 über Vereinbarungen, Beschlüsse und aufeinander abgestimmte Verhaltensweisen von geringer Bedeutung, die nicht unter Artikel 85 Absatz 1 des Vertrages zur Gründung der Europäischen Wirtschaftsgemeinschaft fallen [1970] OJ C64/1 (no English version

only be inferred from its individual decision practice and Block Exemption Regulations.

i. The Decision Practice

The decisions of the 1960s to late 1990s reveal a somewhat inconsistent approach. There are a number of decisions in which the Commission explicitly categorised the investigated agreement as restricting competition by object. These decisions usually did not explain the concept of an object restriction in any detail and rarely referred to the principles established in the case law. The majority of cases in which the Commission specifically described the agreement as restricting competition by object concerned contractual clauses through which the parties aimed to coordinate prices[28] or impede exports to other Member States.[29] The Commission also recognised restrictions by object in a few agreements that imposed trading quotas on the parties,[30] allocated sales outlets or territories[31] and, in one case, stopped distributors from repackaging goods.[32] Strictly speaking, the Commission did not base the finding of anticompetitiveness on the mere form of the contractual clauses in these cases, but on their purpose. For example, it considered the means by which the undertakings in the aforementioned cases intended to limit interstate trade irrelevant. What mattered was the parties' purpose, namely to limit exports to another Member State. The Commission primarily determined this purpose by analysing the terms of the agreement in the context of the overall economic market conditions and the parties' other conduct.

Decisions that explicitly analysed agreements under the aspect of a restriction by effect only were much rarer. In the handful of cases, in which the Commission did engage in such an analysis, it usually assessed the agreement's effects on the parties' commercial autonomy.[33] This was fully in holding with its concept of competitive harm of the time. It tended to prove these effects on the basis of the contractual terms of the parties' agreement alone.

However, the great majority of decisions from this period did not clearly assess the investigated agreements under one or the other concept. Many decisions

available), European Commission, Notice concerning the assessment of the cooperative joint ventures pursuant to Article 85 of the EEC Treaty [1993] OJ C43/2.

[28] *Preserved Mushrooms* (Case IV/27.039) [1975] OJ L 29/26, II.2.a; *Far Eastern Freight Conference* (Case IV/33.218) [1994] OJ L378/17, recitals 43–45; *Coapi* (IV/33.686) [1995] OJ L122/37, recital 37.

[29] eg *Arthur Bell and Sons Ltd* (Case IV/29.440) [1978] OJ L235/15, II.1.c; *BMW Belgium NV and Belgian BMW dealers* (Case IV/29/146) [1978] OJ L46/33, recital 21; *Johnson & Johnson* (Case IV/29.702) [1980] OJ L377/16, recital 29; *John Deere* (Case IV/30.809) [1985] OJ L35/58, recital 25; *Viho/Toshiba* (Case No IV/32.879) [1991] OJ L287/39, recital 20; *Zera/Montedison* (Case IV/31.550) and *Hinkens/Stähler* (Case IV/31.898) [1993] OJ L272/28, recital 116; *The Distillers Company Ltd* (Case IV/28.282) [1978] OJ L50/16, III.2.1 and 2.2; *Sugar beet* (Case IV/32.414) [1990] OJ L31/32, recital 78.

[30] *Preserved Mushrooms* (n 28) II.2.a.

[31] *Preserved Mushrooms* (n 28) II.2.b.

[32] *Bayer Dental* (Case IV/32.877) [1990] OJ L351/46, recitals 10, 11.

[33] *National Sulphuric Acid Association* (Case IV/27.958) [1980] OJ L260/24, recitals 31–34; *Asahi/Saint-Gobain* (Case IV/33.863) [1994] OJ L354/87, recitals 16–22.

simply stated that the investigated agreement had both the 'object and effect' of restricting competition and did not differentiate between these categories in the actual assessment.[34] Others held that the agreement in question had the 'object or effect' of restricting competition.[35] A third category simply stated that the agreement 'restricted competition' and did not refer to the concepts of object or effect at all.[36] Finally, a number of decisions were even vaguer, and do not allow any conclusion as to what type of test the Commission was applying.[37] In line with the decisions that explicitly differentiated between restrictions by object and effect, the key types of harmful effect or purpose identified in these decisions were the restriction of actual and potential competitors' opportunities,[38] obtaining unfair advantages over competitors,[39] the restriction of the parties' commercial autonomy,[40] a reduction in the number of competitors[41] and impediments to interstate trade.[42] Likewise, the key type of evidence relied upon by the Commission for these findings were the terms of the contract. Sometimes, it would additionally rely on instances of actual conduct implementing the agreement, but generally, it did not make much use of empirical evidence.

[34] *Internationales Chininkartell* (Case IV/26.623) [1969] OJ L192/5, recitals 21 ff (no English version available); *Breeders' rights—maize seed* (Case IV/28.824) [1978] OJ L286/23, II.2 and 3; *GERO-fabriek* (Case IV/24.510) [1977] OJ L16/8, II.a.3; *Miller International Schallplatten GmbH* (Case IV/29.018) [1976] OJ L357/40, recital 11; *White lead* (Case IV/29.535) [1979] OJ L21/16, recitals 24–29; *Italian flat glass* (Case IV.29.988) [1981] OJ L326/32, II.A.3; *VBBB/VBVB* (Case IV/428) [1982] OJ L54/36; *National Panasonic* (Case IV/30.070) [1982] OJ L354/28, recital 48; *Milchförderungsfonds* (Case IV/28.930) [1985] OJ L35/35, recital 29; *Velcro/Aplix* (Case IV/4.204) [1985] OJ L233/22, B.II.1; *Fisher-Price/Quaker Oats Ltd—Toyco* (Case IV/31.017) [1988] OJ L49/19, recitals 20, 21; *Konica* (Case IV/31.503) [1988] OJ L78/34, recitals 41–45; *Eco System/Peugeot* (Case IV/33.157) [1992] OJ L66/1, recital 23; *IATA Cargo Agency Programme* (Case IV/32.792) [1991] OJ L258/29, recitals 43–47; *EBU/Eurovision System* (Case IV/32.150) [1993] OJ L179/23, recitals 47–49.

[35] *British Dental Trade Association—BDTA* (IV/31.593) [1988] OJ L233/15, recitals 22–29; *Welded steel mesh* (Case IV/31.553) [1989] OJ L260/1, recital 175; *Soda-ash—Solvay, ICI* (Case IV/33.133-A) [1991] OJ L152/1, recital 60.

[36] *Langenscheidt/Hachette* (Case IV/29.972) [1982] OJ L39/25, recitals 4–11; *AEG-Telefunken* (Case IV/28.748) [1982] OJ L117/15, recital 70; *Nutricia/de Rooij* (Case IV/30.389) and *Nutricia/Zuid-Hollandse Conservenfabriek* (IV/30.408) [1983] OJ L376/22, recitals 25–35; *Distribution system of Ford Werke AG* (Case IV/30.696) [1983] OJ L327/31, recitals 30–32.

[37] *Uniform Eurocheques* (Case IV/30.717) [1985] OJ L35/43, recital 33; *Siemens/Fanuc* (Case IV/30.739) [1985] OJ L376/29, recital 24; *Peugeot* (Case IV/31.143) [1986] OJ L295/19, recitals 33–37; *MELDOC* (Case IV/31.204) [1986] OJ L348/50, recitals 57–69; *Ford Volkswagen* (Case IV/33.814) [1993] OJ L20/14, recitals 19–21; *Schöller Lebensmittel* (Cases IV/31.533 and IV/34.072) [1993] OJ L183/1, recitals 67–71.

[38] eg *Langenscheidt/Hachette* (n 36); *AEG-Telefunken* (n 36); *Distribution system of Ford Werke AG* (n 36); *British Dental Trade Association—BDTA* (n 35); *Siemens/Fanuc* (n 37); *Breeders' rights—maize seed* (n 34).

[39] *Milchförderungsfonds* (n 34).

[40] eg *AEG-Telefunken* (n 36); *Nutricia/de Rooij* (n 36); *Distribution system of Ford Werke AG* (n 36); *Velcro/Aplix* (n 34); *EBU/Eurovision System* (n 34); *Peugeot* (n 37); *Ford Volkswagen* (n 37); *Schöller Lebensmittel* (n 37); *Nederlandse Cement-Handelmaatschappij NV* (Case IV/595) [1972] OJ L22/16; *Italian flat glass* (n 34); *VBBB/VBVB* (n 34).

[41] *Breeders' rights—maize seed* (n 34).

[42] eg *Konica* (n 34); *Eco System/Peugeot* (n 35); *National Panasonic* (n 34).

The Commission's concept of competitive harm during this period and the type of evidence it relied on to support its findings explain why the Commission usually did not take the trouble to distinguish between restrictions by object or effect: it made no difference in practice. Where the Commission was concerned that the agreement restricted the parties' commercial freedom, it inferred both the effect of the agreement on the parties' commercial autonomy and the agreement's purpose of restricting their autonomy from the very terms of the agreement. Likewise, the Commission would infer restrictions of third parties' opportunities from the parties' contractual commitment not to trade with third parties. The distinction between object and effect restrictions only became relevant in a handful of cases in which the parties claimed that they had not actually implemented the agreement containing these restrictions. In these cases, the Commission either disproved this defence by drawing on examples of actual conduct in line with the terms of the agreement, or decided that the agreement had the object of restricting competition, in which case it was irrelevant that the parties had not actually acted upon it.[43]

Evidentiary difficulties were rare and usually only arose in cases in which the Commission needed to prove the existence and terms of a verbal agreement or concerted practice, or to establish whether an individual undertaking had actually participated in such a practice.[44] However, proving the effects or purpose of such agreements, once their terms had been proved, was straightforward, because they were usually inferred straight from the agreement's conditions. Given the ease with which both an agreement's object and effects could be established, the Commission's competitive assessments of this period were very short. They usually only spanned a few paragraphs. Generally, the average length of an Article 101 infringement decision between 1970 and 1998 was around 16 DIN A4 pages,[45] and the actual competitive assessment only took up a very small part of these.

As for individual assessments under Article 101(3), the Commission in theory required the parties to prove that the agreement would generate the benefit in question as well as the other three conditions (pass-on to consumers, indispensability and no complete elimination of competition) in every single case. There were no legal presumptions for inferring either the beneficial effect itself or the other conditions. However, a review of the decision practice reveals that the evidence relied upon in these assessments were often of a speculative rather than an empirical nature, and the standard of proof required by the Commission was often rather low. For example, the Commission regularly allowed exclusive distribution agreements despite their restrictive effects on the parties' freedom and other distributors' opportunities on the basis of the general consideration that a system of exclusive distribution allowed the manufacturer to consolidate its distribution and

[43] eg *Eurocheque—Helsinki Agreement* (n 37) recital 48.
[44] See eg *Welded steel mesh* (n 35) recitals 23–156.
[45] See Annex, Table 1.

not to have to maintain many business contacts.[46] In cases of distribution in other Member States, this was considered a particular advantage because it was assumed that this would make it easier to overcome linguistic and legal barriers.[47] Regarding the second condition of Article 101(3), the pass-on requirement, decisions were usually limited to stating that it had to be assumed that in a competitive environment such advantages would be passed on.[48] These are generic assumptions rather than arguments based on the facts of the individual case. Nonetheless, conceptually, this is a manifestation of a low standard of proof rather than evidence of the use of legal presumptions. In principle, there was no presumption of '*per se* legality' of certain types of agreements under Article 101(3).

ii. Block Exemption Regulations

By contrast, the Commission's early generation of Block Exemption Regulations, which conferred the benefits of Article 101(3) upon entire categories of agreements, contained entirely form-based tests. Block Exemption Regulations were important instruments in the Commission's early enforcement of Article 101, as the Commission held the monopoly for granting exemptions under Article 101(3) until 1 May 2004 and took a broad view of what constituted a restriction of competition within the meaning of Article 101(1). It lies in the nature of a Block Exemption Regulation to use strong rules of thumb, as its very purpose is to facilitate the assessment under Article 101 by eliminating the need to carry out difficult assessments of individual effects. It does so by establishing presumptions of legality for relatively unproblematic cases.

The Block Exemption Regulations of the first 40 years of EU antitrust law tended to be tailored to highly specific forms of agreements, which were often even further limited to specific industries: for example, specialisation agreements,[49] exclusive dealing agreements,[50] exclusive purchasing agreements,[51] motor vehicle distribution and servicing agreements,[52] franchise agreements,[53] agreements concerning joint planning and coordination of schedules, joint operations, consultations on passenger and cargo tariffs on scheduled air services and slot allocation

[46] eg *Goodyear Italiana-Euram* (Case IV/23.013) [1975] OJ L38/10, recital 12.

[47] eg *Duro-Dyne—Europair* (Case IV/560) [1975] OJ L 29/11, III.1.

[48] eg ibid, III.2; *Goodyear Italiana-Euram* (n 46) recital 13; *Bayerische Motoren Werke AG* (Case IV/14.650) [1975] OJ L29/1, recital 29.

[49] Commission Regulation (EEC) No 2779/72 on the application of Article 85(3) of the Treaty to categories of specialization agreements [1972] OJ L292/23.

[50] Commission Regulation 67/67/EEC on the application of Article 85(3) of the Treaty to certain categories of exclusive dealing agreements [1967] OJ 57/849.

[51] Commission Regulation (EEC) No 1984/83 on the application of Article 85(3) of the Treaty to categories of exclusive purchasing agreements [1983] OJ L173/5.

[52] Commission Regulation (EEC) No 123/85 on the application of Article 85(3) of the Treaty to certain categories of motor vehicle distribution and servicing agreements [1985] OJ L15/16.

[53] Commission Regulation (EEC) No 4087/88 on the application of Article 85(3) of the Treaty to categories of franchise agreements [1988] OJ L359/46.

at airports,[54] agreements between undertakings relating to computer reservation systems for air transport services[55] and agreements between liner shipping companies,[56] to mention but a few. These Regulations tended to follow the same structure. They first defined their scope of application by describing the type of agreement and/or industry they were meant to apply to. They then exhaustively listed those contractual clauses within that scope of application that were deemed to fulfil the conditions of Article 101(3).[57] This was known as a 'white list'. The white list was usually followed by a list of exceptions that described circumstances under which the Block Exemption would not apply[58] or further conditions that needed to be met for the exemption to apply.[59]

All in all, these early Block Exemption Regulations relied heavily on form-based tests. They established exhaustive and legally binding presumptions of legality on the basis of the contractual clause's form. In practice, the consequence of this formalistic approach was that legal advisors tended to draft contracts stringently in line with the contractual clauses permitted in the relevant Block Exemption Regulation, regardless of whether this best suited their clients' needs or not. If the contract only contained white listed restrictions, it was generally allowed under Article 101, regardless of the actual effects. The scope for error inherent in this approach was mitigated to some extent by the fact that Block Exemption Regulations usually allowed the Commission to withdraw the effects of the Regulation in individual cases if it transpired that the conditions of Article 101(3) were actually not fulfilled.[60]

iii. Conclusion

In sum, despite recognising the distinction in theory, the Commission did not usually carefully differentiate between the concepts of restriction by object and

[54] Commission Regulation (EC) No 1617/93 on the application of Article 85(3) of the Treaty to certain categories of agreements and concerted practices concerning joint planning and coordination of schedules, joint operations, consultations on passenger and cargo tariffs on scheduled air services and slot allocation at airports [1993] OJ L155/18.

[55] Commission Regulations (EEC) No 2672/88 on the application of Article 85(3) of the Treaty to certain categories of agreements between undertakings relating to computer reservation systems for air transport services [1988] OJ L239/13.

[56] Commission Regulation (EC) No 870/95 on the application of Article 85(3) of the Treaty to certain categories of agreements, decisions and concerted practices between liner shipping companies [1995] OJ L89/7.

[57] eg Regulation No 67/67/EEC (n 50) Art 1(1); Commission Regulation (EEC) No 123/85 (n 52) Arts 1–5; Commission Regulation (EEC) No 4087/88 (n 53) Arts 2 and 3; Commission Regulation (EC) No 870/95 (n 56) Art 3.

[58] eg Commission Regulation (EEC) No 123/85 (n 52) Art 6; Commission Regulation (EC) No 870/95 (n 56) Art 4; Commission Regulation (EEC) No 4087/88 (n 53).

[59] eg Commission Regulation (EC) No 870/95 (n 56) Arts 5 and 6; Commission Regulation (EEC) No 4087/88 (n 53) Art 4.

[60] eg Commission Regulation (EEC) No 123/85 (n 52) Art 10; Commission Regulation (EEC) No 4087/88 (n 53) Art 8.

restriction by effect in its decision practice during the first 40 years of EU antitrust law. This may be explained by the fact that the distinction would not have made a great deal of difference in view of its freedom-based concept of harm and the type of evidence it tended to use to support its assumptions. Individual assessments under Article 101(3) in theory required the parties to demonstrate the beneficial effects in each individual case. There were no presumptions of legality. However, the standard of proof for such effects was often strikingly low. By contrast, the Commission's Block Exemption Regulations of the period contained entirely form-based tests that spelled out in a detailed and exhaustive manner what types of contractual clauses could be presumed to satisfy the conditions of Article 101(3).

C. The Commission's Approach after the Introduction of the More Economic Approach

As explained in Chapter 5, the more economic approach introduced a revised concept of harm to Article 101. While the Commission used to interpret a restriction of competition as meaning a restriction of economic freedom or opportunity, it now only considers such restrictions of competition anticompetitive that result, or are likely to result, in a reduction of consumer welfare. This new concept of harm has made the distinction between restrictions by object and restrictions by effect highly relevant in practice, and has led the Commission to review its formerly relaxed approach in this regard.

i. Soft Law

The Commission's four sets of guidelines on Article 101, introducing the more economic approach to this provision, explained its understanding of how to establish whether competition has been restricted in some detail.[61] All but one have in the meantime been revised and updated in a number of points,[62] but the general principles of assessment remained unchanged. The guidelines follow the premise established by the Court[63] that agreements can either restrict competition by object or by effect, and that once it has been established that an agreement has the object of restricting competition, there is no need to establish its concrete effects.[64] On this conceptual basis, they spell out two distinct tests for these

[61] European Commission, Guidelines on Vertical Restraints [2000] OJ C291/1; Guidelines on the applicability of Article 81 to horizontal cooperation agreements [2001] OJ C3/2; Guidelines on the Application of Article 81 of the Treaty to Technology Transfer Agreements [2004] OJ C101/2; Guidelines on the Application of Article 81(3) of the Treaty [2004] OJ C101/97.

[62] Guidelines on Vertical Restraints [2010] OJ C130/1; Guidelines on the applicability of Article 101 to horizontal co-operation agreements [2011] OJ C11/1; Guidelines on the application of Article 101 to technology transfer agreements [2014] OJ C89/3.

[63] *Consten and Grundig v Commission* (n 13) 342.

[64] Guidelines on the Application of Article 81(3) of the Treaty (n 61) para 20.

two categories of restrictions. In line with the case law, the guidelines explain that object restrictions are those that by their very nature have such a high potential of negative effects on competition that it is unnecessary for the purposes of applying Article 101(1) to demonstrate any actual effects on the market. This presumption is based on the serious nature of the restriction and on the experience that these restrictions are highly likely to produce negative effects on the market. Whether an agreement has such a dangerous nature is first and foremost to be determined on the basis of the agreement's content and its aims. In some cases, it may also be necessary to consider the context in which the agreement is applied and the actual conduct of the parties in the market. The guidelines give two specific examples of what the Commission considers an object restriction: price fixing and market sharing.[65] They also establish the general presumption that the Commission is likely to consider restrictions that are black-listed in Block Exemptions Regulations restrictions by object.[66]

In comparison, the test for assessing whether a (non-object) restriction has the effect of restricting competition is more detailed and complex. According to the Commission's guidelines on Article 101, the assessment of an agreement's actual effects on competition requires establishing that it affects actual or potential competition to such an extent that appreciable negative effects on prices, output, innovation or the variety or quality of goods and services can be expected with a reasonable degree of probability on the relevant market.[67] This first requires defining the relevant market in its product and geographic dimensions.[68] As a second step, it is then necessary to establish that the agreement restricts competition in this market. The Commission takes into account the effects on both inter-brand and intra-brand competition.[69] Finally, it is necessary to establish that the restriction of competition had a negative effect on consumer welfare. This effect can either be demonstrated directly, for example, by proving that the agreement was causal for a price increase. It can also be established indirectly by proving that the parties had market power, which is determined by analysing the market position of the parties, the market position of competitors, the market position of buyers, the existence of potential competitors and the level of entry barriers as to whether the parties are likely to have the power to raise prices.[70]

In sum, the guidelines adhere to the principle that Article 101(1) prescribes two types of test: one that requires the assessment of the agreement's actual effects on competition and consumer welfare, and one that relies on a presumption of illegality based on the agreement's object. This is nothing new. The Court

[65] ibid, para 21.
[66] ibid, para 23.
[67] ibid, para 24.
[68] ibid, para 29.
[69] ibid, para 18.
[70] ibid, paras 25, 26.

established that principle in 1966.[71] If the guidelines' test for assessing restrictions by effect is very different from the test the Commission used to employ prior to the reform, this is because it now assesses a different type of effect than previously. It is the consequence of its new concept of harm. Significantly, the test for assessing an agreement's effects is also substantively very different from the guidelines' test for object restrictions, and it is clear from reading the guidelines that the distinction between these two categories now really matters. One entails a presumption of illegality based on a relatively quick look at the agreement's purpose, and the other requires establishing highly specific effects on competition and on consumer welfare in a detailed and complex assessment of the individual facts.

Somewhat unexpectedly maybe, given the US experience and the polarisation of the 'form v effects' issue in the review process, the more economic approach does not seem to have affected the Commission's understanding of what category of conduct should be considered an object restriction. One might have expected the Commission to abandon a few object categorisations, in the same way the US Supreme Court has moved away from *per se* rules to assessments under the rule of reason. However, the object restrictions listed in the Commission's guidelines are broadly the same as those that the Commission and Court had considered restrictive by object prior to the reform: horizontal price fixing, output limitation and sharing of markets and customers, fixed and minimum resale price maintenance and restrictions providing absolute territorial protection.[72] There is only one noteworthy exception. The guidelines distinguish more carefully between different types of resale price maintenance, and only consider minimum and fixed resale price maintenance restrictive by object, whereas maximum resale price maintenance should be assessed as to its actual effects.[73] This is not a distinction the Commission had previously drawn, and it expressly acknowledged in the case of *Nathan/Bricolux* that it had changed its position on this point.[74]

The assessment under Article 101(3) continues to require the parties to demonstrate that the agreement actually has beneficial effects and that the other conditions for exemption are fulfilled. This premise has not changed. What has changed is the type of benefit deemed capable of offsetting competitive harm, ie economic efficiencies only. Alongside this reinterpretation of the first condition of Article 101(3), the guidelines introduced clearer standards of proof that the Commission expects parties to meet if their efficiency defence is to succeed. According to the guidelines on Article 101(3), the parties are expected to prove in a substantiated manner the nature of the claimed efficiencies, the causality of the agreement for the efficiencies, the likelihood and magnitude of each claimed efficiency, and how and when each efficiency would be achieved.[75] They contain

[71] *Consten and Grundig v Commission* (n 13) 342.
[72] European Commission, Guidelines on the application of Article 81(3) of the Treaty (n 61) para 23.
[73] European Commission, Guidelines on Vertical Restraints (n 62) para 228.
[74] *Nathan-Bricolux* (Case COMP/F.1/36.516) [2001] OJ L54/1, recital 87.
[75] Guidelines on the application of Article 81(3) of the Treaty (n 61) para 51.

detailed guidance as to what type of evidence is considered appropriate. In the case of cost efficiencies, for example, the parties must calculate or estimate the value of the efficiencies as accurately as reasonably possible, and describe in detail how the amount has been computed. They must also describe the methods by which the efficiencies have been or will be achieved. The data submitted must be verifiable so that there can be a sufficient degree of certainty that the efficiencies have materialised or are likely to materialise.[76] The same detail and quality of evidence is expected for proving that the agreement is the least restrictive means for achieving these efficiencies, that the efficiencies passed on to consumers will at least cancel out the harm caused to them and that competition is not eliminated.[77] This seems like a much higher standard of proof than that observed in the decisions of the previous period.

While the guidelines therefore do not contain any form-based presumptions of legality for Article 101(3), they actually contain one rule of thumb that approaches a form-based presumption of illegality. While not excluding *a priori* certain types of agreements from the scope of Article 101(3), the guidelines state that as a matter of principle, restrictions that are black-listed in Block Exemption Regulations or identified as hard-core restrictions in Commission guidelines and Notices are unlikely to fulfil the conditions for exemption.[78]

ii. The Decision Practice

As expected, in view of the assessment principles set out in the Commission's guidelines on Article 101, the decisions practice following the reform now usually distinguishes very carefully between restrictions by object and effect. What may come as somewhat more of a surprise, given the Commission's mission to introduce a more effects-based approach, is the finding that the great majority of infringement decisions since the introduction of the more economic approach have been based on the concept of object restriction. Only a minority of cases actually assessed the investigated agreement as to its effects on competition.

This somewhat counterintuitive finding should not be interpreted as meaning that the Commission has expanded its view on what type of agreement should be presumed illegal under an object rule. If one looks more closely at these infringement decisions, one finds that this phenomenon is the result of a shift in the Commission's case selection. The majority of infringement decisions under Article 101 since the advent of the more economic approach have concerned hard-core cartels in which the parties agreed to fix prices, allocate markets, customers, projects or quotas, or exchange sensitive market information. Between 2000 and July 2015, the Commission thus established 97 cartel infringements[79] as opposed to merely

[76] ibid, para 56.
[77] ibid, paras 73–116.
[78] ibid, para 46.
[79] www.ec.europa.eu/competition/cartels/statistics/statistics.pdf.

11 published Article 101 infringements in non-cartel cases.[80] These numbers reflect the Commission's commitment to focus its resources on pursuing the most dangerous types of agreement after Regulation 1/2003 decentralised the enforcement of Article 101, in the expectation that the national competition authorities would pick up the less dangerous cases.[81] Cartels, however, are restrictive by object, and Commission decisions establishing such infringements therefore infer the anticompetitive nature of such conduct, usually in very few words, without establishing its actual effects on competition and consumer welfare.[82]

In fact, even those infringement decisions that do not concern classical cartel activity but examine more unusual types of agreements rely heavily on the concept of restriction by object. Out of the eight non-cartel infringements since 2004, four exclusively based the liability on a restriction by object. In the cases of *Lundbeck* and *Fentanyl*, for example, the Commission held that paying potential manufacturers of generic pharmaceuticals to delay their entry into the market after the expiry of a drug's IP protection in order to remain the exclusive producer[83] amounted to restrictions by object.[84] Likewise, in *Telefónica/Portugal Telecom*, it found that the agreement between the Spanish and Portuguese telecommunications incumbents not to offer services on each other's markets was restrictive by object.[85] Finally, in *Ordre National des Pharmaciens*, it deemed that the decision by the professional body of pharmacists in France to impose minimum prices on the French market for clinical laboratory tests amounted to a restriction by object.[86]

A further decision, *CISAC*,[87] finds one clear restriction by object[88] but does not clearly categorise the other two investigated restrictions as either a restriction by object or effect. The lack of an explicit assessment of any effects of the second clause, which established exclusive representation, suggests that the Commission in fact also considered it a restriction by object.[89] It examined the third restriction, the territorial delineation of the authority to license, as to its effects on the process of market integration.[90]

[80] See below.

[81] eg M Monti, 'European Competition Policy: Quo Vadis?', Speech/03/195, XX. International Forum on European Competition Policy (Brussels, 10 April 2003) and 'A Reformed Competition Policy: Achievements and Challenges for the Future', Speech/04/477, Center for European Reform (Brussels, 28 October 2004).

[82] See eg *Mushrooms* (Case AT.39965) recitals 24–26; *PO/Elevators and Escalators* (Case COMP/E-1/38.823) recitals 575–83; *Gas insulated switchgear* (Case COMP/F/38.899) recitals 302–08; *Bearings* (Case AT.39922) recitals 51–54; *Automotive Wire Harnesses* (Case AT.39748) recitals 76–78, amongst many others.

[83] The so-called 'pay for delay' strategy.

[84] *Lundbeck* (Case AT.39226) recitals 647–1174; *Fentanyl* (Case AT.39685) recitals 216–372.

[85] *Telefónica/Portugal Telecom* (Case AT.39839) recitals 238–536.

[86] *ONP* (Case 39510) recitals 658–76 (no English version available).

[87] *CISAC* (Case COMP/C2/38.698).

[88] ibid, recital 127.

[89] ibid, recitals 145–52.

[90] ibid, recitals 200–22.

Two further decisions found that the agreements under investigation contained clear restrictions by object,[91] but nonetheless additionally established the agreements' actual effects. In the case of *Groupement des cartes bancaires*, this additional assessment, which proved the agreement's effects on competition and prices, was considerable and added another 50 pages to the decision.[92] The additional assessment in *Peugeot* was less onerous, as the Commission assessed this agreement as to its negative effects on market integration, and the assessment of the agreement's actual effects was therefore limited to demonstrating that exports had declined as a consequence of Peugeot's actions.[93] Finally, in *Mastercard I*,[94] the Commission simply left the point open. It took the view that the agreement presented all the signs of a restriction by object,[95] but decided not to commit itself on the point because it was able to demonstrate (in an extensive analysis) that the agreement in question had actually had the effect of raising prices.[96]

In all of these cases, the Commission assessed the benefits invoked by the parties under Article 101(3) as to their actual effects, and often in great detail.[97] Incidentally, not one of the parties managed to demonstrate these to the Commission's satisfaction.

An analysis of the Commission's many commitments decisions since 2004 reveals a more varied approach. The preliminary assessments sometimes specifically find that there is the likelihood of an object restriction,[98] others specifically engage with the agreement's effects.[99] Others again address both the object and effect of the agreement,[100] and a handful do not distinguish between the two concepts at all, but outline general 'competitive concerns'.[101]

iii. Block Exemption Regulations

The Commission's Block Exemption Regulations also underwent a significant overhaul with the advent of the more economic approach in an attempt to make them less reliant on the conduct's form and to make them more 'effects-based'. Block Exemption Regulations are by their very nature reliant on rules of thumb

[91] *Groupement des cartes bancaires 'CB'* (Case COMP/D1/38606) recitals 193–251; *SEP et autres/Peugeot SA* (Cases F-2/36.623/36.820/37.275) recitals 102–29.

[92] *Groupement des cartes bancaires* (n 91) recitals 252–368.

[93] *SEP et autres/Peugeot SA* (n 91) recitals 130–35.

[94] *MasterCard* (Case COMP/34.579), *EuroCommerce* (Case COMP/36.518), and *Commercial Cards* (Case COMP/38.580) (*'Mastercard I'*), upheld in Case T-111/08 *MasterCard and Others v European Commission* ECLI:EU:T:2012:260, and Case C-382/12 P *MasterCard and Others v European Commission* (n 18).

[95] ibid, recitals 401–07.

[96] ibid, recitals 408–523.

[97] ibid, recitals 666–753; *Groupement des cartes bancaires* (n 91) recitals 375–503; *CISAC* (n 87) recitals 229–55; *Lundbeck* (n 84) recitals 1212–31; *Fentanyl* (n 84) recitals 400–39.

[98] eg *E-BOOKS* (Case AT.39847) recitals 90–93.

[99] eg *Rio Tinto Alcan* (Case AT.39230) recitals 99–103.

[100] eg *Société Air France/Alitalia Linee Aeree Italiane* (Case COMP/38.284/D2) recitals 106–30; *Continental/United/Lufthansa/Air Canada* (Case COMP/AT.39595) recitals 36–52.

[101] eg *Repsol* (Case COMP/B-1/38.348) recitals 20–24.

and legal presumptions. It is their main advantage over an individual assessment under Articles 101(1) and (3). This premise has not changed. However, the Commission has somewhat refined the rules of thumb it uses in these Regulations. The new generation of Block Exemption Regulations no longer contain restrictive white lists of contractual clauses that are deemed to yield more benefits than anticompetitive effects. Instead, they contain a general exemption for all agreements falling within their scope, subject to a number of conditions and limits.

The first condition is that the parties' market shares must remain below a critical threshold. Each Block Exemption Regulation specifies its own market share cap, depending on the type of agreement it aims to exempt.[102] This market share requirement acts as an approximation of the parties' market power, ie their ability to harm consumers, and reflects the Commission's new concept of harm according to which only such restrictions of competition are caught by Article 101(1) that affect consumer welfare in a negative manner. It creates a safe harbour for agreements concluded by undertakings with a relatively low market share.

Secondly, the agreement must not contain any 'hard-core' restraints that have such a high potential for severe anticompetitive effects that they make the entire agreement fall outside the scope of the Block Exemption Regulation.[103] Hard-core restrictions are exhaustively enumerated in each Regulation in a so-called black list. Modern Block Exemption Regulations often also contain a list of less severe but nonetheless worrisome restrictions, that do not make the entire agreement fall outside the scope of the Regulation, but merely exclude that specific restriction from the benefit of the Regulation.[104]

The Commission has also significantly consolidated its Block Exemption Regulations. While the scopes of its previous Block Exemption Regulations were often limited to specific types of contract, it now operates on the basis of Regulations that are broader in scope. For example, instead of using separate Block Exemption Regulations for different types of distribution agreements as it did prior to the reform,[105]

[102] eg Commission Regulation (EU) No 330/2010 on the application of Article 101(3) of the Treaty on the Functioning of the European Union to categories of vertical agreements and concerted practices [2010] OJ L102/1, Art 3; Commission Regulation (EU) No 1217/2010 on the application of Article 101(3) of the Treaty on the Functioning of the European Union to certain categories of research and development agreements [2010] OJ L335/36, Art 4; Commission Regulation (EU) No 1218/2010 on the application of Article 101(3) of the Treaty on the Functioning of the European Union to certain categories of specialisation agreements [2010] OJ L335/46, Art 3.

[103] eg Commission Regulation (EU) No 330/2010 (n 102) Art 4; Commission Regulation (EU) No 1217/2010 (n 102) Art 5; Commission Regulation (EU) No 1218/2010 (n 102) Art 4.

[104] eg Commission Regulation (EU) No 330/2010 (n 102) Art 5; Commission Regulation (EU) No 1217/2010 (n 102) Art 6.

[105] eg Commission Regulation 67/67/EEC (n 5); Commission Regulation (EEC) no 1984/83 (n 51); Commission Regulation (EEC) no 123/85 (n 52); Commission Regulation (EEC) No 4087/88 (n 53).

the majority of vertical agreements are now covered by one general Block Exemption Regulation on Vertical Restraints.[106]

This new generation of Block Exemption Regulations, despite necessarily still relying on approximations, are therefore all in all less formalistic than their counterparts prior to the reform. Contemporary Block Exemption Regulations try to rely on more general rules that transcend specific forms of contracts and contractual clauses and also attempt an approximation of the agreement's likely effects on competition and consumer welfare by means of market share thresholds. The consolidation of several contract-specific Block Exemption Regulations into more general Regulations has also made the system more transparent, which is greatly in the interest of legal certainty.

iv. Conclusion

In sum, even after the reform, the Commission uses both form- and effects-based tests in its assessments under Article 101. The more economic approach has not abolished the concept of restriction by object, either in theory or in practice. Neither has it significantly changed the Commission's understanding of what type of restriction should be considered restrictive by object. In practice, the Commission now even chiefly relies on the concept of object restriction in its infringement decisions under Article 101(1). In individual assessments under Article 101(3), the Commission still requires the parties to demonstrate the (now much narrower) range of beneficial effects that the Commission deems capable of offsetting competitive harm in each individual case. The standard of proof expected from the parties has also become more rigorous. In practice, Article 101(3) defences now rarely succeed.

Block Exemption Regulations continue to operate on the basis of legal presumptions rather than individual assessments. However, the 'more economic' generation of Block Exemption Regulations no longer predicts these effects purely on the basis of the individual restriction's form, but relies on broader categories of restrictions and approximates the agreement's likely effect on consumer welfare by means of market shares.

D. Conclusion on the Changes under Article 101

In conclusion, the more economic approach has not significantly changed the type of test used by the Commission in its assessments under Article 101. As before, the Commission continues to infer the anticompetitive nature of certain types of agreement from their objective, while others need to be assessed as to their likely

[106] Commission Regulation (EU) No 330/2010 (n 102) replacing the first general Block Exemption Regulation on vertical restraints, Commission Regulation (EC) No 2790/1999 [1999] OJ L336/21.

effects. In fact, it now actually uses the object rule more frequently than before. However, this should not be seen as a newfound theoretical preference for form-based over effects-based tests. It is the outcome of a shift in enforcement priorities. Since Regulation 1/2003 decentralised the enforcement of Article 101, the Commission has been focusing its attention on pursuing cartels and similarly serious types of infringements, which tend to contain restrictions by object.

That being said, when the Commission nowadays does exceptionally assess an agreement's actual effects, these assessments have very little in common with the effects-based assessment of the first 40 years of EU antitrust law. This is not because the Commission applies a different type of test, but because it now assesses a different type of effect, ie the effect on competition and consumer welfare rather than on the parties' or third parties' commercial freedom and opportunity. It has also significantly raised its own standard of proof. Both of these developments have made the Commission's assessments far more complex and detailed. Rather than looking at a contract and concluding that the agreement limits the parties' freedom of action (which an agreement is bound to do) in a point that is crucial to competition, the assessment of an agreement's effects now entails defining the relevant market in its product and geographic dimensions, demonstrating a restriction of competition and proving a causal reduction in consumer welfare or at least the presence of market power. The variety and quality of evidence used by the Commission to prove its assumptions has also increased dramatically. Whereas previous decisions relied primarily on the terms of the contract and conjecture, the Commission now attempts to demonstrate the likelihood of harm to competition and consumer on the basis of contemporary economic theories, supported by detailed empirical evidence and often quantitative analysis. Given these developments, the distinction between object and effect restrictions has become much more relevant in practice. As a further curious side effect of these changes, the length of decisions, in particular those that establish the agreement's likely effects, has increased significantly.[107]

Regarding Article 101(3), parties still have to prove the actual beneficial effects in individual assessments. There are no presumptions of legality. However, the Commission's assessments under Article 101(3) have also significantly changed in practice. For one, like under Article 101(1), this is due to the type of effect assessed under Article 101(3) being different.[108] Second, alongside increasing its own standard of proof in assessments under Article 101(3), the Commission has also raised the standard of proof it expects from the investigated undertaking under Article 101(3).

Finally, the theoretical approach of Block Exemption Regulations has changed. They have become somewhat less reliant on form. Instead of prescriptive white lists, they contain restrictive black lists, and attempt to approximate the likely effects on consumer welfare by means of market share thresholds.

[107] This is discussed in more detail in Ch 8.
[108] See Ch 6.

IV. EU Merger Law

The issue of the relevant type of test is relatively straightforward in the area of EU merger control, and does therefore not require many words. Even under the original Merger Regulation, the Commission had always attempted to predict a notified merger's likely effects in an in-depth assessment of the specific market conditions rather than rely on form-based presumptions. It continues to do so after the introduction of the more economic approach to EU merger law.

There has never been an equivalent of an 'object' restriction in the test of EU merger law, and the Commission never read one into it. Regulation 4064/89, the original Merger Regulation, required the Commission to assess whether the notified concentration would create or strengthen a dominant position as a result of which effective competition would be significantly impeded in the common market.[109] It specified that in making this appraisal the Commission was to take into account factors such as the structure of the relevant markets; actual or potential competition from undertakings inside and outside of the Union; the market position of the undertakings concerned and their economic and financial power; the opportunities available to suppliers and users; their access to supplies or markets; any legal or other barriers to entry; supply and demand trends for the relevant goods and services; the interests of the intermediate and ultimate consumers; and the development of technical and economic progress provided that it was to consumers' advantage and did not form an obstacle to competition.[110] The wording of Regulation 4064/89 itself therefore prescribed an individual assessment of the likely effects. Likewise, in practice the Commission never operated on the basis of presumptions of legality or illegality that were inferred from specific contractual terms or formal elements of the transaction, but always assessed every merger as to its individual future effects. It did not even rely on the legal presumption of dominance established by the Court in the context of Article 102, according to which an undertaking with a market share of 50 per cent or more must be presumed dominant.[111] Instead, it always assessed dominance in an individual assessment of the actual market conditions, the merging parties' and their competitors' market shares, potential competition, barriers to entry, countervailing buyer power and other individual factors under Regulation 4064/89.[112]

The test of the new Merger Regulation, Regulation 139/2004, now requires that the Commission establish whether the concentration would lead to a significant

[109] Regulation 4064/89 [1989] OJ L395/1, Art 2(2) and (3).

[110] ibid, Article 2(1).

[111] Case C-62/86 *AKZO Chemie BV v Commission* ECLI:EU:C:1991:286, para 60.

[112] eg *Aerospatiale-Alenia/de Havilland* (Case IV/M.053) [1991] OJ L334/42, recitals 7–71; *Blokker/Toys 'R' Us* (Case IV/M.890) [1998] OJ L316/1, recitals 43–114; *Guinness/Grand Metropolitan* (Case No IV/M.938) [1998] OJ L288/24, recitals 30–182; *General Electric/Honeywell* (Case COMP/M.2220) [2004] OJ L48/1, recitals 9–484.

impediment to effective competition[113] on the basis of the same factors as deemed relevant under Regulation 4064/89.[114] The Commission no more relies on form-based presumptions in assessments under the new Merger Regulation than it did before. What has changed with the advent of the more economic approach is the type of effect assessed, and the quality and type of evidence used to support these findings. This is in line with the developments observed under Article 101. As demonstrated in Chapter 5, the Commission now establishes whether the concentration is likely to have adverse effects on consumer welfare, rather than on the number of competitors in the market. Also, one can observe that the Commission now supports its analyses with more empirical data than it did previously, leading to far lengthier decisions than prior to the introduction of the more economic approach.[115] This being said, analyses under the old Merger Regulation had always been more reliant on empirical data than its early assessments under Article 101, which had primarily been based on the terms of the investigated agreement. Modern merger assessments further frequently incorporate quantitative assessments. However, this is a separate point from the issue of legal presumption v individual assessment, which will be discussed in more detail in Chapter 8 under methodological changes.

V. Article 102

By contrast, the situation under Article 102 is far more complex. Article 102 itself does not explicitly distinguish between conduct that is abusive 'by object' and conduct that is abusive 'by effect' in the manner of Article 101. Nonetheless, an analysis of the decision practice and case law allows the conclusion that both the Court and the Commission have applied form-based tests to certain types of conduct in the past, while assessing others as to their actual effects before making a pronouncement as to their compatibility with Article 102. These form-based presumptions of illegality were subject to a great deal of criticism prior to and during the reform process,[116] and the question of 'form v effects-based tests' therefore was a key issue in the public consultation on the review of Article 102.

[113] Regulation 139/2004 [2004] OJ L24/1, Art 2(2) and (3).
[114] ibid, Art 2(1).
[115] See Ch 8.
[116] eg Vickers, 'Abuse of Market Power' (n 10); G Niels and H Jenkins, 'Reform of Article 82: Where the Link Between Dominance and Effects Breaks Down' (2005) 26 *European Competition Law Review* 605; Ridyard, 'Exclusionary Pricing and Price Discrimination Abuses under Article 82' (n 10); Waelbroeck, 'Michelin II' (n 10); Christiansen and Kerber, 'Competition Policy with Optimally Differentiated Rules Instead of *Per Se* Rules vs Rule of Reason' (n 12), amongst many others.

A. The Commission's Approach Prior to the Introduction of the More Economic Approach

Prior to 2009, the Commission had not issued any soft law instruments explaining its position on how to establish a conduct's abusive nature. Its approach from that period can therefore only be inferred from its decision practice. The Commission's decisions on Article 102 up until the early 2000s show that a competitive assessment under Article 102 generally contained two steps: (1) assessing whether the undertaking had a dominant position, which first required defining the relevant market; and (2) assessing whether the undertaking had abused this position.

The Commission defined dominance in line with the Court's case law as referring to a position of economic strength enjoyed by an undertaking which enabled it to prevent effective competition being maintained on the relevant market, by giving it the power to behave to an appreciable extent independently of its competitors, customers and ultimately of its consumers.[117] It relied heavily on form-based presumptions in its assessments of dominance. Rather than establish the investigated undertaking's actual ability to behave independently of its competitors, customers and consumers, it normally inferred this ability on the basis of a few legal rules.

First, according to the case law of the Court of Justice established in *Hoffmann-La Roche* and *AKZO*, a dominant position may normally be presumed where an undertaking has a 'very large' market share, meaning a share of 50 per cent or more.[118] Although the Commission rarely explicitly cited this case law in support of its approach,[119] the great majority of its Article 102 decisions from the period prior to the review likewise inferred the investigated undertaking's dominant position from its market shares alone.[120] The other presumption applied by the Commission was that an undertaking that held a legal monopoly[121] or an exclusive statutory right[122] had to be presumed dominant. In sum, rather than carry out

[117] Originally defined by the Court in Case 27/76 *United Brands v Commission* ECLI:EU:C:1978:22, para 65, and regularly cited by the Commission, eg in *BPB Industries plc* (Case IV/31.900) [1989] OJ L10/50, recital 114; *Soda-ash—ICI* (Case IV/33.133-D) [1991] OJ L152/40, recital 41.

[118] Cases 85/76 *Hoffmann-La Roche v Commission* ECLI:EU:C:1979:36, para 41; and *AKZO Chemie BV v Commission* (n 111) para 60.

[119] See eg *Warner-Lambert/Gillette and Others* (Case IV/33.440); and *BIC/Gillette and Others* (Case IV/33.486) [1993] OJ L116/21, recital 22.

[120] eg *BPB Industries plc* (n 117) recitals 114–21; *Decca Navigator System* (Cases IV/30.979 and 31.394) [1989] OJ L43/27, recital 96; *Bandengroothandel Frieschebrug BV/NV Nederlandsche Banden-Industrie Michelin* (Case IV/29.491) [1981] OJ L353/3, recital 35; *Tetra Pak II* (Case IV/31043) [1992] OJ L72/1, recitals 99–101; *Eurofix-Bauco v Hilti* (Cases IV/30.787 and 31.488) [1988] OJ L65/19, recitals 66–71.

[121] *British Telecommunications* (Case IV/29.877) [1982] OJ L360/36, recital 26; *HOV SVZ/MCN* (Case IV/33.941) [1994] OJ L104/34, recital 141.

[122] *British Leyland* (Case IV/30.615) [1984] OJ L207/11, recital 25.

a detailed assessment of the undertaking's actual strength, the position of dominance was usually inferred from one objective factor. Only rarely did the Commission take into consideration additional factors for establishing an undertaking's position of dominance.[123]

By comparison, the Commission's approach to assessing whether the investigated undertaking had engaged in abusive conduct was less clear-cut. As Chapter 5 established, the Commission had a broad concept of competitive harm under Article 102 up until the early 2000s. The most important types of harm liable to trigger a finding of abuse were: excluding actual and potential competitors from the market; restricting one's trading partners' commercial freedom; reducing consumers' choice as to where to buy; and undermining the process of market integration. The issue examined in this chapter is how the Commission assessed whether the investigated market conduct actually caused these types of harm. Did it rely on form-based presumptions of abusiveness, did it establish the actual harmful effects in every case, or did it rely on intermediary types of test?

It is in fact very difficult to gain a clear and consistent picture from the Commission's early decision practice. One of the key difficulties in this exercise is that the Commission rarely spelled out the test on which it was basing its assessments. It also did not use uniform language and often took different approaches from one case to the next.

Nonetheless, it is possible to make out a number of cases in which the Commission clearly sought to establish and prove the conduct's actual effects on the values deemed relevant in the day. This was the case, for instance, in the merger cases that the Commission assessed under Article 102 before the first Merger Regulation entered into force, and in which the Commission plainly examined the effects of the acquisition to determine its competitive nature.[124] There were also a few cases of more classical unilateral conduct that it assessed as to its actual effects. In a number of decisions examining discriminatory conduct vis-à-vis trading partners, the Commission not only assessed whether the dominant undertaking had treated similar situations differently, but also examined whether the discrimination had put the trading partner at a competitive disadvantage.[125] Likewise, in *BPB Industries*, it established that BPB's practice of rewarding loyal customers with payments in return for exclusivity actually had had the effect of making it difficult for competitors to access and keep customers.[126] In *British Leyland (BL)*, it proved that the dominant undertaking's refusal to supply traders and individuals wishing to reimport BL vehicles from other Member States with certificates of conformity,

[123] See eg *Soda-ash—ICI* (n 117) recitals 47–52; *Trans-Atlantic Conference Agreement* (Case IV/35.134) [1999] OJ L95/1, recitals 534–538, in the case of a collective dominant position.

[124] eg *Tetra Pak I (BTG licence)* (Case IV/31.043) [1988] OJ L272/27, recitals 45–47; *Warner-Lambert/Gillette* (n 119) and *BIC/Gillette and Others* (n 119) recitals 23–32.

[125] eg *ABG oil companies operating in the Netherlands* (Case IV/28.841) [1977] OJ No L 117/1, B and *GVL* (Case IV/29.839) [1981] OJ L370/49, recitals 49–53.

[126] *BPB Industries plc* (n 117) recitals 123–30.

and later charging excessive and discriminatory fees for this certificate, had had the effect of hindering the reimport of BL vehicles and thus of impeding the process of market integration.[127] In *Magill*, it assessed whether the refusal to supply a key input prevented the development and manufacture of a new product for which there was demand, and established both the demand and the potential of the new product.[128] In *Hugin/Liptons*, another case of refusal to supply, it established whether the conduct seriously injured the undertaking that was refused the input in its business by 'preventing them from continuing to offer a service or to carry on a line of business, thereby ultimately eliminating all competitors independent of the dominant undertaking from the market'.[129] These are not the type of effects the Commission would look at these days, and there is no denying that the standard of proof in these decisions was low. Many of the effects were established in a few sentences on the basis of pure conjecture,[130] or inferred from the evolution of the market shares of the undertakings involved.[131] Sometimes, the standard of proof was indeed so low as to make the assessment of individual effects almost meaningless in practice. Nonetheless, conceptually, the Commission's approach cannot be described as relying on object rules or form-based rules, but as attempting to prove the conduct's actual effects.

By contrast, other decisions can only be understood as applying presumptions of illegality. In *Soda-ash–ICI*, the Commission held that single branding agreements, in which another undertaking agreed to purchase all of its supplies from the dominant undertaking, were 'always abusive' on the part of a dominant undertaking, even if they were concluded at the request of the customer, because they tied the customer to the dominant undertaking and made it impossible for competitors to access the customer.[132] In *GVL*, it held that discrimination on grounds of nationality, which it considered a separate case from other types of discrimination between trading partners, was 'automatically' an infringement of Article 102.[133] In *HOV SVZ/MCN*, it also seemed to take the view that any application of discriminatory conditions to equivalent transactions necessarily constituted an abuse of a dominant position, and did not separately assess the effects on the trading partners.[134] In other cases of 'simple' discrimination, however, it had additionally assessed whether the unequal treatment resulted in an actual competitive disadvantage to the trading partner.[135] Further, the case of *London European–Sabena* suggests that the Commission applied a presumption of illegality to tying, which was

[127] *British Leyland* (n 122) recitals 26–29.
[128] *Magill TV Guide/ITP, BBC and RTE* (Case IV/31.851) [1989] OJ L78/43, recital 23.
[129] *Hugin/Liptons* (Case IV/29.132) [1978] OJ L22/23, II.A.
[130] eg *GVL* (n 125) recital 55.
[131] eg *ABG oil companies* (n 125) B.
[132] *Soda-ash—ICI* (n 117) recital 57.
[133] *GVL* (n 125) recital 46.
[134] *HOV SVZ/MCN* (n 121) recitals 157 ff.
[135] eg *ABG oil companies operating in the Netherlands* (n 125) and *GVL* (n 125) recitals 49–53.

automatically deemed abusive if the dominant undertaking made the conclusion of one transaction dependent on the conclusion of an unrelated transaction.[136]

The Commission's assessments of conduct under the aspect of 'unfair trading conditions' and 'excessive prices' are quite difficult to categorise, but overall fit better in the category of 'per se illegality' or 'abuse by object' than an assessment of its effects. Of course, the qualification of conduct as unfair or excessive also required an individual assessment. However, these assessments were aimed at establishing the moral quality of the conduct, rather than its effects on competition. The Commission commonly considered trading conditions unfair if they did not pursue a legitimate aim or if they were disproportionate (ie dispensable or excessive) to this aim.[137] Prices, in particular, were deemed excessive where there was a great disparity between cost and price, or where the price was discriminatory.[138]

Yet in other cases, the test applied by the Commission amounted to asking whether the dominant undertaking had *intended* to cause harm to competition by means of its conduct, for example by excluding competitors. In *Soda-ash–ICI*, the Commission found decisive that it had been the dominant undertaking's intention and object to tie the customer to itself and to exclude competitors by means of rebates.[139] Likewise, in the famous case of *AKZO*,[140] the Commission found that the intention to exclude was key. *AKZO* was the Commission's first case of suspected predatory pricing. As the parties had argued competently that the Commission should apply the test used in US antitrust law, the Commission, uncharacteristically for this time, went to some lengths to outline a clear theoretical basis for its assessment in this decision.[141] It held that Article 102 prohibited any unfair commercial practice on the part of a dominant undertaking that was intended to eliminate, discipline or deter smaller competitors.[142] Hence, low pricing with the intent to exclude had to be considered *per se* abusive, without regard to its actual effects. The Commission added that there were cases in which the exclusionary consequences of the conduct were so self-evident that it was not even necessary to prove intent.[143] In all other cases, however, intent was key.[144]

[136] *London European—Sabena* (Case IV/32.318) [1988] OJ L317/47, recital 31.

[137] eg *GEMA statutes* (Case IV/29.971) [1982] OJ L94/12, recitals 35–53.

[138] *General Motors Continental* (Case IV/28.851) [1975] OJ L 29/14, recital 8.

[139] *Soda-ash—Solvay, ICI* (n 35) recital 55.

[140] *ECS/AKZO* (Case IV/30.698) [1985] L374/1.

[141] A key argument used by the Commission was that EU (then EEC) antitrust law pursued broader objectives than the 'static and short-term conception of efficiency' guiding the predatory pricing test of US antitrust law (ibid, recital 77).

[142] ibid, recital 74.

[143] ibid, recital 80.

[144] The Court of Justice elaborated on this test in the ensuing action for annulment and ruled that where the dominant undertaking priced below average variable cost, the price had to be presumed irrefutably abusive. Prices below average total costs, that is to say, fixed costs plus variable costs, but above average variable costs, could be regarded as abusive only if they were part of a plan for eliminating a competitor, which the Commission had to prove (Case C-62/86 *AKZO Chemie BV v Commission* (n 111) paras 71, 72.)

Then there were a number of cases in which the Commission neither established the conduct's actual effects nor relied on a clear-cut presumption of illegality based on its form, but assessed whether the conduct in question was 'liable' to cause harm.[145] It is not clear from the decisions of this time what exactly the Commission meant by 'liable' to cause harm. In one decision, it explained that this test amounted to establishing whether 'the foreseeable consequence' of the conduct would be to exclude other undertakings or cause other types of harmful effects.[146] The assessments it carried out under this premise cannot be described as in-depth assessments of the conduct's effects on competition. On the other hand, they went beyond merely inferring the conduct's abusive nature from its form. Instead, they could best be described as taking a cursory look at the conduct and making an educated guess as to whether it was likely to result in harm.

Finally, in a great number of cases, the Commission's legal assessments were so brief and abstract that it is simply not possible to determine what type of test it was applying.[147] They might have been assessments of the conduct's effects that were supported with very little evidence. They might have been based on presumptions of illegality. They might also have been based on non-specified intermediary types of test.

In short, the picture is one of confusion. While the Commission's concept of harm was relatively clear, its theoretical approach to proving this harm was not. What is clear, however, is that even where it assessed conduct as to its actual effects on the relevant values of the day, the standard of proof was low. Conjecture clearly outweighed empirical evidence during this period.

B. The Commission's Approach after the Introduction of the More Economic Approach

i. Soft Law

The issue of what type of test should be used in assessments under Article 102 was a hotly disputed topic during the reform process. The EAGCP came down unequivocally against form based presumptions of legality and illegality, and in favour of assessing the actual effects generated by business behaviour in each individual case.[148] It also proposed abandoning the concept of dominance entirely,

[145] *Napier Brown-British Sugar* (Case IV/30.178) [1988] OJ L284/41, recitals 61–62; *BPB Industries plc* (n 117) recitals 141–47.

[146] *Napier Brown-British Sugar* (n 145) 64.

[147] *Chiquita* (Case IV/26699) [1976] OJ L95/1, II.A.3; British Telecommunications (n 121) recital 32; *Decca Navigator System* (n 120) recitals 97–113; *Eurofix-Bauco v Hilti* (n 120) recitals 74–86; *European sugar industry* (Case IV/26 918) [1973] OJ L140/17, E.1 and 3; *Bandengroothandel Frieschebrug BV/NV Nederlandsche Banden-Industrie Michelin* (n 210) recitals 37–50; *Vitamins* (Case IV/29.020) [1976] OJ L223/27, recitals 22–26.

[148] EAGCP, *An Economic Approach to Article 82* (July 2005) 2, 3, www.ec.europa.eu/dgs/competition/economist/eagcp_july_21_05.pdf.

and suggested that the Commission instead assess the conduct's effects on consumer welfare directly.[149] DG Competition's own Discussion Paper on the reform of Article 102, which formed the basis of the public consultation, had proposed assessing all forms of exclusionary conduct as to whether they were 'likely' to produce anticompetitive foreclosure effects.[150] Dominance was to be established by analysing market shares, barriers to expansion and entry, and the position of buyers specifically for each case.[151] The Discussion Paper made no mention of the rule that market shares above 50 per cent should normally indicate dominance.

The Commission Notice that eventually concluded the reform in February 2009 outlines a similar approach to that of the Discussion Paper. While recognising the relevance of market shares as a useful first indication of the market structure and the relative importance of the various market players, the Guidance proposes a more detailed assessment of the undertaking's economic strength that also takes into account the existence of competitive constraints, such as entry, expansion and countervailing buyer power.[152]

As to the matter of assessing the conduct's actual effects on competition, the Guidance Paper states that the Commission will normally intervene where, on the basis of cogent and convincing evidence, the allegedly abusive conduct is 'likely to lead to anti-competitive foreclosure'. According to the Guidance, it is the Commission's intention to establish this likelihood in every single case on the basis of qualitative and, where possible and appropriate, quantitative evidence, rather than by relying on form-based presumptions.[153] However, it acknowledges that there may be circumstances in which it might not be necessary for the Commission to carry out a detailed assessment of the effects on consumer welfare. Consumer harm may be inferred if it appears that the conduct can only raise obstacles to competition and that it creates no efficiencies. The Guidance explains that this would be considered the case, for example, if the dominant undertaking prevented its customers from testing the products of competitors or provided financial incentives to its customers on condition that they did not test such products, or paid a distributor or a customer to delay the introduction of a competitor's product.[154]

In sum, the Notice outlines a mixed, if effects-heavy approach. In principle, the Commission aims to assess both the conduct's likely foreclosure effects and the likely effects on consumer welfare. In obvious cases, in which it appears that the conduct can only raise obstacles to competition and that it creates no

[149] ibid, 4.

[150] European Commission, DG Competition Discussion Paper on the Application of Article 82 of the Treaty to Exclusionary Abuses, November 2005, paras 5 and 51–256, available at: www.ec.europa.eu/competition/antitrust/art82/discpaper2005.pdf.

[151] ibid, paras 20–42.

[152] European Commission, Guidance on the Commission's enforcement priorities in applying Article 82 of the EC Treaty to abusive exclusionary conduct by dominant undertakings [2009] OJ C45/7, paras 9–18.

[153] ibid, paras 19 and 20.

[154] ibid, para 22.

efficiencies, it will still establish the foreclosure effects, but consumer harm may be inferred. This test is very clear. It is also very different from the tests applied by the Commission in its early decision practice. Not only does it focus on a different type of harm, but it also prescribes an assessment of the conduct's 'likely effects' in every case. There are no more pure presumptions of illegality.

Strictly speaking, this Notice does not claim to explain the Commission's interpretation of Article 102 or outline a legal test for assessing exclusionary abuses. It explicitly distances itself from such an interpretative function, and stresses that it merely aims to outline the Commission's revised enforcement priorities.[155] Formally, therefore, it merely explains how the Commission intends to go about assessing whether a certain type of business conduct is an enforcement priority, rather than whether it fulfils the conditions of Article 102. Nonetheless, it is bound to have a profound impact on the types of cases that are found to infringe Article 102. Only conduct that tests positive under the Guidance Paper's 'priority test' will be assessed and pursued under the appropriate 'legal test' as defined by the Court of Justice,[156] which the Guidance Paper does not engage with in any depth. By contrast, conduct that tests negative under the Guidance's priority test should in principle never even be assessed under the law. The Guidance thus acts as a filter. It is an unusually fine filter. Cases that pass the Guidance Paper's test are highly unlikely not to test positive under the law as well. It is further atypical for a filter in that the test it applies is much more complex than that of the law itself.[157] It requests the Commission to establish each conduct's foreclosure effects, as well as its effects on consumer welfare, unless the latter is so obvious as not to justify a separate assessment, in every individual case on the basis of sound qualitative and quantitative evidence.

ii. The Decision Practice

The next question that arises is whether the Commission has implemented this new effects-based approach in its decision practice. With regard to the issue of assessing the position of dominance, the answer is clear. While recognising the relevance of market shares as a first indicator of dominance, no decision since 2009 has established a position of dominance on the basis of market shares alone. Instead, the Commission now usually carries out a detailed assessment of several individual factors, for example market shares, market concentration, actual and potential competitors, barriers to entry and countervailing buyer power.[158] In fact, this development can already be observed in major Article 102 decisions between 2004 and 2008, when the Commission had already revised its approach to

[155] ibid, para 3.
[156] See Ch 10.
[157] See Ch 10.
[158] *Intel* (Case COMP/C-3 /37.990) recitals 837–912; *Telekomunikacja Polska* (Case COMP/39.525) recitals 640–65; *Motorola—Enforcement of GPRS standard essential patents* (Case AT.39985) 221–70.

Articles 101 and EU merger law, but not yet completed its review of Article 102.[159] It is a clear change from its approach pre-2004, which tended to infer dominance on the basis of large market shares alone.

The Commission's revised approach to assessing the abusive nature of the investigated conduct has taken a little longer to crystallise. Even before it formally concluded its reform of Article 102 with the publication of the Guidance Paper in 2009, the issue of whether it is necessary to prove the actual anticompetitive effects of abusive conduct became highly polarised in the Commission's decision practice and heavily contested in Court. In a number of prominent cases between 2005 and 2008, the Commission therefore chose a two-step-approach. It first assessed the investigated conduct under the relevant legal test established in the case law. These tests tend to be tailored to specific forms of conduct and do not always require demonstrating the actual effects on competition.[160] Having reached the conclusion that the conduct amounted to an infringement of Article 102 within the meaning of the case law, the Commission then 'additionally' proved that the conduct also had actual anticompetitive effects, while stressing that this step was not necessary. In *Prokent-Tomra*, for example, it proved without any difficulty that Tomra's system of exclusivity agreements, quantity commitments and loyalty-inducing discounts, were abusive as such according to the relevant case law. Citing the Court's ruling in *Michelin II*, the Commission emphasised that it was not necessary to establish that the practices had actually foreclosed competition by denying competitors access to customers, because it was sufficient to show that the conduct 'tended' to restrict competition.[161] Nonetheless, it then additionally demonstrated that Tomra's practices had had actual foreclosure effects.[162] Both the General Court and the Court of Justice confirmed on review that the Commission need not have demonstrated the conduct's actual foreclosure effects, because loyalty-inducing conduct on the part of a dominant undertaking was always abusive.[163] The Commission took a similar approach in *AstraZeneca* and *Wanadoo España v Telefónica.* The former investigated a dominant pharmaceutical undertaking's attempts to exclude generic firms from the market and to prevent parallel trade, and the latter investigated a potential margin squeeze. In both cases, the Commission first applied the Court's tests, which did not require evidence of actual anticompetitive effects, and then 'additionally' proved the conduct's effects on competition and consumer welfare in relatively elaborate separate assessments,

[159] eg *AstraZeneca* (Case COMP/A.37.507/F3) recitals 517–601; *Wanadoo España v Telefónica* (Case COMP/38.784) recitals 223–77.

[160] See Ch 10

[161] *Prokent-Tomra* (Case COMP/E-1/38.113) recitals 281–85, citing Case T-203/01 *Manufacture française des pneumatiques Michelin v Commission* ECLI:EU:T:2003:250, para 239.

[162] *Prokent-Tomra* (n 161) recitals 331–44.

[163] Case T-155/06 *Tomra Systems v Commission* ECLI:EU:T:2010:370, para 289, upheld on appeal in Case C-549/10 P *Tomra Systems v Commission* ECLI:EU:C:2012:221.

while emphasising that the law did not require it to do so.[164] Again, the issue of whether it was necessary to establish the actual effects, and whether the Commission had done so in a satisfactory manner, was raised in the subsequent actions for annulment. And again, the Court adhered to its original position according to which it was not necessary to prove actual foreclosure effects, but that it was sufficient to show that the conduct 'tended' to restrict competition or that it was 'capable' of having such an effect.[165] In a similar vein, the Commission had already 'exceptionally' assessed Microsoft's practice of tying as to its actual foreclosure effects in the famous infringement decision of 2004, because it considered the circumstances of the case highly unusual.[166]

Since publication of the Guidance Paper in February 2009, the Commission has enacted four infringement decisions: *Intel*, *Telekomunikacja Polska*, *OPCOM* and *Motorola*.[167] Of these, *Intel* is a borderline case, as the Commission started the investigation before publication of the Guidance Paper, and therefore did not formally apply the Notice to the case. However, the decision states that the Commission considered the assessment to be in line with the 'orientations' set out in the Guidance.[168] *Intel* repeated the approach of the above-mentioned major Article 102 decisions between 2005 and 2008 in that it first assessed the conduct under the case law and then carried out an 'unnecessary' assessment of the conduct's actual effects. The case concerned Intel's practice of granting rebates to customers on condition that they bought all, or almost all, of their requirements in computer chips from Intel. Intel had also made payments to computer manufacturers to delay the launch of specific products containing competitors' computer chips and to limit the sales channels available to these products. The Commission started its competitive assessment by reiterating that, according to the law, it was neither necessary to prove actual foreclosure nor a direct effect on consumer welfare, but that the mere 'capacity' to foreclose was sufficient.[169] It established in a few sentences that all the practices in question tended to remove the freedom of customers to choose their supplier and were therefore capable of foreclosing competition within the meaning of the case law.[170] With regard

[164] *Wanadoo España v Telefónica* (Case COMP/38.784) recitals 543–618; *AstraZeneca* (n 159) recitals 758–72 and 848–59.

[165] Case T-336/07 *Telefónica and Telefónica de España v Commission* ECLI:EU:T:2012:172, para 268, upheld in Case C-295/12 P *Telefónica and Telefónica de España v Commission* ECLI:EU:C:2014:2062. However, the decision in *AstraZenca* was partially annulled by the General Court on the grounds that the Commission had failed to demonstrate to the requisite legal standard that one of the investigated practices was 'capable' of restricting parallel imports in Denmark and Norway (Case T-321/05 *AstraZeneca v Commission* ECLI:EU:T:2010:266, para 856, upheld in Case C-457/10 P *AstraZeneca v Commission* ECLI:EU:C:2012:770).

[166] *Microsoft* (2004) recital 841.

[167] *Intel* (n 158); *Telekomunikacja Polska* (n 158); *Romanian Power Exchange/OPCOM* (Case AT.39984); *Motorola—Enforcement of GPRS standard essential patents* (n 158).

[168] *Intel* (n 158) recital 916.

[169] ibid, recitals 918–23.

[170] ibid, recitals 924–25.

to the rebates, it then demonstrated that, in addition to fulfilling the conditions established in the case law, they were likely to result in anticompetitive foreclosure. While repeating that this was not a legal requirement, the Commissions pointed out that the likelihood of consumer harm meant that the case deserved its particular attention.[171] This additional, quasi-complimentary, assessment was long and complex. It included both qualitative and quantitative analyses and spanned almost 200 pages.[172] In comparison, the Commission's assessment under the Court's test, which it described as being the law, was only a few sentences long. The Commission did not repeat the same exercise for the second type of abuse on the grounds that it did not consider this appropriate.[173]

To date, the infringement decisions after *Intel* have no longer followed this pattern. Instead of first applying the case law and then carrying out a legally 'unnecessary' assessment of the conduct's actual effects, the decisions in *Telekomunikacja Polska*, *Motorola* and *OPCOM* emulated the Court's approach more closely in that they formally assessed whether the conduct in question was 'capable' of producing anticompetitive effects.[174] At first sight, this might suggest that the Commission has abandoned its ambition of carrying out a detailed assessment of the actual effects on competition and consumer welfare in infringement decisions. The decisions seem to be toeing the line of the case law in that they first identified the type of abuse committed, for example, a refusal to supply in *Telekomunikacja Polska* and discrimination on the basis of nationality in the case of *OPCOM*. *Motorola* concerned a new form of abuse.[175] In the first two cases, the Commission then established that the formal requirements of a refusal to supply and discrimination were given. Next, all three decisions stated that according to the case law, it was not necessary for the conduct to have actual anticompetitive effects, and that it was sufficient that they were 'capable' of such effect. Hence, they did not formally carry out an assessment of the conducts' actual effects, but merely assessed whether the behaviour's capacity to have such effects.

However, two observations can be made with regard to these assessments that suggest that the Commission has not given up on introducing a more economic approach to its analyses under Article 102. First, one can note that in *Telekomunikacja Polska* and *OPCOM*, the competitive assessment not only established the capacity to foreclose, as required by the case law, but also the capacity to cause consumer harm.[176] This is in line with the more economic

[171] ibid, recital 925.
[172] ibid, recitals 1002–16.
[173] ibid, recital 1665.
[174] *Telekomunikacja Polska* (n 158) recitals 812–72; *Motorola* (n 158) recitals 308–420; *OPCOM* (n 167) 171–79.
[175] Motorola, an American telecommunications company, had sought and enforced an injunction against another undertaking before German courts to protect a standard-essential patent ('SEP') that it had committed to license on fair, reasonable and non-discriminatory ('FRAND') terms and conditions.
[176] *Telekomunikacja Polska* (n 158) recitals 812–72; *OPCOM* (n 167) recitals 171–79.

approach, but goes beyond what is required by the legal test. Second, the Commission's assessments of the conduct's 'capacity' to have anticompetitive effects in *Telekomunikacja Polska* and *Motorola* were extremely elaborate and in-depth. In *Telekomunikacja Polska*, for example, this assessment included quantitative analyses of the likely effects both on the competitive structure of the market and on consumer welfare.[177] This is more than one could expect under a 'quick look' test. Likewise, in *Motorola*, the Commission established on the basis of a detailed qualitative analysis that the conduct was 'capable' of three different types of anticompetitive effects: a temporary ban on the online sale of another undertaking's products in Germany, the inclusion in the settlement agreement of licensing terms disadvantageous to that undertaking, and a negative impact on standard-setting.[178] If one looks at these assessments, it is difficult to imagine what more the Commission could have done if it had aimed to assess this conduct as to its actual effects. In fact, in all three decisions, the Commission interpreted the Court's expression 'capable of' producing anticompetitive effects as meaning 'likely to' produce anticompetitive effects.[179] This is the same term it uses to describe the standard of proof under Article 101(1) for conduct that needs to be assessed as to its actual effects.[180] Given the detail of the assessments that the Commission carried out in *Telekomunikacja Polska* and *Motorola*, and the fact that it interpreted 'capable' of meaning 'likely', one may conclude that the Commission was assessing these conducts under the same type of test as agreements that are not restrictive by object but need to be assessed as to their effects in the context of Article 101(1).

The assessment in *OPCOM*, by contrast, which concerned a case of discrimination on the basis of nationality and was found to affect parallel trade, was much briefer.[181] There seems to have been little doubt in the Commission's mind that discriminating against trading partners on grounds of nationality was likely to raise barriers to trade between Member States and consequently to the internal market. If this type of behaviour had been carried out by means of an agreement, it would have been considered restrictive by object under Article 101(1). However, *OPCOM* has so far been the odd one out in this regard in the Commission's infringement decisions under Article 102 post-2009. The other three infringement decisions assessed the likely effects of the investigated conduct in great detail.

Finally, the majority of substantive decisions under Article 102 since 2004 have been commitments rather than infringement decisions.[182] These decisions do not carry out complete and final assessments of the conduct's competitive nature, but

[177] *Telekomunikacja Polska* (n 158) recitals 820–72.

[178] *Motorola* (n 158) recitals 308–420.

[179] *Motorola* (n 158) eg heading 8.2.3.2.1 and recitals 365, 371, 372; *Telekomunikacja Polska* (n 158) recitals 701, 702; *OPCOM* (n 167) recitals 172, 185.

[180] eg European Commission, Guidelines on the application of Article 81(3) of the Treaty (n 61) paras 24, 25.

[181] *OPCOM* (n 167) recitals 174–85.

[182] See Ch 5.

merely outline the Commission's initial concerns after a preliminary assessment. They tend not to follow a uniform approach, nor are they always clear on the theoretical approach the Commission would have applied if it had pursued the case till the end. Instead, they usually identify the type of harm the Commission is concerned about and indicate how this harm might be caused.[183] A handful of decisions state the Commission actually carried out detailed calculations to establish these effects.[184] In other cases, the decision merely categorises the conduct as a specific type of potential abuse and indicates that it is likely to fulfil the conditions of illegality set out in the case law.[185] Others are even vaguer than that.[186] However, the summaries of the Commission's concerns in such commitments decisions are not, and do not aim to be, final legal assessments of the conduct's compatibility with Article 102. While they provide some insight into the Commission's theories and concepts of harm, they do not allow any definite conclusions as to what type of legal test the Commission considers appropriate under Article 102.

iii. Conclusion

In sum, the Commission's Guidance and its infringement decisions since 2005 suggest that the Commission is committed to demonstrating business conduct's likely effects both on competition and consumer welfare before finding it abusive within the meaning Article 102. However, it has had difficulties accommodating this commitment with the case law of the Court of Justice, which holds that certain forms of conduct are always abusive regardless of their actual effects because they are by their very nature capable of producing foreclosure effects,[187] and that all other types of conduct merely need to be assessed as to whether they are 'capable' of producing an exclusionary effect.[188]

In a number of infringement decisions between 2005 and 2009, the Commission dealt with this difficulty by first assessing the conduct under the case law, finding that its conditions were met, and then 'additionally' proving the conduct's actual effects in highly elaborate qualitative and quantitative analyses, while stressing that this was not really necessary. Since the conclusion of the reform in February 2009, it has followed another approach. It now reads the Court's case law as requiring an assessment of whether the investigated conduct is 'capable' of producing anti-competitive effects in every case. Significantly, it interprets 'capable' as meaning

[183] eg *Reuters Instrument Codes* (Case AT.39654) recitals 37–45: *CEZ* (Case AT/39727) recitals 21–33.

[184] *Deutsche Bahn I* (Case COMP/AT.39678) and *Deutsche Bahn II* (Case COMP/AT.39731) recitals 48–63; *Microsoft (tying)* (Case COMP/C-3/39.530) recitals 39–58.

[185] *ENI* (Case COMP/39.315) recitals 39–60.

[186] *E.ON Gas* (Case COMP/39.317) recitals 31–41.

[187] eg rebates that are dependent on the customer obtaining all of his supplies from the dominant undertaking (*Hoffmann-La Roche v Commission* (n 118) para 90; reiterated in Case C-95/04 P *British Airways v Commission* ECLI:EU:C:2007:166, paras 61, 62).

[188] eg *British Airways v Commission* (n 187) para 68. This case law, and its compatibility with the Commission's revised approach, are discussed in more detail in Ch 10.

'likely' to produce anticompetitive effects, and thus, seemingly with the blessings of the case law, carries out an assessment of the investigated conduct's likely effects in every case in order to establish whether it is abusive or not. These assessments are usually elaborate, often entail both qualitative and quantitative analyses, and are well supported with evidence. Interestingly, 'likelihood' is the same standard of proof that the Commission applies when it assesses an agreement's effects under Article 101(1). In sum, the Commission's infringement decisions do exactly what the Guidance promised: an assessment of the conduct's likely effects in every individual case. This finding is relativised to some extent by the fact that the majority of Article 102 decisions are not infringement or clearance, but commitments decisions, which do not carry out a conclusive assessment of the conduct's nature, but merely outline the Commission's initial concerns.

C. Conclusion on the Changes under Article 102

Have the Commission's legal assessments become more effects-based under Article 102 after the reform? The answer to this question is not straightforward, but ultimately it has to be answered in the affirmative. Regarding the concept of dominance, the Commission no longer infers this position from the undertaking's market shares or exclusive rights alone, but carries out an individualised assessment of many different factors deemed capable of determining the undertaking's economic power. As to the assessment of the investigated conduct itself, there has also been a marked evolution. The tests applied by the Commission prior to the reform were neither clear nor consistent. In a number of decisions, it seemed to consider specific types of conduct to be automatically abusive, in the vein of abuses 'by object'. In others, it assessed the same type of conduct as to its actual anticompetitive effects, as defined at the time. In yet other cases, it examined whether the conduct was liable to have, or capable of having, anticompetitive effects. In a handful of cases, the undertaking's intention to cause harm was considered the decisive factor. Finally, in many cases, it was simply not clear what type of test the Commission was applying. They could have passed as very poorly substantiated effects analyses, form-based presumptions, or something in between.

The Commission became much more attentive to the issue during the review process, and this is reflected in its enforcement practice since then. The Guidance Paper outlines an approach according to which it is necessary to assess any type of exclusionary conduct at least as to whether it is likely to result in anticompetitive foreclosure effects. There are no more outright presumptions of illegality. While the foreclosure effect is to be established in every single case on the basis of qualitative and where possible quantitative evidence, the effects on consumer welfare may sometimes be inferred when they are obvious. The problem with this Notice, of course, is that it formally does not purport to spell out the Commission's legal interpretation of Article 102. It merely explains how the Commission intends to establish whether a case is an enforcement priority. It is also limited in scope, as it only applies to exclusionary abuses and does not give guidance on exploitative and discriminatory practices.

Likewise, the decision practice shows a much clearer commitment to assessing the conduct's actual or likely effects in each individual case. Since the publication of the Guidance Paper, the Commission has assessed all exclusionary conduct as to whether it is 'likely' to result in anticompetitive foreclosure effects, which is the same standard it employs for effects-based assessments under Article 101(1).

Like in the area of EU merger law, there has been a reduction in the number of decisions making a final finding on the compatibility of the conduct with Article 102. The majority of cases since 2004 have been concluded by means of commitments decisions, which do not contain any in-depth assessments. This has resulted in there being very few actual decisions providing insight into the Commission's practical approach to assessing conduct under Article 102. In combination with the fact that the Commission's Guidance is not an interpretative Notice but one spelling out enforcement priorities, applicable to exclusionary abuses only, this situation has resulted in a fair degree of legal uncertainty.

VI. Conclusion

Is it effect or form for EU antitrust assessments after the introduction of the more economic approach? The answer is less clear than one may have expected given the importance of the matter during the reform.

Beginning with the area of EU merger law, which provides the most straightforward answer, one can say that the Commission has always sought to establish the investigated transactions' likely effects and has never relied on form-based presumptions of illegality or legality. This has not changed with the review. What has changed is the type of effect considered relevant, and the type and quality of evidence used to establish it.

With regard to Article 101(1), the findings are initially somewhat counterintuitive. The great majority of infringement decisions since completion of the reform on Article 101 have actually been cases of object restrictions, which are not assessed as to their actual effects. Their anticompetitive effects are presumed. However, this development is not the result of the Commission having changed its understanding of what constitutes an object restriction and what type of restriction should be examined as to its effects. It is the result of a shift in enforcement priorities and the use of a new type of enforcement instrument. Since decentralisation of the enforcement of Article 101 in 2004, the Commission has focused on pursuing cartels, which have always been and continue to be deemed so dangerous to competition that their anticompetitive effects are presumed. Of the other cases investigated by the Commission, and that would normally have been assessed as to their effects, the great majority have been closed by means of commitments decisions. These decisions only contain a preliminary and usually quite informal assessment that outlines the Commission's concerns. The few decisions in which the Commission has recently carried out an in-depth assessment of the agreements' effects under Article 101 are very different in substance from early effects analysis, because the Commission, in line with its new concept of harm, now assesses different types of effect and uses better evidence to prove these effects. However, one must conclude that there has not been a major shift in the Commission's understanding of what type of conduct should be presumed illegal, and which type of agreement should be scrutinised more closely.

Regarding Article 101(3), parties have always had to prove the actual beneficial effects. This continues to be the case. Again, it is the type of benefit that has changed, and in line with the Commission raising its own standard of proof under Article 101(1), it has also raised the standard of proof expected from the parties under Article 101(3). Article 101(3) defences simply no longer succeed these days. Block Exemption Regulations, by contrast, have become somewhat less formalistic. The Commission abolished the prescriptive white lists, and has attempted to integrate an approximation of the likely effects on consumer welfare by means of a market share threshold.

It is the Commission's current approach to Article 102 that remains the most intriguing. At least it is possible to say with certainty that dominant positions are no longer inferred from the undertaking's market shares alone. Instead, the Commission tends to carry out detailed market power analyses. However, there remains some degree of uncertainty as to the Commission's current position on how to assess whether the dominant undertaking's conduct is abusive. Prior to the reform, its assessments were theoretically inconsistent and often unclear. The Guidance concluding the reform process suggests that the Commission intends to assess potentially exclusionary conduct as to its likely foreclosure effects and effects on consumer welfare in every case. While this seems like a clear enough test, the uncertainty arises from the fact that the Guidance Paper formally only claims to set out enforcement priorities and not legal tests. Secondly, it is limited to exclusionary abuses and does not cover exploitative or discriminatory abuses.

Attempts to establish the Commission's current approach from its decision practice are thwarted by the same phenomenon as encountered under Article 101. The majority of cases have been closed by means of commitments decisions without formal legal assessments. The handful of actual infringement decisions of the past 10 years show a clear commitment to assessing the conduct's actual effects before condemning it, which is, however, constrained by the Court's position that many types of unilateral conduct on the part of a dominant undertaking should be automatically deemed abusive, and that others merely need to be assessed as to their capacity to foreclosure but not their actual foreclosure effects. Between 2005 and 2009, the Commission dealt with this problem by first assessing the conduct under the case law, and then carrying out complex, additional assessments of the conduct's actual effects, while pointing out that this was not really necessary. Paradoxically, these additional, 'unnecessary' assessments were far more elaborate, and presumably much more costly, than the 'necessary' assessment under the legally binding test. Since 2010, infringement decisions have no longer chosen this approach. Instead, they have assessed whether the investigated conduct was likely to result in foreclosure effects and consumer harm. This is the same standard the Commission applies when it assesses agreements as to their effects under Article 101(1).

One noticeable change in the Commission's competitive assessments under all three pillars is that with the new understanding of competitive harm, and hence the new type of effect being assessed, the Commission has also started using different types of evidence than previously. Across the board, its assessments are much better supported with evidence. Whereas many early cases primarily based their conclusions on the terms of the investigated agreements and conjecture, its assumptions are now commonly backed up with solid empirical evidence and recognised economic theories. In addition, all parties now regularly use quantitative analyses and expert economic studies to support their claims. The following chapter takes a closer look at these methodological changes.

8

A More Economic Methodology

I. Introduction

The previous four chapters demonstrated how the key values and aims of economic theory have altered the Commission's interpretation of the prohibition rules of EU antitrust law over the past 15-odd years. While these changes were significant, they were not entirely obvious at first sight. Determining their nature and extent required an in-depth analysis of the Commission's many different enforcement instruments. However, the more economic approach also resulted in a number of methodological changes that are much more visible than the changes in legal interpretation. The Commission now regularly also relies on economic theory and the many practical applications developed by economists in the actual assessments under the newly defined rules. By the same token, it has greatly increased the quality and quantity of evidence to support key assumptions in these assessments.

II. The Use of Economic Theory

Economic theory has gained a great deal of traction in the Commission's substantive assessments under EU antitrust law since the introduction of the more economic approach. Since the early 2000s, the Commission has increasingly turned to economic theory, in particular industrial organisation theory, to understand whether and by what mechanism business conduct is likely to result in specific types of competitive harm or efficiency effects. By contrast, the enforcement practice of the first 40 years, with its freedom-based concept of harm, was typically focused on legal analysis and common economic sense. It was rare for the Commission to draw on expert economic theory during the first 40 years of antitrust enforcement.

A. The Commission's Approach Prior to the Introduction of the More Economic Approach

i. Articles 101 and 102

Prior to the introduction of the more economic approach, the Commission had a broad and predominantly rights-based understanding of competitive harm under Articles 101 and 102. Harm to competition included the restriction of economic freedom or opportunity, the exclusion of competitors, the reduction of choice, discrimination, unfair behaviour, the creation or strengthening of a dominant position and undermining the process of market integration. In its competitive assessments, the Commission rarely established complex chains of cause and effect to prove that the investigated conduct had caused any of these types of harm. For example, to establish that an agreement resulted in the restriction of the parties' freedom, the Commission simply examined the terms of the contract. If it found that the contractual terms restricted the parties' freedom in an important aspect, it concluded that this amounted to a restriction of their freedom and hence to a restriction of competition.[1] The assessment of whether conduct was discriminatory or unfair in other ways was guided by moral rather than economic considerations. The key test in cases of discrimination was whether the undertaking was treating similar situations differently without objective justification.[2]

It is actually difficult to imagine how economic theory could possibly have helped with establishing these types of harm, even if the Commission had had the ambition to rely on such theory. In those cases, in which the Commission additionally assessed whether the unfair or discriminatory conduct placed the victims at a competitive disadvantage, it did not carry out complex economic assessments of this effect either. It normally simply assumed that having to pay a higher price than one's competitors or being treated less favourably in other ways was a disadvantage in the competitive process, hence placing the undertaking at a disadvantage.[3] The effects of export prohibitions and other impediments to intra-Union trade were treated in an equally straightforward manner.

[1] eg *Hennessy-Henkell* (Case IV/26.912) [1980] OJ L383/11, recitals 16–20; *Nederlandse Cement-Handelmaatschappij NV* (Case IV/595) [1972] OJ L22/16, recital 7; *Vereeniging van Cementhandelaren* (Case IV/324) [1972] OJ L13/34, recital 16(b); *ASBL pour la promotion du tube d'acier soudé électriquement* (Case IV/412) [1970] OJ L153/14, II; *SABA's EEC distribution system* (Case IV/29.598) [1983] OJ L376/41, II.C.3; *British Dental Trade Association—BDTA* (Case IV/31.593) [1988] OJ L233/15, recital 23.

[2] eg *Chiquita* (Case IV/26.699) [1976] OJ L95/1, II.A.3.c; *NAVEWA-ANSEAU* (Case IV/29.995) [1982] OJ L167/39, recital 56; *Rabattbeschluss der Interessengemeinschaft der deutschen keramischen Wand- und Bodenfliesenwerke* (Case IV/25107) [1971] OJ L10/15, II.2.b; *ASBL pour la promotion du tube d'acier soudé électriquement* (n 1) II; *Hasselblad* (Case IV/25.757) [1982] OJ L161/18, recital 56; *AEG-Telefunken* (Case IV/28.748) [1982] OJ L117/15, recitals 53 ff.

[3] eg *Napier Brown–British Sugar* (Case IV/30.178) [1988] OJ L284/41, recital 73; *GVL* (Case IV/29.839) [1981] OJ L370/49, recitals 54, 55; *Vitamins* (Case IV/29.020) [1976] OJ L223/27, recital 26.

Without supporting its reasoning with in-depth economic research, the Commission assumed that banning distributors from selling in another Member State resulted in a reduction in trade between Member States.[4]

The Commission's approach to proving that the conduct had restricted third parties' commercial opportunities was usually just as uncomplicated. Where the investigated undertakings had entered into an exclusivity agreement that prohibited one or both of them from dealing with third parties, the Commission inferred that third parties lost the opportunity to deal with the investigated undertakings. This restricted their commercial opportunities.[5] Again, this reasoning is based on common sense rather than sophisticated economic analysis.

The assessments of exclusionary effects, or harm to the structure of competition, were usually equally unscientific. To establish that exclusivity, fidelity and similar rebates could have an exclusionary effect, the Commission again primarily relied on everyday reasoning. It took the view that rebates tied a customer to the dominant undertaking, meaning that it restricted their inclination to obtain their supplies from competing manufacturers. This made it more difficult for existing competitors to sell their products, and also impeded the access of potential competitors to the market.[6] This is not rocket science. More to the point, it is not the product of an expert economic assessment either.

The case of *ECS/AKZO*[7] is an exception to this rule, at least to some degree, in that the Commission engaged in some detail with a cost-based test developed for the purposes of assessing predatory pricing under US law. This test, although developed by two US law professors, draws heavily on economic theory. According to the Areeda and Turner test, only prices below average variable cost should be deemed (*per se*) anticompetitive, because only less efficient firms would be harmed by such prices. Prices above average variable cost should be considered legal.[8] Unusually, for this period, the Commission explicitly engaged with the test and the economic theory underlying it in the competitive assessment.[9] However, it eventually rejected the test as being unsuitable for the purposes of Article 102 on the grounds that EU antitrust law was not guided by efficiency considerations alone but pursued broader objectives than US antitrust law.[10] It was particularly critical of the fact that the test failed to take into account whether the dominant

[4] eg *Theal Watts* (Case IV/28.812) [1977] OJ L 39/19, II.A; *National Panasonic* (Case IV/30.070) [1982] OJ L354/28, recital 48; *Sandoz* (Case IV/31.741) [1987] OJ L222/28, recital 29.

[5] *Rabattbeschluss der Interessengemeinschaft der deutschen keramischen Wand- und Bodenfliesenwerke* (n 2); *Breeders' Rights–Maize Seed* (Case IV/28824) [1978] OJ L286/23, II.3.

[6] eg *Bandengroothandel Frieschebrug BV/NV Nederlandsche Banden-Industrie Michelin* (Case IV/29.491) [1981] OJ L353/3, recital 49; *Soda-ash—Solvay, ICI* (Case IV/33.133-A) [1991] OJ L152/1, recital 53.

[7] *ECS/AKZO* (Case IV/30.698) [1985] OJ L374/1.

[8] P Areeda and DF Turner, 'Predatory Pricing and Related Practices under Section 2 of the Sherman Act' (1975) 88 *Harvard Law Review* 697.

[9] *ECS/AKZO* (n 7) recitals 74, 79.

[10] ibid, recital 77.

undertaking had had the intent to eliminate its competitors, which the Commission considered highly relevant for a finding of abuse.[11]

Market definition under Article 102 also used to be a relatively free exercise. Many early Article 102 decisions defined the relevant market in a few sentences and without providing much of a rationale.[12] In cases in which the dominant position was inferred from a special right held by the undertaking, the Commission would sometimes not define any market at all.[13] As of the mid-1980s, the Commission started defining the relevant market by assessing whether products produced by other manufacturers were interchangeable with the product manufactured by the investigated undertaking.[14] This approach was based on the ruling by the Court of Justice in *Michelin v Commission* of 1983, according to which a market comprises the totality of the products which, with respect to their characteristics, are particularly suitable for satisfying constant needs and are only to a limited extent interchangeable with other products.[15] The Commission's, usually very brief, assessment of the interchangeability of products was primarily based on assumptions that were neither supported by abstract economic theory nor by much empirical evidence.

ii. Merger Control

The previous chapters established that, in many regards, the Commission's assessments under the EU Merger Regulation had always been a little more 'economic' than those it carried out under the other two pillars of EU antitrust law. The same is true, to some extent at least, with regard to its use of economic theory.

The Commission's market definitions under Regulation 4064/89, for example, were consistently more substantial and systematic than the rather sketchy early market delineations under Article 102. However, the main difference between its market definitions under these two provisions lay in the attention to detail and the evidence used to support its assumption, rather than the theory itself. In principle, it applied the same test under both provisions, meaning that it sought to establish whether different products and geographic locations were substitutes for the investigated product and location in the eyes of consumers. It usually did not employ any more sophisticated economic methods for answering this question under the first Merger Regulation than under Article 102. Primarily, its assessments under the Merger Regulation were more thorough and took into account a somewhat wider range of factors, such as product characteristics, function, price, transport cost and local consumption patterns, on the basis of which the Commission made

[11] ibid, recital 80.

[12] *GVL* (n 3) recital 45; *Hugin/Liptons* (Case IV/29.132) [1978] OJ L22/23, II.A.

[13] eg. *General Motors Continental* (Case IV/28.851) [1975] OJ L 29/14.

[14] eg *Soda-ash–ICI* (Case IV/33.133-D) 91/300/EEC [1991] OJ L152/40, recitals 43–46; *HOV SVZ/MCN* (Case IV/33.941) [1994] OJ L104/34, recital 58.

[15] Case 322/81 *Nederlandsche Banden Industrie Michelin v Commission* ECLI:EU:C:1983:313, para 37.

an educated guess as to whether consumers would consider the different products and regions substitutes.[16] These assessments were not only more detailed than its market definitions under Article 102, but usually also better supported with empirical evidence. In a handful of cases, the Commission even used the economic concept of cross-price elasticity of demand, which it took into consideration as an additional factor in its overall analysis of substitutability.[17]

The Commission's assessments of the parties' dominance in the context of merger control clearly also relied on more economic concepts than the corresponding assessments under Article 102. In the context of Article 102, the Commission had primarily inferred the position of dominance from the undertaking's 'very large market shares'. By contrast, its analyses of whether a merger would result in the creation or strengthening of a dominant position under Regulation 4064/89 usually explored a wider variety of factors deemed capable of giving an indication of the parties' economic strength. These assessments always at least analysed the existing barriers to entry and countervailing buyer power in addition to the key players' market shares in order to gain a more precise idea of whether the merged entity would be able to 'act independently of competitors and customers'. Entry and countervailing buyer power are concepts recognised and studied by economists for determining an undertaking's market power.[18]

However, even merger decisions prior to the reform rarely drew on economic theory beyond the aforementioned two concepts. The Commission's early understanding of dominance, guided by the Court of Justice's understanding of the concept, was as a broad and unspecified position of strength. While the parties occasionally retained economic consultants during the investigation and submitted economic studies to support their arguments,[19] there is generally little evidence during this period of the Commission itself using specific theories or principles developed by economists in order to support its assumptions about the potential effects of the merger or the forces that might constrain the merged entity. It usually assessed the potential for future entry by looking at forecast demand, time and cost, regulatory hurdles to entering the market and access to distribution.[20] While these are concepts that economists would also consider relevant in such an assessment, they do not go significantly beyond what common sense would suggest.

[16] eg *Guinness/Grand Metropolitan* (Case No IV/M.938) [1998] OJ L288/24, recitals 8–29; *Blokker/Toys 'R' Us* (Case IV/M.890) [1998] OJ L316/1, recitals 27–41; *Du Pont/ICI* (Case IV/M.214) [1993] OJ L7/13, recitals 10–31.

[17] *Du Pont/ICI* (n 16) recital 28; *Gencor/Lonrho* (Case IV/M.619) [1997] OJ L11/30, recitals 56–59; *Tetra Laval/Sidel* (Case COMP/M. 2416) [2004] OJ L43/13, recital 162.

[18] eg LMB Cabral, *Introduction to Industrial Organization* (Cambridge, Mass, MIT Press, 2000) 160, 252; P Belleflamme and M Peitz, *Industrial Organisation Theory* (Cambridge, Cambridge University Press, 2015) 390.

[19] eg *Aerospatiale-Alenia/de Havilland* (Case IV/M.053) [1991] OJ L334/42, recital 30; *Airtours/First Choice* (Case No IV/M.1524) [2000] OJ L93/1, recital 62.

[20] See eg *Aerospatiale-Alenia/de Havilland* (n 19) recital 54; *Gencor/Lonrho* (n 17) recital 154; *Nestlé/Perrier* (Case IV/M.190) [1992] OJ L356/1, recitals 31–34.

The Commission's approach to assessing countervailing buyer power was less consistent, and often as vague as it was brief.[21]

The same can be said for the less straightforward anticompetitive effects assessed by the Commission, in particular portfolio and leveraging effects. In a number of merger decisions, the Commission had assumed that the combination of the parties' portfolios of products and brands would lead to serious anticompetitive effects on the basis of the hypothesis that market power deriving from a portfolio of brands exceeded the sum of its parts.[22] This assumption was not (at least not explicitly) based on any recognised economic theory, but on the submissions of competitors and customers[23] and general conjecture.[24] Leveraging, on the other hand, refers to the concern that an undertaking which holds a dominant position in one market could leverage this position into an adjacent market where it is active but does not have a dominant position yet, for example by means of bundling or tying. The Commission used to this hypothesis in two merger prohibitions under Regulation 4064/89.[25] Again, it did not support the leveraging theory by any contemporary economic research into the workings and plausibility of such a business strategy other than a passing reference to the somewhat dated 'Cournot effect of bundling' in the *GE/Honeywell* case that had caused such outrage amongst US commentators.[26]

B. The Commission's Approach after the Introduction of the More Economic Approach

This situation changed with the introduction of the more economic approach. The Commission's Green Paper on Vertical Restraints from 1996,[27] one of the first official documents to signal the Commission's intention to rethink its approach to Article 101, was still quite hesitant about the role that economic theory could and should play in competitive assessments. Amongst others, it was concerned that a

[21] eg *Gencor/Lonrho* (n 17) recital 150; *Saint-Gobain/Wacker-Chemie/NOM* (Case No IV/M.774) [1997] OJ L 247/1, recital 180; *Du Pont/ICI* (n 16) recitals 42–44.

[22] *Guinness/Grand Metropolitan* (n 16) recitals 38–45.

[23] Recital 44 of the Commission's decision in *Guinness/Grand Metropolitan* states: 'In response to the Commission's enquiries, competitors and customers recognised the portfolio effect in practice; for example, of ten firms responding to the question 'does possession of a leading brand in all or most spirit categories help sales of spirits in general?' eight replied that it would help a lot'.

[24] ibid, recitals 38, 44.

[25] *Tetra Laval/Sidel* (n 17) recitals 327–400; *General Electric/Honeywell* (Case COMP/M.2220) [2004] OJ L48/1, recitals 96 ff.

[26] *General Electric/Honeywell* (n 25) recitals 374–76; HR Varian, 'In Europe, GE and Honeywell Ran Afoul of 19th Century Thinking' *New York Times* (28 June 2001) C2.

[27] European Commission, 'Green Paper on Vertical Restraints in EC Competition Policy' COM(96) 721 final, of 22 January 1997, available at: www.europa.eu/documents/comm/green_papers/pdf/com96_721_en.pdf.

state of the art economic evaluation of every individual case would be too costly in terms of resources and lead to legal uncertainty.[28]

Despite this initial note of caution, the Commission has made significant use of economic theory and expert economic input in its enforcement practice under all three pillars of EU antitrust law since the mid-2000s. This is hardly surprising. With the more economic concept of harm, ie restrictions of competition that lead to a reduction of consumer welfare in the form of higher prices, lower output or other forms of consumer harm, the chain of causation between the conduct and the harmful effect has become longer and more complex. For example, while an exclusivity contract used to be considered anticompetitive if it restricted the parties' economic freedom and restricted the opportunities of others to deal with them, the Commission now considers exclusivity contracts anticompetitive only if they result in anticompetitive foreclosure. Rather than merely showing that the terms of the contract restrict the parties' freedom (and this will always be the case), and that the logical consequence of the exclusivity agreement is that other undertakings will not be able to deal with the parties (this will also always be the case), it now needs to prove that an exclusivity agreement will result in the foreclosure of competition, which in its turn needs to result in higher prices, lower output, lower quality products, lower levels of innovation or other detrimental effects on consumer welfare. Proving these effects is much more complex and requires more economic know-how than merely concluding from an exclusivity agreement that the parties have committed not to deal with anyone else. The Commission therefore now regularly relies on economic theory and expert economic input both for developing the general assessment principles outlined in its soft law and for individual assessment.

To this end, DG Competition has had to boost its economic expertise. Generally, the ratio of economists to lawyers working within DG Competition has significantly increased since the turn of the millennium.[29] Since 2003, DG Competition has also had the input of the Chief Competition Economist and his team of industrial economists, whose role is to provide independent guidance on methodological issues of economics and econometrics in the application of the competition rules and to foster the economic debate within DG Competition.[30] The Chief Competition Economist is supported by the European Advisory Group on Competition Policy (EAGCP), whose role is to support DG Competition in improving the economic reasoning in competition policy analyses.[31]

This growing participation of economists in the work of DG Competition is clearly reflected in the Commission's preparatory documents, guidelines and other soft law instruments. They usually explain the theory underlying their approach clearly and in detail. While the final Notices or Communications tend not to cite

[28] ibid, paras 13 and 86.
[29] See Ch 2, s IV.
[30] www.ec.europa.eu/dgs/competition/economist/role_en.html.
[31] www.ec.europa.eu/dgs/competition/economist/eagcp.html.

any precise academic sources for their theories, they use concepts such as inter-brand and intra-brand competition,[32] market power,[33] foreclosure,[34] Herfindahl-Hirschman Index levels,[35] cross-price elasticities and diversion ratios,[36] economies of scale and scope,[37] qualitative efficiencies,[38] free-riding,[39] hold-up problems,[40] externalities,[41] long-run average incremental cost,[42] and demand-related advantages such as network and learning effects,[43] to mention but a few. These are all concepts of economic theory and worlds removed from the Commission's early assessments under the antitrust rules, where the Commission normally limited itself to looking at whether the agreement or unilateral conduct affected the parties' or a third parties' freedom. In individual assessments under Article 101, the Commission previously did not even use to define a market or take into account the parties' economic power in any form whatsoever. A Notice now sets out common principles for defining the relevant market for the purposes of assessments under the EU antitrust rules. These principles integrate key economic concepts such as demand- and supply-side substitutability,[44] the small but significant and non-transitory increase in price (SSNIP) or hypothetical monopolist test,[45] and price elasticities,[46] amongst many others.

The Commission also makes regular use of these theoretical concepts in its decision practice under all three pillars of EU antitrust law. Market definition, for example, has evolved considerably, especially in assessments under Article 102. From the few paragraphs that were deemed sufficient for defining a relevant market in the 1970s and 1980s, often with no attempt at explaining the finding in question,[47] the Commission now regularly carries out extensive market definitions that are not only much more in-depth, meticulous and better supported with evidence, but use the economic concepts set out in the Commission's diverse

[32] European Commission, Guidelines on the Application of Article 81(3) of the Treaty [2004] OJ C101/97, para 17.

[33] ibid, para 25.

[34] ibid, para 26.

[35] Guidelines on the assessment of horizontal mergers under the Council Regulation on the control of concentrations between undertakings [2004] OJ C31/5, paras 19–21.

[36] *Supra*, para 29.

[37] Guidelines on the Application of Article 81(3) (n 32) paras 64–68.

[38] ibid, paras 69–72.

[39] Guidelines on Vertical Restraints [2010] OJ C130/1, para 107(1).

[40] ibid, para 107(4).

[41] ibid, para 107(6).

[42] European Commission, Guidance on the Commission's enforcement priorities in applying Article 82 of the EC Treaty to abusive exclusionary conduct by dominant undertakings [2009] OJ C45/7, para 26.

[43] ibid, para 24.

[44] European Commission, Notice on the definition of the relevant market for the purposes of Community competition law [1997] OJ C372/5, para 13.

[45] ibid, paras 16, 17.

[46] ibid, para 39.

[47] See eg *GVL* (n 3) recital 45; *Hugin/Liptons* (n 12) II.A; *ABG oil companies operating in the Netherlands* (Case IV/28.841) [1977] OJ L117/1, I.D.

guidelines.[48] Market definitions in merger decisions follow the same principles and use the same economic concepts. They are usually even more detailed than those now carried out for Article 102.[49]

The competitive assessments as such, especially those that establish the investigated conduct's actual or likely effects, also generally make ample use of the economic principles set out in the interpretative Notices from 2004 onwards. Across the board, they deal with market power,[50] establish foreclosure effects,[51] apply Herfindahl-Hirschman Index levels,[52] consider cross-price elasticities of demand,[53] economies of scale and scope,[54] other types of efficiencies,[55] free-riding,[56] participation externalities[57] and network externalities,[58] long-run average incremental cost,[59] network and learning effects[60] and customer lock-in effects.[61] The Commission occasionally cites and engages with economic literature to justify the use of certain econometric models or when examining the validity of an economic study submitted by the parties, although this tends to be the exception rather than the rule.[62] All in all, the language of these decisions is very different from that of decisions of the first 40 years, which used classical legal rights-based terminology and dealt with concepts of freedom, individual opportunity and fairness.

III. The Use of Quantitative Analysis

The more economic approach has not only introduced abstract concepts of economic theory, but also a wide variety of practical applications developed by economists. A quantifiable concept of competitive harm, ie a reduction in consumer welfare, and a quantifiable concept of countervailing effects, ie consumer

[48] eg *Motorola—Enforcement of GPRS standard essential patents* (Case AT.39985) recitals 181–220; *Telekomunikacja Polska* (Case COMP/39.525) recitals 579–639.

[49] eg *Ryanair/Aer Lingus* (Case COMP/M.4439) recitals 41–334; *Ryanair/Aer Lingus III* (Case COMP/M.6663) recitals 39–422; *Olympic/Aegean Airlines* (Case COMP/M.5830) recitals 41–377.

[50] eg *Olympic/Aegean Airlines* (n 49) recital 84; *Intel* (Case COMP/C-3 /37.990) recital 837.

[51] eg *España v Telefónica* (Case COMP/38.784) recitals 564 ff; *Microsoft (tying)* (Case COMP/C-3/39.530) recitals 39–54.

[52] eg *Ryanair/Aer Lingus* (n 49) recital 342; *Ryanair/Aer Lingus III* (n 49) 475; *De Beers* (Case COMP/B-2/38.381) recital 24; *Morgan Stanley/Visa International and Visa Europe* (Case COMP/D1/37860) recitals 167.

[53] *AstraZeneca* (Case COMP/A. 37.507/F3) recital 366.

[54] *Intel* (n 50) recitals 1635, 1636; *Ryanair/Aer Lingus III* (n 49) recitals 565–83.

[55] *Intel* (n 50) recitals 1637, 1638; *Olympic/Aegean Airlines* (n 49) recitals 1775–809.

[56] *Groupement des cartes bancaires* 'CB' (Case COMP/D1/38606) recitals 420–26; *Morgan Stanley/Visa International* (n 52) recitals 203–76.

[57] *Deutsche Börse/NYSE Euronext* (Case No COMP/M.6166) recital 1261.

[58] *Telekomunikacja Polska* (n 48) recital 865.

[59] *Wanadoo España v Telefónica* (Case COMP/38.784) recitals 316–24.

[60] *Telekomunikacja Polska* (n 48) recital 604; *Wanadoo España v Telefónica* (n 59) recital 177.

[61] *Reuters Instrument Codes* (Case AT.39654) recital 10; *Motorola* (n 48) recitals 231–36.

[62] See eg *Olympic/Aegean Airlines* (n 49) Annex I; *Ryanair/Aer Lingus III* (n 49) Annex II.

welfare-enhancing efficiency effects, downright invite quantitative analysis, and the Commission decisions of the past 10 years do not disappoint in this respect.

A. The Use of Quantitative Analysis in the Commission's Decision Practice

Prior to the reform, quantitative analysis was very rare in the Commission's decision practice. In a handful of assessments under the old Merger Regulation, the Commission had carried out price correlation analyses for the purposes of establishing the substitutability of two products in the context of market definition.[63] Very occasionally, the parties would submit econometric studies to support their defence in merger cases, none of which the Commission ever found convincing or relevant.[64]

By contrast, the guidelines spelling out the more economic approach to Article 101 and the EU Merger Regulation, as well as the Guidance on the Commission's new enforcement priorities to Article 102, explicitly state that the Commission may make use of quantitative analysis in certain cases, although they do not describe this as being compulsory.[65] The merger guidelines also strongly recommend that the investigated undertakings demonstrate efficiencies and the resulting benefit to consumers in quantitative analyses when making an efficiency defence.[66]

The use of quantitative analysis in individual assessments has since become common practice under all three pillars of EU antitrust law, in particular in major infringement and prohibition decisions. Econometric techniques do not directly determine the competitive nature of conduct. However, they allow the Commission to prove quantifiable facts and causal relationships that are relevant in the assessment of the conduct. It is therefore an evidentiary instrument, rather than one that takes the place of the legal assessment. Following the US Antitrust Revolution, econometrists developed many such tools specifically for the purposes of antitrust assessments, ranging from relatively 'simple' correlation analyses to highly complex econometric procedures, simulations and laboratory experiments.[67] Since the introduction of the more economic approach, these instruments have also found

[63] *Gencor/Lonrho* (n 17) recital 53; *Nestlé/Perrier* (n 20) recital 16.

[64] *Guinness/Grand Metropolitan* (n 16) recital 126; *Airtours/First Choice* (n 19) recital 154.

[65] eg Guidelines on 81(3) (n 32) para 109; Guidance on the Commission's enforcement priorities in applying Article 82 (n 42) paras 19, 27, 45.

[66] Horizontal merger guidelines (n 35) para 86.

[67] See eg S Bishop and M Walker, *The Economics of EC Competition Law: Concepts, Application and Measurement*, 3rd edn (London, Sweet and Maxwell, 2010) pt 3; P Davis and E Garcés, *Quantitative Techniques for Competition and Antitrust Analysis* (Princeton, Princeton University Press, 2010); DL Rubinfeld, 'Quantitative Methods in Antitrust' (2008) 1 *Issues in Competition Law and Policy* 723; I Lianos and C Genakos, 'Econometric Evidence in EU Competition Law: an Empirical and Theoretical Analysis' *CLES Working Paper Series* 6/2012.

their way into the Commission's assessments under the EU antitrust rules. Over the past 10 years, the Commission has thus used quantitative analysis to prove the costs of an undertaking;[68] the substitutability of services or products in the eyes of consumers,[69] that the acquired undertaking exercised an important competitive constraint on the acquiring undertaking's pricing policy;[70] that a certain conduct was likely to result in foreclosure[71] or affect prices;[72] that an undertaking had the incentive to foreclose;[73] and that an equally efficient competitor could operate profitably if it were to meet the dominant undertaking's prices,[74] amongst others. Regression analyses are the type of quantitative analysis most commonly used by the Commission.

Indeed, quantitative analysis has now become such common practice that the Commission saw the necessity to justify itself for not using any quantitative tools in the case of *Deutsche Börse/NYSE Euronext*. The parties had criticised the Commission for failing to use any of the 'many quantitative instruments in its tool box', such as cross-price elasticity analysis, critical loss analysis, regression analysis, price correlation analysis, stationarity tests, shock analysis, co-integration analysis, merger simulation, own-price elasticity analysis, analysis of survey evidence, natural experiment analysis and supply-side substitution analysis.[75] The Commission therefore explained in some detail why it did not consider any of these tools appropriate in this case.[76]

Finally, the parties themselves now also regularly hire economic consultants to support their defence by means of econometric analyses. The Commission tends to engage with these studies in detail in final decisions, and normally analyses them as to the validity of the model and data used. In fact, the parties appear to commission and use econometric analyses in support of their arguments more often than the Commission itself.[77] DG Competition therefore issued a Staff working paper on how best to present economic evidence in antitrust proceedings.[78] That being

[68] *Sea-Invest/EMO-EKOM* (Case COMP/M.3848) recital 41.

[69] *Ryanair/Aer Lingus III* (n 49) recital 111 and Annex I.

[70] *Ryanair/Aer Lingus III* (n 49) recitals 607–24, Annex III; *Ryanair/Aer Lingus I* (n 49) recitals 463–68, 481, 488, Annex IV; *IAG/BMI* (Case No COMP/M.6447) recital 283.

[71] *Telekomunikacja Polska* (n 48) recitals 820 88.

[72] *MasterCard* (Case COMP/34.579) *EuroCommerce* (Case COMP/36.518), and *Commercial Cards* (Case COMP/38.580) ('Mastercard I') recitals 425–36; *Telekomunikacja Polska* (n 48) recitals 820–72; *Volvo/Scania* (Case No COMP/M.1672) [2001] OJ L143/74, recitals 72–74.

[73] *TomTom/Tele Atlas* (Case COMP/M.4854) recitals 221–28.

[74] *Wanadoo España v Telefónica* (n 59) recitals 325–542, and *Intel* (n 50) recitals 1156–576.

[75] *Deutsche Börse/NYSE Euronext* (n 57) recital 247.

[76] ibid, recitals 247–52.

[77] eg *Intel* (n 50) recitals 1065 ff; *AstraZeneca* (n 53) recitals 347 ff; *Wanadoo España v Telefónica* (n 59) recitals 606 ff; *Prokent-Tomra* (Case COMP/E-1/38.113) recitals 364–90; *Groupement des cartes bancaires* 'CB' (n 56) recitals 433–45; *Mastercard I* (n 72) 252 ff; *Olympic/Aegean* (n 49) recitals 227–49; *Ryanair/Aer Lingus I* (n 49) recitals 433 ff.

[78] European Commission, 'DG Competition Staff working paper on Best Practices for the submission of economic evidence and data collection in cases concerning the application of Articles 101 and 102 TFEU and merger cases', www.ec.europa.eu/competition/antitrust/legislation/best_practices_submission_en.pdf.

said, the Commission is rarely convinced by the econometric studies submitted by the parties. In none of the above-cited cases did the Commission find the parties' quantitative analyses convincing. In *UPS/TNT*, in which the parties submitted five econometric studies, the Commission even used the evidence contained in these studies to prove that the planned merger would result in price increases, which led it to prohibit the merger as incompatible with the internal market.[79]

B. The Significance of Quantitative Analysis in the Commission's Decision Practice

The above findings do not mean that quantitative analysis has entirely replaced qualitative analysis in the Commission's analyses. In the beginning, the Commission was even hesitant to accord any weight to its quantitative studies at all. In the *Volvo/Scania* case from 2001, for example, the Commission requested an econometric study from two economic experts, which pointed to 'serious competition problems' in the relevant market. Nonetheless, the Commissions decided not to use the findings of this merger simulation because the parties contested its validity and because it recognised that using this type of study was a 'relatively new development in European merger control'.[80]

In subsequent years, however, it increasingly began to rely on quantitative analyses in addition to qualitative assessments. In *Ryanair/Aer Lingus I* and *Ryanair/Aer Lingus III*, for example, it carried out substantial price regression analyses and found that these 'confirmed and complemented' the findings of the qualitative analysis.[81] In other cases, it carried out both qualitative and quantitative assessments of relevant chains of causation, and left their respective weight open, as they both reached the same conclusions.[82] It is rare, but not unprecedented, that the Commission relies on quantitative analysis alone to establish a relevant fact. This was the case in *Wanadoo España vs Telefónica*, where the Commission carried out complex econometric calculations to establish whether an equally efficient competitor would have been excluded from the market as a consequence of the dominant undertaking's pricing.[83] The outcome of this exercise was decisive for the Commission finding the conduct abusive. Likewise, in *TomTom/Tele Atlas*, the Commission relied exclusively on its calculations to conclude that a foreclosure

[79] *UPS/TNT Express* (Case COMP/M.6570) recitals 725–40.

[80] *Volvo/Scania* (n 72) recitals 72–75.

[81] *Ryanair/Aer Lingus I* (n 49) recital 489; *Ryanair/Aer Lingus III* (n 49) recital 625. In *Ryanair/Aer Lingus I*, it discounted the findings of its cross-section regression analyses on the grounds that they were not sufficiently robust (*Ryanair/Aer Lingus I* (n 49) recital 468).

[82] *Telekomunikacja Polska* (n 48) recitals 820–28; *MasterCard I* (n 72) recitals 425–36; *IAG/BMI* (n 70) recital 283.

[83] *Wanadoo España v Telefónica* (n 59) recitals 325–542.

strategy would not be profitable and that the undertaking in question was therefore unlikely to pursue it.[84] However, in the majority of cases in which the Commission carried out quantitative assessments, it supported the relevant findings with both quantitative and qualitative analyses.

While the use of quantitative analysis is thus no longer a rarity in antitrust decisions, the Commission does not employ it in every case, and not even in every prohibition decision. There is not actually a great deal of scope for econometric analysis in the competitive assessment of cartels, the key type of case pursued by the Commission these days, because their anticompetitive effects are presumed. In the context of cartels, quantitative analysis could theoretically be used for the purposes of calculating the fine, but the Commission itself tends not to use sophisticated quantitative techniques to determine the fine.[85] Even in cases in which the Commission assesses the investigated conduct as to its actual or likely effects, ie mergers, agreements that are not restrictive by object and abusive conduct, it does not always use econometric analysis. To date, the Commission has prohibited five mergers on the basis of the new Merger Regulation. It carried out quantitative assessments to establish key facts in three of these.[86] In the other two cases it did not, although it engaged with the calculations submitted by the parties in great detail.[87] Out of the four Article 102 infringement decisions since 2009, two made use of quantitative analysis to establish relevant facts.[88] The other two did not.[89] Finally, only one of the 11 non-cartel infringement decisions under Article 101 since 2000 used econometric analysis to prove key facts.[90] The other 10[91] primarily relied on qualitative analysis and did not use any econometric tools beyond organising quantitative information in tables.[92] That being said, the majority of these 11 non-cartel cases concerned object restrictions,[93] which the Commission does not assess as to its actual effects. Again, this greatly reduces the scope for quantitative analysis.

[84] *TomTom/Tele Atlas* (n 73) recitals 211–30.

[85] By contrast, parties have been known to submit econometric studies for the purpose of calculating the fine, which the Commission engaged with in the decision (eg *Copper Plumbing Tubes* (Case COMP/E-1/38.069) recitals 632, 655–66).

[86] *Ryanair/Aer Lingus III* (n 49) recitals 607–24, Annex III; *Ryanair/Aer Lingus I* (n 49) recitals 463–68, 481, 488, Annex IV; *UPS/TNT Express* (n 79) recital 934.

[87] *Olympic/Aegean* (n 49) and *Deutsche Börse/NYSE Euronext* (n 57).

[88] *Telekomunikacja Polska* (n 48) recitals 820–72; *Intel* (n 50) recitals 1156–576.

[89] *Romanian Power Exchange/OPCOM* (Case AT.39984); and *Motorola—Enforcement of GPRS standard essential patents* (n 48).

[90] *Mastercard I* (n 72) recitals 425–36.

[91] *Glaxo Wellcome and others* (Case IV/36.957/F3); *Souris–Topps* (Case COMP/C-3/37.980) recital 48; *CISAC* (Case COMP/C2/38.698); *Morgan Stanley/Visa International and Visa Europe* (Case COMP/D1/37860); *Telefónica/Portugal Telecom* (Case AT.39839); *Lundbeck* (Case AT.39226); *Fentanyl* (Case AT.39685); *ONP* (Case 39510); *SEP et autres/Peugeot SA* (Cases F-2/36.623/36.820/37.275).

[92] However, in *Groupement des cartes bancaires*, the Commission also calculated the additional cost imposed on new entrants by the agreement (*Groupement des cartes bancaires* (n 56) recitals 265–77).

[93] See Ch 7.

IV. More Empirical Evidence

When comparing Commission decisions from the period prior to the more economic approach with the decisions of the last 15 years, there is one further change in methodology that cannot be ignored. Today's assessments are far better supported with empirical evidence than assessments from the 1960s–90s. Whereas competitive assessments under Article 101 and 102 in particular used to rely primarily on the terms of the investigated agreements,[94] the Commission nowadays supports its assumptions and predictions more thoroughly and carefully with a wide array of empirical evidence.[95]

This is a clear change in methodology that occurred around the time of the introduction of the more economic approach. Nonetheless, the author hesitates to qualify this development as a purely economic phenomenon that would not, and could not, have been achieved in the absence of the changes of interpretation introduced by the more economic approach. Any legal assessment, regardless of the concept of harm and test, should be based on solid evidence, and this always requires empirical evidence rather than pure conjecture. The General Court made this very clear in the three annulment judgments of 2002, when it not only criticised the decisions' vagueness and logical inconsistencies, but also the lack of cogent evidence.[96] The Commission made the necessary changes. This is a very positive development. However, it is a change that could theoretically also have been achieved without adopting the consumer welfare aim, reinterpreting key concepts and using quantitative methods of assessment. An economic interpretation of the law is not a prerequisite for an adequate standard of proof. Any legal assessment should always be well supported with evidence.

[94] eg *Nederlandse Cement-Handelmaatschappij NV* (Case IV/595) [1972] OJ L22/16, recitals 7, 8; *SABA's EEC distribution system* (Case IV/29.598) [1983] OJ L376/41, II.A.2; *British Dental Trade Association–BDTA* (Case IV/31.593) [1988] OJ L233/15, recitals 22, 23; *Miller International Schallplatten GmbH* (Case IV/29.018) [1976] OJ L357/40, recitals 9–17; *Continental/Michelin* (Case No IV/32.173) [1988] OJ L305/33, recitals 13–16.

[95] See eg, in comparison, *Groupement des cartes bancaires* (n 56) recitals 193–374; *Mastercard I* (n 72) recitals 400–665; *AstraZeneca* (n 53) recitals 512–862; *Motorola* (n 48) recitals 179–420.

[96] In *Airtours*, the Court described the Commission's description of the competitive situation as being 'elliptical', and held that, as well as being vitiated by errors of assessment and incompatible with economic theory, it was insufficiently supported with evidence (Case T-342/99 *Airtours plc v Commission* ECLI:EU:T:2002:146, paras 75, 120, 174 and 295). In *Schneider-Legrand*, it found that the Commission had committed multiple errors in the analysis of the concentration's impact, and that it had, once again, failed to provide convincing evidence in support of key assumptions, which the Court deemed to be of 'undoubted gravity' (Case T-310/01 *Schneider Electric SA v Commission* ECLI:EU:T:2002:254, para 404). Finally, in *Tetra Laval*, it struck down the Commission's prohibition decision because of manifest errors of assessment and a 'lack of cogent evidence' (Case T-5/02 *Tetra Laval BV v Commission* ECLI:EU:T:2002:264, paras 137, 214, 235, 251, 261, 275, amongst many others).

V. The Length of Decisions

Finally, all of the developments described in this and the previous chapters have had one further, very visible consequence. The new, quantifiable concepts of harm and countervailing effects, the more complex chains of cause and effect, and the commitment to demonstrating these effects in every single case by means of quantitative qualitative assessments supported by a wide variety of evidence have resulted in much longer decisions. While the average length of an Article 101 decision of the 1970s was just under 10 DIN A4-pages, a non-cartel infringement decision post-2004 now averages 157 pages.[97] The same trend can be observed under the other two pillars. The average length of an Article 102 infringement decision between 1971 and 1998 was around 19 pages.[98] Since the beginning of the reform in 2005, Article 102 infringement decisions have averaged 216 pages.[99] Merger prohibitions in the 1990s were on average just under 36 pages long,[100] whereas prohibition decisions on the basis of the new Merger Regulation have spanned an average of 465 pages to date.[101] These are impressive leaps. They are most likely mirrored by equally impressive increases in the amount of resources that go into preparing and writing these decisions.

VI. Conclusion

In addition to changing the interpretation of the EU antitrust rules, economic theory has also provided the Commission with a number of practical tools for carrying out assessments under the newly defined rules. In comparison to its decisions of the first 40 years, the Commission now regularly makes use of abstract economic theory to design its secondary legislation and soft law, and to support its theories of harm individual cases. It also frequently employs econometric tools in individual assessments to prove key facts and chains of causation, in particular in cases in which it assesses the effects of the relevant conduct on competition and consumer welfare. Finally, it is noticeable that the quantity and quality of empirical evidence used by the Commission in support of its assumptions has greatly improved since 2002. Altogether these changes have resulted in greatly increasing the dimensions of infringement decisions.

[97] See Annex, Tables 1 and 2.
[98] See Annex, Table 3.
[99] See Annex, Table 4.
[100] See Annex, Table 5.
[101] See Annex, Table 6.

Conclusions on Part II

What then is the more economic approach to EU antitrust law? The more economic approach can be defined as the Commission's interpretation and application of the EU antitrust rules in a way that is guided by the key values, theoretical concepts and practical applications of contemporary mainstream economics. It has led the Commission to make significant changes to its interpretation of the law and its assessment methods.

The key to the Commission's more economic interpretation of the law lies in its new understanding of the antitrust rules' purpose. During the first 40 years of EU antitrust law, the Commission did not operate on the basis of a clearly and exhaustively defined legal objective. On the contrary, it took the view that the aims of EU antitrust law could not be encapsulated by one sole objective, but that it pursued a multitude of economic, political and social aims, including market integration, economic growth, the competitiveness of the European economy, the fairness of the competitive process, the protection of individual commercial freedom, the protection of the democratic process against the abuse of private economic power, the interests of society as a whole, the interests of consumers, industrial policy aims, employment, the fundamental Union objectives and, as of the mid-1980s, also innovation and efficiency. The more economic approach changed this position radically. It is based on the principle that EU antitrust law should be guided by the objective of economic theory, namely the creation of economic wealth, to the exclusion of any other aim. However, the Commission chose to adopt a more restrictive concept of economic wealth than that favoured by economic theory, and decided that EU antitrust law should be guided by the aim of enhancing consumer welfare rather than total welfare. This decision reflects a social choice that is not entirely in line with pure economic theory. The Commission also made a further compromise that is not entirely compatible with a pure economic welfare objective: in addition to the consumer welfare aim, the objective of market integration remains a separate objective of EU antitrust law.

This development, while raising many fascinating philosophical questions, is not only of interest to politicians and the ivory tower. It has led the Commission to make significant changes to its interpretation of key legal concepts under all three pillars of EU antitrust law.

First, it changed its understanding of what makes conduct anticompetitive and adopted new concepts of competitive harm, at least under Article 101 and the EU Merger Regulation. Prior to the reform, the Commission used to consider agreements anticompetitive within the meaning of Article 101 if they restricted competition, which it considered to be the case if the agreement restricted any market participant's commercial freedom or opportunity. Since adopting the (almost) exclusive consumer welfare aim, the Commission reads Article 101 as prohibiting only such restrictions of competition that are likely to result in a tangible reduction of consumer welfare, in the form of higher prices, less output, less choice, lower quality or lower levels of innovation. Restrictions of competition that impede cross-border trade, and are therefore deemed to obstruct the process of market integration, also remain caught by Article 101. The Commission's concept of competitive harm under EU merger law was conceptually unclear prior to the introduction of the more economic approach. Now, in line with its new reading of Article 101, it deems mergers anticompetitive only if they result in a lessening of competition that will or is likely to result in consumer harm. At least in the context of non-horizontal mergers, it had previously deemed the mere exclusion of competitors sufficient to make the transaction anticompetitive. In sum, the Commission has read a consumer harm requirement into both Article 101 and the EU Merger Regulation.

The situation under Article 102 is more complicated. The Commission clearly had the aspiration to introduce the same changes to this provision. Prior to the review, it had had a broad understanding of what constituted competitive harm under Article 102, in line with its early reading of Article 101. The exclusion of actual or potential competitors from the market, discriminatory and unfair conduct, and the creation of obstacles to market integration were all deemed instances of competitive harm within the meaning of the provision. In order to bring its interpretation of Article 102 into holding with its more economic reading of Articles 101 and the EU Merger Regulation, it would have had to read a consumer harm requirement into Article 102 as well. The ambition was clearly there. However, putting it into action was complicated by the fact that the European Court of Justice repeatedly ruled that direct consumer harm is not a requirement of this provision. Instead of changing its interpretation of Article 102, as it did under the two other pillars, the Commission therefore ended up revising its enforcement priorities. It will simply no longer enforce Article 102 in cases in which consumer welfare is not likely to be negatively affected. In practice, this achieves the same result as a reinterpretation of the provision: business conduct that is not likely to affect consumer welfare will no longer be prohibited and fined, even if it affects competitors.

The second change in interpretation concerns the types of benefit the Commission deems capable of offsetting the investigated conduct's anticompetitive effects. As a consequence of adopting the consumer welfare objective, the Commission now takes the view that competitive harm can be offset by economic efficiency effects that are passed on to consumers to such an extent as to cancel out the reduction in consumer welfare. If that is the case, the conduct should not be deemed anticompetitive. In the context of Article 101, this balancing exercise is carried out by using the mechanism of Article 101(3). In EU merger review, economic efficiencies are now considered one of the many relevant factors that should be taken into account in the overall assessment to determine whether the merger is likely to result in an impediment to effective competition. In the context of Article 102, the Commission uses the concept of an objective justification.

This is an important change in interpretation. Prior to the reform, the Commission had been undecided as to whether it was legally permissible to take into consideration efficiency effects as countervailing factors in merger assessments. In practice, it had never recognised an efficiency defence as founded in the handful of cases in which the parties attempted such a defence, and even considered the creation of efficiencies anticompetitive in a number of cases. By contrast, under Article 102 it had always recognised, in principle at least, that abusive conduct could be objectively justified on the basis of an open-ended list of legitimate aims. However, in practice, only one efficiency defence had ever been attempted under Article 102, unsuccessfully at that, prior to the reform. Under Article 101(3), the Commissions had often taken into account efficiencies as countervailing factors, without necessarily using the technical term 'efficiency', alongside a wide variety of other socially, economically and environmentally beneficial effects even prior to the review. Insofar, the idea that efficiency effects should be able to offset an agreement's anticompetitive effects was not new under Article 101. However, the innovation was that the more economic approach made efficiencies the only type of beneficial effect capable of offsetting competitive harm under Article 101(3). The Commission now no longer takes into account any other benefits than quantifiable cost or qualitative efficiencies under this provision. The Commission's current legal position on non-efficiency effects as countervailing factors under Article 102 is somewhat unclear. The Guidance, while not an interpretative document, suggests that the Commission formally continues to deem public policy benefits capable of justifying abusive conduct in principle, but that it is unlikely to consider them indispensable in practice. Again, the Commission's reform of Article 102 has formally not gone as far as that of Article 101. In practice, however, a public policy defence is just as unlikely to succeed under Article 102 as it is under Article 101 and the Merger Regulation.

The third change in interpretation relates to the type of test used to assess whether the investigated business conduct is likely to produce the relevant harmful or beneficial effects. The agenda of the more economic approach had promised to move away from form-based presumptions of illegality to establishing the actual effects of the conduct on the basis of the individual circumstances of each case. The findings on this point are partially quite unexpected. There have been no major changes on this point in the area of EU merger law. Both on the basis of Regulation 4064/89 and Regulation 139/2004, the Commission has always aimed to establish a merger's likely effects and has never relied on form-based presumptions. What has changed is the type of effect investigated, in line with the new concept of harm and countervailing effects, and the type and quality of evidence that the Commission uses to prove these effects. Under Article 101(1), the Commission continues to use both the concept of restriction by object, in which case the anticompetitive effect is presumed, and restrictions by effect, in which case the Commission will assess the likely effects before condemning them. The great majority of types of agreement that were clearly considered restrictive by object prior to the reform continue to be deemed restrictive by object. There has been no major 'overruling' of previous object classifications in the Commission's decision practice under Article 101, as was the case under US antitrust law after the Antitrust Revolution. What is more, the vast majority of infringement decisions since the reform of Article 101 have been cases of object restrictions, in which the Commission presumed the agreements' anticompetitive nature rather than assessed its effects. However, one should not draw the conclusion from this finding that the Commission has broadened its understanding of what constitutes an object restriction and has thus done the exact opposite of what it set out to do in its reform. This phenomenon is better explained as being the result of a combination of other factors: a shift in enforcement priorities and the advent of commitments decisions. Since the decentralisation of the enforcement system in 2004, the Commission has focused on pursuing cartels and other particularly serious restrictions, which have been and continue to be considered restrictions by object. The great majority of other cases investigated by the Commission have been closed by means of commitments decisions, which do not make final assessments under Article 101. In sum, the more economic approach has not significantly affected the Commission's view of what type of restriction should be presumed anticompetitive, and which type of restriction needs to be assessed as to its actual effects under Article 101.

It is under Article 102 that the changes are most significant in practice. They are also the most ambiguous in law. At least it is possible to say with certainty that, in contrast to the situation prior to the reform, the Commission in practice no longer infers the dominant position from the undertaking's market shares or exclusive rights alone. Instead it tends to carry out a detailed analysis of the undertaking's economic strength that takes into account many different factors relevant in determining whether the undertaking will be restrained in the exercise of its economic power. Even if does not always explicitly refer to this as a market power analysis, the assessment contains all the elements of such as analysis in substance. Insofar, its assessments of the position of dominance are now less reliant on legal presumptions.

However, there is a fair degree of uncertainty as to the Commission's current understanding of what type of test Article 102 requires to establish the abuse. Prior to the reform, the Commission's approach to assessing whether conduct was abusive was inconsistent and often unclear. Sometimes, it assessed the conduct as to its effects (on the other undertakings' freedom, opportunities and ability to stay in the market), whereas in other cases, similar types of conduct seemed to be deemed automatically abusive. In yet other cases, the undertaking's intent was deemed crucial. Finally, in many cases, it was simply unclear what type of test the Commission was applying.

Trying to establish the Commission's current approach is complicated by the fact that the Notice concluding the reform of Article 102 is not an interpretative instrument, but only claims to spell out enforcement priorities. At least, it makes very clear that the Commission intends to assess each conduct's likely foreclosure effects in order to decide whether it is an enforcement priority and does not intend to rely on legal presumptions. The infringement decisions of the past 10 years are conceptually somewhat less clear. Again, this is explained by the fact that the Court of Justice considers certain types of exclusionary conduct on the part of a dominant undertaking to be abusive 'by object', and that others merely need to be assessed as to their capacity to foreclose. Despite this case law, DG Competition has clearly been keen to prove the investigated conduct's effects at least in major cases rather than rely on presumptions of illegality. Between 2004 and 2009, it attempted to straddle the line by first assessing the conduct under the test developed in the case law and finding it abusive under these criteria. It then demonstrated in long and complex 'additional' assessments that the conduct also actually had the presumed effects, while emphasising that this additional assessment was not necessary. Since 2010, infringement decisions no longer follow this approach. Instead, they take the view that it is necessary to demonstrate in every case that the investigated conduct is 'capable' of producing anticompetitive effects. They interpret capacity as meaning likelihood, and on that basis carry out very substantial assessments of the conduct's likely effects. This standard is the same as the one the Commission applies when assessing agreements as to their effects under Article 101(1).

Finally, in addition to changing the legal interpretation of the antitrust rules, economic theory has provided the Commission with a number of practical tools for carrying out its assessments under the reinterpreted rules. The Commission now regularly relies on abstract principles of economic theory, in particular industrial organisation, to support its theories of harm and countervailing effects in the design of its soft law and secondary legislation, and in its individual assessments. It now also routinely makes use of econometric tools and other practical applications developed by economists in individual assessments to prove key facts and chains of causation.

The more economic approach has transformed the Commission's competitive assessments to the point of unrecognisability. When reading the Commission's assessment of rebates under Article 102 in *Intel* from 2009, for example, it is very difficult to believe that this emanates from the same institution that assessed the rebate system in *Virgin/British Airways* under the same provision only 10 years earlier.[102] Likewise, if one compares a typical assessment under Article 101 from the first 30 years to a current assessment of an agreement's effects, one will be hard pressed to find many similarities. The Commission operates on the basis of a different concept of harm, a different concept of countervailing effects and uses different tools to prove the former. It has reduced the scope of the prohibitions, the scope of the exemptions and partly changed the nature of the relevant tests. As a result, decisions are also substantially longer. Remarkably, the Commission introduced all of these significant changes by means of soft law and decision practice, rather than formal amendment of the legal rules.

Part III of this book evaluates these changes. It looks at the advantages of the Commission's more economic approach and the concerns that it raises, in particular with regard to its compatibility with the case law.

[102] *Virgin/British Airways* (Case IV/D-2/34.780) [2000] OJ L30/1.

Part III

9

Advantages

I. Introduction

Having identified the key features of the more economic approach and the changes it made to the Commission's enforcement practice, what remains to be done is to cast a critical eye upon the new approach. How sound is it? This chapter starts the process by identifying the strong points of the more economic approach. The following two chapters will look at a number of its weaknesses.

II. Logic and Internal Consistency

The logic and internal consistency of the theoretical principles underlying the more economic approach are compelling. It proposes one concept of harm for all three pillars of EU antitrust law: a lessening of competition that results in a reduction of consumer welfare. It also operates on the basis of the same theories of harm for all three pillars. A lessening of competition likely to result in consumer harm can occur either as a result of coordination between competitors or as a consequence of foreclosure. Moreover, only pro-competitive effects can offset a conduct's anticompetitive effects according to the more economic approach. It defines pro-competitive effects as the polar opposite of anticompetitive effects, namely as the creation of economic welfare that is passed on to consumers. Where the increase in consumer welfare is equal to or exceeds the reduction in consumer welfare, the overall effect must be considered neutral or even pro-competitive, so that there is no reason to prohibit the conduct in question.

This interpretation of the rules is not only internally consistent. It also avoids a number of logical shortcomings of the previous approach. According to the Commission's original interpretation of the antitrust rules, an agreement was restrictive of competition if it restricted the parties' commercial freedom. But do not agreements always restrain the parties' commercial freedom? It is the very purpose of a contract to make the parties' commitments to act (or forebear to act) in a certain way legally binding. A legally binding contract therefore necessarily restricts the parties' freedom to act as they see fit on the points covered by the agreement. If one therefore applied the Commission's early position to the letter, any agreement would be restrictive of competition. In order to make this approach work, one would have to add a limiting factor, for example, require the restriction of the parties' commercial freedom to relate to aspects that are fundamental to competition. However, that only raises the further question of how to determine what elements of an undertaking's commercial autonomy are fundamental to competition. Pricing, output and choice of customers come to mind. However, this kind of approach would amount to relying on primarily form-based rules again, with all the shortcomings (lack of precision and loopholes) that these entail. An understanding of competitive harm that is dependent on a specific, measurable outcome in the market avoids these problems.

That being said, in practice, the Commission's more economic approach is not 100 per cent consistent with the highly logical principles outlined above. First, there is the problem of Article 102. Reality is that the Commission has not achieved the same results in its reform of Article 102 as it did with regard to Article 101 and EU merger law. It has not officially changed its legal interpretation of Article 102, but has merely adapted its enforcement priorities. It dutifully cites the old legal concepts developed by the Court, which are incompatible with the more economic approach, but then does something quite different in substance. This significantly undermines the consistency of the approach as it stands. Second, the more economic approach does not faithfully adhere to an exclusive consumer welfare objective. It still considers market integration an additional aim of EU antitrust law, at least under Articles 101 and 102. Consequently, it continues to deem practices that are aimed at discouraging cross-border trade within the European Union restrictive of competition, regardless of their effects on consumer welfare. This also undermines the credibility of the exclusive consumer welfare aim and the general consistency of the approach. Why make an exception for the objective of market integration, but not for any of the many other Treaty objectives?

III. Accuracy

The more economic approach has the potential to achieve very precise results. It operates on the basis of clear and largely quantifiable concepts of harm and countervailing effects. Changes in consumer welfare, at least insofar as they occur in the form of higher prices and lower output, are quantifiable in theory. Deteriorations in the quality of products may also be measurable to some extent. Quantifying a decline in innovation, the fourth parameter of consumer welfare used by the Commission, may be more difficult. However, in particular in the case of price increases and output reductions, the new consumer welfare-based concept of harm makes it possible for the enforcement agency to gain a relatively accurate idea of the magnitude of the restriction's impact, at least when it assesses the conduct as to its actual effects rather than relying on 'object' rules. What is more, economists have developed many econometric tools designed for predicting and quantifying exactly these types of effects.

This comes in particularly useful, for example, when balancing anticompetitive effects against countervailing effects. Cost efficiencies can also be expressed in monetary terms, and in practice the Commission is normally only prepared to take cost savings into account where they have been quantified by the parties. Accurately translating qualitative efficiencies into monetary terms may be less straightforward. However, at least when balancing a restriction of competition that could be expected to result in higher prices against cost efficiencies that are passed on to consumers, one should be able to expect an accurate result as to whether consumers are suffering a loss as a result of the conduct in question. By contrast, such precision seems nigh impossible under the old approach. How does one accurately balance a restriction of individual economic freedom against, say, cost savings or environmental benefits?

This being said, even the Commission's reformed approach has its limitations in terms of accuracy. First, as mentioned before, not every instance of consumer harm found by the Commission consists in a price increase. Its understanding of consumer harm is broader, and also includes decreases in variety, quality, choice and levels of innovation.[1] It further considers barriers to market integration a form of competitive harm regardless of the actual effects on consumer welfare. These forms of competitive harm are less easily quantified, and less easily balanced accurately against cost savings. Also, not every efficiency is a cost efficiency. Balancing qualitative efficiencies against price increases is less straightforward than balancing potential price increases against cost savings.

Moreover, even the use of mathematics does not necessarily guarantee the 'correct' result. Not every econometric model is beyond doubt, as the Commission's decision practice amply demonstrates. It is very common for the parties to submit detailed quantitative studies prepared by respectable economic experts, which the Commission's own economic experts find entirely unconvincing.[2] In fact, the Commission and parties usually fail to agree on the quantification of the diverse effects already, and tend not even to reach the stage of balancing them against each other. As demonstrated in Chapter 8, there is not a single documented case under any of the three pillars of EU antitrust law, in which the Commission had serious competition concerns and found the parties' quantification of efficiency effects sufficiently convincing to take them into account. The situation is

[1] See eg Guidelines on the application of Article 81(3) of the Treaty [2004] OJ C101/97, para 24; *Microsoft* (Case COMP/C-3/37.792), recitals 693–701; *Deutsche Börse/NYSE Euronext* (Case No COMP/M.6166) recitals 527–31.

[2] eg *Ryanair/Aer Lingus III* (Case No COMP/M.6663) recital 114, Annex II; *Intel* (Case COMP/C-3/37.990) recitals 1065 ff; *AstraZeneca* (Case COMP/A.37.507/F3) recitals 461–87; *Wanadoo España v Telefónica* (Case COMP/38.784) recitals 607–09; *Prokent-Tomra* (Case COMP/E-1/38.113) recitals 364–90; *Groupement des cartes bancaires* 'CB' (Case COMP/D1/38606) recitals 433–45; *Olympic/Aegean* (Case COMP/M.5830) recitals 232–68.

no different in the United States, where quantitative analysis has been used on a regular basis since the 1990s, and where it is equally common that both sides present apparently sound but entirely contradictory analyses.[3] Finally, even where it is possible for economists to agree on the correct theoretical model, a quantitative analysis can only yield the correct result if the data used captures the real market situation. Outcomes can easily be manipulated by using selective data.[4] In other words, even the use of econometric tools does not necessarily guarantee the correct, let alone an undisputed, result.

IV. More Empirical Evidence

The improvement in the quality and quantity of evidence used by the Commission to support its assumptions in competitive assessments under all three pillars of EU antitrust law can only be applauded. However, as argued in the previous chapter, while this development happened around the same time as the increased reliance on the aims and tools of economic theory, the use of empirical evidence is not dependent on a welfare-based interpretation of the law or the use of econometric tools. It is not a consequence of 'more economics' and therefore not a benefit that is specific to the more economic approach.

V. Reduction in the Number of Cases Caught by the Antitrust Provisions

The Commission's more economic approach has had the effect of reducing the number of cases caught by the EU antitrust provisions. It has reinterpreted Article 101 and the EU Merger Regulation restrictively by reading a market power requirement into their prohibition provisions. While it has not explicitly done the same for Article 102, it has achieved the same result in practice by reformulating its enforcement priorities in a restrictive manner: it simply no longer applies Article 102 in cases in which the dominant undertaking's conduct is not likely to result in consumer harm. Hence, fewer cases are now caught by the EU antitrust rules than prior to the reform. Interestingly, the introduction of the more economic approach happened around the time when the Commission,

[3] D Scheffmann and M Coleman, 'FTC Perspectives on the Use of Econometric Analysis in Antitrust Cases' in JD Harkrider and D Rubinfeld (eds), *Econometrics: Legal, Practical and Technical Issues* (Chicago, ABA Publishing, 2005).

[4] L-H Röller, 'Economic Analysis and Competition Policy Enforcement in Europe' in PAG van Bergeijk and E Kloosterhuis (eds), *Modelling European Mergers* (Cheltenham, Edward Elgar, 2005).

overstretched with the enforcement of Article 101, initiated a review of the procedural rules in order to ease the administrative burden.[5]

The procedural reform addressed the issue by decentralising public enforcement to a greater degree than had been the case previously.[6] Regulation 1/2003, the 'Modernisation Regulation', empowered the national competition authorities to enforce both Article 101 and Article 102 in their entirety alongside the Commission. Simultaneously, the Commission announced its intention to refocus its resources on pursuing the most serious infringements.[7] The enforcement of the Merger Regulation, however, remains the sole prerogative of the Commission.

The substantive reform brought about by the more economic approach, which reduced the scope of the provisions, further helped alleviate the burden of the Commission—as well as that of the national enforcement authorities, by reducing the number of cases caught by the EU antitrust provisions. Using limited public resources efficiently by focusing the enforcement on the most serious cases is sensible. Also, as argued previously, under the Commission's early freedom-based approach, almost any contract between undertakings was doomed to be caught by Article 101(1). This was an unreasonable result and clearly not what Article 101 intended.

That being said, adopting a welfare-based concept of harm is not the only possible way of filtering out less serious cases. In fact, even prior to the reform, the Commission corrected the consequences of its broad freedom-based concept of harm by means of a restrictive interpretation. The *de minimis* rule serves the very purpose of excluding cases that are likely to have only a negligible impact on competition and inter-state trade from the scope of Article 101. Since the Court established the principle in 1969,[8] it has become a standard instrument in the Commission's decision practice. The Commission has since issued successive sets of guidelines that have attempted to quantify the concept of insignificance for the purposes of Article 101, and have created increasingly generous safe harbours for agreements between undertakings with relatively low market shares and turnovers.[9] While market shares and turnovers are blunt instruments for making

[5] European Commission, 'White Paper on modernisation of the rules implementing Articles 85 and 86 of the EC Treaty' [1999] OJ C132/1, paras 5 and 6.

[6] Prior to the reform, the national competition authorities had had the power to apply Art 101(1), but not Art 101(3), which was the prerogative of the Commission. This procedural peculiarity made the enforcement of Art 101(1) by the national authorities impracticable.

[7] European Commission, White Paper on modernisation of the rules implementing Articles 85 and 86 of the EC Treaty (n 5) paras 9 and 10; European Commission, *Report On Competition Policy (2004) Vol 1* 14.

[8] Case 5/69 *Völk v Vervaecke* ECLI:EU:C:1969:35, paras 5–7.

[9] European Commission, Bekanntmachung der Kommission vom 27. Mai 1970 über Vereinbarungen, Beschlüsse und aufeinander abgestimmte Verhaltensweisen von geringer Bedeutung [1970] OJ C64/1; Commission Notices concerning agreements of minor importance of 19 December 1977 [1977] OJ C 313/3; of 3 September 1986 [1986] OJ C 231/2; of 19 December 1997 [1997] OJ C 372/13;

predictions about whether a conduct will have merely insignificant effects on the market, they have the advantage of being relatively easy and cheap to apply. Assessing whether an agreement is likely to result in consumer harm, by contrast, is a less straightforward exercise.

In sum, while the reduction in the scope of Article 101 and the Merger Regulation may have had the welcome effect for the Commission of reducing the number of cases potentially caught by these provisions and thus reducing its enforcement burden, this result could also be achieved by other means, for example, the intellectually less scintillating but highly practicable *de minimis* rule or enforcement priorities. In fact, the Commission has retained the *de minimis* safe harbours despite having adopted a more restrictive concept of competitive harm.

VI. Approximation with US Antitrust Law

The Commission's reform has brought its interpretation and application of the EU antitrust rules more into line with the approach of the US antitrust authorities than was the case prior to the reform. As outlined in the previous chapters, US antitrust law has been guided by the consumer welfare aim since the late 1970s,[10] and the US antitrust authorities have considered consumer harm an indispensable component of competitive harm since the 1980s. At least, this is the case under section 1 of the Sherman Act and section 7 of the Clayton Act: if an agreement or merger does not affect consumer welfare in a negative manner, the US FTC and DoJ do not consider it anticompetitive.[11] Their current position on section 2 of the Sherman Act, which outlaws anticompetitive unilateral conduct is somewhat less clear, as there are no interpretative guidelines and the US antitrust authorities have enforced the provision only sparingly since the Antitrust Revolution. Moreover, the US antitrust authorities only consider economic efficiencies capable of counterbalancing anticompetitive effects to the exclusion of any other desirable effect.[12] Again, the more economic approach has brought the Commission's interpretation of the EU

of 22 December 2001 [2001] OJ C368/13; Notice on agreements of minor importance which do not appreciably restrict competition under Article 101(1) of the Treaty on the Functioning of the European Union (De Minimis Notice) [2014] OJ C291/1.

[10] eg *Reiter v Sonotone Corp*, 442 U.S. 330, 343 (1979); *Brooke Group Ltd v Brown & Williamson Tobacco Corp* 509 U.S. 209, 221 (1993); *NCAA v Board of Regents of the University of Oklahoma*, 468 U.S. 85, 107 (1984) for the US Supreme Court. Likewise, *Broadcom Corp v Qualcomm Inc*, 501 F.3d 297, 308 (2007); *Rebel Oil Company, Inc, Auto Flite Oil Company, Inc v Atlantic Richfield Company* 51 F.3d 1421, 1433 (1995).

[11] See eg US Federal Trade Commission and US Department of Justice, Antitrust Guidelines for Collaborations Among Competitors (issued April 2000) s 2.2, and Horizontal Merger Guidelines (issued 19 August 2010) s 1.

[12] US FTC and US DOJ, Antitrust Guidelines for Collaborations Among Competitors (n 11) s 3.36, and Horizontal Merger Guidelines (n 11) s 10.

antitrust rules more or less into line with this position. Finally, the use of econometric analysis, now a standard tool of assessments under EU antitrust law, has been common practice in US antitrust enforcement since the 1980s.[13] In sum, the more economic approach emulated many of the changes that the Antitrust Revolution had brought to US antitrust law 30 years previously. The Commission's interpretation of the EU antitrust rules and its assessment techniques are nowadays much closer to that of its US counterparts than prior to the review.

Irrespective of the substantive merits of the more economic approach, the harmonisation of EU and US antitrust law may have advantages of its own. The United States and European Union are each other's main trading partners.[14] US companies export to and import from Europe. Likewise, European businesses export to and import from the United States. Given the extra-territorial reach of both EU and US antitrust law, this type of business conduct is likely to fall within the scope of both jurisdictions.[15] It is particularly likely in digital markets.

In view of this situation, similar substantive tests, standards and assessment techniques in both jurisdictions create greater legal certainty for the businesses of each jurisdiction. Familiar rules and a clear understanding of what is allowed and what is prohibited may have a positive effect on undertakings' incentives to engage in vigorous competition in the other jurisdiction. Also, given that one and the same business conduct, be it a merger, an agreement or unilateral practice, may caught by both the US and EU antitrust rules, similar substantive standards reduce the chances that the US and EU antitrust authorities will take a different view of the conduct's competitive nature. In theory, at least, it makes another clash à la *GE/Honeywell* less likely. Given the political tension that ensued between the United States and the European Union during that and similar conflicts,[16] this can only be considered a good thing. Indeed, despite a number of parallel investigations into the same conduct by the US and EU antitrust authorities, there have not

[13] See eg L Kaplow, 'Antitrust, Law and Economics, and the Courts' (1987) 50 *Law and Contemporary Problems* 181; DL Rubinfeld, 'Econometrics in the Courtroom' (1985) 85 *Columbia Law Review* 1048, and 'Quantitative Methods in Antitrust' in (2008) 1 *Issues in Competition Law and Policy* 723.

[14] See eg the Commission's Impact Assessment Report on the future of EU-US trade relations of 2013 (European Commission Staff Working Document SWD(2013) 68 final, Impact Assessment Report on the future of EU-US trade relations), and Centre for Economic Policy Research, *Reducing Transatlantic Barriers to Trade and Investment, An Economic Assessment, Final Project Report* (London, March 2013) www.trade.ec.europa.eu/doclib/docs/2013/march/tradoc_150737.pdf. For the most recent figures, see European Commission, Directorate-General for Trade, 'European Union, Trade in goods with USA', available at: www.trade.ec.europa.eu/doclib/docs/2006/september/tradoc_113465.pdf.

[15] Over the past years, the European Commission has investigated the practices of many major US businesses, eg Apple (*E-BOOKS* (Case AT.39847)); Microsoft (*Microsoft* (*tying*) (Case COMP/C-3/39.530)); Google (Cases COMP/C-3/39.740, COMP/C-3/39.775 & COMP/C-3/39.768); and Motorola (CASE AT.39985), to name but a few.

[16] eg the dispute over the *Boeing/McDonnell Douglas* merger in 1997, and later the conflicting approaches to the first *Microsoft* case in 2004 (see Ch 1).

been any outrageously incompatible decisions since the introduction of the more economic approach. This is not to say that such a clash cannot and will not happen again in the future, but similar substantive standards and tests, in theory at least, reduce the likelihood of this happening.

VII. Conclusion

The Commission's more economic approach thus presents a number of real advantages over its prior interpretation and application of the same rules. First and foremost, its key principles are in theory highly logical and consistent. The approach is guided by one well-defined objective, the enhancement of consumer welfare. The concept of competitive harm is clear and quantifiable in that it presupposes a reduction in consumer welfare. The only type of effect that can offset a reduction of consumer welfare is the exact opposite effect: an increase in consumer welfare. Again, this is in theory a quantifiable effect. This interpretation, combined with the commitment to assess a conduct's actual effects before prohibiting it instead of relying on rough rules of thumb, promises great accuracy and minimal errors.

The reality is somewhat less perfect. The Commission makes an exception from the exclusive consumer welfare objective insofar as it still considers the aim of market integration a separate aim of EU antitrust law. Consequently, impediments to market integration remain illegal under the antitrust provisions, regardless of their effects on consumer welfare. This somewhat mars the ideological coherence of the approach. The second problem relates to Article 102, under which the Commission has not implemented the approach to the same degree as under Article 101 and the Merger Regulation. Instead of reinterpreting the law, it has set new enforcement priorities that are bound to achieve the same result in practice. However, it has resulted in a fair degree of legal uncertainty.

Two further consequences of the approach are that it has reduced the scope of the antitrust provisions in a logical manner, and that it has brought the Commission's approach more into line with that of its US counterparts. The former is presumably a very welcome effect for the Commission, which was dealing with an unmanageable caseload prior to the reform. The latter is a positive development insofar as it reduces the likelihood of opposite outcomes in parallel investigations by the EU and US antitrust authorities, thus avoiding political conflict and encouraging international trade.

The following two chapters now to turn to the drawbacks and concerns one may have about the Commission's more economic approach in its current form.

10

Compatibility with the Case Law

I. Introduction

A key concern is the compatibility of the Commission's new approach with the case law of the European Court of Justice. As argued in Part II of this book, the Commission has introduced significant changes to its interpretation of all three provisions of EU antitrust law. It has done so primarily by means of soft law and individual decision practice. However, while the Commission is the primary enforcement body at EU level, it is not the only relevant EU institution in the area of antitrust law. The European Court of Justice has the power to review and strike down Commission decisions in individual actions for annulment.[1] While it grants the Commission a margin of appreciation in matters of economic assessment,[2] it carries out a full review of whether the Commission interpreted the law correctly. The Court also has the task of giving preliminary rulings on the correct interpretation of EU law at the request of national courts.[3] These are binding *erga omnes*, meaning that they are binding on individuals, Member States and the other EU institutions, including the Commission. The Court has established key principles of EU antitrust law in such judicial actions, including the concepts of dominance, special responsibility and other theories that the Commission has been trying to distance itself from because they are not compatible with a welfare-based interpretation of the law.

The question therefore arises in how far the Commission's new interpretation of the law is compatible with the Court's interpretation. This chapter examines the Court of Justice's understanding of the four legal concepts reinterpreted by the Commission: the consumer welfare aim, the consumer welfare-based concepts of harm and countervailing effects, and the rejection of form-based presumptions of illegality under Article 102. It shows that, in contrast to the US Supreme Court, the Court of Justice of the European Union has not fully embraced the exclusive

[1] TFEU, Art 263.

[2] eg Case T-102/96 *Gencor v Commission* ECLI:EU:T:1999:65 paras 164 and 165; Case T-342/99 *Airtours v Commission* ECLI:EU:T:2002:146, para 64; T-175/12 *Deutsche Börse v Commission* ECLI:EU:T:2015:148, para 65.

[3] TFEU, Art 267.

welfare aim and its consequences for the interpretation of the law. The chapter concludes with a few reflections on the implications of this difference of opinion.

II. The Aims of EU Antitrust Law in the Case Law

While there are no cases in which the definition of the legal objective was the main issue, there are a great number of judgments in which the Court referred to the antitrust rules' purpose as a basis for interpreting their wording. From these judgments, it is possible to establish one principle relatively easily: according to the Court, all three prohibition provisions of EU antitrust law pursue the same legal objective.[4] So much is clear. However, what is this common objective? The answer to that question is less straightforward. The Court uses a number of different definitions in its judgments, albeit with recurring themes.

The earliest judgment touching on the legal objective of Article 101 dates from 1966. In *Italian Republic v Council and Commission*, the Court stated that Article 101 aimed to 'bring about the activities of the Community' laid down in former Article 3 EEC, in particular the institution of a system ensuring that competition in the common market was not distorted, as the latter was necessary for realising the common market. It further held that Article 101 should be read in the context of the Treaty's preamble, in particular with reference to its provisions on the 'elimination of barriers' and 'fair competition', both of which it also deemed necessary for achieving a common market.[5] The emphasis in this judgment thus clearly lay on Article 101's role in the creation of a common market. However, the first part of the Court's statement could also be read as meaning that the antitrust rules aimed to facilitate the achievement of all the activities listed in ex Article 3 EEC. In 1966, this list already contained a range of different activities, even if the spectrum was by far not as broad as nowadays. In addition to establishing a system ensuring that competition in the internal market was not distorted, the activities in question included: the coordination of economic policies of Member States; addressing disequilibria in their balances of payments; creating a European Social Fund in order to improve employment opportunities of workers and contribute to the raising of their standard of living; establishing a European investment bank to facilitate the Union's economic expansion; jointly promoting economic and social development; and adopting a common policy in the sphere of agriculture and transport. With each successive Treaties amendment, new, increasingly non-economic activities were added to this list. In 2001, in the version of the Treaty of Nice, Article 3 EC listed 21 very diverse activities. In addition to the original

[4] Case 6/72 *Europemballage and Continental Can v Commission* ECLI:EU:C:1973:22, para 25; Joined Cases 46/87 and 227/88 *Hoechst v Commission* ECLI:EU:C:1989:337, para 25.

[5] Case 32/65 *Italian Republic v Council and Commission* ECLI:EU:C:1966:42, 405.

activities, closely related to the creation of a common market, it included social policy, environmental policy, the strengthening of the competitiveness of Community industry, promoting research and technological development, contributions to the attainment of a high level of health protection, education, training, the flowering of the cultures of the Member States and the strengthening of consumer protection, development cooperation, and measures in the spheres of energy, civil protection and tourism.[6] If the Court's statements in *Italian Republic* were to be understood as meaning that the EU antitrust rules aimed to facilitate all of these activities, they would have had an extraordinarily broad range of legal objectives.

In *Walt Wilhelm*,[7] another antitrust case from the very early days of the Union, the Court was asked to give a ruling on whether national competition authorities were allowed to apply their national antitrust provisions to a situation that the Commission was already investigating under EU antitrust law. The Court held that the application of the EU antitrust rules did not generally preclude the parallel assessment of the situation under the Member States' national rules, because Union and national law considered cartels 'from different points of view'.[8] Whereas Union law regarded them in the light of obstacles that could result for trade between Member States, each body of national legislation proceeded on the basis of considerations peculiar to it and considered cartels only in that context.[9] Article 101's primary objective was to eliminate the obstacles to the free movement of goods within the common market and to confirm and safeguard the unity of that market. In addition, it permitted the Union authorities to carry out certain positive, though indirect, action with a view to 'promoting a harmonious development of economic activities within the whole Community' in accordance with ex Article 2 EEC.[10] Again, the emphasis lay on the internal market project. However, the ruling suggests that Article 101 was also guided by the aim of promoting a harmonious development of economic activities in the Member States. According to ex Article 2 EEC, market integration and the progressive approximation of the Member States' economic policies were the key tools for achieving this aim.[11] The Court used the same definition in two further key judgments of the 1970s. Both in *Commercial Solvents* and in *Hoffmann-La Roche*, it held that prohibitions of Articles 101 and 102 had to be interpreted and applied both in the light of ex Articles 3 EEC's aim of instituting a system ensuring that competition in the common market was not distorted and the aim of promoting a harmonious

[6] Art 3 EC in the version of the Treaty of Nice [2002] OJ C325/33 (consolidated version).

[7] Case 14/68 *Walt Wilhelm and others v Bundeskartellamt* ECLI:EU:C:1969:4.

[8] It qualified this dictum by adding the proviso that the parallel application of the national and the EU antitrust rules must not prejudice the uniform application of the Union antitrust rules throughout the internal market and the full effect of the Commission's decision in the individual case; ibid, para 4.

[9] ibid, para 3.

[10] ibid, para 5.

[11] Case 167/73 *Commission v French Republic* ECLI:EU:C:1974:35, para 18.

development of economic activities throughout the Union.[12] Given the origins of the European Union, and the original tasks of the European Economic Community, this focus on the key tasks of economic integration and harmonisation is hardly surprising.

Other judgments of the first 40 years simply defined the objectives of EU antitrust law by reiterating the wording of ex Article 3 EEC. In these cases, the Court held that the antitrust provisions were 'applications of the general objective of the activities of the Community laid down by Article 3(f)/(g) of the Treaty', ie the institution of a system ensuring that competition in the common market was not distorted.[13] This line of case law is only marginally helpful. While it makes clear that the aim of the antitrust rules is to protect competition, it does not indicate why competition is worth protecting, meaning that the ultimate aim of the rules remains unclear.

In the early 1980s, the Court introduced a new formula to the existing canon. In *National Panasonic*, it held that the function of the Treaty's rules on competition were to prevent competition from being distorted 'to the detriment of the public interest, individual undertakings and consumers', and explained that this interpretation followed from the fourth recital of the preamble to the EEC Treaty, according to which the essential objective of the Union was to improve the living and working conditions of its peoples, from ex Article 3(f) EEC and Articles 101 and 102 themselves.[14] Subsequent cases added to this formula that by preventing competition from being distorted to the detriment of the public interest, individual undertakings and consumers, the antitrust rules ensured 'economic well-being' in the Union.[15] This is a very broad definition of the antitrust rules' aims. Not only does it include the interests of those immediately involved in the economic activity in question, ie consumers and producers in the relevant markets, but it also comprises the public interest and the economic well-being of the entire Union.

In sum, while the Court's list of legal objectives of the first 40 years was less varied than that of the Commission, it was broad and open-ended. It included the creation of a common market, the harmonious development of economic activities throughout the Union, competition as such, the public interest, individual undertakings, consumers and the general economic well-being of the European Union. None of these recurring formulas explicitly designated consumer welfare as the exclusive aim of EU antitrust law. This is not to say that the Court did not

[12] Joined Cases 6/73 and 7/73 *Istituto Chemioterapico Italiano and Commercial Solvents v Commission* ECLI:EU:C:1974:18, para 5; and Case 85/76 *Hoffmann-La Roche v Commission* ECLI:EU:C:1979:36, para 125.

[13] *Europemballage Corporation and Continental Can Company Inc v Commission* (n 4) paras 23–25; Case 27/76 *United Brands v Commission* ECLI:EU:C:1978:22, para 63; *Hoffmann-La Roche v Commission* (n 12) para 38; Case 322/81 *NV Nederlandsche Banden Industrie Michelin v Commission* ECLI:EU:C:1983:313, para 29; *Gencor Ltd v Commission* (n 2) para 8.

[14] Case 136/79 *National Panasonic v Commission* ECLI:EU:C:1980:169, para 20; Joined Cases 46/87 and 227/88 *Hoechst AG v Commission* ECLI:EU:C:1989:337, para 25; Case 374/87 *Orkem v Commission* ECLI:EU:C:1989:387, para 19; Case 85/87 *Dow Benelux NV v Commission* ECLI:EU:C:1989:379, para 36; Case T-65/99 *Strintzis Lines Shipping SA v Commission* ECLI:EU:C:2003:336, para 40.

[15] Case C-94/00 *Roquette Frères* ECLI:EU:C:2002:603, para 42; Case C-52/09 *Konkurrensverket v TeliaSonera Sverige* ECLI:EU:C:2011:83, para 22.

consider the protection of consumer welfare an objective of the EU antitrust rules. Consumer welfare was included in the *National Panasonic* line of case law, according to which the antitrust rules protected competition from being distorted to the detriment of the public interest, individual undertakings and consumers. However, one may also conclude that the Court did not consider consumer welfare, measured in terms of price, output, quality and levels of innovation, the exclusive aim of the EU antitrust rules. Essentially, the Court's and the Commission's views on the antitrust rules' objectives were more or less in line during the first 40 years.

This raises the question whether the Court followed the Commission when the latter restricted its understanding of the antitrust rules' objectives around the turn of the millennium to economic consumer welfare and market integration only. The short answer is that it did not. There was a point in 2006, when the General Court actually seemed willing to embrace the new consumer welfare aim. In its judgment in *GlaxoSmithKline*, it agreed with the Commission that the objective assigned to Article 101 was to prevent undertakings from 'reducing the welfare of the final consumer of the products in question'.[16] In the same judgment it also followed the Commission's 'more economic' interpretation of Article 101 according to which there can be no harm to competition unless the conduct is also at least likely to affect the welfare of final consumers.[17] However, the delight that supporters of the more economic approach may have felt in response to this judgment must have been short-lived. On appeal, the Court of Justice ruled that the objective of the antitrust provisions was to protect 'not only the interests of competitors or of consumers' but also the 'structure of the market and, in so doing, competition as such'.[18] Consequently, it also held that the General Court had committed an error in law when ruling that only those agreements that deprived consumers of certain advantages could have an anticompetitive object.[19]

One can draw several conclusions from the Court of Justice's ruling in *GlaxoSmithKline*. First, one can infer from the statement that the antitrust rules aim to protect both competitors and consumers. The second conclusion one can draw is that the protection of competitors and consumers are not the only aims. Another aim of the antitrust rules is to protect the structure of the market, and, in so doing, competition as such. It is not evident what exactly the Court means by 'structure of the market' and 'competition as such'. The structure of the market is likely to refer to the number of undertakings present in the market, their market shares and the market concentration, although the Court does not explain what type of market structure is considered competitive. This makes it difficult to establish whether the market structure has been affected in a way that makes the conduct anticompetitive. 'Competition as such' may refer to the competitive process, regardless of a specific

[16] Case T-168/01 *GlaxoSmithKline v Commission* ECLI:EU:T:2006:265, para 118.

[17] ibid, para 119.

[18] Joined cases C-501/06 P, C-513/06 P, C-515/06 P and C-519/06 P *GlaxoSmithKline v Commission* ECLI:EU:C:2009:610, para 63.

[19] ibid, paras 63, 64.

outcome for any of the stakeholders. Both of these concepts need serious clarification to make them workable in practice. Be this as it may, while there is no doubt that the protection of consumer welfare is included in the Court's understanding of the antitrust rules' purpose,[20] it is equally clear that the Court does not consider consumer welfare their exclusive purpose. In its view, the antitrust rules also aim to protect the interests of competitors and competition as such.

This definition has since been the Court's standard formula in cases that refer to the objectives of the EU antitrust rules,[21] although in *TeliaSonera*, it reverted to the prior, even broader, concept, according to which the function of the antitrust rules is to prevent competition from being distorted to the detriment of the public interest, individual undertakings and consumers, thereby ensuring the well-being of the European Union.[22] It also continues to consider the general Treaty aim of market integration an objective of antitrust law.[23]

In conclusion, the Court has not embraced the Commission's 'more economic' understanding of the antitrust rules' legal objective. While both institutions agree that the objectives of market integration and consumer welfare are key values in the interpretation of the antitrust rules, the Commission considers them the only relevant values, while the Court does not. It takes the position that the antitrust rules protect competition as such in the interests of a broader range of actors, including undertakings and the public interest. Insofar, the Commission's more economic approach is not compatible with the Court's interpretation of the law.

III. The Concept of Harm in the Case Law

Having established that the Court has always had and continues to have a broad understanding of the aims of competition law, the next question that arises is how this objective translates into its concept of competitive harm. In practice, the concept of harm is far more relevant than the definition of the provision's legal objective, although, in theory, the former should follow from the latter.

A. The Court's Concept of Harm under Article 101

An analysis of the Court's judgments on Article 101 of the first 40 years reveals no general and abstract definition of competitive harm. The Court established

[20] See eg Joined cases C-468/06 to C-478/06 *Sot Lélos and Others v GlaxoSmithKline* ECLI:EU:C:2008:504, para 68.

[21] T-357/06 *Koninklijke Wegenbouw Stevin v Commission* ECLI:EU:T:2012:488, para 111; Case C-8/08 *T-Mobile Netherlands BV* ECLI:EU:C:2009:343, para 38; Case T-461/07 *Visa Europe Ltd and Visa International Service v Commission* ECLI:EU:T:2011:181, para 126.

[22] *Konkurrensverket v TeliaSonera Sverige* (n 15) para 22.

[23] *Sot Lélos and Others v GlaxoSmithKline* (n 20) para 65.

early on that agreements that had the object of restricting competition could be presumed anticompetitive,[24] and that all other agreements had to be assessed as to their effects on competition.[25] However, it did not define in a general manner what constituted a restriction of competition.

The early case law gave some guidance as to what type of restriction was deemed restrictive by object, for example, price fixing, market allocation and export restrictions, but rarely explained in any detail what type of harm was expected from these practices that led the Court to consider them anticompetitive. The Court's key rationale for deeming price fixing and market allocation restrictive (by object) in these early decisions was that these practices were explicitly named in Article 101.[26] It was somewhat more expansive with regard to the type of harm caused by export restrictions. In *Consten and Grundig*, it held that clauses establishing absolute territorial protection distorted competition in the common market because they aimed at artificially maintaining separate national markets, thus frustrating one of the most fundamental objectives of the Union.[27] One can conclude that, like the Commission, the Court considered impediments to the process of market integration competitive harm within the meaning of Article 101. It subsequently relied on the more general principle that any agreement prohibiting or discouraging exports by their very nature restricted competition, usually without any further rationalisation.[28]

Agreements that do not have the object of restricting competition need to be assessed as to their effects on competition. The Court established this principle in *Suiker Unie* in 1973.[29] It explained that agreements that were to be assessed as to their concrete effects needed to be considered in the context in which they took place, that is to say in their surrounding economic and legal circumstances within which they could, together with other factors, have a cumulative effect on competition. However, it did not define or explain in any way what constituted a detrimental effect on competition. The following paragraph of the judgment suggested that the competitive assessment should aim to establish the extent to which agreements were likely to restrict 'free trade',[30] but again did not define what constituted a restriction of free trade. Subsequent judgments were rarely more explicit. In a number of cases examining the legality of vertical agreements, the Court indicated

[24] Joined Cases 56 and 58/64 *Établissements Consten S.à.R.L. and Grundig-Verkaufs-GmbH v Commission* ECLI:EU:C:1966:41, 342.

[25] Joined Cases 40 to 48, 50, 54 to 56, 111, 113 and 114/73 *Coöperatieve Vereniging 'Suiker Unie' UA and others v Commission* ECLI:EU:C:1975:174, para 548.

[26] eg Case 8/72 *Vereeniging van Cementhandelaren v Commission* ECLI:EU:C:1972:84, para 18; Case 73/74 *Groupement des fabricants de papiers peints de Belgique and others v Commission* ECLI:EU:C:1975:160, para 9; Joined Cases 43/82 and 63/82 *Vereniging ter Bevordering van het Vlaamse Boekwezen, VBVB, and Vereniging ter Bevordering van de Belangen des Boekhandels, VBBB, v Commission* ECLI:EU:C:1984:9, para 9.

[27] *Établissements Consten S.à.R.L. and Grundig-Verkaufs-GmbH v Commission* (n 24) 340, 343.

[28] Case 19/77 *Miller International Schallplatten GmbH v Commission* ECLI:EU:C:1978:19, para 8.

[29] *Coöperatieve Vereniging 'Suiker Unie' UA and others v Commission* (n 25) para 548.

[30] ibid, para 549.

that assessing the effects of the agreement on competition required examining the effects on the opportunities of competitors to gain access to the market or to increase their market share.[31] This is in line with the Commission's understanding of competitive harm prior to the more economic approach.

While the Court thus did not exhaustively define the concept of competitive harm in its case law of the first 40 years, one may infer from its judgments reviewing the Commission's decisions of this period that it did indeed share the Commission's early understanding of competitive harm. Although it sometimes found fault with the Commission's standard of proof and annulled decisions on the grounds that the Commission had not proved the infringement to the required legal standard,[32] it never objected to the Commission's legal concept of harm. It thus upheld numerous decisions in which the Commission equated restrictions of the contract parties' or third parties' economic autonomy or opportunity with a restriction of competition. In particular, it found no fault with competitive assessments in which the Commission based the restriction of competition on the fact that the agreement restricted the parties' freedom to determine the volumes of their sales,[33] to whom they could sell,[34] where they could sell[35] or to determine their own levels of production.[36] It also did not criticise the Commission's concept of harm in cases in which the Commission found that an agreement restricted competition because it restricted (actual or potential) competing manufacturers' or distributors' opportunities to enter a market.[37] Finally, it upheld decisions in which the Commission found agreements to be incompatible with Article 101 because of their discriminatory nature.[38]

[31] Case T-7/93 *Langnese Iglo GmbH v Commission* ECLI:EU:T:1995:98, para 99; Case C-234/89 *Stergios Delimitis v Henninger Bräu* ECLI:EU:C:1991:91, para 15; Case T-65/98 *Van den Bergh Foods Ltd v Commission* ECLI:EU:T:2003:281, para 83.

[32] eg Joined Cases T-68/89, T-77/89 and T-78/89 *Società Italiana Vetro SpA, Fabbrica Pisana SpA and PPG Vernante Pennitalia SpA v Commission* ECLI:EU:T:1992:38, partially annulling *Italian flat glass* (Case IV.29.988) [1981] OJ L326/32; or Joined Cases 29/83 and 30/83 *Compagnie Royale Asturienne des Mines SA and Rheinzink GmbH v Commission* ECLI:EU:C:1984:130, partially annulling *Rolled zinc products and zinc alloys* (Case IV/29.629 [1982] OJ L362/40.

[33] *Vereeniging van Cementhandelaren* (Case IV/324) [1972] OJ L13/34, recital 15; upheld in Case 8/72 *Vereeniging van Cementhandelaren v Commission* ECLI:EU:C:1972:84, paras 24 and 25.

[34] *Distribution system of Ford Werke AG* (Case IV/30.696) [1983] OJ L327/31, recital 30; upheld in Joined Cases 25 and 26/84 *Ford-Werke AG and Ford of Europe Inc v Commission* ECLI:EU:C:1985:340; *Hasselblad* (Case IV/25.757) [1982] OJ L161/18, recital 59, upheld in Case 86/82 *Hasselblad (GB) Limited v Commission* ECLI:EU:C:1984:65, para 46.

[35] *Rolled zinc products and zinc alloys* (n 32) III.A.1, upheld in Joined Cases 29/83 and 30/83 *Compagnie Royale Asturienne des Mines SA and Rheinzink GmbH v Commission* (n 32) para 24.

[36] *Rolled zinc products and zinc alloys* (n 32) III.A.1, upheld in Joined Cases 29/83 and 30/83 *Compagnie Royale Asturienne des Mines SA and Rheinzink GmbH v Commission* (n 32) para 33.

[37] eg *Theal Watts* (Case IV/28.812) [1977] OJ L 39/19, II.A, upheld by the Court in Case 28/77 *Tepea BV v Commission* ECLI:EU:C:1978:133.

[38] *NAVEWA-ANSEAU* (Case IV/29.995) [1982] OJ L167/39, recital 56, upheld in Joined cases 96–102, 104, 105, 108 and 110/82 *NV IAZ International Belgium and others v Commission* ECLI:EU:C:1983:310, paras 10, 11.

In sum, despite the absence of a clear and unequivocal definition of competitive harm in the case law, one can conclude that the Court shared the Commission's broad concept of competitive harm prior to the more economic approach, according to which a restriction of individual economic freedom and opportunity, discrimination, lack of fairness as well as impediments to cross border trade all amounted to restrictions of competition. This makes sense in view of the Court's equally broad understanding of the objectives of EU antitrust law during this period.

Again, this raises the question whether the Court has accepted the Commission's revised understanding of competitive harm under Article 101, which requires that the agreement not only restrict competition but also result in a reduction of consumer welfare. The case law is relatively scarce on the issue. Over the past 10 years, the Commission has focused its enforcement on pursuing cartels,[39] which do not give rise to many questions of competitive harm, as they are presumed to be anticompetitive. The great majority of non-cartel cases over the past 10 years have been solved by means of commitments decisions that contain no formal legal assessment. This trend has greatly reduced the likelihood of the Court being asked to pronounce itself on the concept of competitive harm under Article 101. Nonetheless, the opportunity arose in the aforementioned case of *GlaxoSmithKline*.

In 2001, the Commission had found that GlaxoSmithKline, a major global pharmaceutical company, had infringed Article 101 by operating a dual pricing system in Spain.[40] GlaxoSmithKline had required its Spanish wholesalers to pay a higher price for products that they exported to other Member States than for products that they resold on the Spanish market. GlaxoSmithKline did not dispute that this dual pricing system was intended to prevent distributors from other Member States, where GlaxoSmithKline charged higher prices for the same product, from buying these pharmaceuticals at the lower price in Spain. According to the Commission, the dual pricing system discouraged parallel trade in a manner similar to an export ban and therefore had the object of restricting competition.[41] For the sake of completeness, it also carried out an assessment of the agreement's effects and found that the dual pricing system also had the effect of restricting competition by excluding or limiting the possibilities of parallel trade.[42] GlaxoSmithKline brought an action for annulment, arguing amongst others that the Commission had not taken into account that consumers would not be directly affected as a consequence of the agreement because the cost for the products in question were primarily covered by the different national health insurance systems. The General Court agreed with this argument and held that the mere fact that the agreement in question was intended to limit parallel trade and partition

[39] See Ch 5, section II.B.ii.

[40] *Glaxo Wellcome* (Case IV/36.957/F3); *Aseprofar and Fedifar* (Case IV/36.997/F3); *Spain Pharma* (Case IV/37.121/F3); *BAI* (Case IV/37.138/F3); *EAEPC* (Case IV/37.380/F3) [2001] OJ L302/1.

[41] ibid, recitals 116–25.

[42] ibid, recitals 126–44.

the single market was not sufficient to make the agreement restrictive by object. The Commission should also have taken into account whether the agreement had the object of preventing, restricting or distorting competition on the relevant market to the detriment of the final consumer.[43] As the Commission had failed to take into account whether final consumers could be affected at all, the General Court found that the Commission's finding that the agreement had the object of restricting competition could not be upheld. However, it failed to see any manifest errors of assessment in the Commission's analysis of the agreement's actual effects, in which the Commission had also considered the effects on the welfare of final consumers.[44] This ruling seemed to signal that the EU judiciary was prepared to follow the Commission's new welfare-based approach and even go beyond it, insofar as it required the potential for a reduction on consumer welfare even in cases in which the agreement harmed market integration by partitioning the market along national borders.

Both GlaxoSmithKline and the Commission appealed the judgment, Glaxo SmithKline pleading that the General Court had erred in holding that the agreement had the effect of restricting competition, and the Commission pleading that the General Court had been wrong to condemn the Commission's conclusion that the agreement had the object of restricting competition. The Court of Justice strongly disagreed with the General Court's position on the relevance of consumer harm. It held that there was nothing in the provision of Article 101 to indicate that only those agreements that deprived consumers of certain advantages could have an anticompetitive object. Further, like the Treaty's other competition rules, Article 101 aimed to protect not only the interests of competitors and consumers, but also the structure of the market and, in so doing, competition as such. It was therefore not necessary that final consumers be deprived of the advantages of effective competition in terms of supply or price for an agreement to be restrictive by object. The Court of Justice concluded that the General Court had committed an error of law by requiring proof that the agreement entailed disadvantages for final consumers as a prerequisite for a finding of anticompetitive object.[45]

While the ruling in *GlaxoSmithKline* that a reduction in consumer welfare is not necessary for a restriction of competition explicitly only refers to object restrictions, it must be understood as applying to the concept of restriction of competition in general when read in conjunction with other key statements in the judgment. The Court based its conclusion that object restrictions do not require consumer harm on the wording of Article 101 and on its understanding of Article 101's objective. Indeed, Article 101 does not state that consumer harm is a necessary prerequisite for a restriction of competition by object. The same is true for restrictions by effect. Further, the Court took the view that Article 101 aimed to protect not only

[43] *GlaxoSmithKline v Commission* (n 16) para 119.
[44] ibid, paras 147–92.
[45] *GlaxoSmithKline v Commission et al* (n 18) paras 63, 64.

the interests of competitors or of consumers, but also the structure of the market and thereby competition as such. If this broad definition of the provision's legal objective allowed the Court to conclude that restrictions by object do not require consumer harm, the same should also be true for restrictions by effect. Restrictions of competition by object and restrictions of competition by effect do not refer to different types of competitive harm. The distinction relates to different tests and a different standard of proof. Restrictions of competition by object are restrictions that are so obvious that it would amount to a waste of resources to prove the actual anticompetitive effect. Restrictions of competition by effect are less obvious restrictions, in which the anticompetitive effect needs to be assessed and established in the individual case. However, the concept of what amounts to a restriction of competition should be the same. In sum, *GlaxoSmithKline* must be understood as meaning that the Court of Justice does not consider consumer harm an essential requisite of competitive harm within the meaning of Article 101(1). This makes the Commission's new understanding of competitive harm under Article 101(1) incompatible with the case law.

B. The Court's Concept of Harm under EU Merger Law

The Court's concept of harm under Regulation 4064/89 was as broad and open-ended as that of the Commission at the time. The original Merger Regulation prohibited mergers that were likely to create or strengthen a dominant position as a result of which effective competition would be significantly impeded in a substantial part of the common market.[46] The Court defined dominance under Regulation 4064/89 in line with the concept of dominance under Article 102 as a position of economic strength which would enable the merged entity to prevent effective competition from being maintained in the relevant market by giving them the opportunity to act to a considerable extent independently of their competitors, their customers and, ultimately, of consumers.[47] As argued in Chapter 5, this definition describes a very broad and generalised position of strength that does not specify the type of harm that the entity holding this position would be expected to cause. It is, at any rate, not limited to the ability to affect consumer welfare.

The case law on Regulation 4064/89 does not reveal a general definition of what amounted to a significant impediment to effective competition in the eyes of the Court. However, one can at least infer from judgments reviewing the Commission's assessments of non-horizontal mergers under Regulation 4064/89 that, like

[46] Council Regulation (EEC) No 4064/89 on the control of concentrations between undertakings [1990] OJ L257/13, Art 2(3).

[47] eg *Gencor Ltd v Commission* (n 2) para 8; Case T-210/01 *General Electric Company v Commission* ECLI:EU:T:2005:456, para 114.

the Commission itself, the Court did not consider consumer harm a prerequisite of competitive harm under the original Merger Regulation. Both institutions considered the likely foreclosure of competitors sufficient to find a merger anticompetitive. This was demonstrated in the case of the contentious *GE/Honeywell* merger. The Commission had prohibited the merger because of its likely foreclosure effects.[48] It did not examine whether the exclusion of competitors was likely to affect consumer welfare, which was one of the key bones of contention in the subsequent spat between the US and EU antitrust authorities.[49] On appeal, the General Court found that the Commission's assessment of potential vertical effects was vitiated by manifest errors of assessment insofar as it failed to meet the high standard of proof required for predicting uncertain future effects.[50] However, it did not criticise the Commission's concept of harm as such. In sum, one can conclude that the Court shared the Commission's early understanding that consumer harm was not a prerequisite of competitive harm under the original Merger Regulation.

The Commission changed its position on this issue when the new Merger Regulation entered into force, and now takes the view that only mergers that are likely to reduce consumer welfare should be deemed anticompetitive.[51] This change of interpretation is most relevant in cases of mergers leading to foreclosure. Whereas the Commission used to consider foreclosure effects as such sufficient to make a merger anticompetitive, it now only deems 'anticompetitive foreclosure', ie foreclosure resulting in consumer harm, incompatible with the Merger Regulation.

What about the Court? Has it gone along with this change? In fact, the Court's current concept of competitive harm under Article 2(3) of Regulation 139/2004 is not clear, although there are signs that the Court may be nudging closer to accepting a welfare-based concept of harm under EU merger law. The key problem in trying to determine the Court's current position is that there have been very few judgments on the new Merger Regulation in recent years. To date, the Commission has only prohibited five mergers on the basis of Regulation 129/2004,[52] of which only two have been reviewed by the General Court at the time of the writing of this book.[53] Both concerned horizontal mergers. The Commission's prohibition decisions in *Ryan Air/Aer Lingus I* and *Deutsche Börse/NYSE Euronext*[54]

[48] *General Electric/Honeywell* (Case COMP/M.2220) [2004] OJ L48/1, recitals 342 ff.

[49] See Ch 1, s IV.

[50] *General Electric v Commission* (n 47) para 312. Ultimately, the General Court upheld the decision because it agreed with the Commission's assessment of the concentration's likely horizontal effects.

[51] See Ch 5.

[52] *Ryanair/Aer Lingus* (Case No COMP/M.4439); *Olympic/Aegean Airlines* (Case No COMP/M.5830); *Ryanair/Aer Lingus III* (Case No COMP/M.6663); *Deutsche Börse/NYSE Euronext* (Case No COMP/M.6166); *UPS/TNT Express* (Case No COMP/M.6570).

[53] Case T-342/07 *Ryanair v Commission* ECLI:EU:T:2010:280; *Deutsche Börse v Commission* (n 2). The appeal against *UPS/TNT Express* (Case T-194/13 *United Parcel Service v Commission*) is currently still pending.

[54] *Ryanair/Aer Lingus* (n 52); *Deutsche Börse/NYSE Euronext* (n 52).

were themselves relatively vague on the underlying concept of harm, citing old concepts of dominance and other concepts established in the case law, while in reality being clearly concerned about the effects on consumer welfare.[55] As argued in Chapter 5, this conceptual caginess may very well have been intentional to pre-empt being criticised for an entirely welfare-based concept of harm on appeal. In fact, the judgment reviewing the decision in *Deutsche Börse/NYSE Euronext* is just as vague on the concept of harm as the decision itself. It does not engage with or even mention any possible effects on consumers in its review of the Commission's assessment of the merger's anticompetitive effects. The Commission itself had formally based its assessment on the concept of a dominant position, and the Court merely reviewed whether the Commission had committed manifest errors in its assessment of diverse competitive constraints, without specifying what type of harm these restraints were expected to prevent.

In *Ryanair v Commission*, the applicant explicitly pleaded that the Commission had failed to demonstrate that the merger would lead to consumer harm. One could have hoped to find a clear statement on the necessity of consumer harm in the judgment. Unfortunately this is not the case. The General Court merely held that the Commission had in fact explained in detail why the concentration would 'eliminate current competition between Ryanair and Aer Lingus to the detriment of customers'.[56] This statement is ambiguous. If taken literally, it merely rejects the applicant's contention that the Commission had not taken into account the effects on consumers. One might be tempted to read into it that, because it did not dispute the necessity of demonstrating consumer harm, the General Court implicitly recognised that such harm needs to be established. This, however, is not an imperative conclusion.

In addition to the two prohibition decisions, the Court has also had the opportunity to review a few actions for annulment brought by competitors against Commission decisions clearing a concentration.[57] The most recent of these judgments is of interest with regard to the issue of competitive harm. In *Cisco Systems and Messagenet v Commission*, the General Court reviewed the Commission's decision to allow Microsoft, a major designer and manufacturer of software, to acquire Skype, a provider of internet-based communications services and software.[58] The Commission assessed the proposed acquisition as to both potential horizontal and conglomerate effects, and found that neither type of effect was likely. It is the analysis of conglomerate effects that is particularly interesting in relation to

[55] See Ch 5, s III, and A Witt, 'From *Airtours* to *Ryanair*: Is the More Economic Approach to EU Merger Law Really about More Economics?' (2012) 49 *Common Market Law Review* 217.

[56] Case T-342/07 *Ryanair v Commission* (n 53) paras 223–27.

[57] Case T-282/06 *Sun Chemical Group et al v Commission* ECLI:EU:T:2007:203; Case T-151/05 *NVV et al v Commission* ECLI:EU:T:2009:144; Case T-237/05 *Éditions Odile Jacob v Commission* ECLI:EU:T:2010:224; Case T-79/12 *Cisco Systems and Messagenet v Commission* ECLI:EU:T:2013:635.

[58] *Microsoft/Skype* (Case No COMP/M.6281).

the concept of harm. The Commission had followed its theoretical approach outlined in the non-horizontal merger guidelines and had examined whether (1) the merged entity would have the ability and incentive to foreclose competitors and (2) whether this foreclosure could be expected to reduce consumer welfare.[59] It found that neither of these conditions was fulfilled. In the application for annulment, the applicant submitted that not only would the merged entity have the incentive and ability to foreclosure, but the foreclosure would also result in a lessening of consumer welfare. The General Court focused its review on the Commission's assessment of the merged entity's ability and incentive to foreclose, in which it could not find any manifest errors.[60] It added, in a few sentences, that it could not find any manifest errors in the Commission's assessment of the effects of a potential foreclosure strategy on consumers either.[61] Again, the General Court did not positively state that a reduction in consumer welfare was a requisite of anticompetitive foreclosure. On the other hand, it also did not outright state that consumer harm was irrelevant, and that foreclosure in itself was sufficient to make a merger anticompetitive. In the cases of Article 101, and 102 in particular, it has in the past not hesitated to point out that it is not necessary to assess the effects on consumers.[62] This uncharacteristic reticence might lead one to wonder whether the General Court might not be inclined to accept a purely welfare-based concept of harm under the new Merger Regulation. An alternative explanation is that it simply wanted to avoid pronouncing itself on the issue in those cases. What speaks against the assumption that the General Court considers consumer harm a prerequisite of anticompetitive foreclosure is that this would result in it having a different concept of competitive harm under Regulation 139/2004 than it does under Articles 101 and 102. In sum, none of the judgments under Regulation 139/2004 to date allows a definite conclusion as to the Court's concept of harm under this pillar of EU antitrust law.

C. The Court's Concept of Harm under Article 102

By contrast, the Court's position on the necessity of consumer harm under Article 102 does not leave much room for speculation. In short, the Court did not consider consumer harm an indispensable element of competitive harm under Article 102 prior to the Commission's review, and it does not consider it an indispensable element now. While it considers consumer harm one possible form of competitive harm under Article 102 in the context of exploitative abuses, it does not consider it the only type of competitive harm. According to the Court, the

[59] ibid, recitals 142–70; 214–22; European Commission, Guidelines on the assessment of non-horizontal mergers [2008] OJ C265/6, paras 18, 32.

[60] Case T-79/12 *Cisco Systems and Messagenet v Commission* (n 57) paras 115–33.

[61] ibid paras 134, 135.

[62] See ss III.1 and 3 of this chapter.

foreclosure of competitors as such is sufficient to make a dominant undertaking's behaviour anticompetitive.

Article 102 is only addressed to undertakings in a dominant position. As pointed out in the previous section, the Court defines dominance as a

> position of economic strength enjoyed by an undertaking which enables it to hinder the maintenance of effective competition on the relevant market by allowing it to behave to an appreciable extent independently of its competitors and customers and ultimately of consumers.[63]

This concept is too broad to be compatible with the exclusively welfare-based interpretation of the antitrust rules that the Commission has been trying to achieve over the past 15 years. If one aimed to interpret Article 102 as protecting consumer welfare only, it would make sense to read dominance as meaning market power, ie the ability to raise prices or affect other parameters of consumer welfare. Alternatively, one could abandon the criterion of dominance entirely and simply assess in each individual case whether the conduct was likely to lead to consumer harm.[64] However, despite the Commission's mission to introduce such a welfare-based interpretation of the EU antitrust rules since the early 2000s, the Court of Justice has unerringly insisted on adhering to the broad formula coined in *United Brands* almost 50 years ago.[65]

The second key concept in Article 102 is that of abuse. Like the Commission, the Court distinguishes between exploitative, discriminatory and exclusionary abuses. An exploitative abuse is conduct that directly exploits consumers. This type of abuse therefore per definition requires the presence of consumer harm. Excessive pricing is an example of exploitative abuse.[66] The Court does not dispute that exploitation of consumers can only occur if consumers have suffered some form of harm. Actually, it is the Commission's position on exploitative abuses that is much less clear at present, as the Guidance Paper does not cover this type of abuse and the Commission has been focusing on its enforcement activities on exclusionary practices over the past years. It is the treatment of these exclusionary abuses, so-called because they result in the exclusion of competitors, that is more contentious.

In *Hoffmann-La Roche*, the Court defined exclusionary abusive behaviour as

> the behaviour of an undertaking in a dominant position which is such as to influence the structure of a market where, as a result of the very presence of the undertaking in

[63] Case 27/76 *United Brands v Commission* (n 13) para 65; *Hoffmann-La Roche v Commission* (n 12) para 38.

[64] The EAGCP favoured this approach in its Report 'An Economic Approach to Article 82' (2005) 4, available at: www.ec.europa.eu/dgs/competition/economist/eagcp_july_21_05.pdf.

[65] eg Case C-202/07 P *France Télécom v Commission* ECLI:EU:C:2009:214, para 103; Case C-280/08 P *Deutsche Telekom v Commission* ECLI:EU:C:2010:603, para 170; Case C-549/10 P *Tomra v Commission* ECLI:EU:C:2012:221, para 38; *Konkurrensverket v TeliaSonera* (n 15) para 79.

[66] See eg *United Brands v Commission* (n 13) paras 250–52.

> question, the degree of competition is weakened and which, through recourse to methods different from those which condition normal competition in products or services on the basis of the transactions of commercial operators, has the effect of hindering the maintenance of the degree of competition still existing in the market or the growth of that competition.[67]

This became the Court's standard definition of exclusionary abuse in subsequent cases.[68] A welfare-based interpretation of abusive behaviour, such as that favoured by the Commissions, would require that the exclusionary conduct result in consumer harm for it to be deemed anticompetitive. However, the Court's definition in *Hoffmann-La Roche* did not require this. It did not even mention consumers. Instead, the Court's definition suggests that the relevant effect was the impact on the 'structure of the market' as long as this happened by methods different from those governing normal competition. This is reminiscent of the Court's understanding of competitive harm under Article 101, both before and after the Commission's reform.[69] In line with this position, the Court regularly held that Article 102 prohibited a dominant undertaking from eliminating a competitor and thereby strengthening its position by recourse to means other than those based on competition on the merits.[70] While the case law did not define the concept of competition on the merits, one may assume that it relates to attracting customers by offering better quality products, better service or lower prices, as long as these are not predatory.

In fact, the Court also considered an unsuccessful attempt to eliminate a competitor abusive on the part of a dominant undertaking[71] because the latter had a 'special responsibility' not to allow their conduct to impair genuine undistorted competition.[72] The concept of special responsibility makes little sense from an economic point of view, according to which only conduct that results in consumer harm should be considered anticompetitive. Either an undertaking's conduct affects prices, or it does not. In the former case the conduct is anticompetitive, in the latter it is not. There is no room for 'special responsibilities' in an interpretation of the law that is guided by the aims of welfare maximisation only.

[67] *Hoffmann-La Roche v Commission* (n 12) para 91.

[68] eg *Nederlandsche Banden Industrie Michelin v Commission* (n 13) para 70; Case C-62/86 *AKZO v Commission* ECLI:EU:C:1991:286, para 69; T-151/01 *Duales System Deutschland v Commission* ECLI:EU:T:2007:154, para 120; T-228/97 *Irish Sugar v Commission* ECLI:EU:T:1999:246 para 111; T-203/01 *Michelin v Commission* ECLI:EU:T:2003:250, para 54, amongst many others.

[69] *GlaxoSmithKline v Commission et al* (n 18) paras 63, 64.

[70] *United Brands v Commission* (n 13) para 201; *AKZO v Commission* (n 68) para 70; Case T-83/91 *Tetra Pak International v Commission* ECLI:EU:T:1994:246, para 147; Case T-228/97 *Irish Sugar plc v Commission* (n 68) para 111; *Van den Bergh Foods v Commission* (n 31) para 157.

[71] Cases T-340/03 *France Télécom v Commission* ECLI:EU:T:2007:22, para 196; T-228/97 *Irish Sugar v Commission* (n 68) para 191; T-24/93 *Compagnie maritime belge transports and Others v Commission* ECLI:EU:T:1996:139, para 149.

[72] eg *Nederlandsche Banden Industrie Michelin v Commission* (n 13) para 57; *Tetra Pak International v Commission* (n 70) para 114; Joined cases C-395/96 P and C-396/96 P *Compagnie maritime belge transports et al* ECLI:EU:C:2000:132, para 85, amongst many others.

The Court's key concern about the exclusion of competitors therefore was that such exclusion affected the structure of the market. In some cases, it also referred to the effects on the 'structure of competition'[73] or an 'effective competition structure'.[74] These terms appear to have been synonymous in its language. The case law did not define what constituted an effective competition structure. All one could infer from the fact that the exclusion of a competitor was considered harmful to the structure of a market or competition is that 'more was better'. While the Commission's concern about exclusionary effects under Article 102 prior to the reform was expressed more in terms of the effects on individuals' opportunities and economic freedoms, rather than safeguarding a competitive market structure, both institutions agreed on the practically relevant point that the exclusion of a competitor by means other than those of competition on the merits made a dominant undertaking's conduct anticompetitive. There was no need for consumers to be affected as a consequence of such exclusion.

Since the Commission's reform, the Court and the Commission no longer see eye to eye on this point. While the Commission nowadays only considers such instances of exclusion anticompetitive that result in consumer harm, the Court has not changed its original position. After the Commission had introduced its welfare-based interpretation of Article 101 and EU merger law, undertakings repeatedly attempted to challenge Article 102 prohibitions on the grounds that the Commission had failed to prove that the allegedly exclusionary conduct was likely to result in consumer harm. So far, these types of plea have not been successful. In each case, the Court ruled in no uncertain terms that the exclusion of competitors as such was sufficient to make the conduct abusive, as long as it was achieved through means other than competition on the merits.[75] The Court has also steadfastly adhered to the broad definition of abuse established in *Hoffmann/La Roche*[76] and the concept of special responsibility[77] in recent case law.

[73] eg *Hoffmann-La Roche v Commission* (n 12) para 123; 22/78 *Hugin v Commission* ECLI:EU:C:1979:138, para 17; 75/84 *Metro SB-Großmärkte v Commission* ECLI:EU:C:1979:138, paras 88, 89; T-201/04 *Microsoft v Commission* ECLI:EU:T:2007:289, para 1054; Case C-23/14 *Post Danmark III A/S v Konkurrencerådet* ECLI:EU:C:2015:651, para 72.

[74] See eg 6/72 *Europemballage and Continental Can v Commission* (n 4) para 12; C-95/04 P *British Airways v Commission* ECLI:EU:C:2007:166, para 106; *France Télécom v Commission* (n 65) para 105; T-286/09 *Intel v Commission* ECLI:EU:T:2014:547, para 105.

[75] *British Airways* (n 74) para 106; *France Télécom v Commission* (n 65) para 105; T-321/05 *AstraZeneca v Commission* ECLI:EU:T:2010:266, para 353; *TeliaSonera Sverige* (n 15) para 24; *Intel v Commission* (n 74) para 105. The appeal in *Intel* is currently pending (Case C-413/14 P: Appeal brought on 28 August 2014 by Intel Corporation against the judgment in Case T-286/09 *Intel Corporation v European Commission*).

[76] eg *Tomra v Commission* (n 65) para 17; *TeliaSonera Sverige* (n 15) para 27; Case C-457/10 P *AstraZeneca v Commission* ECLI:EU:C:2012:770, para 74; *Post Danmark v Konkurrencerådet* (n 73) para 26; Case C-170/13 *Huawei Technologies v ZTE* ECLI:EU:C:2015:477, para 45, amongst many others.

[77] eg Cases T-155/06 *Tomra Systems v Commission* ECLI:EU:T:2010:370, para 207; *France Télécom v Commission* (n 65) para 105; C-280/08 P *Deutsche Telekom v Commission* ECLI:EU:C:2010:603, para 176; C-457/10 P *AstraZeneca v Commission* (n 76) para 134; *Post Danmark A/S v Konkurrencerådet* (n 73) para 71; T-398/07 *Kingdom of Spain v Commission* ECLI:EU:T:2012:173, para 92.

In 2012, the Court seemed to have taken a step towards a more welfare-based interpretation of Article 102 in the case of *Post Danmark I*.[78] This case was based on a reference for a preliminary ruling by a Danish court, which had asked the Court of Justice for clarification on the concept of exclusionary abuses. In particular, the Danish Court had sought to clarify whether, and if so under what circumstances, selective low pricing on the part of a dominant undertaking, aimed at its competitors' major customers but which did not fulfil the conditions of predatory pricing, could amount to an abuse within the meaning of Article 102. The Court of Justice's ruling began by reiterating many of the old-established principles, ie that Article 102 not only covered those practices that directly caused harm to consumers but also practices that caused consumers harm through their impact on competition,[79] and that a dominant undertaking had a special responsibility not to allow its behaviour to impair genuine, undistorted competition on the internal market.[80] However, it also held that Article 102 did not seek to ensure that competitors less efficient than the dominant undertaking should remain on the market.[81] This is something it had already hinted at in two previous judgments on predatory pricing practices.[82] In *Post Danmark I*, it drew the further consequence from this principle that not every exclusionary effect was necessarily detrimental to competition. Competition on the merits could, by definition, lead to the departure from the market or the marginalisation of competitors that were less efficient and therefore less attractive to consumers from the point of view of price, choice, quality or innovation.[83] The Court concluded that Article 102 prohibited a dominant undertaking from adopting pricing practices that had an exclusionary effect on competitors considered to be *as efficient as it is itself* and strengthening its dominant position by using methods other than those that are part of competition on the merits.[84] The Court further held that the fact that the dominant undertaking engaged in price discrimination was in itself not sufficient evidence of an exclusionary abuse.[85]

The Court's explanations in *Post Danmark I* suggest that not any exclusion of competitors should be deemed anticompetitive, but only the exclusion of competitors that are at least as efficient as the dominant undertaking itself. The exclusion of less efficient competitors would consequently not be deemed anticompetitive. This understanding of an exclusionary abuse would indeed be a major adjustment of the Court's traditional concept of harm, which had not distinguished between equally or less efficient competitors but deemed the exclusion of any competitor

[78] Case C-209/10 *Post Danmark I v Konkurrencerådet* ECLI:EU:C:2012:172.
[79] ibid, para 20.
[80] ibid, para 23.
[81] ibid, para 21.
[82] *Konkurrensverket v TeliaSonera Sverige* (n 15) para 39; C-280/08 P *Deutsche Telekom v Commission* ECLI:EU:C:2010:603, para 177.
[83] *Post Danmark I v Konkurrencerådet* (n 78), para 22.
[84] ibid, para 24.
[85] ibid, para 30.

anticompetitive because it caused harm to the structure of competition. In *Post Danmark I*, the Court did not mention the structure of competition, or the structure of the market, but defined exclusionary abuses as conduct that caused harm to consumers indirectly through their impact on competition. The emphasis of this definition clearly lies on the protection of consumers, and could even be interpreted as meaning that consumer harm is the ultimate form of competitive harm. If this truly were the Court's new understanding of an exclusionary abuse, it would require the enforcement agencies to assess in every case whether the excluded competitors were as efficient as the dominant undertaking before being able to conclude that the exclusionary conduct was abusive. These statements were widely considered a major step towards the Court accepting the consumer welfare aim.[86]

However, in the final answer to the Danish Court's question, the Court did not mention the requirement that the excluded competitor had to be as efficient as the dominant undertaking. It 'merely' ruled that Article 102 had to be interpreted as meaning that a policy by which a dominant undertaking charged low prices to certain major customers of a competitor could not be considered to amount to an exclusionary abuse merely because the undertaking charged one of those customers a price that was below average total cost but above average incremental cost. Rather, in order to assess the existence of anticompetitive effects in such circumstances, it was necessary to consider whether that pricing policy, without objective justification, produced an 'actual or likely exclusionary effect to the detriment of competition and, thereby, of consumers' interests'. This final answer was surprisingly vague, given the relatively strong statements in the judgment itself on the relevance of the excluded competitor's efficiency.

Shortly after the ruling in *Post Danmark I*, another Danish court therefore made a further reference for a preliminary ruling and specifically asked whether an assessment of potentially exclusionary rebates required the competition authority to carry out an 'as-efficient-competitor' test. This case, which concerned another pricing practice by the incumbent Danish postal operator, became known as *Post Danmark III*.[87] The ruling in *Post Danmark III*, which followed three years after *Post Danmark I*, is more conservative and in line with the case law of the first 40 years. It opens with the old *Hoffmann-La Roche* formula from 1979,[88] according to which Article 102 refers to conduct which is such as to 'influence the structure of a market' where, as a result of the very presence of the undertaking in question, the degree of competition is already weakened and which has the effect of hindering the maintenance of the degree of competition still existing in the market or the growth of that competition.[89] There is no mention of the effects on consumers.

[86] See eg E Rousseva and M Marquis, 'Hell Freezes Over: A Climate Change for Assessing Exclusionary Conduct under Article 102 TFEU' (2013) 4 *Journal of European Competition Law & Practice* 32.

[87] *Post Danmark v Konkurrencerådet* (n 73).

[88] *Hoffmann-La Roche v Commission* (n 12) para 91.

[89] *Post Danmark v Konkurrencerådet* (n 73) para 26.

The Court of Justice further held that when assessing the likelihood of an anticompetitive effect, it was necessary to examine whether the rebate tended to remove or restrict the buyer's freedom to choose his sources of supply, to bar competitors from access to the market, to apply dissimilar conditions to equivalent transactions with other trading parties or to strengthen the dominant position by distorting competition.[90] Again, there is no mention of consumers. Instead, the focus lies on concepts of freedom, the ability of competitors to access or remain in the market, as well as discrimination.

To add insult to injury, from an economic point of view, the Court also ruled that there was no room for a *de minimis* rule under Article 102. It reiterated the principle that dominant undertakings had a special responsibility not to allow their behaviour to impair genuine, undistorted competition on the internal market. Since the structure of competition had already been weakened by the presence of the dominant undertaking, any further weakening of this structure could constitute an abuse. The abusive conduct was by its very nature liable to give rise to not insignificant restrictions of competition.[91]

Regarding the contentious issue of the as-efficient-competitor test, the ruling in *Post Danmark III* also seems to take a step back from the position expressed in *Post Danmark I*. First, the Court stressed that the Commission's Guidance, which contains an as-efficient-competitor test, merely set out the Commission's administrative practice for choosing cases and was hence neither binding on national courts or administrative authorities.[92] Second, it held that it was not possible to infer from either Article 102 or the Court's previous case law that an assessment of a rebate scheme's competitive nature had to be based on the as-efficient-competitor test.[93] It stressed that it did not want to exclude recourse to such a test in cases involving rebate schemes on principle. It was, in theory, one possible tool amongst others for the purposes of assessing, whether a rebate scheme was abusive.[94] However, in a case such as the one under consideration, in which the dominant undertaking had a very large market share and structural advantages conferred upon it by a statutory monopoly, the test was inappropriate because the structure of the market had made the emergence of an as efficient competitor practically impossible.[95] In conclusion, the Court of Justice's final answer to the Danish Court's question was that it was not necessary to apply an as-efficient-competitor test to rebate schemes under Article 102.[96]

In sum, *Post Danmark I* seemed to signal a certain degree of willingness on the part of the Court of Justice to re-examine its traditional concept of harm insofar as it suggested that not every exclusionary effect made a dominant undertaking's

[90] ibid, para 64.
[91] ibid, paras 70–74.
[92] ibid, para 52.
[93] ibid, para 57.
[94] ibid, paras 58 and 61.
[95] ibid, para 59.
[96] ibid, para 62.

conduct abusive, but that the exclusion of competitors that were less efficient than the dominant undertaking could not be deemed anticompetitive. The subsequent ruling in *Post Danmark III* relativised this ruling. Not only did the Court hold that Article 102 did not require the enforcement authorities to apply an as efficient competitor test. It also ruled than in certain cases such a test would be inappropriate, because the market structure prevented the emergence of equally efficient competitors, in which case a less efficient competitor had to be considered better than none. In any event, it is clear from the case law of the past 10 years that, the Commission's change of heart notwithstanding, the Court does not consider consumer harm an essential precondition of exclusionary abusive conduct under Article 102.

D. Conclusions on the Court's Concept of Harm

To conclude, the Court has not made the same adjustments to its concept of competitive harm as the Commission. While the Court's concept of harm under the Merger Regulation remains somewhat hazy, it has ruled repeatedly both under Articles 101 and 102 that consumer harm is not an essential requisite of anticompetitive conduct since the Commission introduced its welfare-based interpretation of the EU antitrust rules. This point is particularly relevant in cases of exclusionary conduct. According to the Commission's more economic approach, exclusionary effects should only be considered anticompetitive if they are likely to result in consumer harm. However, according to the existing case law, the Court considers the likelihood of exclusionary effects as such sufficient to make an agreement or unilateral conduct anticompetitive.

IV. The Relevance of Non-economic Policy Goals in the Case Law

The more economic approach is based on the notion that efficiency effects should be capable of offsetting the anticompetitive effects of business conduct under all three pillars of EU antitrust law. Under Article 101 and EU merger law, at least, the Commission now further takes the view that efficiencies are the only type of effect capable of offsetting an agreement's or merger's anticompetitive effects.

The Court essentially seems to take the same view with regard to assessments under the EU Merger Regulation. It shares the Commission's current theoretical position that efficiencies should be taken into account as countervailing factors in the overall assessment under Article 2(3) of the Regulation 139/2004,[97] and there

[97] Case T-342/07 *Ryanair v Commission* (n 53) paras 386 ff.

is no judgment that indicates that the Court has ever considered it appropriate to take into consideration any other types of benefit in merger assessments.

Likewise, there are no major disagreements under Article 102. The Court agrees with the Commission's current position that efficiencies are a type of benefit capable of justifying the anticompetitive effects caused by a dominant undertaking's abusive conduct.[98] It has never pronounced itself conclusively on what other types of beneficial effect it considers capable of justifying abusive behaviour in addition to such efficiency effects. The fact that it relies on the general concept of an objective justification suggests that, in theory, at least any legitimate aim should be capable of outweighing the anticompetitive effects, as long as it is proportionate to the harm caused. It has thus repeatedly held that abusive conduct can be justified if it is necessary to protect the dominant undertaking's own legal or economic interests.[99] However, in practice, these defences tend to fail on the requirement of proportionality. Further, the judgments in *Hilti* and *Tetrapak* suggest that the Court deems public health and safety capable of justifying an abuse in principle. Again, the Court did not consider the conduct in question necessary for the protecting of these values in either case.[100] In another case, it considered 'the task and method of financing of public service undertakings' capable of justifying an abuse under Article 102 in theory.[101] One can conclude that, in principle at least, the Court takes a broad view of the type of benefit capable of outweighing the anticompetitive effects caused by a dominant undertaking's abusive behaviour that is not limited to economic efficiency effects. That being said, the Commission's revised approach to Article 102, unlike its more economic approach to Article 101 and EU merger law, has not formally limited the type of benefit capable of justifying abusive conduct to efficiencies only. In theory at least, it still takes the view that benefits other than economic efficiencies, for example the protection of public health, could justify an abuse, as long as the abuse is proportionate to this aim. While it has indicated that non-economic benefits are in practice probable to fail on the criterion of proportionality because private action is unlikely to be necessary,[102] this is in line with the Court's approach in previous cases.

The situation is more problematic under Article 101. The Commission primarily takes countervailing effects into account under Article 101(3), but whereas it used to take a broad view of the types of benefits capable of outweighing a restriction of competition under this provision,[103] it now interprets it as referring

[98] *British Airways v Commission* (n 74) para 86; *Microsoft v Commission* (n 73) para 1159; and *Tomra and Others v Commission* (n 77) para 224.

[99] eg *United Brands v Commission* (n 13) para 189; *Microsoft* (n 73) paras 688–91; *France Télécom v Commission* (n 65) paras 46, 47; *Tomra and Others v Commission* (n 77) para 207.

[100] Case T-30/89 *Hilti v Commission* ECLI:EU:T:1991:70, paras 115–19; *Tetra Pak* (n 70) para 138.

[101] Case C-52/07 *Kanal 5 Ltd and TV 4 AB v Föreningen Svenska Tonsättares Internationella Musikbyrå* ECLI:EU:C:2008:703, para 47.

[102] European Commission, Guidance on the Commission's enforcement priorities in applying Article 82 [2009] OJ C45/7, paras 28, 29.

[103] See Ch 6.

to economic efficiencies only. The Court, on the other hand, appears to interpret Article 101 more broadly.

In *Continental Can*, the Court held that the Treaty allowed certain restraints of competition because of the need to harmonise the various objectives of the Treaty.[104] The General Court reiterated this principle as recently as 2012.[105] This general statement already suggests that the Court does not consider the enhancement of consumer welfare the only beneficial effect that should be taken into account in assessments under Article 101. An analysis of the Court's case law on Article 101 confirms that this is the case. There are two key mechanisms by which the Court balances the aim of protecting competition against the other Treaty objectives: a broad interpretation of Article 101(3) and a restrictive interpretation of Article 101(1).

While the Court unquestionably includes efficiencies in the range of benefits it considers capable of offsetting competitive harm under Article 101(3),[106] it does not regard them as the only eligible type of benefit. On the contrary, there are a number of cases in which the Court explicitly held that wider public policy aims had to be considered in assessments under Article 101(3). For example, it repeatedly ruled that the 'provision of employment', ie the protection or creation of jobs, fell within the framework of objectives that could be considered under Article 101(3) because it improved the general conditions of production, especially when market conditions were unfavourable.[107] In *Métropole television*, the General Court held more generally that the Commission was entitled to base itself on 'considerations connected with the pursuit of the public interest' under Article 101(3).[108] In that case, the public interest in question was the obligation to provide varied programming including cultural, educational, scientific and minority programmes of little commercial appeal and to cover the entire national population irrespective of the cost.[109] In *Der Grüne Punkt—DSD*, the General Court found no fault with the Commission's decision to exempt an agreement because it 'enabled environmental objectives to be met'.[110]

Admittedly, the last of these cases dates from 2003. The Court has not had the opportunity to pronounce itself on the issue of non-efficiency benefits under Article 101(3) since then. There is therefore the possibility that it would decide differently if a similar case arose today. However, there are two reasons that make this

[104] *Europemballage and Continental Can v Commission* (n 4) para 24.

[105] Case T-352/09 *Novácke chemické závody a.s. v Commission* ECLI:EU:T:2012:673, para 235.

[106] eg *GlaxoSmithKline v Commission* (n 16) paras 147–262.

[107] Cases 26/76 *Metro SB-Großmärkte v Commission* ECLI:EU:C:1977:167, para 43; 75/84 *Metro SB-Großmärkte v Commission* ECLI:EU:C:1986:39, para 65; 42/84 *Remia and others v Commission* ECLI:EU:C:1985:327, para 42.

[108] Cases T-528/93, T-542/93, T-543/93, T-546/93 *Métropole télévision and others v Commission* ECLI:EU:T:1996:99, para 118.

[109] ibid, para 116.

[110] Case T-289/01 *Der Grüne Punkt—Duales System Deutschland v Commission* ECLI:EU:T:2007:155, para 38.

unlikely. First, the Court consistently defines the first condition of Article 101(3) as referring to 'appreciable objective advantages of such a kind as to compensate for the resulting disadvantages for competition'.[111] Not unlike its concept of harm, this is a broad definition. Nothing in it suggests that the appreciable objective advantages are limited to quantifiable increases in consumer welfare in the form of lower prices or better quality product. In fact, the Court's definition does not even specify that the advantages in question must be of an economic nature. It last used this definition in the case of *GlaxoSmithKline* in 2009,[112] when it ruled that consumer harm was not a prerequisite of a restriction of competition under Article 101(1). Second, given that the Court does not consider the enhancement of the consumer welfare the exclusive aim of Article 101 and does not consider consumer harm necessary to make conduct anticompetitive, there is no compelling reason why it should limit countervailing benefits to consumer welfare-enhancing effects only. In sum, the Commission's revised interpretation of Article 101(3) is difficult to reconcile with the Court's case law.

In addition to considering a broad range of benefits under Article 101(3), the Court sometimes takes economic and non-economic benefits into account under Article 101(1) already. According to the Court, not every agreement that restricts the parties' freedom of action necessarily falls within the prohibition of Article 101(1).[113] Instead it takes the view that any competitive assessment must first establish the overall context of the agreement and its objectives, and must then consider whether the agreement's restrictive effects on competition are inherent in the pursuit of those objectives and proportionate to them.[114] Based on this principle, the Court has in the past excluded agreements from the scope of Article 101(1) because they pursued legitimate policy goals. In *Albany, Brentjens* and *Drijvende Bokken*, for example, it held that agreements concluded in the context of collective bargaining between management and labour and aimed at improving employment conditions had to fall outside the scope of Article 101(1), because any other view would seriously undermine the pursuit of social policy aims through the dialogue between management and labour. The latter was explicitly encouraged by the Treaty.[115] Likewise, in the case of *Wouters*, it held that a regulation adopted by the Bar of a Member State, that prohibited partnerships of its members with

[111] *Consten and Grundig v Commission* (n 24) pt 13; C-279/95 P *Langnese-Iglo v Commission* ECLI:EU:C:1998:447, para 180; T-17/93 *Matra Hachette v Commission* ECLI:EU:T:1994:89, para 135; *Van den Bergh Foods v Commission* (n 31) para 139.

[112] P *GlaxoSmithKline v Commission* (n 18) para 92.

[113] C-67/96 *Albany International* ECLI:EU:C:1999:430, para 59; Case C-219/97 *Maatschappij Drijvende Bokken* ECLI:EU:C:1999:437, para 47; Joined cases C-115/97 to C-117/97 *Brentjens' Handelsonderneming* ECLI:EU:C:1999:434, para 57; Joined Cases T-217/03 and T-245/03 *Fédération nationale de la coopération bétail et viande (FNCBV) and Others v Commission* ECLI:EU:T:2006:391, para 98.

[114] Case C-309/99 *Wouters v Algemene Raad van de Nederlandse Orde van Advocaten* ECLI:EU:C:2002:98, para 97; C-519/04 P *David Meca-Medina and Igor Majcen v Commission of the European Communities* ECLI:EU:C:2006:492, para 42.

[115] *Albany International* (n 133) para 64; *Drijvende Bokken BV* (n 113) para 51; *Brentjens* (n 113) para 61.

members of other liberal professions, did not infringe Article 101(1) as it was necessary for the proper practice of the legal profession.[116] In *Meca-Medina*, the Court decided that the anti-doping rules adopted by the International Olympic Committee did not necessarily infringe Article 101(1) because they pursued the legitimate objective of preserving the fairness and integrity of competitive sport, and because their restrictive effect on the athletes' freedom of action was inherent in the organisation and proper conduct of competitive sport.[117]

On the face of it, this line of case law seems wide in scope and suggests that the Court's test for excluding an agreement from the scope of Article 101(1) because of legitimate objectives contains only three conditions, ie that the agreement pursue a legitimate aim; that the restriction of competition be inherent in the pursuit of this aim; and that the restriction be proportionate. However, the Court's subsequent ruling in *Pavlov*[118] suggests that things are not quite as straightforward. In *Pavlov*, the Court refused to apply the rule established in *Albany* to a collective agreement concluded by members of the liberal professions. Even though the agreement in question pursued a legitimate social policy objective, namely to guarantee its members a minimum pension level, the Court held that the situation was not comparable to that in *Albany*. In contrast to collective bargaining between management and labour, agreements amongst the self-employed were neither specifically encouraged by the Treaty nor could they be made compulsory by the public authorities for all the members of the profession in question.[119] This ruling suggested that the Court limits its restrictive interpretation of Article 101(1) to agreements or decision made in pursuit of objectives specifically encouraged by the Treaty, and possibly even to agreements made by entities that have regulatory or quasi-regulatory powers. If the latter were true, agreements concluded by 'ordinary' market participants could never benefit from this exception. In the recent case of *FNV Kunsten Informatie en Media*, however, in which the Court confirmed the rule that agreements amongst the self-employed did not benefit from the *Wouters* exception, it exclusively based the distinction on the fact that the Treaty did not explicitly encourage such agreements in the way it did for agreements between employers and workers.[120] It did not refer to the issue of regulatory powers at all. While there is thus some uncertainty as to the exact scope of the *Wouters* line of case law, it remains a valid method for taking into account beneficial non-efficiency effects of anticompetitive agreements. The Commission's guidelines on the interpretation of Article 101, incidentally, do not mention this mechanism at all.

[116] *Wouters* (n 114) paras 97–110.

[117] *David Meca-Medina* (n 114) para 45.

[118] C-180/98 to C-184/98 *Pavel Pavlov and Others v Stichting Pensioenfonds Medische Specialisten* ECLI:EU:C:2000:428.

[119] *Pavlov* (n 118) paras 68 and 69.

[120] Case C-413/13 *FNV Kunsten Informatie en Media v Netherlands* ECLI:EU:C:2014:2411, paras 25–30.

In sum, the Court takes a wider view of what type of benefit is capable of offsetting and justifying restrictions of competition under Article 101 than the Commission.

V. Form- v Effects-based Tests in the Case Law

As explained in Chapter 7, the Commission has not made major changes to the types of test it uses for assessing conduct under Article 101 and Article 2(3) of the Merger Regulation. What has changed is the type of effect it considers relevant, but this is a matter of the concept of harm and not of whether effects must be presumed or assessed in each individual case. Even though the Court and the Commission disagree on the concept of harm underlying these analyses, there are no major disagreements on the issue of the correct type of test. They both take the view that mergers need to be assessed as to their effects in each individual case. Regarding Article 101, it is the Court that established the rule that the anticompetitive effects of agreements could be presumed if they had the object of restricting competition, and that less obviously dangerous agreements needed to be assessed as to their likely effects in the individual case.[121] The Commission has always followed and continues to follow this approach.[122] The two institutions do not even seem to diverge much in their understanding of what type of agreement should be considered restrictive by object. Mostly, the Commission appears to follow the Court's case law on this point, which considers horizontal price fixing,[123] output reduction,[124] customer allocation,[125] market allocation and bid-rigging[126] restrictive by object. As far as vertical agreements are concerned, the Court will presume the anticompetitive effects of absolute territorial protection and restrictions of parallel trade[127] as well as resale price maintenance.[128] The latter is the only category of restriction on which there might be a certain degree of discrepancy, although even this is not certain. Since the introduction of the more economic approach, the Commission differentiates more carefully between different types of resale price maintenance. While it continues to deem minimum and fixed resale price maintenance restrictive by object, it now takes the view that maximum

[121] *Établissements Consten S.à.R.L. and Grundig-Verkaufs-GmbH v Commission* (n 24) 340, 342; *Coöperatieve Vereniging 'Suiker Unie' UA and others v Commission* (n 25) 174, para 548.

[122] See Ch 7.

[123] Case T-47/10 *Akzo Nobel v Commission* ECLI:EU:T:2015:506, para 230.

[124] Case C-209/07 *Beef Industry Development Society (BIDS)* ECLI:EU:C:2008:643, para 40.

[125] eg *Akzo Nobel v Commission* (n 123) para 230.

[126] Case T-208/08 *Gosselin Group NV v Commission* ECLI:EU:T:2011:287, para 67.

[127] *GlaxoSmithKline v Commission* (n 18) para 59.

[128] Case 161/84 *Pronuptia de Paris* ECLI:EU:C:1986:41, para 25; Case 243/83 *Binon v Agence et messageries de la presse* ECLI:EU:C:1985:284, para 44.

resale price maintenance needs to be assessed as to its actual effects.[129] There is actually no case in which the Court has had the opportunity to pronounce itself on maximum resale price maintenance specifically. However, the language it used in cases dealing with fixed resale price maintenance was very broad. In *Pronuptia*, for example, it held that provisions which impaired the franchisee's freedom to determine her own prices were restrictive of competition by object, so long as these were not mere recommendation.[130] In *Binon*, it ruled that provisions which fixed the prices to be observed in contracts with third parties constituted, of themselves, a restriction on competition within the meaning of Article 101(1).[131] One could conclude from the ruling in *Pronuptia*, in particular, that the Court of Justice considers any type of resale price maintenance restrictive by object. However, given that the two cases in question concerned fixed resale price maintenance, this is not imperative.

Once again, Article 102 is the problem child. Since the review of its approach to Article 102, the Commission has been assessing potentially abusive conduct as to its likely effects in every case. The Court, by contrast, takes an approach that is reminiscent of its reading of Article 101. While the wording of Article 102 does not distinguish between abuses by object and abuses by effect, an analysis of the case law shows that the Court differentiates between types of conduct that it presumes to be abusive and conduct that needs to be assessed more carefully as to whether it is 'capable' of restricting competition. It thus takes the view that exclusivity arrangements, for example, are always abusive on the part of a dominant undertaking.[132] Likewise, it considers that fidelity rebates, ie rebates that are dependent on the customer buying all or almost all of its requirements from the dominant undertaking, always amount to an abuse of a dominant position.[133] According to this case law there is no need to assess the actual or potential foreclosure effects of the exclusivity contract or fidelity rebate, let alone the effects on consumer welfare.

The Court's approach to assessing predatory pricing is a little more intricate. It deems low prices abusive if they are below average variable cost, while it takes the view that prices below average total costs but above average variable costs are only abusive if it can be proved that the undertaking had an intention to eliminate competitors.[134] According to the Court, there is no need to carry out an individual assessment of actual foreclosure effects in either case. Neither is it necessary to assess the likelihood that consumers will be affected negatively by demonstrating

[129] European Commission, Guidelines on Vertical Restraints [2010] OJ C130/1, paras 223 –29.

[130] *Pronuptia de Paris* (n 128) para 25.

[131] *Binon v Agence et messageries de la presse* (n 128) para 44.

[132] eg *Tetra Pak International v Commission* (n 70) para 137; *Hoffman-La Roche v Commission* (n 12) para 89.

[133] *Tomra Systems and Others v Commission* (n 65) para 70; *Nederlandsche Banden Industrie Michelin v Commission* (n 13) para 71.

[134] *France Télécom v Commission* (n 65) para 33; Case C-333/94 P *Tetra Pak v Commission* ECLI:EU:C:1996:436, para 41; *AKZO v Commission* (n 68) paras 71 and 72.

that the undertaking would have the ability to recoup the losses it made while pricing below cost.[135] In sum, this is a type of intermediary test. The anticompetitive nature of the conduct is not simply inferred from the mere form of the undertaking's behaviour, but the Court does not require the enforcement agency to assess the actual effects on competition either.

According to the case law, all other types of conduct on the part of a dominant undertaking need to be assessed as to whether they are 'capable' of having or 'liable' to have a negative effect on competition as understood by the Court, ie a foreclosure effect in the case of exclusionary conduct. 'Capacity' and 'liability' seem to be used interchangeably in this line of case law. The Court applies this type of test, amongst other, to discounts other than fidelity rebates[136] and refusals to supply. With regard to the latter, the Court holds that the refusal by an undertaking occupying a dominant position to meet the orders of an existing customer constitutes an abuse of that dominant position under Article 102 where, without any objective justification, that conduct is 'liable' to eliminate a trading party as a competitor.[137] The most recent case law on margin squeezes suggests that this type of conduct also needs to be assessed as to whether it is capable of foreclosure effects.[138] There is some uncertainty about the Court's current position on tying. In the case of *Hilti* in 1991, the General Court had ruled that an undertaking abused its dominant position if it refused to supply certain products separately, put pressure on independent distributors to cause them to adopt its discriminatory practices and refused to honour the guarantee attaching to its tools where they have been used with consumables produced by other manufacturers.[139] According to this ruling, there was no need to assess whether the conduct had actual or likely foreclosure effects. In *Microsoft*, however, the only other plain tying case examined by the EU judiciary to date, the General Court held that the Commission was correct to assess the practice's foreclosure effects before deciding to consider it abusive. According to this test, the practice needed to fulfil three formal conditions (ie the tying and tied products had to be separate products; the undertaking concerned had to be dominant in the market for the tying product; and the undertaking concerned must not have given customers a choice to obtain the tying product without the tied product) and be 'capable of foreclosing competition'.[140] This ruling would suggest that tying has moved from the category of conduct that is presumed to be abusive because of its nature to the category of conduct that needs to be assessed as to its capacity to foreclose competitors.

[135] *France Télécom* (n 65) para 37.

[136] *Post Danmark v Konkurrencerådet* (n 73) para 27; *Tomra Systems and Others v Commission* (n 65) para 70; *Nederlandsche Banden Industrie Michelin v Commission* (n 13) para 71.

[137] *Sot Lélos kai Sia EE and Others v GlaxoSmithKline* (n 20) para 34; *Istituto Chemioterapico Italiano and Commercial Solvents v Commission* (n 12) para 25; *United Brands v Commission* (n 13) para 183.

[138] *Konkurrensverket v TeliaSonera Sverige* (n 15) paras 60–74.

[139] *Hilti v Commission* (n 100) pt 5.

[140] *Microsoft v Commission* (n 73) para 868.

This raises the question what the Court actually means by capacity to foreclose. The concept was relatively mysterious for many years. Earlier cases explained that this effect did 'not necessarily relate to the actual effect' of the abusive conduct, but that it was sufficient to show that the abusive conduct 'tended' to restrict competition.[141] In *Post Danmark III* of 2015,[142] the Court of Justice was finally asked to clarify the concept. The Court reviewed its previous case law and held on this basis that the relevant effect of removing or restricting the buyer's freedom to choose his sources of supply, or of barring competitors from access to the market, could not be of purely hypothetical nature. On the other hand, it found that the case law had established that the effect did not have to be concrete either, but that it was sufficient to demonstrate that there was an anticompetitive effect that could potentially exclude competitors. On this basis, the Court concluded that the anti-competitive effects had to be 'likely'.[143]

This brings the Court's conceptual approach to Article 102 very close to that it employs under Article 101. Under both provisions, the Court presumes the anticompetitive effects of certain types of conduct. Others need to be assessed as to their effects. Under Article 102, the Court now requires that these effects be 'likely'. While the Court has never specified the standard for proving anticompetitive effects under Article 101, 'likelihood' is the standard used by the Commission for assessing restrictions by effect. The Court has never objected to this standard on review. Finally, both under Article 101 and Article 102, it submits a number of practices to intermediary types of test that do not automatically infer their effects from their objective, but do not require an in-depth assessment of their likely effects either. That is the case of predatory pricing under Article 102 and selective distribution under Article 101.

VI. Compatibility of the Commission's More Economic Approach with the Case Law and Consequences

A. The Points of Divergence

The above allows the conclusion that the Commission's more economic approach is at odds with the Court's interpretation of the antitrust rules on several points.

First, the Commission's new understanding of the objectives of EU antitrust law is narrower than that of the Court. For the past 15 years, the Commission has

[141] eg Cases T-203/01 *Manufacture française des pneumatiques Michelin v Commission* ECLI:EU:T:2003:250, para 239; *British Airways v Commission* (n 74) para 293; *Tomra v Commission* (n 65) para 289.

[142] *Post Danmark v Konkurrencerådet* (n 73).

[143] ibid, paras 64–67.

taken the view that the EU antitrust rules aim to protect consumer welfare and the process of market integration exclusively. The Court has not embraced this narrower object, but adheres to a broader position. In its view, the EU antitrust rules protect not only consumer welfare, but competition as such in the interest of consumers, competitors, other businesses and the well-being of the European Union in general.

Second, in line with its broader understanding of the law's objective, the Court has also retained a broader concept of competitive harm than the Commission. Since the introduction of the more economic approach, the Commission has only considered such conduct anticompetitive that is likely to result in consumer harm. The Court does not consider direct consumer harm a requisite of competitive harm. It also considers the mere foreclosure of competitors anticompetitive.

Third, at least under Article 101, the Court takes a broader view than the Commission of the types of benefits capable of offsetting competitive harm. While the Commission nowadays only deems economic efficiency effects capable of offsetting competitive harm, the Court is willing to take into consideration a broad array of Treaty objectives subject to the principle of proportionality.

Fourth, the Court deems certain types of unilateral conduct abusive 'by object' under Article 102, meaning that it infers the anticompetitive effects from the conduct's form, rather than require an assessment of its effects in the individual case. By contrast, the Commission's Guidance Paper prescribes an assessment of all exclusionary practices' likely effects in each case.

B. Consequences

How problematic is this divergence? With regard to a number of these points, the Commission's position appears clearly incompatible with the case law. This is the case of the Commission's new, limited understanding of the aims of the EU antitrust rules, its requirement of anticompetitive foreclosure under Article 101 and the EU Merger Regulation, and its position that only efficiency effects can offset competitive harm under Article 101.

The compatibility of the Commission's revised approach to Article 102 with the case law is more difficult to evaluate, because of the indirect manner in which the Commission introduced the more economic approach to this provision. Unlike the guidelines on Article 101 and the EU Merger Regulation, the Communication on Article 102 does not formally reinterpret the provision as only prohibiting exclusionary conduct likely to result in consumer harm and prescribing an assessment of the investigated conduct's likely effects in every case. This would have been plainly incompatible with the case law, and is presumably the very reason the Commission chose not to introduce its reformed vision of Article 102 by means of interpretative guidelines. Instead, it issued a Communication that redefines the Commission's enforcement priorities and explains how the Commission intends to assess whether a case is such a priority. In essence, the Commission will only consider a case a priority if an individual assessment of its effects shows that the exclusionary conduct is likely to result in anticompetitive foreclosure. If it does not, the Commission will not consider the case a priority and simply not enforce Article 102. In practice, this pragmatic solution has solved many of the Commission's problems. While not formally contradicting and disregarding the Court's interpretation of the law, it achieves the desired result of no longer applying Article 102 to cases that are not anticompetitive according to the principles of the more economic approach.

This roundabout and rather ingenious solution may cause an instinctive sense of unease because it pushes through the welfare-based approach to Article 102 while paying lip service to the views of the institution that has been consistently resisting a welfare-based interpretation of Article 102. The Guidance Paper opening by reiterating the key principles established in the case law, which make no sense from the point of view of the welfare-based assessment that follows, is little more than window dressing. But is it legally objectionable?

The Guidance Paper has no direct legal effect, as confirmed repeatedly by the Court.[144] It merely sets out enforcement priorities that are not binding on anybody but the Commission itself, until it decides to change its decision practice. Furthermore, the Commission is in principle entitled to set enforcement priorities in order to use its limited resources in the most efficient manner possible. In *Automec II*, a case predating the Commission's review process, the General Court examined the Commission's practice of determining the priority of cases based on their degree of 'Union interest',[145] which the Commission had developed in order to prioritise the use of its resources.[146] It held that it was an inherent feature of administrative activity for an authority entrusted with a public service task to take all the organisational measures necessary for the performance of that task, including priority setting within the limits prescribed by the law where those priorities have not been determined by the legislature. It recognised that this was particularly necessary where an authority had been entrusted with a supervisory and regulatory task as extensive and general as that assigned to the Commission in the field of competition. Consequently, it held that the Commission applying different degrees of priority to the cases submitted to it in the field of competition was compatible with the Treaty, as long as it set the priorities in accordance with the law.[147] When relying on the criterion of Union interest, in particular, the Commission should balance the significance of the alleged infringement with regard to the functioning of the internal market, the probability of establishing the existence of the infringement and the scope of the investigation required in order to fulfil,

[144] See eg *Post Danmark v Konkurrencerådet* (n 73) para 52.
[145] 'Community interest' in the original.
[146] European Commission, *Seventeenth Report on Competition Policy 1987*, 23 and 24.
[147] T-24/90 *Automec v Commission* ECLI:EU:T:1992:97, para 77.

under the best possible conditions, its task of ensuring that Articles 101 and 102 were complied with.[148]

The first question one might ask oneself therefore is whether the Guidance Paper's enforcement priorities exceed the limits of the law. *De facto*, if not *de lege*, the Guidance Paper reduces the scope of Article 102 in a manner that is incompatible with the Court's interpretation of the provision. In practice, it is irrelevant whether the Commission formally reinterprets the wording of Article 102 as prohibiting only conduct that is welfare-reducing, or whether it lays down in a general and abstract manner that it shall no longer pursue conduct that does not result in consumer harm. The practical effect is the same. Likewise, it is immaterial in practice whether the Commission reinterprets Article 102 as requiring an assessment of the conduct's likely effects in every case, or whether it decides not to enforce Article 102 anymore unless an individual assessment of the investigated conduct shows that it is likely to result in anticompetitive effects.

Moreover, the Guidance Paper's priorities are different from standard administrative priorities, which are normally guided by the aim of using scare resources in the most efficient manner possible. This is not the primary aim of the Guidance Paper. It is the last step in a comprehensive and systematic reform of EU antitrust law that introduced a new legal objective and concept of harm to Article 101 and EU merger law. The Guidance on Article 102, the outcome of a four-year reform process, aimed to bring this last pillar into line with the Commission's revised approaches to Article 101 and the Merger Regulation. It explains over the course of 14 pages how to carry out a consumer welfare- and effects-based assessment of exclusionary conduct under Article 102. It is drafted in a way that is similar in style to that of the Commission's interpretative guidelines on Article 101 and merger control. The language outlining the Commission's approach to specific practices is indistinguishable from that used in the guidelines outlining the Commission's interpretation of Article 101 and the Merger Regulation. After the introduction, it no longer mentions enforcement priorities. If one disregards the Guidance Paper's title and opening statements, the Communication in fact reads exactly like interpretative guidelines. This impression is heightened by the fact that the Commission has outlined its priorities under separate headings relating to the individual legal conditions of Article 102, merging its own explanations with well-known passages of key Court rulings. In sum, in the eyes of the stakeholders, the Guidance Paper is likely to carry the same weight and fulfil the same function as the Commission's interpretative guidelines. This conclusion is supported by the fact that undertakings regularly invoke the Guidance Paper's principles as the relevant authority in proceedings before the European Court of Justice[149] and also in national proceedings.[150]

[148] ibid, para 86.

[149] See eg Opinion of Advocate General Kokott in Case C-109/10 P *Solvay v Commission* ECLI:EU:C:2011:256, para 20; Opinion of Advocate General Mazák in *Tomra v Commission* (n 65) para 36.

[150] See eg in a case before the German enforcement authority (Bundeskartellamt): *Deutsche Post AG* (Case B9-128/12) decision of 2 July 2015, para 195.

The Commission's soft law in the area of EU antitrust law generally carries considerable weight, and has a strong persuasive effect both for individuals and national courts. As the Commission is the main enforcement body, its understanding of the law as well as its enforcement priorities are of great importance to market participants. Although formally the Court has the ultimate word in matters of legal interpretation, only few undertakings will in reality consider it worth their while to run counter to the Commission's express recommendations in order to challenge its policy in lengthy, costly and risky appeal proceedings. Likewise, it will be tempting for national courts and specialised enforcement agencies to rely on the ready-made and detailed rules spelled out in the Guidance when carrying out legal assessments under Article 102. In fact, there is evidence that both national courts[151] and enforcement authorities[152] refer to the principles of the Guidance in their legal assessments under Article 102 as if the Guidance were a statement of the law rather than a tool for prioritising cases. In actual fact, the Commission memorandum accompanying the publication of the Guidance Paper emphasised that the document was intended to provide guidance to the business community and competition law enforcers at the national level on how the Commission articulates an effects-based approach to exclusionary conduct under Article 102.[153]

All in all, the Guidance is likely to have a very different effect from a standard set of enforcement priorities, such as the Commission's criteria for determining Union interest. One can expect that its principles will eventually evolve into legal interpretation. This may well have been the Commission's long-term expectation and intention in publishing the Paper. The above-mentioned memorandum also explicitly states that the Paper is intended to contribute to the 'process of introducing a more economics based approach' to Article 102, already formulated and implemented in the area of Article 101 and EU merger law.[154] While they are presented as enforcement priorities, their substance and effect are that of interpretative guidelines, which are not compatible with the Court's interpretation of the law.[155]

[151] eg Opinion of Advocate General Mazák in Case *Konkurrensverket v TeliaSonera Sverige* (n 15) para 17; Opinion of Advocate General Kokott in *Post Danmark* (n 77) para 58.

[152] See eg the German competition authority (Bundeskartellamt) in *Deutsche Telekom* (B7-11/09), decision of 6 August 2009, para 65; the French competition authority (Autorité de la Concurrence) in decision 13-D-07 of 28 February 2013 *E-kanopi*, para 39; the Belgian competition authority (Autorité Belge de la Concurrence) in décision no ABC-2015-P/K-09-AUD of 26 March 2015 (Affaire CONC-P/K-09/0002) *Lampiris v Electrabel*, para 104, and the former UK Office of Fair Trading (OFT) in a decision on an alleged abuse of a dominant position by Flybe Limited (Case MPINF-PSWA001) of 5 November 2010, s 3.3; and the OFT decision on an alleged abuse of a dominant position by CH Jones Limited (Case reference: CE/9278/10) of 1 October 2013, s 3.5.

[153] DG Competition MEMO/08/761 of 3 December 2008, para 1, available at: www.europa.eu/rapid/.

[154] ibid.

[155] See eg A Witt, 'The Commission's Guidance Paper on Abusive Exclusionary Conduct—More Radical than it Appears?' (2010) 35 *European Law Review* 214. Similarly, L Lovdahl Gormsen, 'Why the European Commission's Enforcement Priorities on Article 82 EC Should be Withdrawn' (2010) 31 *European Competition Law Review* 45.

However, even if one takes the view that the Guidance Paper remains within the limits of the law, and that the Commission is not overstepping its powers by persisting with an interpretation of Article 102 that the Court consistently opposes, the situation is not desirable from the point of view of legal certainty. The principle of legal certainty requires that the law be clear. This is all the more important in the context of prohibition rules the non-observance of which is liable to fines. These fines can be considerable. In 2009, for example, the Commission fined Intel €1,060,000,000 under Article 102.[156] However, currently, we have a situation in which the two key institutions have a different concept of competitive harm and a different understanding of whether the harmful effects, however defined, may be inferred or should be established in the individual case. While the Commission pays lip service to the case law, it operates on the basis of a different interpretation in practice. This is not in the interest of legal certainty and undermines the credibility of the institutions', and in particular the Commission's, commitment to the rule of law.

Finally, unlike the Guidance Paper, the Commission's individual decisions applying Article 102 do have direct legal effect. As demonstrated in Chapters 6 and 7, the Commission started introducing the more economic approach to individual decisions under Article 102 around 2004. While its prohibition decisions between 2004 and 2009 did so by first assessing the conduct under the Court's case law and then carrying out an 'additional and unnecessary' assessment of the conduct's effects on consumer welfare, several prohibition decisions since 2009 no longer take this roundabout approach, but assess the effects on consumer welfare as if it were business as usual. They are therefore based on a concept of harm that is not that of the Court of Justice. On appeal, the Court would presumably not find this a reason for annulling a finding of illegality, as the assessment of consumer harm is a 'plus' that does not call into question the conduct's foreclosure effects, which the Court deems sufficient to make a practice abusive. Nonetheless, they are based on a legal interpretation that is not compatible with the Court's interpretation of the law.

VII. Conclusion

In sum, it is clear that the Court has not fully embraced the Commission's revised legal objective and interpretation of the EU antitrust rules. The Court has a wider view of the aims of EU antitrust law and a broader understanding of competitive harm. Under Article 101, it also seems willing to take into consideration other Treaty aims than the enhancement of consumer welfare when it comes to balancing conflicting effects. Finally, with regard to Article 102, it considers certain types

[156] *Intel* (Case COMP/C-3 /37.990).

of conduct abusive 'by object' in the sense that it infers their illegality from their form.

In practice, the two institutions' differences are most significant in cases of exclusionary conduct, be it unilateral, the result of an agreement or the possible consequence of a merger. While the Court considers the exclusion of competitors as such anticompetitive, the Commission nowadays only considers such instances of exclusion anticompetitive that is likely to result in consumer harm, and is committed to establishing the likelihood of such consumer harm before finding an infringement of the antitrust rules.

This is a remarkable situation. The Commission does much more than it is legally required to prove the anticompetitive nature of business conduct. Establishing the actual or likely effects of a certain practice on the ability of competitors to enter and remain in the market, and then additionally establishing the effects on prices or other parameters of consumer welfare, is more difficult, time-consuming and hence more costly than inferring it from the conduct's objective or form. This raises the question as to why an institution would act in such a manner if it could instead choose the easier route and clearly remain within the law. The only rational explanation is that this situation is the result of the personal convictions of the officials working in DG Competition, who believe that an interpretation of the antitrust rules in the light of an exclusive consumer welfare aim and an assessment of these effects in each individual case is the best approach and thus in the general interest, even in the face of the Court's resistance.

11

Other Concerns

I. Introduction

The previous chapter identified a major weakness of the European Commission's more economic approach: a few of its key principles are not consistent with the Court of Justice's interpretation of the law. This chapter puts this issue to one side, and reflects on the drawbacks of the approach as such. While the more economic approach undoubtedly has a number of inherent strengths, as argued in Chapter 9, it is not without its shortcomings.

II. Consistency

How consistent is the Commission's more economic approach as it stands? The key principles on which it is based are wonderfully logical and coherent: one single, quantifiable legal objective (consumer welfare) that results in clear, quantifiable concepts of harm (restrictions of competition that result in consumer harm) and countervailing effects (consumer welfare-enhancing efficiency effects). However, in reality, there are a number of points on which the Commission's approach currently falls short of this premise.

First, the Commission does not fully follow the premise that EU antitrust law is guided by the exclusive aim of enhancing economic consumer welfare. While the aim of consumer welfare clearly dominates the decision practice and interpretative guidelines, the Commission also recognises and relies on the aim of market integration and the corresponding concept of harm, at least under Article 101.[1] Further, harm to the process of market integration is usually inferred and not established on the basis of actual evidence.[2] This undermines the internal consistency of the approach, and also the credibility of the claim that EU antitrust law is now informed by one single, non-political aim.

[1] European Commission, Guidelines on Article 81(3) [2004] OJ C101/97, para 13.
[2] *Glaxo Wellcome and others* (Case IV/36.957/F3) [2001] OJ L302/1, recitals 124, 125.

Second, the Commission has not officially introduced the restrictive concepts of harm and countervailing effects on which its reformed approach to Article 101 and the Merger Regulation are based to Article 102. It legally requires consumer harm under Article 101 and merger law for business conduct to be anticompetitive, but officially does not do so under Article 102. In sum, it operates on the basis of different concepts of harm and countervailing effects under the different pillars. As explained in Chapter 10, the reason for this discrepancy is clear enough. While the Commission would have liked to bring its approach to Article 102 into line with its revised interpretation of Article 101 and the EU Merger Regulation, an interpretation of Article 102 as requiring consumer harm in the case of exclusionary conduct would have been clearly incompatible with the case law.

Third, while the Commission's more economic approach recognises the theory that efficiencies are capable of offsetting competitive harm, efficiency defences tend not to succeed in practice. The Commission has not once recognised an efficiency claim in a case in which it had identified serious competitive concerns. In this aspect, the Commission's theory and practice are out of sync.

Fourth, the Commission's more economic approach is based on a very broad concept of consumer harm, that not only comprises quantifiable price increases and output reductions, but also negative effects on the variety of products, product quality and levels of innovation.[3] In *Motorola*, the Commission even considered the practice's negative impact on standard-setting in the telecommunications industry to be a form of consumer harm, because undermining confidence in the standard-setting process would deprive consumers of its benefits.[4] This broad understanding of consumer harm undermines the advantages of the precise, single aim informing an equally precise concept of harm. Also, the effects on innovation and product quality are not as easily quantifiable as price increases and output reductions. One of the attractions of a concept of harm that equals a reduction in economic welfare is that it can be measured, quantified and accurately balanced against countervailing efficiency effects. It is one of the great advantages over a freedom-based concept of harm. Including welfare factors in this concept that cannot be quantified greatly diminishes that advantage.

III. Clarity

The Commission's reform of its approach to Article 102 has led to a fair degree of legal uncertainty. Having introduced a new interpretation of Article 101 and the Merger Regulation by means of interpretative guidelines, the Commission's decision to complete the reform by means of a Guidance Notice that formally

[3] European Commission, Guidelines on the application of Article 81(3) [2004] OJ C101/97, para 24.
[4] *Motorola—Enforcement of GPRS standard essential patents* (Case AT.39985), recital 312.

proclaims to spell out enforcement priorities, but in substance explains in great detail how the Commission envisages a consumer-welfare guided assessment of Article 102, has truly muddied the waters. It has resulted in a situation that is confusing and full of contradictions.

In the eyes of the addressees, ie the business community, their legal advisors, the national enforcement bodies and courts, this Guidance Paper, following in the steps of the Article 101 and merger guidelines, is bound to take the place of substantive guidelines, especially as the Commission refers to its principles in its decisions' substantive assessments. However, the Guidance Notice emphatically claims not to contain interpretative guidelines, because formulating its principles in such terms would have amounted to spelling out an interpretation that is not compatible with the case law. The Communication's solution of reiterating the Court's old-established principles in the introduction, and then spelling out a conflicting approach in the main body under the guise of enforcement priorities, is highly confusing. It is not all clear what the Commission's current legal interpretation of Article 102 is. This is not a desirable situation.

IV. Difficulty of Application

The more economic approach requires an assessment of the investigated conduct's effects on competition and consumer welfare, unless these effects may exceptionally be inferred because of their inevitability, for example in the case of hard-core cartels under Article 101. Ideally, both the anticompetitive and pro-competitive effects should be quantified. Both the Commission and parties now frequently use econometric tools to prove the likelihood of such effects. While such an approach promises a high if not complete degree of accuracy,[5] establishing and quantifying such effects is not a straightforward approach. This raises a number of problems.

A. Manageability for Courts

While the Commission may have the resources and know-how to prove the effects of a specific conduct on competition and prices or other parameters of consumer welfare, the specialised enforcement authorities of the smaller or less prosperous Member States might find this more difficult to do. Even more doubtful is the ability of generalist courts to carry out such assessments. There are several ways in which EU and national courts can be required to apply EU antitrust law to a specific case. First, courts review the decisions of the public enforcement authorities. The ability of the European Courts to carry out meaningful judicial review of

[5] See Ch 9.

the Commission's enforcement decisions is all the more important because of the structure of EU antitrust enforcement. Unlike in the United States, the EU enforcement authority not only investigates the case. It also takes the final decision. It thus combines prosecutorial and adjudicating functions. In fact, in view of its substantive review of EU antitrust law by means of soft law instruments over the past 15 years, which has led it to make important changes in interpretation, it also has also taken on quasi-legislative functions in the area of EU antitrust law. Given this concentration of powers in the hands of one institution, judicial review of the Commission's decisions is particularly important. Second, national courts are responsible for applying the EU antitrust rules in cases of claims for compensation by parties injured by an antitrust infringement. They also review the decisions of the national competition authorities enforcing Articles 101 and 102. Judges must therefore be able to apply the EU antitrust rules.

However, if one looks at the Commission's ideal of how the EU antitrust rules should be interpreted and applied, as spelled out in the Guidance on Article 102 for instance, this requires a great deal of economic know-how. For example, the most fundamental principle underlying the Guidance is that of anticompetitive foreclosure. According to the Guidance, anticompetitive foreclosure is to be assessed by determining whether effective access of actual or potential competitors to supplies or markets is hampered as a result of the conduct of the dominant undertaking whereby the dominant undertaking is likely to be in a position to increase prices profitably to the detriment of intermediate or final consumers. The identification of such harm can rely on qualitative and quantitative evidence.[6] Specifically, with regard to price-based exclusionary conduct, the Commission additionally suggests assessing whether the conduct concerned is capable of hampering competition from competitors who are as efficient as the dominant undertaking. To establish whether the competitor is as efficient as the dominant undertaking, the Commission will examine economic data relating to cost and sales prices, and in particular whether the dominant undertaking is engaging in below-cost pricing. The cost benchmarks it proposes to use are average avoidable cost (AAC) and long-run average incremental cost (LRAIC).[7] These types of assessments, two amongst many others that the Guidance Paper suggests as standard tests, are likely to exceed the abilities of many lawyers. The same is most likely true of the complex econometric analyses which the Commission now frequently produces to prove key anticompetitive effects produced by the investigated conduct under all three pillars of EU antitrust law.

Inevitably, judges are more likely to be experts in law than in economics. Even in the United States, where the exclusive economic welfare aim is almost universally

[6] European Commission, Guidance on the Commission's enforcement priorities in applying Article 82 of the EC Treaty to abusive exclusionary conduct by dominant undertakings [2009] OJ C 45/7, para 19.

[7] ibid, paras 23–27.

accepted, and econometrics have played a significant role in antitrust proceedings since the advent of the Chicago school in the 1970s, many commentators are sceptical about the ability of generalist judges to handle complex econometric assessments.[8] Even Richard Posner, a staunch Chicagoan and one of the fathers of the economic approach to US antitrust law, takes the view that econometrics is such a difficult subject that it is unrealistic to expect the average judge or juror to be able to understand all the criticisms of an econometric study, no matter how skilful the econometrician is in explaining a study to a lay audience.[9] The American Bar Association expresses similar concerns.[10] However, if the law is too difficult for a judge to apply, because it requires complex economic assessments that are beyond the ability of even very competent lawyers, this makes the law unsuitable to fulfil its function. Recourse to a neutral, court-appointed expert economic witness who advises the judge on specific points might be a solution, although this raises a whole new set of problems.[11] Ideally, a judge would be able to apply the law himself in the majority of cases, and not routinely have to call on an expert to make key decisions for him.

B. Manageability for Undertakings

Courts and enforcement authorities are not the only entities that must be able to apply the law. The individuals to whom the rules are addressed also need to be able to understand the law and self-assess their conduct under the rules in order to determine whether their conduct is legal. This is required by the principle of legal certainty, and is all the more important if, like in the area of antitrust law, an infringement is punishable.

While a court that is called to determine whether an investigated conduct produced anticompetitive effects during a specific period may deal with the difficulties of having to carry out complex economic assessments by appointing an independent expert, this is not a realistic option for an undertaking's ongoing self-monitoring process. Can a business really be expected to predict with certainty on a continuous basis whether its behaviour is likely or not to result in a non-transitory increase of prices to a supra-competitive level or affect other parameters of consumer welfare in a similar manner? This question has to be answered in the negative.

[8] MR Baye and JD Wright, 'Is Antitrust Too Complicated for Generalist Judges? The Impact of Economic Complexity and Judicial Training on Appeals' (2011) 54 *Journal of Law and Economics*.

[9] RA Posner, 'The Law and Economics of the Economic Expert Witness' (1999) 13 *The Journal of Economic Perspectives* 91, 96.

[10] www.americanbar.org/content/dam/aba/migrated/antitrust/at-reports/01_c_ii.authcheckdam.pdf.

[11] See eg JG Sidak, 'Court-appointed Neutral Economic Experts' (2013) 9(2) *Journal of Competition Law & Economics* 359, 363–64.

C. Cost

Finally, another consequence of carrying out difficult individual economic assessments in the manner favoured by the more economic approach, instead of relying on simpler rules of thumb, is that it increases the cost and length of proceedings. This is true for the costs of enforcement authorities, the courts and the investigated undertakings. Economic expertise does not usually come for free for any of these entities.[12] The great increase in length of the Commission's infringement decisions since the introduction of the more economic approach reflects the greater effort that the Commission puts into assessing business conduct under the new approach. The average merger prohibition decision under the old approach was 36 pages long. Since the reform, merger prohibitions average 465 pages. This is a significant change. The same development can be observed under Articles 101 and 102.[13] The additional cost will eventually be partially borne by taxpayers and passed on to consumers. This effect needs to be carefully weighed against the benefits of the more economic approach, ie primarily its potential for greater accuracy.

A further consequence of the increased cost for the enforcement authorities is that, unless resources are increased accordingly, it is bound to result in fewer cases being decided in this elaborate manner. This is likely to explain the Commission's heavy use of commitments decisions since 2004, and possibly even its current attempts to encourage private enforcement, which would shift the enforcement burden to individuals and national courts in the case of standalone actions. Chapter 9 identified as one of the benefits of the more economic approach that it had reduced the scope of the antitrust provisions and thus reduced the Commission's enforcement burden. The incredibly elaborate methods of assessment introduced by the more economic approach have somewhat counteracted this effect. It raises the question whether avoiding infringement decisions because they have become too costly to issue in great numbers really achieves the aim of protecting competition to the desired standard, and whether the more economic approach currently strikes the right balance between accuracy and assessment costs.

D. Conclusion

In sum, the more complex and demanding tests championed by the more economic approach have a number of drawbacks. While they may increase the chance of achieving accurate results, the economic know-how they presuppose makes them difficult to apply for those who are not economic experts.

[12] See eg the data collected by Damien Neven, who found in 2005 that the annual turnover of the main economic consultancy firms had increased by a factor of 20 since the early 1990s, amounting to around 15% of the aggregate fees earned in EU antitrust cases (DJ Neven, 'Competition Economics and Antitrust in Europe' (2006) 21 *Economic Policy* 741).

[13] See Tables 1 to 6 in the Annex.

This affects judges and undertakings in particular. The former are not able to carry out meaningful judicial review of enforcement decisions or assess the legality of many types of conduct without the input of economic experts, and the latter are not able to self-assess the legality of their conduct with certainty. Moreover, the need for expert economic input, in particular in order to carry out econometric studies, increases the cost and length of proceedings.

Incidentally, the Commission's Green Paper on Vertical Restraints from 1996, which first discussed the possibility of a more economics-based approach, identified exactly these dangers and was cautious about the role that economic theory should play in the future Commission policy. It clearly stated that economic theory could not be the only factor in the design of policy, and this for a number of reasons. For one, economic theory was just one of several relevant sources of policy, which had to be applied in the context of the existing legal texts and jurisprudence. Second, economic theories were necessarily based on simplifying assumptions often obtained in the context of stylised theoretical models that could not take into account all the complexities of real life cases. Third, a full economic analysis of every case would be very costly and might not be justified by gains in identifying market situations and restraints that were detrimental to competition. In those circumstances, competition policy should resort to relatively simple rules of thumb and do without a full economic analysis of every case, as the costs in terms of uncertainty for enterprises and resources needed to do this analysis would not be justified by the expected economic gains of this approach.[14] The Green Paper on Vertical Restraints dates from the period of Monti's predecessor Karl van Miert. The concerns it outlines seem to have taken a back seat during his successors' offices.

V. Consumer Welfare as the Only Relevant Value

While the difficulty of application for businesses and courts is the most practical concern, there is another, equally important even though more theoretical question one may ask about the validity of the more economic approach. This concerns the claim that the exclusive value underlying the EU antitrust rules should be the enhancement of consumer welfare. What is the basis for choosing this particular value to the exclusion of all others, save the aim of market integration? Why should the aim of enhancing economic consumer welfare take the place of and even trump over such fundamental values as individual economic freedom, fairness and democracy?

One practical reason for choosing consumer welfare as the exclusive value of antitrust law could be that an economic welfare aim can be translated into a clear

[14] European Commission, 'Green Paper on Vertical Restraints in EC Competition Policy' COM(96) 721 of 22 January 1997, para 86.

concept of competitive harm, provided that one defines welfare concisely enough. For example, if one defines consumer welfare as a situation in which prices are low, then an increase in prices amounts to consumer harm. This is a tangible and quantifiable concept of competitive harm that can be proved on the basis of qualitative and quantitative evidence. The same goes for output reductions. This makes for a very workable concept of competitive harm. By contrast, translating the aim of protecting individual freedom or even the democratic process into a logical, workable concept of harm is less straightforward. However, the Commission's understanding of consumer welfare and its concept of competitive harm are not as clear-cut as that proposed by economists. The Commission's understanding of consumer welfare is broader, and includes product quality, consumer choice and innovation, amongst others. Likewise, it considers reductions in quality, consumer choice and levels of innovation instances of competitive harm. These forms of harm are not as easily captured and quantified as prices increases.

While a quantifiable concept of harm is a great advantage, as long as the method for assessing such harm remains within the grasps of the stakeholders, it cannot be the only determinative argument in this debate. Whether consumer welfare, as determined by economic theory, is the only objective of antitrust law also raises fundamental substantive questions. Many commentators take the view that economic consumer welfare should not be the be-all and end-all, but that the many other legal values of Western society should not be entirely excluded from assessments under the antitrust rules.[15] This author generally sympathises with that position, as long as the balancing process is done in a predictable, logical and proportionate manner. Low prices are important, but not the only relevant aim. Individual freedom, the protection of the democratic process and an inhabitable ecosystem are fundamental values without which low prices are meaningless.

Setting aside the issue of personal values, is there any legal basis for making consumer welfare the only relevant value of EU antitrust law? Is it even compatible with primary EU law? If one looks at the Treaties, there is in fact very little support for the assumption that the EU antitrust rules aim at the enhancement of economic consumer welfare only. The antitrust provisions themselves do not define their purpose as protecting consumer welfare.[16] Article 2 TEU lists the key values of the European Union. While it includes the above-mentioned values of freedom, democracy, equality, the rule of law and respect for human rights, there is no

[15] R Pitofsky, 'The Political Content of Antitrust' (1979) 127 *University of Pennsylvania Law Review* 1051; T E Kauper, 'The "Warren Court" and the Antitrust Laws: Of Economics, Populism, and Cynicism' (1968–69) 67 *Michigan Law Review* 325; ME Stucke, 'Reconsidering Antitrust's Goals' (2012) 53 *Boston College Law Review* 551; B van Rompuy, *Economic Efficiency: The Sole Concern of Modern Antitrust Policy? Non-Efficiency Considerations under Article 101 TFEU* (Alphen aan den Rijn, Kluwer, 2012); C Townley, *Article 81 EC and Public Policy* (Oxford, Hart Publishing 2009); L Lovdahl Gormsen, *A Principled Approach to Abuse of Dominance in European Competition Law* (Cambridge, Cambridge University Press, 2010).

[16] See Ch 4.

mention of consumer welfare, let alone consumer welfare defined in terms of product prices, output, diversity, quality or levels of innovation. Article 3 TEU contains the list of the Union's aims. These include, amongst others, the promotion of peace, the Union's values and the well-being of its peoples, the establishment of an internal market, a sustainable development based on balanced economic growth and price stability, a highly competitive social market economy, aiming at full employment and social progress, and a high level of protection and improvement of the quality of the environment. The Union shall combat social exclusion and discrimination, and shall promote social justice and protection, equality between women and men, solidarity between generations and protection of the rights of the child. It shall promote economic, social and territorial cohesion, and solidarity among Member States, while respecting its rich cultural and linguistic diversity, and ensuring that its cultural heritage is safeguarded and enhanced. Once more, the enhancement of consumer welfare specifically is not amongst those aims.

What is more, the Treaties contain the general principle that no Union policy or law shall operate in isolation. According to Article 7 TFEU, the Union shall ensure consistency between its policies and activities by taking into account all of its objectives. Article 9 TFEU re-emphasises this general principle when it states that the Union shall always take into account requirements linked to the promotion of a high level of employment, the guarantee of adequate social protection, the fight against social exclusion and a high level of education, training and protection of human health in defining and implementing its policies and activities. Articles 12 and 167(4) TFEU contain similar reminders for the aims of consumer protection and cultural policy respectively. There is no provision in the Treaties that exempt the antitrust rules from this general principle. The premise of the more economic approach that the EU antitrust rules should be guided by the aim of enhancing economic consumer welfare exclusively, in the image of US antitrust law, therefore stands on very shaky feet from a legal point of view. This is not to say that consumer welfare is not one of the values protected by EU antitrust law, and even a very important one. However, there is no basis in the law that makes it the only relevant value and objective.

VI. Conclusion

In sum, the partial incompatibility with the Court of Justice's interpretation is not the only weakness of the Commission's more economic approach. It is not as internally consistent as it may seem as first sight, and its legal interpretation of Article 102 is currently unclear. There also seems little basis in EU law for considering consumer welfare the only relevant objective of EU antitrust law.

Conclusion

In 1988, Barry Hawk prophesied that the US Antitrust Revolution would not be replicated in Europe because the Union would never abandon its distributive concerns, social goals and values of fairness and freedom in favour of efficiency.[1] As it turns out, he was partially right, but also partially wrong. These days, the story of EU antitrust law is very much a tale of two institutions.

The European Commission has almost fully embraced the agenda of the US Antitrust Revolution, with a few internal market twists of its own. It has adopted consumer welfare as the exclusive objective of EU antitrust law although it makes an exception from this principle for the aim of market integration, which it continues to consider a valid aim. It has changed its interpretation of the EU antitrust rules accordingly by adapting its concepts of competitive harm and countervailing effects, at least under Article 101 and the EU Merger Regulation. Under these two provisions, it now takes the view that business conduct should only be considered anticompetitive if it is likely to result in consumer harm, and that the only types of effect capable of offsetting such harm are efficiency effects that are passed on to consumers to such an extent as to outweigh the reduction in consumer welfare. This is a significant change in interpretation, in particular with regard to Article 101. While the Commission's concept of harm under the original Merger Regulation had been conceptually unclear, it had previously equated restrictions of competition within the meaning of Article 101 with restrictions of economic freedom and opportunity, harm to the structure of the market, and unfair conduct. Under Article 101 it had also regularly taken into account a broad array of beneficial effects other than economic efficiencies as countervailing factors.

The Commission's revised approach to Article 102 is somewhat less straightforward as it did not officially amend its interpretation of Article 102 to bring it into line with its current understanding of Article 101 and EU merger law. Instead, it chose to implement the consumer welfare aim by reformulating its enforcement priorities. In the case of exclusionary abusive behaviour at least, it will only enforce Article 102 if the conduct is likely to result in consumer harm. In practice, this achieves the same result as reinterpreting the provision as legally requiring consumer harm.

The Commission has made a further significant change to assessing exclusionary conduct under Article 102. Not only does it take the view that only such

[1] B Hawk, 'The American (Anti-trust) Revolution—Lessons for the EEC?' (1988) 9 *European Competition Law Review* 53.

instances of exclusion should be pursued that are harmful to consumers, it also intends to assess the likely effects on competition and consumer welfare in every individual case rather than rely on form-based presumptions of anticompetitiveness as it had previously done for specific types of conduct. By contrast, it has not, officially at least, abandoned or even substantially amended its categories of object restrictions that are presumed illegal under Article 101. This is a noteworthy difference from the US Antitrust Revolution, a key feature of which had been the shift away from rules of *per se* illegality to rule of reason assessments under section 1 of the Sherman Act.

In addition to these changes in legal interpretation, the European Commission has also embraced many of the tools that economics has to offer for evidentiary purposes. It now uses both abstract economic theory and quantitative analyses to support its assumptions. All in all, it has considerably increased its standard of proof since the introduction of the more economic approach.

These changes in interpretation and methodology have had a number of practical implications. Commission decisions that carry out final competitive assessments are nowadays more complex and significantly longer than previously, and hence presumably more costly. Not surprisingly, there have been on average far fewer final decisions than prior to the introduction of the more economic approach. The great majority of cases are nowadays closed by means of commitments decisions without a final legal assessment.

The Court, by contrast, is not on board with all of the Commission's interpretative changes. It has so far resisted the notion that consumer welfare and market integration should be considered the only valid objectives of antitrust law. It takes a broader view of the reasons for protecting competition. Consequently, it does not deem consumer harm an indispensable requirement of competitive harm either but considers that harm to competition as such, in the form of harm to the structure of the market, can be sufficient to make business conduct anticompetitive under all three pillars of EU antitrust law. In practice, this difference of opinion is most relevant in cases in which the investigated conduct is likely to result in the exclusion of competitors. While the Court deems the likelihood of exclusion as such sufficient to make the conduct anticompetitive, the Commission nowadays only considers exclusionary effects anticompetitive if they are ultimately likely to result in higher prices or affect other parameters of consumer welfare. Also, the Court does not take the view that only efficiency effects should be capable of offsetting competitive harm under Article 101. It is prepared to take into account a broader range of benefits both under Article 101(1) and Article 101(3). Finally, the Court adheres to its original position that certain types of conduct on the part of a dominant undertaking may be presumed abusive under Article 102, regardless of its actual effects.

This development reveals a remarkable shift in institutional dynamics. During the first two decades of EU antitrust law, it had been the Court that took the leading role in shaping the substance of the antitrust rules by developing key concepts in broad rulings. During this period, the Commission mostly took its cue from the case law. It has been argued that the Court gave up its role as intellectual leader in the mid-1980s already, when it stopped developing general principles in a forward-looking manner and started resolving cases at a much lower level of abstraction.[2] This change went hand in hand with a change in the Court's methodology. It relied less on teleological interpretation and drew increasingly on concepts that it had developed in previous cases. Even members of the Court could only speculate on the exact reasons for this change. One view is that the arrival of a new generation of judges in the 1980s, less imbued with *une certaine idée de l'Europe* than their predecessors, and the addition of judges from common law systems may have played a role.[3] It has further been suggested that the Court cut back its role around that time because it realised that the Union's political institutions had been strengthened to a point that its leadership position was no longer called for.[4]

Around the turn of the millennium, these dynamics underwent a further noticeable shift. The Commission took up the reins and began to reshape key concepts of EU antitrust law of its own accord, while the Court started applying the brakes. The reasons for the Commission's new activism seem a little more obvious than the Court's reasons for scaling back its former leading role. In the mid-1990s, the internal market was formally in place, and the Commission was able to turn its attention to other tasks. Its antitrust policy had been subject to much criticism in the literature. Its assessments were unfavourably compared to the approach of its US counterparts, especially after the two jurisdictions reached different conclusion in the assessment of a few cases with transatlantic dimensions. The appointment of an economist with a mission as Commissioner for Competition Policy did the rest. Not only did he see through the review of Articles 101 and the EU Merger Regulation by means of interpretative guidelines, he also set in motion the review of Article 102. Maybe just as importantly, he significantly increased the ratio of economists within the permanent staff of DG Competition, which had been previously dominated by lawyers.

Undoubtedly, the outcome of the Commission's long review process presents many advantages. The key theoretical principles of the more economic approach are wonderfully logical. Even more importantly, it is possible to translate the underlying legal objective into a consistent, tangible and quantifiable concept

[2] See eg DJ Gerber, *Law and Competition in Twentieth Century Europe* (Oxford, Clarendon Press, 1988) 371; G Mancini, 'The Making of a Constitution for Europe' (1989) 26 *Common Market Law Review* 595.

[3] P Pescatore, 'The Doctrine of Direct Effect—An Infant Disease of Community Law' (1983) *European Law Review* 155, 157. Likewise, G Mancini and DT Keeling, 'Language, Culture and Politics in the Life of the European Court of Justice' (1995) 1 *Columbia Journal of European Law* 397, 401; U Everling, 'Court of Justice as a Decisionmaking Authority' (1984) *Michigan Law Review* 1292, 1301.

[4] Mancini, 'The Making of a Constitution for Europe' (n 2).

of harm, namely a restriction of competition that results in the reduction of consumer welfare. This is a far less straightforward task if the legal objective is the protection of freedom, commercial opportunities and democracy, or even competition as such.

However, the more economic approach is not without its drawbacks. In practice, the Commission has not (yet) implemented all of its principles in a manner that is entirely consistent. The market integration aim breaks the intellectual coherence of the more economic approach, and even more seriously, the Commission has not implemented the consumer welfare aim and the ensuing legal concepts under Article 102 in the same way it has done under the other two pillars. In theory, it still adheres to its former interpretation of the provision, which is not compatible with its current interpretation of Article 101 and the EU Merger Regulation and has resulted in different legal objectives and concepts of harm under these provisions. Moreover, it is not at all clear what the Commission's current position on discriminatory and exploitative abuses is.

A further concern is that the assessments required by the Commission's more economic approach are so complex that they require the input of economic experts. This seriously calls into question their suitability for the very individuals to whom the antitrust rules are addressed and for the judges who are called to apply them on appeal or in standalone actions for compensation. It also raises the question whether this approach strikes the right balance between the accuracy of assessment in individual cases and the level of enforcement. The number of infringement decisions has dropped significantly since the introduction of the more economic approach.

A particular worry is that many of the more economic approach's key principles are not compatible with the case law. DG Competition is bound to be aware of this situation. It is the only reasonable explanation for why it chose to implement the revised approach to Article 102 in such an indirect manner. Nonetheless, it perseveres with the more economic approach. It is a rather curious situation. The key enforcement body is carrying out far more complex and labour-intense assessments than required by the law. Assessing the competitive nature of business conduct according to the Court's principles is generally much easier, and thus quicker and cheaper, than according to the Commission's more economic approach, in particular where exclusionary conduct is concerned. Under Article 102, for example, the Court takes the view that certain types of exclusionary conduct on the part of a dominant undertaking may be presumed anticompetitive and that it is not necessary to prove the conduct's actual effects on competition, let alone its effects on consumer welfare. One might assume that an administrative body operating with limited resources would jump at the opportunity of applying these relatively straightforward tests. Nonetheless, the Commission persists with its much more complex approach, which results in assessments that are hundreds of pages long. Why does it do this? One can only assume that the staff of DG Competition persevere with the approach because they consider it better.

This is not only a remarkable situation. It is also worrying. It is not in the interest of legal certainty and the rule of law that the two key institutions in the area of EU antitrust law interpret the law in significantly different and incompatible ways. Undertakings, national enforcement bodies and courts need to be able to ascertain the relevant legal rules. This is not possible if the Commission says A and the Court says B. It is also not in the interest of the rule of law that one institution ignores the interpretation of the institution that is supposed to have the final word in matters of interpretation because it considers its approach to be better. As unfashionable as the Court's approach may be, the Commission should not spell out an interpretation in guidelines or other types of Communications that is incompatible with the Court's interpretation. This is not to say that the Court should not reflect on the validity of its own interpretation and consider whether it might be worth making a few adjustments.

What matters is that both institutions get back onto the same page. This may happen by one side backing down, or both meeting somewhere in between the two current positions. Finding this common position will first require both institutions to gain clarity on the purpose of protecting competition. Is it really about consumer welfare in terms of prices only, or does competition serve a wider purpose? On that basis, one can then establish workable rules. These should not rely on overly blunt form-based presumptions in every case, but should not require such in-depth economic analyses either that individuals are unable to self-assess their conduct, judges cannot carry out meaningful judicial review and the enforcement authorities have to invest so many resources into competitive assessments that they can only afford to do so in select cases.

Annex: Tables on Decision Length

Table 1: Length of Article 101 infringement decisions between 1970–98

Cases (in chronological order)	**Page length**
CARREAUX CERAMIQUES	8
JULIEN/VAN KATWIJK	4
NEDERLANDSE CEMENT-HANDELSMAATSCHAPPIJ	14
VERENIGING VAN CEMENTHANDELAREN	10
CIMBEL	17
GISA	5
WEA-FILIPACCHI MUSIC	4
CEMENTREGELING VOOR NEDERLAND	11
PITTSBURGH CORNING EUROPE-FORMICA BELGIUM-HERTEL	5
CHAUFFAGE CENTRAL	10
KALI UND SALZ/KALI-CHEMIE	5
DEUTSCHE PHILIPS GMBH	5
GAS WATER-HEATERS AND BATH-HEATERS	5
SCPA–KALI UND SALZ	4
ENTENTE FR. JAP ROULEMENTS À BILLES	8
FRUBO	16
ADVOCAAT ZWARTE KIP	4
PAPIERS PEINTS DE BELGIQUE	9
MANUFACTURERS OF GLASS CONTAINERS	17
AOIP/BEYRARD	8
BOMÉE-STICHTING	5
IFTRA	14
STOVES AND HEATERS	7
PRESERVED MUSHROOMS	5
GERO-FABRIEK	5
THEAL/WATTS	9
MILLER INTERNATIONAL SCHALLPLATTEN GMBH	4

(continued)

Table 1: ***(Continued)***

Cases (in chronological order)	**Page length**
PABST AND RICHARZ/BNIA	6
REUTER/BASF	11
BMW BELGIUM	12
VEGETABLE PARCHMENT	15
SPICES	6
DISTILLERS COMPANY LIMITED	18
VIDEOCASSETTE RECORDERS	6
CAULIFLOWERS	9
CENTRAAL BUREAU VOOR DE RIJWIELHANDEL	10
COBELPA/VNP	10
KAWASAKI	8
WHITE LEAD	9
WANO SCHARZPULVER	10
BREEDERS' RIGHT—MAIZE SEED	15
ARTHUR BELL AND SONS LTD	5
TEACHER AND SONS	5
CSV	22
FEDETAB	17
PIONEER	18
RENNET	8
FLORAL	13
BP KEMI—DDSF	21
VAESSEN/MORIS	5
ITALIAN CAST GLASS	8
HENNESSSY-HENKELL	8
JOHNSON AND JOHNSON	12
IMA-RULES	22
NAVEWA-ANSEAU	14
HASSELBLAD	17
MOET ET CHANDON	5
VBBB/VBVB	15
ITALIAN FLAT GLASS	12
AROW/BNIC	19

(continued)

Table 1: *(Continued)*

Cases (in chronological order)	**Page length**
TOLTECS–DORCET	11
ROLLED ZINC PRODUCTS AND ZINC ALLOYS	13
CAFETEROS DE COLOMBA	5
NATIONAL PANASONIC	8
SSI	39
AEG–TELEFUNKEN	14
NUTRICIA	8
IPTC BELGIUM	4
FORD WERKE AG	9
CAST IRON AND STEEL ROLLS	19
VIMPOLTU	8
WINDSURFING INTERNATIONAL	22
ALUMINIUM	77
WOODPULP	53
JOHN DEERE	7
GROHE SALES SYSTEM	9
IDEAL-STANDARD SALES SYSTEM	8
MILCHFÖRDERUNGSFONDS	8
FIRE INSURANCE (D)	15
PEROXYGEN PRODUCTS	20
ZINC PRODUCER GROUP	19
FLAT-GLASS (BENELUX)	10
POLISTIL/ARBOIS	7
SIEMENS/FANUC	10
SPERRY NEW HOLLAND	8
BREEDERS'S RIGHTS	10
VELCRO-APLIX	11
EATE LEVY	10
FATTY ACIDS	10
MELDOC	16
PEUGEOT	9
ROOFING FELT	19
POLYPROPYLENE	67
FISHER PRICE/QUAKER OATS LTD–TOYCO	5

(continued)

Table 1: *(Continued)*

Cases (in chronological order)	**Page length**
KONICA	10
SANDOZ	7
TIPP-EX	12
LDPE	24
PVC	20
PUBLISHERS ASSOCIATION/NET BOOK AGREEMENTS	24
FLAT GLASS	30
HUDSON' S BAY/DANSK PELSDYRAVLERFORENING	7
BLOEMENVEILINGEN AALSMEER	18
BRITISH DENTAL TRADE ASSOCIATION	10
SUGAR BEET	14
BAYO-N-OX	9
WELDED STEEL MESH	45
ANSAC	7
SODA-ASH–SOLVAY/CFK	5
SODA-ASH–SOLVAY/ICI	16
BAYER DENTAL	5
ECO SYSTEM/PEUGEOT	13
VIHO/TOSHIBA	5
GOSME/MARTELL-DMP	8
SCREENPORT/EBU MEMBERS	13
IJSSELCENTRALE AND OTHERS	15
ASTRA	17
LANGNESE–IGLO GMBH	19
SCHÖLLER LEBENSMITTEL GMBH AND CO.KG	19
FORD AGRICULTURAL	5
DISTRIBUTION OF PACKAGE TOURS 1990 WORLD CUP	12
SCOTTISH SALMON BOARD	9
VIHO/PARKER PEN	6
EUROCHEQUE: HELSINKI AGREEMENT	18
NEWITT/DUNLOP SLAZENGER	18
U.K. TRACTOR REGISTRATION EXCHANGE	5
BUILDING AND CONSTRUCTION IN THE NETHERLANDS	30
CNSD	7

(continued)

Table 1: ***(Continued)***

Cases (in chronological order)	**Page length**
ZERA/MONTEDISON AND HINKENS/STÄHLER	18
FAR EASTERN FREIGHT CONFERENCE	20
TRETORN AND OTHERS	9
CIMENT	158
TRANSATLANTIC AGREEMENT	56
PVC	22
CARTONBOARD	78
SCK/FNK	11
BASF LACKE+FARBEN AG, AND ACCINAUTO SA	18
COAPI	14
NOVALLIANCE/SYSTEMFORM	11
FERRY OPERATORS	12
FENEX	9
ADALAT	81
PREINSULATED PIPES	70
BRITISH SUGAR	62
VW–AUDI	49
Average length	*16.24*

Table 2: Length of Article 101 (non-cartel) infringement decisions since 2004

Cases (in chronological order)	**Page length**
SEP ET AUTRES/PEUGEOT SA	79
SOURIS–TOPPS	42
MASTERCARD I	242
GROUPEMENT DES CARTES BANCAIRES 'CB'	170
MORGAN STANLEY/VISA INTERNATIONAL AND VISA EUROPE	84
CISAC	78
ONP	150
TELEFONICA/PORTUGAL TELECOM	116
FENTANYL	147
LUNDBECK	464
Average length	*157.2*

Table 3: Length of Article 102 infringement decisions between 1971–98

Cases (in chronological order)	**Page length**
GEMA I	15
CONTINENTAL CAN COMPANY	15
ZOJA/CSC-ICI	8
GENERAL MOTORS CONTINENTAL	6
CHIQUITA	20
VITAMINES	13
ABG/OIL COMPANIES	16
HUGIN/LIPTONS	15
GVL	11
MICHELIN	15
BRITISH TELECOMMUNICATIONS	7
BRITISH LEYLAND	6
ECS/AKZO CHEMIE	27
EUROFIX–BAUCO/HILTI	26
DECCA NAVIGATOR SYSTEM	22
MAGILL TV GUIDE/ITP, BBC AND RTE	9
BPB INDUSTRIES PLC	23
LONDON EUROPEAN-SABENA	8
TETRA PAK I (BTG-LICENCE)	20
NAPIER BROWN/BRITISH SUGAR	19
SODA-ASH–ICI	14
SODA-ASH–SOLVAY	19
TETRA PAK II	68
IRISH SUGAR	32
AFS/ADP	32
FRANKFURT AIRPORT	35
Average length	*19.2*

Table 4: Length of Article 102 infringement decisions since 2005 (beginning of the reform)

Cases (in chronological order)	**Page length**
ASTRAZENECA	214
PROKENT–TOMRA	163
WANADOO ESPAÑA V TELEFÓNICA	233
GERMAN ELECTRICITY WHOLESALE MARKET	170
INTEL	518
TELEKOMUNIKACJA POLSKA	243
ROMANIAN POWER EXCHANGE/OPCOM	69
MOTOROLA	106
Average length	*214.5*

Table 5: Length of merger prohibition decisions on the basis of Regulation 4064/89

Cases (in chronological order)	**Page length**
1. AEROSPATIALE-ALENIA/DE HAVILLAND	39
2. NESTLÉ/PERRIER	31
3. DU PONT/ICI	23
4. MSG MEDIA SERVICE	25
5. RTL/VERONICA /ENDEMOL	36
6. SAINT-GOBAIN/WACKER-CHEMIE/NOM	46
7. GENCOR/LONRHO	54
8. KESKO/TUKO	42
9. GUINNESS/GRAND METROPOLITAN	31
10. BLOKKER/TOYS "R" US	25
11. BERTELSMANN/KIRCH/PREMIERE	41
12. DEUTSCHE TELEKOM/BETARESEARCH	20
13. AIRTOURS/FIRST CHOICE	52
Average length	*35.7*

Table 6: Length of merger prohibition decisions on the basis of Regulation 139/2004

Cases (in chronological order)	**Page length**
RYANAIR/AER LINGUS I	515
OLYMPIC/AEGEAN AIRLINES	451
DEUTSCHE BÖRSE/NYSE EURONEXT	447
UPS/TNT EXPRESS	380
RYANAIR/AER LINGUS III	532
Average length	*465*

BIBLIOGRAPHY

Ahlborn, C and Grave, C, 'Walter Eucken and Ordoliberalism: An Introduction from a Consumer Welfare Perspective' (2006) 2(2) *Competition Policy International* 197

Akman, P, 'Article 82 Reformed? The EC Discussion Paper on Exclusionary Abuses' (2006) *Journal of Business Law* 816

——, 'Searching for the Long-Lost Soul of Article 82 EC' (2009) 29 *Oxford Journal of Legal Studies* 267

Andrews, EL, 'Boeing, Threatened, Sees Trade War' *New York Times* (New York, 21 May 1997)

Areeda, P and Turner, DF, 'Predatory Pricing and Related Practices under Section 2 of the Sherman Act' (1975) 88 *Harvard Law* Review 697

Art, J-Y and McCurdy, G, 'The European Commission's Media Player Remedy in its Microsoft Decision: Compulsory Code Removal despite the Absence of Tying or Foreclosure' (2004) 25 *European Competition Law Review* 694

Arthur, TC, 'A Workable Rule of Reason: A Less Ambitious Antitrust Role for the Federal Courts' (2002) 68 *Antitrust Law Journal* 337

Averitt, NW and Lande, RH, 'Using the Consumer Choice Approach to Antitrust Law' (2007) 74 *Antitrust Law Journal* 175

Badura, P, *Wirtschaftsverfassung und Wirtschaftsverwaltung* (Tübingen, Mohr Siebeck, 2008)

Bailey, D, 'Restrictions of Competition by Object under Article 101 TFEU' (2012) 49 *Common Market Law Review* 559

Bain, JS, *Barriers to New Competition: Their Character and Consequences in Manufacturing Industries* (Cambridge Mass, Harvard University Press, 1956)

Baker, DI 'Vertical Restraints in Times of Change: From White to Schwinn to Where?' (1975) 44 *Antitrust Law Journal* 537

Baker, JB, 'Economic and Politics: Perspectives on the Goals and Future of Antitrust' (2013) 81 *Fordham Law Review* 2175

Basedow, J, 'Konsumentenwohlfahrt und Effizienz—Neue Leitbilder der Wettbewerbspolitik?' (2007) 57 *Wirtschaft und Wettbewerb* 712

Bavasso, A, 'The Role of Intent under Article 82 EC: from "Flushing the Turkeys" to "Spotting Lionesses in Regent's Park"' (2005) 26 *European Competition Law Review* 616

Baxter, S, Dethmers, F and Dodoo, N, 'The GE/Honeywell Judgment and the Assessment of Conglomerate Effects: What's New in EC Practice?' (2006) 2 *European Competition Journal* 141

Baye, MR and Wright, JD, 'Is Antitrust Too Complicated for Generalist Judges? The Impact of Economic Complexity and Judicial Training on Appeals' (2011) 54 *Journal of Law and Economics* 1

Becker, G, 'Economic View Point: What US Courts Could Teach Europe's Trust Busters' *Business Week* (6 August 2001) 20

Belleflamme, P and Peitz, M, *Industrial Organisation Theory*, 2nd edn (Cambridge, Cambridge University Press, 2015)

Berghahn, VR, 'Ludwig Erhard, die Freiburger Schule und das "Amerikanische Jahrhundert"' *Freiburger Diskussionspapiere zur Ordnungsökonomik* 10/1

Bermann, GA, 'The Single European Act: A New Constitution for the Community' (1989) 27 *Columbia Journal of Transnational Law* 529

Biro, Z and Parker, D, 'A New EC Merger Test? Dominance v Substantial Lessening of Competition' (2002) 1 *Competition Law Journal* 157

Bishop, S, 'Pro-competitive Exclusive Supply Agreements: How Refreshing!' (2003) 24 *European Competition Law Review* 229

—— and Ridyard, D, 'E.C. Vertical Restraints Guidelines: Effects Based or *per se* Policy?' (2002) 23 *European Competition Law Review* 35

—— and Walker, M, *The Economics of EC Competition Law: Concepts, Application and Measurement*, 3rd edn (London, Sweet & Maxwell, 2010)

Blair, RD and Sokol, D, 'The Rule of Reason and the Goals of Antitrust: An Economic Approach' (2012) 78 *Antitrust Law Journal* 471

Bloom, M, 'The Great Reformer: Mario Monti's Legacy in Article 81 EC and Cartel Policy' (2005) 1 *Competition Policy International* 55

Blumenberg-Lampe, C, *Das wirtschaftspolitische Programm der 'Freiburger Kreise'* (Berlin, Duncker & Humblot, 1973)

Böge, U, 'Der "more economic approach" und die deutsche Wettbewerbspolitik' (2004) 54 *Wirtschaft und Wettbewerb* 726

——, 'Reform der Europäischen Fusionskontrolle' (2004) 54 *Wirtschaft und Wettbewerb* 138

Böhm, F, 'Das Problem der privaten Macht—Ein Beitrag zur Monopolfrage' (1928) 3 *Die Justiz*, reprinted in E-J Mestmäcker, *Franz Böhm—Reden und Schriften* (Karlsruhe, CF Müller, 1960) 25

——, *Wettbewerb und Monopolkampf* (Cologne, Carl Heymann, 1933)

Bork, R, 'The Rule of Reason and the *Per Se* Concept: Price Fixing and Market Division [I]' (1965) 74 *Yale Law Journal* 775

——, 'Legislative Intent and the Policy of The Sherman Act' (1966) 9 *Journal of Law and Economics* 7

——, 'The Rule of Reason and the *Per Se* Concept: Price Fixing and Market Division [II]' (1966) 75 *Yale Law Journal* 373

——, 'The Goals of Antitrust Policy' (1967) 57 *American Economic Review* 242

——, *The Antitrust Paradox: A Policy at War With Itself* (New York, Basic Books Inc, 1978)

Buccirossi, P, *Handbook of Antitrust Economics* (Cambridge, Mass, MIT Press, 2008)

Buch-Hansen, H and Wigger, A, *The Politics of European Competition Regulation* (Abingdon, Routledge, 2011)

Budzinski, O, 'Towards an International Governance of Transborder Mergers?—Competition Networks and Institutions between Centralism and Decentralism' (2004) 36 *New York University Journal of International Law and Politics* 1

Bundeskartellamt, 'Reply to the Green Paper on the review of Regulation (EEC) No 4064/89'—Competition Law Forum, 'Debate on Reform of Article 82: A Dialectic on Competing Approaches' (2006) 2 *European Competition Journal* 211

Burgess, J, 'Europeans Come down Hard on Microsoft' *Washington Post* (Washington, DC, 25 March 2004)

Burnside, A and Botteman, Y, 'Networking Amongst Competition Agencies' (2004) 10 *International Trade Law & Regulation* 1

—— and Crossley, H, 'Cooperation in Competition: a New Era?' (2005) 30 *European Law Review* 234

Cabral, LMB, *Introduction to Industrial Organization* (Cambridge, Mass, MIT Press 2000)

Camesasca, PD, *European Merger Control: Getting the Efficiencies Right* (Antwerp, Intersentia, 2000)
Carlton, DW, 'Does Antitrust Need to be Modernized?' (2007) 21 *Journal of Economic Perspectives* 155
Centre for Economic Policy Research, 'Reducing Transatlantic Barriers to Trade and Investment, An Economic Assessment' Final Project Report March 2013, available at: www.trade.ec.europa.eu/doclib/docs/2013/march/tradoc_150737.pdf
Chalmers, P, 'EU Threatens Boeing/McDonnell Douglas Deal' *Reuters News* (4 July 1997)
Christiansen, A, 'Die "Ökonomisierung" der EU-Fusionskontrolle: Mehr Kosten als Nutzen?' (2005) 55 *Wirtschaft und Wettbewerb* 285
—— and Kerber, W, 'Competition Policy with Optimally Differentiated Rules Instead of "*Per Se* Rules v Rule of Reason"' (2006) 2 *Journal of Competition Law & Economics* 215
Coleman, B, 'Clinton Hints U.S. May Retaliate if EU Tries to Block Boeing-McDonnell Deal' *Wall Street Journal* (New York, 18 July 1997) A2
——, 'EU Still Threatening To Vote Down Boeing-McDonnell Douglas Deal' *Dow Jones Business News* (New York, 21 July 1997)
Competition Law Forum Article 82 Review Group, 'The Reform of Article 82: Recommendations on Key Policy Objectives' (2005) 1 *European Competition Journal* 179
Davis, P and Garcés, E, *Quantitative Techniques for Competition and Antitrust Analysis* (Princeton, Princeton University Press, 2010)
de Zwaan, JW, 'The Single European Act: Conclusion of a Unique Document' (1986) 23 *Common Market Law Review* 747
Doern, GB and Wilks, S (eds), *Comparative Competition Policy: National Institutions in a Global Market* (Oxford, Clarendon Press, 1996)
Dolmans, M and Graf, T, 'Analysis of Tying under Article 82 EC: the European Commission's Microsoft Decision in Perspective' (2004) 27 *World Competition* 225
Drauz, G, 'Unbundling GE/Honeywell: The Assessment of Conglomerate Mergers under EC Competition Law' (2001) 25 *Fordham International Law Journal* 885
——, 'Unbundling GE/Honeywell: The Assessment of Conglomerate Mergers under EC Competition Law' in B Hawk (ed), *International Antitrust Law and Policy 2001, Annual Proceedings of the Fordham Corporate Law Institute* (New York, Juris Publishing, 2002) 183–203
—— and Reynolds, M (eds), *EC Merger Control—A Major Reform in Progress* (Oxford, Oxford University Press, 2003)
Dreher, M and Adam, M, 'Abuse of Dominance under Reform—Sound Economics and Established Case Law' (2007) 28 *European Competition Law Review* 278
Drexl, J (ed), *The Future of Transnational Antitrust—From Comparative to Common Competition Law* (Berne/The Hague, Staempfli Publishers/Kluwer Law International, 2003)
——, 'International Competition Policy after Cancún: Placing a Singapore Issue on the WTO Development Agenda' (2004) 27 *World Competition* 419
——, Enchelmaier, S, Leistner, M, Mackenrodt, M-O and Conde Gallego, B, 'Comments of the Max Planck Institute for Intellectual Property, Competition and Tax Law on the Directorate-General Competition Discussion Paper of December 2005 on the Application of Art.82 of the EC Treaty to Exclusionary Abuses' (2006) 37 *International Review of Intellectual Property and Competition Law* 558
——, Kerber, W, Podszun, R (eds), *Competition Policy and the Economic Approach—Foundations and Limitations* (Cheltenham, Edward Elgar, 2011)

Easterbrook, F, 'Is There a Ratchet in Antitrust Law?' (1982) 60 *Texas Law Review* 705
——, 'The Limits of Antitrust' (1984) 63 *Texas Law Review* 1
——, 'Workable Antitrust Policy' (1986) 84 *Michigan Law Review* 1701
Ehlermann, C-D and Atanasiu, I (eds) *European Competition Law Annual 2003—What is an Abuse of a Dominant Position?* (Oxford, Hart Publishing, 2006)
—— and Laudati, L (eds), *European Competition Law Annual 1997—Objectives of Competition Law* (Oxford, Hart Publishing, 1997)
Eilmansberger, T, 'How to Distinguish Good From Bad Competition under Article 82 EC: In Search of Clearer and More Coherent Standards for Anticompetitive Abuses' (2005) 42 *Common Market Law Review* 129
Elhauge, E, 'Harvard, Not Chicago: Which Antitrust School Drives Recent U.S. Supreme Court Decisions?' (2007) 3 *Competition Policy International* 59
Elzinga, KG, The Goals of Antitrust: Other than Competition and Efficiency, What Else Counts? (1977) 125 *University of Pennsylvania Law Review* 1191
Eucken, W, 'Staatliche Strukturwandlungen und die Krisis des Kapitalismus' (1932) 84 *Weltwirtschaftliches Archiv* 297
——, *Die Grundlagen der Nationalökonomie* (Jena, Gustav Fischer, 1940)
——, *Konzernentflechtung und Kartellauflösung, Gutachten des Comité d'Etudes Economiques* (Freiburg, 1947), partially reprinted in E Günther, 'Entwurf eines deutsehen Gesetzes gegen Wettbewerbsbeschränkungen' (1951) 1 *Wirtschaft und Wettbewerb* 17
——, 'Die Wettbewerbsordnung und ihre Verwirklichung' (1949) 2 *ORDO* 1
——, *Grundlagen der Nationalökonomik*, 9th edn (Berlin, Springer, 1989)
Evans, DS, 'The New Trustbusters, Brussels and Washington May Part Ways' (2002) 81 *Foreign Affairs* 14
——, 'How Economists Can Help Courts Design Competition Rules: A EU and US Perspective' (2005) 28 *World Competition* 93
—— and Salinger, M, 'Competition Thinking at the European Commission: Lessons from the Aborted GE/Honeywell Merger' (2002) 10 *George Mason Law Review* 489
—— and Padilla, AJ, 'Demand-side Efficiencies in Merger Control' (2003) 26 *World Competition* 167
—— and ——, 'Tying under Article 82 EC and the Microsoft Decision: a Comment on Dolmans and Graf' (2004) 27 *World Competition* 503
Everling, U, 'Court of Justice as a Decisionmaking Authority' (1984) *Michigan Law Review* 1292
Ezrachi, A, *Research Handbook on International Competition Law* (Cheltenham, Edward Elgar, 2012)
Farrell, J and Katz, ML, 'The Economics of Welfare Standards in Antitrust' (2006), www.escholarship.org/uc/item/1tw2d426
Federico, G, 'When are Rebates Exclusionary?' (2005) 26 *European Competition Law* Review 477
Fisher, F, 'Economic Analysis and "Bright-Line" Tests' (2007) *Journal of Competition Law and Economics* 129
Fox, EM, 'The Modernization of Antitrust: A New Equilibrium' (1981) 66 *Cornell Law Review* 1140
——, 'Antitrust Regulation Across National Borders: The United States of Boeing Versus the European Union of Airbus' (1998) 16 *Brookings Review* 30
——, 'Mergers in Global Markets: GE/Honeywell and the Future of Merger Control' (2002) 23 *University of Pennsylvania Journal of International Economic Law* 457

——, 'US and European Merger Policy—Fault Lines and Bridges—Mergers that Create Incentives for Exclusionary Practices' (2002) 10 *George Mason Law Review* 471
—— and Sullivan, L, 'Antitrust—Retrospective and Prospective: Where Are We Coming From? Where Are We Going?' (1987) 62 *New York University Law Review* 936
—— and Crane, DA (eds), *Antitrust Stories* (New York, Foundation Press, 2007)
——, Fingleton, J and Mitchell, S, 'The Past and Future of International Antitrust: Gaps, Overlaps and the Institutional Challenge' in D Lewis (ed), *Building New Competition Law Regimes* (Cheltenham, Edward Elgar, 2013) 163
Frotscher, W, Wirtschaftsverfassungs- und Wirtschaftsverwaltungsrecht (Munich, Beck, 2008)
Furse, M, 'Article 82, Microsoft and Bundling, or "The Half Monti"' (2004) 3 *Competition Law Journal* 169
Gavil, AI and First, H, *The Microsoft Antitrust Cases* (Cambridge, MA, MIT Press, 2014)
Geiger, A and Meibom, W von, 'A World Competition Law as an Ultima Ratio' (2002) 23 *European Competition Law Review* 445
Geradin, D and Petit, N, 'Price Discrimination under EC Competition Law: Another Antitrust Doctrine in Search of Limiting Principles?' (2006) 2 *Journal of Competition Law and Economics* 479
Gerard, D, 'Merger Control Policy: How to Give Meaningful Consideration to Efficiency Claims?' (2003) 40 *Common Market Law Review* 1367
Gerber, DJ, *Law and Competition in Twentieth Century Europe* (Oxford, Clarendon Press, 1998)
——, 'The European Commission's GE/Honeywell Decision: US Responses and their Implications' (2003) 1 *Zeitschrift für Wettbewerbsrecht* 87
——, 'Competition Law and the WTO: Rethinking the Relationship' (2007) 10 *Journal of International Economic Law* 707
Ginsburg, DH, 'Originalism and Economic Analysis: Two Case Studies of Consistency and Coherence in Supreme Court Decision Making' (2010) 33 *Harvard Journal of Public Policy* 217
Global Competition Review, 'European Commission's Directorate General for Competition' (London, 15 June 2015)
Goldschmidt, N, 'Die Entstehung der Freiburger Kreise' (1997) 4 *Historisch-Politische Mitteilungen* 1
—— (ed), *Wirtschaft, Politik und Freiheit* (Tübingen, Mohr Siebeck, 2005)
Goyder, J, 'Cet obscur objet: Object Restrictions in Vertical Agreements' (2011) 2 *Journal of European Competition Law and Practice* 327
Graham, C, 'Methods for Determining whether an Agreement Restricts Competition: Comment on Allianz Hungaria' (2013) 38 *European Law Review* 542
Günther, E, 'Entwurf eines deutsches Gesetzes gegen Wettbewerbsbeschränkungen' (1951) 1 *Wirtschaft und Wettbewerb* 17
Gyselen, L, 'Vertical Restraints on the Distribution Process: Strength and Weakness of the Free Rider Rationale Under EEC Competition Law' (1984) 21 *Common Market Law Review* 647
Harkrider, JD and Rubinfeld, D (eds), *Econometrics: Legal, Practical and Technical Issues* (Chicago, ABA Publishing, 2005)
Hawk, B, 'The American (Anti-Trust) Revolution: Lessons for the EEC?' (1988) 9 *European Competition Law Review* 53

——, 'System Failure: Vertical Restraints and EC Competition Law' (1995) 32 *Common Market Law Review* 973
—— (ed), *International Antitrust Law & Policy: Fordham Corporate Law Institute 2001* (New York, Juris Publishing, 2002)
—— (ed), *International Antitrust Law & Policy: Fordham Corporate Law Institute 2003* (New York, Juris Publishing, 2004)
Hildebrand, D, *The Role of Economic Analysis in the EC Competition Rules* (Alphen aan den Rijn, Wolters Kluwer, 2002)
Houck, S, 'The EC Decision Against Microsoft: Windows on the World, Glass Houses, or Through the Looking Glass?' *The Antitrust Source* (September 2004)
Hovenkamp, H, *The Antitrust Enterprise: Principle and Execution* (Cambridge, Mass, Harvard University Press, 2008)
——, 'Implementing Antitrust's Welfare Goals' (2013) 81 *Fordham Law Review* 2471
ICN Merger Working Group, 'The Role of Economists and Economic Evidence in Merger Analysis' Presented at the 12th Conference of the ICN (Warsaw, 24–26 April 2013) www.internationalcompetitionnetwork.org/uploads/library/doc903.pdf
——, Recommended Practices for Merger Analysis, www.internationalcompetitionnetwork.org/uploads/library/doc316.pdf
ICN Unilateral Conduct Working Group, Report on the Objectives of Unilateral Conduct Laws, Assessment of Dominance/Substantial Market Power, and State-created Monopolies (2007) www.internationalcompetitionnetwork.org/uploads/library/doc353.pdf
——, Unilateral Conduct Workbook Chapter 1: The Objectives and Principles of Unilateral Conduct Laws, www.internationalcompetitionnetwork.org/uploads/library/doc827.pdf
——, Unilateral Conduct Workbook Chapter 3: Assessment of Dominance, www.internationalcompetitionnetwork.org/uploads/library/doc752.pdf
International Antitrust Working Group, Draft International Antitrust Code from 1993 (reprinted in 'Draft International Antitrust Code as a GATT-MTO-Plurilateral Trade Agreement 10 July 1993' (1993) 5 *World Trade and Arbitration Materials* 126)
Ivaldi, M, Jullien, B, Rey, P, Seabright, P, Tirole, J, 'The Economics of Tacit Collusion' Final Report for DG Competition, European Commission (March 2013), www.ec.europa.eu/competition/mergers/studies_reports/the_economics_of_tacit_collusion_en.pdf.
James, CA, 'Statement on the EU's Decision Regarding the GE/Honeywell Acquisition' (3 July 2001)
——, 'International Antitrust in the 21st Century: Cooperation and Convergence' OECD Global Forum on Competition (Paris, 17 October 2001)
Jenkins, HW, 'Business World: What's a Little Antitrust between Friends?' *Wall Street Journal* (New York, 28 January 1997)
Jones, A, 'Left Behind by Modernisation? Restrictions by Object under Article 101(1)' (2010) 6 *European Competition Journal* 649
Kallaugher, J and Sher, B, 'Rebates Revisited: Anti-competitive Effects and Exclusionary Abuse under Article 82' (2004) 25 *European Competition Law Review* 263
Kaplow, L, 'Antitrust, Law and Economics, and the Courts' (1987) 50 *Law and Contemporary Problems* 181
Kauper, TE, 'The "Warren Court" and the Antitrust Laws: Of Economics, Populism, and Cynicism' (1968) 67 *Michigan Law Review* 325
Kennedy, K, *Competition Law and the WTO: Limits of Multilateralism* (London, Sweet & Maxwell, 2001)

Kerber, W, 'An International Multi-Level System of Competition Law: Federalism in Antitrust' in J Drexl (ed), *The Future of Transnational Antitrust—From Comparative to Common Competition Law* (Berne/The Hague, Staempfli Publishers/Kluwer Law International, 2003) 269

King, S, 'The Object Box: Law, Policy or Myth?' (2011) 7 *European Competition Journal* 269

Kirkwood, JB, 'The Essence of Antitrust: Protecting Consumers and Small Suppliers From Anticompetitive Conduct' (2013) 81 *Fordham Law Review* 2425

Klein, J, 'Anticipating the Millennium: International Antitrust Enforcement at the End of the Twentieth Century' Fordham Corporate Law Institute, 24th Annual Conference on International Law and Policy (New York, 9 November 2000)

Klump, R, 'Der Beitrag der Freiburger Kreise zum Konzept der Sozialen Marktwirtschaft' in N Goldschmidt (ed), *Wirtschaft, Politik und Freiheit* (Tübingen, Mohr Siebeck, 2005) 383–401

Kolasky, WJ 'Conglomerate Mergers and Range Effects: It's a Long Way from Chicago to Brussels' (2002) 10 *George Mason Law Review* 533

——, 'GE/Honeywell: Continuing the Transatlantic Dialogue' (2002) 23 *University of Pennsylvania Journal of International Economic Law* 513

Korah, V, 'EEC Competition Policy—Legal Form or Economic Efficiency' (1986) 39 *Current Legal Problems* 85

——, 'The Judgment in Delimitis: A Milestone towards a Realistic Assessment of the Effects of an Agreement—or a Damp Squib?' (1992) 14 *European Intellectual Property Review* 167

——, 'The Paucity of Economic Analysis in the EEC Decisions on competition: Tetra Pak II' (1993) 46 *Current Legal Problems* 148

Kovacic, WE, 'The Intellectual DNA of Modern U.S. Competition Law for Dominant Firm Conduct: The Chicago/Harvard Double Helix' (2007) *Columbia Business Law Review* 1

—— and Shapiro, C, 'Antitrust Policy: A Century of Economic and Legal Thinking' (2000) 14 *Journal of Economic Perspectives* 43

Kroes, N, 'The International Competition Network—Achievements and Goals' International Competition Network Annual Conference (Moscow, 30 May 2007)

——, 'European Competition Policy in the Age of Internationalisation—Towards a Global Competition Order?' (FIW, Innsbruck, 7 February 2008)

——, 'Exclusionary Abuses of Dominance—the European Commission's Enforcement Priorities' Fordham University Symposium (New York, 25 September 2008)

Kühn, K-U, Stillman, R and Caffarra, C, 'Economic Theories of Bundling and their Policy Implications in Abuse Cases: an Assessment in Light of the Microsoft Case' (2005) 1 *European Competition Journal* 85

Kyriazis, N and Gyselen, L, 'Article 86 EEC: the Monopoly Power Measurement Issue Revisited' (1986) 11 *European Law Review* 134

Lande, R, 'A Traditional and Textualist Analysis of the Goals of Antitrust: Efficiency, Preventing the Theft from Consumers, and Consumer Choice' (2013) 81 *Fordham Law Review* 2349

Levy, N, 'Dominance versus SLC: A Subtle Distinction?' in G Drauz and M Reynolds (eds), *EC Merger Control—A Major Reform in Progress* (Oxford, Oxford University Press, 2003)

Lewis, D (ed), *Building New Competition Law Regimes* (Cheltenham, Edward Elgar, 2013)

Lianos, I and Genakos, C, 'Econometric Evidence in EU Competition Law: an Empirical and Theoretical Analysis' *CLES Working Paper Series* 6/2012

Lofaro, A and Ridyard, D, 'Beyond Bork: New Economic Theories in Merger Cases' (2002) 23 *European Competition Law Review* 151

Löffler, B, 'Soziale Marktwirtschaft und administrative Praxis: das Bundeswirtschaftsministerium unter Ludwig Erhard' (2003) 162 *Vierteljahrschrift für Sozial- und Wirtschaftsgeschichte* 72

Lovdahl Gormsen, L, *A Principled Approach to Abuse of Dominance in European Competition Law* (Cambridge, Cambridge University Press, 2010)

——, 'Why the European Commission's Enforcement Priorities on Article 82 EC Should be Withdrawn' (2010) 31 *European Competition Law Review* 45

Lowe, P, 'Current Issues of E.U. Competition Law: the New Competition Enforcement Regime' (2004) 24 *Northwestern Journal of International Law & Business* 567

——, 'DG Competition's Review of the Policy on the Abuse of Dominance' in B Hawk (ed), *International Antitrust Law & Policy: Fordham Corporate Law 2003* (New York, Juris Publishing, 2004) 163

——, 'Consumer Welfare and Efficiency—New Guiding Principles of Competition Policy?' 13th International Conference on Competition (Munich, 27 March 2007)

Lugard, P and Hancher, L, 'Honey, I Shrunk the Article! A Critical Assessment of the Commission's Notice on Article 81(3) of the EC Treaty' (2004) 25 *European Competition Law Review* 410

Maier-Rigaud, F, 'Article 82 Rebates: Four Common Fallacies' (2006) 2 Supp (Special issue) *European Competition Journal* 85

—— and Parplies, K, 'EU Merger Control Five Years after the Introduction of the SIEC Test: What Explains the Drop in Enforcement Activity?' (2009) 30 *European Competition Law Review* 565

Majoras, DP, Speech before the Antitrust Law Section State Bar of Georgia (29 November 2001), www.justice.gov/atr/speech/ge-honeywell-us-decision

Mancini, G, 'The Making of a Constitution for Europe' (1989) 26 *Common Market Law Review* 595

—— and Keeling, DT, 'Language, Culture and Politics in the Life of the European Court of Justice' (1995) 1 *Columbia Journal of European Law* 397

Marsden, P, A Competition Policy for the WTO (London, Cameron May, 2003)

Mason, ES, 'Monopoly Law in Law and Economics' (1937) 47 *Yale Law Journal* 34

——, 'The Current State of the Monopoly Problem in the United States' (1949) 62 *Harvard Law Review* 1265

——, *Economic Concentration and the Monopoly Problem* (New York, Atheneum, 1964)

Meese, AJ, 'Debunking the Purchaser Welfare Account of Section 2 of the Sherman Act: How Harvard Brought us a Total Welfare Standard and Why We Should Keep It' (2010) 85 *New York Law Review* 659

Melamed, D and Rubinfeld, DL, '*U.S. v. Microsoft*: Lessons Learned and Issues Raised' in EM Fox and DA Crane (eds), *Antitrust Stories* (New York, Foundation Press 2007) 287–310

Mestmäcker, H-J, *Franz Böhm—Reden und Schriften* (Karlsruhe, C F Müller, 1960)

——, 'Die Interdependenz von Recht und Ökonomie in der Wettbewerbspolitik' in Monopolkommission (ed), Zukunftsperspektiven der Wettbewerbspolitik (Baden-Baden, Nomos-Verlag, 2005) 19–35

Miksch, L, *Wettbewerb als Aufgabe* (Stuttgart, Kohlhammer, 1937)

Millon, D, 'The Sherman Act and the Balance of Power' (1988) 61 *Southern California Law Review* 1219

Monopolkommission, *Zukunftsperspektiven der Wettbewerbspolitik* (Baden-Baden, Nomos, 2005)

Monti, G, 'The Concept of Dominance in Article 82' (2006) 3 *European Competition Journal* 31
Monti, M, 'Deposit, Credit and Interest Rate Determination under Alternative Bank Objective Functions' in GP Szegö and K Shell (eds), *Mathematical Methods in Investment and Finance* (Amsterdam, North-Holland Publishing, 1972)
——, 'A Competition Policy for Today and Tomorrow' (2000) 23 *World Competition* 1
——, 'Antitrust in the US and Europe: A History of Convergence' General Counsel Roundtable American Bar Association (Washington, DC, 14 November 2001)
——, 'EU Competition Policy' Fordham Annual Conference on International Antitrust Law and Policy (New York, 31 October 2002)
——, 'Merger Control in the European Union: A Radical Reform' European Commission/IBA Conference on EU Merger Control (Brussels, 7 November 2002)
——, 'European Competition Policy: Quo Vadis?' XXth International Forum on European Competition Policy (Brussels, 10 April 2003)
——, 'EU Competition Policy after May 2004' Fordham Annual Conference on International Antitrust Law and Policy (New York, 24 October 2003)
——, 'The New Shape of European Competition Policy' Inaugural Symposium of the Competition Policy Research Center (Tokyo, 20 November 2003)
——, 'Competition Policy in a Global Economy' (2004) 7 *International Finance* 495
——, 'The New EU Policy on Technology Transfer Agreements' (École des Mines, Paris, 16 January 2004)
——, 'Convergence in EU-US Antitrust Policy Regarding Mergers and Acquisitions: an EU Perspective' UCLA Law First Annual Institute on US and EU Antitrust Aspects of Mergers and Acquisitions (Los Angeles, 28 February 2004)
——, 'A Reformed Competition Policy: Achievements and Challenges for the Future' Center for European Reform (Brussels, 28 October 2004)
——, 'Comments to the Speech of Hew Pate at the Conference "Antitrust in a Transatlantic Context"' (Brussels, 7 June 2004) www.ec.europa.eu/comm/competition/speeches
Möschel, W, 'Competition Policy from an Ordo Point of View' in A Peacock and H Willgerodt (eds), German Neo-Liberals and the Social Market Economy (London, Palgrave Macmillan, 1989) 146
Motta, M, 'E.C. Merger Policy and the Airtours Case' (2000) 21 *European Competition Law Review* 199
——, *Competition Policy* (Cambridge, Cambridge University Press, 2004)
—— and Polo, M, 'Leniency Programs and Cartel Prosecution' (2003) 21 *International Journal of Industrial Organization* 347
Müller, E and Böge, U, 'From the Market Dominance Test to the SLC Test: Are there any Reasons for Change?' (2002) 23 *European Competition Law Review* 495
Muris, TJ, 'The Rule of Reason after California Dental' (2002) 68 *Antitrust Law Journal* 527
Muysert, P, 'Price Discrimination—an Unreliable Indicator of Market Power' (2004) 25 *European Competition Law Review* 350
Nazzini, R, 'The Wood Began to Move: An Essay on Consumer Welfare, Evidence and Burden of Proof in Article 82 EC Cases' (2006) 31 *European Law Review* 518
Neven, DJ, 'Competition Economics and Antitrust in Europe' (2006) 21 *Economic Policy* 741
——, 'Competition Economics in Europe' (2007) *The Handbook of Competition Economics* 4
——, D, Papandropoulos, P and Seabright, P, 'Trawling for Minnows. European Competition Policy and Agreements between Firms' (Center for Economic Policy Research, 1998)

—— and Röller, L-H, 'Consumer Surplus vs. Welfare Standard in a Political Economy Model of Merger Control' (2005) 23 *International Journal of Industrial Organization* 829

Niels, G and Jenkins, H, 'Reform of Article 82: Where the Link between Dominance and Effects Breaks Down' (2005) 26 *European Competition Law Review* 605

O'Donoghue, R and Padilla, AJ, *The Law and Economics of Article 82 EC* (Oxford, Hart Publishing, 2006)

—— and ——, *The Law and Economics of Article 102*, 2nd edn (Oxford, Hart Publishing, 2013)

Odudu, O, 'A New Economic Approach to Article 81(1)?' (2002) 27 *European Law Review* 100

——, 'The Wider Concerns of Competition Law' (2010) 30 *Oxford Journal of Legal Studies* 599

OECD Global Forum on Competition, Policy Roundtable on Crisis Cartels (2011) www.oecd.org/competition/cartels/48948847.pdf

Orbach, B, 'The Antitrust Consumer Welfare Paradox' (2011) 7 *Journal of Competition Law and Economics* 133

——, 'How Antitrust Lost Its Goal' (2013) 81 *Fordham Law Review* 2253

Pardolesi, R and Renda, A, 'The European Commission's Case Against Microsoft: Kill Bill?' (2004) 27 *World Competition* 513

Pate, RH, 'Antitrust in a Transatlantic Context—From the Cicada's Perspective' (Brussels, 7 June 2004) available at: www.usdoj.gov/atr/public/speeches/203973.htm

Pathak, AS, 'Articles 85 and 86 and Anti-competitive Exclusion in EEC Competition Law: Part 1' (1989) 10 *European Competition Law Review* 74

——, 'Articles 85 and 86 and Anti-competitive Exclusion in EEC Competition Law: Part 2' (1989) 10 *European Competition Law Review* 256

Patterson, DE and Shapiro, C, 'Transatlantic Divergence in GE/Honeywell: Causes and Lessons' (2001) 16 *Antitrust* 18

Peacock, A and Willgerodt, H (eds), *German Neo-Liberals and the Social Market Economy* (London, Palgrave Macmillan, 1989)

Peeperkorn, L, 'E.C. Vertical Restraints Guidelines: Effects Based or *per se* Policy?—a Reply' (2002) 23 *European Competition Law Review* 38

Peritz, RJR 'The Microsoft Chronicles' in L Rubini (ed), *Microsoft on Trial* (Cheltenham, Edward Elgar, 2010) 205–57

Pescatore, P, 'The Doctrine of Direct Effect—An Infant Disease of Community Law' (1983) *European Law Review* 155

Peukert, H, 'Die wirtschafts- und sozialpolitischen Zielsetzungen der Freiburger Kreises' in N Goldschmidt (ed), *Wirtschaft, Politik und Freiheit* (Tübingen, Mohr Siebeck, 2005) 267–87

Pflanz, M and Caffarra, C, 'The Economics of G.E./Honeywell' (2002) 23 *European Competition Law Review* 115

Pitofsky, R, 'The Political Content of Antitrust' (1979) 127 *University of Pennsylvania Law Review* 1051

Porter, ME, 'Competition and Antitrust: A Productivity-Based Approach to Evaluating Mergers and Joint Ventures' (2001) 46 *Antitrust Bulletin* 919

Posner, R, 'Antitrust Policy and the Supreme Court: An Analysis of the Restricted Distribution, Horizontal Merger and Potential Competition Decisions' (1975) 75 *Columbia Law Review* 282

——, 'The Rule of Reason and the Economic Approach: Reflections on the Sylvania Decision' (1977) 45 *University of Chicago Law Review* 1
——, 'The Law and Economics of the Economic Expert Witness' (1999) 13 *The Journal of Economic Perspectives* 91
——, *Antitrust Law*, 2nd edn (Chicago, Chicago University Press, 2001)
——, *Economic Analysis of Law*, 9th edn (The Hague, Wolters Kluwer, 2014)
Priest GL and Romani, F, 'Antique Antitrust: The GE/Honeywell Precedent' *Wall Street Journal* (New York, 21 June 2001) 6
Ridyard, D, 'Economic Analysis of Single Firm and Oligopolistic Dominance under the European Merger Regulation' (1994) 15 *European Competition Law Review* 255
——, 'Exclusionary Pricing and Price Discrimination Abuses under Article 82—An Economic Analysis' (2002) 23 *European Competition Law Review* 286
——, 'Compulsory Access under EC Competition Law—a New Doctrine of "Convenient Facilities" and the Case for Price Regulation' (2004) 25 *European Competition Law Review* 669
——, 'Tying and Bundling—Cause for Complaint?' (2005) 26 *European Competition Law Review* 316
——, 'Exclusive Contracts and Article 82 Enforcement: an Effects-based Perspective' (2008) 4 *European Competition Journal* 579
Riley, AJ, 'EC Antitrust Modernisation: The Commission Does Very Nicely—Thank You! Part 1' (2003) 11 *European Competition Law Review* 604
——, 'EC Antitrust Modernisation: The Commission Does Very Nicely—Thank You! Part 2' (2003) 11 *European Competition Law Review* 657
Röller, L-R, 'Der ökonomische Ansatz in der europäischen Wettbewerbspolitik' in Monopolkommission, *Zukunftsperspektiven der Wettbewerbspolitik* (Baden-Baden, Nomos, 2004)
——, 'Antitrust Economics—Catalyst for Convergence?' George Mason Law Review Symposium (Washington, DC, 20 September 2005)
——, 'Economic Analysis and Competition Policy Enforcement in Europe' in PAG van Bergeijk and E Kloosterhuis (eds), *Modelling European Mergers* (Cheltenham, Edward Elgar, 2005) 11
—— and Buigues, P, 'The Office of the Chief Competition Economist at the European Commission' (2005) 8 *Global Competition Review* 3
Romano, F, 'General Electric/Honeywell—Victory of the Commission … or Failure?' (2007) 3 *International Business Law Journal* 368
Rousseva, E, 'Modernizing by Eradicating: How the Commission's New Approach to Article 81 EC Dispenses with the Need to Apply Article 82 EC to Vertical Restraints' (2005) 42 *Common Market Law Review* 587
—— and Marquis, M, 'Hell Freezes Over: A Climate Change for Assessing Exclusionary Conduct under Article 102 TFEU' (2013) 4 *Journal of European Competition Law & Practice* 32
Rubinfeld, DL, 'Econometrics in the Courtroom' (1985) 85 *Columbia Law Review* 1048
——, 'Quantitative Methods in Antitrust' (2008) 1 *Issues in Competition Law and Policy* 723
Salop, SC, 'Question: What Is the Real and Proper Antitrust Welfare Standard? Answer: The True Consumer Welfare Standard' (2010) 22 *Loyola Consumer Law Review* 336
Schaub, A, 'Continued Focus on Reform: Recent Developments in EC Competition Policy' in B Hawk (ed), *International Antitrust Law and Policy 2001, Annual Proceedings of the Fordham Corporate Law Institute* (New York, Juris Publishing, 2002) 31

Scheffmann, D and Coleman, M, 'FTC Perspectives on the Use of Econometric Analysis in Antitrust Cases' in JD Harkrider and D Rubinfeld (eds), *Econometrics: Legal, Practical and Technical Issues* (Chicago, ABA Section of Antitrust Law, 2005)

Schmidt, A, 'Wie ökonomisch ist der "more economic approach"? Einige Anmerkungen aus ordnungsokonomischer Sicht' (2006) *Freiburger Diskussionspapiere* 06/10

—— and Voigt, S, 'Der "more economic approach" in der Mißbrauchsaufsicht' (2006) 56 *Wirtschaft und Wettbewerb* 1097

Schmidt, ILO, 'The Suitability of the More Economic Approach for Competition Policy: Dynamic vs. Static Efficiency' (2007) 28 *European Competition Law Review* 408

Schulze, R and Hoeren, T (eds), *Dokumente zum Europarecht, Kartellrecht, Volume 3* (Berlin, Springer, 2000)

Schuman, R, Declaration of 9 May 1950, available at: www.robert-schuman.eu/en/doc/questions-d-europe/qe-204-en.pdf

Schwartz, L, '"Justice" and Other Non-Economic Goals of Antitrust' (1979) 127 *University of Pennsylvania Law Review* 1076

Selvam, VSV, 'The EC Merger Control Impasse: Is there a Solution to this Predicament?' (2004) 25 *European Competition Law Review* 52

Sher, B, 'The Last of the Steam-Powered Trains: Modernising Article 82' (2004) 25 *European Competition Law Review* 243

Sidak, JG, 'Court-appointed Neutral Economic Experts' (2013) 9 *Journal of Competition Law & Economics* 359

Spagnolo, G, 'Leniency and Whistleblowers in Antitrust' in P Buccirossi, *Handbook of Antitrust Economics* (Cambridge MA, MIT Press, 2008) 259

Stock, EJ, 'Explaining the Differing U.S. and EU Positions on the Boeing/McDonnell-Douglas Merger: Avoiding Another Near-Miss' (1999) 20 *University of Pennsylvania Journal of International Economic Law* 825

Streit, M and Wohlgemuth, M, 'Walter Eucken und Friedrich A. von Hayek: Initiatorien der Ordnungsökonomik' Max-Planck-Institut zur Erforschung von Wirtschaftssystemen Discussion Paper No 9911 (1999)

Stucke, ME, 'Reconsidering Antitrust's Goals' (2012) 53 *Boston College Law Review* 551

Szegö, GP and Shell, K (eds), *Mathematical Methods in Investment and Finance* (Amsterdam, North-Holland Publishing, 1972)

Taylor, M, *International Competition Law: A New Dimension for the WTO?* (Cambridge, Cambridge University Press, 2006)

Temple Lang, J, and O'Donoghue, R, 'Defining Legitimate Competition: How to Clarify Pricing Abuses under Article 82 EC' (2002) 26 *Fordham International Law Journal* 83

The Concise Oxford English Dictionary, 11th edn (Oxford, Oxford University Press, 2008)

The Economist, Editorial, 'Brussels v Boeing' (London, 17 July 1997)

——, Editorial, 'Distrustful' (London, 26 July 1997) 60

Tom, WK and Pak, C, 'Toward a Flexible Rule of Reason' (2000) 68 *Antitrust Law Journal* 391

Torres, A, 'EU Issues Tough Warning over Boeing-McDonnell Merger' *Reuters News* (15 July 1997)

Townley, C, *Article 81 EC and Public Policy* (Oxford, Hart Publishing, 2009)

van Bergeijk, PAG and Kloosterhuis, E (eds), *Modelling European Mergers* (Cheltenham, Edward Elgar, 2005) van den Bergh, R, 'Modern Industrial Organisation versus Old-Fashioned European Competition Law' (1996) 17 *European Competition Law Review* 75

van Rompuy, B, *Economic Efficiency: The Sole Concern of Modern Antitrust Policy? Non-Efficiency Considerations under Article 101 TFEU* (Alphen aan den Rijn, Kluwer, 2012)

Vanberg, VJ, 'Consumer Welfare, Total Welfare and Economic Freedom—on the Normative Foundations of Competition Policy' in J Drexl, W Kerber, R Podszun (eds), *Competition Policy and the Economic Approach—Foundations and Limitations* (Cheltenham, Edward Elgar, 2011) 44

Varian, HR, 'In Europe, GE and Honeywell Ran Afoul of 19th Century Thinking' *New York Times* (New York, 28 June 2001) C2

Veljanovski, C, 'EC Merger Policy After *GE/Honeywell* and *Airtours*' (2004) 49 *Antitrust Bulletin* 153

Venit, JS, 'Article 82: The Last Frontier—Fighting Fire With Fire?' (2005) 28 *Fordham International Law Journal* 1157

Verouden, V, Bengtsson, C and Albaek, S, 'The Draft EU Notice on Horizontal Mergers: A Further Step toward Convergence?' (2004) 49 *Antitrust Bulletin* 243

Vezzoso, S, 'The Incentives Balance Test in the EU Microsoft Case: a Pro-innovation "Economics-based" Approach?' (2006) 27 *European Competition Law Review* 382

Vickers, J, 'Competition Economics and Policy' (2003) 24 *European Competition Law Review* 95

——, 'How to Reform the EC Merger Test?' in G Drauz and M Reynolds, *EC Merger Control—A Major Reform in Progress* (Oxford, Oxford University Press, 2003)

——, 'Merger Policy in Europe: Retrospect and Prospect' (2004) 25 *European Competition Law Review* 445

——, 'Abuse of Market Power' (2005) 115 *The Economic Journal* 244

——, 'Market Power in Competition Cases' (2006) 2 *European Competition Journal* 3

Voigt, S and Schmidt, A, 'Der "more economic approach" in der Mißbrauchsaufsicht' (2006) *Wirtschaft und Wettbewerb* 1097

Völker, SB, 'Mind the Gap: Unilateral Effects Analysis Arrives in EC Merger Control' (2004) 25 *European Competition Law Review* 395

Waelbroeck, D, 'Michelin II: A *Per Se* Rule Against Rebates by Dominant Companies?' (2005) 1 *Journal of Competition Law and Economics* 149

Wagner-von Papp, F, 'Competition Law and Extraterritoriality' in A Ezrachi, *Research Handbook on International Competition Law* (Cheltenham, Edward Elgar, 2012) 21–59.

Wall Street Journal, Editorial, 'A "Dangerous" Merger?' (New York, 21 July 1997)

——, Editorial, 'Europe to GE: Go Home' (New York, 15 June 2001) A14

Weiler, JHH, 'The Transformation of Europe' (1991) 100 *Yale Law Journal* 2403

Weitbrecht, A, 'From Freiburg to Chicago—The First 50 Years of European Competition Law' (2008) 29 *European Competition Law Review* 81

Wesseling, R, *The Modernisation of EC Antitrust Law* (Oxford, Hart Publishing, 2002)

Whish, R, *Competition Law*, 5th edn (Oxford, Oxford University Press, 2003)

Wilks, S and McGowan, L, 'Competition Policy in the European Union: Creating a Federal Agency' in GB Doern and S Wilks (eds), *Comparative Competition Policy: National Institutions in a Global Market* (Oxford, Clarendon Press, 1996)

Witt, AC, 'The Commission's Guidance Paper on Abusive Exclusionary Conduct—More Radical than it Appears?' (2010) 35 *European Law Review* 214

——, 'From *Airtours* to *Ryanair*: Is the More Economic Approach to EU Merger Law Really about More Economics?' (2012) 49 *Common Market Law Review* 217
——, 'Public Policy Goals Under EU Competition Law—Now is The Time to Set the House in Order' (2012) 8 *European Competition Journal* 443
Wolf, J, 'Boeing-McDonnell Merger Plan is Closer to Rejection in Europe' *Wall Street Journal* (New York, 16 July 1997) B4.
Wray, R, 'Microsoft Ruling is 'First Shot in Trade War'' *Guardian* (London, 26 May 2004) 17.
Wright, JD and Ginsburg, DH, 'The Goals Of Antitrust: Welfare Trumps Choice' (2013) 81 *Fordham Law Review* 2405
Zimmer, D (ed), *The Goals of Competition Law* (Cheltenham, Edward Elgar, 2012)

INDEX

abusive conduct
'as-efficient-competitor' test 278, 279, 280, 281
assessments of abusive conduct 216–19, 222–5, 226, 227, 228, 229, 249, 250
case law 275–81
Commission's concept of harm 144, 145, 146
'competition on the merits' 276, 277
exclusionary abuse 151, 275–6, 277, 278–9, 280, 281, 295
exploitative abuse 275
legal tests 287–9
academic criticism of EU antitrust law 10–11
lack of economic analysis 10, 11
academic debate about the Commission's reform agenda 69–70, 72–3
economic efficiency effects 72–3
form- and effects-based tests 72
opposing views 73
relevance of consumer welfare 72
accuracy of the more economic approach 260
limitations to 255–6
quantifiable concepts of harm and countervailing effects 254–5, 260
advantages of the more economic approach 307–8
accuracy 260
limitations to 255–6
quantifiable concepts of harm and countervailing effects 254–5, 260
empirical evidence
increased use of 256
harmonisation of EU and US antitrust law 258–60
logic and internal consistency 253–4, 260
competitive harm 253, 254, 260
countervailing effects 253, 260
reduction in the number of cases caught by the antitrust provisions 256–8, 260
focusing on the most serious infringements 257–8
Airtours/ First Choice proposed merger 28
errors of assessment 28–9
Andriessen, F. 34
Annual Reports on Competition Policy
Commission's concept of harm 142
objectives of EU antitrust law 93–4, 102, 107–8
consumer interests 97–8
democracy 99
economic growth 96
efficiency 100–101
employment policy 99–100
equality of opportunity 99
fairness 98–9
fighting inflation 97
individual freedom 99
industrial adaptability 96–7
innovation 100
interests of society as a whole 98
market integration 94–5
preventing the concentration of economic power 95–6
protection of constitutional rights 99
safeguarding the competitiveness of the European economy 97
strategy for achieving the Union's fundamental objectives, as 101–2
anticompetitive agreements
Commission's changed understanding of 246–7
'Areeda and Turner' test 91, 233–4
Areeda, P. 81, 91, 233–4
Article 101
review of
approach to assessing vertical agreements 40–41
Block Exemption Regulation for vertical agreements 45
Guidelines on the Application of Article 81(3) 58
interpretative guidelines 43–5
more economic approach 41
public consultation 49–50
Article 102
Commission's revised approach to 290–94
legal uncertainty after reform 228, 254, 260, 294, 297–8
review of 42, 43, 183–4
Commission documents 59
EAGCP report 42, 71, 106, 146–7, 184, 219–20
guidance on enforcement priorities 46–7

more economic approach 42–3
public consultation 51–2
'as-efficient-competitor' test 278, 279, 280, 281

Bain, J. 80
Block Exemption Regulations
countervailing effects 160–62, 166–7
legal objectives of EU antitrust law 91–2
legal tests 202–3, 204, 209–11, 212
vertical agreements 45
Boeing / McDonnell Douglas crisis
dual investigation of proposed merger 11–14
Böhm, F. 83, 86
Bork, R. 64, 66, 67, 79, 81, 82
Borschette, A. 34
Breyer, S. 81
Brittan, L. 34

cartel settlement procedure 2
case law
compatibility with the Commission's more economic approach 294–5, 306, 308
Commission's revised approach to Article 102 290–94
consequences of divergence 290, 294
exclusionary conduct 295
legal certainty 294
points of divergence 289–90
concept of harm, Court's
abusive conduct 275–81
after the more economic approach 269–71, 272–4
Article 101 266–271
Article 102 274–281
'as-efficient-competitor' test 278, 279, 280, 281
compatibility with the Commission's early understanding of harm 268–9, 272
compatibility with the Commission's more economic approach 290
'competition on the merits' 276, 277
consumer welfare 269, 270, 271, 272, 273, 274, 277, 279, 281
dominance 271, 275
EU Merger Law 271–4
exclusionary abuse 275–6, 277, 278–9, 280, 281
exploitative abuse 275
market structure 276, 277
prior to the more economic approach 266–9, 271–2
restrictions by effect 267–8, 270, 271
restrictions by object 267, 270, 271
'special responsibilities' 276, 277
countervailing effects, Court's view of 281–6
compatibility with the Commission's more economic approach 290
consumer welfare 284
efficiency effects 281–2
harmonisation with other objectives 283
legitimate policy goals 284–5
objective justification 282
public policy 282, 283
legal objectives, Court's understanding of
after the more economic approach 265–6
compatibility with the more economic approach 266, 289–90
market integration 266
prior to the more economic approach 262–5
protection of competitors, consumers, and market structure 265–6
legal tests, Court's view of
abusive conduct 287–9
compatibility with the Commission's more economic approach 290
form and effects-based tests 286, 289
intermediary tests 289
restrictions by object 286–7
Chicago school of thought 81
Chief Competition Economist
creation of position 48, 55
role of 48, 55–6, 237
Commissioner for Competition Policy
appointment of an economist to the position of 7, 34
backgrounds of 34
see also **Monti, M.**
Commission's approach to legal tests after the introduction of the more economic approach
Article 101
Block Exemption Regulations 209–11, 212
countervailing effects 206–7, 211, 212
decision practice 207–9
form-based presumption of illegality 207
length of decisions 209, 212
restrictions by effect 204, 205, 206, 207, 209, 212, 248
restrictions by object 204, 205, 206, 207, 208, 209, 211, 212, 248, 249
soft law 204–7
standard of proof 206–7, 211, 212
Article 102
assessments of abusive conduct 222–5, 226, 227, 228, 249, 250
assessments of dominance 221–22, 227, 249
decision practice 221–6, 227, 229–30
detailed assessments 225, 226, 227
legal uncertainty 228
soft law 219–21
standard of proof 227

EU merger law 213
effects-based tests 213–14, 248
length of decisions 214
Commission's approach to legal tests prior to the introduction of the more economic approach
Article 101
Block Exemption Regulations 202–3, 204
decision practice 199–202, 203–4
length of decisions 201
restrictions by effect 199, 203–4
restrictions by object 199, 203–4
soft law 198
standard of proof 201, 202, 204
Article 102
assessments of abusive conduct 216–19, 249
assessments of dominance 215–16
decision practice 215–19
length of decisions 219
soft law 215
standard of proof 217, 219
EU merger law 213
effects-based tests 213, 248
Commission's concept of harm after the introduction of the more economic approach
Article 101 156
commitments decisions, use of 122
consumer welfare 118, 119, 120, 121, 123, 125, 126, 156
de minimis market share threshold 121
decision practice 121–5
freedom and opportunities 123–4
hard-core cartels 121–2
interpretative guidelines 118–21, 126
market integration 124, 125, 156
Article 102 146, 157–8
Commission Notice 147–9, 155, 157–8
commitments decisions 149–50
consumer welfare 147, 148, 149, 151, 152, 154, 155, 158
decision practice 149–55, 155–6, 158
discrimination on the grounds of nationality 153
exclusion of competitors 151
infringement decisions 150–54
rejection decisions 154–5
safeguarding the 'competitive process' 147
soft law 146–7
EU merger law 156
consumer welfare 135–7, 138–9, 140, 141, 156, 157
coordinated effects and non-coordinated effects 135, 136, 138, 140
Council Regulation 139/2004 133–5
decision practice 137–40
dominance 134, 135, 137, 139
interpretative guidelines 135–7
significant impediment to effective competition 134, 135
Commission's concept of harm prior to the introduction of the more economic approach
Article 101
decision practice 114–18
exclusive dealing contracts 112
freedom and opportunities 114–17, 118, 125
interpretative Notices 111–14
joint ventures 113
market integration 118
Article 102 146, 155, 157
abuse 144, 145, 146
Annual Reports on Competition Policy 142
decision practice 142–6
dominance 143, 155
freedom 142, 144
'special responsibility' 145
EU merger law 132
consumer welfare 131
Council Regulation 4064/89 127
decision practice 128–32
distinction between horizontal and non-horizontal mergers 131–2
dominance 129
freedom of action 128
interpretative Notices 127–8
Commission's understanding of countervailing effects after the introduction of the more economic approach
Article 101
Block Exemption Regulations 166–7
consumer welfare 166, 174
cultural protection 171–2, 173
decision practice 167–73
economic efficiency 166, 167, 169, 171, 173, 174, 190, 247, 248
environmental benefits 170–71
industrial or social policy benefits 168, 169
interpretative guidelines 165–6
public health and safety 172–3
Article 102
consumer welfare 189
decision practice 186–8
efficiency effects 184, 185, 186, 187, 188, 189, 190, 191
'objective necessity' 186–7, 188, 189, 247
public policy 185, 189, 191, 248
soft law 184–6
efficiency defences, cost and success of 191–2
EU merger law
consumer welfare 180

Council Regulation 139/2004 177
decision practice 178–9, 180
economic efficiency 177, 178, 179, 180, 190, 247
guidelines 177–8

Commission's understanding of countervailing effects prior to the introduction of the more economic approach
Article 101
Block Exemption Regulations 160–62
decision practice 162–5
distressed industries, aiding 163–4
environmental benefits 164, 165
increased economic welfare 162, 163, 165
increased number of competitors 162, 163, 165
interpretative Notices 160
social benefits 164, 165
Article 102
decision practice 181–3
efficiency effects 183, 188, 191
protection of consumers and the general public 182–3, 188
protection of the dominant undertaking's own rights or interests 181–2, 188
efficiency effects 247–8
EU merger law
Council Regulation 4064/89 174–5
decision practice 175–6
economic efficiency 175, 176, 177, 190

commitments decisions
use of 2, 3

common market *see* **internal market**

'competition on the merits' 276, 277

competitive harm
Article 101 111
Article 102 141, 142
unfairness 141–2
Commission's broad concept of consumer harm 297
Commission's changed understanding of 247
concept of 110
different concepts of harm under the different pillars 297
logical and consistent approach to 253, 254, 260
quantifiable concept of 254–5, 260
US Antitrust Law
concept of harm 65
see also **case law; Commission's concept of harm after the introduction of the more economic approach; Commission's concept of harm prior to the introduction of the more economic approach**

competitiveness of the European economy, safeguarding
objective of EU antitrust law 97

concentration of economic power, preventing
objective of EU antitrust law 95–6

constitutional rights, protection of
objective of antitrust laws 83–6
EU antitrust law 99

consumer welfare
academic debate on relevance of 72
Commission's broad understanding of 303
Commission's concept of harm, and 118, 119, 120, 121, 123, 125, 126, 131, 135–7, 138–9, 140, 141, 147, 148, 149, 151, 152, 154, 155, 156, 157, 158
Commission's understanding of countervailing effects, and 166, 174, 180, 189
Court's concept of harm, and 269, 270, 271, 272, 273, 274, 277, 279, 281
Court's view of countervailing effects, and 284
objective of antitrust laws 64, 68, 69, 81–2
objective of EU antitrust law 97–8, 104, 105, 106, 107, 109, 246
exclusivity of aim 302–4
legal basis for 303–4

countervailing effects
academic debate on 72–3
concept of 159
conditions to fulfill 159–60
different concepts of countervailing effects under the different pillars 297
legal basis
Article 101 159–60
Article 102 181
legal tests 198, 206–7, 211, 212, 229
logical and consistent approach to 253, 260
quantifiable concept of 254–5, 260
see also **case law; Commission's understanding of countervailing effects after the introduction of the more economic approach; Commission's understanding of countervailing effects prior to the introduction of the more economic approach**

cultural protection 171–2, 173

decentralising public enforcement 257

decision practice
countervailing effects 162–5, 167–73, 175–6, 178–9, 180, 181–3, 186–8
economic theory, use of 238–9
harm 114–18, 121–5, 128–32, 137–40, 142–6, 149–55, 155–6, 158
legal tests 199–202, 203–4, 207–9, 215–19, 221–6, 227, 229–30

Delors, J. 10

democracy
objective of antitrust laws 83, 86
EU antitrust law 99

Directorate General for Competition Policy (DG Competition)
Discussion Paper on Article 102 59, 146, 147, 184, 220
public consultation on the document 71–2
General Court striking down decisions because of serious errors of assessment 27, 28, 32–3
Airtours / First Choice proposed merger 28–9
Schneider Electric / Legrand proposed merger 29–30
Tetra Laval SA / Sidel proposed merger 30–32
increasing the number of economists in 47–9, 237
dominance
assessments of dominance 215–16, 221–22, 227, 229, 249
Commission's concept of harm 129, 134, 135, 137, 139, 143, 155
Court's definition of 271, 275
drawbacks of the more economic approach 308, 309
difficulties of application 298, 301–2
cost and length of proceedings 301
courts 298–300
undertakings 300
enhancement of consumer welfare
Commission's broad understanding of 303
exclusivity of aim 302–4
legal basis for 303–4
inconsistency
broad concept of consumer harm 297
different concepts of harm and countervailing effects under the different pillars 297
market integration aim as well as the aim of enhancing economic consumer welfare 254, 260, 296
theory and practice of efficiency effects 297
legal uncertainty and the rule of law 309
Article 102 reform 254, 260, 297–8
need for compromise and review 309

EAGCP *see* **European Advisory Group for Competition Policy**
Easterbrook, F. 81
economic efficiency
countervailing effects 166, 167, 169, 171, 173, 174, 175, 176, 177, 178, 179, 180, 190, 247, 248, 281–2, 297
objective of EU antitrust law 100–101
economic growth
objective of EU antitrust law 96
economic theory 231, 245
Commission's use of after the introduction of the more economic approach 236–9, 250
decision practice 238–9
DG Competition, role of economists in 237
Green Paper on Vertical Restraints in EC Competition Policy 236–7
soft law instruments 237–8
Commission's use of prior to the introduction of the more economic approach
'Areeda and Turner' test 233–4
Articles 101 and 102 232–4
detailed assessments 234–5
EU merger law 234–6
lack of complex analysis 232–3, 234
concerns over use of 302
ECSC 8
empirical evidence
increased use of 244, 245, 256
employment policy
objective of EU antitrust law 99–100
environmental benefits 164, 165, 170–71
equality of opportunity
objective of antitrust laws 83, 86
EU antitrust law 99
Erhard, L. 85
EU 'antitrust law'
concept defined 3
EU merger law
review of 41
guidelines 41–2, 46, 58–9
public consultation 50–51
role of the Commission 45–6
Eucken, W. 83
Euratom 8–9
European Advisory Group for Competition Policy (EAGCP)
economic approach to Article 102 42, 71, 106, 146–7, 184, 219–20
creation of 48
role of 48, 237
European Atomic Energy Community (Euratom) 8–9
European Coal and Steel Community (ECSC) 8
European Court of Justice
powers of 261
principles of EU antitrust law 261
see also **case law**
European Economic Community
competition rules 9
economic integration 9
exclusionary abuse 151, 275–6, 277, 278–9, 280, 281, 295
exploitative abuse 275

fairness
objective of antitrust laws 83, 86
EU antitrust law 98–9
Freiburg school of thought *see* **ordoliberalism**

General Electric Company (GE) / Honeywell International Inc
dual investigation of proposed merger 14–15
different analyses 15, 17–18
EU Investigation 15–16
merger's effects on competitors / consumers welfare 17, 18
reaction to EU prohibition of the transaction 16, 17, 18
US Investigation 15
Germany
instrumental role in creating the EU's competition rules 85–6, 127

Hallstein, W. 86
Harvard school of thought 80, 81
Hawk, B. 10, 11, 305

inconsistency in the more economic approach
broad concept of consumer harm 297
different concepts of harm and countervailing effects under the different pillars 297
market integration aim as well as the aim of enhancing economic consumer welfare 254, 260, 296
theory and practice of efficiency effects 297
individual freedom
objective of antitrust laws 83, 84, 86
EU antitrust law 99
industrial adaptability
objective of EU antitrust law 96–7
industrial policy benefits 163–4, 168, 169
inflation, fighting
objective of EU antitrust law 97
innovation, stimulating
objective of EU antitrust law 100
internal market
completion of 7–10
International Competition Network (ICN) 37–8
Unilateral Conduct Working Group 79, 83, 86
international cooperation
increased cooperation and exchange of best practices 36, 37
International Competition Network (ICN) 37–8
OECD Competition Committee 37
OECD Global Forum on Competition 37
UNCTAD Competition and Consumer Policies Programme 37
introduction of the more economic approach to EU antitrust law
Commission documents introducing the more economic approach 57–60, 73–4
implications of 306
lead role in shaping the antitrust rules 306–7
overview of 305–6
soft law instruments 1, 43, 52
three pillars of EU antitrust law
Article 101 40–41
Article 102 42–3
EU merger law 41–2

joint ventures 113

Kaysen, C. 81
Kroes, N. 38

legal certainty 309
Commission's interpretation of Article 102, and 228, 254, 260, 294, 297–8
legal objectives of antitrust laws 86–7
balancing conflicting policy goals 87
enhancement of economic welfare 80–83
consumer welfare 81–2
total welfare 80–81
protection of fundamental constitutional rights and values 83–6
democracy 83, 86
equality of opportunity 83, 86
fairness 83, 86
individual freedom 83, 84, 86
single / multitude of policy aims 88
see also **legal objectives of EU antitrust law; US Antitrust Law**
legal objectives of EU antitrust law
Commission's understanding of, according to the more economic approach 109, 246
achieving the political objectives, contributing to 108
Annual Reports on Competition Policy 107–8
Commission Notices 106
efficiency 104, 105, 106, 107
enhancement of consumer welfare 104, 105, 106, 107, 109, 246
interpretative guidelines 104–7
legal provisions' identification of objectives 103–4
market integration 104, 105, 106, 107, 109, 246
Merger Regulations' objectives 103–4, 105–6
protection of the competitive process 106, 108

Commission's understanding of, prior to the more economic approach 108–9, 246
Annual Reports on Competition Policy 93–102
Block Exemption Regulations 91–2
Commission Notices 92–3
legal provisions' identification of objectives 89–91
legally binding enforcement instruments 91–2
market integration 90
Merger Regulations' objectives 89–90
soft law instruments 92–3
Court's understanding of
after the more economic approach 265–6
compatibility with the more economic approach 266, 289–90
market integration 266
prior to the more economic approach 262–5
protection of competitors, consumers, and market structure 265–6
importance of identifying 77, 79
interpretation of law 77–9
legal tests
Article 101
agreements that have the effect of restricting competition 197, 229
agreements that have the object of restricting competition 196–7, 228
countervailing effects 198, 229
intermediary rules 197–8
standard of proof 229
Article 102
assessments of abusive conduct 229
assessments of dominance 229
form v. effects-based tests 214
'unnecessary' assessments 229–30
EU merger law
form v. effects-based tests 228
form v. effects-based tests 193, 194–6
academic debate on 72
types of evidence 230
US antitrust law
per se rules / rule of reason, use of 65–8, 69, 194
see also **case law; Commission's approach to legal tests after the introduction of the more economic approach; Commission's approach to legal tests prior to the introduction of the more economic approach**
length of decisions 1, 201, 209, 212, 214, 219, 245, 250, 301, 310–17
leniency programme 2
market integration
objective of EU antitrust law, as 90, 94–5, 104, 105, 106, 107, 109, 246, 254, 260, 266, 296
obstacles to 118, 124, 125, 156
market structure 265–6, 276, 277
Mason, E. 80
methodology 231
empirical evidence
increased use of 244, 245, 256
length of decisions 245
quantitative analysis 239–40
evidentiary instrument, as 240
limitations of 255–6
other parties use of 241–2
prior to the more economic approach 240
significance of in decision practice 242–3
use of in decision practice 240–42
see also **economic theory**
Microsoft
dual investigation of business practices 18–19
academic criticism of analysis 25
effects on competitors rather than consumer welfare 25
EU Investigation 21–24
reaction to EU decision 24
US Investigation 19–21
Miksch, L. 83
Monti, M. 135
background 34
Commissioner for Competition Policy, as 34
'Great Reformer' 35
increasing the ratio of economists in DG Competition 47–8
more economic approach 34, 35
public statements on 54–6
reform proposals 33, 35
more economic approach to EU antitrust law
concept defined 246
Müller-Armack, A. 85

ordoliberalism 83–6
Organisation for Economic Cooperation and Development (OECD)
Competition Committee 37
Global Forum on Competition 37

Posner, R. 67, 69, 81, 300
Post-Chicago school of thought 82
procedural reform 1
public consultation
reform process 49–52, 53, 70, 71, 72
public policy
countervailing effects 172–3, 185, 189, 191, 248, 282, 283

quantitative analysis 239–40
evidentiary instrument, as 240
limitations of 255–6
other parties use of 241–2
prior to the more economic approach 240
significance of in decision practice 242–3
use of in decision practice 240–42

restriction of competition by effect 197, 199, 203, 204, 205, 206, 207, 209, 212, 229, 248, 267–8, 270, 271
restriction of competition by object 196–7, 199, 203, 204, 205, 206, 207, 208, 209, 211, 212, 228, 248, 249, 267, 270, 271, 286–7

Sassen, M. 34
Schneider Electric / Legrand proposed merger 29
errors of assessment 29–30
Schuman, R. 8
single market *see* **internal market**
soft law instruments 1, 43, 52
standard of proof 201, 202, 204, 206–7, 211, 212, 217, 219, 227, 229
substantive review process 1
Sutherland, P. 34

teleology 77–8
terminology of the book 3–4
Tetra Laval SA / Sidel proposed merger 30–31
errors of assessment 31–2
Turner, D. 81, 91, 233–4

United Nations Conference on Trade and Development (UNCTAD)
Competition and Consumer Policies Programme 37
US antitrust law
competitive harm
concept of 65
key substantive principles of 61–2
objectives of
changes to 62–4
consumer welfare 64, 68, 69
enhancing economic welfare 63–4
freedom of small companies to compete 62–3
per se rules / rule of reason, use of 65–8, 69, 194
US antitrust law and EU antitrust law
conflict between 11, 26–7
Boeing / McDonnell Douglas crisis 11–14
GE / Honeywell merger 14–18
interpretation of antitrust rules 25–6
Microsoft business practices 18–25
protection of businesses or consumers 26, 61
harmonisation of EU and US antitrust law 258–60
'US Antitrust Revolution' 56, 63, 64, 69, 74
Commission's more economic approach, and 69

van Miert, K. 34, 302
vertical agreements
Block Exemption Regulations 45
criticism of EU approach to 10–11, 40–41
economic approach to assessing vertical agreements 41, 45
Green Paper on Vertical Restraints in EC Competition Policy 35, 41, 49, 50, 57, 236–7, 302
guidelines on vertical restraints 58, 104, 105
von der Groeben, H. 34, 85, 86
Vouel, R. 34

White Paper on Modernisation of the Rules Implementing Articles 85 and 86 of the EC Treaty 57–8
World Competition 54

www.ingramcontent.com/pod-product-compliance
Ingram Content Group UK Ltd.
Pitfield, Milton Keynes, MK11 3LW, UK
UKHW020132290926
15471UKWH00003B/445

9 781509 927951